W9-CQK-532

Teaching Music
through Performance
in Band
Volume 2

G-4889

Teaching Music through Performance in Band

Volume 2

Larry Blocher
Eugene Corporon
Ray Cramer
Tim Lautzenheiser
Edward S. Lisk
Richard Miles
Jack Stamp

Compiled and Edited by Richard Miles

GIA Publications, Inc.
Chicago

G-4889

Copyright © 1998 GIA Publications, Inc.
7404 S. Mason Ave.
Chicago, IL 60638
ISBN: 1-57999-028-2
All rights reserved
Printed in the United States of America

Table of Contents

PART II: The Band Conductor as Music Teacher

ACKNOWLEDGEMENTS

The following Research Associates are
gratefully acknowledged for outstanding scholarly contributions to the "Teacher
Resource Guides:"

Susan Creasap
Assistant Director of Bands
Morehead State University • Morehead, Kentucky

Jeff Emge
Assistant Director of Bands
East Texas State University • Commerce, Texas

Mitchell J. Fennell
Director of Wind Studies
California State University/Fullerton • Fullerton, California

Robert E. Foster, Jr.
Associate Director of Bands
Texas Christian University • Fort Worth, Texas

Otis French
U.S. Army Field Band
Ft. Mead, Maryland

Brad Genevro
Assistant Director of Wind Studies
University of North Texas • Denton, Texas

Jay W. Gilbert
Director of Bands
Doane College • Crete, Nebraska

Robert Halseth
Director of Wind Studies
California State University • Sacramento, California

Edward Harris
Director of Bands
California State University/Stanislaus • Turlock, California

Glen J. Hemberger
Doctoral Associate
University of North Texas • Denton, Texas

Patricia J. Hoy
Director of Bands
Northern Arizona University • Flagstaff, Arizona

Keith Kinder
Associate Professor of Music
McMaster University • Hamilton, Ontario, Canada

Jim Klages
Professor of Trumpet
Ft. Lewis College • Durango, Colorado

Kenneth Kohlenberg
Director of Bands
Sinclair Community College • Dayton, Ohio

Brian Lamb
Director of Instrumental Studies
Southwest Baptist University • Bolivar, Missouri

Alan Lourens
Doctoral Associate
Indiana University • Bloomington, Indiana

Rich Lundahl
Doctoral Associate
Indiana University • Bloomington, Indiana

Matthew Mailman
Director of Bands
Oklahoma City University • Oklahoma City, Oklahoma

Jennifer McAllister
Berkner High School • Richardson, Texas

Keelan McCamey
Heritage of American Band
Langley Air Force Base • Hampton, Virginia

Matthew McInturf
Director of Wind Studies
Florida International University • Miami, Florida

Robert Meunier
Director of Bands
Drake University • Des Moines, Iowa

Doug Norton
Director of Bands
American School in London • London, United Kingdom

James Popejoy
Doctoral Associate
University of North Texas • Denton, Texas

Edwin Powell
Conducting Associate
McLennan Community College • Waco, Texas

Jeffrey Renshaw
Director of Bands
University of Connecticut • Storrs, Connecticut

Rodney C. Schueller
University Bands
Northern Illinois University • De Kalb, Illinois

Robert Spittal
Director of Bands
Gonzaga University • Spokane, Washington

Jack Stamp
Conductor of University Bands
Indiana University of Pennsylvania • Indiana, Pennsylvania

Scott A. Stewart
Doctoral Associate
Indiana University • Bloomington, Indiana

Lawrence F. Stoffel
Assistant Professor of Music/Director of Huskie Bands
Northern Illinois University • De Kalb, Illinois

Yoshiaki Tanno
Doctoral Associate
Indiana University • Bloomington, Indiana

Ibrook Tower
Director of Bands
Elizabethtown College • Elizabethtown, Pennsylvania

Jason Worzbyt
Assistant Professor of Music
Morehead State University • Morehead, Kentucky

Introduction

Larry Blocher

A good friend of mine in graduate school was from a small, southern town. Returning to his hometown during a "break," Martin took the opportunity to visit his uncle. Now Martin had not seen his uncle for quite a while, and his uncle was anxious to "catch up" on what was happening in Martin's life. The conversation began something like this: "Hey Martin, you still studying that music stuff? Well hell, son, there's only eight notes!"

Eight notes. It sounds so simple. Many music teachers—band directors—have spent and continue to spend countless hours learning about and teaching those "eight notes" (and, of course many other "things") to students in band. Today, as never before, there is a growing wealth of material designed to assist band directors—music teachers—in helping those students learn about music.

This volume of *Teaching Music through Performance in Band* represents the continuation of a project designed to add to this resource material. Like the first book in this *Teaching Music* series, it is written for music teachers, prospective music teachers, and other music professionals who interact with students in band rehearsals. The text is divided into two parts. Part I is a series of independent "chapters" that address issues and/or techniques basic to teaching music to students in band. Part II contains resource guides for one hundred band works, Grades Two through Six. The resource guide included for each selection includes analytical and historical information "units" designed for integration into regular band rehearsals.

This project continues to be a team effort. We are grateful to the many wonderful music teachers who have touched and continue to touch our lives and the lives of music teachers and students everywhere in positive ways. It is our sincere hope that this *Teaching Music* series will continue to be a useful resource for band directors desiring to teach music through performance in band.

PART I

THE TEACHING
OF MUSIC

CHAPTER 1

Teaching Music

Larry Blocher

*"A teacher affects eternity; he can never
tell where his influence stops "*
··· Henry Adams ···

Introduction

What an *incredible* time to be teaching music! While it is likely that most readers, especially those who are currently teaching music, may not need to reach for their personal edition of *Webster's* to define the word "incredible" as it applies to their particular situation, a quick look in my *New World* version defines "incredible" as "seemingly too unusual to be possible." "Incredible" may, indeed, describe what it is like to teach music in today's schools.

The first part of this chapter takes a brief look at some of the "new" challenges facing music teachers at all levels. The second part of this chapter looks at teaching students about music through performance, in this case in band. In today's schools, becoming aware of, understanding, and being able to respond to the issues presented in the first part of this chapter may be necessary in order to *have* students to teach about music through performance.

Information Management

In his 1982 book *Megatrends*, John Naisbitt described "ten new directions," or trends, that were shaping the 1980s. One of the trends that Naisbitt described was a shift from an industrial society to an information society. Naisbitt suggested, at that time, that we were "drowning in information."[1] Additionally, Naisbitt stated that "trends, like horses, are easier to ride in the direction they are already going."[2] It appeared that learning to deal with increased amounts of information was going to be a way of life for all of us, music teachers included, as we dealt with the present and headed into the future.

In 1990, *Megatrends 2000* confirmed that many of the earlier "shifts" were continuing "pretty much on schedule," and reiterated the information overload theme, stating that "in fewer than ten years, the growth of information has only quickened."[3] Naisbitt and his colleagues suggested that all this information might just "whiz right by" us if we were not careful. As music teachers, the task of "keeping up" with and organizing—managing—the vast amounts of data that come our way each day or that are available to us on a daily basis seems to be one of our most incredible challenges.

School Reform Information

Change has become a way of life in today's schools. Becoming aware of, understanding, and responding to reform issues can be an incredible task for music teachers. Many school music teachers are currently involved in sorting out lots of new information as a basis for decision making on a variety of issues. Attempting to provide an up-to-date list of these reform issues is not practical given the current climate of school change (change is on-going). However, a brief overview of recent professional literature dealing with school reform provides at least a "starting point" for becoming aware of current school reform ideas.

Higher standards • benchmarks • rubrics • outcome-based learning; curriculum frameworks • authentic assessment • site-based management • cooperative learning • integrated curriculum • heterogeneous grouping • charter schools • vouchers and choice plans • inclusive schools • work-based learning • alternate use of school time • national standards

Many of these issues have their own vocabulary. Alternate use of school time, for example, involves special terms such as block, double-blocked, pure, full, 4x4, modified, accelerated, hybrid, intensive, split, imbedded, expanded, skinnies, oreo cookie, zero hour, Copernican Plan, etc.[4] The scheduling "jargon"—part of the information important to understanding the alternate use of school time issue—seems to grow on a regular basis. Special jargon is a part of many school reform issues—more information. Additionally, many changes that are a part of school reform are often accompanied by anecdotal evidence and, depending on the nature and the "newness" of the reform issue, supporting research that hopefully will lead to additional formal research and more information for responding to school reform issues in an informed way. Incredible!

The Path of School Reform

"Signs of frustration with the progress of reform and the direction it should take seem to be on the increase. Shouldn't we know by now what works?"[5] The idea of school reform is not new. Conversations with "veteran" music teacher colleagues and/or perusal of professional literature generally confirms this as "fact". "Next to "All children can learn at high levels," the

most frequently heard phrase in education reform these days seems to be "This too shall pass."[6] Time may be an important factor.

In recent years schools have "taken it on the chin."[7] In *The Manufactured Crisis*, David Berliner and Bruce Biddle state that "Good-hearted Americans have come to believe that the public schools of their nation are in a crisis state because they have so often been given this false message by supposedly credible sources."[8] True messages or false messages—the collective jury may still be out on this one. Nevertheless, the last several years have seen the publication of a number of national reports on education. Driven by: a) a genuine interest in students and a sincere desire to improve teaching and learning in the schools; b) political rhetoric (short-sighted decisions that are made during election years)[9]; c) budgetary constraints (there are probably not too many music teachers with budgets that are too large or who are making too much money); d) all of the above; or, e) none of the above (you provide your own answer), these national reports appear to be blazing the current reform path.

Michael Mark, in a summary of these national reports, states that "arts educators were pleased to note that most of the reports that were based on research and informed reflection supported the arts."[10] In a helpful discussion on historical foundations of music education, Mark offers the following conclusion about change and the music education profession: "Almost everything new that has happened from the 1970s to the 1990s has been the result of social issues that originated outside of the music education profession. The issues include the national standards and goals, professional certification of music educators, muticulturalism, children-at-risk, practical application of the subject in the real-life world of society, assessment, technology, and decentralization and privatization of schools."[11] Clearly our professional "homework" is spelled out.

School Expectations

As of this writing, our educational system has roughly 50 million students, 2.6 million teachers, and more the 15,000 school districts.[12] Given the size of our educational system, the assumption that we could get everyone to agree on any aspect of the entire system is probably wishful thinking. Many people, however, will agree that schools are "different" today than they used to be—a time-worn cliché. Part of this perceived difference may be in expectations for schools. According to one source, public schools in America today are expected to:

> Teach good nutrition habits; train students in pulmonary-coronary resuscitation; give specialized instruction for the hard of hearing, the blind, and the neurologically impaired; treat the emotionally impaired; train the mentally retarded; teach the gifted; do eye test-

ing; give inoculations; teach first aid procedures; provide pregnancy counseling; assist in disease prevention; inculcate morals, ethics, and values; stress information about drug, alcohol, and tobacco abuse; help students develop political know-how; develop civic responsibility; provide sex education; maintain birth information and age certification data; provide instruction in good health care; teach driver training; provide civil rights and racial tolerance; foster integration; teach the principles of free enterprise; assist in career planning; provide career information; detect and report child abuse; teach telephone manners and etiquette; eradicate head lice, scabies, and other parasites and diseases; assist in charity fund-raising; provide vocational training; build economic awareness; serve hot lunches and breakfasts; dispense surplus milk; do job placement; stress bicycle safety and pedestrian safety; promote physical fitness; assist bilingual language development; counsel delinquents; foster metric education; provide transportation; teach consumer education; counsel students with problems; follow due process procedures; protect student privacy; teach humanness and individual responsibility; eliminate sex discrimination; develop an appreciation of other people and other cultures; promote the uses of information; develop the ability to reason; build patriotism and loyalty to the ideals of democracy; promote an understanding of the heritage of our country; build respect for the worth and dignity of the individual; develop skills for entry into a specific field; teach management of money, property, and resources; develop curiosity and thirst for learning; develop skills in the use of leisure time; teach pride in work; build a feeling of self-worth or self-respect; avoid religion; and teach Reading, Writing, and Arithmetic.[13]

The above school expectations are not presented as a definitive list, or intended to be universal. They are presented as food for thought about the role of schools in our contemporary society. Some of the language could probably be adjusted to more accurately reflect current school situations. Selected ideas could probably be added, others deleted. Additionally, even the most conservative "core" curriculum would hopefully include additional academic subjects. Nonetheless, public expectations for schools—both academic and social—are presenting challenges for all teachers, music teachers included.

Student Expectations

Fifty million students? Incredible! One of the reported "changes" that has taken place in schools in the past two decades is "the shift in the relative proportion of engaged and disengaged students."[14] So ends the first chapter of

Beyond the Classroom, a 1996 publication by Laurence Steinberg. Steinberg and his colleagues spent ten years systematically studying more than 20,000 teenagers—high school students—and their families in nine different American communities. The primary goal of the research was to describe "the ways in which parents, peers, and communities influence students' commitment to school."[15] The term "engagement" as used in their studies refers to how "connected"—interested, committed—students are to what is going in the classroom. Major findings of these studies suggested that:

- An extremely high percentage of students do not take school seriously.
- Student time out of school seldom reinforces what is learned in class.
- Many students "demean" academic success.
- Parents are just as "disengaged" from school as their children.[16]

Steinberg and his colleagues suggest that high school teachers today are faced with a much greater percentage of students who have "checked out" than did teachers twenty years ago.[17] What students "bring" to the contemporary school experience may, in many cases, be "new."

Challenges seem to come in many forms for music teachers at all levels. There is nothing new about that idea. Welcome to the world of school music. What may be new—information overload, school reform initiatives, and different expectations for schools and from students—will ultimately result in new expectations from school music teachers. What an incredible time to teach music!

Teaching Students about Music

During the past year, I have had the opportunity to interact with music teachers and music students from several states in a number of formal and informal settings. In every case, I have learned a great deal from these special folks. Some of the most important ideas have come at unexpected times. Recently, sitting on a bus in Missouri following a day of adjudication, I overheard one of my favorite colleagues discussing what she had heard during the day. The comments were "typical" until I heard her say, "We don't just teach music, we teach students—real live people—about music through performance." Teaching students about music through performance. The words had a familiar sound with an important focus: *students*.

Can we teach students about music through performance in band? The answer is *yes!* We can teach students about music through performance in band. We have done it. We have seen it done. Some of the resources that could be used to teach music through performance in band are included in this book series.

How can we teach students about music through performance in band?

There are probably as many "techniques" as there are music teachers reading this chapter. The "how" of teaching is one of the most individual and enjoyable parts of the teaching/learning process.

Throughout the first part of this chapter, the importance of awareness, understanding, and response (application) was presented as one "paradigm" for managing information. These ideas may also apply to the teaching/learning process in music. Bennett Reimer offers the following example: "In music, a person able to 1) notice the common features of the sounds of Beethoven's music, 2) give the proper name to that noticing ('that's Beethoven'), and 3) do so regularly whenever a piece of Beethoven is played can be assumed to have the concept of 'Beethovenness.' And so on for all concepts no matter how simple or complex."[18] Teaching for musical "understanding"—the "big ideas," the concepts, the essence of music—*may* involve teaching for student awareness of any musical idea (skill or knowledge), some type of understanding of the idea, and opportunities for students to apply the information learned in similar situations.[19]

Band directors must teach for musical understanding and still produce acceptable performances. "If the band does not sound good, the band does not sound good."[20] However, Robert Garofalo cautions that "performing group participation has little effect on musical behavior other than the acquisition of performance skills, unless there is a planned effort by the teacher to enrich the performing experience with additional kinds of musical understanding."[21] Teaching for musical understanding must become a part of a band director's daily rehearsal process.

The first book in this series suggests that teaching for musical understanding in band requires band director desire, planning, and resources. While none of these ideas is "new," each idea is important. Each idea is also personal. Reviewing the nine units included with each composition in the Teacher Resource Guides in this series reveals a wealth of quality literature and information available at all levels (more homework of a different kind). This is a very small part of what is out there. A key question that was a part of an earlier chapter continues to drive both the music selection and the daily rehearsal process for band directors: "What is it that I want my students to learn and remember from their rehearsal and performance experience in band?" No doubt most band directors already have the answer to this question. Armed with the answer, band directors *may* choose to incorporate *some* or *all* of the following information into their *regular rehearsals*: information about the composer (Unit 1); information about the composition and its place in history (Units 2 and 3); technical and stylistic considerations (Units 4 and 5); information about how various elements work (Unit 6); and, ideas about the form and structure of the musical selection (Unit 7). Band directors may choose to use Units 8 and 9 for additional study, incorporating this information into their regular teaching. The material contained in each unit is a sug-

gested "point of departure," designed to serve as a resource for teaching information about music that might lead to increased musical understanding.

In deciding how much information to include during rehearsals, each band director must carefully consider his or her specific teaching situation. Starting in your teaching where the students "are" in their musical understanding, and taking them, over the time that you have, to where you want them to be would be one "plan of attack." For example, if band students have little or no idea of what "form" is, a place to start would be to teach during rehearsal for awareness of the idea of form, a "gentle" understanding of what form or the form is, and then provide additional opportunities for students to see that other musical selections also have form.

An important part of teaching students about music through performance is to use performance—the music making—as a central part of your teaching for understanding. The goal is to integrate musical skills and musical knowledge—product and process—during each rehearsal.

A Next Step

Will it really make any difference to the students if we teach them about music through performance in band? The "answer" to this question is a bit more tentative. It should make a difference. But it should make a difference not just because we want it to make a difference or because we think that it should make a difference. Additional research designed to systematically investigate the complex issues involved in the teaching/learning process in group performance settings seems warranted. "We'd like to break down the old model where, historically, people at the university are expected to do research and publish so the university is the producer of knowledge, and the school-based people are the consumers of knowledge. We'd like to break that down so we are studying together."[22] What an incredible and challenging time to be teaching music!

Notes

1 John Naisbitt, *Megatrends* (New York: Warner Books, 1982), 17.

2 John Naisbitt and Particia Aburdene, *Megatrends 2000* (New York: William Morrow and Company, 1990), 12.

3 Naisbitt, *Megatrends*, xxxvi.

4 Richard Miles and Larry Blocher, *Block Scheduling: Implications for Music Education* (Springfield, IL: Focus on Excellence, 1996), 3.

5 Chris Pipho, "Fix It or Reinvent It," *Phi Delta Kappan* 78 (November 1996): 188.

6 Anne Lewis, "Staying with the Standards Movement," *Phi Delta Kappan* 78 (March 1997): 487.

7 Pauline Gooch, "The News in Chains," *Phi Delta Kappan* 78 (September 1996): 4.

8 David Berliner and Bruce Biddle, *The Manufactured Crisis* (Reading, MA: Addison Wesley Publishing, 1995), 3.

9 Pipho, "Fix It or Reinvent It," 462.

10 Michael Mark, *Contemporary Music Education* (New York: Schirmer Books, 1996), 23.

11 Ibid., 25.

12 Pipho, "Fix It or Reinvent It," 189.

13 "The Litany," Anonymous.

14 Laurence Steinberg, *Beyond the Classroom* (New York: Simon & Schuster, 1996), 28.

15 Ibid., 12.

16 Ibid., 18-19.

17 Ibid., 28.

18 Bennett Reimer, *A Philosophy of Music Education* (Englewood Cliffs, NJ: Prentice Hall, 1989), 83.

19 Larry Blocher, Richard Greenwood, and Bentley Shellahamer, "Teaching Behaviors Exhibited by Middle School and High School Band Directors in the Rehearsal Setting," *Journal of Research in Music Education* (in press).

20 Thomas Goolsby, "Verbal Instruction in Instrumental Rehearsals: A Comparison of Three Career Levels and Preservice Teachers," *Journal of Research in Music Education* 45 (Spring, 1997): 36.

21 Charles Benner, "Teaching Performing Groups: From Research to the Music Classroom," in Robert Garofalo, *Blueprint for Band* (Ft. Lauderdale, FL: Meredith Music Publications, 1976), vii.

22 *Dayton Educator* 1 (Spring, 1997): 11.

CHAPTER 2

The Rehearsal—Mastery of Music Fundamentals

Edward S. Lisk

*"The notes of a composition do not exist in isolation;
the movement of harmonic progressions, melodic contours
and expressive colorations provide each interval with a specific
sense of belonging and/or direction."*

··· Pablo Casals ···

Introduction

As the world of education continues its transformation, our teaching responsibilities are expanding into many more areas of music making with very limited schedule time. State and national music standards suggest that students be able to sing, play an instrument, improvise melodies, compose, read and notate music, listen and analyze musical compositions, and evaluate and understand music in relation to history and culture. This is no small undertaking and requires considerable planning, especially when redesigning curriculum, instruction, and rehearsal content.

With so many new expectations, what will the instructional priorities be for a "successful" band program? The answer to such a question can lead us in many directions. Most important, a successful program represents quality wind literature that is supported through an efficient, sequential instructional program emphasizing music performance fundamentals.

A band program must have intrinsic meaning for student participants. For "meaning" to occur beyond the usual activities of a program (performance, travel, etc.), students must be mentally active and involved in a musical task that results in a "product" created through their application of knowledge and developed skill (skill level determined by age). Larry Blocher, Richard Greenwood, and Bentley Shellahamer presented a "Triad of Meaning" in their 1993 research paper, *Teaching Behaviors Exhibited by Middle School and High School Band Directors in a Rehearsal Setting*. The Triad of Meaning states: 1) the student must become an independent performer and understand concepts; 2)

the student should have musical experiences that allows him/her to become a consumer of quality music; and 3) the instructional experience must also provide the student with performance skills they will need to be successful in the next performance. The Triad of Meaning identifies the outcome of a successful band program: *musical literacy and musical independence*.

Early in my career, I found myself in search of a "special" method book that would surely turn my students into master musicians and solve all musical problems. Moreover, this elusive publication would certainly allow my students to perform all the wonderful wind masterworks, without restrictions or part modifications! I quickly discovered it was not the method book that held the answers nor would it develop superb musicians. It was the instrumental teacher's rehearsal planning and prescriptive strategies based upon keen listening skills, knowledge, experience, and efficient teaching techniques that would lead to successful learning.

It is extremely important when developing rehearsal warm-up plans that all music and performance fundamentals be *connected and integrated*. The rehearsal warm-up process can easily become disconnected or disjointed from any musical meaning when not connected to the literature being prepared. Moreover, performance fundamentals should originate from a single musical source, or seed. When designing an instructional or rehearsal program through a *connected*, *integrated* approach (originating from a single source) and *linked* to the literature in preparation, meaning occurs and provides opportunities for success without any imposed instructional restrictions.

The type and quality of band literature determines *what* will be accomplished within a given rehearsal time. Too often, performance fundamentals (dynamics, articulation, etc.) are re-taught with every composition. Be careful not to create a rehearsal situation supported through mindless repetition. Mindless repetition plays havoc with programs as it is easy to become consumed with the next performance, especially with limited rehearsal time. It is important to look beyond immediate needs and become sensitive to the number of times particular skills are re-taught throughout the year. Remember, each instance of re-teaching can imply a weakness within the instructional process and eventually inhibit student potential.

Sequential Development of Technique

Earlier I spoke about performance fundamentals originating from a single musical source. I consider this single and most important musical source or seed to be SCALES! Scales provide the student musician with an all-inclusive foundation for becoming a literate performer in any type of instrumental ensemble. Scale knowledge expands the musical options for technique development, melodic and harmonic understanding, intonation, and improvisation. Along with technique, scales develop the *ear* to hear key tonality

and maintain a pitch center within a particular key. This becomes quite noticeable when a solo line is played by a student *conditioned* to tuning only one note. *Listening and tuning* must be conditioned and centered around keys and harmonic tonality.

Composers write music in *all* keys and have no restrictions with chord content or harmonic direction. Key signatures are merely a guide and do not indicate the number of keys or scales being used in a particular composition. Accidentals indicate a new key or harmonic structure not indicated by key signature. Students must be trained to respond to such key changes rather than the typical response of "You missed the C-sharp." This is a "bit and piece" approach with no relevance to key or harmonic progression. Rather than stating the C-sharp was missed, try a statement that has connected meaning and scale relevance, such as, "You are in the key of D major or D minor." Place importance upon scale/key knowledge and not an isolated accidental.

Introducing the Grand Master Scale

When establishing scales as the source or foundation for all performance fundamentals and warm-ups, it is necessary to move away from playing a single scale as we have had students do for so many years. Furthermore, move away from using the performance of scales for things having nothing to do with music making, such as seat assignments. These conditions disassociate scales from any meaningful connected value with literature, sight reading, intonation, or other important performance expectations. Too often, when using scales for other extrinsic non-musical needs, a "negative halo" is created around scale performance, thus hindering the potential of student musicians (much like trying to read a book without knowing the ABC's).

Knowledge and performance of *all* scales (major, minor, and chromatic scales) should be a high priority for all student musicians (and directors). This may require breaking some old scale habits. When eliminating the single scale performance approach, students play the twelve major scales in a predesignated rhythm pattern as a single exercise. I coined the term "Grand Master Scale" for such an extended scale. The Grand Master Scale makes important connections with *all* literature demands by playing in *all* keys and not just a limited few. This avenue leads to the mastery of technical skills.

The Grand Master Scale is built upon a row of pitches based upon the interval of the fourth (C-F-Bb-Eb-Ab-Db[C#]-Gb[F#]-Cb[B]-E-A-D-G-C). To clarify any misunderstandings, the traditional circle of fifths moves in a clockwise direction starting with C and continues with pitches based upon the interval of the fifth. The Grand Master Scale moves with the interval of the fourth (C to F, etc.), although if playing C down to F, we have the interval of the fifth. At this time it is not important for the student to be concerned whether they play *up* the interval of the fourth or *down* the interval of the fifth.

14

Grand Master Scale Row of Pitches (Fourths)

Flats →

$$\overset{5}{\underset{4}{D^b}} - \overset{6}{\underset{5}{G^b}} - \overset{7}{\underset{6}{C^b}} \overset{(Fb)}{(7)}$$

$$\overset{1}{\underset{}{C}} - \overset{2}{\underset{}{F}} - \overset{3}{\underset{}{B^b}} - \overset{4}{\underset{}{E^b}} - \overset{}{\underset{}{A^b}}$$ or   or   or $$\overset{4}{\underset{4}{E}} - \overset{3}{\underset{}{A}} - \overset{2}{\underset{}{D}} - \overset{1}{\underset{}{G}}$$ ← Sharps

(B#) (E#) (A#) (D#) (G#)
7   6   5   4   3

$$\overset{7}{\underset{2}{C^\#}} - \overset{6}{\underset{1}{F^\#}} - \overset{5}{\underset{}{B}}$$

The top number indicates the number of flats or sharps in that particular scale.
The bottom number indicates the correct order of flats or sharps.

To acquaint the students with the row of pitches, simply have them play the letter pitches (whole notes) starting with their assigned (transposed) pitch and continue through the row as outlined below. Students should be instructed to play mid-range notes.

B-flat Instruments: C-F-B♭-E♭-A♭-D♭(C♯)-G♭(F♯)-C♭(B)-E-A-D-G-C
E-flat Instruments: G-C-F-B♭-E♭-A♭-D♭(C♯)-G♭(F♯)-C♭(B)-E-A-D-G
F Instruments: F-B♭-E♭-A♭-D♭(C♯)-G♭(F♯)-C♭(B)-E-A-D-G-C-F
C Instruments: B♭-E♭-A♭-D♭(C♯)-G♭(F♯)-C♭(B)-E-A-D-G-C-F-B♭

After playing through the row of pitches using various note durations, rhythm patterns, dynamics, and/or chord qualities, proceed to playing the Grand Master Scale (see section on *Playing Scales without Notation*).

Grand Master Scale

Note the asterisk* on the last note of each scale. It is at this point the student prepares by *thinking* of the next scale's key signature. This is a departure from the single conventional performance of scales. This mental preparation *conditions the thought process* to move in tempo to the next key rather than coming to rest and becoming inactive on the last note of a scale. Students quickly become conditioned to move *thoughtfully* through all keys. This introductory scale performance experience is vital for developing improvisatory skills.

The rhythm pattern, tempo, and variation determines the amount of time consumed (forty-five seconds to two-plus minutes) during the rehearsal warm-up.

Understanding Chord Progressions

The Grand Master Scale Row of Pitches provides instructional opportunities emphasizing important learning connections. Expanding this row of pitches to chord progressions becomes very simple for students to understand. Any pitch in the row can be considered a dominant chord resolving to the next pitch that is treated as a major chord (e.g., C7 resolves to F or V7 to I).

Taken to the next level of harmonic understanding, any pitch can be considered a II minor chord, moving to the next pitch in the row as a V7, and resolving the V7 to the next pitch as a major chord (Cm—F7—BbM). This process provides the basic chord progression of II—V7—I that is easily understood and connected to scales or notes used in the chord progression (extremely valuable when teaching improvisation).

I found early in my career that when my band students were taught to play the Grand Master Scale, my program exploded with musical performance skills and knowledge. My daily warm-up included some form of scale, chord, or rhythm pattern (connected to the literature to be rehearsed) played through the row of pitches (Circle of Fourths). This daily musical occurrence continually reinforced technique development, harmonic understanding, and listening. I quickly learned that the Grand Master Scale was the single most important connecting link for all music making (performance and theory). No longer was it necessary to select literature based upon individual or section weaknesses.

The Octave of Reason

To further establish your reliance upon the Grand Master Scale as the doorway for sequential performance development, consider my "Octave of Reason" for making the Grand Master Scale and its unlimited variations a part of your daily rehearsal warm-up process.

The Grand Master Scale also provides a logical, sequential approach for

all forms of minor scales and chromatics. The graphic illustration makes the many important musical connections surrounding the Grand Master Scale.

The Grand Master Scale will:

1. *Establish new musical value and worth for scale knowledge.*

Scales make music. It is for this reason alone that students should experience the value of scale knowledge. Notice that I stated "experience" rather than using the word "teach." Frequently when scales or other music fundamentals are taught, students fail to make connections to the larger whole of music making and become isolated from a reason for learning. When experiencing scales in the larger context of music making, an awareness and value for such knowledge receives greater importance for application. Scales make music—any three or more notes in a diatonic pattern imply a key. A considerable amount of repetition will be necessary if such diatonic patterns are not recognized or taught when reading musical notation (see #4 below).

Scales should only be related to music making and not chair placement or other non-music needs.

2. Establish a spontaneous reaction to all keys.
The ability to spontaneously relate musical notation to keys, chords, intervals, and rhythm patterns is a priority for sight reading success. Responding to the letters in the row of pitches creates an expanded awareness for a pitch or combination of pitches. The mind creates connections as it thinks and processes the letter name as being a part of something such as a note within a scale, melody, chord quality, or chord progression; these are all important relationships when considering and exercising musical decisions. The warm-up for rehearsal improves considerably when students are able to exercise their "thought/listening" process without musical notation (presented later in this chapter).

3. Significantly improve technique throughout all sections of the band.
Performance restrictions (musical and literature) are placed upon band programs when technical skills are not consistently developed within all sections of the band. Literature standards are often compromised to overcome such weaknesses. Literature selected to accommodate a strong trumpet section and weak low brass section would be a typical example of such a compromise. Rhythm, articulation, and tempo weaknesses are eliminated by playing Grand Master Scale variations daily in the warm-up process.

4. Eliminate mindless repetition of technical passages.
Any diatonic passage (three or more notes) implies a scale or key. There are no musical reasons to require students to practice diatonic passages found in solo or ensemble literature without "connecting" the passage with a scale. Unfortunately, for too many years students have played scales with limited variations (tonic to tonic in a standard rhythm pattern) and fail to recognize other scale patterns in solo or ensemble literature. Students who play scales through such a memorized habit are usually unable to apply such knowledge to literature if the scale passage does not start on the keynote with the practiced rhythm pattern. This creates a serious void in a student's musical skill development (forming a scale habit without application forms no connected meaning).

5. Provide a meaningful approach to sight reading.
Sight reading is a visual reaction to notation coupled with the spontaneous association of something previously learned with error-free application (hopefully). Or, it is the result of teaching techniques that provide students the opportunity to apply their prior knowledge

and learned skill successfully (intelligent performance).

Scanning a piece of music and associating various technical passages through "scale fragments" or keys eliminates a note-by-note reading process. A note-by-note reading process often produces note errors and poor rhythmic response. The eye scans and only transmits the symbol to the brain for interpretation and timed response. Scale patterns and interval recognition are important for accuracy and reading comprehension.

The application of scale knowledge with sight reading is much like having the necessary vocabulary for reading prose. Scale knowledge is part of our performance vocabulary for musical reading comprehension. Playing a lot of music does not increase reading ability. It is the analysis process coupled with the application of learned musical skills that provides successful reading.

Instruct your students, when scanning for sight reading, to identify any technical diatonic passage (three or more notes) as scale fragments implying a scale or key which they have previously learned.

6. *Provide a foundation for harmonic understanding, analysis of band literature, and a foundation for improvisation.*

The state and national music standards addressing improvisation, composing, notating music, and the analysis of music extend teaching responsibilities and rehearsal content. The Grand Master Scale serves this purpose. It is framed in the whole of musical performance through scale, key, and harmonic relationships. Its variations and combinations allow student musicians to easily understand (hear) chord qualities and progressions, intervals, and unique composer voicings (literature analysis), as well as being an intelligent approach to classical and jazz improvisation (creativity and musical imagination).

7. *Provide a foundation for solo and ensemble intonation (playing in a "pitch center").*

Scales and playing an instrument in tune are inseparable. Playing the Grand Master Scale is critical in establishing the in-tuneness of a melodic line: a tonality, feeling/hearing, an in-tuneness for a particular key or its relationship to other keys. A soloist without the skill of scale performance has difficulty playing in tune with a band or any other form of accompaniment. The intonation problems encountered when trying to play in tune are a result of listening to notes out of key context or *harmonic relationship*. In-tune playing is a result of

pitch and melodic line being a part of a given key tonality or harmonic support. Students must be taught to realize that intonation is more than the tuning note.

8. Provide access to a full range of band literature.
It is no longer necessary to compromise quality literature due to students' inability to play in various keys or scales. Too often music publications are limited to the keys of F, B-flat, and E-flat. Unfortunately such limitations restrict a program's musical development. The Grand Master Scale and its variations provide the necessary technical skill to play all the selected literature found in this publication and Volume 1. Such a "musical diet" provides the important "vitamins" that assure the young musician a long, healthy, vibrant musical life.

Learning Process for Scale Mastery

The suggested learning process for scale mastery is based upon a natural learning process (similar to the way we learn to speak, read, and write). Many early scale performance problems are eliminated when this learning process is introduced as a part of the first scale exercise in the beginning method book.

Part 1: Introducing the Process

Most students are familiar with the musical alphabet. Before applying this procedure with scales, the student (or students) recites the musical alphabet in the following manner:

1. Ascending (in a tempo of quarter=60)
   A-B-C-D-E-F-G-A-B-C-D-etc.
2. Ascending (forward) and descending (backward)
   A-B-C-D-E-F-G-A-G-F-E-D-C-B-A
3. Start on a scale pitch and recite without accidentals
   D-E-F-G-A-B-C-D-C-B-A-G-F-E-D
4. Recite with scale accidentals such as two sharps for D major.
   D-E-F♯-G-A-B-C♯-D-C♯-B-A-G-F♯-E-D

Hesitation usually occurs when reciting the letters in reverse. This is a temporary situation because traditionally, students have been trained to play scales by memorizing musical notation without application of the musical alphabet. This approach often neglects the fundamental understanding of note names and their order to achieve scale mastery.

The instructional process establishes an important *mind/body connection* that mentally processes the "signal" (note name and order) to produce error-free scale performance immediately and without mindless repetition. It is important to maintain a steady tempo (quarter=60) when reciting scales and accidentals.

Once students are comfortable with this process, apply the outlined procedures below with instruments.

Part 2: Applying the Process with Instrument

Scale Mastery
Instructional Process

Process...Awareness Level

1. **Recite Pitch Names*** ————————————➤ **Mental**
      (ascend & descend)

2. **Recite & Dictate to Fingers** ————————➤ **Mental - Physical**
      (fingering instrument)

3. **Mental Recitation & Play Instrument** ————➤ **Mental - Physical - Auditory**
      (silent/internal recitation
      while playing instrument)

4. **Mental Recitation - Play Instrument - Read Notation** ———➤ **Mental - Physical**
      (silent/internal recitation while playing instrument   **Auditory - Visual**
      and reading musical notation)

* It is important to maintain a steady tempo (quarter = 60) without hesitation or repeating letters.

Step 1 is the recitation process necessary in making a mental connection for intelligent *application of new knowledge*.

Step 2 employs the recitation process (intelligent application of knowledge) while dictating note accuracy to the fingers. This recitation and "telling the fingers what to do" establishes the important mind/body connection leading to error-free scale performance.

Step 3 expands the process to make an auditory connection. The mind silently recites to the fingers while playing the instrument to create an auditory connection that "hears" the scale error-free.

Step 4 is the final step for connecting the mind/fingers/ear to the written notation. This final event solidifies learning connections (meaning) for retention and recall with band literature.

This simple process is applied with all new scales. Within one school year, your entire band will be playing all scales without error.

Playing Scales without Notation

One of the most important performance priorities with the Grand Master Scale is having students play scales without written notation. This may cause concern or questions. Let me assure you such an uneasy reaction is natural. Most of the students' musical training (up to this point) has been from method books and solo and ensemble literature with *total reliance* upon notation. The departure from notation is part of the natural learning process (as children we didn't learn to read and write before we were able to speak). Playing scales without notation places an important *reliance upon the thought/listening* process (as outlined with instructional process for Scale Mastery) rather than a visual reaction to printed notes. This is not to say notation is not important. The purpose is to have ensemble members respond spontaneously to any key or scale. Before students are able to develop such spontaneity, the instructional program must recognize and provide rehearsal opportunities to exercise such performance skills. Without such learning opportunities, students are unable to realize their musical potential.

To create a comfortable, non-threatening situation, students play the *known scales* and, for any *unknown scale*, they sustain the keynote for the duration of that scale. This pattern is followed through the entire row of pitches. I've found when scales become a part of the daily warm-up process, students realize the priority for scales and quickly learn scales through the Scale Mastery Learning Process.

Grand Master Scale Variations

Examples of scale variations (adjust patterns to grade level):

1. Ascending—Descending

2. Ascending only

3. Descending only

4. Ascend the first and descend the next

5. Descend the first and ascend the next scale

6. Ascend scale and descend chromatic scale

7. Ascend chromatic scale and descend major scale

8. Mixed meter scale (7/8)

Scales are played with various articulation patterns from band literature being prepared.

Developing Articulation through Five-Note Scales

Articulation clarity and uniformity—in sections as well as in the ensemble—are best developed through five-note scale patterns. Playing the Grand Master Scale will exercise articulation patterns through *all* keys. The pattern should be adjusted (eighths or quarters) to accommodate grade level of band.

1. Slur

2. Slur 2, tongue 2

3. Tongue 2, slur 2

4. Slur 3, tongue 1

5. Tongue 1, slur 3

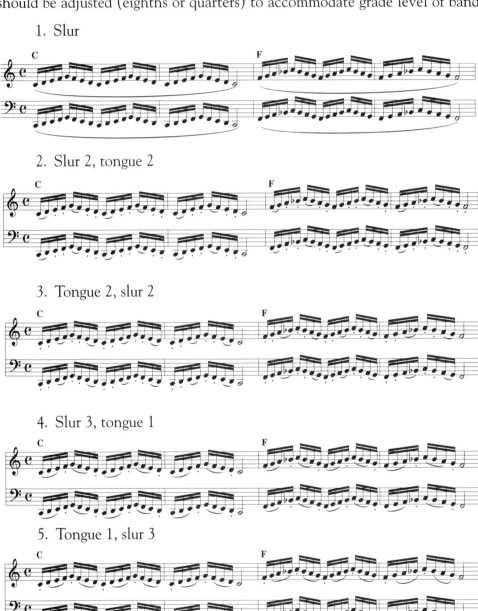

Warm-up exercises should also include other articulation patterns found in literature under preparation (connected learning).

Scales Played in Harmony

Scales may be performed in any type of harmonic interval by following the row of pitches. Instruments may be assigned starting pitches based upon any chord qualities or intervals (major, minor, etc.). This is a departure from the usual unison/octave playing and provides many new "sound colors" for scale performance. The new sound colors expand listening awareness and sensitivity, which eliminates many of the conventional monotonous approaches with scales.

The variations and possibilities are important for technique development in that they will always create a newness to something that perhaps became boring with other types of scale patterns.

Experiment with different intervals by using the grouping assignments found in Leonard Smith's *Treasury of Scales* (CPP/Belwin), W. Francis McBeth's *Effective Performance of Band Music* (Southern Music Company), and *The Creative Director Series* (Meredith Music Publications).

Suggested Grouping Assignments
for Middle and High School Bands

The Grouping Assignments provide a variety of approaches and sound colors for scale variations, rhythm patterns, chords, and other warm-up exercises. The groups are determined by the part a student plays in band. Adjust and balance grouping assignments relative to band size and instrumentation.

WOODWIND CHOIR

Group 1	Group 2	Group 3	Group 4
Piccolo	2nd Flute	3rd Clar.	Bass Clar.
E-flat Clar.	2nd Clar.	Alto Clar.	1st & 2nd Bassoon
1st Oboe	2nd Oboe		
1st Flute	2nd Alto Sax	Tenor Sax	Bari Sax
1st Clar.			
1st Alto Sax			

BRASS CHOIR

Group 1	Group 2	Group 3	Group 4
1st Cornet/Trpt.	2nd Cornet	3rd Cornet	Bari./Euphonium
1st Fr. Horn	2nd Fr. Horn	2nd Trumpet	Tuba
1st Trombone	2nd Trombone	3rd Trombone	
		3rd/4th Fr. Horn	String Bass

PERCUSSION

Group 1	Group 2	Group 3	Group 4
Vibraphone	Xylophone	Marimba	Timpani

Examples of Chord Voicing with Group Assignments

The instrument groups are assigned a starting pitch based upon a chord quality (major, minor, dominant, etc.) and played through the row of pitches (B-flat, E-flat, and F instruments start on transposed pitch). The process provides learning/listening opportunities for all types of chord qualities. Examples of major and dominant chord qualities are as follows:

Major Chords
  Group 1 = B-flat   **Group 2** = D   **Group 3** = F   **Group 4** = B-flat

Dominant Seventh Chords
  Group 1 = A-flat   **Group 2** = D   **Group 3** = F   **Group 4** = B-flat

The chord variations provide unlimited possibilities for rehearsal warm-up. You are encouraged to experiment with grouping assignments by applying the unique composer chord voicings found in selected literature.

Listening: Balance, Blend, and Intonation

Balance, blend, and intonation—high priorities for superior band programs. The simple three-step process for balance, blend, and intonation provides students an *integrated* learning experience when making decisions about tone and musical quality. They have the responsibility for determining the ensemble's tone quality. This eliminates a situation that often creates a passive student/player waiting to be told what adjustments to make.

The three-step process is a form of "silent questioning" students follow to determine the quality of sound they are producing. The director prompts the sequence of questions with the student making the final decision/adjustment. It is important to listen for the musical answer and not accept a verbal answer. The verbal answer is of little importance if the students are unable to demonstrate through playing what they are listening for in ensemble tone quality. A valuable learning experience is lost if students are not allowed to shape their musical decisions (correct or not) that determine the ensemble's tone quality.

The sequence is important when teaching ensemble listening. It is impossible to tune poor tone quality or an overblown pitch. The student must understand that balance (volume) and blend (tone quality) precede intonation.

Students' Responsibility for Balance, Blend, and Intonation

The student's silent questioning sequence is as follows:
"If you hear yourself...., one of three things is happening...."

1. To determine balance, the silent question is: If you hear yourself above all others in your section or band, you are overpowering or overblowing. Make an adjustment to volume by playing softer; lose your identity by making your tone become a part of the section and/or ensemble!

2. To determine blend, the silent question is: If you still hear yourself and you made the volume adjustment in #1, you are playing with poor tone quality. Adjust embouchure, breath support, or posture. Poor tone quality will not blend with your section or band; lose your identity by making your tone become a part of the section and/or ensemble!

3. To determine intonation, the silent question is: If you still hear yourself and you made the adjustments to balance and blend, you are playing out of tune. Adjust the length of your instrument.

The outlined process shifts the listening responsibilities for individual and ensemble musical quality away from the director and onto the students. It is the individual musician who creates the sound and must be held responsible for the tone quality (balance, blend, intonation) of the organization. The director only teaches the specifics of listening and then allows the student to exercise or apply their musical decisions.

Conclusion

I hope that perhaps some of these outlined procedures will contribute to the excellence of your band program. The musical priorities addressed the need for providing instructional opportunities that ultimately develop individuals who are musically literate and musically independent.

Throughout my career, I have tried to communicate the need to recognize an instrumental program as being a vital component to a student's educational experience, a unique learning experience which students cannot be without. We must look beyond entertainment or service and acknowledge the academic responsibilities of playing a musical instrument. "Performing in an instrumental ensemble requires an intricate combination of visual, intellectu-

al, physical, and auditory control coupled with a perceptive decision making process" (*The Intangibles of Musical Performance*, Meredith Music Publications).

When developing an effective curriculum for a superior instrumental program, its foundation must be built upon the masterworks of wind literature. Our professional responsibilities extend well beyond many of the superficial underpinnings often encountered when building an instrumental program. Instrumental music is a form of communicating meaning and feeling through the signs and symbols of musical notation. A successful band program provides students with opportunities to become *active participants* in this life-long learning experience through musical performance, communication, and appreciation. To be future consumers of wind literature, students first must experience the masterworks of wind literature. This is best accomplished through the wind literature being presented in this text and Volume 1.

Notes

The instructional techniques and musical examples found in this chapter are from The Creative Director Series *and used with permission from Meredith Music Publications, 170 N.E. 33rd St., Ft. Lauderdale, FL 33334.*

CHAPTER 3

Performing Music of Multicultural Diversity

Ray Cramer

Introduction

Not so many years ago, instrumental music educators probably felt if they performed marches, overtures, tone poems, suites, and an occasional solo with band accompaniment they were doing their part in contributing to a student's diversified education. In one sense they were, by providing music of variety and character. Please do not misunderstand me, this is still important today at any level of band participation and programming. How well I remember some of my early band experiences during the decade of the '50s, when the band would perform some of the "new" works by John Morrisey, Paul Yoder, Clifton Williams, Frank Erickson, and, of course, those really strange pieces by Persichetti, Gould, and Grainger. I had not yet even heard the Hindemith Symphony. Some band composers of that era would introduce multimovement works which carried titles aimed at representing music from different periods or countries and use rhythmic devices one would associate with other cultures.

My reason for relating these early band experiences is not to point a disapproving finger at the people entrusted to teaching and leading my early development in instrumental music. They were excellent teachers and conductors who inspired, motivated, and produced outstanding results in the small rural community of Knoxville, Illinois. In fact, I should mention the names of Don Zimmerman, my first trombone teacher and director, and Charles Knapp, my last high school teacher and director. Both of these gentlemen were excellent role models for all of us and brought great success to our small school during a time when most music programs were struggling to find identity and direction. Our fine band was exposed to the best literature available at the time. We were encouraged to strive for excellence in performance and challenged as people and musicians. During my high school education there were numerous opportunities to hear professional musicians especially

when they were invited to perform with our band. It was also an honor to be conducted by respected university directors and to hear concerts by such noted bands as the University of Illinois, University of Iowa, and Northwestern University. There were many other fine university bands during this period but it was just too difficult to travel to their campuses.

I point all of this out only to bring a strong message to conductors everywhere at every level. These same goals and opportunities exist in abundance today through videos, CDs, CD-ROM, and various computer programs which are easily obtained and affordable. However, we must never arrive at the point where we think, *only* these products will help our students achieve our desired goals. Personal interaction with professionals, attendance at live performances, inspired teaching, and energetic leadership will inevitably make the most positive impressions on young musicians. Teachers and conductors with vision and creativity will continue to produce effective programs and students who wish to continue in the footsteps of their mentors. However, there is a larger picture today which can have a dynamic impact on our programs. One of the means to ensure future growth and support of music education as we move into the twenty-first century is by exploring the challenges of performing music of multicultural diversity.

Communication

Information sharing is quick and easy today. I grew up on a farm with a crank telephone on the dining room wall and our phone number was two shorts and a long. It is rather amazing to me how quickly you can communicate via e-mail with a computer sitting on your desk. Even more astounding is the information available on almost any subject at the touch of a finger. The very concept of these two books, *Teaching Music through Performance in Band*, is to put information about compositions, composers, style, form, historical perspective, technical considerations, musical elements, and even suggested listening into the hands of conductors preparing these pieces for performance. How easy it becomes for conductors to incorporate this information into the daily rehearsal. Our whole responsibility as conductors is to *share* information with our students through gesture and verbal skills. You might think your students will not hold still for these lecture sessions. It is not intended for a conductor to share all of this information at one time, but rather to creatively bring these facts into the rehearsal procedure. It is astonishing just how much information is retained by eager students. They need to understand communication as a basic human need. It's just that we do it in different ways and need to teach this to our students so they embrace diversity instead of finding differences.

All of this serves as an introduction to a popular movement in education today which involves bringing diversity to programming and exposing our stu-

dents to the various aspects of world music. This concept is not possible with-out *your* sincere interest and vision in sharing music of multicultural diversi-ty. In a real sense, conductors have been engaged in this practice all along, but more recently the emphasis has been on carefully reproducing colors and styl-istic trends inherent to the country or culture being represented. As you may well suspect, this is not always easy, especially in terms of finding out just what is involved in securing instruments to accurately produce the desired sounds. However, if only in a few circumstances you can bring to your students and audiences these special sounds and styles, their concert experience will have been enhanced.

Symbolism

In music, just as in art and literature, interpretation is left up to the individual who is listening, looking, or reading. Creatures of the world are in a constant state of struggle for survival with each other for sustenance, lead-ership, and territorial domain. However, they do not struggle for things which *stand* for sustenance, leadership, or domain. In the arts, on the other hand, we constantly examine *symbols* which *represent* different things as individuals respond through aural and visual perceptions. From early civilization, symbols have caused great confusion in deciding just what they represent. By the very nature of the meaning, symbols are used or regarded as representing *something else*. One can understand why there has been, and will continue to be, great confusion over exactly what a pictograph meant when discovered on a cave wall. Admittedly, when I listen to some concerts where music I know well is being performed, I am confused by what I know is marked in the score and what I am hearing from the ensemble. In music, symbols are taken for grant-ed, but the crux of the musical process is obviously in the interpretation of these symbols by the conductor. A conductor's musical achievement rests solely on his or her realization of those symbols in manipulating sound. This is our primary function as a conductor: to control sound. Without this funda-mental process, the re-creation of the composer's intent and the stylistic trends representing the country or culture, cannot be successfully achieved.

Student Involvement

You may ask, "Just what benefit is there in attempting to bring various aspects of world music to my students?" All of us, from time to time, become involved in various kinds of performance pressures and a general "get-the-notes-learned" mentality. Is it all that important? Of course we want our bands to play correct notes, but the real answer to that question depends on your own personal attitude. An individual who is curious about discovering new things and places will usually be inclined to share this excitement with others.

Young people are tremendously inquisitive by nature. With proper guidance and motivation, new subjects, topics, and musical elements of different cultures can become quite an exciting project. One thought which immediately comes to mind is the preparation of a program where music and art can join in a presentation of one or more cultures in a single event. Art could be displayed throughout the lobby with appropriate information written about paintings or sculptures. Perhaps a student could be assigned to each display information about food, dance, clothing and housing of the culture it represents. A brief pre-concert lecture could be given by students or faculty explaining various aspects of the musical program to follow. Perhaps a video or slide presentation could accompany the music. Included in this would be specific examples of musical elements or sounds on which the audience could focus their attention. I can see a tremendous event where many areas of the school would be represented. This collaboration would result in a win/win situation for everyone involved.

How do we learn about other cultures without the opportunity of living there? Of course, it would be ideal if everyone could experience living in a different culture. Most of us must rely on the usual forms for education about a country or culture, namely through its literature, art, music, or by viewing video resources. Through these various media presentations, we have a fantastic opportunity to produce a very special event through our own gifts, talents, and research.

The Elements of Music

The widely accepted elements of music today are still rhythm, melody, harmony, and timbre. These elements are vividly described and discussed in the wonderful book by Aaron Copland, *What to Listen for in Music*. As one begins to explore the parameters of performing music from other cultures, these four basic elements of music must remain in the forefront of a conductor's preparation. The realization of the performance, as always, develops in the interpretation of the *symbols*.

In 1984 our Indiana University Symphonic Band traveled to Japan to perform at the ABA/JBA joint convention. As one would expect, we deemed it appropriate to include on our program numbers written by Japanese composers. Additionally, we invited two Japanese directors to guest conduct these works in concert. Needless to say, this proved to be highly educational for me and for the band. While the notes and technical demands of the compositions had been carefully prepared, it quickly became apparent there were other musical considerations which I would have known only by growing up in their culture.

Knowledge

One of the compositions was *Asuka* by Tensunosuke Kushida. This wonderful piece depicts a traditional ceremony which takes place in an ancient temple in Japan. The score called for a "bell tree" and "wood block" as special colors used in various sections of the music. In fact, they were scored in such a manner that they became focal points of the piece. As our guest conductor was rehearsing the number, after the place where these "color" instruments were being used, he immediately stopped the band and gave a very strange look towards the percussion section. It was obvious he was not pleased with the kinds of sounds our percussionists were produceing. The conductor must have anticipated this happening for he had carried an athletic bag to the rehearsal. He proceeded to unzip the bag and motioned for me to come forward. He then gave me a present which consisted of Japanese "wood blocks" that looked like giant claves. They were made of extremely hard wood and were approximately three inches wide, two inches thick, and twelve inches long. He next gave the percussion section a lesson on how to achieve the exact sound he was seeking, which was quite deep and piercing. Finally, I was given a pair of traditional Japanese "bell trees." These bell trees looked like miniature Christmas trees with a handle and tiny bells hung around the outside of the tree. Shaking them produced the most unusual jingle I've ever heard. These traditional Japanese instruments totally changed the nature of *Asuka*. Years later, when my wife and I lived in Japan for a time, we had several opportunities to hear these instruments as they were played in temple ceremonies. Perceiving the use and sound of these instruments, I realized how misinformed I was in my concept of performance practice. With proper research I could have attained the knowledge to achieve the interpretation the composer intended.

A similar instance happened a few years ago when a fine young composer on our Indiana University faculty, David Dzubay, wrote a piece for the Indiana University Wind Ensemble titled *Incantations*. This piece is also about a Japanese shrine ceremony in which different types of drums are used in the ritual. For our American premiere, because I did not have access to traditional Japanese drums, we used regular bass drums and tom-toms of various sizes to produce the multi-pitches required. Now, after having lived in Japan and observing the culture, I know these drums were not what would be used in a Japanese shrine ceremony. Unfortunately, our school did not have the drums necessary for use in the premiere. A year later when I returned to Japan to conduct the Musashino Academy of Music Wind Ensemble, we performed this work using traditional Japanese horizontal drums. These drums produced the kind of sound one would hear in visiting a shrine ceremony. When adding the Japanese drums I also asked the percussion section to employ the proper performance technique required in playing these instruments. To further

enhance the concert the percussionists were clad in the attire one would see in such a ceremony. With the utilization of the proper equipment, correct playing techniques, and traditional attire, this fine work took on a whole new expression.

During the 1995 MidWest Clinic, the Musashino Academy of Music Wind Ensemble performed *Methuselah II* which features the percussion section. This is quite an exciting number which can be performed on a wide variety of percussion instruments found in any part of the world. However, this performance was unique because it used traditional Japanese drums performed with established Japanese drumming techniques. The performers again wore traditional attire of the country and the performance brought about a spectacular response. The performance was overwhelming because it was beautifully performed *and* the students embodied the spirit, culture, and traditions of a rich heritage.

These kinds of experiences are possible for any group at any level, given the proper guidance and direction. You should choose material carefully and bring information to the students about the music and the style and culture from which it is derived. Is it possible to conclude that expression is a basic need, as is hunger, warmth, pain, love? Yes, it just comes in different forms. The ability of a student to appreciate the differences in expression will lead them to a life of tolerance, respect, and open-mindedness. The inclusion of music from other cultures and bringing attention to the beauty of the different forms and techniques brings our students closer to the complete acceptance of humanity.

Included in this publication are many pieces of multicultural diversity. I would like to point out several of these compositions in each grade level and encourage you to explore the cultural diversity. Since all are included in the "Teacher Resource Guides" I will not add any further information except to point out the national origin of the piece. Some are written by composers who are actually from the represented countries while other works are written to represent other styles and cultures.

GRADE TWO

Composition	Composer	Country
Sandy Bay March	Brian West	Australia
The New ANZACS	Brian Hogg	Australia
A Little French Suite	Pierre LaPlante	France
Old Scottish Melody	Charles Wiley	Scotland
Three on the Isle	Hugh M. Stuart	England
Korean Folk Song Medley	James Ployhar	Korea

GRADE THREE

Composition	Composer	Country
Fantasy on "Sakura, Sakura"	Ray Cramer	Japan
Retreat and Pumping Song	David Stanhope	Australia
Brazilian Folk Dance Suite	Arr. William E. Rhoads	South America
Renaissance Suite	Tielman Susato/Curnow	Germany
Rhosymedre	R. Vaughan Williams	Wales
An Irish Rhapsody	Clare Grundman	Ireland

GRADE FOUR

Composition	Composer	Country
Trail of Tears	James Barnes	Native American
Japanese Tune	Soichi Konagaya	Japan
Autumn Walk	Julian Work	African American
Variations on "Scarborough Fair"	Calvin Custer	England
Dreamcatcher	Walter Mays	Native American
Africa: Ceremony, Song, and Ritual	Robert W. Smith	African American

GRADE FIVE

Composition	Composer	Country
Four Scottish Dances	Malcolm Arnold/Paynter	Scotland
The Solitary Dancer	Warren Benson	America
Paris Sketches	Martin Ellerby	France
Ricarcare a 6	J. S. Bach/Fennell	Germany
Russian Christmas Music	Alfred Reed	Russia

GRADE SIX

Composition	Composer	Country
Gazebo Dances	John Corigliano	America
Huntingtower Ballad	Ottorino Respighi	Scotland
Winds of Nagual	Michael Colgrass	Central America
Dance Movements	Philip Sparke	England
Dance of the New World	Dana Wilson	America
Circus Polka	Igor Stravinsky	America

Conclusion

There are many popular songs with titles expressing the joy one finds in the experience of music. For example, "Music, Music, Music," "Say It with Music," "Music Makes the World Go 'Round," "The Sound of Music," or "The Music Will Not End." Music is the *message*, the *medium*, and the *motivator*. The world becomes smaller and more intimate every day. Distant places and cultures are no longer something we see and read about only in the *National*

Geographic. The concert band, as we know it in the Western Hemisphere, has gained in popularity around the globe. The increased presence of bands has spawned a new generation of international composers who have given us compositions that add significantly to the rich depth of our literature. All too often wind literature has received undue criticism from those who point to orchestral literature as having such great depth of repertoire. There is no question a tremendous wealth of material exists for this medium. The orchestra has enjoyed a long and distinguished heritage.

Since 1950, however, the amount and quality of material written for the band is unsurpassed. The most respected composers from around the world have written and will continue to write for the band medium knowing full well their music will be performed and at a high level of execution. The music will be well received and will become immediately accessible to bands everywhere. Review a list of Pulitzer Prize winners in music over the past twenty-five years and note the number of composers who have written compositions for band. The wind band has made astounding advancements during the second half of the twentieth century. Band directors must carefully prepare in order to guide their ensembles into the twenty-first century. The key to success, as always, depends on the material we put before our bands. We must all believe everything we accomplish in our programs is through the music we choose. It is the music which brings goals into focus, is inspirational, and brings discipline and personal growth to our students.

In this publication you will find a list of one hundred compositions, divided into five grade levels, with twenty selections in each grade. This chapter contains a chart with six works from each level which represent different countries and/or cultures. There are many others on the list which also represent music of multicultural diversity. As you choose material which represents other cultures you must become well informed about sounds, timbres, stylistic trends, and the equipment needed to achieve authentic performances.

Music is a journey. The band is our vehicle and the literature we choose to place before our students is the fuel which enables us to travel from one adventure to another. Perhaps the most important rule for directors to follow is to choose only literature which you respect. We cannot expect our students to become excited about what they are performing if they sense we do not respect the music. Will Rogers once said, "Even if you're on the right track, you'll still get run over if you just sit there." The *music* will keep us and our programs moving in the right direction. As we approach the twenty-first century the possibilities for incorporating various aspects of world music into our programs will only add high-test fuel for greater power and efficiency in the operation of our instrumental programs. Above all else, have fun with your students as you share the excitement and enthusiasm for *making music through performance in band.*

CHAPTER 4

Teaching Music from a Historical Perspective

Richard Miles

What does it mean to be literate in the arts? Does it mean that students not only should receive the signal system we call the arts, but also be content in sending aesthetic signals too? Can one be literate with only the capacity to appreciate the arts, and not the ability to communicate meaningfully with others?

Children not only need to know the isolated facts; they need to see connections that bridge the disciplines and discover how ideas are connected. Without a comprehension of larger patterns, we prepare our students not for wisdom but for a game of Trivial Pursuit.[1]

··· Ernest L. Boyer ···

Introduction

The purpose of this chapter is to provide information on the teaching of music literature from a historical perspective. Making connections to other disciplines and cultures through a historical perspective can lead to deeper valuing, understanding, and fulfillment in music making. Therefore, by emphasizing these elements a greater musical literacy, accountability, and alignment with current educational direction can be achieved.

This chapter identifies the need for a strong justification for "academic" standing in the school curriculum for band classes, provides information about the *National Standards for Art Education,*[2] encourages a comprehensive and cyclic approach in the teaching of music through literature and performance, and provides resources to enable the teaching of a historical perspective with the music literature being rehearsed and performed. The historical resources include an outline of the development of Western music by period, and a comparative historical chronology of representative people, and events in history, the arts, and daily life.

The "Academic" Label

Academic accountability is considered by many to be the main thrust of today's education. Teachers are constantly searching for the best and most effective delivery techniques; for authentic assessment with measurable achievement; and ultimately, for a way to convince parents, administrators, and politicians that students have gained in knowledge and have progressed toward higher national test scores. This emphasis on the "academic" leads educators to define what subjects should be taught during the school day and what qualifies as an appropriate academic subject. In addition, many educators are seeking to distinguish clearly between the "academic/curricular" subjects and roles for those areas that may be "co-curricular" and/or "extra-curricular."

The "academic" labeling becomes a most sensitive issue when financial concerns and/or a lack of sufficient time to teach current subjects arise in schools. When problems do occur, reductions are often necessary. Areas which *border* on being academic/curricular and/or those areas which may not be "essential" often end up as targets for reduction, removal from the regular school day offerings, and elimination.

The role of band as an academic music class in today's curriculum finds varying interpretations and definitions from curricular (only during school time) to entirely extra-curricular (all rehearsals and performances after the normal school day). Whether the role is curricular, co-curricular, or extra-curricular, participation in music should still be academic. This system of labeling necessitates a strong justification and basis for band to remain in the daily curriculum.

As an academic subject, band must be more than just teaching the correct notes, going on trips, gaining in social values, and having great fun. All are important and serve a vital role; however, *the teaching of musicianship through performance should be our "academic/curricular" goal.* Music instruction (band) in today's schools must also *be accountable and have clearly defined goals and objectives to justify consecutive semesters and years of study in the school curriculum.* We do that best by teaching about the music through the music while working to perform the music. Teaching with a historical perspective can assist in this development.

Guidelines for Academic Development
from the National Standards for Art Education

In 1992 the Consortium of National Arts Education Associations developed comprehensive guidelines to help define competence in instruction and academic experiences in the arts. These directives were presented in the publication *National Standards for Arts Education—What Every Young American Should Know and Be Able to Do in the Arts.*[3] By the time American students

complete secondary school, all should know and be able to do the following:

- They should be able to communicate at a basic level in the four arts disciplines: dance, music, theatre, and the visual arts. This includes knowledge and skills in the use of the basic vocabularies, materials, tools, techniques, and intellectual methods of each arts discipline.

- They should be able to communicate proficiently in at least one art form, including the ability to define and solve artistic problems with insight, reason, and technical proficiency.

- They should be able to develop and present basic analyses of works of art from structural, historical, and cultural perspectives, and from combinations of those perspectives. This includes the ability to understand and evaluate work in the various arts disciplines.

- They should have an informed acquaintance with exemplary works of art from a variety of cultures and historical periods, and a basic understanding of historical development in the arts disciplines, across the arts as a whole, and within cultures.

- They should be able to relate various types of arts knowledge and skills within and across the arts disciplines. This includes mixing and matching competencies and understandings in art-making, history, and culture, and analysis in any arts-related project.

  As a result of developing these capabilities, students can arrive at their own knowledge, beliefs, and values for making personal and artistic decisions. In other terms, they can arrive at a broad-based, well-grounded understanding of the nature, value, and meaning of the arts as a part of their own humanity.[4]

The following outlines the seven specific competencies and standards for those in music grades 9-12:

> Every course in music, including performance courses, should provide instruction in creating, performing, listening to, and analyzing music, in addition to focusing on its specific subject matter.

1. Content Standard: Singing, alone and with others, a varied repertoire of music.

2. Content Standard: Performing on instruments, alone and with others, a varied repertoire of music.

3. Content Standard: Improvising melodies, variations, and accompaniments.

4. Content Standard: Composing and arranging music within specified guidelines.

5. Content Standard: Reading and notating music.

6. Content Standard: Listening to, analyzing, and describing music.

7. Content Standard: Evaluating music and music performances.

8. Content Standard: Understanding relationships between music, the other arts, and disciplines outside the arts.

9. Content Standard: Understanding music in relation to history and culture.[5]

It is also important to note that in *Goals 2000, Educate America Act*,[6] public law 103-227 (March, 1994) acknowledged "core subjects" in the school curriculum. The arts are defined as a core subject, as important to our education as mathematics, English, and science.

Content Standards 8 and 9 of the National Standards make the point clear that it should be our goal and objective as comprehensive music teachers (band directors) to convey the relationship, in our teaching and performances (marching, concert, jazz, and other ensembles), to history, culture, and disciplines in and outside the arts.

Teaching Comprehensive Music: Developing a Curriculum

There are numerous curricular resources available. For a review of several curricular models based on literature selection, see Chapter 7, in Volume I of *Teaching Music through Performance in Band* (1996).[7] The "four-year hybrid cycle" (pages 54-56) presents one of the strongest literature and comprehensive music outlines to support a student's enrollment in band for eight consecutive semesters in high school. The teaching of music from a historical perspective is one of the major components.

Two other sources are highly recommended and will assist the teaching of comprehensive music and curriculum development in more detail. See Robert Garofalo's *Blueprint for Band* (1983)[8] and Joseph LaButa's *Teaching Musicianship in the High School Band* (revised 1997).[9]

Resources

The following section identifies resources that will help the student and

teacher make comparisons and discover relationships while studying the development of Western music. These resources provide basic information concerning major music periods with more details outlined from the Baroque era to the present along with listings of representative composers. Also presented are examples that reveal general characteristics, basic styles, and performance practices common to each period.

Historical information can be presented in a variety of ways. "Units of the Teacher Resource Guides" in Chapter 5, Volume I, *Teaching Music through Performance in Band* suggests historical information can be presented entirely at one time, integrated with other information, presented as an individual concept skill, or preferably, presented in one- to two-minute segments over an extended period while preparing the music for performance.

For an extensive review of the historical development of music and comparative historical chronology, readers should consult the following which are credited as the direct sources for all of the information included in the following sections:

Apel, Willi. *Harvard Dictionary of Music*. Cambridge, MA: The Belknap Press of Harvard University Press, 1972.

The ASBDA Curriculum Guide. Compiled by the American School Band Directors Association. Pittsburgh: Volkwein Bros., 1973.

Cyclopedia. Second Edition. Philadelphia, PA: Running Press Book Publishers, 1995.

Elledge, Chuck, Jane Yarbrough, and Bruce Person. *Music Theory and History Workbook*. San Diego, CA: Neil A. Kjos Music Company, 1993.

Fennell, Frederick. *Time and the Winds*. Kenosha, WI: Leblanc Educational Publications, Classroom and Studio Study Texts— Number P-81.

Gelpi, Lynn Ruth. "College Wind Band Programming: A Suggested Curriculum for Undergraduate Training." Diss., University of Northern Colorado, 1985.

Grout, Donald J. and Claude V. Palisca. *A History of Western Music*. Fifth ed. New York: W.W. Norton & Company, 1996.

Grun, Bernard. *The Timetables of History*. Third revised edition. New York: Simon & Schuster, 1991.

Hickok, Robert. *Exploring Music*. Fourth edition. Dubuque, IA: Wm. C. Brown Publishers, 1989.

Labuta, Joseph. *Teaching Musicianship in the High School Band*. Revised edition. Ft. Lauderdale, FL: Meredith Music Publications, 1997.

Machlis, Joseph. *The Enjoyment of Music*. New York: W.W. Norton & Company, 1963.

Miles, Richard, ed. *Teaching Music through Performance in Band*. Chicago: GIA Publications, Inc., 1997.

Moore, Douglas. *A Guide to Musical Styles*. New York: W.W. Norton & Company, 1962.

Morgan, Robert. *Twentieth-Century Music*. New York: W.W. Norton & Company, 1991.

Sadie, Stanley, ed. *The New Grove Dictionary of Music and Musicians*. Twenty vols. London: Macmillan, 1980.

Stolba, K Marie. *The Development of Western Music*. Dubuque, IA: William C. Brown Publishers, 1990.

Whitwell David. *A Concise History of the Wind Band*. Northridge, CA: WINDS, 1985.

Historical Outline

Antiquity (3000 B.C.-400 A.D.)

GENERAL CHARACTERISTICS

Egyptians were prominant in the development of music, especially for use in ceremonies. The harp, lyre, and lute families were the primary instruments. Greek influences included the study of sound by Pythagoras, who established mathematical (acoustical) descriptions of pitch, and Plato, who advocated the philosophy that music influenced personality and emotions. A scale system was developed based on the use of tetrachords. It was during this period that tones were given specific letter names.

The Romans were strongly influenced by Greek culture. Early Roman music served mostly for ceremonial, military, and social engagements and the early brass instruments were very important especially for these uses. The Roman music consisted of pure melodic lines which were based on simple rhythms.

Middle Ages (400 A.D.-1450)

GENERAL CHARACTERISTICS

The Middle Ages saw the development of more structure to the independent melodic line (monophony). Medieval music theory was still based on theory principles from the ancient times. Only a few fragments of Greek or

Roman music have been found from this entire period.

During the Middle Ages, the sacred music of the Catholic Church consisted primarily of vocal chants which were sung in unison and without accompaniment. The secular music was mostly Plainsong.

Counterpoint was developed which incorporated the use of several parts or melodies sounding at the same time (polyphony). Polyphonic forms of music included organum and the motet along with the use of counterpoint and canons. Secular music became more popular and was performed by musicians known as troubadours and trouvères in France and Minnesingers and Meistersingers in Germany.

Medieval instruments included the harp, vielle or fiedel, organistrum, psaltery, lute, flute, recorder, shawms, natural trumpet and horn, bagpipes, drums, and great organs in churches.

Renaissance Period (1450-1600)
GENERAL CHARACTERISTICS

During the Renaissance, there was a "reviving" of the human spirit and of the cultures of ancient Greece and Rome. Individuality became increasingly respected and revered. This movement, known as Humanism, reinfluenced the development of music.

The sound of the music of the Renaissance became more rich and full with clearer voicing. Rhythms moved in a steady and flowing manner. The rhythmic flow included basic meters with only agogic accents. Melodies were mostly modal with the harmony involving chords, sometimes found in first inversions. Homophonic texture began which involved both accompaniment to the melody with singers and/or instruments. Imitation was used often and included three to six polyphonic voices. Some singers (Meistersingers) incorporated dynamic contrasts using different numbers of voices. The architectural structure of vocal and instrumental music became more developed with the use of many forms such as the mass, motet, madrigal, chanson, frottola, lauda, toccata, concerto, canzona, ricercar, fantasia, ground variations, masque, and others.

The first attempts at music printing came shortly after the appearance of Gutenberg's Bible (c. 1455). The first book of music ever printed is a Gradual; the date (probably c. 1473) and the name of the printer are unknown. Petrucci adapted Gutenberg's process of printing and published music quickly became more available throughout Europe.

The primary focus during the Renaissance was music for the voice; however, instrumental music became more popular. Most instruments were built in sets or families of graduated sizes with soprano to bass voicing. The basic types of instrumental music included those derived from vocal compositions, dance music, variations, and freely composed and quasi-improvisatory works.

Instruments in use during the Renaissance included guitars, recorders,

flutes, shawms, cromornes, cornettos, natural trumpets, trombones, viols, organ, lutes, and percussion instruments (drums, bells, bell chimes, castanets, etc.). Many churches in Italy used one large organ and one small organ. New instruments included those in the violin family, large copper timpani, and the harpsichord and clavichord.

REPRESENTATIVE COMPOSERS
 Binchois, Gilles (1400-1460)
 Byrd, William (1543-1623)
 Cabezón, Antonio de (1510-1566)
 Dunstable, John (1390-1453)
 Du Fay, Guillaume (1400-1474)
 Frescobaldi, Girolamo (1583-1643)
 Gabrieli, Giovanni (1553-1612)
 Hassler, Hans Leo (1562-1612)
 Josquin des Prez (1440-1521)
 Lassus, Orlande de (1532-1594)
 Marenzio, Luca (1553-1599)
 Monteverdi, Claudio (1567-1643)
 Obrecht, Jacob (1450-1505)
 Ockeghem, Johannes (1410-1497)
 Palestrina, Giovanni Piegluigi da (1525-1594)
 Tallis, Thomas (1505-1585)
 Tavener, John (1490-1545)
 Tye, Christopher (1505-1572)
 Victoria, Thomás Luis de (1548-1611)
 Willaert, Adrian (1490-1562)

BAROQUE PERIOD (1600-1750)
GENERAL CHARACTERISTICS

 The Baroque Era was known as the continuo period by some music scholars. A continuo bass line was often used and included a harmony instrument with two performers (keyboard with cello or bassoon). Vocal music featured the use of two practices: old style Renaissance counterpoint in which the music dominated the text, and modern style in which the text was of prime importance. Church, chamber, and theater performing styles were dominant and instrumental music became more important. New purely instrumental forms evolved as well.

 Composers of vocal music attempted to musically portray the expressions or interpretation on the texts. The new music exhibited a polarity of florid treble and firm bass. Filler harmonies, not notated, were improvised as the accompanists realized the figured *basso continuo* line. Two types of rhythm pre-

vailed: the regular metrical rhythm vital to dance music and a flexible, unmetrical rhythm founded on speech. Music notational practices included the use of figured bass, barlines, meter, and key signatures. New printing methods were produced and by the end of the eighteenth century, rounded noteheads appeared.

The Baroque period was divided into three distinct developmental time frames: Early, Middle, and Late.

Early Baroque (1600-1650)

- In the early Baroque Period two attitudes toward music performance predominated:
  > *Prima Prattica* (the first practice)—the church conservative *Stile Antico*, the sober style which was a continuation of the Palestrinian style of overlaid voices; and the Progressive—chamber and or ornamented "Luxuriant Style."

  Vocal music still dominated. The madrigal text carried over, influencing expression of emotion within a single piece. The melody was harmonically supported and they created all kinds of intervals such as an augmented fourth. Dissonance was permitted when the harmony was stable. Motives would contrast with smooth, long lines and quick moving, spastic melodic lines. *"Parlando"* was used to enunciate a text of ornamentation of long notes.

- The harmony was diatonic. Chromaticism was used for emotion and expressions of the text. Harmonies were generated by the bass line (basso continuo, or thoroughbass). Chords above the root position bass were usually single chords. Harmony was non-functional; that is, not tending toward tonic.

- Text was declamatory and expressive with a strong, regular pulse. Rhythm was dance inspired.

- Texture of the music was two-part, a continuo bass and melodic line; trio texture was two upper melodic parts with bass (the middle part filled in, imitating the higher part through parallel thirds, sixths).

- Chamber duets were found in instrumental music.

- Chamber theater style was used.

- Forms of music included multi-section (*Ritornello*) variations (*ostinato*, strophic), and solo song (monody) with accompaniment.

- Dynamics were essentially loud and soft. Very few markings were present.

- Early keyboard styles were the canzona, ricercar, and toccata.

Middle Baroque (1650-1700)

- Text-dominated vocal music began to die out.

- Short, shifting sections began to expand into larger sections. "Parts" were all supported by the harmony of the time, and now relationships resulted between the chords.

- Definite styles and forms developed, which included aria types. Instrumental forms were the sonata, suite, and overture (which affected later instrumental form development). There were two overture types: Italian (three distinct sections) and French (two sections, each repeated).

- Rhythm began to stabilize and more stylized dance patterns resulted in sonatas, suites, and overtures.

Late Baroque (Early 1700-1750)

- Instrumental music began to overshadow vocal writing.

- Trumpets and timpani were placed at the top of instrumental scores; strings and continuo were added above the horn and flute.

- A continuo orchestration was developed.

- Range and technical abilities were expanded.

- More structure and tone color developed.

- Melodic lines began to expand in length; normal long, extended, continuous lines resulted; themes were incomplete (fugue subject ending), and repetition and sequence were common.

- Harmony: root movements by fifths were planned; moving bass line; chords changed quickly with IV, V, or vi chords changing frequently per measure which resulted in faster harmonic rhythm.

- Two kinds of fast harmonic rhythms were used: free improvisatory (preludes, toccata, or introductory sections), and patterns, repetitions, or recurring rhythmic patterns, mechanical rhythm.

- The texture was consistent throughout; "luxuriant" ornamented counterpoint.

- Musical forms were controlled by continuous expansion and were non-sectional; fugal-type development; binary form was the exception—rounded binary form prevailed (e.g., Bach Italian suites [partitas], and English and French suites); sonatas dominated ensemble music.

Baroque Instrumental Music

- There were four principal instrumental types: dance music or stylized dance music intended for listening; quasi-improvisatory pieces; variations; and contrapuntal works (ricercar and ensemble canzona types).

- Stylized instrumental dance music evolved into the suite; the basic format was allemande, courante, sarabande, gigue (with additional movements optional anywhere within the sequence).

- The fugue grew out of organ ricercar and the ensemble canzona eventually became the sonata da chiesa.

- Principal types of organ music were quasi-improvisatory pieces (usually named toccatas), the fugue, and the chorale prelude which included the chorale fantasia, chorale partita, and chorale prelude.

- Composers of organ works were Girolamo Frescobaldi and Bernardo Pasquini in Italy and Dietrich Buxtehude in Germany.

- There were three principal instrumental compositions for ensembles: the *sonata da chiesa* and related forms, the suite (*sonata da camera*) and related forms, and the concerto.

- Some sonatas were written for solo instrument with basso continuo, but most sonatas written during the last third of the seventeenth century were primarily trio sonatas; a few were written for unaccompanied solo violin.

- Construction of instruments in the violin family flourished (Amatis, Stradivarius, and Guarneri).

- Baroque instruments included the harpsichord, organ, pianoforte, violin, viola da gamba, cello, timpani, natural horn and natural trumpet, recorder, oboe, bassoon, transverse flute, trombone, and percussion.

REPRESENTATIVE COMPOSERS
    Bach, Johann Sebastian (1685-1750)
    Corelli, Arcangelo (1653-1713)
    Couperin, Francois (1688-1733)
    Frescobaldi, Girolamo (1583-1643)
    Froberger, Johann Jakob (1616-1667)
    Gabrieli, Giovanni (1553-1612)
    Handel, George Fredrick (1685-1759)
    Lully, Jean-Baptiste (1632-1687)
    Monteverdi, Claudio (1567-1643)
    Pachelbel, Johann (1653-1706)
    Purcell, Henry (1659-1695)
    Rameau, Jean-Philippe (1683-1764)
    Scarlatti, Domenico (1685-1757)
    Schütz, Heinrich (1585-1672)
    Telemann, Georg Philipp (1681-1767)
    Vivaldi, Antonio (1678-1741)

Classical Period (1750–1820)—The Age of Enlightenment
GENERAL CHARACTERISTICS

The Classical period, known as the Age of Enlightenment, brought about many changes in the style of music performance and the form of music construction. Unlike those works composed during the Baroque period, which frequently emphasized improvisational or ornamental techniques (figured bass, ornamentation, trills, etc.), compositions of the Classical period emphasized tuneful, simple, singable melodies, simple harmony, major and minor modes, strict formal structure, and contrasting dynamics. "Classical" music became more formal, light in texture, and considered by many to be more enjoyable. Instrumental music became more important. The following characterizes this development and provides additional information regarding the Classical period:

- A large portion of the music in this period was instrumental.

- The principle genres of instrumental music composed between c. 1770 through c. 1820 were the symphony, sonata, solo concerto, chamber music, and opera.

- The structural principal most often used for a movement was sonata form, or a variant thereof (sonata-rondo, sonata form used in a concerto, abridged sonata).

- The use of theme and variation form continued to develop in the Classical period.

- The Viennese Classical idiom, an important part in the development of this period, was a synthesis of *galant, empfindsamer,* and learned styles. In the 1770s this Viennese Classical style was firmly established, especially in the instrumental music of Haydn.

- The middle works of Haydn were characterized by clarity, balance, and restraint. The same traits were present in the late works of Mozart and the early works of Beethoven and Schubert.

- Haydn and Mozart developed the characteristic style of the string quartet, each composing sets of quartets.

- Mozart used a three-movement overall scheme for his piano concertos. The first movement utilized sonata form; the second movement of the piano concerto was usually an instrumental aria; the third movement a type of rondo.

- Other instrumental forms included the symphonie concertante, divertimenti, cassation, nocturno, and serenade.

- Although the exact number is not known, Mozart composed approximately fifty symphonies and twenty-six string quartets.

- Etude books appeared in Paris after 1785. The earliest publications were for flute and violin. Piano étude books were published in the early nineteenth century.

- Haydn considered himself to be primarily a composer of vocal music. He wrote numerous operas, masses, and other sacred and secular vocal works; he also composed 104 symphonies.

- Considered by many to be Haydn's most significant contribution were his two oratorios, *The Creation* and *The Seasons,* his symphonies, and his string quartets.

- Gluck worked to reform opera in his *Orpheus and Euridice.*

- Beethoven was an innovator with his development of the form of the symphony. His innovations included commencing a symphony in a key other than its tonic and modulations to a key a third removed.

- Singing schools were started in America to improve the quality of singing in church.

- The first native-born American to compose a secular song is considered to be Francis Hopkinson.

- Francis Hopkinson (1737-1791), James Lyon (1735-1794), William Billings (1746-1800), and John Antes (1740-1811) all flourished in the second half of the eighteenth century as the first native-born North American composers.

BASIC CLASSICAL STYLE

According to Joseph LaButa in *Teaching Musicianship in the High School Band* (1997),[10] Classical melodies were basically diatonic with simple construction and were tuneful, folk-song-like, and very singable. The musical phrases were short, mostly symmetrical, and cadenced frequently. Harmony was mostly simple and included seventh chords, limited chromatic alteration, and modulations to closely related keys. Harmonic rhythm was slow and evenly spaced. Simple meters were dominant with barline regularity, the emphasis being on the measure rather than the beat as in the Baroque period. The texture was largely homophonic. Dynamics allowed sudden changes in volume with *crescendos* and *diminuendos* suddenly moving from *pianissimo* to *fortissimo*.

BASIC CLASSICAL PERFORMANCE PRACTICE

Music of the Classical period included light, thin, restrained, gay, and delicate qualities. The performance style required the use of light, precise, restrained articulation along with *staccatos* performed lightened and separated. The brass were to generally underplay the volume and use refined dynamics in comparison to the woodwinds and strings.

REPRESENTATIVE CLASSICAL COMPOSERS

Bach, Carl Philipp Emanuel (1714-1788)
Beethoven, Ludwig van (1770-1827)
Gluck, Christoph Willibald (1714-1787)
Haydn, Franz Joseph (1732-1809)
Mozart, Wolfgang Amadeus (1756-1791)
Salieri, Antonio (1750-1825)

Classicism to Romanticism

GENERAL CHARACTERISTICS

The latter years of the eighteenth century involved many changes in cultural and political events. The French Revolution led the way to most of these changes. Many musical compositions were composed with heroic attributes emphasized. Musical drama and dramatic tension began to increase. Instrumental ensembles became important for massed ceremonial and commemorative activities.

- The Paris *Conservatoire* and the National Guard Band were established.

- National archives began to include collections of valuable instruments.

- Many works were written for commemorative purposes and for massed ensembles, thus leading to the development of wind band instrumental music and ensembles.

- At the time of the French Revolution there were several important European composers. The London school of pianist-composers included J. B. Cramer, Muzio Clementi, Jan L. Dussek, John Field, and George Pinto.

- Leading Bohemian composers active in Vienna were Václav Jan Tomásek, Jan Václav Vorísek, and Johann Nepomuk Hummel (Beethoven's chief rival in Vienna).

- Hummel's style was Mozartean, a restrained Classicism, neat and delicate, with emphasis on fluent technique and textural clarity.

- Beethoven contributed many important developmental procedures, among them thematic transformation, fugue, and variation.

- Beethoven's best-known symphony, *Symphony No. 5*, marks the first use of trombones in a symphony.

- Much of the nineteenth-century Romantic music was rooted in Beethoven's music.

- The doctrine of nationalism gained strength in the middle quarter of the nineteenth century.

Romantic Period (1820-1900)

GENERAL CHARACTERISTICS

The Classical era evolved into a newer period in which many "classical" aspects were altered, expanded, and enhanced. This was a time when music and the other arts emphasized expressive elements, many based on emotion and feeling, along with spiritual aspects. Thus, variety in sound, instrumentation, and expression prevailed. The following characterize the development:

- The Romantic period brought about musical characteristics that emphasized lyricism, chromatic themes, long sequences, chromatic harmony, harmonic color, and new instrumental color.

- The major musical forms included: symphonic poem, music drama (e.g., *opéra comique*, *Leitmotif*), symphonic variations,

symphony development, art songs for voice, character pieces for piano, and the concerto.

- Nationalism in music became important in the second half of the nineteenth century as composers began to utilize native folk songs or emphasized some national or ethnic element in their music.

- Along with the freedom of form development and variety in sounds came the extension and added length to many musical works.

- The orchestra grew in size and instrumentation.

- "Program music" incorporated ideas to express, refer, or describe something, or to tell a story (e.g., Beethoven's *Pastoral Symphony*, Berlioz' *Symphonie Fantastique*).

- Many new instruments were invented and new ways of performing (fingerings, key systems, valves, mouthpieces, reeds, etc.) were developed.

- Instrumental innovations included the Albert system for the clarinet, the Heckel system for the bassoon, and the Boehm system for the flute and clarinet.

- Machine-tuned timpani were developed.

- Instrumental music compositions for winds and performances of instrumental ensembles increased.

- Chopin, Mendelssohn, and Schumann were early Romantic period leaders in the development of character pieces for piano.

- Schumann's main musical contributions were Lieder and piano music.

- Paganini advanced violin playing through his virtuosic performances and innovative bowing and fingering techniques, thus improving orchestral string performances.

- There were two primary types of music in America during the Romantic period: native/popular and art music.

- Lowell Mason pioneered music education and established music in the curriculum in the Boston schools in 1837. He was also a prolific hymn writer who composed and/or arranged over 1,600 hymns.

- Stephen Foster was America's principal song writer; he composed more than 150 songs of varying style.

- The New York Philharmonic (Philharmonic Symphony Society of New York) was the first permanent American symphony orchestra (1842).

- Singing schools in America continued with two main leaders: William B. Bradbury (1816-1868) and Lowell Mason (1792-1872).

- Wagner composed and produced many great works, particularly his music dramas. He utilized large ensembles, and many of his works were of great length.

- Verdi composed twenty-eight operas and other instrumental and vocal compositions.

- Liszt composed secular cantatas and oratorios and has been credited as the originator of the symphonic poem.

- Brahms is considered by many to have been the most inventive and accomplished nineteenth-century composer.

- Anton Bruckner composed eleven symphonies and other instrumental and vocal works. He wrote fine sacred choral music. The *Ninth Symphony* has been considered his best orchestral work.

- Five major composers in Russia led the way for nationalism in music (frequently referred to as the Russian Five): Mily Balakirev, César Cui, Modest Musorgsky, Nikolai Rimsky-Korsakov, and Alexander Borodin.

- The symphonic suite was first developed by Rimsky-Korsakov (e.g., *Scheherazade*).

BASIC ROMANTIC STYLE

Lyricism and the use of long sequences were emphasized. Musical lines were both diatonic and chromatic and stated in either major or minor modes. Melodies were singable with more expressive emotion than those of the Classical period. The instrumental and vocal colors were expanded with the increase of instrumentation and/or voices and size. The harmonic elements often emphasized seventh, ninth, and eleventh chords along with the use of chromatic progressions. Wide dynamic ranges were common. Scoring sometimes varied from monophony to large masses of sound. Instruments included complete families, thus adding to the orchestral color.

BASIC ROMANTIC PERFORMANCE PRACTICE

The Romantic Period involved many changes in style. Variety included many contrasts: loud/soft volume, heavy/light articulation, thick/thin texture, dark/light sonority, intense/relaxed expression, complex/simple color, and programmatic/absolute development.

REPRESENTATIVE ROMANTIC COMPOSERS

Balakirev, Mily (1837-1910)
Berlioz, Louis-Hector (1803-1869)
Bizet, Georges (1838-1875)
Borodin, Alexander (1833-1887)
Brahms, Johannes (1833-1897)
Bruckner, Anton (1824-1896)
Chopin, Frédéric (1810-1849)
Cui, César (1835-1918)
Dvořák, Antonin (1841-1904)
Fauré, Gabriel (1845-1924)
Foster, Stephen Collins (1826-1864)
Franck, César (1822-1890)
Glinka, Mikhail (1804-1857)
Liszt, Franz (1811-1886)
Mahler, Gustav (1860-1911)
Mendelssohn (Bartholdy), Felix (1809-1847)
Mussorgsky, Modest (1839-1881)
Paganini, Niccolò (1782-1840)
Puccini, Giacomo (1858-1924)
Rimsky-Korsakov, Nikolai (1844-1908)
Rossini, Gioacchino (1792-1868)
Saint-Saëns, Camille (1835-1921)
Schubert, Franz Peter (1797-1828)
Schumann, Robert (1810-1856)
Scriabin, Alexander (1872-1915)
Sibelius, Jean (1865-1957)
Smetana, Bedrich (1824-1884)
Strauss, Richard (1864-1949)
Tchaikovsky, Peter (1840-1893)
Verdi, Giuseppe (1813-1901)
Wagner, Richard (1813-1883)
Weber, Carl Maria von (1786-1826)
Wolf, Hugo (1860-1903)

Contemporary Period (1900-present)
GENERAL CHARACTERISTICS

The development of music continued with a growing reaction to Romanticism. Many varieties of change, alteration, and experimentation resulted. Composers chose many styles of writing which have included impressionism, nationalism, neoromanticism, neoclassism, serialism, pointillism, minimalism, experimentalism (determinant and indeterminant forms), electronic, jazz, popular (country, rock and roll, rap, alternative) and others. This period has been known as "The Age of Diversity." The following characterize the development and musical styles:

- *Impressionism*: the Contemporary period started with this movement. The music emphasized an atmosphere of vague sounds, lack of precise formal development, and varied musical color. Tonality was still prevalent with the use of irregular phrases, nontraditional harmony, dissonances which were not resolved, parallel chords which utilized altered tones, and special selected instruments that portrayed special images.

  Claude Debussy and Maurice Ravel were the leaders of French Impressionism. Other composers of Impressionism were Florent Schmitt, Ottorino Respighi, and Frederick Delius.

- *Nationalism*: the movement began in the late nineteenth century and continued into the twentieth century. Composers utilized native folk songs or emphasized some national or ethnic element in their music. Leaders were the Russian and Czechoslovakian composers, and concepts of the nationalistic movement continue today. Composers incorporating nationalism in some of their works included Mikhail Glinka, Bedřich Smetana, Jean Sibelius, Edward Elgar, Ralph Vaughan Williams, Béla Bartók, Zoltán Kodály, Heitor Villa-Lobos, Carlos Chávez, and George Gershwin.

- *Neoromanticism*: some contemporary composers chose to incorporate older musical elements of the Romantic period into new music of the twentieth century. These elements included more emphasis on melodic writing, tonal centers or tendencies toward tonality, and use of similar construction forms. Expressive performance emphasis was again highlighted. The music of David Del Tredici incorporated many of these elements.

- *Neoclassicism*: similar in concept to neoromanticism, neoclassicism in twentieth century music incorporated

seventeenth- and eighteenth-century musical elements into contemporary composition. The concepts of contrapuntal writing, as used by J. S. Bach, were particularly used along with a reuse of other particular construction styles and forms (suite, toccata, madrigal, opera, etc.). Neoclassicism was incorporated by composers such as Igor Stravinsky, Paul Hindemith, Sergei Prokofiev, and a group of French composers known as Les Six: Georges Auric, Louis Durey, Arthur Honegger, Darius Milhaud, Francis Poulenc, and Germaine Tailleferre.

- *Serialism*: Arnold Schoenberg, and his students Alban Berg and Anton Webern are credited with developing a new style of music construction. The new style, known as twelve-tone music or dodecaphony, used all twelve chromatic pitches (pitch classes) contained in an octave, with each tone equally emphasized. The sound was actually "a tonic" or atonal, meaning without tonality. A special system to organize the order and style of the use of these twelve tones was created. This system involved the use of a "tone row" or "series of tones" within a basic pattern. From this established tone row, the series could appear in different forms such as forward (prime), backward (retrograde), inverted, inverted backward (retrograde inversion), and/or in different transpositions. This construction system allowed for as many as forty-eight variations. Multiple tones sounding together created new harmonic sounds. Many current composers use serialistic elements combined with other contemporary writing techniques.

- *Pointillism*: Anton Webern is credited with the adaptation of this painting concept to music. Composing athematic music, isolated notes were constructed in a very pointed or disjunct manner and blended to create certain tone colors and variations of timbres; for example, a musical line would appear with wide leaps and extreme intervals and could call for varying articulations, volumes, registers, mutes, and other special effects. Both Webern and Schoenberg used this construction technique. Currently, many composers utilize pointillistic techniques.

- *Minimalism*: in the late 1960s a musical construction technique used "repetition," an ostinato-type concept. This repetition was of short figures, based on a specific rhythm or series of tones, or both elements were used together, which served as the basis of the entire work. Many early minimalistic works were quite lengthy with static harmonies. Today, many composers incorporate this construction technique along with other contemporary techniques to reiterate musical ideas in their works. Major composers utilizing minimalism as a dominant construction technique include La Monte Young, Philip Corner, Terry Riley, Philip Glass, and Steve Reich.

- *Experimentalism* (determinant and varying indeterminant forms): experimentalism has often been referred to as "chance music" and "aleatoric music." John Cage led the way with this form of compositional creativity. Music that was predetermined and scored in such a manner as to allow performers to vary such elements as length, volume, tone sequences, form, etc., was referred to as the "determinant" form of chance music. When musicians were given the opportunity to decide independently on the choices of sounds (not necessarily scored) such as the length, volume, tone sequences, form, etc., this form of chance music was called "indeterminant." Although these forms of chance music involved different sounding performances, more variation was possible with the indeterminant forms.

- *Electronic music:* since the invention of recording devices in the late nineteenth century, sound technology has significantly improved and has allowed varying forms of stored sounds, manipulated sounds, and produced sounds. From the early use of magnetic tape to those generated by computer and synthesizer, many new techniques have been utilized by composers. Contemporary composers who have utilized this medium include Philip Glass, Pierre Schaeffer, Karlheinz Stockhausen, John Cage, Pauline Oliveros, and Luciano Berio.

BASIC CONTEMPORARY STYLE

Contemporary—also called "modern" or "twentieth-century"—style involves a variety of musical characteristics. No particular set of restraints applies to the many types and styles as addressed in the categories above. Some characteristics include the use of fragmented melodies, dissonance, wide ranges of expression, extreme range demands, varied instrument choices, special effect sounds, and linear melodic lines. Other characteristics are polyrhythms, atonality, polytonality, multiple meter changes, asymmetric rhythms and meters, densities of sound (i.e., layers of sonorities and intensities), and new sounds artificially generated.

BASIC CONTEMPORARY PERFORMANCE PRACTICE

To interpret contemporary performance practices properly, the music of this period requires research into the composer's life and compositional style. Rhythms, meters, and segmentation of notes seem to have greater emphasis than in earlier periods of music. Performers should follow written musical notation and interpretation marks precisely. Dissonances serve a most important role and need proper balance. Performance accuracy is essential to make the special effect sounds and sections convincing.

REPRESENTATIVE CONTEMPORARY COMPOSERS

Auric, Georges (1899-1983)
Babbitt, Milton (b. 1916)
Bartók, Béla (1881-1945)
Berg, Alban (1885-1935)
Berio, Luciano (b. 1925)
Britten, Benjamin (1913-1976)
Brown, Earl (b. 1926)
Cage, John (1912-1992)
Chávez, Carlos (1899-1978)
Cowell, Henry (1897-1965)
Copland, Aaron (1900-1990)
Crumb, George (b. 1929)
Debussy, Achille-Claude (1862-1918)
Del Tredici, David (b. 1937)
Durey, Louis (1888-1979)
Elgar, Edward (1857-1934)
Gershwin, George (1898-1937)
Glass, Philip (b. 1937)
Hanson, Howard (1896-1981)
Hindemith, Paul (1895-1963)
Holst, Gustav (1874-1934)
Honegger, Arthur (1892-1955)
Ives, Charles (1874-1954)
Kodály, Zoltán (1881-1967)
Ligeti, György (b. 1929)
Messiaen, Olivier (1908-1992)
Milhaud, Darius (1892-1974)
Musgrave, Thea (b. 1928)
Nono, Luigi (1924-1996)
Oliveros, Pauline (b. 1932)
Orff, Carl (1895-1982)
Penderecki, Krzystof (b. 1933)
Piston, Walter (1894-1976)

Poulenc, Francis (1899-1963)
Prokofiev, Sergei (1891-1953)
Ravel, Maurice (1875-1937)
Reich, Steve (b. 1936)
Riley, Terry (b. 1935)
Schaeffer, Pierre (b. 1910)
Schoenberg, Arnold (1874-1951)
Shostakovich, Dmitry (1906-1975)
Still, William Grant (1895-1978)
Stockhausen, Karlheinz (b. 1928)
Stravinsky, Igor (1882-1971)
Tailleferre, Germaine (1892-1983)
Varèse, Edward (1883-1965)
Villa-Lobos, Heitor (1887-1959)
Williams, Ralph Vaughan (1872-1958)
Webern, Anton (1883-1945)
Young, La Monte (b. 1935)

Comparative Historical Chronology

The following serves as a resource to assist in making connections as out-lined in the *National Standards for Arts Education—What Every Young American Should Know and Be Able to Do in the Arts.*

8. Content Standard: *Understanding relationships between music, the other arts, and disciplines outside the arts*
9. Content Standard: *Understanding music in relation to history and culture*[11]

The primary sources for the comparative historical chronology include the following: *The Timetables of History* (1991), *Cyclopedia* (1995), *A History of Western Music* (1996), *Exploring Music* (1989), *The Development of Western Music* (1990), *The Enjoyment of Music* (1963), and *Teaching Music through Performance in Band* (1997). When these sources provided conflicting information, every reasonable attempt was made to verify the dates listed as closely as possible.

Please note the following code for the comparison area:

H	Historical Event
A	Artistic Contribution
DL	Daily Life
SI	Scientific Contribution or Invention

1600-1750   BAROQUE PERIOD

Date	Person/Event/Invention/Artistic Contribution	Area
1500-1780	The Reformation	H
1600-1700	American Colonization	H
1600	*Hamlet* (William Shakespeare)—Theater	A
1600	*The Merry Wives of Windsor* (William Shakespeare)—Theater	A
1600	Wigs and dress trains became popular	DL
1602	"Laws of Gravitation and Oscillation" investigated (Galilei Galileo)	SI
1603	Plague outbreak in England	DL
1604	*Othello* (William Shakespeare)—Theater	A
1605	*Don Quixote* (Part 1) (Miguel de Cervantes)—Literature	A
1606	*Macbeth* and *King Lear* (William Shakespeare)—Theater	A
1607	*L'Orfeo* (Claudio Monteverdi)—Music (Opera)	A
1607-1609	Founding of Jamestown Colony, Jamestown, Virginia	H
1608	First bank checks used in the Netherlands	DL
1609	Baptist Church founded, Amsterdam (John Smythe)	H
1611	King James Version of the *Bible* made available—Literature	A
1615	*Canzoni et Sonate* (Giovanni Gabrieli)—Music	A
1618	Beginning of the Thirty Years' War	H
1620	Mayflower Compact—Pilgrims arrive at Cape Cod	H
1625	Europeans start to use "full-bottomed wigs"	DL
1627	*Dafne* (Heinrich Schütz) (First German Opera)—Music	A
1636	Harvard College founded	H
1637	*Le Cid* (Corneille)—Theater	A
1638	*Lycidas* (John Milton)—Literature	A
1640	*Bay Psalm Book* published—Music	A
1642	"The Night Watch" (Rembrandt Van Rijn)—Painting	A
1643	King of France, Louis XIV	H
1644	Barometer invented (Evangelista Torricelli)	SI
1648	Society of Friends (Quakers) founded (George Fox)	H
1654	"Bathsheba" (Rembrandt Van Rijn)—Painting	A
1657	Pendulum clock invented (Christiaan Huygens)	SI
1666	Great Fire of London	H
1667-74	*Paradise Lost* (John Milton)—Literature	A
1675-1710	St. Paul's Cathedral re-construction begins (Christopher Wren)—Architecture	A
1682	Peter the Great begins reign	H
1687	*Principiae Mathematica* (Isaac Newton)	H
1689	*Dido and Aeneas* (Henry Purcell)—Music (Opera)	A
1692	Salem Witchcraft Trials	H
1700	Vaccination against smallpox (Edward Jenner)	SI
1700-1850	Industrial Revolution begins	H

1702	Beginning of the War of the Spanish Succession	H
1707	Billiards introduced in Berlin	DL
1709	Pianoforte first built (Bartolomeo Cristofori)	A
1714	Mercury thermometer invented (Gabriel Fahrenheit)	SI
1718	Machine gun invented (James Puckle)	SI
1719	*Robinson Crusoe* (Daniel Defoe)—Literature	A
1720	Wallpaper popular in England	DL
1721	*The Brandenburg Concertos* (J. S. Bach)—Music	A
1725	*The Seasons* (Antonio Vivaldi)—Music	A
1726	*Gulliver's Travels* (Jonathan Swift)—Literature	A
1729	*St. Matthew Passion* (J. S. Bach)—Music	A
1729	Methodist Church founded, England (John Wesley)	H
1735	"The Rake's Progress" (William Hogarth)—Painting	A
1742	*Messiah* (George Frederick Handel)—Music	A
1748	*The Royal Fireworks Music* (George Frederick Handel)—Music	A
1749	Sign language for the deaf invented	DL

1750-1820 | **CLASSICAL PERIOD** | |
1752	Discoveries in electricity (Benjamin Franklin)	SI
1756	Seven Years' War, French and Indian War	H
1762	*Orpheus and Euridice* (Christoph Willibald Gluck)—Music (Opera)	A
1765	Potato is most popular European food	DL
1765-1783	U. S. War of Independence	H
1766	First paved sidewalk (London)	DL
1769	Steam engine patented (condenser model) (James Watt)	SI
1770	Factory system begins	SI
1770	Spinning jenny invented (James Hargreaves)	SI
1770	First restaurant for public (Paris)	DL
1773	Boston Tea Party at Boston Harbor	H
1774	Electrical telegraphy invented (Georges Lesage)	SI
1776	U. S. Declaration of Independence	H
1776	Submarine invented (David Bushnell)	SI
1776	Bolshoi Ballet founded in Moscow	A
1776-88	*Decline and Fall of the Roman Empire* (Edward Gibbon)—Literature	A
1781-82	*Serenade No. 10 in B Flat K. 361* (Wolfgang Amadeus Mozart)—Music (Winds)	A
1781	*Critique of Pure Reason* (Immanuel Kant)—Literature	A
1784	First school for the blind (Paris)	DL
1786	*The Marriage of Figaro* (Wolfgang Amadeus Mozart)—Music (Opera)	A
1787	*Don Giovanni* (Wolfgang Amadeus Mozart)—Music (Opera)	A

1787	U. S. dollar currency founded	DL
1789	George Washington, first U. S. president	H
1789-99	French Revolution	H
1789	National Guard Band formed (French Revolution)	H
1791	U. S. Bill of Rights	H
1793	Cotton gin invented (Eli Whitney)	SI
1798	*Essay on Population* (Thomas Malthus)—Literature	A
1799	*Symphony No. 1 in C Major* (Ludwig van Beethoven)—Music	A
1799	Pestalozzi School opened (Switzerland)	DL
1800	Electric battery invented (Alessandro Volta)	SI
1800-1815	Napoleonic Wars	H
1803	*Eroica Symphony* (*Symphony No. 3 in E-flat*) (Ludwig van Beethoven)—Music	A
1803	U. S. Louisiana Purchase	H
1804	Napoleon proclaimed Emperor	H
1805-1844	Joseph Smith founds the Church of the Latter Day Saints (Mormons) in U.S.	H
1808	*Symphony No. 5 in C Minor* (Ludwig van Beethoven)—Music	A
1808	*Faust*, Part 1 (Johann Wolfgang von Goethe)—Drama	A
1808	Pigtails in men's hair no longer fashionable	DL
1810	Food canning begins (Nicolas Appeet)	SI
1810-1826	Spanish-American Wars of Independence	H
1813	Waltz is most popular dance in ballrooms (Europe)	DL
1813	*Pride and Prejudice* (Jane Austen)—Literature	A
1814	Steam locomotive invented (George Stephenson)	SI
1815	Battle of Waterloo (Napoleon defeated)	H
1816	Metronome invented (J. N. Maezel)	SI
1816	Fire extinguisher invented (George Manby)	SI
1816	*The Barber of Seville* (Gioachino Rossini)—Music (Opera)	A
1818	Prussia divided into ten provinces	H
1819	"The Raft of the Medusa" (Théodore Géricault)—Painting	A
1819	*Ivanhoe* (Scott)—Literature	A
1819-24	*Don Juan* (Lord Byron)—Literature	A
1820-1900	**ROMANTIC PERIOD**	
1821	*Der Freischütz* (Carl Maria von Weber)—Music (Opera)	A
1823	Monroe Doctrine	H
1823	*Symphony No. 9* (Ludwig van Beethoven)—Music	A
1824	*Overture for Winds*, Op. 24 (Felix Mendelssohn-Bartholdy)—Music (Band)	A
1824	Completion of the Erie Canal	H
1825	First world passenger railroad (Stockton-Darlington)	SI
1825	Buckingham Palace, London (John Nash)—Architecture	A

1826	*Last of the Mohicans* (James Fenimore Cooper)—Literature	A
1828	First commercial railroad in United States	SI
1830	Ladies' dress—dresses shorter, decorated hats, large sleeves	DL
1830	Men's dress—use of stiff collars	DL
1830	*Symphonie Fantastique* (Hector Berlioz)—Music	A
1831	Electric generator invented (Michael Faraday)	SI
1834	Braille invented (Louis Braille)	SI
1835	Revolver hand gun (single-barreled pistol) invented (Samuel Colt)	SI
1835	Paper photography from negative invented (William Fox Talbot)	SI
1835-72	*Fairy Tales* (Hans Christian Anderson)—Literature	A
1837-38	*Oliver Twist* (Charles Dickens)—Literature	A
1837	Reign of Queen Victoria begins	H
1839	Bicycle invented (Kirkpatrick Macmillan)	SI
1839	Vienna Philharmonic founded	A
1840	Saxophone invented (Adolphe Sax)	A
1840	*Grande Symphonie* (*Funèbre et Triomphale*) (Hector Berlioz)—Music (Band)	A
1840-1914	Period of European nationalism	H
1841	First university degrees received by women in America	DL
1841	*Essays* (Ralph Waldo Emerson)—Literature	A
1842	Polka dance becomes popular	DL
1844	First paper made of wood pulp (Friedrich Gottlob Keller)	SI
1844	*Trauermusik* (Richard Wagner)—Music (Band)	A
1845	*Tannhäuser* (Richard Wagner)—Music (Opera)	A
1845	*The Count of Monte Cristo* (Alexander Dumas)—Literature	A
1848	*Communist Manifesto* published (Karl Marx)	H
1848	First Gold Rush in America (California)	DL
1849	*Requiem Mass* (Anton Bruckner)—Music	A
1850	*Lohengrin* (Richard Wagner)—Music (Opera)	A
1851	Sewing machine invented (Isaac Singer)	SI
1851	*Moby Dick* (Herman Melville)—Literature	A
1853	*La Traviata* (Giuseppe Verdi)—Music (Opera)	A
1853	Japan opened to the West	H
1854	*Walden* (Henry David Thoreau)—Literature	A
1854	*Les Préludes* (Franz Liszt)—Music (Symphonic Poem)	A
1855	*Leaves of Grass* (Walt Whitman)—Literature	A
1859	*Tristan und Isolde* (Richard Wagner)—Music (Opera)	A
1860	First recorded baseball game in America (San Francisco, California)	DL
1860	Imperial Russian Ballet (Kirov Ballet) (St. Petersburg)	A
1861-1866	United States Civil War	H

1862	Rapid-fire gun invented (R. J. Gatling)	SI
1862	Refrigerator invented (James Harrison)	SI
1862	*Les Misérables* (Victor Hugo)—Literature	A
1862	*La Forza del Destino* (Givseppe Verdi)—Music (Opera)	A
1863	Baha'i faith founded in Persia (Mirza Hosein Ali)	H
1863	Battle of Gettysburg (Civil War)	H
1863	Abraham Lincoln's Gettysburg Address	H
1863-69	*War and Peace* (Leo Tolstoi)—Literature	A
1864	*Alice in Wonderland* (Lewis Carroll)	A
1865	Salvation Army founded (William Booth)	H
1865	Abolition of slavery in United States (Civil War ends)	H
1865	President Abraham Lincoln assassinated	H
1865	Antiseptics invented (Joseph Lister)	SI
1865	*Apollo March* (Anton Bruckner)—Music	A
1866	Christian Science founded (Mary Baker Eddy)	H
1866	Citizenship to African Americans (U. S. Civil Rights Act)	H
1867	Dynamite invented (Alfred Nobel)	SI
1868	Primitive typewriter invented (Christopher Sholes)	SI
1869	*Occident et Orient*, Op. 25 (Camille Saint-Saëns)— Music (Band)	A
1870	Italy united	H
1870	Plastics invented (John Wesley Hyatt)	SI
1870	Electric motor (DC) invented (Zenobe Gramme)	SI
1872	"Impression: Sunrise" (Claude Monet)—Painting	A
1872	*Around the World in Eighty Days* (Jules Verne)—Literature	A
1874	*Pictures at an Exhibition* (Modest Mussorgsky)—Music	A
1876	Telephone invented (Alexander Graham Bell)	SI
1877	Gramophone invented (Thomas Edison)	SI
1877	First public telephones in United States	DL
1877	*Swan Lake* (Peter Tchaikovsky)—Theater/Ballet	A
1879	Electric light invented (incandescent) (Thomas Edison)	SI
1880	Canned meats and fruits introduced in stores	DL
1881	Boston Symphony founded	A
1882	Berlin Philharmonic founded	A
1882	First rodeo (U. S.)	DL
1883	Skyscraper, Chicago (William Jenney)—Architecture	H
1885	New York Metropolitan Opera founded	A
1885	Gasoline engine invented (Karl Benz)	SI
1885	Rabies vaccination (Louis Pasteur)	SI
1885	*Symphony No. 4 in E minor* (Johannes Brahms)—Music	A
1887	First "Sherlock Holmes" story (Arthur Conan Doyle)— Literature	A
1888	*Scheherazade* (Nikolai Rimsky-Korsakov)—Music	

	(Symphonic poem)	A
1888	"The Sunflower" (Vincent Van Gogh)—Painting	A
1889	Electric oven invented (Bernina Hotel, Switzerland)	SI
1889	"The Thinker" (Auguste Rodin)—Sculpture	A
1890	Punch card machine (Herman Hollerith)	SI
1891	*The Nutcracker* (Peter Tchaikovsky)—Theater/Ballet	A
1893	New Zealand is first country to grant women the right to vote	H
1894	*New World Symphony (No. 5)* (Antonin Dvořák)—Music	A
1894	*Prelude to the Afternoon of a Faun* (Claude Debussy)—Music	A
1895	X-Ray invented (Wilhelm Röntgen)	SI
1895	First United States professional football game (Pennsylvania)	DL
1895	*Till Eulenspiegel's Merry Pranks* (Richard Strauss)—Music	
	(Symphonic Tone Poems)	A
1896	First modern Olympics (Athens)	DL
1896	*La Bohéme* (Giacomo Puccini)—Music (Opera)	A
1897	*The Stars and Stripes Forever* (John Philip Sousa)—	
	Music (Band)	A
1898	Tape recorder invented (Vlademar Poulsen)	SI

1900-1997   CONTEMPORARY PERIOD

1900	Cake Walk dance becomes popular	DL
1900	Loudspeaker invented (Horace Short)	SC
1901	Jazz "Ragtime" develops in U.S.	A
1903	First successful flight of powered airplane (Orville	
	and Wilbur Wright)	SI
1903	Twenty-mile-an-hour speed limit set in Britain	DL
1903	Ford Motor Company founded	DL
1904	Helen Keller graduated from Radcliffe College	DL
1905	First neon light signs	DL
1907	Electric washing machine invented (Alva J. Fisher,	
	Hurley Machine Company)	SI
1908	Model "T" Ford (Ford Motor Company)	SI
1909	*First Suite in E-flat* (for Military Band) (Gustav Holst)—Music	A
1909	Permanent waves for hair started (London)	DL
1912	S.S. *Titanic* sinks	DL
1914-1918	World War I	H
1914	Panama Canal opened	H
1915	General "Theory of Relativity" (Albert Einstein)	SI
1915	Motorized taxis appear	DL
1920	*The Symphonies of Wind Instruments* (Igor Stravinsky)—	
	Music (Band)	A
1920	First air mail service (United States)	DL
1923	U.S.S.R. established	H

1924	*English Folk Song Suite* (Ralph Vaughan Williams)— Music (Band)	A
1924	*Toccata Marziale* (Ralph Vaughan Williams)—Music (Band)	A
1924	First Winter Olympics (Chamonix)	DL
1925	Television invented (John Logie Baird)	SI
1925	Charleston dance becomes popular	DL
1926	First all-sound film	DL
1927	First solo air flight across Atlantic (Charles Lindbergh)	DL
1928	Antibiotics/penicillin (Alexander Fleming)	SI
1928	Amelia Earhart becomes first woman to fly solo across Atlantic	DL
1928	"Jazz Singer" - first major talking film	DL
1929	U. S. Stock Exchange collapses; world economic crisis begins	DL
1930	*Lincolnshire Posy* (Percy Aldridge Grainger)—Music (Band)	A
1930	*Hammersmith* (Gustav Holst)—Music (Band)	A
1930	Photoflash bulb used	DL
1933	Electron microscope invented (M. Knoll and E. Ruska)	SI
1933-1945	Holocaust	H
1935	Rumba dance becomes popular	DL
1939	Nylon stockings first worn	DL
1939-1945	World War II	H
1941	Japan bombed Pearl Harbor	H
1941	Color television invented (Peter Carl Goldmark)	SI
1942	Nuclear reaction invented (First nuclear chain reaction) (Enrico Fermi)	SI
1942	*Circus Polka* (Igor Stravinsky)—Music (Band)	A
1943	*Theme and Variations*, Op. 43a (Arnold Schoenberg)— Music (Band)	A
1944	D-Day: Normandy Landings, World War II	H
1944	*Appalachian Spring* (Aaron Copland)—Music (Ballet)	A
1945	*Suite Française* (Darius Milhaud)—Music (Band)	A
1945, May	Germany surrendered	H
1945, Aug.	Atomic bombs: Hiroshima and Nagasaki, Japan	H
1945, Aug.	Japan surrendered	H
1945-1994	The Cold War	H
1947	Microwave oven invented (P. Spencer)	SI
1948	State of Israel established	H
1948	Velcro invented (George de Mestral)	SI
1948	Electronic computer invented (Frederick Williams)	SI
1949	North Atlantic Treaty Organization (NATO) formed	H
1950	*George Washington Bridge* (William Schumann)— Music (Band)	A
1950-1953	Korean War	H

1951	*Amahl and the Night Visitors* (Gian Carlo Menotti)— Music (Opera)	A
1951	*Symphony in B-flat* (Paul Hindemith)—Music (Band)	A
1951	Color television introduced in the United States	DL
1953	*Kontra-Punkte* (Karlheinz Stockhausen)—Music	A
1954	Unification Church founded (Sun Myung Moon)	H
1954-1975	Vietnam War	H
1955	Disneyland opened (California)	DL
1956	Video recorder patented (Ampex Corp.)	SI
1956	*Symphony No. 6 for Band*, Op. 69 (Vincent Persichetti)—Music (Band)	A
1956	*The Diary of Anne Frank* (Goodrich and Hackett)—Theater	A
1957	U.S.S.R. launches *Sputnik I and II* satellites	SI
1958	National Aeronautics and Space Administration (NASA) founded	SI
1960	Laser invented (Theodore Mailman)	SI
1960	Mini computer invented (Digital Corporation)	SI
1961	*Sinfonietta* (Ingolf Dahl)—Music (Band)	A
1962	*To Kill a Mockingbird* (Harper Lee)—Cinema	A
1963	President John F. Kennedy assassinated	H
1963	*Variants on a Medieval Tune* (Norman Dello Joio)— Music (Band)	A
1964	United States intervenes in Vietnam War	H
1964	*In C* (Terry Riley)—Music (Band)	A
1964	*Emblems* (Aaron Copland)—Music (Band)	A
1965	Hare Krishna movement founded (Bhaktivedanta Swami Prabhupada)	H
1965	Word processor invented (IBM)	SI
1967	Heart transplant (Christiaan Barnard)	SI
1968	Martin Luther King, Jr. assassinated	H
1969	United States launches *Apollo 11* and puts first man on moon	H
1969	*HPSCHD* (John Cage)—Music	A
1969	*Music for Prague 1968* (Karel Husa)—Music (Band)	A
1970	Computer floppy disk invented (IBM)	SI
1973	Cease-fire in Vietnam	H
1973	Microcomputer invented (Trong Troung)	SI
1973	Oil embargo and energy crisis	DL
1974	First Ronald McDonald House opened (Pennsylvania)	DL
1974	President Nixon resigns	H
1977	*and the mountains rising nowhere...* (Joseph Schwantner)— Music (Band)	A
1977	*Star Wars* (George Lucas)—Cinema	DL

1978	Compact Disc (CD) invented (Netherlands: Phillips)	SI
1978	*Paradise Lost* (Krzystof Penderecki)—Music (Opera)	A
1981	Space Shuttle program begins (NASA)	SI
1981	Acquired Immune Deficiency Syndrome (AIDS) first reported in United States	SI
1981	Sandra Day O'Connor becomes first woman Supreme Court Justice (U.S.)	H
1983	*The Color Purple* (Alice Walker)—Theater	A
1987	The Trail of Tears becomes U. S. National Monument	H
1990	*The Piano Lesson* (August Wilson)—Theater	A
1990	"Good Defeats Evil" (Zurab Tsereteli)—Sculpture	A
1991	Commonwealth of Independent States replaces U.S.S.R.	H
1991	Desert Storm (Gulf War)	H
1993	Bill Clinton elected U. S. President	H
1993	*Jurassic Park* (Steven Spielberg)—Cinema	A
1994	Janet Reno becomes first woman Attorney General (U. S.)	H
1996	Oklahoma Bombing, Oklahoma City	H
1997	Scientists at Roslin Institute announce ability to clone sheep through nuclear transfer from somatic cells (UK)	SI
1997	Hale-Bopp Comet appears	SI
1997	Probe lands on Mars and sends photographs back to Earth	SI

Notes

1 American Council for the Arts, "The Arts and School Reform: Making the Connections" by Ernest L. Boyer (New York: American Council for the Arts Books, 1989), 23, 27.

2 Consortium of National Arts Education Associations. *National Standards for Arts Education - What Every Young American Should Know and Be Able to Do in the Arts* (Reston, VA: Music Educators National Conference, 1994).

3 Ibid.

4 Ibid, 18-19.

5 Ibid, 59-63.

6 *Goals 2000, Educate America Act* (Washington, D.C.: U.S. Department of Education).

7 Richard Miles, ed., *Teaching Music through Performance in Band* (Chicago: GIA Publications, Inc., 1997), 44-56.

8 Robert Garofalo, *Blueprint for Band* (Ft. Lauderdale, FL: Meredith Music Publications, Revised 1983).

9 Joseph LaButa, *Teaching Musicianship in the High School Band* (Ft. Lauderdale, FL: Meredith Music Publications, Revised 1997).

10 Ibid.

11 Consortium of National Arts Education Associations, 62-63.

CHAPTER 5

Whole Brain Listening

Eugene Corporon

Introduction

When I was a boy scout of eleven I set out on a hike during a camping trip with two companions in the rocky foothills of the California desert. Through a stroke of blind luck we happened on a cave that had once served as a home for a group of nineteenth-century Native Americans. The three of us found, among other things, a large pot which was still intact after 150 years! We knew we had to bring the find off the mountain. That task proved difficult. We carried the fragile vessel in shifts and had to literally hand it from person to person down what could best be described as a series of rough, four-foot-high vertical steps that descended from the hill like some giant stone staircase. We traveled approximately four miles back to the base camp with our new-found treasure. It took awareness, will, and trust to bring that artifact down the ravine in one piece. It occurred to me just recently that this experience could be thought of as a metaphor for music making. The collaboration has shifted to conductor and players, the treasure has become the musical composition left by the composer, and the journey has come to represent the actual process of "musicing." We donated the pot to the San Diego Museum of Natural History, and because we had made a map on the way out we were able to guide a team of archeologists and naturalists back to excavate the site the next weekend. All in all it was a true "Indiana Jones" adventure for a youngster to experience. The artifact remains in the museum's collection to this day, where it continues to be enjoyed by all who visit the exhibits. I had no way of knowing at the time how that encounter would prepare me for the life of music making that awaited me. I continue to be committed to the search and to doing my utmost to give away everything I find in my ongoing process of exploring and discovering the treasure that is music.

Recently, I have become consumed by the challenges of developing deeper meaning and building character in my own musicing while improving my

abilities to illuminate the path to greater creativity and expressivity for all those involved. The question is, how do we infuse the music we make with our spirit while revealing the essence of the composer? Listening both inwardly and outwardly seems to be the answer. Comparing what you hear inside as the ideal aural model to the reality of what is actually sounding outside is key. We accomplish our goals by following this three-step process:

1. Develop the sound image (inward hearing).
2. Compare and evaluate the image and the actual (outward hearing).
3. Teach the sound image and effect a change (transferred hearing).

Musicing is full of contradictions, the biggest of which is that making right is not the same as making music. It is important to be right; however, it is crucial to avoid cranked-out rightness. You must pay careful attention to the composer's instructions knowing full well that the written symbols, no matter how literally followed, are merely a hint to what lies buried in the work of art. You must be in tune, but you have to be willing to adjust or match pitch to create the illusion of in-tune-ness. You must keep a steady tempo, but the tempo should always remain flexible. You must balance the work, but every hall requires a different mix of sound. You must rely completely on sight, while at other times hearing is all that can be counted on. You must find room for individual feelings and ideas to be expressed without doing damage to those of the composer's. And on it goes.

It is clear that our teaching style or method should develop musical understanding, emotional sensitivity, and technical proficiency. All too often we fall prey to teaching music as a series of facts while overlooking the ideas and feelings that music captures and preserves. We must keep in mind that musicing is one of the things that most clearly defines the human experience. It is computers that deal with facts, and humans who deal with ideas and emotions. We need to continually amplify the human aspects of musicing and learn how to fix problems without dehumanizing the experience. There is entirely too much flat-line, spiritless music making, devoid of feeling, which is done in the name of correctness. The music we make should come from our heart and soul as well as our brain. I have observed far too many musicians "frozen in the headlights" of someone else's opinion or methodology. We cannot allow the development and implementation of our teaching technique, which is admittedly very necessary, to *ruin* our artistry. While input from others is essential to growth, it is important that we learn to rely on our own intuition and experiences rather than imitating the ideas and decisions of those who have taught us or those we admire. It is incumbent upon us to learn to count on our own musicianship in order to develop self-expression and a unique voice. In short, we have to discover ways to listen and teach for ourselves. The work we do must be a reflection of *our* personal vision and aural

imagination, no one else's. While teachers, guides, and allies contribute in very beneficial ways to our development, we must eventually learn to do our own work without them. In this context the definition of a great teacher might just be someone who makes themself obsolete in the student's learning process.

Conducting involves converting feelings and knowledge into meaningful movement that can be perceived by a body of musicians as readable and pre-dictable silent messages. The goal is to reveal or uncover the work of art through directing the listening of others. Much like a sculptor, we have two possible ways of working. We can keep chipping at the rock with the hope that something will appear, or we can see the creation in the rock and remove what does not belong. We must be able to perceive the composer's creation in our imagination in order to take away what does not belong. If we acknowl-edge that conducting is a silent language, then it becomes essential to develop the nonverbal skill to facilitate understanding and hearing. We also become obligated to teach the vocabulary and syntax of our silent language to those we lead. We must insist that the musicians follow the signs that we give. They must be convinced that we *mean what we show*. We have to be able to reveal *what* to feel and *how* to listen in addition to *when* to play. Our silent language should become more and more descriptive of the listening process as we refine our aural and technical skills. We are too often tempted to conduct only what we see on the page or happen upon as problems rather than allow-ing our imagined ideal concept of the work to guide us and be revealed to others. A clear image develops a primary understanding of when to lead, when to follow, and when to get out of the way.

The conductor's role in the music-making process is truly unique in the arts. A single performer or chamber group is coached. A dance is choreo-graphed. A play or movie is directed. Unlike any of these related endeavors the conductor remains an integral part of the creative process from inception to completion. Because we conductors continue to guide the creative decision making and listening while the performance is in progress, we have a very unique relationship to the work of art, the performers, and the audience. Just as the coach, choreographer, or director has a responsibility to bring something of themselves to their work, we must bring compassion, positive honesty, expressivity, and creativity to our musicing. We are responsible for creating the environment—a biosphere, if you will—which nurtures and encourages those same attributes in other musicians. The creation of this greenhouse takes energy, time, thought, dedication, and, above all, patience. The conductor's life must be brought to the music in order to bring the music to life. Luckily, the quick fix does not exist. Therefore, it becomes important to spend regular time in our study place, the place we go to make contact with the spirit of the composer and to develop an inner concept of the work. Success in our endeavors requires a commitment to a lifetime of personal and

professional growth as well as a willingness to share without hesitation all that we discover and hear. In other words, commitment only truly reveals itself through action. It is essential to develop our ability to *give* clear listening instructions, *make* astute listening observations, *create* an understanding of the listening goals, and *establish* listening priorities. All of these listening skills allow us to facilitate an encounter with the composer and an interaction with their work of art.

Listening

A basic premise of this book is *the more you know about the music, the greater your achievement and enjoyment will be*. While there are a number of important issues which go into successful musicing, none is more central or crucial than listening. The ability to *hear what is so* is key to learning and teaching a composition. As the person in charge we are responsible for creating, molding, and shaping the listener's perceptions of the work of art. There is no doubt that our decision making influences what our performers and audiences *hear*. We must be able to help others hear what we hear and catch sight of our imagined vision. In other words, what is heard in the "mind's ear" and seen in the "mind's eye" must be transmitted in order to guide the listening and seeing of others. Before we can teach people how to play the piece, we have to teach them how to hear the music. Webster's dictionary defines the word "listen" as "to make a conscientious effort to hear." "Hear" is defined as "to become aware of, to notice, to pay attention to, to learn about." The goal is to help people *hear* what they are *listening* to.

The numerous listening adjustments that are made by the conductor during the process of musicing can be very easily compared to an optometrist who is searching for just the right lens combination that allows us to see our best. The doctor places a machine that resembles a futuristic set of glasses in front of the eyes. These "bionic glasses" allow the examiner to make literally hundreds of adjustments offering a multitude of lens combinations until just the right one "clicks in" and the eye chart becomes beautifully clear from across the room. What we do with sound is not so different. In a very real way we are putting a set of supersonic headphones on the listener. These "bionic headphones" allow the conductor to control the mix of sound and silence with endless variety until the composition "clicks in" from across the room. There is that glorious moment when everything becomes absolutely clear and you hear better than ever before what has always been there on the page. Some people presume that this type of clarity in performance is a matter of acoustical luck. It is not about luck! Luck is what happens when *preparation meets opportunity*. You create your own luck or acoustic success through thorough investigation, diligent attention to detail, and informed decision making. Clarity is not an illusion, it *evolves* in the ensemble; it does not just *appear*.

It is my belief that *every* note in the score has a right to be heard. The true challenge is to discover the relationship of the notes on the page to one another and to make those relationships clear to whomever is listening. Once the relationships become audible the piece becomes clear. The conductor must continually be in the question of "Do they hear what I see?" Establishing the priorities of any given event or time frame in the work of art and making those priorities clearly audible are primary tasks of the conductor.

When musicing, we are simultaneously engaged in two important endeavors: *subjective listening* and *objective doing*. From the outside one activity appears to be passive and the other active, but this is not so. It goes without saying that engaged thought or thinking is a prerequisite to success in musicing. Surely we are active when engaged in thought. Maintaining a balance between "doing" and "listening to others do" for the musicers keeps the energy flowing during the process and leads to more interesting and productive rehearsals and performances. Obviously it is much easier to monitor what someone is *doing* than it is to evaluate what they are *hearing*. The only way we can evaluate what they are hearing is through paying close attention to what they are doing. For anything meaningful and lasting to be accomplished everyone must remain intellectually *engaged* and intuitively *responsive* when "doing" or "listening to others do." This can be represented as follows:

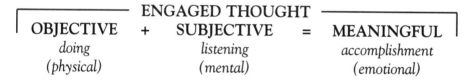

The goal in rehearsal is to help the *musicians* hear what is so. The goal in performance is to help the *audience* hear what is so. The composer has provided a symbolic representation of the thoughts, ideas, feelings, and memories that make up the composition. The page is full of symbols which contain literal as well as implied meaning. The musicer's role is to discover and make clear those meanings. What we do makes it possible for listeners to attach their listening to the events and moments of the work of art and to hear the relationships which exist in the music. The listeners' experience can be guided, focused, or targeted through what I call "Directed Listening Instructions." These instructions seek to facilitate the understanding of:

WHO to listen for.
WHAT to listen to.
WHERE to direct the listening.
WHEN to shift the listening.
WHY to listen at all.
HOW to make sense of what is heard.

A balanced interaction of *participating and receiving information* facilitated by

Directed Listening Instructions can lead to a greater understanding of and appreciation for the work of art. This relationship can be represented as follows.:

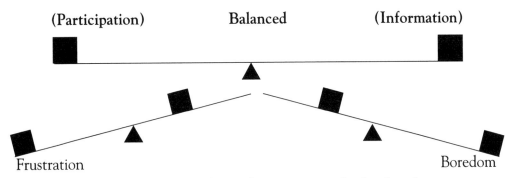

(Participation)　　　**Balanced**　　　**(Information)**

Frustration　　　　　　　　　　　　　　　　　　　　Boredom

Too much "waiting to do" with no action can lead to boredom.
Too much "doing" with no information leads to frustration.

Musicers can become bored or frustrated when the balance of the two activities gets weighted too heavily to one side or the other. "Bore" can be defined as "to weary by being dull, uninteresting or monotonous." "Frustrate" is defined as "to cause to have no effect, bring to nothing, counteract, to prevent from achieving." The goal, of course, is to strike the proper balance between "facilitating participation" and "giving information." These two endeavors need not always be done separately. A great conductor is able to send silent messages which contain essential and valuable information to the musicians while they are participating. We strive to help people enjoy the experience of understanding and appreciating the work of art. To this end, getting musicers to participate, whether they are doing or waiting to do, is the "meat of the matter."

One of the most delicate issues of musicing is finding a way to turn passive listening into active participation. Even though musicers can be physically active or inactive when playing they must always remain mentally involved. In fact, when engaged, the mind can produce physical responses in the musicians even if they are not making sounds. It is no secret that musicians enjoy participating. They did not take up the instrument to hear someone explain its sounds. Musicers want to make the sound. The true joy of music can only be fully experienced through thoughtful participation. Making the sounds is what it is all about. Musicing is a visceral and magical experience. We use air to create the essence of a human spirit, bringing to life the thoughts, feelings, ideas, and memories of the composer.

Exposing the craft in the work of art is an important component of a successful rehearsal. Equally central is revealing the inspiration of the creator. We must be deeply involved in the music in order to involve others. It is not enough for the music to be of quality and significance. It must also resonate

within you. In other words we must only teach and conduct music that we value and believe in. Because we spend untold hours preparing and presenting a piece, we have a responsibility to choose music that is worth the musicians' time and energy. If you cannot find *craft* in the work, do not waste their time. If you cannot find *inspiration* in the work, do not waste their spirit! Remember the hours invested are compounded not only by the number of performers but also by the number of listeners who will experience the composition along the way.

It will come as no surprise that involving people in the process who are just listening at various moments in the rehearsal is more difficult than involving those who are physically participating. It is imperative that we guide and direct the listening attention of the musicians who are not playing at any given point in time as well as those who are. There is one other very disturbing possibility: we cannot assume that *anyone* is listening. Yes, it is possible for someone to *do* and not *listen*. It happens all the time in even the best of ensembles. Because of this we must find ways to monitor and verify "listening in progress."

The listening process is an additive one. Each rehearsal and performance experience increases the perception and understanding of the musicians and listeners. Achieving this involves keeping people objectively active and subjectively attached. There must be something going on in their inner space as well as in the outer space. The rehearsal and performance involve a process that occurs in time and must be balanced between intellect and intuition. Balancing intellect and intuition requires in-depth listening which can yield perception and insight. Perception and insight lead to developing the key element in successful music making: musical memory. In his *Introduction to Music*, Hugh Miller helps to clarify these relationships.

> Any moment in music must be grasped as it goes by, and must be related to all that has gone before and what is yet to come....When the performance of a piece is finished, one must see the whole composition in retrospect... thus the development of musical memory is essential to appreciation....

Our challenge while rehearsing and performing is to create active listening skills in the players which help them to stay physically involved and mentally engaged in the musical process. In doing so we help the musicians build a memory of the work. Each musician flies into the musical universe in his or her own shuttle craft. The goal is to get them all to dock at the same "space station" and stay connected while we transfer the cargo. They must understand that they can always be doing something, especially if they are not playing. That "something" is *listening*. There are six important listening tools

which can help us focus and direct the listening and reveal what is going on in the work of art:

1. **Isolate** the time frame (*sub-phrase, phrase, section, page*)
2. **Dissect** the structures (*disassemble complex events*)
3. **Catalog** the component parts (*number of events*)
4. **Collate** the timbral groups (*scoring of events*)
5. **Prioritize** the texture (*order of importance of events*)
6. **Communicate** the decisions (*make the relationships clear*)

There are several different focuses that listening can take. For example we can listen *horizontally* for melody, *vertically* for harmony, *diagonally* for texture. We can also listen *physically* for the impact of pulse, *intellectually* for the purity of form, or *imaginatively* for the sound paintings we call timbre. We can attach our listening to the specifics of *sound* or to the specifics of *silence*. It is crucial to make the silences in a composition as important as the sounds. Arrhythmic playing is often the result of uneven silences, not uneven sounds. An understanding of when sound ends and when silence begins is a necessity in creating a balance of sound and silence in one's music making. The interaction of sound and silence creates the perception of time. The goal is not to keep time as much as it is to use time. Pulse in music must be internalized. Time is created where the musician meets the instrument, in the fingers and hands, not the foot! While steady pulse is important, the music must also have a certain elasticity. Time must remain flexible, expanding and contracting to meet the musical design of the work. The outline found below (Diagrams 1 and 2) seeks to serve as a listening guide that will provide an approach to teaching and developing Directed Listening Skills. In great music it is literally impossible to run out of things to listen for, and therefore equally difficult to categorize all of the listening elements. The guide provides a basic approach to breaking down each listening component into smaller and more focused issues. This allows the musicians to become aware of the multiple levels of activity in each area and to work with more manageable listening goals.

Listening Relationships

In order to develop good musicianship we must also develop good listenership. When we listen, what do we hear? What should we notice? What should capture our attention? What is important? These are crucial questions which should guide our approach to the music-making process. In his introduction to Aaron Copland's book *What to Listen for in Music*, William Schuman offers the following:

Listening to music is a skill that is acquired through experience and learning. Knowledge enhances enjoyment....The destiny of a piece of music, while basically in the hands of the composer and performer, also depends on the attitude and ability of the listener.

DIRECTED LISTENING SKILLS

CORE ELEMENTS
The Interaction of sound and silence in time with intent. The four basic materials of any musical composition.

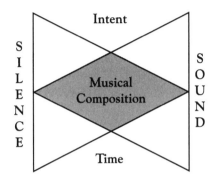

LISTENING COMPONENTS

I. Compositional Elements
- Pulse
- Melody
- Harmony
- Timbre
- Texture

II. Formal Elements
- Unity
- Contrast
- Statement
- Digression
- Return
- New
- Repeated
- Varied
- Developed

III. Structural Elements
- Work
- Movement
- Section
- Sub-section
- Double Period
- Period
- Phrase
- Sub-phrase
- Motive
- Note

IV. Interpretive Elements

Sound	Silence
• Energy	• Energy
• Volume	• Impact
• Speed	• Effect
• Length	• Length
• Timbre	• Quality
• Texture	• Clarity
• Morphology	• Morphology
• Growth	• Purpose
• Note Grouping	• Rests
• Resonance	• Resonance
• Direction/Repose	• Direction/Repose
• Tension/Release	• Tension/Release
• Anticipation	• Anticipation
• Resolution	• Resolution

Diagram 1

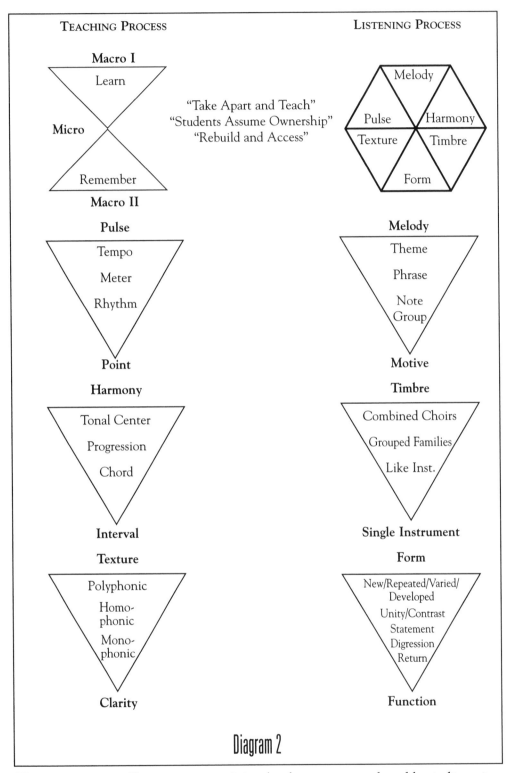

Diagram 2

The importance of having our musicing lead us to comprehend basic listening relationships cannot be overstated. Directed, focused listening allows us to

develop perceptions and understandings that facilitate the transfer of the work of art from the page to the listener. It is through our *objective instructions* which ask musicians to see, understand, and remember, and our *subjective suggestions* which encourage them to feel, hear, and imagine that we create the comprehension and memory of the complex relationships which exist in the work of art. It is all about experiencing the music. A number of wonderful relationships emerge or are made known during the process of bringing a work to life. Some of the relationships that can be pointed out and should be investigated include:

sound—silence	*primary—secondary*	*varied—developed*
cause—effect	*simultaneous—successive*	*new—repeated*
whole—part	*shape—movement*	*intent—execution*
form—function	*simple—complex*	*tension—release*
unity—variety	*convergent—divergent*	*direction—repose*
compare—contrast	*internal—external*	*departure—arrival*
written—implied	*design—structure*	*anticipation—resolution*

The music we choose to study and perform must present us with opportunities to discover and discuss these types of meaningful and interesting related interactions. Quality repertoire that speaks to our own soul is our most important ally in this endeavor. When we choose literature to study and perform it is incumbent upon us as professionals to make informed decisions which are based on value and worth. You simply cannot develop musicianship without using music of serious artistic merit! The music must be about something. I am not suggesting that the music has to have a story. I am referring to its significance and substance, not its programmatic or absolute nature. In his writing about the music of John Harbison, Richard Dyer offered this eloquent and concise description of music which has meaning:

> Like all music that is meaningful to us, it creates and confounds , attracts on first hearing, rewards repeated listening and study; it says things that could find expression in no other way....above all, it is genuine music born of necessity; it had to be written.

If this premise is so, then it is fair to ask what elements qualify a piece to be considered worthy, significant, artistic, meritorious, and meaningful. In their repertoire research, Acton Ostling Jr. and Jay Gilbert have offered and used a set of criteria that can serve as a guide to determining quality, worth, and value in a composition. These criteria are:

1. The composition has form—not a form but form—and reflects a proper balance between repetition and contrast.
2. The composition reflects shape and design, and creates the impression of conscious choice and judicious arrangements on

the part of the composer.

3. The composition reflects craftsmanship in orchestration, demonstrating a proper balance between transparent and tutti scoring, and between solo and group colors.

4. The composition is sufficiently unpredictable to preclude an immediate grasp of its musical meaning.

5. The route through which the composition travels in initiating its musical tendencies and probable musical goals is not completely direct and obvious.

6. The composition is consistent in its quality throughout its length and in its various sections.

7. The composition is consistent in its style, reflecting a complete grasp of technical details, clearly conceived ideas, and avoids lapses into trivial, futile, or unsuitable passages.

8. The composition reflects ingenuity in its development, given the stylistic content in which it exists.

9. The composition is genuine in idiom, and is not pretentious.

10. The composition reflects a musical validity which transcends factors of historical importance, or pedagogical usefulness.

Every program I design is made up of works that I hold accountable to these ten principles. While choosing quality literature does not necessarily ensure success, playing literature of poor quality will undoubtedly guarantee failure. As professionals, every time we design a program we are implying that a belief system based on good judgment and lasting value has been applied to the selection process. We must seek out and become familiar with models in which we not only believe but to which we aspire. While the models may be too difficult or inappropriate for our present situation, they can serve as a basis for comparison and define the standards for true artistic merit in the works we feel are appropriate to perform. It is important to build a thorough knowledge of a diverse repertoire of works of varied difficulties in order to be considered a complete professional. As our teaching improves and our students get better as a result, we can only hope that the day will come when the out-of-reach model becomes a necessary component of our everyday repertoire. We must guard against allowing our musical and personal development to be tied directly to our current position. As Richard Bach says in *Illusions*, "argue for your limitations and surely they will be yours." Our quest for knowledge must reach beyond our circumstances in order to propel us towards new levels of achievement and understanding.

The Sound Canvas: Multidimensional Viewing

One of our most important tasks in musicing is to take on the identity of the music, to literally become the music. We must animate the score and bring

the music alive, creating characters, settings, incidents, actions, and events that impact lives. On a recent trip to Amsterdam I had the opportunity to see Rembrandt's painting "The Night Watch" in the Rijks Museum. As I looked at the painting I became acutely aware of a number of issues that are essential to painting that might also apply to making music. This experience led me to the thought that musicing might be compared in some ways to this related art form. We in fact use much of the same vocabulary, albeit with a musical twist. Music has been called a painting in sound on a canvas of silence framed by the element of time. In painting, even though the canvas is flat, the illusions of depth and dimension are very strong. Music has a similar analogy. I believe that we can create a multidimensional sound canvas that can envelop the listener. We can move sound around the room much the way a painter can move characters around on the canvas. Just as a painter can influence the impact of a particular subject through placement and shading, so too can we bring a sound into the foreground or move it to the background. We can make a sound seem closer to or farther away from the ear, just as a painter does with the eye. Obviously there is a fundamental difference in this analogy. While a painting is concrete and to a certain extent static, sound is in constant motion. The relationships on the sound canvas can change moment to moment, phrase to phrase, or even note to note.

Rembrandt had an exceptional way of using light to focus the viewers' attention. In music we highlight (*bring out*) or cover (*suppress*) a sound in order to have it emerge from or hide in the texture. We perceive sounds in various places: left, right, center, forward, back, high, low, depending on the *tessitura* as well as the textural and timbral combinations. You learn very quickly in musicing that range, size, or placement is not always related to importance. The highest, biggest, or closest element is not always meant to be the most important sound on the canvas. We can position the elements on the canvas in any number of ways; we decide what should be primary and for how long. We mix the timbre to an infinite variety of colors. We prioritize events in the texture to create various shades. An awareness of texture creates a sense of proportion in the work of art. Multidimensional viewing requires the perception of individual lines that combine to create layers of activity. Once we have observed the entity or event on the page we have an obligation to make it audible to the listener. All of this must be accomplished while protecting the interests of the composer to the best of our ability. It is incumbent upon us to discover the threads that weave their way through the fabric of the work and hold it together. We also have to be careful not to disrupt the organic unity by pulling any single thread too hard. Conducting or rehearsing one frayed issue, no matter how well, to the exclusion of all others risks unraveling the entire tapestry that is the work of art. Timbre and texture are to sound what color and depth are to painting. We must continuously preserve and transmit to the listener the tone painting in progress that is called scoring.

The diagram below may help clarify these points.

ART	paint	color	depth	canvas	frame	brush stroke
MUSIC	sound	timbre	texture	silence	time	baton movement

The Sound Stage: Multidimensional Listening

The goal of multidimensional listening is to facilitate a creative interpretation which is tempered with correct performance practice and recreates the composer's very essence. The worst thing that can possibly happen is that we find ourselves replicating a product and not creating a work of art. The composition should be thought of as an artistic entity which is in a state of constant metamorphosis and continues to grow with every hearing. I think we spend entirely too much time looking down into the score and not enough time looking across the score. We need to get the notes to stand up and move around, grouping themselves according to function and placing themselves on the sound stage according to their importance. Sometimes events are successive, sometimes they are simultaneous; in either case music is about the placement of sound in motion. In order to develop a sense of imagery we need to become more aware of the scoring choices a composer makes, and allow those choices to guide our decision making.

Early in my preparation of the world premiere of John Harbison's dance piece *Olympic Dances*, I received a piano reduction to study while he was completing the scoring of the work. The fully instrumented or colorized version followed several weeks later. This experience has become one of the most valued of my life. Circumstance had provided the opportunity to reaffirm the unbelievable importance and impact that scoring has on creating the rich timbre that is so crucial to any piece of music. The piano score could only be compared to the black and white opening of the *Wizard of Oz*. All of the characters or notes were there but none of them were in costume. The vivid, breath-taking use of color was yet to reveal itself. Once I received the completed score I became instantly aware of the impact timbre was to have on the perception of texture. Timbre facilitates the clear separation of musical events in the texture and allows the listeners to group images and events in their imagination.

A second marvelously unique aspect to the premiere was the addition of the dance theatre company Pilobolus. Musicians turn something that is seen into something that can be heard while dancers turn something that is heard into something that can be seen. The impact of the choreographer's vivid imagination and the dancers' movement on the sound was astonishing. While the piece stands strongly on its own, I will never be able to conduct the concert version of *Olympic Dances* without seeing the dancing of Pilobolus in my mind's eye. Although the image of motion need not be so literal in every

piece, I do believe that some image of motion must be present in the minds of the musicians in order to create a sense of flow and growth in their performance!

Creating Partnerships through Expanded Listening

As we work to deepen and broaden our listening, we begin to realize the value of targeting our attention on specific issues which contribute to creating something of significance and value. We must attach ourselves to something in the music in order to create character and deepen our perception. It is important to find something to focus on every moment. We must pay attention to the musical process and the flow of events. In addition to connecting with the work of art we also have to connect with the people who bring it to life. Guided listening and facilitated individual discovery are essential tools in making that connection. The rehearsal should not just be about *our* ideas. Players should be encouraged to have and express *their* ideas and play the music the way *they* think it should go. We need to make room in the process for others to be creative and interactive. All must be encouraged to become integrally involved in working to understand the relationships, feelings, and ideas that are inherent in the work. Musicing provides opportunities for *all* to be creative and expressive, not just the conductor. The process becomes much easier when we realize that we do not have to have all the answers. We just need to keep asking the right questions. We must create partnerships which work to find creative solutions to musical challenges while allowing *everyone* to feel free to discover and express their ideas and feelings.

When musicing, it is important that we focus on the piece rather than the problems. The goal is to *conduct* the piece while *solving* the problems. The dichotomy of the process is that we need to stay aware of the mundane problems which interfere with our ability to reach the "ethereal plane" of great musicing. We must do our best to solve "terrestrial bumps" quickly and return to our true purpose: "celestial music making." Rehearsing is as much about viewing life in progress as it is about fixing problems. The rehearsal can be thought of as a "walking tour" during which we observe and investigate a living, breathing ecosystem which is in a continuous state of change and growth. The goal is to become an explorer, not a fixer and to stay on the path so that we do not damage the fragile relationships in the environment. As the music is in a state of metamorphosis, so too are the musicians. The rehearsal presents ongoing opportunities to turn ideas and feelings into sound, through action. Our actions should facilitate and encourage growth through a balance of objective and subjective instructions which lead people to learn and appreciate everyone's part rather than just their own. Putting the parts together to create a whole is what we should be about when rehearsing and performing.

Musicing is a "gift-giving" experience, one that is cumulative as well as

additive. Paradoxically, it is a present that cannot be given away. Every time we try something comes back in return. When we play a work we are presented with an opportunity to give and receive the gifts of increased awareness and greater appreciation. Something from every work we perform remains with us as well as goes out to others as an invaluable gift. It becomes a part of who we are musically and personally. It goes without saying that I am writing of music that has something to offer and give, and not all music does. Great music, well presented, can be one of the most personal, precious, and lasting gifts of all.

Musical Topography: Mapping through Phrasing

Phrasing can be defined most simply as the organization of musical thought. Every composer begins with a musical idea that seeks to express their feelings. A piece of music can be said to represent the purest essence of a person's thoughts and feelings. When musicing the goal is to create active and engaged listeners who know how to traverse the terrain and target their attention in a way that focuses them on the composer's thoughts and feelings which are inherent in the work. Musicians must develop an awareness of what is going on both inside and outside the composition. Creating a map or chart of the "musical topography" can do just that. In his book *What to Listen for in Music*, Aaron Copland said:

> every good piece must give a sense of flow...a sense of continuity from first note to last...a great work is a man-made Mississippi down which we irresistibly flow from the instant of our leave taking to a long foreseen destination...every composition must have a beginning, a middle, and an end.

Charting that sense of flow or the journey opens up the new world presented by a piece to a lifetime of exploration and discovery. This process allows us to become aware of the currents that run through the work and carry us along. "Mapping" can be defined as "arranging or planning in detail; surveying or exploring for the purpose of making a map." "Charting" can be defined as "mapping a body of water to show the depths, currents, and coastlines." "Topography" can be defined as "an accurate and detailed description of a place; a drawing or representation of the surface features of a region including hills, valleys, caves, bridges, roads, waterways, cities, towns, etc." All of these words pertain directly to creating a visual representation of what is going on inside and outside a piece of music. Copland continues;

> The only thing that one can do for the listener is to point out what actually exists in the music itself and reasonably explain the wherefore and the why of the matter. The listener must do the rest!

Mapping or charting helps us to direct the listener's attention to important

points of interest along the way. While the map does need to point out the location of the mine fields, it is worthless if it does not guide us to the treasure. All too often we spend a majority of our time reacting to and repairing the explosive damage we encounter on our journey and not enough time exploring the essence of the work of art.

MAPPING THE MUSICAL TERRAIN
The Interaction of Shape and Movement

CREATE A LANDSCAPE

	Scan	Survey	Conceive	Plan
Fly Over				
Walk About	Observe	Chart	Prepare	Practice
Explore	Interact	Discover	Implement	Rehearse
Make Known	Reveal	Enlighten	Present	Perform

MUSICAL TOPOGRAPHY

Vertical	**Horizontal**
Peaks	Paths
Valleys	Roads
Hills	Rivers
Caves	Bridges

A phrasal outline is the first step in creating a topographical map of the musical surface.

The conductor is the map maker and the landscape architect.

Diagram 3

The above diagram (Diagram 3) depicts the process of mapping the musical terrain. It includes a number of words that might be used to describe the over-

all approach to discovering the interaction of shape and movement which create growth and flow in a composition. Movement tends to function horizontally by either staying put, going forward, or holding back. Shape, on the other hand, functions more vertically, staying static or rising and falling to create, in the words of Pablo Casals, "a series of rainbows one within the other." Words that describe horizontal concepts might include: path, road, river, bridge. Vertical concepts could include: peak, valley, hill, cave. It is important to have a concept of how phrases are shaped. The drawing below represents a common shape attributed to phrases.

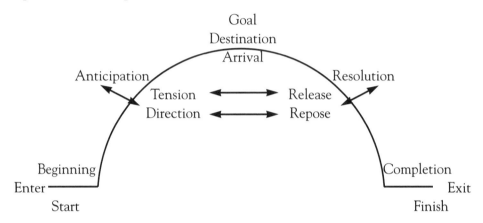

The start, arrival, and finish are the most obvious points within the phrase. Less obvious, but perhaps most important, is the area found between the beginning and the goal, called the anticipation, and the area found between the goal and the completion, called the resolution. The distance between the entrance and the destination should be filled with anticipation, which creates tension and direction. The distance between the destination and the exit is often used to reach a resolution, which creates a sense of release and repose before the phrase concludes. These areas are respectively the most exciting and sensitive moments in musicing. They must be carefully attended to if the music is to have impact and expression. It should be noted that phrases are not always so arch-like. They can assume any number of very interesting linear curved shapes, including multiple goals within the same phrase. The anticipation, goal, and resolution, which function quite often as a unit, can move freely about on the continuum between the entrance and the exit. An inexhaustible variety of shapes occur in the process of creating phrases within a composition!

A comprehensive interaction with the composition requires continually telescoping our attention in and out of the phrases being observed. Initially we fly over the terrain scanning to create a general survey. We then touch down so that we can walk about a chosen site and chart a specific area. Our investigation eventually becomes more localized. We begin to explore in a particular quadrant. What we discover can change the perception of the isolated terrain as well as enhance the understanding of the entire work of art. Last, we reveal what we have discovered to others who have not had the benefit of a thorough investigation or, in many cases, who have not even been there before.

At a basic level, phrasal awareness will allow us to guide the ears of the musicians and listeners. We must focus on the structure in order to make it perfectly clear where we think the listening should be directed. Our best ally in this endeavor is the phrase. Phrases create the architectural stability in a work. It is the phrases that hold the piece together, like the cables on a suspension bridge. The various thicknesses and lengths provide strength and flexibility, allowing the musical structure to bend and sway without breaking. Phrase points and ellisions can also serve as signposts which guide us through the musical map. Phrasal awareness is a basic tenet of great music making. Phrasal elasticity—expanding and contracting the phrase—allows us to change the shape of the music. In effect, we sculpt the phrases to create a sense of shape and movement in the music. This keeps the music alive and in a state of constant growth and flow.

If we are to lead others through the exploration and discovery process, it is incumbent upon us to create a map as we traverse the musical terrain. Diagramming the phrasal structure of the work is a way of charting the ideas and chronicling the events that we encounter along the way. Once our skeletal map is created we have a much better chance of guiding others though the musical journey in a thoughtful and knowing way. Each time we lead an expedition we collect more and more information which helps us to fill in the details of the map. As the guides we are expected to know where we have been, where we are, and where we are going. We become the listeners' link and the composer's representative on the journey. Informed, attentive musicians are the listeners' only hope for a successful "walkabout."

All music has some story to tell. In order to perceive the music's story you must be able to break it down into its component parts or layers. Helping musicians and listeners to do that is a primary task of the conductor. Phrasing creates the grammar, syntax, and rhetoric of music. Becoming aware of the phrase structure, or organization of musical thought is an important first step in creating an understanding of the composer's ideas and emotions. Keep in mind that all notes depend upon context for meaning. At the most basic level it is the phrase that creates the context and the sense of flow that is so important to establishing continuity and understanding. The following comparison to literary elements may help to clarify what goes into the construction of a musical work.

BOOK	Chapter	Paragraph	Sentence	Phrase	Word	Letter
COMPOSITION	Movement	Section	Phrase	Sub-phrase	Motive	Tone

Creating a visual representation of the phrasal structure always helps to deepen and broaden our concept of the whole. Phrases help us to create an outlined memory of the piece. A sample diagram (Diagram 4) of the theme from Schoenberg's *Theme and Variations* can be found below. The goal is to create a visual representation that can function as a map which will lead you back again and again to the caves, hills, peaks, and valleys of the work. This allows us to effectively and efficiently revisit important spots in the music at will so that we can continue to refine concepts and explore the work in greater and greater detail. Whether we use letters, symbols, brackets, arches, graphs, numbers, or colors to develop an outline is unimportant. What really matters is that we find a way to visually represent the process. This helps us create a memory of the work and continue to investigate where the trails lead and currents flow.

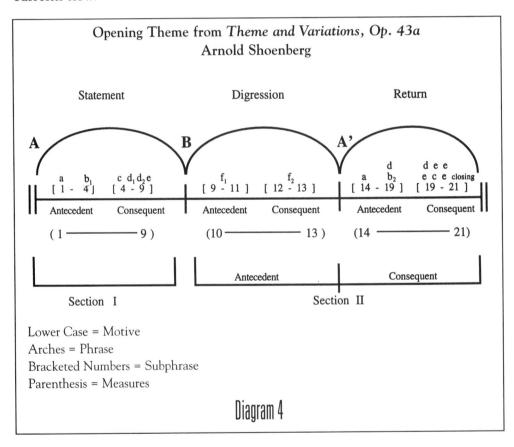

Diagram 4

Playing Smart

In the first volume of this series I offered a four-part approach to preparation for the teacher called "The Quantum Conductor." The "Playing Smart" diagram (Diagram 5) found below represents an attempt to extend this four-step approach to the musicians. The information seeks to clarify the differences between planning, practicing, rehearsing, and performing from the viewpoint of the player. Great performances are achieved through paying careful attention to the issues found in the diagram at all stages of develop-

Playing Smart

Plan - Method - With Mentors	Time Continuum
• Wanting to be successful • Mental organization • Set short and long term goals • Keep a journal to chronicle progress • Continuously revise and redesign • Determine what needs work, now and next • Budget time to achieve goals • Map musical topography	(Space represents time invested) Develop a flexible plan which establishes priorities and helps you act thoughtfully and knowingly
Practice - Part - On Own • Taking action to be successful • Physical activity • Develop craft • Build muscle and musical memory • Repetition slow and controlled • Time intensive • Work on what you cannot play • Target attention on problem solving • Use a metronome and tuner • Solve individual problems • Develop consistency	Nobody knows what you cannot play better than you. The doing that qualifies you to attend rehearsals. A well prepared part is something you bring to rehearsal, not something you develop in rehearsal.
Rehearse - Piece - With Others • Interrupted process • Broken energy flow • Learning more formal • Verbal and visual • Informal environment, ensemble is the audience • Directed listening and adjusting • Discover composer's intent • Multiple zooms in and out • Critical listening • Search for the implied meaning • Solve group problems • Evaluate during the process • Apply consistency	Doing things together that cannot be done alone. You do not come to rehearsal to learn your part, you come to learn everyone else's.
	Coming to rehearsal without practicing is like coming to a drama or dance run-through without knowing your lines or steps. Preparation allows us to take musical direction, not just technical instruction.
Perform - Work - For Others • Continuous process • Non-stop energy flow • Learning more intuitive • Nonverbal and visual • Self monitored listening and adjusting • Formal environment with outside audience • Suspend time and achieve ethereal plane • Culmination of study and experience • Spontaneous creation • Focus and target attention • Transcend problems • Evaluate following the process • Access consistency	A collaboration between conductor and player which represents the collective musical understanding. Unlike dance or drama, the teacher is on stage with the player throughout the creative process. Present a gift that comes from the heart and inspires the soul (Space represents the amount of accountability to others) **Responsibility Continuum**

Diagram 5

ment. If music has not been made and consistency has not been developed during practice and rehearsal, it will not suddenly appear like magic at a performance. In other words, if it has not happened in rehearsal it cannot happen in performance. This diagram will, I hope, allow for comparing and contrasting the musical processes of the player with the musical process of the conductor. While the first two stages are quite different for the player, the third and fourth are shared with the conductor. I must reiterate that the ongoing goal is to increase the enjoyment and appreciation of the work of art. The diagram is offered merely as food for thought. Please feel free to expand the points under each category. It is my hope that this information can help to demystify the growth process of players while calling attention to the responsibilities inherent in playing in an ensemble.

Conclusion

I believe the value of our musicing can be quantified by how much of the musical experience stays with us. All too often in music education we rely on the number of trophies in the case or first-division ratings received to demonstrate the value of our programs to others. We must remember that the trophies and rating sheets remain in the rehearsal room while the experiences go with the students. It is the wonderful memories of musicing as well as enhanced knowledge and appreciation of music that the students take with them that define the true value of our work as teachers.

Not too long ago I was conducting the California All-State High School Band. On a lunch break, I was sitting at a table in the hotel restaurant, studying a score and not paying too much attention to what was going on around me. "Mr. Corporon?" I heard my name very faintly and looked up to see my waitress standing at the table with tears in her eyes. In a flash I recognized her as a former horn player, Debbie, who had played in my first band twenty years earlier. This was a young lady whom I had switched from trumpet to horn and on the same day handed her the first part to *La Fiesta Mexicana*—a very difficult work, especially for the horn—by H. Owen Reed. Before I could even say hello or apologize for all of the extra responsibility I had heaped on her two decades earlier, Debbie began to recount her experiences in band as though they had just happened. Every word she uttered had to do with the music. "Do you remember *La Fiesta*? I'll never forget *Suite Francaise*. Is John Paynter still arranging music? Do people play the Holst suites anymore? Did you ever get a better score to *Lincolnshire Posy*?" I began to cry with her. It all came back: the early morning master classes, the evening orchestra rehearsals, the after-school sectionals, the concert tour to Catalina Island, but above all, the great music and the great moments we had shared as a family. Debbie explained to me how she made a point of playing our old vinyl recordings for her daughter and how proud she was of those records. We visited for a long while and caught up. She had not touched her horn for several years but the memories of her other life as a musician were as vivid as any she held in her mind. While Debbie had been a member of a division one, trophy-winning band, the memories she treasured most were of the feelings and emotions that great music making had evoked in her. As a teacher it was a defining moment in my life. Debbie had continued to be an avid consumer of art and was still listening to and appreciating great music. She helped me to remember why I love this profession so much. The memories of the music, the people, and the experiences remain with all of us. They are our gifts to give, keep, and treasure for a lifetime. They never can be taken away, they can only be given away. The quality of those experiences impacts the quality of life for every musician and society at large. Once you have become a musician you will always be one whether or not you continue to perform. There can be no doubt musicing impacts and changes lives for the better and forever!

CHAPTER 6

Composing Music That Educates

Jack Stamp

I have never taught. I share music with my students.

··· Vincent Persichetti ···

Introduction

Works of art used specifically for pedagogical purposes? This is a concept with which the great master composers rarely had to deal. Though some instructional music was written, the majority of the compositions written before the advent of institutionalized music education were strictly artistic in nature. These compilations were made by composers such as C. P. E. Bach (*The True Art of Playing the Keyboard*) and J. J. Quantz (*On Playing the Flute*), who were able performers on the featured instruments in these compositions. Most of these works were received by an "educated" public, artistically attuned to the music of their time. This is not to say that there were no controversial or poorly received works. One only needs to read excerpts from Nicolas Slonimsky's *Lexicon of Musical Invective* to realize that new works, now considered standard repertoire, often struggled for identity following their premieres. However, we also know that following its premiere, subsequent performances of *Le Sacre du Printemps* were well received! Nonetheless, the early patrons of art music were well-educated and somewhat sophisticated in the musical genres of their time.

The specific education of composers during the common practice period was achieved through apprenticeships. We are all well aware of stories of the apprentice hand copying scores and parts for the great master and learning his art via this process. Musicians studied composition in order to learn, not so that they could be employed. But this was not just an eighteenth- and nineteenth-century ideal. Twentieth-century American composers flocked to Fontainebleau to study with the master teacher, Nadia Boulanger. No degrees were offered, but incredible insights into the compositional process were shared.

How does one become a composer? The image of a composer to most non-composing musicians or laypersons is one of mystery. In his book *What to Listen for in Music*, Aaron Copland states that "the composer, in short, is a [person] of mystery to most people, and the composer's workshop an unapproachable ivory tower."[1]

Copland further states that the layman tends to forget that "composing to a composer is like fulfilling a natural function." Elizabeth Swados, in her book *Listening Out Loud*, concurs with Copland, stating that "the passion for organizing sounds and the desire to own and shape them are characteristic of all composers."[2]

Probably, the questions most often asked of a composer are, "Where do you get your idea or inspiration for a work?" and "How do you begin?" I rarely begin composing with the first measure of a piece, though Joan Tower, outstanding composer and recipient of the prestigious Grawmeyer Award, does just that, beginning with measure one and composing in sequence until the work is completed. In the initial stages of a work, coming up with "an idea" can be excruciating. It may start with a melodic motive, harmonic progression, or rhythmic pulsation. Whatever the material, it must be shaped, formed and developed from a "seedling" into a carefully devised series of musical events we call a composition.

If we agree that music should appeal to our emotions and intellect, then surely the music being written for educational purposes must meet the same criteria. Early works written for the American wind band exhibit these qualities. *George Washington Bridge* (Schuman), *Tunbridge Fair* (Piston), *Lincolnshire Posy* (Grainger), *Canzona* (Mennin), *Suite Française* (Milhaud), *Divertimento for Band* (Persichetti), and *Symphony for Band* (Gould) have qualities that both touch our hearts and engage our minds. These works, however, predate the real push in educational music of the 1960s, 1970s, and 1980s. In fact, many of these works, originally written for high school band, are quite demanding and unplayable by many of today's secondary school ensembles. I chuckle when I read Darius Milhaud's inscription in the score of *Suite Française* about the "moderate" difficulty of his composition. Nonetheless, these early compositions are the forerunners of educational literature and should serve as the models for the band literature written today. Yet the advent of institutionalized music education and the business of music education has sometimes produced educational products which are less than artistically viable. The incredible availability of instruments, music, and instruction in our culture is unparalleled. Yet the concept of assembly line or mass production seems to encourage music which is more functional than inspired.

The question for the educational composer is simple. I paraphrase Frank Battisti (conductor of the New England Conservatory of Music Wind Ensemble) when I ask, "Is our job to create music that teaches both intellectually and emotionally, or is our job to compose music that will sound good?"

When I was a child, television programs always referred to castor oil as a remedy for any illness. Its horrible taste was legendary, though no one I knew had actually tasted the elixir. A commercial, advertising a new children's medicine stated, "Medicine doesn't have to taste bad to be good!" And so it is with music; it need not be difficult to be good music.

If we were asked to give a few words describing the major qualities in the music of Bach, Beethoven, and Brahms, one might say:

Bach: counterpoint, clarity

Beethoven: structure, contrasts

Brahms: melody, scoring, rhythm

Notice that when we think of the great masters' music, those elements that come to mind are not technical aspects of performance. Therefore, technique, range, and instrumentation should not impede the creation of meaningful, educational literature. It seems as if these limitations have stripped much music of the basic elements of composition. None of these basic elements has technical demands, yet all can be found in the music of the great masters.

If we approach the music we compose and perform with our ensembles as a type of diet, then we must provide high-protein, low-fat, and low-cholesterol music. Music of little substance—whether it lacks emotional and intellectual depth or is absent of craft—adds hollow "musical calories" to students' perception of art music. An "addiction" to this type of music can develop so that actual teaching is no longer the focus and instead feeding this musical addiction keeps the ensemble alive. We have heard conductors say that their bands don't like a particular work and "won't play it!" Does the public school English teacher ever not read Shakespeare in fear of students' initial reaction? Most school systems have guidelines and requirements for the selection of literature in English classes. Sadly, the same cannot be said for the instrumental music programs in a majority of our secondary schools. It is, therefore, each individual music teacher's responsibility to select the "Shakespeares" for his/her medium and students' level of ability.

It is also the educational music composer's responsibility to write works that model the great compositions for our medium. The music need not be a clone or watered-down version of a famous piece, but it should possess the qualities in its craft and use of techniques that are characteristic of all great music including those works of the twentieth century. Composer Paul Hindemith was attuned to this concept. His approach to composing "educational music" was termed *Gebrauchsmusik*, a classification Hindemith disliked. Nonetheless, the concept was founded in strong pedagogical and musical principles. Hindemith "stressed the need for new works in a contemporary style which children and beginners could use to familiarize themselves with new styles of composition and thus come nearer to understanding them."[3] Qualities common to all great music include:

- a variety of keys or key centers
- use of non-diatonic melodies
- use of non-triadic harmony
- accompaniment not restricted to *ostinato*
- texture (transparent and full)
- contrasts and unpredictability
- counterpoint
- transitions
- rhythmic variety including *hemiola* and meter changes

It is my goal when composing educational works to strive to expose the performers to a wide variety of compositional techniques explored not only by Bach and Beethoven, but by twentieth-century composers as well. This requires craft! I then must homogenize those techniques, filtering them through my own personality. It is at this point that I must appeal to the listener's emotions. Once a composer has the ability to do this, he/she acquires an identifiable style. The works may sound different, but there is something that suggests the identity of the composer. This is not to say that the music has repetitive clichés and a cloned predictability. On the contrary, the composer must continually bring fresh ideas to an individualized and identifiable style. It is not difficult to recognize a work by Debussy, Hindemith, or Copland. The music of J. S. Bach, though not innovative or unique for his time, is highly recognizable for its sheer quality and perfection. Therefore, the music of educational composers should retain those qualities of individuality and strive for the perfection achieved by the masters. As composers, it is our duty to both music and our students to provide the very best we have to offer as musicians and composers.

Realistically, the composer cannot bear the entire responsibility for the musical education of students. The band conductor must take an active role in the creation of new works via the commissioning process.

Creating a Repertoire: Commissioning

As few as twenty years ago, the idea of a school band commissioning a new work was an isolated event. The concept was unimaginable for most teachers; a project only for the exceptionally gifted and financially endowed ensemble. This misconception was mostly based on a lack of understanding of the commissioning process. Thankfully, in more recent years the commissioning of new works has become a regular activity of many school band programs. Through commissioning, the ensemble has the opportunity to contribute quality literature to the existing repertoire while having an individual interaction with a living composer. The process benefits the medium as well as the individuals of the ensemble. Therefore, a careful and responsible commissioning project will provide years of benefits not only to the commissioning party,

but to all those ensembles which eventually perform the work.

When approached about the commissioning process, the following questions are most often asked:

1. *How do I commission a piece?*
2. *Whom should I commission?*
3. *What type of piece do I commission?*
4. *How much will it cost?*
5. *How do I pay for it?*
6. *What is a consortium?*
7. *What are my rights in the process; what are the composer's rights?*
8. *Are there any alternatives to the commissioning process?*

1. How do I commission a piece?

The actual timetable for a commissioned work may extend up to two years. A composer must be chosen with an agreement on the price, type of work, part copying, and deadline for a work. This is best done through a contractual agreement. A composer usually prefers at least a year's notice for a commission. Some work with computers, so the parts may be included in the price of the commission. Others score in manuscript, so the extraction of parts may be an additional cost. Some composers request half of their fee when they begin the work, receiving the balance upon delivery of the completed score.

2. Whom should I commission?

The choice of the composer is usually the responsibility of the music director. Determining factors are usually based upon how much the commissioning party can afford and/or the type of work requested. Many composers are chosen based upon their previous work, usually in the band genre. Many of these commissions are superb works, while others are mere clones of previously popular pieces. If commissioning a noted band composer, making a request for a work which varies from the composer's normal musical approach (whether it be in form, length, instrumentation, or movement structure) can produce a fresh new work as well as provide an impetus for the composer to branch out into new areas of composition.

Another suggestion is to commission a composer who has not written widely for band. This type of commission usually provides a work free of the clichés associated with band music and one that is adventuresome in the area of scoring.

If cost is a concern, canvas the local area for a retired composer or arranger. The local college surely will have a theorist/composer on its faculty. Usually a local composer will negotiate a fee which is workable for both parties. If price is still an issue, then approach a student composer at the local college. I have found several student pieces which are well-suited to school ensembles. Most of these young composers are eager to write a commissioned

work and are very affordable (depending upon how far they are from home, a few home-cooked meals could serve as a down payment!).

3. What type of piece do I commission?

Using resources in the community always rallies support for the project and often produces wonderful works. Using the words of a local poet set to music for solo voice or chorus and band is one suggestion. Requesting a work for narrator and band based on speeches by a town's founder and performed with the local state representative as narrator is sure to attract the public eye. A work for a soloist and band featuring local talent or a non-traditional band instrument as soloist (e.g., violin, harp, accordion, harmonica, organ, synthesizer, guitar, string quartet) is unique to the genre and sure to be a welcome addition to the repertoire. Be inventive and creative in the process, not only serving the students, but also furthering the medium.

4. How much will it cost?

Commission fees can range from $500 to $25,000, depending upon the status of the composer and the length of the work. Many composers charge a fee based upon their interest in composing such a work. Others base their fee upon a "per minute of music" rate. Above all, be up front with a composer concerning how much budget is available. Don't be upset if the composer refuses, nor surprised if he or she is willing to work within the commissioning party's means.

5. How do I pay for it?

Obviously, the typical fund-raising activities, as well as band parents' projects, will be the seed money for such an endeavor. Depending upon the type of work requested, community corporate support is highly probable. Local arts councils may have funding available. Finally, Meet the Composer, Inc. has a fund entitled "New Music in Our Schools" which funds commissions for school music programs. More details can be obtained by writing directly to:

> Meet the Composer, Inc.
> 2112 Broadway, Suite 505
> New York, NY 10023
> Phone: (212) 787-3601

6. What is a consortium?

A consortium commission is one of the fastest growing ways to commission and finance a project. The consortium is a "group" commission. Several schools get together and pool their resources to co-commission a work. This drastically reduces the price to each individual party. A consortium can be as few as two parties or up to thirty! Of course, this process takes careful planning and coordination. It also takes music educators that are interested in the process. In a consortium commission it is difficult to hold the premiere. However, the combining of groups for the performance, or the establishment

of a "premiere week" in which all of the groups perform the work at their respective institutions, are viable methods of dealing with the first performance.

7. What are my rights as a commissioner?

It is my belief that the commissioning party has the right to dictate the type of work requested. This may include instrumentation, use of soloists, style, and length of the work. In addition, the commissioning organization can request the inscription as well as a period of exclusivity, during which only the commissioning party may perform the work.

8. Are there any alternatives to the commissioning process?

I am constantly amazed at the amount of money band programs spend on a variety of projects. Though commissioning fine composers can be expensive, there are less expensive alternatives to the commissioning process. Why do we limit composer interaction with students to those band festivals where only a portion of the school's instrumental students are involved? Bringing a composer to a school is an inexpensive way to provide students with hands-on experience with a living composer. Not all composers are dead! Preparing a variety of already published works by the composer and presenting a concert of their music with them present is highly educational and provides truly meaningful experiences for students.

A Composer's Perspective on Conductors and Interpretations

At the advent of large instrumental ensemble music, the composer played an important and essential role in bringing the work to performance. The composer would assume the duties of manager, promoter, and agent as well as musical director and conductor. In numerous letters of Mozart we find reference to "conducting," on several instances from the keyboard. In fact, the first conductors in history were composers. It was not until the latter part of the nineteenth century that the non-composer/conductor emerged. Many composer/conductors also flourished in that century including Mendelssohn, Liszt, Wagner, Mahler, and Strauss. However, there were many composers who were not as adept with the baton as they were with the pen. In his treatise *Traité d'Instrumentation*, Hector Berlioz addressed this issue when he stated that many times composers "imagining they know how to conduct, innocently ruin their best scores."[4]

I can distinctly remember discovering Stravinsky. On spring break, I went to the local record store and bought a big silver boxed set entitled *Nine Masterpieces Conducted by the Composer*. Stravinsky was conducting his own works! Upon my return to campus, I rushed into my major professor's studio and exclaimed my musical find. His reaction totally dumbfounded me at the

time. "That's too bad," he said. "Stravinsky was not known as the best inter-
preter of his own works." It took years for me to understand his statement. Not
until I had worked with composers, conducted their music, and composed
myself did I realize the truth of his comment. Although the composer can lend
great insights to the structure, direction, and meaning of a work, he/she also
brings the "architectural baggage" to the podium. There are few composers
who can separate the role of creator from the responsibility of re-creator.
Baton and rehearsal technique aside, an independent voice can bring energy
and new perspective to a work. Most conductors are intuitively drawn to a
work before they are intellectually stimulated by it. This lends itself to a reac-
tionary interpretation, motivated by the very elements the composer hopes
will stimulate the listener.

Many composers give tedious and detailed instruction for the performance of their own works. These guidelines are extremely helpful but somewhat confining in nature. I tend to agree with Arthur Weisberg who states the
following in *The Art of Wind Playing*:

> We do not reproduce music; we interpret it. If it were simply a mat-
> ter of reproducing it, there would only be one way to play each piece
> and the world of music would be incredibly dull. Fortunately we are
> not faced with this situation, except in the area of electronic music,
> because no two people play alike, and, what is more important, the
> composer is at best only able to put down on paper about thirty
> percent of his intentions. The rest is left to the interpretation of the
> performer.[5]

The great composer and friend of bands, Vincent Persichetti, concurred:

> One of the things I encounter very often that really bothers me is a
> false respect for the composer's intentions. They [conductors] try to
> be slaves to what the composer has written. There are some things
> that can be written; we can write ritards and accelerandos. But there
> are times when we cannot write accelerandos and ritards, but we
> mean them, when a phrase has to shape itself, and you must give and
> take. There has to be flexibility. Too many conductors are almost too
> afraid to show a disrespect for the composer.[6]

Therefore, composers expect and implicitly request interpretation of their
music. The issue becomes interpretation versus poetic license. No composer
wants his/her music distorted at the hands of an egocentric conductor.
Exploring new or bold and daring interpretations for the purpose of being different or noticed does not serve the composer, the students, or the music well.
The conductor should be, in Erich Leinsdorf's terms, "the composer's advocate." He/she should be subservient to the music. Just as the same clothing
looks different on different individuals, so can performances of the same work

by different conductors legitimately sound different, as long as they are all rooted in careful study, thorough preparation, and honest feelings. Composers welcome interpretations and look forward to hearing different performances of their works. However, it should be noted that the degree of interpretation is directly proportional to the quality of the musical work chosen. Therefore, a work of high compositional integrity will lend itself to interpretation more easily than a work of lesser quality.

Impromptu Composing for the School Ensemble

The process of composing should not be limited to those trained in the art, or those who are published in a particular genre. The basic techniques of composition can be taught to students via the school ensemble.

The concepts of motivic development, retrograde, augmentation, diminution, octave displacement, and melody as harmony can easily be taught in a half-hour session with a school ensemble. I will outline the process as follows:

1. To immediately involve the ensemble in the process, ask for a pitch from four or five individuals in the group. Write them on the board as follows:

   G   F-sharp   B-flat   A

2. Then, write the B-flat, E-flat, and F transpositions under the original. Depending upon the age level of the group, I label the row by the transposition or by the instruments involved (e.g., B-flat or clarinet, tenor sax, trumpet, treble clef baritone):

(C Instruments)	G	F-sharp	B-flat	A
(B-flat instruments)	A	G-sharp	C	B
(E-flat instruments)	E	D-sharp	G	F-sharp
(F instruments)	D	C-sharp	F	E

3. Have the students play the row, one note at a time. Once they get it in their ear, have them play it backwards!

4. It is here that you begin to experiment with different permutations of the row. Do not actually build a work yet, but have the ensemble experiment (à la Schoenberg) with the four notes as follows:

   a. Pick one note of the row and sustain it as a *fermata*; do that four times with each student changing their note until they have played all four.

   b. Have the students play the four notes, one time, in a fast, unison treatment à la four sixteenth notes at quarter note=120. Have them repeat it backwards.

   c. Have the students play the row forward, taking one of the notes and changing the octave either higher or lower.
   d. Free for all! Have the students play the row repeatedly, as fast as they can.
   e. Terrace the performance of the row, either canonically or via rhythmic values:
      i. divide the ensemble via transposition, spatial arrangement, or range and perform the row as a canon at one or three beats.
      ii. divide the ensemble via transposition, spatial arrangement, or range and perform the row with one group playing half notes, one group playing quarter notes, and one group playing eighth notes, each beginning at a different time.
   f. A percussion cadenza is always fun; make sure the timpani are tuned to the four pitches and all of the keyboard percussion instruments are being covered.

5. Now that the students have experienced the various permutations of the original row, it is time to string these segments together into a composition. Having the students write the sequence down on a piece of notebook paper usually helps to avoid the numerous "train wrecks" that can happen.

A composition may be put together in steps as follows:
1. Unison forward at *forte* (#3)
2. Unison backward at *piano* (#3)
3. Sustain chords (#4a)
4. One time fast sixteenths forwards (#4b), one time fast sixteenths backwards
5. Terracing via rhythm (#4e-ii)
6. Repeat step 1
7. Percussion cadenza (#4f)
8. Octave displacement (#4c)
9. Canon at three beats (#4e-i)
10. Free for all (#4d)
11. Repeat step 3, beginning *forte* with a *diminuendo* to *piano*

Obviously, each permutation does not have to be included and the order of the events can be varied. However, note that the above exercise is ordered in a type of rondo, with the unison original anchoring the more adventurous episodes.

Other permutations of the given row can include individual improvisations and/or the teaching of "pointillism." The students can choose one of the

notes and play it as the conductor points to them.

I have used this exercise successfully with a wide variety of age groups and musical abilities. Though it is not an exercise that should be used daily or even weekly, it does break up the monotony of a typical rehearsal as well as open the students' ears and eyes to the compositional process.

Conclusion

Educational composers and music educators should rededicate themselves not only to their students but to their involvement in the music-making process. We must realize that the immortality of music lies in its aesthetic power and its meticulous construction. These are both elements that we must share with our students.

Jamie Aebersold was interviewed on a CBS Sunday Morning program several years ago. He told the story of a salesman who canvassed an entire community for a week trying to sell his wares, only to come up emptyhanded. At the end of the week, he reported his dismal sales record to his boss, detailing the number of houses he had approached and lamenting, "Well, I guess it's like the old adage: you can lead a horse to water, but you can't make him drink." The boss looked over his desk at the young salesman and replied, "There is where you are wrong, young man. Our job is not to make them drink; our job is to make them thirsty!" It is our job to make our students thirsty for music. We can achieve this through the careful selection and composition of quality music, enriched by the craft of the past masters, yet exploring the freshness of contemporary techniques.

Notes

1　Aaron Copland, *What to Listen for in Music* (New York: McGraw-Hill Book Company, 1957), 24-26.

2　Elizabeth Swados, *Listening Out Loud* (New York: Harper & Row Publishers, 1988), 2-3.

3　Geoffrey Skelton, *Paul Hindemith: The Man Behind the Music* (London: Victor Gollancz Ltd., 1975), 16.

4　Hector Berlioz, *Treatise on Instrumentation*, enlarged by Richard Strauss, translated by Theodore Front (New York: E. F. Kalmus, 1948), 4.

5　Arthur Weisberg, *The Art of Wind Playing* (New York: Schirmer Books, 1975), 118-119.

6　Robert E. Page, "In Quest of Answers: An Interview with Vincent Persichetti," *Choral Journal* (November 1973): 7.

CHAPTER 7

Successful Music Advocacy

Tim Lautzenheiser

*Musical training is a more potent instrument than any other (for education)
because rhythm and harmony find their way into the inward places
of the soul, on which they mightily fasten, imparting grace, and
making the soul of him who is rightly educated graceful, or of him who
is ill-educated ungraceful.*

··· Plato ···

Introduction

Within the last two decades—specifically starting in the early '80s—music advocacy has come to the forefront of the music education world. The focus is on *the value of music* in the educational development of our children. Many professional leaders have contributed to the ever-growing wealth of knowledge. Scientific research continues to point to music as a key factor in the development the human mind. We no longer have to justify music with platitudes or personal notions; the hard-copy facts and figures are now available. The horizon is bright for the world of music education, but only if we fulfill our roles as the stewards of the good news, delivering it to the right people and in the right context.

This chapter is not a definitive laundry list of specific suggestions or instructions, such as developing the parent phone tree, sample letters to the School Board, etc. Detailed advocacy kits are available and can be attained by contacting the organizations listed at the end of the chapter. These advocacy blueprints, offering success-proven techniques, are priceless and you are encouraged to obtain them and share them with your music supporters. I see your position as a leader, guiding and directing your music advocates and serving as an enthusiastic role model, much as you would direct your ensemble. Therefore, this chapter is devoted to a more holistic approach to advocacy, an

overall perspective, a viewpoint that is specifically applicable to the music educator who is responsible for creating, developing, sustaining, and nurturing an advocacy organization.

The entire school year could easily be devoted to promoting the program, educating the administrators, informing the parents, and so forth. However, the primary responsibility of the music educator is *to teach music*. Keeping this in mind, and also being crucially aware of the importance of the advocacy component, "Successful Music Advocacy" approaches the advocacy responsibility through the eyes of the music teacher. For many it will be a shift in attitude, from an intense point of convergence based on creating a flawless performance to a larger perspective, one of comprehending and understanding that the process of learning music is more valuable than the final product. Strangely enough, when the mind is willing to accept this reality, the performance aspect of the ensemble inevitably improves. It is not just the awareness of the academic value of music, it is an acceptance of this reality and the integration of the knowledge (knowing) in the daily teaching habits. When this realization takes place, advocacy is no longer something we do, it is something *we are*.

The one common characteristic of programs of excellence is a strong and healthy advocacy constituent. The director/leader realizes the importance of music as an academic core subject and insists on sharing the information with everyone who has a vested interest in the music program, and, likewise, makes certain *everyone* is aware of their vested interest.

As a suggestion to the reader, do not simply peruse the chapter looking for some quick-fix solution or the hopeful discovery of a cute idea guaranteed to generate excitement about the band. You will be sorely disappointed. Read a paragraph and then apply it to your situation, reframe it to fit your needs, let it simmer in your mind, then reread it and mentally outline how you could adopt and adapt the information to benefit your program. Come back to the chapter time and time again; it is a reference, not a patented prescription.

Above all, approach the material with an open mind. In all too many instances we have become our own worst enemy by our unwillingness to shift, change, and conform to the present-day educational perspective. We, as music educators, offer students the most valuable educational training in the school; we give students the tools to manifest success in every phase of their lives. It's time to share the good news, to let our words accompany our music, and let the world know about the immeasurable value of music education through "Successful Music Advocacy."

Successful Music Advocacy: Communication Is the Answer

Educational reformation is a way of life in the American society. Politicians are eager to include education as a mainstay of their campaign platforms. Teachers know the curriculums must be in constant transition to accommodate the ongoing growth of modern technology. Parents are keenly aware of the importance of the learning atmosphere and are eager to see their children experience a positive learning culture. In the midst of this evolution, music, as well as the other fine arts, has come to the educational forefront and our nation is embracing the arts as a basic subject for every child.

In 1990 the Music Educators National Conference (MENC), the National Association of Music Merchants (NAMM), and the National Association of Recording Arts and Sciences, Inc. (NARAS) joined forces in establishing the National Coalition for Music Education. The first priority of the organization: *to garner the support of people who are aware of the importance of music in our schools and begin a dialogue with state, regional, and district officials to promote music education and to avoid any kind of program reduction or omission based on budgetary decisions.* The state and local coalitions are effective if they have strong leadership and the inclusive involvement of teachers, parents, administrators, and community patrons. As with any organization, success is measured by the strength of its membership.

Advocacy, by definition, means: "1. To push; 2. To bolster; 3. To further a cause." As teachers of music, band directors, we often allow advocacy responsibilities to slip to the bottom of the priority list. The daily responsibilities—ranging from selecting repertoire for the upcoming solo-ensemble festival to negotiating with the drama teacher for access to the concert hall—take precedence over any formally designed program of music advocacy. Directors contend that there simply is not enough time, and yet it is ever apparent that the outstanding band programs integrate advocacy in all aspects of the organization. It is not viewed as a separate responsibility, but is synthesized as part of the musical climate; it is a focused commitment, an ongoing sharing of the value of music in the growth of *every* child.

Granted, in years past, most colleges did not include a class in "Advocacy" as a requisite to the completion of the music degree. Even today advocacy is often combined with a general methods class, or included as an amendment to a preparatory class in student-teaching. The point is, many directors are clearly aware of the need for advocacy, but feel a great sense of inadequacy in creating, developing, and maintaining an ongoing advocacy agenda. As a result we are depriving the students, the parents, the school, the community, and ourselves of many benefits that add artistic richness to the musical experience. As with any template of educational growth, the greatest form of learning is *by doing*. We can no longer point the finger of blame at anyone; it is time to take action, shift the paradigm, and eagerly include advocacy in our teaching philosophies. It is time *to do, to take action*, to become active music advocates.

Music Advocacy: A Realistic Approach

When asked, "What is music advocacy?" thoughts of a school board meeting attended by several hundred supportive band parents with placards in hand loudly shouting their support for the director come to mind. While there have been such scenes (more for dramatic effect than for effective advocacy), this chapter is devoted to a more subtle and sophisticated approach focusing on pro-action rather than reaction. Instead of operating out of crisis mode to save the program from administrators' sharpened fiscal pencils, let us perceive advocacy as an opportunity to build alliances to secure the present program and become a participant in the future policy making. We must demonstrate a commitment to the ongoing exchange of data emphasizing the legitimacy of the core subject: music. Based on the amount of positive information available through the National Coalition Library (see reference page) and the ongoing research material surfacing daily through the efforts of MENC, NAMM, and NARAS, we are not lacking for convincing statistics highlighting the importance of music education; the challenge lies in the *communication* of the information. Any individual mildly interested in the education of our youth will quickly jump on the Arts Bandwagon after he/she has been exposed to the facts and figures concerning the impact of music in the human potential development process, i.e., *learning*. What is the most effective and efficient way to educate every one concerning the necessity of *music for every child?* That is the question: not *what* to do, but *how* to do it.

Advocacy Begins with the Director: You

Music advocacy begins with the director, it begins with a complete *knowing and understanding* of the mission, it begins with you. As stated in all the MENC materials, *"Just as there can be no music without learning; no education is complete without music."*[1] Herein lies the foundation of the music educator's professional mission statement: the belief/knowing that learning music is a part of every young person's birthright. It is easy to lose sight of this truth in the heat of performance deadlines; however this truth is the basis of every action taken, a fundamental truth that determines the prosperity of every program from beginning to end. We must first be believers before we can ethically engage others in our quest. "Why music?" is not an unfair question, but one deserving of a clear, concise, easily understood answer.

PHILOSOPHICALLY:

1. *Music is intrinsic*, and in every individual; it is connected to the human spirit and creative mind. We cannot duplicate it through any other form of expression, we cannot quantify it. It exists for its own sake.

INTELLECTUALLY:
2. *Music opens the mind.* Ongoing brain research continues to link excelled learning skills with music. The breakthrough work of Dr. Gordon Shaw (University of California-Irvine) and his colleagues affirms every musician's inherent knowing, but (until now) not scientifically proven theory, of access to higher levels of creativity in every form of learning based on musical understanding.

EDUCATIONALLY:
3. *Music teaches more than music.* While these characteristics are not specifically tied to the study of music, they are a by-product of the process:
    A. The establishment of high achievement standards transferable to other academic subjects.
    B. Development of keen problem-solving patterns.
    C. Establishment collaborative teamwork habits through communication skills.
    D. Understanding flexible thinking and adapting the known to the unknown.
    E. Improvement of reading comprehension, motor proficiency, spatial awareness, and listening ability.
    F. Mastery of a given challenge while expanding the realm of understanding and pushing beyond self-inflicted limits (raising of personal standards).
    G. Increasing self-esteem, self-confidence, and self-discipline.

GLOBALLY:
4. *Music is the universal language.* The shrinking globe dictates the need for establishing relationships with every world culture. Cross-civilization communication continues to be at the forefront of our very existence. Music creates sensitive individuals dedicated to dispelling prejudices that jeopardize the harmony of mankind.

This is all well and good, but means little to present-day programs unless it is disseminated in an intelligent, understandable fashion to parents, school officials, political decision-makers, and even the students themselves. There is more to this music learning experience than renting an instrument and participating in band; it is focused on the preparation of the individual for a life of personal success and happiness.

The First Step:
To Convince Others, We Must First Convince Ourselves

The perspective of the educator who is a music advocate is shaped by a deep personal conviction. Just as the person of a given faith interprets the

world through the filters of a chosen belief system, likewise the teacher who is a confirmed music advocate embraces his/her professional catalogue of responsibilities influenced by the realization that music education reaches far beyond producing a fine concert. It is not enough to bring the ensemble on stage and demonstrate beautiful intonation, clear articulation, and an expressive rendition of the music. While it is imperative we strive for these musical goals, they only represent one segment of the overall goal. The auditorium must be filled with enthusiastic parents, proud administrators, and appreciative community patrons. It requires more than just a few publicity tricks to guarantee a sold-out house; it is a reflection of those in attendance who understand, through careful educational guidance, the importance of music as an essential element of life. It will not happen by accident; it is the fruit of a solid, active advocacy program constantly fed by the director and his/her support team.

Communicating to the Right Audiences

The Students

The greatest stage for advocacy is the rehearsal room. Who needs to understand the value of music more than anyone? *The students.* It will be of little use to convince others if the students are not privy to the benefits of music as it relates to their development.

Speak to the students concerning music as an expressionistic language. School, for the most part, is *impressionistic*—an exercise in memorizing various bits of information in preparation for the test. However music offers the opportunity to involve the heart and mind in a process of personal *expression*, to reach beyond the notes on the page. Encourage the connection of the students' inner thoughts to the music, constantly remind them of the need to "be the music" and not just "play the music." The zenith experience for any musician is *to be one with the music*. With proper instruction this could easily happen at the beginning level of music learning with the first note, and it should. Advocacy, at the level of students, is supporting their love of music and their desire to continue their journey of self-exploration. Conversely, if the student associates band (orchestra, choir, etc.) with a negative connotation, then all other advocacy efforts are of little consequence. First and foremost, the students must sense the teacher's dedication to music as an art form.

The Parents

The parents are more than just a body of people who raise funds for additional equipment, or meet monthly for an update of the ensemble's planned activities. The parents have a vested interest in the program, and the director, in turn, has a responsibility to create an open line of communication that serves as a busy network of exchange relating the valuable impact music has

on *every* student. Caution: when the parents/boosters are only an avenue to financial gains, the participation will be meager. If, however, the parent organization embraces the educational worth of music, the allegiance will evidence a notable increase in membership and active involvement.

Communication is the answer. It must be frequent, sincere, selfless, and dedicated to the parents' greatest concern: *the welfare of their child.* With the arrival of e-mail, the internet, web pages, etc., communication to an unlimited number of people is available at the touch of a computer key. Communication is not a luxury, it is a necessity. There is an endless supply of positive data ready to be shared with the parents; the challenge is to offer it to them in a user-friendly format. *Communication is the answer* and the key to all successful advocacy efforts.

Constantly reinforce the importance of music aside from the obvious; playing the clarinet, marching in the local parade, or performing at the annual holiday concert are tangible measurements of music education, but we know it is only the tip of the iceberg. Remind the parents that music *builds critical thinking skills, prepares students for the rigors of higher education, invigorates the process of learning, and pushes the mind to an advanced level of competence.* The excitement of the concert will be short lived, but the awareness of the long-range advantages of music education will serve as a strong influence for future parental decision making.

The Administrators

Administrators, in almost every case, are former classroom teachers. They made a career choice to contribute to the education of children by assuming a set of new challenges. Like everyone, their administrative choices are based on available information. With rare exception the administrator will do what is best (in his/her perception) for the positive educational growth and development of the students. To assume the administrator is aware of the benefits of music education is professional naiveté. In many cases the principal, supervisor, superintendent, etc., only sees/evaluates the results of the music classes at a basketball game (the pep band), at graduation (the band without seniors), or the July Fourth parade (summer band with the new eighth graders). This is hardly a fair assessment of a teacher's academic worth. In many instances the music wing of the school is at the opposite end of the building; administrators and directors can go weeks, even months without seeing one another. This creates, by proximity, a void in communication; remember, *communication is the answer.*

Paying frequent visits to the administrator's office offering important music information is as vital as tuning the band before the rehearsal begins. Inviting the administrators to come to class (rehearsal) is always an eye-opening experience for all. Student leaders can serve as messengers of good news concerning the program by requesting monthly update meetings with

administrators. Parents should be encouraged to seek various ways to include administrators in the booster meetings and events. Create a partnership with the administrator and the music program; by doing so the administrator becomes a music advocate via the inclusion process.

The Colleagues

The word "colleague" generally refers to music colleagues. Consider other teachers in the school as your advocate-colleagues. The human is infamous for polarizing with its own ilk or likeness, and education is no exception; English teachers talk to one another, coaches stick together, elementary educators chat with other elementary teachers, and music educators are no different. It is difficult to garner the support of interdisciplinary colleagues if we only communicate with other music educators. Advocacy is based on outreach. It is difficult to convince anyone of anything if we wait for people to come to us. We cannot afford to idly sit in the music office hoping others will have a sudden artistic revelation. When a music teacher says, "There isn't enough time to get to know the other teachers in the school," it demonstrates a shortsightedness that builds a certain communication barrier. In truth we must know *every* teacher in the school; these colleagues are key members of the advocacy team.

Over thirty percent of college graduates participated in their high school music program. One could easily conclude that one out of every three teachers in the school has participated in band, orchestra, or choir. It is time to *bring them back to music* and they will become new advocate-leaders for other faculty members. Invite your colleagues to play in a concert, work with a sectional, travel with the ensemble, be a soloist at a concert, serve as the announcer, become part of the music program. The dormant but enthusiastic adult musician is simply waiting for an opportunity to rejoin the band. It is very likely that a third of the school faculty are already music advocates; tap this powerful source of support.

The Community Leaders

It is true: *if the quality of student education diminishes, the community's lifestyle will also diminish.* The Athenians were well aware of the crucial balance between education and community welfare (music was also a required subject in the Greek educational system). Our forefathers insisted on an education for every child (represented by our public schools) for they knew it would secure America's position as a world leader. This theme is evident at the national, state, regional, and local levels. In smaller communities, the music teacher *is* the focal point of arts education, and the people of the community look to this individual (you) for advice, direction, and all expertise dealing with music. They must be included in the communication loop; otherwise they will assume music education is what they hear on the radio and see on television.

These people are taxpayers, voters, members and friends of the Board of Education, golfing partners with your administrators and colleagues. The conversations they have with their friends and acquaintances must positively support music education, and the most persuasive voice in the community *is* the music director.

The opportunities for community participation are endless, literally at the limits of the imagination, but the thoughts must be directed to mine the gems hidden within the local population. Does the editor of the area newspaper play trombone? Is the grocery store owner a percussionist? Did your doctor, minister, insurance agent sing in a choir? Even if they do not want to perform, rest assured they will want to contribute in some fashion, for they know the value of a solid music education. Reach out to them and invite them to be an active member of your advocacy organization; they will eagerly join.

Most successful business people are eager to support education. They realize their own achievements are a product of their knowing, their education. You can count on them for contributions of financial support if you can demonstrate through advocacy what their help will mean to the youth of the community. Do not expect the potential philanthropists to seek out the music program; you must go to them. It is the responsibility of the music advocate to make the first move. *Communication is the answer.*

The General Public

Contrary to popular thought, the general public is very much in favor of music education. The overwhelming opinion of American people is very pro-music, pro-art. Karl Bruhn, former Director of Market Development for the National Association of Music Merchants, was a key figure in the establishment and organization of the National Coalition. In one of his many essays, "On Preaching to the Choir: The Good News and the Bad News," he states (in reference to the 1992 Harris poll prepared at the request of the American Council for the Arts): *"More than nine out of ten polled, for example, said it was important for children to learn about the arts and to develop artistic interests in school."* He goes on to say:

> What the results of the Harris poll really mean is that we have to redouble our efforts to make sure the right message gets to the right people. We have to tell the decision makers not just that education in music and other arts has intrinsic value, or that it is the "right thing to do," but this is what the people in their community and in their state—in large numbers—want their children to learn.[2]

Much of the groundwork is in place for advocacy; the missing link to the puzzle appears to be leadership at the local level. Advocacy begins with the music educator. While it is possible to delegate individual duties along the

way, the advocacy wellspring is, and will always be, part of the mission of every music teacher. There is an army of support ready and eager to come forward. They are already convinced the arts/music have a place in the educational framework of our youth. Take the lead, become the focal point for pro-music advocacy within your community.

Guidelines to Successful Music Advocacy

The first part of this chapter has been devoted to the big picture of music in our schools: the whys and wherefores of music education. Where do we start? What is the first step? What are the key factors in making certain the invested time and energy produces the results needed? Of course every individual will discover his/her particular style of advocacy as time goes on, but there are many tried-and-true road signs that will aid along the advocacy journey.

Cooperation, Not Competition

Never promote the music program at the expense of another organization. Music must stand on its own and should not compete with any other aspect of the school's programs. Creating a situation where an individual is forced to choose is not only unfair to the one who chooses, but has no educational foundation. When an either-or situation appears, the students will always lose. Music advocacy is a benefit to the entire school and community; it must live in harmony with the existing curriculum.

Advocacy Is Student-Oriented

Music education is centered around students, children, the musicians. If the theme of the advocate is self-serving, then the charade will be short lived, as it should be. While there may be teaching positions retained or even added because of advocacy programs, this certainly is not the priority-theme. The emphasis is *music education for every child*. It must not be disguised to save one's job or buy a new amplification system for the jazz band; it must be focused on the academic importance of arts education. It is about students, not adults.

Think "Everyone Is a Musician"

Potentially every student in school could be in the band, the orchestra, and/or the choir. When discussing music advocacy, *everyone* is a student, not just those enrolled for the semester. Should we be satisfied with the participation of ten percent of the school? Are we simply trained to accept the fact that only a chosen few will be involved in music? Should we be content with enough good players for one showcase group? Why are we limiting our scope? Are we the living echo of "it's always been this way"? Every student walking the hallways of the school is a potential music-maker. Bringing this attitude to

advocacy makes the message very potent.

Developing Relationships Is Advocacy in Action

"What are your thoughts about the importance of music education for our children?" Ask the question, then *listen*. (Remember, you wanted their opinion; they didn't inquire about yours.) You don't have to agree or disagree, simply discover what people know or don't know about music education. Thank them and extend genuine appreciation for their time. Follow up with a short note of acknowledgment and include some of the latest information about music research. Developing trust relationships is the basis for group support.

Share Music with Everyone

When a member of your musical ensemble performs, it's newsworthy. When the band plays, everyone needs to know. Publicity is often an afterthought. Telling the students to "bring parents to the concert" will not pack the house. Studying and knowing the musical scores is crucial in conducting a successful performance; creating and developing the audience is equally as crucial. One cannot be at the expense of the other; both exist in an exemplary music program.

It is not essential to engage in every aspect of the publicity campaign, but it is necessary to guide those who are in charge and reinforce the theme of music education as the foundation of the program. They must be aware of the inherent values that music offers the performer as well as the listener. It is more than just creating a large audience, it is the chance to involve more people in the support of music.

Open the Forum

Invite guests to share in the musical harvest. Add a local politician to the concert to welcome the audience and speak about the importance of the arts. Bring other music teachers in the system and in the area to conduct and perform. Acknowledge in the written concert program and at the performance the music teachers who were part of the lives of the students on stage. Extend appreciation to everyone who plays a role in the music community; it is amazing what will get accomplished when others receive the credit.

Learn, Learn, Learn

It is tempting to slip into the we've-always-done-it-this-way rut. Life becomes a series of habits and complacency takes over creative thinking. For your own continuing growth, invite a respected colleague to review your program and make suggestions for future growth and improvement. Talk honestly and openly with your principal, supervisor, superintendent and mutually agree upon a plan to accomplish short-range and long-range goals. Open your

ears to the thoughts and opinions of your students and be appreciative of their candor, even though you may not agree. Continue your professional growth by attending workshops, reading professional journals and magazines, and—above all—listening to outstanding music performed by the finest musicians of the day. Keep your ears, your eyes, your thoughts, and your mind open. And, above all, enjoy the journey. We live in a country that knows the importance of the arts; we have only scraped the surface of possibilities. The opportunities are infinite. *Communication is the answer.* Let the music begin.

Strike Up the Band!

For more in-depth information, contact:

The National Coalition for Music Education
5140 Avenida Encinas, Carlsbad, CA 92008
(703) 860-4000, or (619) 438-8001
or visit the website of the American Music Conference,
http://www.AMC-Music.com

Music Educators National Conference
1902 Association Drive
Reston, VA 22091
(703) 860-4000

Notes

1 "Growing Up Complete, The Imperative for Music Education," (Music Educators National Conference, Reston, Virginia, March, 1991), p. 37.
2 Bruhn, Karl T., "On Preaching to the Choir: The Good News and the Bad News," *Southwestern Musician* (Texas Music Educators Association, March, 1993), p. 60.

PART II

THE BAND CONDUCTOR AS MUSIC TEACHER

Teacher Resource Guides

Grade Two

Teacher Resource Guide

As Torrents in Summer
Sir Edward Elgar
(1857–1934)

arranged by
Albert Oliver Davis (b. 1920)

Unit 1: Composer

Edward Elgar was one of the few English composers to enjoy wide international acclaim during the Romantic period. His music began the trend of nationalism in England during the late nineteenth century. Yet his works do not use folk song or other characteristics typically found in national music writing. They do, however, reflect British speech patterns in the melodic contour with wide leaps and descending patterns. Elgar's best known works are his symphony *Enigma Variations* (1899) and the oratorio *The Dream of Gerontius* (1900).

Unit 2: Composition

As Torrents in Summer is from Elgar's cantata *Scenes from the Saga of King Olaf*, completed in 1896. The libretto comes from the poem *Tale of a Wayside Inn*, written by the composer's favorite poet, Henry Wadsworth Longfellow. The story is one of a young musician's hero, Olaf Tryggvasson, whose early successes were finally overwhelmed by his enemies. *As Torrents in Summer* is taken from the Epilogue, and sung by unaccompanied chorus:

> As torrents in summer, half dried in their channels
> Suddenly rise, though the sky is still cloudless,
> For rain has been falling far off at their fountains;
> So hearts that are fainting grow full to o'erflowing.
> And they that behold it marvel, and know not
> That God at their fountains far off has been raining!

This arrangement was tastefully scored for band by Albert Oliver Davis in 1988 and is approximately three minutes in length.

Unit 3: Historical Perspective

Choral works continue to offer great musical depth and beauty found in both the music and the chosen text. Elgar's masterful craft through motivic writing paired with Longfellow's timeless poetry offers a look into this relatively unknown work. Written during Elgar's early years, the many different scenes of *King Olaf* provided the young composer an opportunity to develop his compositional skill. Thus, each section could be completed independently before being compiled into a full-length work. This technique proved successful with the completion of his first large orchestral work, *Enigma Variations*, three years later. Albert Oliver Davis's works continue to offer the young band quality literature that is both interesting and readily accessible. *As Torrents in Summer* is no exception.

Unit 4: Technical Considerations

The technical demands for *As Torrents in Summer* are relatively few with comfortable ranges for all instruments. The work is in triple meter with a tempo of *Adagio* (quarter note=76). The tonal area centers around the key of E-flat major throughout the piece. Accurate performance of triplet figures along with eighth-note subdivision is necessary. Three independent trumpet, French horn, and trombone parts all require specific attention by individual performers. Percussion parts include bells, chimes, triangle, and timpani.

Unit 5: Stylistic Considerations

The stylistic demands for this work are formidable. Dynamic nuance and *legato* style require careful attention. The arranger has skillfully reproduced the song-like melodic lines through detailed articulation and phrasing. The melody should be performed in cantabile style with precise rhythmic accompaniment as a foundation.

Unit 6: Musical Elements

Davis has given a true representation of Elgar's choral writing within the musical content of *As Torrents in Summer*. The melody is quite simple with traditional triadic harmonies below. The difficulty of the work is found with the phrasing and melodic contour. This setting offers bands the opportunity to work on balance, blend, and intonation through listening in the comfortable key of E-flat major.

Unit 7: Form and Structure

Strophic with repetition

Section	Measures	Scoring
introduction	1-11	*tutti*
verse 1/a theme	12-21	woodwinds
verse 2/b theme	22-31	*tutti*
verse 3/c theme	32-39	trumpets/*tutti*
transition	40-43	*tutti*
verse 4/a theme	44-53	*tutti*
verse 5/b theme	54-61	*tutti*
verse 6/c theme	62-72	woodwinds/*tutti*

Unit 8: Suggested Listening

James Barnes, *Yorkshire Ballad*
Aaron Copland, *Down a Country Lane*
Edward Elgar, *Scenes from the Saga of King Olaf*
Frank Ticheli, *Amazing Grace*

Unit 9: Additional References and Resources

Dvorak, Thomas L., Cynthia Crump Taggart, and Peter Schmaltz. *Best Music for Young Band*. Brooklyn, NY: Manhattan Beach Music, 1986.

Dvorak, Thomas L., Robert Grechesky, and Gary Ciepluch. *Best Music for High School Band*. Brooklyn, NY: Manhattan Beach Music, 1993.

Grout, Donald J. and Claude V. Palisca. *A History of Western Music*, 5th ed. New York: W.W. Norton & Company, 1996.

Kreines, Joseph. *Music for Concert Band*. Tampa, FL: Florida Music Service, 1989.

Miles, Richard, ed. *Teaching Music through Performance in Band*. Chicago: GIA Publications, Inc., 1997.

Moore, Jerrold Northrop. Compact disc notes, *Scenes from the Saga of King Olaf*, London Philharmonic Orchestra and Choir, EMI Digital 7-47659-8, 1987.

Rehrig, William H. *The Heritage Encyclopedia of Band Music*. Edited by Paul E. Bierley. Westerville, OH: Integrity Press, 1991.

Sadie, Stanley, ed. *The New Grove Dictionary of Music and Musicians*. 20 Vols. London: Macmillan, 1980. S.v. "Edward Elgar," by William W. Austin.

Smith, Norman and Albert Stoutamire. *Band Music Notes*. Lake Charles, LA: Program Note Press, 1989.

Contributed by:
Rich Lundahl
Indiana University
Bloomington, Indiana

Teacher Resource Guide

Early English Suite

William Duncombe
(1737/8–1819)

James Hook
(1746–1827)

arranged by
Walter Finlayson (b. 1919)

Unit 1: Composer

William Duncombe is credited with having composed three of the four melodies that have been arranged for band in *Early English Suite*. Although Duncombe was born in 1737 or 1738 and died in 1819, biographical references concerning this composer are not prevalent. His works for keyboard instruments frequently appear in collections for the piano, harpsichord, and organ. McAfee Publishing Corporation has published a set of piano works that bear the title *A Collection of Easy Marches and Airs from Early America*. The "Trumpet Minuet" from the *Early English Suite* appears in this volume.

The third movement bears the name James Hook who was born in Norwich, England on June 3, 1746. He composed songs, concertos for organ, sonatas for flute and pianoforte, cantatas, an oratorio, and music for dramatic pieces. He lived in London and was the organist/composer at Marylebone Gardens (1769-1773) and Vauxhall Gardens (1774-1820). Hook married a Miss Madden and had two sons: James (1772-1826) who was dean of Worcester, and Theodore (1788-1841) who was a novelist and musician. Hook died in Boulogne in 1827.

Walter Alan Finlayson was born in Burlington, Vermont on March 2,

1919. He earned a Bachelor of Science in Music Education from Ithaca College (1941) and a Master of Arts degree in Music from Columbia University (1957). He studied composition with Norman Lockwood. Although Finlayson is known as a composer/arranger, he is also a professional artist who illustrated the covers of children's piano pieces for Boosey and Hawkes. His career as a music educator includes the chairmanship of the Katonah-Lewisboro School music department. He retired in 1974.

Unit 2: Composition

The *Early English Suite* is a setting of four movements: "Trumpet Menuet," "Sonatina," "Menuet," and "Hunting Jig." Only the "Menuet" is credited to James Hook while the remaining three movements are attributed to William Duncombe. The work is 112 measures in length, not including repeats, and has a performance time of approximately five minutes.

Unit 3: Historical Perspective

The minuet (*menuet*, French) has a lengthy history, having developed from an ancient dance found in different parts of France. While the original *menuet* was rustic and lively, it may have been Lully who was the first to compose a more stately rendition adapted to the stage and ballroom. According to Jeffrey Pulver, the modified *menuet* showed "the artificiality, the snobbery, the arrogance, and the affectation of the Eighteenth Century;...the little steps that gave the dance its name (*menu*, small) pictured the mincing gait of the affected dandy; and the humble curtsey of the lady heightened by its very humility her haughty self-complacency" (151-152). The typical *menuet* is written in 3/4 and has two sections of four or eight measures that are repeated. Only the later forms of the dance employed the first and second *menuet* and these generally were instrumental versions.

The sonatina is usually a simplified sonata associated with the piano and often used as a teaching device. While it employs fewer movements than the sonata, the sonatina's movements are typically shorter in length. The sonatina in this band work appears to be an arrangement of a piano work. A simple melody is set over a basic quarter- and half-note harmonic accompaniment.

Although the jig (*gigue*, Italian) is known as an English dance form, the earliest references to the *gigue*, found in a mid-twelfth-century German poem, indicate that the term applied to a musical instrument. This was also the case in France where an instrument with three strings played with a bow was called a *gigue*. By the late sixteenth century, England had a dance called the *Gigue*, or Jig, and during this same time period the word was also applied to a kind of ballad. This particular type of ballad was a metrical composition performed by a clown who typically sang the song, and then danced to the tune accompanied by tabor and pipe. It is probable that this light-hearted dance was the predecessor of the jig since by the mid to late sixteenth century the term can be traced to Northern England in reference to the dance accompanying the ballad. The jig, written in almost any triple meter, replaced the older Galliard. By Handel's time, the term "jig" was applied to the closing movement of a formal suite and was no longer associated with a dance. The dotted rhythms of the early jig were altered when the jig became popular in Italy. The Italians smoothed out the rhythm so that when the jig returned to English soil, this newer, smoother rhythm was reconstructed as running triplets in eight-measure sections.

Unit 4: Technical Considerations

The first movement, "Trumpet Minuet," is in E-flat major, contains no accidentals, and is harmonically based in I-IV-V chords. The meter signature is 3/4 with a tempo indication of *Moderato*. All rhythms are simple combinations of eighth, quarter, half, and dotted half notes, the only exception being an eighth-note triplet in the first trumpet part. While all parts fall easily within the capabilities of most young players, the horn parts may provide a bit of a challenge in comparison. Although these parts are doubled in other voices, the horn writing requires that the students have a command of the range from B-flat just below the staff to fourth-line D. The third clarinet part does not cross the break.

The second movement, "Sonatina," is a setting of a simple melody over a sustained chordal accompaniment in 2/4 meter. The key signature of B-flat major coupled with the rhythmic and harmonic simplicity of the movement makes this an excellent vehicle for teaching balance. Although the melody employs a diatonic eighth-note triplet, it poses no fingering problems for any of the melodic instruments, except perhaps the third clarinets who are above the break on the unison melody with the first and second clarinet.

The third movement, "Menuet," is scored in F major in 3/4 meter for woodwinds with no cornets, trombones, or tubas, and limited horn and baritone parts. Only the bells are used in the percussion. While the rhythms are simple combinations of eighth, quarter, half, and dotted half notes, the vertical alignment of these rhythms is more complicated than the other movements. In addition the flutes and first clarinet have a dotted eighth-sixteenth. The instrumentation includes an independent alto clarinet part but this is cued in the tenor saxophone. The minuet is written in two sections, both repeat, and there is a *da capo*. The first section in F major is contrasted by the second theme in C major. This shift in tonality occurs through the use of the appropriate accidentals.

The final movement, "Hunting Jig," is an *allegro* romp in 6/8 meter. The key signature of B-flat major, traditional triadic harmonies, and the lack of accidentals makes this quite accessible for the young band. The rhythms are the standard 6/8 combinations of eighth, quarter, dotted quarter, and dotted half notes. This is the only movement that employs accents and crescendos in the wind parts.

Unit 5: Stylistic Considerations

Care should be taken to preserve the integrity of the dance style in the minuets and jig, thereby keeping the tempo rather rigid and addressing the vertical alignment of the rhythms. While the minuets are more stately, the jig should be lively, light, and bouncy. The "Sonatina," with its simple melody and accompaniment, should convey grace and dignity. Keep in mind that this may have been a training or recital piece for a young pianist and maintain its simplistic nature.

Unit 6: Musical Elements

The *"Trumpet Menuet"* has two contrasting melodic themes. The first theme consists of two four-measure phrases while the second theme is eight bars in length. Use this phrasing difference to enhance the differences in these musical ideas. In addition, note that the first theme is based on a *forte* triadic trumpet fanfare that clearly supports the title of the movement while establishing the style. The B theme is more lyrical and uses terrace dynamics. The percussion parts include snare drum, bass drum, crash cymbals, and timpani.

An eight-measure phrase is the rule in the "Sonatina." Strive to maintain this same phrasing in the accompanying quarter/half-note harmonies. Because the melody tends to be scored for fewer voices than the accompaniment, it will be important to establish good balance. Although the melody is always marked at least one dynamic level louder than the other voices, the density of the harmonic texture could easily overpower the tune.

The *"Menuet"* provides an excellent opportunity to develop the tone color of the woodwind section. With the virtual absence of brass parts, this movement is sure to please most of the woodwind players. The alto saxophone section has the least to do. The melody consists of two four-bar phrases. As in the previous movement, proper balance will insure a musical performance. Keep this minuet lyrical and *legato* while maintaining a softer dynamic range. The bells play for two measures, all other percussion instruments are tacet.

The lively "Hunting Jig" is a fine introduction to 6/8 meter. The rhythms are relatively simple and the phrases are broken into four-measure segments. The two-measure crescendo from *piano* to *forte* in the brass parts will provide a challenge to young players, especially at the *allegro* tempo. Work to keep the articulations consistent throughout the movement. The percussion parts include timpani, triangle, snare drum, and bass drum.

Unit 7: Form and Structure

"Trumpet Minuet"   This movement is in ABAA form with a repeat of the BAA. A four-bar triadic trumpet fanfare states the opening theme to be joined by full band with the A' half of the phrase. The contrasting B theme maintains the trumpet melody with a *legato* woodwind accompaniment figure. The A theme returns as initially presented and is followed by yet another statement of this theme with the entire brass section playing the trumpet fanfare. This BAA section repeats with a *ritardando* in the final two measures to indicate the ending.

"Sonatina"   This movement is also a combination of two themes creating an ABAA form. Although both themes are *legato* and lyrical in nature, different rhythmic and melodic material create the contrast. There are no repeats and a *ritardando*.

"Menuet"   This movement is in ABA form. The A and B themes both repeat with a *da capo* to the opening A section.

"Hunting Jig"   This movement is in ABA form with a repeat of the BA.

Unit 8: Suggested Listening

Malcolm Arnold/Johnstone, *English Dances*
Frank Erickson, *Suite of Early Marches*
Clare Grundman, *Little English Suite*
Handel/Gordon, "Menuet" (from *Almira*)
John Kinyon, *Air and Dance*
Robert Jager, *Colonial Airs and Dances*

Unit 9: Additional References and Resources

Apel, Willi. *Harvard Dictionary of Music*, 2nd ed. Cambridge, MA: The Belknap Press of Harvard University Press, 1970.

ASCAP *Biographical Dictionary*, 4th ed. New York: Jaques Cattell Press, 1980.

Boosey and Hawkes Music Publishers, New York.

Brown, James D. and Stephen S. Stratton. *British Musical Biography*. New York: Da Capo Press, 1971.

Pulver, Jeffrey. *A Dictionary of Old English Music and Musical Instruments*. New York: E.P. Dutton and Company, 1923.

Rehrig, William H. *The Heritage Encyclopedia of Band Music*. Westerville, OH: Integrity Press, 1991.

World's Greatest Sonatinas for Piano. Van Nuys, CA: Alfred Publishing Co., 1994.

Contributed by:
Susan Creasap
Assistant Director of Bands
Morehead State University
Morehead, Kentucky

Teacher Resource Guide

Fanfare Ode and Festival

Bob Margolis
(b. 1949)

Unit 1: Composer

Bob Margolis was born in April, 1949 in New York. He studied music at Brooklyn College before transferring to the University of California at Berkeley (UCB), where he studied design. After completing his study at UCB, he returned to Brooklyn College, and completed a Bachelor of Arts degree in speech and television production. Honored twice in composition contests by the American Bandmasters Association, he is one of a few composers who uses musical settings and ideas from the Renaissance period in his compositions. He is founder of Manhattan Beach Music.

Unit 2: Composition

Fanfare Ode and Festival for concert band is based on the popular old French dance music originally written for a small Renaissance wind band. The work is very rhythmic and tuneful. Students are able to enjoy the musical experience. The suite is approximately four minutes long.

The three-movement suite was first performed by the Eau Claire Summer Concert Band at the University of Wisconsin under the direction of Donald S. George on July 21, 1982.

Unit 3: Historical Perspective

This suite of popular dances is based on music published by Pierre Attaignant found in a six volume collection, *Danceries*. "Fanfare" is a *branle simple* from Volume VI (1555) of the *Danceries*; "Ode" is a *branle gay* ("Marie songeois l'aultre iour") from Volume II (1547); "Festival" is a *branle de*

Champaigne II from Volume VI. (The various types of *branle*—*simple*, *gay*, and *de Champaigne*—refer to differences in the dancing steps. The *branle de Champaigne*, or Burgundian brawl, is the liveliest, and was danced by the youngest dancers.) Pierre Attaignant employed Claude Gervaise as his editor. No composer is listed for the *branle gay*, yet it is likely that Gervaise was the arranger. He is credited as the composer of the *branle simple* and the *branle de Champaigne* (both published after Attaignant's death in 1552).

A different arrangement of the *branle simple* may be seen in Pierre Phalèse's collection of dances, published in Antwerp in 1583. The same *branle* is again found, under the title "Petite Marche Militaire," in the 1935 *Suite Française (d'après Claude Gervaise)* by Francis Poulenc for two oboes, two bassoons, two trumpets, three trombones, percussion, and harpsichord. (*Adapted from notes by Bob Margolis.*)

Unit 4: Technical Considerations

The ensemble should be familiar with the G Aeolian, G Dorian, and F major scales. The phrases with accent, *staccato*, *tenuto*, and slur markings demand precise articulation for making this work as dance music. Percussion parts seem simple but great dynamic control is required throughout this work.

Unit 5: Stylistic Considerations

Accent markings marked *forte* tend to be overplayed. The ensemble should remember this work is dance music from the sixteenth century.

Establishing the difference between *fortissimo* and *forte*, and *forte* and *mezzo forte* requires great sensitivity from all players. Examine the percussion parts carefully, especially the use of the snare drum. The use of both regular and piccolo snare drums is suggested to add more color to the performance.

Unit 6: Musical Elements

Fanfare, Ode and Festive features strong but simple motivic ideas. Rhythms are rather vertical and phrasings are clearly organized. "Fanfare" includes two motivic ideas. The first motive emphasizes eighth-note figures while the other emphasizes quarter-note figures. Dynamic levels (*f-ff*) suggest brilliant sounds throughout the movement. Contrasting ideas and sounds appear in the "Ode." The motivic idea is still simple (all quarter- and half-note figures). However, it suggests more horizontal gestures rather than vertical. The sound reminds one of traditional sacred chorale music. "Festival" features a motivic idea throughout with a contrasting mood in measures 22 through 32. From measure 59, the same motive repeats and the tempo becomes faster towards the end.

Unit 7: Form and Structure

MEASURES	SECTION	KEY	EVENTS
MOVEMENT I:			
1-12	Motive A	G minor (G Aeolian)	Brass section is featured
13-23	Motive B	G Dorian	Woodwinds are featured
24-35	Motive A	G minor (G Aeolian)	Melody in trumpets with fragments played by wood-winds and horns
35-38	Coda	G major	Short closing material in percussion section
Movement II:			
1-8	Intro. (motive A)	G minor (G Aeolian)	Melody in trumpet and clarinets
9-24	Motive A	G Aeolian	Melody in flutes and clarinets
25-46	Motive B	G Aeolian	Melody appears alternately between brass and woodwind sections
47-57	Motive A	G Aeolian	Woodwind section is featured
Movement III:			
1-4	Intro.	F major	Every instrument plays F
5-21	Motive A	F major	First melody in trumpets and second melody in flutes and oboes
22-31	Motive B (modified A)	F major	Melody in clarinets and first trumpets
32-47	Motive C (modified A)	F major	Melody in piccolo, flutes, and trumpets
48-66	Motive A	F major	All instruments are featured in unison or alternately
67-73	Coda	F major	Fragments of motive A in piccolo, flutes, trumpets, trombones, euphoniums, and tubas

Unit 8: Suggested Listening

Bob Margolis, *Terpsichore, Belle Qui Tien Ma Vie*
Jan Bach, *Praetorious Suite*
Norman Dello Joio, *Variants on a Medieval Tune*
Ron Nelson, *Medieval Suite*

Unit 9: Additional References and Resources

Rehrig, William H. *The Heritage Encyclopedia of Band Music*. Edited by Paul
   E. Bierly. Westerville, OH: Integrity Press, 1991.

Whitwell, David. *A Concise History of the Wind Band*. Northridge, CA:
   WINDS, 1985.

Contributed by:

Yoshiaki Tanno
Indiana University
Bloomington, Indiana

Teacher Resource Guide

In the Bleak Midwinter

Gustav Holst
(1874–1934)

arranged by
Robert W. Smith (b. 1958)

Unit 1: Composer

Gustav Holst was born on September 21, 1874 in Cheltenham, England. He graduated from the Royal College of Music and performed as a professional trombonist. Holst served as music director of St. Paul's Girls School in London, taught at Morley College, the Royal College of Music, and Harvard University. During World War I Holst was a bandmaster and close friend to Ralph Vaughan Williams. Strongly influenced by English folk song and Hindu mysticism, Holst composed works that display sensitivity to text. He has the distinction of having written three major works for band that were later arranged for orchestra: *First Suite in E-flat* (1909), *Second Suite in F* (1911), and *Hammersmith* (1930). Holst died in London on May 25, 1934.

Unit 2: Composition

Gustav Holst composed *In the Bleak Mid-Winter* (H73, No. 1) in 1904/5 as a result of a commission to write a hymn for the new English hymnal. He selected a text by Christina Rossetti (1830-1894) and set to work. The completed project was published by the Oxford University Press in 1906 but the whereabouts of the original manuscript are unknown. Since its publication, *In the Bleak Mid-Winter* has been published in the *Oxford Book of Carols*, *Pilgrim Hymnal* (United Church of Canada), *Episcopal Hymnal* (1940), *Methodist Hymnal* (1935), *Church Hymnary* (Church of Scotland), *Songs of Praise* (1925), and other similar collections.

This lovely setting for concert band by Robert W. Smith bears the dedication "for Ben, Chuck, and Susan, in loving memory of their Mother, Alta Sue Hawkins." The choice of the hymn-tune was suggested to Smith by Alta Sue Hawkins who unfortunately did not live to hear its premiere. The initial statements of the melody are significant in their instrumentation. Alta Sue Hawkins was a clarinetist, hence the clarinet solo presentation of the complete melody. The second verse is scored for clarinets, solo horn, solo baritone, with the addition of a second horn midway through the melody. This choice of scoring is well conceived since Ben and Susan are hornists and Chuck is an equally professional baritone player. Set in three main sections, it bears tempo markings that range from 52 to 104 for the quarter note, unlike the Holst tempo of moderately, quarter note=100. The original key of F has been transposed to E-flat which allows all instruments to remain within a comfortable range. The seventy-eight-measure composition is approximately four and one-half minutes in length.

Unit 3: Historical Perspective

The English hymn dates from the late fifteenth and sixteenth centuries when sacred ballads and carols were sung apart from the usual religious meetings. A translation of Martin Luther's hymn, "Vom Himmel hoch," appeared in John Wedderburn's *Gude and Godlie Ballates* sometime in the mid-sixteenth century. Due to a variety of factors, the English Psalters tended to be less musical than their French and German counterparts and so by 1725 a majority of English congregations typically sang most hymns to fewer than ten tunes. With the advent of a new style of hymn texts by Isaac Watts (1674-1748) and Charles Wesley (1707-1788), more tunes were composed. It was not until the mid-nineteenth century that hymns began to appear in four-part harmony. The collection *Hymns Ancient and Modern* (1861-1950) published these part songs and the tradition of unison hymn singing was changed. This opened the door for more of the new-style hymns, hence the commission to Holst (and others, particularly to Holst's close friend, Ralph Vaughan Williams) to compose such a work for the soon-to-be-published *English Hymnal* (1906). The Robert W. Smith arrangement of *In the Bleak Midwinter* is a fine addition to the ever-expanding list of band settings based on hymn tunes, chorales, and folk songs.

Unit 4: Technical Considerations

The work remains in concert E-flat major with few accidentals. The rhythms include multiple common combinations of sixteenth notes that are generally diatonic for the woodwinds and arpeggiated in the brass. These rhythms must be cleanly articulated. Although the clarinet solo is not technically demanding, the phrasing, tonal, and musical concerns will be most effective in the hands of a fine player. This is also true for the solo horn and baritone players. The open scoring of the first two statements of the hymn tune must be carefully rehearsed to establish proper balance and expressiveness. The musicality of the ensemble will be challenged by the phrasing requirements of the melody coupled with the moderate tempos and dynamic extremes of the composition. Dynamic aspects of the piece will be best expressed by the band that has learned to perform at the *pianissimo* and triple *forte* levels with clarity and control of both individual and ensemble tone color. Because the selection has several tempo changes, it is important to rehearse all transitional areas while making sure to establish each new tempo as indicated by the arranger.

Unit 5: Stylistic Considerations

The seven-measure introduction is fanfare-like in character. Since the words to the first verse of the hymn are, "In the bleak midwinter frosty wind made moan," it is appropriate that the band arrangement opens with a wind-like effect. This haunting sound is produced by a *sforzando-piano* in the clarinets and flutes, while other voices crescendo-decrescendo on an airy "sh", to the accompaniment of wind chimes. The horns and trombones establish the fanfare theme and are quickly joined by the trumpets. It will be important to establish proper articulations and balance throughout this brief introduction while pacing the dynamic shifts from *piano* to *forte* and back to *mezzo piano*. This is the perfect place to teach pyramid dynamics as discussed by W. Francis McBeth in *Effective Performance of Band Music*. The composition consists of sections that are contrasting in style. While parts of the piece are *legato* and lyrical, other areas are majestic, accented, and noble. Not only do these contrasting stylistic areas promote musical interest, they provide excellent educational material. In the span of seventy-eight measures the style changes to include fanfare-like statements, solos, lyrical and flowing sections, a woodwind choir setting, and full band with strong articulations and running sixteenth notes. The challenge is to convey the unique character of each section while creating a cohesive and musical performance of the complete composition.

Unit 6: Musical Elements

Although the primary tonality of the work is E-flat major, the harmonic structure is both quartal and triadic. After the initial solo statement of the hymn tune, the texture of the second verse is contrapuntal. Contrasting textures in this work are as prevalent as the variety of styles and dynamic levels.

Unit 7: Form and Structure

The composition has four statements of the hymn melody, one for each verse of text.

MEASURES	EVENTS AND SCORING
1-7	Introduction, brass fanfare motive
8-15	Hymn tune, verse 1, clarinet solo
16-23	Clarinet solo continues with mallets
24-31	Verse 2, first clarinets, solo horn and solo baritone
32-39	Add second horn
40-42	Transition, brass fanfare motive
43-52	Verse 3, full band, melody in horns and baritone, slight rhythmic variation
53-61	Woodwind choir
62-74	Verse 4, partial statement of hymn tune, full band, melody harmonized in brass, upper woodwind rhythmic counter-melody
75-78	Coda, full band to clarinet solo and "sh"

Unit 8: Additional Listening

J.S. Bach, *Come Sweet Death*
James Barnes, *Yorkshire Ballad*
Robert Foster, *Fantasia on a Hymn by Praetorious*
David Holsinger, *On a Hymn Song of Philip Bliss, On a Hymn Song of Lowell Mason, A Childhood Hymn, On an American Spiritual*
Claude T. Smith, *Overture on an Early American Folk Hymn*
Frank Ticheli, *Amazing Grace*
Charles "Pete" Wiley, *Old Scottish Melody*

Unit 9: Additional References and Resources

Apel, Willi. *Harvard Dictionary of Music*, 2nd ed. Cambridge, MA: The Belknap Press of Harvard University Press, 1970.

Belwin Mills, c/o CPP Belwin, Inc.

Grout, Donald J. *A History of Western Music*, 3rd ed. New York: W.W. Norton & Company, 1980.

McBeth, W. Francis. *Effective Performance of Band Music*. San Antonio, TX: Southern Music, 1972.

Miles, Richard B., ed. *Teaching Music through Performance in Band*. Chicago: GIA Publications, Inc., 1997.

Mitchell, Jon C. Telephone interview. 10 June 1997.

Rehrig, William H. *The Heritage Encyclopedia of Band Music*. Westerville, OH: Integrity Press, 1991.

Routley, Erik. *Twentieth Century Church Music*. New York: Oxford University Press, 1964.

Contributed by:
Susan Creasap
Assistant Director of Bands
Morehead State University
Morehead, Kentucky

Teacher Resource Guide

Korean Folk Song Medley
James D. Ployhar
(b. 1926)

Unit 1: Composer

James D. Ployhar was born in Valley City, North Dakota and received the Bachelor of Science degree from Valley City State College. He received a Master of Arts degree from Northern Colorado University and pursued further graduate study in composition at California State University at Long Beach with Morris Hutchins Ruger, and later with Knud Hovalt of the Danish Royal Philharmonic Orchestra. He taught in the public schools for over twenty years and has over 350 publications for young bands in print. Ployhar is in demand as a clinician and conductor throughout the United States and Canada.

Unit 2: Composition

This Grade Two composition uses three Korean folk songs—"Beteul Norae", "Odoldogi", and "Arirang"—in one, continuous movement. The "Arirang" is the same folk song used by John Barnes Chance in his *Variations on a Korean Folk Song*. The Ployhar work would serve as an excellent introduction to Korean folk music for young bands. This piece, like most others by Ployhar, is published by Belwin Publishing Company and is approximately four minutes in length.

Unit 3: Historical Perspective

The educational band works of James Ployhar are similar musically to those of Frank Erickson and John Edmundson. Use of folk songs by composers of educational music has become commonplace. *Korean Folk Song Medley* uses three ancient folk songs. Ployhar keeps the melodies intact, unlike most folk or native song use in a theme and variations setting (e.g., Ployhar's *Variations on a Sioux Melody*).

Unit 4: Technical Considerations

The most technically demanding aspects of the work are the varying tempos and the ability to make smooth transitions between the three different folk songs. It does use both 3/4 and 6/8 meters, but no rhythms that are difficult for this level. The upper range for most of the ensemble is not a problem and should be fine for all high school and most junior high school bands. Percussion writing is simple and requires a woodblock, gong, snare drum, bass drum, suspended cymbal, and triangle.

Unit 5: Stylistic Considerations

A majority of the melody in the work appears in the upper woodwinds with the brasses often accompanying with block chords. The melody of the first and third sections should flow almost as though it is effortless. The accompaniment and percussion should remain light.

Unit 6: Musical Elements

This piece, even though in the Grade Two category, is very fresh and colorful. The "Beteul Norae" is a very simple tune that contains two phrases. With so many playing the melody it is important for the conductor to listen carefully to insure good intonation. The varying articulations, including slurs and *staccatos*, provide musical contrast. Balance will be a concern in the final section as the accompaniment cannot become overbearing for the melody. Phrasing usually falls into four-bar segments with an occasional break within the phrase. Students need to know when to breathe and how to handle the ends of phrases.

Unit 7: Form and Structure

The piece is in three contrasting sections and is divided as follows:

SECTION	MEASURES	EVENTS AND SCORING
Introduction	1-4	Full ensemble introduction which lead directly to the first folk song.
Beteul Norae	5-27	Melody resides in the upper woodwinds with blocked chord accompaniment in the brasses. The section ends with a ritardando and a C minor *fermata*. There are two repeats in this section.
Transition	28-29	This short transition takes us from 3/4 to 6/8 time, remaining in C minor.

| Odoldogi | 30-47 | This section is set up similar to the first with two repeats. It is in 6/8 time and once again keeps the melody in the upper voices with blocked chord accompaniment. It ends with a *fermata*, a V chord of the new key in the next section. |
| Arirang | 48-end | The meter moves back to 3/4 and we are now in B-flat major tonality. The melody lies in the alto sax and trombone and eventually makes its way through the rest of the group. At rehearsal G, a fugue is presented, with the flute, cornets, and saxes beginning the melody and the trombones and horns picking it up a bar later. This section has one repeat and ends with a *ritardando* in the last four bars before closing on a B-flat concert chord and a *fermata*. |

Unit 8: Suggested Listening

James Barnes, *Chorale and Jubiloso*
John Barnes Chance, *Variations on a Korean Folk Song*
James D. Ployhar, *Devonshire Overture*
James D. Ployhar, *Variations on a Sioux Melody*

Unit 9: Additional References and Resources

Kreines, Joseph. *Music for Concert Band.* Tampa, FL: Florida Music Service, 1989.

Smith, Norman and Albert Stoutmire. *Band Music Notes.* Rev. ed. San Diego, CA: Kjos., 1979.

Contributed by:

Rodney C. Schueller
Indiana University
Bloomington, Indiana

Teacher Resource Guide

A Little French Suite

Pierre La Plante
(b. 1943)

Unit 1: Composer

Pierre La Plante was born in Milwaukee, Wisconsin and is of French-Canadian descent. He received his formal training at the University of Wisconsin at Madison where he earned Bachelor of Music Education and Master of Music degrees. While an undergraduate, he studied arranging with Jim Christensen. Yet he became interested in publishing his compositions only after teaching, when he recognized the limited repertoire available for young band. La Plante resides in Blanchardsville, Wisconsin where he teaches K through 6 General Music and Beginning Band in the Pecatonica Area School District. In addition to teaching full time, La Plante plays bassoon with the Beloit-Janesville Symphony Orchestra. Other works for band include *Overture on a Minstrel Theme* (1978), *Prospect* (1978), *Lakeland Portrait* (1987), *A March on the King's Highway* (1988), *All the Young Sailors* (1988), *American Riversongs* (1990), *Nordic Sketches* (1994), and *Come to the Fair* (1995).

Unit 2: Composition

A Little French Suite was completed in 1987 and is based upon four traditional French folk songs. The work has three contrasting movements that develop this rich yet playful folk material. Movement One, "March," is based on a popular song of the 1700s, "J'ai du bon tobac." The second theme is based on the very familiar French folk song, "Sur le Pont d'Avignon." The slow and beautiful second movement, "Serenade," uses the song "Cadet Rouselle," which is about a happy-go-lucky young man as he reflects. The last movement, "Finale," concludes brilliantly using the song "Il etait un bergère." This folk song is a "humorous round about a shepherdess whose mischievous cat gets into the delicious cheese she has just made." The work is approximately six and one-half minutes in duration.

Unit 3: Historical Perspective

Traditional music of the provinces in France is referred to as *chansons populaires* or popular songs. These *chansons* were sung unaccompanied except for a fiddle or lone instrument doubling the melody. According to the composer, the *chansons* used in *A Little French Suite* were often sung as part of a game or round dance. Folk music has always been a source of rich tradition, valuable to culture and the society which it represents. Darius Milhaud's *Suite Française* (1945) incorporated French folk songs in each movement that were unique to the provinces that they represented. Percy Grainger (1882-1961) dedicated his life to the collection and presentation of folk music through various musical media. The collection of folk songs found in his *Lincolnshire Posy* has become a staple of the wind repertoire. Béla Bartók (1881-1945) was another twentieth-century composer who traversed the countryside of what was then Hungary, in search of the music of "the people."

Unit 4: Technical Considerations

A Little French Suite centers around the tonal areas of E-flat, A-flat, and B-flat major. The first movement's rhythmic demands are numerous, using sixteenth-note lines across the ensemble within a moderate tempo. The second movement's triple-meter melody falls within a comfortable range and presents no technical problems. Facility in 6/8 meter is necessary for successful performance of the last movement. The bright tempo (dotted quarter note=126) and contrapuntal writing offers challenging parts for all players. Young band scoring calls for instruments in pairs: bassoons, clarinets, alto saxophones, trumpets, horns, and trombones. All other instruments have single parts.

Unit 5: Stylistic Considerations

The French *chanson populaire* folk style requires song-like interpretation in each movement. The composer pays great attention to detail through articulation and dynamic nuance. The rhythmically complex first theme in the "March" requires a light and buoyant interpretation while the middle theme is *legato* and connected. The second movement, "Serenade," requires seamless connection of notes, especially in the accompaniment. The melody should be performed without break as it is passed among instrument groups. The theme of "Finale" should be separated and never heavy or connected until the theme is presented in augmented form. At this point, the original theme in the woodwinds remains light and joyous above the augmented theme in the brass which is *legato* and sonorous.

Unit 6: Musical Elements

The first movement contains two separate themes. The initial theme is presented in E-flat major with upper woodwinds as a contrapuntal counter-melody is heard in the first trumpet. The second theme, "Sur le Pont d'Avignon," is heard with oboe and flute in the key of A-flat major. Euphonium and bassoon then carry the melody to the return of the first theme. The second movement develops the beautiful song "Cadet Rouselle," initially with solo flute and then tutti woodwinds. Phrasing must be addressed to successfully perform this musically demanding movement. The final movement is back in A-flat major with the statement of the 6/8 melody. The next section moves to B-flat major with the melody now in augmented form with contrasting dynamics and style. The next section moves through a fugal treatment of the original theme stated in four different instrument groups. The final section combines the augmented theme, presented by brass, and an *obbligato* variation of the original theme, found in upper woodwinds.

Unit 7: Form and Structure

Three-movement suite

SECTION AND EVENTS	MEASURES	SCORING
"March"—ABA form		
theme A	1-16	*tutti*
theme B	17-24	oboe/flute
motivic extension	25-32	trumpet/saxophone/flute
theme B	33-40	bassoon/euphonium
transition (fragment from theme A)	41-48	*tutti*
theme A	49-52	trumpet counterpoint
	53-end	*tutti*
"Serenade"—Strophic song form		
introduction	1-4	low woodwinds
theme A	5-20	solo flute
	21-39	flute/oboe/saxophone
repeat of theme A	40-55	oboe/clarinet/saxophone
	56-63	*tutti*
	64-end	flute/saxophone/trumpet

"Finale"—Theme and variations

theme A	2-11	woodwinds
repeat of theme A	12-20	*tutti*
motivic extension	21-28	*tutti*
theme A1 (augmented variation of theme A)	29-46	upper woodwinds
transition (fragments of theme A)	47-54	low woodwinds
theme A2 (varied)	55-70	multiple fugal entrances
theme A3 (combination of theme A1 with woodwind obbligato)	71-88	*tutti*
coda (theme A melodic fragments)	89-end	various low winds/tutti

Unit 8: Suggested Listening

Béla Bartók/Phillip Gordon, *Three Hungarian Songs*
Albert Oliver Davis, *Rhenish Folk Festival*
Martin Elersby, *Paris Sketches*
Percy Grainger, *Lincolnshire Posy*
Clare Grundman, *An Irish Rhapsody*
Pierre La Plante, *American Riversongs*
Darius Milhaud, *Suite Française*
Hugh Stuart, *Three Aires from Gloucester*

Unit 9: Additional References and Resources

Dvorak, Thomas L., Cynthia Crump Taggart, and Peter Schmaltz. *Best Music for Young Band*. Brooklyn, NY: Manhattan Beach Music, 1986.

Dvorak, Thomas L., Robert Grechesky, and Gary Ciepluch. *Best Music for High School Band*. Brooklyn, NY: Manhattan Beach Music, 1993.

Grout, Donald J. and Claude V. Palisca. *A History of Western Music*, 5th ed. New York: W.W. Norton & Company, 1996.

Kreines, Joseph. *Music for Concert Band*. Tampa, FL: Florida Music Service, 1989.

Miles, Richard, ed. *Teaching Music through Performance in Band*. Chicago: GIA Publications, Inc., 1997.

Rehrig, William H. *The Heritage Encyclopedia of Band Music*. Edited by Paul E. Bierley. Westerville, Ohio: Integrity Press, 1991.

Smith, Norman and Albert Stoutamire. *Band Music Notes*. Lake Charles, LA: Program Note Press, 1989.

Contributed by:
Rich Lundahl
Indiana University
Bloomington, Indiana

Teacher Resource Guide

The New ANZACS

Brian Hogg
(b. 1953)

Unit 1: Composer

Australian composer Brian Hogg developed his musicianship through the Salvation Army. As a performer, composer, and conductor, he has gained a fine reputation and remains in demand as a clinician. His works for British-style brass band and for concert band have been performed throughout the world. Brian Hogg has twice received the Australian Band and Orchestra Directors Association (ABODA) "Composer of the Year" award.

Unit 2: Composition

The New ANZACS is based upon musical motifs found throughout ANZAC Day in Australia. The opening motive is from "The Last Post," a bugle call played as the flag moves from half mast. This idea is developed into a march-like section that signifies the ANZAC Day parade seen in many Australian and New Zealand cities. The closing theme is based on the hymn "St. Anne," whose first verse is always heard on ANZAC Day:

> O God, our help in ages past,
> Our hope for years to come,
> Our shelter from the stormy blast,
> And our eternal home.

The New ANZACS is approximately two minutes and ten seconds in duration, and is published by Brolga Music.

Unit 3: Historical Perspective

The word ANZAC is an acronym for "Australian and New Zealand Army Corps," and was the name given to troops from the antipodes that sailed to Europe during World War I. The ANZAC tradition was established on the beaches of Gallipoli in Turkey, where the troops struck at what First Sea-Lord Winston Churchill described as "The Soft Underbelly of Europe." After a murderous charge on well-defended beaches on April 25th, 1915, the ANZACS were repulsed after months of heavy fighting that took many lives.

The Beaches of Gallipoli established a reputation of bravery for the fighting men of the young nations of Australia and New Zealand as brave fighting men. ANZAC Day remains one of the most important days in both countries, a day replete with memorials and services when those who have died in all wars are remembered. The motto of the day is "Lest We Forget."

April, 1990 saw the seventy-fifth anniversary of ANZAC Day. The return of some of the surviving soldiers to the beaches of Gallipoli served to remind Australians and New Zealanders of "In Memorium," traditionally sung on ANZAC Day:

> They shall not grow old,
> As we that are left grow old.
> Age shall not weary them,
> Nor the years condemn.

Unit 4: Technical Considerations

Listed by the publishers as Level 1.5, *The New ANZACS* offers players few technical difficulties. The opening measures are for solo trumpet and snare drum. Bar 9 sees a tempo change to a march tempo, the only tempo change in the work. The work includes some sixteenth notes, scalic in motion, and does not vary from the key of E-flat major, with the exception of two chords. The bass line is doubled in the bass clarinet, baritone, saxophone, euphonium, tuba, and string bass.

Percussion writing is extensive, with three percussion parts. Part one is for snare drum/bass drum, part two is for crash cymbal, suspended cymbal and triangle, with part three as a timpani part.

Unit 5: Stylistic Considerations

The outer sections are flowing, the first in a slow tempo, the last in a two feel (marked *legato*) that moves back to four-four. The middle section is march-like, with a very martial feel. This section contains some very pointed moments, and a constantly moving bass line. The woodwind countermelody, when it appears at rehearsal 30, is comprised mostly of longer notes and flowing lines.

146

Unit 6: Musical Elements

The important musical elements include the move from the slow opening section, and the return to the hymn at measure 39. The melody is somewhat rhythmically asymmetrical with a regular accompaniment that includes repeated eighth notes. When the melody returns at 24, it includes a pyramid effect and an abrupt hiccup in the melody. At 49, it is a challenge for the ensemble to maintain a sense of direction through the melody (the hymn "St. Anne"), now comprised of half notes. The full range of dynamics appears in this skillfully constructed and interesting work for young band.

Unit 7: Form and Structure

SECTION	MEASURES	SCORING
"The Last Post"	1-8	trumpet/snare/low brass
Introduction	9-12	full band
A	13-19	trumpet melody / low brass
B	20-23	full band
A	24-29	full band
A1	30-36	trumpet melody/woodwind counterline
B	37-40	full band
A	41-44	full band
"The Last Post"	45-48	trumpet/percussion/low brass
Hymn	49-56	upper/middle woodwinds
Hymn Variant	57-61	full band
Coda	62-end	full band

Unit 8: Suggested Listening

Traditional bugle call, *The Last Post*

Unit 9: Additional References and Resources

Rehrig, William H. *The Heritage Encyclopedia of Band Music*. Editor Paul E. Bierley. Westerville, OH: Integrity Press, 1991.

Smith, Norman and Albert Stoutamire. *Band Music Notes*. Third ed. Lake Charles, LA: Program Note Press, 1979.

Contributed by:
Alan Lourens
Indiana University
Bloomington, Indiana

Teacher Resource Guide

Old Scottish Melody
Charles A. Wiley
(1925–1992)

Unit 1: Composer

Charles A. (Pete) Wiley was born in Abeline, Texas and began studying clarinet at the age of nine but soon thereafter switched to oboe. He received an undergraduate degree from Texas Tech and a Master of Music degree from the University of Texas in 1949. In 1962, he completed a Doctor of Education degree from the University of California. His father, Dewey, was known as the "father of Texas bands" and his uncle, Russell, was Director of Bands at the University of Kansas. His son, Jim Wiley, now owns TRN (That's Really Nice) music publishing company which was founded by Charles in 1974. His teaching career began with the Austin High School Band after service in the Navy during World War II. He was appointed director of bands at Lamar University in 1952 where he built a program of over 500 students. His other works for band include *El Palo Duru pasodoble* (1972), *Antonito pasodoble* (1973), *Earl's March* (1981), *Big Red March* (1982), and *Lowlands March*.

Unit 2: Composition

Old Scottish Melody is a simple setting for band of the folk song "Auld Lang Syne." This well-known tune was written by the famous Scottish poet and song writer Robert Burns (1759-1796). This setting is brilliantly scored for young band, yet is musically very demanding in its expressive requirements. The text offers insight to the lyrical adaptation of the familiar song:

> For auld lang syne, my dear
> For auld lang syne,
> We'll take a cup o'kindness yet

> For auld lang syne!
> Should auld acquaintance be forgot,
> And never brought to mind?
> Should auld acquaintance be forgot,
> And days of auld lang syne!

This tasteful arrangement by Charles A. Wiley was completed in 1977 and is approximately four minutes in duration.

Unit 3: Historical Perspective

Robert Burns's name is not affixed to "Auld Lang Syne," yet there is no doubt it is chiefly his own. This famous Scottish poet discussed the song that dates from 1788:

> This old song and tune has often thrilled through my soul...the air is but mediocre but the song of itself...the song of the olden times, and which has never been in print, until I took it down from an old man's singing, is enough to recommend any air.

While the text is Burns's, the melody itself is actually the old Scottish air of "Can ye labour lea" which is now universally identified with "Auld Lang Syne." This folk music of Scotland continues to be a source of rich tradition and provides a depth of harmonic color from which a composer may draw. Charles Wiley's skillful arrangement of this simple melody brings out the sonorous quality found in the folk music of Scotland.

Unit 4: Technical Considerations

Old Scottish Melody remains in F major throughout the work. Though rhythmically quite simple, the slow tempo presents several challenges to the young ensemble. Independent melodic writing and other contrapuntal techniques demand confidence by all players through eighth-note pulse. Full instrumentation, including multiple clarinet (three), trumpet (five), French horn (four), and trombone (three) parts, is needed for successful performance. Required ranges are extended for clarinet, French horn, euphonium, and trumpet.

Unit 5: Stylistic Considerations

The style of *Old Scottish Melody* should be song-like and as connected as possible. The folk style of the melody suggests that it should always be brought forth. Yet within this work, the ever-moving countermelody plays an equal role. Great attention to articulation detail as well as dynamic contrast has been made by the composer. Use of *rubato* will further add to the expressive quality of the composition.

Unit 6: Musical Elements

The slow tempo and *legato* style of *Old Scottish Melody* make the musical aspects the most difficult to address. Phrasing demands of the melody are also challenging with the slow development of the musical line. The melody begins in low woodwinds and brass with a beautiful countermelodic figure in the first cornet. Several textural variations follow creating different colors from instrument choirs and combinations. An eighth-note contrapuntal line offers harmonic tension that is finally resolved on the final F major chord.

Unit 7: Form and Structure

Song-Form - Strophic

Event	Measures	Scoring
theme	1-8	low woodwinds/euphonium, trombone with cornet countermelody
chorus	9-16	*tutti*
repeat of theme	17-24	woodwind choir/cornet with clarinet *obbligato*
chorus	25-32	*tutti* with French horn, saxophone *obbligato*
repeat of chorus	33-end	*tutti* with multiple obbligato lines

Unit 8: Suggested Listening

James Barnes, *Yorkshire Ballad*
Timothy Broege, *Sinfonia Six*
Aaron Copland/Patterson, *Down a Country Lane*
Edward Elgar/Davis, *As Torrents in Summer*
Brian Hogg, *Llwyn Onn*
Thomas Root, *Polly Oliver*
Hugh Stuart, *Three Aires from Gloucester*

Unit 9: Additional References and Resources

Robert Burns—The Ploughman Poet (database on-line); available from http://calligrafix.co.uk/burns/biography.html; accessed 12 April 1997.

Dvorak, Thomas L., Cynthia Crump Taggart, and Peter Schmaltz. *Best Music for Young Band*. Brooklyn, NY: Manhattan Beach Music, 1986.

Dvorak, Thomas L., Robert Grechesky, and Gary Ciepluch. *Best Music for High School Band*. Brooklyn, NY: Manhattan Beach Music, 1993.

Grout, Donald J. and Claude V. Palisca. *A History of Western Music*, 5th ed. New York: W.W. Norton & Company, 1996.

Kreines, Joseph. *Music for Concert Band*. Tampa, Florida: Florida Music Service, 1989.

Miles, Richard, ed. *Teaching Music through Performance in Band*. Chicago: GIA Publications, Inc., 1997.

Rehrig, William H. *The Heritage Encyclopedia of Band Music*. Edited by Paul E. Bierley. Westerville, Ohio: Integrity Press, 1991.

Smith, Norman and Albert Stoutamire. *Band Music Notes*. Lake Charles, LA: Program Note Press, 1989.

Contributed by:
Rich Lundahl
Indiana University
Bloomington, Indiana

Teacher Resource Guide

Peregrin: A Traveler's Tale

Douglas Akey
(b. 1957)

Unit 1: Composer

Douglas Akey is Music Department Chairman at Hendrix Junior High School in Chandler, Arizona. He was the 1985 recipient of the American School Band Directors Association's Stanbury Award as the outstanding young elementary/junior high school band director in the United States, and is active as a clinician and guest conductor at the junior and senior high level. In addition, he maintains an active career as a performer and is currently principle horn with the Tempe Symphony Orchestra.

Unit 2: Composition

According to *Webster's International Dictionary*, *Peregrin* comes from the Latin root *peregrinari*, meaning "to travel in foreign lands." The title was inspired by an image of the pioneers crossing the country to homestead in the great west. In the words of the composer, "there are moments of discovery, trepidation, and joy throughout the piece, the uncertainty of pulling up roots and the excitement of discovery." This work was commissioned by and premiered at the 1993 Parade of Bands Festival in Peoria, Arizona. As the closing feature, the festival requested a piece which could be performed by "mass band" with the high school and several junior high schools together on stage.

Unit 3: Historical Perspective

Peregrin represents a culmination of two twentieth-century musical movements. Although not strictly programmatic like Berlioz's *Symphonie fantastique* (1830), this work was conceived to conjure up images and emotions from the listener and performer alike, a task mastered by today's film composers. John Williams (*Indiana Jones Trilogy, Star Wars, Jaws*), Danny Elfman (*Batman*), and Gerry Goldberg (*Star Trek, Planet of the Apes*), are just a few such composers. An individual whose music has come to define the spirit of American adventure and idealism which inspired *Peregrin*, is Aaron Copland (*Billy the Kid*, 1938, and *Rodeo*, 1942). Copland's use of widely spaced intervals and empty octaves and fifths helped to create his unique sound. Akey has used similar open intervals in Theme 2 of *Peregrin* to elicit a similar effect.

Unit 4: Technical Considerations

The scales of F, E-flat, and B-flat major are required for all wind and mallet players in eighth notes at 160 beats per minute. Upper woodwinds and xylophone should have facility at this tempo in sixteenth notes in F major. Piccolo, flute, and clarinet must be comfortable with B-flat major arpeggios in eighth notes at 144 beats per measure. *Peregrin* is in 4/4 meter with several 2/4 measure extensions on the ends of phrases, and there is some chromatic alteration in places of harmonic transition. Syncopation is created through tied notes, and quarter-note triplets provide a layer of rhythmic complexity. A variety of articulations is used. Ranges are within the parameters of the Queenwood Young Band Series. One exception to this is in the third clarinet part which does cross over the break, although these sections are during unison with the rest of the section. In the percussion at m. 29, Akey suggests percussion I use two brushes in each hand for better balance. Also, in m. 103, the composer substitutes a tam-tam hit instead of the suspended cymbal roll. The section at m. 133 to the end poses the most technically challenging music with alternating 3/4 and 4/4 measures, a syncopated theme with an upper woodwind five-note scalic motive in sixteenth notes, and *forte-piano* dynamics. The composer has included specific rehearsal suggestions in the preface to the score.

Unit 5: Stylistic Considerations

Peregrin begins slowly and gains momentum which drives to the end. In the opening section, bass clarinet, tuba and string bass should use a *legato* tongue (bow) on a continuous air stream to create a pulsing effect. As each instrument enters, players should make every effort to blend, subtly changing the timbre with soft entrances. The theme at m. 15 should be declamatory but not accented or clipped, giving shape and direction to the four-measure phrase. The *andante* requires sustained, controlled playing to effectively execute the dynamics written. In the "Twice as Fast" section, careful attention should be paid to the clarinet line m. 83 to "chime" the notes and play inside the chime sound in the percussion. At this same place, bassoon and brass may wish to slightly separate their repeated notes for clarity. This style should remain constant for all accented notes. The flute *staccato* theme should be light without clipping the eighth notes. Balance is of chief concern at the *Allegro vivo*, m. 111, where Theme 1 must be heard under the woodwind flourishes.

Unit 6: Musical Elements

There are two primary themes in this work. The first is firmly stated in F major, m. 15, and cascades down through the entire ensemble, giving every section a subphrase of the melody. The dominant tonal centers are F major and E-flat major, although these shift, especially during transitional sections, and touch on D-flat and B-flat tonal centers. Measure 79 appears to be in B-flat major according to the key signatures; however, the pedal E-flat aurally centres it in E-flat major without actually using the fourth scale degree. Theme 2 first appears in half notes, measure 29, and later appears in rhythmic diminution in quarter notes. There is a return to theme 1 at the *Allegro vivo*, before the *coda* harmonically digresses to A-flat and finally returns to F major.

Unit 7: Form and Structure

SECTION	MEASURES	EVENTS AND SCORING
Intro.	1-4	Pulsing rhythmic motive in bass clarinet, tuba and string bass over sustained F tonic in bassoon, baritone saxophone, and timpani
	5-14	Pyramid of open intervals (foreshadow Theme 2) builds harmonic tension by increasing dynamics which creates the expectation of an arrival
A	15-24	Theme 1, four-measure melody started in cornet and orchestrated in two measure units throughout the ensemble
	25-28	Harmonic shifting with some chromatic alterations
	29-36	Theme 2, in third clarinet, alto clarinet, tenor saxophone, horns, and mallet percussion
	37-42	*Crescendo* and retransition
	43-52	Theme 1, exact repetition of mm. 15-24
	53-55	*Rallentando*, modulation to E-flat

B	56-62	*Andante*, introduction-like section with open intervals and pyramiding harmonic structures
	63-66	Flute and oboe motive foreshadow m. 79 arpeggiated figures
	67-71	Theme 2 returns in diminution in clarinets, counter melody in saxophones, horns, baritone, and low woodwinds, flute motive suggests m. 87
	72-78	Canonic entrances in clarinet, cornet, and horn
C	79-82	"Twice as Fast," *arpeggio* motive in clarinet
	83-86	"Chime" *arpeggios*, add low brass and bassoon, beginning layering effect
	87-90	Flute staccato *arpeggio* motive added to layers
	91-98	Theme 2 in saxes and horns
	99-102	Flute motive out, brass sustained, "un-layering" effect
	103-106	Chiming out, clarinet, horn and flute pyramid open intervals to harmonic structure over sustained brass
	107-110	Transition, opening rhythmic pulsation returns in alto and tenor saxophone, horn, trombone, and baritone, increase in motion with sixteenth-note flourishes in flute, oboe, and alto sax
A′	111-120	Recapitulation of Theme 1, now with woodwind and mallet sixteenth-note layer
Coda	121-123	Quarter-note triplet figure in low wood winds, saxes, and brass
	124-127	Upper woodwinds enter with open intervals

128-132	Oboe and clarinet *arpeggio* figure reminiscent of mm. 71 and 79
133-139	Syncopated line in brass and low woodwinds, upper woodwinds sixteenth-note flourishes build to decisive accented fortissimo conclusion

Unit 8: Suggested Listening

Hector Berlioz, *Symphonie fantastique*
Michael Colgrass, *The Winds of Nagual*
Aaron Copland, *Rodeo, Billy the Kid, An Outdoor Overture*
Danny Elfman, soundtrack to *Batman*
Nancy Galbraith, *With Brightness Round About It.* (Carnegie Mellon
    Wind Ensemble, 1995)
John Williams, soundtrack to *Raiders of the Lost Arc, Star Wars*

Unit 9: Additional References and Resources

Akey, Douglas. Interview with the composer, April, 1997.

Duarte, Leonard P., Daniel S. Hiestand, Carol Ann Prater, Doy E. Prater. *Band Music That Works*. Volume 1. California: Contrapuntal Publications, 1987.

Duarte, Leonard P., Daniel S. Hiestand, Carol Ann Prater, Doy E. Prater. *Band Music That Works*. Volume 2. California: Contrapuntal Publications, 1988.

Grout, Donald J. and Claude V. Palisca. *A History of Western Music*, 4th ed. New York: W.W. Norton & Company, 1988.

Miles, Richard, ed. *Teaching Music through Performance in Band*. Chicago: GIA Publications, Inc., 1997.

Rehrig, William H. *The Heritage Encyclopedia of Band Music*. Edited by Paul E. Bierley. Ohio: Integrity Press, 1991.

Thomas, Tony. *Film Score: The Art and Craft of Movie Music*. California: Riverwood Press, 1991.

Contributed by:

Jennifer McAllister
University of North Texas
Denton, Texas

Teacher Resource Guide

Polly Oliver

Thomas Root
(b. 1947)

Unit 1: Composer

Thomas Root was born in Redwood Falls, Minnesota in 1947. He received his undergraduate and master's degrees from the University of Minnesota and his Doctorate in Music Composition from Michigan State University. Root was previously on the faculties of the University of Minnesota, Saginaw Valley State University, and California State University-Long Beach. Currently, he is Director of Bands and Chairman of the Music Theory Department at Weber State University. Root won the 1997 Utah Composers Guild competition with his commissioned work, *Chorale Prelude on "Sleepers Awake"* (to be published in late 1997). He also took top honors in 1995 for *Lithuanian Rhapsody* for symphonic band which was written for Vitatis Landsbergis, former president of Lithuania. Other well-known works for band include *Let Us Break Bread* (1980), *Ballad for Kristin* (1980), *The Lone Wild Bird* (1984), and *Prelude and Giocoso* (1985).

Unit 2: Composition

Polly Oliver was composed in 1972 but not published until 1977 after numerous revisions and editing done by the composer. The work continues to be Root's most popular piece to date and enjoys wide critical acclaim. *Polly Oliver* is considered by many to possess substantial musical merit and should be "core" repertoire for the young band. It was recently selected as one of the ten most important works for young band by contributors to the American Band College. The work is approximately five minutes in duration.

Unit 3: Historical Perspective

The source of the melody from which the piece is constructed comes from a folk song of Welsh background. The melody was discovered by the composer in a book of simple pieces while he was teaching junior high trumpet students. Although completed in 1972, Root almost did not submit the work for publication. Between 1972 and 1977, it accompanied him in a box until editing and revisions for publication were complete. Folk music has always been a source of rich tradition, valuable for culture and the society which it represents. Percy Grainger (1882-1961) dedicated his life to the collection and presentation of folk music through various musical media. The collection of folk songs found in his *Lincolnshire Posy* has become a staple of the wind repertoire. Béla Bartók (1881-1945) was another twentieth-century composer who traversed the countryside of what was then Hungary in search of the music of "the people." Thomas Root's setting of this Welsh folk song demonstrates the musical depth from which composers may draw.

Unit 4: Technical Considerations

Polly Oliver is developed around the tonal area of E-flat major. The middle *Allegretto* moves through several key centers including C major, A and B minor, and G-flat major, using accidentals. Required ranges are moderate with few exceptions, including French horn and euphonium where strong players are needed. Sensitive solo clarinet playing is needed in the opening statement of the theme. The set of variations found in the *Allegretto* provides several rhythmically complex melodic lines found primarily in upper woodwinds. Cross-rhythms, accidentals, various meter changes, and independent melodic writing offer the greatest challenge in this work.

Unit 5: Stylistic Considerations

The opening and concluding sections of *Polly Oliver* are *legato* while the middle *Allegretto* incorporates both *legato* and *staccato* requirements. Great attention to detail as it relates to articulation has been provided by the composer. Dynamic nuance also plays an important role, especially through the creation of textural color and balance. Elasticity of tempo through the original theme should be incorporated as musical gesture and phrasing warrants.

Unit 6: Musical Elements

After a brief introduction, the folk-like theme is presented by solo clarinet atop a static but sonorous harmony described by the composer as "indefiniteness." What follows is a more rich harmonization of the sixteen-bar melody to conclude the "modified" exposition of a sonata form. The development section then proceeds at a brisk pace with a series of variations on the original theme. Contrapuntal writing, thin textures, and various key centers make this section the most difficult to perform successfully. The recapitulation then brings back the theme in its original form but with dynamic and textural alteration. The theme is now supported by the earlier horn countermelody as well as a new woodwind countermelody. A *coda* concludes the work with a static C major triad over which upper woodwinds provide a beautiful eighth-note "unwinding" effect.

Unit 7: Form and Structure
Modified sonata form

SECTION AND EVENTS	MEASURES	SCORING
Exposition:		
introduction	1-7	*tutti*
theme	8-19	solo clarinet
	20-23	*tutti*
transition	24-27	woodwinds/low brass
theme	28-42	harmonized woodwinds, French horn countermelody
Development:		
variation 1 of theme	43-60	trumpets with various rhythmic motives as countermelody
transition	61-69	various melodic fragments
variation 2 of theme	70-81	French horn with woodwind countermelody
	82-88	French horn/trombone with various countermelody
transition	89-91	trombone
variation 3 of theme	92-108	woodwinds with French horn countermelody
Recapitulation:		
return of theme	109-126	*tutti*
Coda	127-end	upper woodwinds

Unit 8: Suggested Listening

James Barnes, *Yorkshire Ballad*
Timothy Broege, *Sinfonia Six*
Albert Oliver Davis, *Rhenish Folk Festival*
Brian Hogg, *Llwyn Onn*
Thomas Root, *The Lone Wild Bird*
Hugh Stuart, *Three Aires from Gloucester*

Unit 9: Additional References and Resources

Dvorak, Thomas L., Cynthia Crump Taggart, and Peter Schmaltz. *Best Music for Young Band*. Brooklyn, NY: Manhattan Beach Music, 1986.

Dvorak, Thomas L., Robert Grechesky, and Gary Ciepluch. *Best Music for High School Band*. Brooklyn, NY: Manhattan Beach Music, 1993.

Grout, Donald J. and Claude V. Palisca. *A History of Western Music*, 5th ed. New York: W.W. Norton & Company, 1996.

Kreines, Joseph. *Music for Concert Band*. Tampa, FL: Florida Music Service, 1989.

Miles, Richard, ed. *Teaching Music through Performance in Band*. Chicago: GIA Publications, Inc., 1997.

Rehrig, William H. *The Heritage Encyclopedia of Band Music*. Edited by Paul E. Bierley. Westerville, OH: Integrity Press, 1991.

Smith, Norman and Albert Stoutamire. *Band Music Notes*. Lake Charles, LA: Program Note Press, 1989.

Contributed by:

Rich Lundahl
Indiana University
Bloomington, Indiana

Teacher Resource Guide

Rhenish Folk Festival

Albert Oliver Davis
(b. 1920)

Unit 1: Composer

Albert Oliver Davis was born in Cleveland, Ohio in 1920. He received his compositional training with a degree from Arizona State University and additional studies at the Cleveland Institute of Music. He has published over 400 works including solos, works for orchestra, jazz band, marching band, and concert band. He served as arranger and accompanist to Thomas L. Thomas with *The Voice of Firestone* for more that twenty years and was an arranger for the Paul Burton Orchestra for thirty-seven years. Several well-known original works for band include *From Shire and Sea* (1968), *Fantasie on a Danish Theme* (1967), *Ladies, Lords, and Gypsies* (1986), *Songs of Wales* (1970), and the arrangement of Elgar's *As Torrents in Summer* (1988).

Unit 2: Composition

Rhenish Folk Festival was completed in 1983 and inspired by the scenic Rhine River in western Germany. The three-movement work is based upon folk songs about the Rhine and its adjoining regions. The first movement, "O You Beautiful, Wonderful Rhine," is a delightful waltz in a moderate tempo. The next movement, "The Lorelei," is the familiar German song and legend. This beautiful 6/4 melody moves effortlessly from woodwind choir to brass choir, changing only in texture and color. The final movement, "What Does the Grapevine Bring Us?" is a lively and spirited march that moves through several tonal centers. The technical facility and musical brilliance of this movement concludes *Rhenish Folk Festival* as "joyful music, brimming with life and good fun."

Unit 3: Historical Perspective

Folk music has always been a source of rich tradition, valuable for culture and the society which it represents. Percy Grainger (1882-1961) dedicated his life to the collection and presentation of folk music through various musical media. The collection of folk songs found in his *Lincolnshire Posy* has become a staple of the wind repertoire. Béla Bartók (1881-1945) was another twentieth-century composer who traversed the countryside of what was then Hungary in search of the music of "the people."

Albert Oliver Davis has taken three German folk songs that are of vibrant musical quality and set them brilliantly for young band. His careful attention to detail and musical craft retain the vitality and original character of each folk song. The contrasting movements convey the song-like quality found in the music of the Rhine regions of Germany.

Unit 4: Technical Considerations

The tonal centers of B-flat, E-flat, and A-flat major are incorporated throughout the movements of *Rhenish Folk Festival*. The first movement's technical demands are quite reasonable within the context of triple meter (dotted half note=60). Difficulties that may be encountered in the slow second movement (*Lento*, quarter note=96) are limited to rhythmic alignment of eighth notes with melody above. The third movement is by far the most technically demanding. This fast march (quarter note=135) moves through three keys and uses dotted rhythms as well as sixteenth notes frequently. The euphonium countermelody is especially demanding and requires a strong player or section.

Unit 5: Stylistic Considerations

A folk style through song-like interpretation is needed in each movement. The composer pays great attention to detail through articulation and dynamic nuance. The first movement is a light and buoyant waltz and should be felt as one. The second movement is *legato* throughout yet never becomes heavy as wind instrument choirs exchange textural color. Articulation and rhythmic precision provide the vibrant march quality of the concluding movement.

Unit 6: Musical Elements

The theme of the first movement is a lilting waltz in B-flat major, first presented in upper woodwinds. An *obbligato* euphonium line is then added during a variation of the melody as it returns twice to conclude the movement. The second movement's slow 6/4 theme begins with brass choir and alternates with woodwind choir. The tonality centers around E-flat major with very little chromatic alteration. The final movement begins in B-flat major with the theme presented in woodwinds. A demanding euphonium *obbligato* offers a delightful countermelody. A new theme in E-flat major is then introduced in low woodwinds and clarinets. The work concludes by moving to yet another key (A-flat major) with upper woodwinds providing a sixteenth-note countermelody above the established theme.

Unit 7: Form and Structure

Three-movement suite

SECTION AND EVENTS	MEASURES	SCORING
Movement I: "O You Beautiful, Wonderful Rhine"		
introduction	1-8	*tutti*
theme a	9-24	upper woodwinds
theme b	25-40	low woodwinds/euphonium countermelody
theme b varied	41-end	low woodwinds/euphonium melody, upper woodwinds countermelody
Movement II: "The Lorelei"		
theme a	1-8	brass choir
	9-12	woodwind choir
	13-16	brass choir
theme a varied	17-24	woodwind choir
transition	25-28	*tutti*
theme a	29-end	combined choirs
Movement III: "What Does the Grapevine Bring Us?"		
introduction	1-8	tutti
theme a	9-16	woodwinds with euphonium *obbligato*
repeat	17-26	
theme b	27-34	clarinet/low woodwind
repeat	35-42	
theme b	43-54	*tutti*

theme b	55-62	low woodwind/brass with woodwind *obbligato*
coda	63-end	*tutti*

Unit 8: Suggested Listening
Béla Bartók/Phillip Gordon, *Three Hungarian Songs*
Albert Oliver Davis, *From Shire and Sea*
Percy Grainger, *Lincolnshire Posy*
Clare Grundman, *An Irish Rhapsody*
Hugh Stuart, *Three Aires from Gloucester*

Unit 9: Additional References and Resources
Dvorak, Thomas L., Cynthia Crump Taggart, and Peter Schmaltz. *Best Music for Young Band*. Brooklyn, NY: Manhattan Beach Music, 1986.

Dvorak, Thomas L., Robert Grechesky, and Gary Ciepluch. *Best Music for High School Band*. Brooklyn, NY: Manhattan Beach Music, 1993.

Grout, Donald J. and Claude V. Palisca. *A History of Western Music*, 5th ed. New York: W.W. Norton & Company, 1996.

Kreines, Joseph. *Music for Concert Band*. Tampa, FL: Florida Music Service, 1989.

Miles, Richard, ed. *Teaching Music through Performance in Band*. Chicago: GIA Publications, Inc., 1997.

Rehrig, William H. *The Heritage Encyclopedia of Band Music*. Edited by Paul E. Bierley. Westerville, OH: Integrity Press, 1991.

Smith, Norman and Albert Stoutamire. *Band Music Notes*. Lake Charles, LA: Program Note Press, 1989.

Contributed by:
Rich Lundahl
Indiana University
Bloomington, Indiana

Teacher Resource Guide

Sandy Bay March

Brian West
(b. 1959)

Unit 1: Composer

Brian West is a native of Australia. He studied Music Education at the Tasmanian Conservatorium of Music (Hobart) in the late 1970s. It was during this time that he began composing and arranging for young bands. Thirteen years of teaching high school band gave West an even greater appreciation of the needs of both young players and developing bands. With more than a dozen published original works for the young band to his credit, West has established himself as an advocate of music education. He and two other Australian composers, Brian Hogg and Ralph Hultgren, were instrumental in the production of the Aussie Band Concert Curriculum. This program is designed to provide the band director with three complete concert repertoires for the first year of a band's concert performance. The music provides concert pieces that are both technically and conceptually accessible to young musicians. West is the winner of the 1991 Brolga Music Composition Contest and presently teaches Music and Audio Design at Rosny College in Hobart, Tasmania, Australia.

Unit 2: Composition

Sandy Bay is a on the river Derwent in the Tasmanian City of Hobart. The march is a short work for young band that opens in the "patrol" genre, with voices being added to the texture to simulate the arrival of a band. It was written for the Combined Primary Schools Concert Band of Hobart, which incorporates students of one and two years experience. The work is a lively one that is ideal for teaching syncopation, the use of D.S., *coda,* and repeats.

Unit 3: Historical Perspective

The form of the march has been connected with wind music since the time of the Ancient Greeks. Drum and bugle calls have been used by military commanders to identify units and communicate with troops. March music is "essentially an ornamentation of a fixed, regular and repeated drum rhythm" intended to help the army move from one place to another. In the early nineteenth century, the role of the march changed from the purely military entity to the "popular" march. Early examples include Beethoven's *Yorck'scher March*. These marches continued to be inspired by war, however, and the marches of Johann Strauss, Sr. (e.g., *Radetsky March*) and Claudio S. Grafulla (e.g., *Washington Grays*) were inspired by the Austrian Revolution and the American Civil War. The "Golden Age of Bands" following the American Civil War, and social upheaval in Europe saw the mainstay of modern marches written between the middle of the nineteenth century until the end of World War I. This period includes the major output by Sousa and Alford, and many notable marches by Bagley, Goldman, Klohr, King, J.F. Wagner, and others. The twentieth century has for the most part seen a decline in the popularity of the march, although the older marches continue to be very popular. The main exception to this decline have been marches that entered the repertory through successful musical, film, and television scores, such as Rodgers's *Victory at Sea*, Coates's *The Dam Busters*, and Goodwin's *633 Squadron*.

Unit 4: Technical Considerations

This is listed as a Level Two work. The main teaching elements are syncopation, *staccato* markings, slurs, D.S., *coda*, repeats, and, for many parts, eighth-note rests. The work has a moderate range for all parts. It is firmly in B-flat major, with some secondary dominants (and thus accidentals) in the B and C sections.

The percussion writing, while straightforward, offers interest for young percussionists, and includes parts for mallets, snare and bass drum, crash cymbals, triangle and timpani.

Unit 5: Stylistic Considerations

Marches present students with a unique style. This march is very rhythmical, with the syncopated figure highlighting the underlying beat. The composer has made extensive use of *staccato* to emphasize the separated articulations so prevalent in the march form.

Unit 6: Musical Elements

Sandy Bay March includes the syncopated eighth/quarter/eighth figure in all parts, and features *staccato* markings. Dynamic range throughout the work helps make the repeats interesting, as does the "layering" effect at the opening.

The work includes a *dal segno* and *coda.*

Unit 7: Form and Structure

Section	Measure	Scoring
A, repeated	1	clarinets, alto saxophone two times
A	11	full ensemble
A1	19	full ensemble
B, repeated	27	full ensemble
A	43	brass and low reeds
C, repeated	51	emphasis on low brass, though full ensemble
DS		
A	11	full ensemble
A1 1 (To *Coda* at 27)	9	full ensemble
Coda	69	*Coda* (four bars based on A)

Unit 8: Suggested Listening

Kenneth J. Alford, *Colonel Bogey*
Ludwig van Beethoven, *Yorck'scher Marsch*
John Philip Sousa, any march

Unit 9: Additional References and Resources

Begian, Harry. "Behold the Lowly March." *The Instrumentalist*, June, 1986.

Byrne, Frank. *"Sousa Marches: Principles for Historically Informed Performance."* The Wind Ensemble and Its Repertoire, edited by Frank J. Cipolla and Donald Hunsberger. Rochester, NY: University of Rochester Press, 1994, 141-67.

Perrins, Barrie. "More Marches, Please!" *Brass Band Digest*, Baldocks, Herts, UK: Egon Publishing, 1984, 111-112.

Rehrig, William H. *The Heritage Encyclopedia of Band Music.* Editor Paul E. Bierley. Westerville, OH: Integrity Press, 1991.

Rehrig, William H. "Marches, The Original Band Music." *The Heritage Encyclopedia of Band Music*. Editor Paul E. Bierley. Vol. 2, Westerville, OH: Integrity Press, 1991, 873-874.

Contributed by:
Alan Lourens
Indiana University
Bloomington, Indiana

Susan Creasap
Assistant Director of Bands
Morehead State University
Morehead, Kentucky

Teacher Resource Guide

Suite from Bohemia

Vaclav Nelhybel
(1919–1997)

Unit 1: Composer

Vaclav Nelhybel is a composer and conductor, well known for his works for band, as well as ballets, operas, and much chamber music. Born in Czechoslovakia in 1919, he studied at the university and conservatory in Prague. Later he studied musicology at Fribourg University. He held various conducting posts including the Czech. Philharmonic (1945-46), Swiss Radio (1946-50), and Radio Free Europe (1950-57). He emigrated to the U.S. in 1957, and became a citizen in 1962.

Unit 2: Composition

Suite from Bohemia is in four movements written specifically for younger bands. Technical demands have been kept to a minimum. Each of the (short) movements has a programmatic title, which will help the players and audience understand the spirit and character of the music. The publisher is E. C. Kerby Ltd., Toronto.

Unit 3: Historical Perspective

Suites of folk music are important for the understanding they provide of the life of peoples from other places and times. The various dance, ceremonial, work songs, laments, and joy help bring an intuitive sense of how life was and is for others. The movements bring to life four differing snapshots of Bohemia. The first movement is a stately "Procession to the Castle." It is followed by a story, "Folk Tale," a "Tournament," and the work concludes with a "Round Dance."

170

Unit 4: Technical Considerations

The work is well crafted for the young band. There are frequent rests for the brass players, and *tessitura* is appropriate. The various parts are kept interesting by having differences in what the various players in the section are asked to do. The woodwind writing is conservative also. Dynamics range from *ppp* to *ff*. Slurred and accented notes are called for, as well as mordents in the woodwind parts. The key signatures for the various movements are in two or three flats (concert pitch), and the melodic content is modal. The notation is constructed primarily from eighth and quarter notes.

Unit 5: Stylistic Considerations

Choosing the correct tempo for the various movements is essential for the successful performance of this piece. The articulations and dynamics are clearly marked, and will bring out the character of each movement. The composer has been careful to bring contrasting bodies of sound into juxtaposition. It is important that the players keep the character of the music going as the sound changes.

Unit 6: Musical Elements

The melodic materials are folk-like, and the accompaniments often move in parallel intervals (fourths or fifths) or with *ostinato* patterns. The percussion parts are interesting and independent.

Unit 7: Form and Structure

I. "Procession to the Castle:" *Allegro marcato*, 4/4 time

Starting with the full band, an eight-measure theme is presented by the brass and answered by the woodwinds. The brasses are accented, the woodwinds *legato*. The woodwind and brass choirs alternate these materials until the entire band comes together at m. 48 to lead to an *allargando* closing section at m. 56. The percussion parts bring drive to the movement.

II. "Folk Tale:" *Moderato*, common time

This movement is in two short sections, each starting with a six-measure theme for solo woodwind.

The clarinet starts the first section with a six-measure melody in the lowest register, after an introductory two measures of half notes in open fifths by the low woodwinds and brass. As the line progresses, more players are added until the entire woodwind choir is playing. The brass choir comes in on the last measure and takes over in a variant of the opening clarinet melody—*forte* and *marcato*. The woodwinds join in *agitato*, and after a unison modal cadential formula by the brass, the band cadences on a unison G.

The second section is marked *Tranquillo molto* and starts with solo flute. The melody is fragmented into one-measure units and passed back and forth

between the saxophones and the clarinets. The entire band closes with the half-note figure which opened the movement.

III. "Tournament:" *Con fuoco*, cut time

This movement starts with snare drum and trumpet. The fourteen-measure theme stated by the trumpet is repeated throughout the movement in progressively larger and more complex settings. After the initial statement, it is played in duet with the horn, then in three parts. After the entire brass section comes in at the key change (measure 55), clarinet choir takes over. The next statement is in the trombones, accompanied by horns and muted trumpets. At m. 86 the key returns to two flats, and a rhythmic figure with emphasis on the third beat is stated first in the woodwinds and then in the brass. At m. 96 this is combined with the opening theme to bring the movement to a dramatic close.

IV. "Round Dance:" Allegretto, 3/4

The Round Dance starts softly with the percussion section. The bells state the melody on which the movement is constructed. On the second time through the clarinet comes in with the next section. This is followed by a *ritornello* section which is eight measures long and played by the brass. The round is played again twice by the woodwinds, then the movement is concluded by the *ritornello* which is repeated *accelerando al fine*.

Unit 8: Suggested Listening

Antonín Dvořák, *Slavonic Dances*
Karel Husa, *Music for Prague 1968*

Unit 9: Additional References and Resources

Paul Johnson. *Modern Times: The World from the Twenties to the Eighties*. New York: Harper & Row Publishers, 1983.

Contributed by:

Jim Klages
Indiana University
Bloomington, Indiana

Teacher Resource Guide

They Led My Lord Away

Adoniram J. Gordon
(1836–1895)

arranged by
Fred J. Allen (b. 1953)

Unit 1: Composer

Adoniram Judson Gordon was born in New Hampton, New Hampshire on April 19, 1836. He attended Brown University and upon graduation entered the ministry. His first position was that of pastor at the Baptist Church in Jamaica Plain, Massachusetts. In 1869 Gordon moved to Boston where he was the pastor of the Clarendon Street Baptist Church. Gordon was the editor of *The Service of Song for Baptist Churches* (1871), and a year later published the collection *The Vestry Hymn and Tune Book*. He further distinguished himself by serving on the Board of Trustees of Newton Theological Institution and on the Board of Fellows of Brown University. In 1878 Gordon was awarded an Honorary Doctor of Divinity degree from his alma mater. He was the author of *In Christ, or the Believer's Union with His Lord* (1872), *Congregational Worship* (1872), *Grace and Glory* (1880), *Ministry of Healing* (1880), and *The Two-Fold Life* (1883). Gordon composed a number of hymn tunes of which four have been employed in the twentieth century: "Gordon," "Caritas," "Love," and "My Jesus I Love Thee." He died in Boston on February 2, 1895.

Unit 2: Composition

The early American hymn tune "They Led My Lord Away" is beautifully scored for band by Fred J. Allen. The arranger discovered this lovely melody in a collection of hymns among the holdings of the North Texas State University Library. He made a copy of it and several years later decided to arrange it for concert band. It was Charles "Pete" Wiley (1925-1992) who

173

attributed the hymn to Adoniram J. Gordon. From the opening statement of the melody, the piece exudes dignity, grace, power, and hope. The plaintive call of the refrain, "oh tell me where to find him," in the solo trumpet does much to preserve the call-response characteristics of the original hymn spiritual. The work was premiered in 1984 in its prepublication version at a summer band camp in Abilene, Texas. Published in 1990, *They Led My Lord Away* is thirty-nine measures in length and has a performance time of approximately three and one-half minutes.

Unit 3: Historical Perspective

The American hymn has its roots in the mid-eighteenth century when James Lyon published the tune book *Urania* (1761). Other New England composers quickly followed suit, and by 1800 the number of tune books had grown to more than 130. With the Great Revival of 1800 in Kentucky came the religious revival meetings where preaching, praying, and singing abounded. From these settings emerged a new type of hymn, the spiritual song, which was less complex than the traditional hymn and had text repetitions or a call-response structure. It appears that "They Led My Lord Away" was composed in this tradition.

Unit 4: Technical Considerations

The composition is scored for standard instrumentation and employs much doubling of parts. There are few exposed lines, although the first trumpet has two solos, both written on the staff. Although the score lists four separate horn parts, the first and second horns frequently are doubled, as are the third and fourth horns. The horns only expand into three parts for three measures and never have four parts. The baritone part typically doubles one of the trombone parts. The composition calls for timpani, chimes, triangle, and suspended cymbal. Flutes and clarinets have two beats of diatonic sextuplets.

Unit 5: Stylistic Considerations

Keeping with the simplistic style of the hymn spiritual, the setting is lyrical and straightforward. The phrasing is clearly marked, but the length of the phrase coupled with the tempo indication of *andante* indicates that this composition requires an ensemble with good breath control. Frequent tempo shifts give the sensation of *rubato*, while the markings—*stringendo*, *sostenuto*, and *with fervor*—help to convey the style and the emotional content of the work. Be aware that the arranger indicates that this work lends itself to a variety of interpretations; therefore it is appropriate for each conductor to follow his/her heart in preparing this piece for performance.

Unit 6: Musical Elements

The tonality of the work is E-flat major with a triadic and traditional harmonic structure. A variety of textures and dynamic levels contribute to the effectiveness of this composition and provides an excellent resource for teaching balance. The simple hymn tune melody must remain predominant throughout the piece and generally should convey a quiet dignity and strength. Strive to develop expressiveness in all parts, particularly at m. 29 where the full band is marked *fortissimo*. In the prepublication version of the work, the trumpet solo in mm. 16-18 was scored for horn. This solo is now cued for horn and may be performed by that instrument.

Errata: Measure 24, Trombone 3, change all G's to G-flat.

Unit 7: Form and Structure

MEASURES	EVENTS
1-8	Melody in flutes and first clarinet, generally woodwind texture with horn and baritone, andante
9-16	Melody to trumpets and trombones with woodwind echo
17-24	Call-response, solo trumpet to woodwinds, solo trumpet to full band
25-28	Transition, clarinet/bassoon duet to full band, *poco stringendo*
29-36	Final statement of melody, full band, *sostenuto* and *fortissimo*, *diminuendo*
37-39	Ending, melody in flutes with accompaniment in all clarinets

Unit 8: Suggested Listening

James Barnes, *Yorkshire Ballad*
Johannes Brahms/Buehlman, *Blessed Are They*
Larry D. Daehn, *As Summer Was Just Beginning*
David Holsinger, *On a Hymn Song of Philip Bliss, On a Hymn Song of Lowell Mason, A Childhood Hymn*
Gustav Holst/Robert W. Smith, *In the Bleak Midwinter*
Paul Tschesnokoff, *Salvation Is Created*
Frank Ticheli, *Amazing Grace*
Charles "Pete" Wiley, *Old Scottish Melody*

Unit 9: Additional References and Resources

Apel, Willi. *Harvard Dictionary of Music*, 2nd ed. Cambridge, MA: The Belknap Press of Harvard University Press, 1970.

Companion to the Hymnal, a Handbook to the 1964 Methodist Hymnal. New York: Abington Press, 1970.

de Charms, Desiree and Paul F. Breed. *Songs in Collections.* Detroit: Information Service Inc., 1966.

Diehl, Katharine Smith. *Hymns and Tunes—An Index.* New York: The Scarecrow Press, Inc., 1966.

Hitchcock, H. Wiley. *Music in the United States: A Historical Introduction*, 3rd ed. Englewood Cliffs, NJ: Prentice Hall, 1988.

Hughes, Charles W. *American Hymns Old and New.* New York: Columbia University Press, 1980.

Rehrig, William H. *The Heritage Encyclopedia of Band Music.* Westerville, OH: Integrity Press, 1991.

TRN Music Publisher, Ruidoso, New Mexico.

Contributed by:

Susan Creasap
Assistant Director of Bands
Morehead State University
Morehead, Kentucky

Teacher Resource Guide

Three Hungarian Songs

Béla Bartók
(1881–1945)

arranged by
Phillip Gordon (1894–1983)

Unit 1: Composer

Béla Bartók synthesized the elements of the peasant folk music of Hungary and Romania with the Austro-German tradition. In making use of these folk melodies, harmonies, and rhythms, he was able to forge his own unique nationalistic style in the early twentieth century. He was a collector of folk music, a virtuoso pianist, and an active teacher.

Unit 2: Composition

These three pieces are accessible by most beginning band groups. They represent the simplest folk melodies collected by Bartók. *Three Hungarian Songs* was arranged by Phillip Gordon (1894-1983), a pioneer composer/ arranger of school band and orchestral music.

Unit 3: Historical Perspective

The twentieth-century search for a creative, new voice which did not follow the Schoenbergian path of serialism resulted in a variety of different styles and genres. Nationalism and interest in the folk music of world cultures was one such interest of many composers. As a result, many compositions for orchestra and wind ensembles began to contain actual folk materials or musical ideas informed by folk materials. Bartók implemented both methods, publishing over two thousand folk tunes from Hungary and surrounding areas, and incorporated much of the musical ideas into the symphonic forms of his time.

Unit 4: Technical Considerations

I.   The key is B-flat major. Melodic material is diatonic and within standard range. Parts are doubled and cues appear to assist with accompaniment. A muted trumpet (m. 9) is the only solo voice.

II.   The key is centered in D (minor). The horns carry the first half (cued in the trumpets), and the trumpets and high woodwinds take the second. Accompaniment consists of block chords and some chromatically altered moving lines. Some low register clarinet playing and horn leaps may present challenges.

III. The key is G minor, although the sections modulate. Melodic motion is basically diatonic once again, and accompaniment is blocked. The xylophone part doubles the upper woodwinds.

Unit 5: Musical Considerations

I.   The weak-beat accompanying voices must agree on note length. All voices must participate in phrasing, not just the melody. Muted trumpet and flute at m. 9 will need to tune carefully.

II.   All accompanying long notes should follow the contour of the melody played by the horns in the first phrase and by the trumpets and woodwinds in the second.

III. Accents should be played with air increases, not harder articulation. The accented quarter notes must be matched for uniform length. Light, staccato playing of eighth notes must be exhibited by the horns at m. 10 and the upper woodwinds at m. 17.

Unit 6: Musical Elements

Three Hungarian Songs features regular phrase structures, symmetry, tonality, folk songs, and major and minor modality.

Unit 7: Form and Structure

The overall structure of the piece is fast-slow-fast, with the following formal divisions among movements:

I.   ABBA repeated

II.   CDCD

III. EFGHGHGH with brief coda

Unit 8: Suggested Listening
Pieces by Bartók:
Mikrokosmos
Music for Strings, Percussion, and Celesta

Other pieces influenced by folk music:
Antonín Dvořák, *Slavonic Dances*
Percy Grainger, *Lincolnshire Posy*
Gustav Holst, *Second Suite in F*
Ralph Vaughan Williams, *English Folk Song Suite*

Unit 9: Additional References and Resources
Rehrig, William H. *The Heritage Encyclopedia of Band Music.* Westerville,
    OH: Integrity Press, 1991.

Stevens, Halsey. *The Life and Music of Béla Bartók.* New York: Oxford
    University Press, 1953.

Contributed by:
Scott A. Stewart
Indiana University
Bloomington, Indiana

Teacher Resource Guide

Three on the Isle
Hugh M. Stuart
(b. 1917)

Unit 1: Composer
Active as a school instrumental music teacher and supervisor for thirty-three years in Maryland and New Jersey, Hugh M. Stuart brings a wealth of experience to the field of educational band music. Born in Harrisburg, Pennsylvania, Stuart received degrees from the Oberlin Conservatory and Columbia Teachers College. He has also done graduate study at Rutgers, Newark State College, and the University of Michigan. In addition to composing, teaching, and guest clinician work, he was also an active studio musician, working on radio, television, and in jazz groups before his retirement. His catalogue of compositions include over a hundred works for band, orchestra, small ensembles, solos, and instrumental teaching. He now lives in Albuquerque, New Mexico.

Unit 2: Composition
Three on the Isle is a three-movement composition inspired by the sound and feel of folk songs from different areas of Britain. The melodies are not settings of actual folk songs, but compositions original to this piece. The first movement, "Song from Wolking Castle," is a light *Allegretto* which the score notes is reminiscent of songs from that area's countryside. The second tune, "Ayre for Betws-y-Coed," was inspired by the Welsh town of the same name, and is a plaintive *Moderato* in triple meter. The third and final movement is entitled "A Tune from County Antrim," and reflects the mingled Scottish and Irish musical heritage of that area.

Unit 3: Historical Perspective

Though there is great variation in the definitions of the term "folk song," authorities agree on one aspect which forms a vital and distinctive part of any folksong: that it evolves through oral transmission rather than through musical notation. This gives a folk song great flexibility, as performers are not tied to printed notes and can interpret with much more freedom. Folk songs are thus rarely performed exactly the same way twice—in text and notes as well as artistic rendering—even by the same performer. Many versions of the same song exist; tunes usually vary from place to place, as do lyrics. How this historical concept should inform current performance practice is often a matter of debate.

Since most English folk song is syllabic (one syllable to one note), melody is strongly tied to the poetic form of its lyrics: a four-line stanza equates to a four-phrase musical form. This is one element clearly heard in *Three on the Isle*.

English folk song found strong influence in the works of many composers of this century, Ralph Vaughn Williams, Gustav Holst and Percy Grainger among them. Through their on-site research of folk tunes, transcriptions and settings of tunes, or through their assimilation of the language and style of the folk song into their personal compositional style, the folk song has made a lasting impression upon the musical direction and focus of the twentieth century.

Unit 4: Technical Considerations

True to most of Hugh Stuart's compositions for young band, technical concerns are minimal in *Three on the Isle*. Scoring is rich, including four horn parts and three trombone parts for bands strong in those voices, but also with ample doubling and/or cueing for bands short on brasses. Rhythms are straightforward yet varied, and meters include common, cut time, and two types of triple meter. Ranges are well within the scope of most junior high groups, and the percussion writing requires four players to cover the parts. There are no mallet parts beyond a simple chimes part in the second movement, so some additional doubling of treble parts may be needed to keep a large section active.

Unit 5: Stylistic Considerations

Because of their roots in the style of folk tunes, the melodies of *Three on the Isle* should have a lilting graceful quality, yet also have an underlying energy and pulse. Careful attention should be paid to achieving a unified articulation throughout sections, especially on the *tenuto* and *staccato* quarter notes in the melody of the first movement. Obvious though it may sound, take the cut-time marking seriously; don't attempt a fast four (or even a moderate four for that matter). The melody pulses in two beats, not four.

In the second movement, Stuart has provided ample phrase markings, some of which may stretch your players' lung capacities. Balance tempo with need for long phrases, and strive for a seamless quality to the lines. A light, detached style in the third movement will keep the pulse moving forward—almost a march style, but without the aggression. Consider a space between the prominent rhythmic pair of dotted eighth and sixteenth (where not slurred, of course).

Unit 6: Musical Elements

This composition uses a tonality scheme of A-B-A, with the first and third movements in the keys of F major, and the second in the key of C minor (with a brief shift to C major in the B theme). At the end of the first movement, there is a sudden shift from cut time to common time—the bass line must follow the conductor carefully to make the change possible for the whole band. A *caesura* and *rallentando* set up the close of the second movement. The third movement uses the *D.S. al coda* to close the form.

Unit 7: Form and Structure

SECTION AND EVENTS	MEASURES
"Song from Wolking Castle"	
Introduction	1-4
A Section	5-28
B Section (repeated)	29-37
A Section return	38-45
Coda	46-48
"Ayre for Betws-Y-Coed"	
A Section	
(four eight-bar phrases)	1-32
B Section	33-40
A Section (with elongation)	41-59
"A Tune From County Antrim"	
Introduction	1-7
A Section	8-23
B Section	24-39
C Section	40-46
D.S. back to A Section	8-22
Coda up to C Section	
(repeated)	47-54
Coda/Finale	55-60

Unit 8: Suggested Listening

Clare Grundman, *English Folk Song Suite*
Gordon Jacob, *Old Wine in New Bottles*
Gordon Jacob, *More Old Wine in New Bottles*
Hugh M. Stuart, *Three Ayres From Gloucester*
Ralph Vaughan Williams, *Sea Songs*

Unit 9: Additional References and Resources

Duarte, Leonard P., Daniel S. Hiestand, Carol Ann Prater, Doy E. Prater. *Band Music That Works*. Volume 1. Burlingame, CA: Contrapuntal Publications, 1987.

Duarte, Leonard P., Daniel S. Hiestand, Carol Ann Prater, Doy E. Prater. *Band Music That Works*. Volume 2. Burlingame, CA: Contrapuntal Publications, 1988.

Dvorak, Thomas L., Robert Grechesky, and Gary Ciepluch. *Best Music For High School Band*. Bob Margolis, ed. Brooklyn, NY: Manhattan Beach Music, 1993.

Dvorak, Thomas L., Cynthia Crump Taggart, and Peter Schmaltz. *Best Music for Young Band*. Bob Margolis, ed. Brooklyn, NY: Manhattan Beach Music, 1986.

Randel, Don, ed. *New Harvard Dictionary of Music*. Cambridge, MA: Harvard University Press, 1986.

Sadie, Stanley, ed. *New Grove Dictionary of Music and Musicians*. London: Macmillan Publishers Limited, 1980.

Sadie, Stanley, ed. *Norton/Grove Concise Encyclopedia of Music*. NY: W.W. Norton and Co., 1988.

Contributed by:

Doug Norton
Director of Bands
American School in London
London, United Kingdom

Teacher Resource Guide

Three Pieces for American Band Set No. 2

Timothy Broege
(b. 1947)

Unit 1: Composer

Timothy Broege was born in Belmar, New Jersey and received a Bachelor's of Music with Highest Honors in June, 1969 from Northwestern University where he studied composition and harpsichord. He taught for a number of years in the public schools of Chicago and New Jersey. Currently Broege is organist and director of music at First Presbyterian Church in Belmar, and a faculty member at Monmouth Conservatory of Music, Red Bank, New Jersey. A prolific composer, he has written over thirty compositions for band including the *Sinfonia* series, *Three Pieces for American Band Set No. 1*, *Dreams and Fancies*, and *Sonata for Trumpet and Band*. Broege received the Goldman Award at the 1994 ASBDA Convention for his works for school bands.

Unit 2: Composition

Three Pieces for American Band Set No.2 was commissioned and premiered in 1978 by the Gilbert S. Lance Junior High School Band of Kenosha, Wisconsin under the direction of Larry Simons. The outer movements of Broege's work, "Fanfare" and "Fantasia," serve as a prelude and a postlude to the central work, "Pavan to a Ground," which combines a chaconne with a Renaissance court dance. Originally each movement was subtitled "The Jewel in the Grass," "The Queen in the Lake," and "The Door in the Tree," respectively. These titles came from Steven Millhauser's *Edwin Mullhouse: The Life and Death of an American Writer* and were not intended to be programmatic. In the words of the composer, they were, "just added for spice...they gave the audience something to think about." These subtitles are not present in the score published by Bourne Co. Together the three movements are approximately seven minutes long.

Unit 3: Historical Perspective

Completed in 1978, *Three Pieces for American Band Set No. 2* is based on musical gestures found in the sixteenth and seventeenth century, encased within twentieth-century harmony. Broege found his inspiration for these pieces in the *Fitzwilliam Virginal Book,* an English manuscript collection of keyboard pieces for harpsichord written around the reign of Queen Elizabeth I. These manuscripts contained not only traditional dances of the time, such as the pavane, but pieces called fantasias as well. William Byrd's *Pavana Lachrymae* is a well known work from this period. The chaconne developed during the same period from French courtly dances and was based upon a harmonic *ostinato* or *ground bass*. Other works for winds which draw their inspiration from this period in history are Gordon Jacob's *William Byrd Suite*, Tielman Susato's *The Battle Pavane* arranged by Bob Margolis, and *First Suite in E-flat* by Gustav Holst.

Unit 4: Technical Consideration

This work is centered around the tonal area of D, alternating between D major and D natural minor. Students should be familiar with both scales, as well as C major and F major. There is some chromatic alteration throughout each movement in all voices. Idiosyncratic of its Renaissance roots, the three movements are in duple meter with straightforward quarter- and eighth-note divisions. Syncopation through accents, entrances after rests, and tied-note figures are prevalent throughout the work. One variation of the "ground," or "chaconne," utilizes a dotted eighth-sixteenth figure and the ensemble should be comfortable tonguing eighth notes at 144 beats per measure. Warm, sustained playing is required of the low woodwinds and brass to establish the chaconne in the second movement, and from the entire ensemble at the *coda* of the final movement. The low brass range drops to F2 in the baritone and third trombone, and G1 in the tuba. Horn I reaches a G5 and the upper woodwinds may reach one step beyond a beginner's comfortable range. *Three Pieces for American Band Set No. 2* is scored for a full wind ensemble.

Unit 5: Stylistic Considerations

Broege orchestrates from a pipe organ, and as such, he thinks in terms of choirs of instruments according to their register. This work contrasts choirs of instruments, adding, subtracting, and alternating them throughout the work, much as an organist changes manuals and stops. As a result, timbral unity within each choir, and timbral contrast between them is important. A full sonorous "organ" sound is necessary, especially in the chorale sections where the composer would like "huge golden brass tones" led by the trumpets. Prolific use of *ostinato* requires a steady pulse. In keeping with renaissance dance influences, articulations should be smooth and light, not heavy. The *staccato* eighth notes at m. 63 should be lifted, not too short, with a "da" or other softer syllable. In general, long sustained pitches should not cover moving parts (especially at m. 20 in Movement III), and careful attention should be paid to the dynamics as the composer is very specific about marking them with ensemble balance in mind.

Unit 6: Musical Elements

In the "Fanfare" there are two basic themes. The first is based upon the interval of a second expanding to a seventh. The second theme is reminiscent of Gregorian chant with twentieth-century syncopation. This movement is centered around D, and moves to a D major final chord. "Pavan to a Ground" is based on the contrast between the pavan theme, which alternates between D major and F major, and the chaconne, which is resolutely in D minor. In the words of the composer, "these musical worlds overlap...with the *ground* winning out," as it is the final theme presented in the movement, creating suspensions which resolve to a D major chord. The "Fantasia" begins with an introduction quoting fragments of the four main themes heard from the previous movements. A new theme in F major is heard over a two-measure *ostinato* in the accompaniment. In keeping with the free treatment of fantasias in the sixteenth and seventeenth century, this theme is varied through rhythmic augmentation as note values are doubled and the harmony turns minor. The final *coda* is a chorale which modulates back to a D major final chord.

Unit 7: Form and Structure

SECTION	MEASURES	EVENTS AND SCORING
"Fanfare"		
A	1-4	Theme 1 in brass centered around G-A second expanding to a seventh
	5-6	Woodwinds repeat opening theme a semitone higher
	7-10	Transition to B, syncopation introduced in the brass
B	11-16	Theme 2 first stated in piccolo, bass clarinet, and timpani in D and then by solo cornet with tambourine
	17-22	Development of Theme 2 and retransition back to A, m. 22 exact repeat of transition m. 10

A'	23-26	Return to theme 1, varied
	27-30	Transition same as mm. 7-10, now *tutti*, establishes G pedal, the dominant of C major
Coda	31-35	Thinner texture, chorale style, to *tutti* D major final chord

"Pavan to a Ground"
   A—Chaconne (Ground)

	1-6	First statement of harmonic pattern (ground) in brass and low woodwinds (theme A), centered in D
	7-12	Chaconne varied rhythmically, add saxophones
	13-18	Cornet I solo with melody

   B—Pavan

	19-22	"Pavan" theme (B) in upper woodwinds
	23-26	Second statement of B theme with piccolo, oboe, E-flat and third clarinet
	27-32	Third statement of B theme, add saxophones and changes harmony

   C—Development

	33-37	Theme B in upper woodwinds, theme A in brass and low woodwinds
	38-42	*Forte, tutti* ensemble, theme B varied in woodwinds and cornet I & II, brass and low woodwinds with theme A in dotted rhythm
	43-46	Theme B in brass with tenor drum
	47-50	Theme A in woodwinds, theme B in brass centered in G
	51-55	Theme B in saxes with tenor drum
	56-58	Theme B varied in upper brass
Coda	59-62	"Pavan" theme B as in mm. 19-22

	63-68	Theme A returns in *staccato* eighth notes, final chord resolves from suspensions to D major

"Fantasia"

Introduction	1-10	
	3-4	Fragment of "Fanfare" Theme 1
	5-6	"Fanfare" Theme 2 fragment
	6-7	"Pavan" Theme A
	8-9	"Pavan" Theme B
A	11-14	New theme in F major, cornet melody over *ostinato*
	15-19	Theme varied, split between a different choir each measure, dynamic contrast
Repeat	11-19	Add piccolo to cornet melody, woodwinds to sax *ostinato*
B	20-29	A varied through rhythmic augmentation, "minor" tonality
Coda	30-37	Chorale with bassoons, saxes, horns, and low brass, ground bass of Theme A returns, final chord is D major

Unit 8: Suggested Listening

Timothy Broege, *Three Pieces for American Band Set No.1*, *Sinfonia V*, *Peace Song*, *The Headless Horseman*
William Byrd, *Lachrymae Pavane*
Gustav Holst, *First Suite in E-flat*
Gordon Jacob, *William Byrd Suite*
Bob Margolis, *The Battle Pavane*

Unit 9: Additional References and Resources

Battisti, Frank. *The Twentieth Century American Wind Band/Ensemble: History, Development, and Literature*. Fort Lauderdale: Meredith Music Publications, 1995.

Broege, Timothy. "*Timothy Broege Speaks about Three Pieces for American Band Set No. 2.*" Audio recording for Gilbert S. Lance Junior High School Symphonic Band, 1978.

California State University—Fullerton. *The University Wind Ensemble*. DAT recording, 1990-91.

Cummings, David, ed. *International Who's Who in Music and Musicians Directory*, 13th ed. Cambridge: Melrose Press Limited, 1992.

Grout, Donald J. and Claude V. Palisca. *A History of Western Music*, 4th edition. New York: W.W. Norton & Company, 1988.

Miles, Richard, ed. *Teaching Music through Performance in Band*. Chicago: GIA Publications, Inc., 1997.

Millhauser, Steven. *Edwin Mullhouse: The Life and Death of an American Writer*. New York: Knopf Publishing, 1972.

Palisca, Claude V. *Baroque Music*, 3rd ed. New Jersey: Prentice-Hall, 1991.

Contributed by:
Jennifer McAllister
University of North Texas
Denton, Texas

Teacher Resource Guide

Two Grieg Songs
Edvard Grieg
(1843–1907)

arranged by
Andrew Balent (b. 1934)

Unit 1: Composer

Scandinavian native Edvard Grieg received his musical education first from his mother, a gifted pianist, and then attended the Leipzig Conservatoire, where he contracted a lung disease which plagued him all of his life. He was highly attracted by Norwegian folk songs, and spent a good deal of time composing mostly songs and short works (and a few large symphonic works) based on those idioms, in addition to having a busy piano-playing and conducting career. Among his output are the *Piano Concerto in A Minor*, the *Peer Gynt Suite*, the *Lyric Pieces* for piano, and 120 songs.

Andrew Balent has completed degrees at Syracuse University and the University of Michigan. He served as Director of Bands in public schools in New Haven, Connecticut; Utica, New York; and Warren, Ohio. Retired from teaching since 1986, Balent has composed or arranged well over 400 works for beginning bands.

Unit 2: Composition

Both selections have been taken from Grieg's *Lyric Pieces* for piano. The first, "Norwegian Dance" (op. 35, no. 2), is a charming duple dance in ABA: a light *allegretto* and a more fleeting *allegro*, followed by a return to the opening section. The second, "Sailor's Song" (op. 68, no. 1), is a light modal tune in ABBA form.

Unit 3: Historical Perspective

National independence became an icon of the late Romantic era of Western philosophy. This passion for individual and national freedom gave rise to many struggles in the late nineteenth century: Greece and Turkey, Poland and Russia, Czechoslovakia and Austria, and Norway and Sweden. Throughout Europe, people as members of specific cultures were becoming cognizant of their history, arts, character, and future. The musical movement known as "nationalism" arose from this line of thought, and folk music became infused into operas, symphonic pieces, and songs. Edvard Grieg often deliberately broke the traditional rules of common-practice harmony and form (using sharped fourths in both major scales as well as bass drones), and in doing so developed a fresh, new, easily recognized Norwegian style.

The piano miniature blossomed late in Brahms's career, and saw a great proliferation in literature in the works of Grieg, Dvořák, Balakirev, Mussorgsky, Franck, Chabrier, and Fauré. The "miniature" was a brief work which conveyed a single, particularly pointed emotion in its unadulterated form—an intense, intimate, meaningful snapshot type of communication. These stood in stark contrast to the grandiose symphonies, cantatas, tone poems, and operas of the late Romantic era.

Unit 4: Technical Considerations

The opening section of the "Norwegian Dance" contains melodic challenges for the flute, alto saxophone, and trumpet, who should practice the melody both on their own time and together, if possible. There are no loud markings in this entire opening, so players should phrase within the context of *mezzo piano*. The *allegro* marks a change in tempo, volume, and articulation. The flute, bass clarinet, tenor and baritone saxophones, and euphonium all have technically challenging passages at m. 24 as well as the end of the section, where accidentals will present some opportunities for a modulation study. The "Sailor's Song" presents little technical challenge, but demands confident sectional playing in the middle section.

Unit 5: Stylistic Considerations

In the "Norwegian Dance," melodic parts should rehearse a light, bouncy, almost comical style. Downbeats and afterbeats must agree on note length and should phrase with the melody, not just play the same dynamic intensity throughout. All percussion parts are important, and should be played with taste. At the *allegro*, all quarter notes should be nicely spaced, and all accents should be observed (emphasized with space and breath, not tongue). Style must still be quite light and forward-moving. The four sixteenth notes at the *fermata* prior to the *da capo* may present some precision problems—be sure that the last notes are the same length and type of release (air). The "Sailor's

Song" tutti sections must be carefully balanced so that the "Grieg-like" chords can be heard. Note lengths (regular, *marcato*, *legato*, *staccato*) must be well-differentiated in all sections. Careful tuning must be observed (always!) in the saxophone family, bass clarinet, and trombone section.

Unit 6: Musical Elements

These elements are incorporated: use of folk music in symphonic idioms, formal construction (AB, etc.), Norway, modulation, *da capo al fine*, opus.

Unit 7: Form and Structure

SECTION		MEASURES	EVENTS AND SCORING
"Norwegian Dance," op. 35, no. 2			
A		1-12	
	a	1-4	trumpet melody with upbeat/downbeat accompaniment (tuba/baritone saxophone with clarinet/tenor saxophone/horn and percussion coloring), E-flat
	b	5-8	two-measure repeated phrase, flute melody
	c	9-12	closing statement, flute, alto saxophone, trumpet melody trombones add to upbeats, horn/second trumpet counterline
A'		1-12	repeated
	a	1-4	flute melody with upbeat/downbeat accompaniment
	b	5-8	flute melody
	c	9-12	closing statement, cadence in E-flat major, pianissimo
B		16-39	
	d	16-19	tutti marcato figures, forte
	e	20-23	flute melody, light sixteenths with soft accompaniment
	e	24-27	bass clarinet/tenor saxophone/baritone saxophone/trombone/baritone/bassoon melody, trumpet accompaniment
	d	28-31	*tutti marcato* figures, *forte*

| e | 32-35 | flute melody repeats |
| e | 36-39 | low voice melody repeats, sudden cadence on F dominant |

Da capo

| A | 1-12 | (third ending-*Fine*) cadence in E-flat |

"Sailor's Song," op. 68, no. 1

A	1-8	two four-bar phrases, largely homophonic scoring with moving bass line (low woodwinds/low brass), full percussion battery playing, B-flat major to C major, *forte* (second time, upper woodwinds added)
B	9-16	second phrase, scored in bass clarinet/ saxophone family/ horn/ trombone/ triangle only, pianissimo, F major to unstable C minor-minor ninth in first inversion
B'	17-24	varied melody and accompaniment, but taken from B material (minor thirds), same scoring as above B extension of cadence, addition of *tutti* in m. 23 with crescendo, F major to C major over bass F
A'	25-28	A material, now accompanied *tutti* in block chords and marching quarter notes (low saxophones and low brass), B-flat major
B	9-16	repeat
B'	17-24	repeat
A'	25-28	repeat, second ending, cadence in B-flat major

Unit 8: Suggested Listening
Compositions by Edvard Grieg:
Concerto in A Minor, Op. 16
Peer Gynt Suite, Op. 46, No. 1
Norwegian Dances
Symphonic Dances
Lyric Suite
Holberg Suite

Songs (e.g., "Ich Dich Liebe")

Other settings using national folk songs or folk song idioms:
Aaron Copland, *El Salon Mexico*
Percy Grainger, *Lincolnshire Posy*
Clare Grundman, *American Folk Rhapsody Nos. 1 and 2*
Alfred Reed, *Armenian Dances* (Sets I and II)
Ralph Vaughan Williams, *English Folk Song Suite*

Unit 9: Additional References and Resources
Forlag, Johan Grundt Tanam. *Contemporary Norwegian Orchestral and Chamber Musicians*. Norway: Society of Norwegian Composers, 1970.

Randel, Don Michael, ed. *The New Harvard Dictionary of Music*. Cambridge, MA: The Belknap Press of Harvard University Press, 1986.

Contributed by:
Scott A. Stewart
Indiana University
Bloomington, Indiana

Teacher Resource Guide

Westridge Overture

James Barnes
(b. 1949)

Unit 1: Composer

As a member of both the Band and Theory-Composition faculties at the University of Kansas, James Barnes teaches orchestration, arranging, and composition, and conducts the Wind Ensemble and Concert Band. He also teaches graduate conducting and band and orchestral literature classes. His numerous compositions for concert band are extensively performed in the United States, Europe, and the Pacific Basin. His works have been performed at Tanglewood, Lincoln Center, Carnegie Hall, and the Kennedy Center in Washington, D.C. Barnes has twice received the coveted American Bandmasters Association Ostwald Award for outstanding contemporary wind band music. He has been the recipient of numerous ASCAP awards for composers of serious music, the Kappa Kappa Psi Distinguished Service to Music Medal, and a number of other honors and grants. He has completed three commercial compact disc recordings of his music with the famed Tokyo Kosei Wind Orchestra. In recent years he has been commissioned to compose works for all five of the major military bands in the Washington, D.C. area. Barnes has traveled extensively as a guest composer, conductor, and lecturer throughout the United States, Australia, and Japan. He is a member of the American Society of Composers, Authors, and Publishers, the American Bandmasters Association, and numerous other professional organizations and societies. Since 1984, his music has been published exclusively by Southern Music Company of San Antonio, Texas.

Unit 2: Composition

Westridge Overture is an original composition for band written in the early 1980s for Andy Clark, who at that time was president of the Norman Lee Publishing Company. The piece serves as a wonderful opener for young bands and is about four and one-half minutes in length. In general, the scoring is thick which helps young performers feel more secure. Although this piece was originally published by Norman Lee, it is now available from Southern Music Company.

Unit 3: Historical Perspective

This Grade Two original band work was written in the early 1980s and apparently has no programmatic features. The piece is similar to the many educational band works from composers such as Frank Erickson, James Ployhar, and Hugh Stuart.

Unit 4: Technical Considerations

This piece is tonally centered in E-flat major with the B section in the dominant key of B-flat major. Conductors should make sure young performers are familiar with both of the scales involved. Rhythmic considerations include the dotted quarter, eighth, and two sixteenths, and the rhythmic pattern of four sixteenths for the percussionists. Most instruments are written well within their range. Percussion instrumentation includes timpani, snare drum and triangle (one player can cover this part), crash and suspended cymbals, and bass drum. Conductors may use as many as six percussionists or as few as four.

Unit 5: Stylistic Considerations

Westridge Overture features two sections of stylistic contrast. The opening and closing *Allegro Moderato* allows the performers to play mostly step-wise eighth-note lines with varying articulations and dynamics. The conductor should strive for energy and rhythmic precision. Included in this section are nice melodic lines in the woodwinds; thus good balance is needed. The middle *Moderato* once again features the woodwinds, namely the flutes, but the clarinets and oboes as well. The brasses provide the accompanying lines and this needs to balance the lyrical *solo* or *soli* melodic line in the flute(s) and other woodwinds. The *coda* once again displays the vivacity of the concert band and should be played with much energy and clarity for a rousing close to the work.

Unit 6: Musical Elements

When asked about the musical elements of the work, the composer responded:

> When I write works for youngsters, I try to write for them in a way
> that challenges them musically and that teaches them a couple of

things about technique, phrasing, counting, or what have you. All educational music should have some sort of agenda of this kind. The harmony is conventional on purpose because I don't know how one plans to teach youngsters to play with good style, good tone, and good intonation if they are playing tone clusters. I don't write tone clusters for children at an age when I believe that they need to work on important musical concepts that are best taught with conventional tertian harmony.

Unit 7: Form and Structure

SECTION	MEASURES	EVENTS AND SCORING
Introduction	1-9	Full band intro using thematic material that appears in the rest of the work; nine-measure phrase, leads to opening theme in flutes and clarinets
A	10-55	E-flat major; primary theme (four-measure phrase) in flutes and clarinets; horns and saxes are added in third phrase; ensemble provides accompaniment; number 3 presents a new melodic line in oboe, clarinet, and tenor sax; continues into transition to B section
Transition	56-59	Slowing of tempo, clarinets, flutes, and alto sax provide eighth-note lines with chordal accompaniment in the brasses; meter and key change for B section
B	60-102	B-flat major; theme appears in flutes (option of solo flute); chordal accompaniment in saxes and low brass; modulates back to B-flat major
A	103-148	E-flat major; return of A material, presentation as before
Coda	149-156	Eight measures in length; moves from dominant to tonic, full ensemble with new material to close.

Unit 8: Suggested Listening

James Barnes, *Chorale and Jubiloso, Trail of Tears, Yorkshire Ballad*
Frank Erickson, *Toccata*

Unit 9: Additional References and Resources

C.L. Barnhouse Publishing Company, Oskaloosa, Iowa (Norman Lee).

Southern Music Company, San Antonio, Texas.

Contributed by:

Rodney C. Schueller
Indiana University
Bloomington, Indiana

Teacher Resource Guide

With Trumpets Sounding
Ralph Hultgren
(b. 1953)

Unit 1: Composer

Ralph Hultgren remains one of Australia's foremost composers of music for bands. A recipient of several Outstanding Composition awards from the Australian Band and Orchestra Directors Association, Hultgren is extremely active as a conductor both within Australia and beyond. Although much of his music has been for young bands, Hultgren has been extremely active in works at all levels, including the first published *Symphony for Band* by an Australian composer. Hultgren is currently conductor of the Wind Symphony at the Queensland University of Technology in Brisbane, Australia.

Unit 2: Composition

A work for very young band, *With Trumpets Sounding* features the trumpet section yet has a great amount of work for all members of the ensemble. In the form of a majestic march, the work provides contrasting sections, and some light scoring to balance the full ensemble work. *With Trumpets Sounding* is around two minutes in duration, published by Brolga Music.

Unit 3: Historical Perspective

With Trumpets Sounding was written in the late 1980s, at the time of the fall of the Iron Curtain and the emergence of new opportunities for peace. At the front of the score, the composer states: "An age of peace, of reason and understanding, is heralded in this work for elementary band. The new age begins 'With Trumpets Sounding' ".

Music played an extremely symbolic role in the fall of the Iron Curtain, with the finale of Beethoven's Ninth Symphony being appropriated for several important concerts across Europe, one of the most famous being the Berlin Philharmonic's appearance with Leonard Bernstein in Brandenberg Square in Berlin.

Unit 4: Technical Considerations

Listed by the publisher as a Level One work, the technical considerations in this score are minimal. The work falls firmly in the key of E-flat major, with only three bars including accidentals. As the title suggests, the melody falls to the trumpet section a great deal, although the melody consists mostly of fourths and fifths above middle C. An optional clarinet part doubles the trumpet lines.

Rhythmically, the work includes no rhythm smaller than eighth notes, with the exception of grace notes in the snare. Dynamics have been used to great effect in the work, and vary from *mezzo forte* to *fortissimo*. Articulation marks include accents and slurs.

The percussion is written in three parts. The mallet part is written for glockenspiel, Percussion I for snare and bass drum, and Percussion II for crash cymbals.

Unit 5: Stylistic Considerations

This march-like work includes three distinct stylistic sections. The opening main theme is martial in character, while the low brass melody at rehearsal 29 is more emphatic in nature. The third style is the flowing counterline of 37 that is skillfully intertwined with the opening theme at 45.

Unit 6: Musical Elements

This work gives all sections in the ensemble a chance to shine. While the trumpets carry the weight of the main melody, all other sections have a melody at some stage. The contrasting nature of the three ideas offers an opportunity to teach several musical styles in a march-like setting. There is some use of accents in the upper parts during the bass melody at 29, and several slurs are used at 37.

Unit 7: Form and Structure

SECTION	MEASURES	SCORING
Introduction	1	Brass melody/woodwind accompaniment
A	5	Trumpet melody/rest of band stop-time
B	13	Woodwind melody/low brass accompaniment

A	21	Trumpet melody/rest of band stop-time
B1	29	Low brass melody/accompaniment stop-time
C	37	Clarinet/alto saxophone melody/snare
C/A	45	Woodwinds continue C/brass and percussion A
Coda	51	Full band

Unit 8: Suggested Listening
Ludwig van Beethoven, "Finale," *Symphony No. 9*
Higgs, *Sussex by the Sea*
Kenneth J. Alford, *Colonel Bogey*

Unit 9: Additional References and Resources
Rehrig, William H. *The Heritage Encyclopedia of Band Music*. Editor Paul E. Bierley. Westerville, OH: Integrity Press, 1991.

Smith, Norman and Albert Stoutamire. *Band Music Notes*, 3rd ed. Lake Charles, LA: Program Note Press, 1979.

Contributed by:
Alan Lourens
Indiana University
Bloomington, Indiana

Grade Three

Teacher Resource Guide

Adagio for Winds

Elliot Del Borgo
(b. 1938)

Unit 1: Composer

An ASCAP award-winning composer, Elliot Del Borgo has taught instrumental music in the Philadelphia Public Schools, and currently is Associate Professor of Music at the Crane School of Music at the State University of New York at Potsdam. He received degrees from the State University of New York, Temple University in Philadelphia, and the Philadelphia Conservatory. Del Borgo studied theory and composition with Vincent Persichetti and Gilbert Johnson, and has written songs and etudes as well as having written extensively for band, orchestra, choir, and chamber groups.

Unit 2: Composition

"*Adagio for Winds* is in the harmonic and melodic framework of the Romantic era, with song-like melodic lines prominently set within a simple, uncluttered accompaniment. The piece moves slowly, and gently builds to a climax toward the end before coming to a quiet close."

Unit 3: Historical Perspective

An "adagio" is a composition with a slow tempo, often specified by the term *adagio* (but not always) itself. It can be the slow movement of a symphony, sonata, or can stand on its own. Perhaps the most well known of these such pieces is the *Adagio for Strings* by Samuel Barber.

Unit 4: Technical Considerations

The piece is centered in E-flat major, although chromatic harmonization takes the listener to distant key areas throughout the piece. There are no technical/fingering challenges, with the exception of some wide-interval leaps in clarinets and trumpets which need to be rehearsed for fluidity of line. The primary challenge is in keeping the intensity of phrasing alive with well-controlled air at a slow tempo. Doubling and jolting chromatic melodies will require careful listening for blend and intonation by different instrument families. Rhythms are simple, and use of percussion involves only a suspended cymbal.

Unit 5: Stylistic Considerations

Phrases are well marked, and must match in both manner of release and contour, most probably with a sense of taper and air release. Phrasing must be uniform in moving voices, and chromatics must both tune well and fit in the overall harmonic scheme. The rising broken *arpeggios* should not leap out at the top of the line; instead, care should be taken to make sure that the figure is smooth and even in intensity. Articulation of the chords must be mostly air/least tongue, and require a good breath preparation. Players must strive for horizontal (not vertical) line in every phrase throughout the piece. The composer allows for *rubato* "at appropriate places," and suggests that solo lines should be played with "warmth and expression," while accompanying instruments should remain "relaxed and blended."

Unit 6: Musical Elements

Adagio, legato, phrase marking, fluidity/flowing/smoothness, *a2,* "*largo e sostenuto.*"

Unit 7: Form and Structure

Section	Measures	Scoring
Introduction	1-9	Establishment of harmonic structure— low brass/ bassoons/low clarinets, add clarinets, add flutes/low saxophones, then reduce back to low voices with horns
First section	10-16	Alto saxophone solo, woodwind accompaniment
Second section	17-22	Upper woodwind melody clarinet counterline, add baritone and bassoon
Third section	23-29	Trumpet, alto/tenor saxophone melody (material from first section), flute/oboe/ clarinet countermelody, brass block chords
Fourth section	30-39	Trumpet melody, bass clarinet/baritone, saxophone/baritone rising and falling

		broken chords, add flute/oboe/clarinet/ alto and tenor saxophone on counter-line to climax, cadence on E-flat major with slight *ritardando*
Fifth section	40-46	D-flat major established, alto saxophone solo, held chords in clarinet family/horns/ low brass, clarinet *tutti*, harmonic progression to G major
End	47-50	G major held, upper woodwinds continue progression to cadence in E-flat major, brasses drop out for last measure

Unit 8: Suggested Listening

Representative works by Elliot Del Borgo:
Do Not Go Gentle into That Good Night
Festive Ode
Modal Song and Dance
Music for Winds and Percussion
Overture for Winds
Prologue and Dance
Symphonic Essay

Other Adagios:
Samuel Barber, *Adagio for Strings*
Rodrigo, *Adagio para orquesta de instrumentos de viento*

See also *Adagios* by Albinoni, Boccerini, Fiocco, Janaceck, Leclerc, and Tartini. They are frequently paired with an *Allegro* movement (to create the title "Adagio and Allegro") as seen in compositions of Bach, Haddad, Handel, Haydn, Mozart, Nehlybel, Schumann, von Weber, and many others.

Unit 9: Additional References and Resources

Randel, Don M. *The New Harvard Dictionary of Music*. Cambridge: The Belknap Press of Harvard University Press, 1986.

Rehrig, William H. *Encyclopedia of Band Music*. Edited by Paul Bierley. New York: Integrity Press, 1991.

Contributed by:

Scott A. Stewart
Indiana University
Bloomington, Indiana

Teacher Resource Guide

Americana Folk Suite

Barry Kopetz
(b. 1951)

Unit 1: Composer

Barry Kopetz was born in Morristown, New York in 1951. He is current-ly Director of Bands at the University of Utah, where he supervises all aspects of the program. He conducts the Wind Symphony, oversees the graduate conducting program, and teaches undergraduate conducting classes and the secondary instrument ensemble. Kopetz received his undergraduate and mas-ter's degrees from Ohio State University and his doctorate from Indiana University, where he studied with Frederick C. Ebbs. He has held positions at Roosevelt Junior High School (Columbus, Ohio), Franklin High School (Strasburg, Ohio), Bowling Green State University (Ohio), University of Minnesota, and University of Utah. Kopetz has also written numerous musi-cological treatises on major band works and has contributed many articles to music journals. His memberships include the Music Educators National Conference, the College Band Directors National Association, the National Band Association, Phi Beta Mu, and Kappa Kappa Psi.

Unit 2: Composition

Americana Folk Suite is a three-movement work based on the folk tunes "The Young Man Who Wouldn't Hoe Corn," "Sweet Nelly," and "The Little Old Sod Shanty." The composer describes these three movements as "cowboy-like," "a love song," and a "hoe-down." The impetus for this work was both the composer's interest in folk songs from different countries, as well as his belief that more folk suites needed to be written for young band. Kopetz's setting of these folk melodies suits the appropriate level of difficulty for young bands and is both interesting and enjoyable.

Unit 3: Historical Perspective

Composers have collected and used folk songs in their compositions for generations. Grainger, Holst, and Vaughan Williams are perhaps the most important and influential collectors of folk tunes, as this was the source material for a large number of their compositions. The means by which they collected these tunes varied as well. Composers such as Grainger and Holst would literally venture out into the fields and record people singing their native songs. *Americana Folk Suite* follows this long tradition of folk song collecting, as it was inspired by Barry Kopetz's gathering of folk tunes from various song books.

Unit 4: Technical Considerations

Americana Folk Suite utilizes three main key areas including F major, E-flat major, and B-flat major. Knowledge of these scales by the ensemble is essential. The rhythmic demands placed on the ensemble are basic, including dotted eighth/sixteenth-note figures and some syncopated rhythms. The tempo indications have a wide range with the understanding that it is acceptable for the tempos to vary according to the ability level of the ensemble.

Unit 5: Stylistic Considerations

Americana Folk Suite is an adaptation of American folk songs; therefore, careful consideration should be taken to recreate a song-like quality throughout each movement. This work often demands that the ensemble play the same melodic material in many different styles. Therefore, the song-like melodies in this composition demand constant attention in regard to changes in phrasing, articulation, dynamics, and expression. In addition, the accompanimental figures must be played in a lilted style without sacrificing the clarity of the melodic line.

Unit 6: Musical Elements

The key centers in the first movement are F major and E-flat major. The harmony is standard tertian harmony with the addition of two polychords in mm. 77 and 79. The melodic design often carries a standard periodic phrase structure, with the use of an occasional extension such as m. 73 in the first movement. The latter two movements reflect periodic phrasing as well, and are essentially homophonic in texture. The key areas of the second movement are A-flat major and B-flat major, while the last movement is centered around F major and B-flat major.

Unit 7: Form and Structure

SECTION   MEASURES   EVENTS AND SCORING

I. "The Young Man Who Wouldn't Hoe Corn"

Section	Measures	Events and Scoring
Introduction	1-35	Horns and trumpets boldly proclaim the melodic content above a B-flat pedal point.
Theme (1x)	36-53	First statement in the cornet and horn in F major with an accompanimental figure in the low brass and percussion. A consequent answer in the flute and woodwinds follows in m. 43 to complete the phrase.
Bridge	54-58	Key change from F major to E-flat major. This serves as a transition to the second statement of the theme.
Theme (2x)	59-72	Second statement in the clarinet in E-flat major. Accompaniment has moved to low reeds, horns, and euphonium. Consequent phrase begins in m. 66 after a "Surprise!" on beat two of the previous bar.
Codetta	73-82	An extension of the consequent melodic material begins at m. 73 and is followed by two polychords. These chords create a brief harmonic instability until a unison E-flat is played at the end of the movement.

II. "Sweet Nelly"

Section	Measures	Events and Scoring
Theme (1x)	1-16	First statement in A-flat major; cornet presents the melody (a love song) with brass accompaniment.
Theme (2x)	17-32	Second statement of love song in B-flat major; upper woodwinds have the melody
Coda	33-36	Brief closure in woodwinds in B-flat major.

III. "The Little Old Sod Shanty"

Introduction	1-4	Repeated rhythmic pattern with octave leaps in flute and xylophone; solidifies F major.
Theme (1x)	5-20	First statement of theme (representing a barnyard hoedown) in clarinet over an F pedal with rhythmic *ostinato* in flute and xylophone; accented notes in horns, saxophone, and tambourine add to excitement.
Theme (2x)	21-38	Second statement of theme in cornet with accompaniment in low brass and percussion.
"Barnyard Fiddler" Theme	39-54	New material that is not part of the original tune; it is based on a "fiddle approach" to the barnyard dance; announced in piccolo, flute, and oboe; accentuated by temple blocks and xylophone.
Theme (3x)	55-70	Third statement that combines original theme (clarinet) and "barnyard fiddler" theme (flute).
Theme (4x)	71-86	Fourth statement in cornet and horn with alto sax and flute simulating string crossings.
Dissolution	87-91	Afterthought as the dance winds down.
Coda	97-103	"Barnyard fiddler" idea comes back; it represents someone saying "Let's hear it one more time!"

Unit 8: Suggested Listening

Other works by Barry Kopetz:
Afton River Fantasy, *Climb Ev'ry Mountain*, *Do-Re-Mi*, *The Duke of Bedford*, *Greenland March*, *Camperdown Way*

Other works:
Stan Applebaum, *Irish Suite*
Ralph Vaughan Williams, *English Folk Song Suite*

Percy Grainger, *Lincolnshire Posy*
Gustav Holst, *Suite No. 1 for Military Band, Suite No. 2 for Military Band*

Unit 9: Additional References and Resources
Barry Kopetz, interview by author, Denton, TX, 22 April 1997.

"The Basic Band Curriculum: Grades I, II, III." *BD Guide*,
September/October 1989, 2-6.

Duarte, Leonard P., Daniel S. Hiestand, Carol Ann Prater, and Doy E.
Prater. *Band Music That Works*. Volume 1. Burlingame, California:
Contrapuntal Publications, 1987.

Duarte, Leonard P., Daniel S. Hiestand, Carol Ann Prater, and Doy E.
Prater. *Band Music That Works*. Volume 2. Burlingame, California:
Contrapuntal Publications, 1988.

Dvorak, Thomas L., Cynthia Crump Taggart, and Peter Schmaltz. *Best
Music for Young Band*. Edited by Bob Margolis. Brooklyn, New York:
Manhattan Beach Music, 1986.

Garofalo, Robert J. *Instructional Designs for Middle/Junior High
School Band*. Fort Lauderdale, FL: Meredith Music Publications, 1995.

Kreines, Joseph. *Music for Concert Band*. Tampa, FL: Florida Music Service,
1989.

Rehrig, William H. *The Heritage Encyclopedia of Band Music*. Edited
by Paul E. Bierley. Westerville, OH: Integrity Press, 1991.

Contributed by:
Keelan McCamey
Heritage of America Band
Langley Air Force Base
Hampton, Virginia

Teacher Resource Guide

Brazilian Folk Dance Suite

William E. Rhoads
(1918–1990)

Unit 1: Composer
William Earl Rhoads was born in Harvey, Illinois, and received a degree in Education from the University of Michigan. He served in the U. S. Signal Corps during World War II, and after his discharge he was appointed Director of Bands in the Alamogordo, New Mexico public schools. In 1953, he became Director of Bands at the University of New Mexico, also serving as Chairman of the Music Department from 1973 to 1977. He published over 100 works for band, orchestra, and wind ensemble, and study books for the alto and bass clarinet. He was active as an adjudicator, clinician, and conductor throughout the United States and Canada, and was the recipient of many ASCAP awards.

Unit 2: Composition
The *Brazilian Folk Dance Suite* consists of three folk songs freely adapted for concert band and set in dance forms native to Brazil: the bossa nova, the beguine, and the quickstep march. Published by Kjos Music Company in 1986, the approximate performance time of the three movements is six minutes and twenty-five seconds. The first movement is written in a bossa nova style and entitled "The Painter of Cannahay;" the second movement, "A Picture to Remember," is written in the style of a bequine; while the third movement, "Fiesta Quickstep!" brings the work to a rousing conclusion with an up-tempo march style. William Rhoads composed and arranged many works using Latin music styles in his career, including *El Aguanieve, Mexican Dance, Jamaican Holiday, Latin Elegy, Pete's Bossa Nova, A Time to Beguine,* and *Tres Danzas de Mexico.*

Unit 3: Historical Perspective

The suite was an important instrumental form of the baroque music era, consisting of a number of movements, each in the character of a dance. The suite became practically extinct after 1750, but was revived in the late 1800s with the establishment of a modern suite in which the traditional dances were replaced by a free succession of movements of different character. Particularly common were orchestral suites arranged for operas and ballets. The neoclassical movement of the twentieth century led to a deliberate revival of the abstract (non-operatic) suite. Composers of music for the concert band in the twentieth century have been quite successful using suites to explore the folk music of various cultures.

Unit 4: Technical Considerations

The piece utilizes the keys of C minor, F minor, B-flat major, and E-flat major. Key signatures are used with occasional accidentals indicated. With the three movements based on Latin dance styles, establishing a strong accompaniment "groove" is essential for a successful performance of this composition. The first two movements are written in common time, with the third movement exclusively in 2/4 meter. Tempos range from quarter note=84 to quarter note=126, and are clearly indicated. The only solo material is a two-measure trumpet line near the end of the second movement. The third movement has the upper woodwinds opening with a trill and the trumpets using straight mutes. Most of the ensemble will have at least some sixteenth notes to play and several syncopated rhythms to learn. The percussion parts will require at least four players performing on snare drum, bass drum, high hat cymbal, claves, guiro, suspended cymbal, and tambourine.

Unit 5: Stylistic Considerations

Each movement requires strong rhythmic precision in order to perform the proper dance styles. The parts are clearly notated with articulations and phrase markings. As would be expected, the suite utilizes various styles throughout. Ensemble members will at times be required to play contrasting styles at the same time, such as a flowing, *legato* melody over a light, *staccato*-like accompaniment. Providing listening opportunities of authentic Brazilian dance music would be an important element in teaching this style.

Unit 6: Musical Elements

Each of the three movements begins with an introduction that presents the mood and character of the particular folk tune of that movement. These introductions also typically allow the accompaniment figures to be established for each dance style. The first two movements utilize the dark minor tonal centers of C minor and F minor, while the third movement presents a brighter sound with the keys of B-flat and E-flat major. Many of the accompaniment

figures and melodic lines require the performance of close chordal harmonies, while playing unison rhythmic patterns and articulations. The syncopated rhythms in the percussion and wind accompaniment parts will provide a greater challenge than much of the thickly scored melodic material.

Unit 7: Form and Structure

SECTION	MEASURES	EVENTS AND SCORING
Movement I (bossa nova)		
Introduction	1-8	Slow opening statement by unison trumpets, answered by full ensemble. This is followed with an immediate tempo change to moderato to set up the accompaniment figures.
A	9-18	Clarinet and low woodwind unison melody with established accompaniment. Flute and oboe counterline on repeat.
B	19-34	Flute, oboe, and trumpet unison melody followed by horn and trombone melody.
A	35-42	Flute, oboe, alto and tenor saxophone melody.
Coda	43-48	Flute, oboe, alto and tenor saxophone continue melody. Movement ends with a soft, rhythmic figure in low brass and woodwinds, bass drum.
Movement II (beguine)		
Introduction	1-8	Flute, oboe, clarinet, alto and tenor saxophone chordal melody.
A	9-24	Flute, clarinet melody over established beguine accompaniment. Alto and tenor saxophone counterline is added at m. 15.
B	25-40	Trumpet and horn melodic line, expanded to include flute, oboe, and clarinet in m. 33.
B'	41-58	Key change from C minor to F minor. Alto and tenor saxophone, trumpet, and horn melody with flute, oboe, and

		clarinet counterline. Flute, oboe, clarinet, alto and tenor saxophones take over melodic line at m. 49. Two-measure trumpet solo in m. 55 begins transition to the end of the movement.
Coda	57-64	Ensemble passes two-measure melodic line around as full ensemble *diminuendos* to *pianissimo*.

Movement III (march)

Introduction	1-10	Upper woodwind trills and percussion rolls with trumpet melody. Rest of ensemble helps emphasize melodic line. Measures 9 and 10 feature trumpet and percussion set up for the main section.
A/B	1-74	Alternation every eight measures of two melodic lines taken through several variations and instrumentations. Includes rhythmic background accompaniment responsibilities for all sections. Melodic material is chiefly found in the upper woodwinds, trumpets, and bells.
C	75-90	Key change from B-flat major to E-flat major. Introduction of new melodic material presented by upper woodwinds and trumpets. Counterline in low brass and woodwinds along with traditional march accompaniment.
D	91-108	Horn and trombone melody with full ensemble accompaniment figures for first eight measures. Upper woodwinds and trumpets take over for last half of melodic material. Entire section repeats to m. 75.
Coda	109-114	Low brass and woodwinds have final statement with percussion tag ending.

Unit 8: Suggested Listening

Robert Russell Bennett, *Suite of Old American Dances*
Leonard Bernstein/arr. Krance, "Danzon" from *Fancy Free*
Albert Ginastera/arr. John, "Danza Final" from *Estancia*
Frank Perkins/arr. Werle, *Fandango*
Heitor Villa-Lobos/arr. Reed, *Suite* from *Bachianas Brasileiras No. 4*
Heitor Villa-Lobos/arr. Herbert, *Aria* from *Bachianas Brasileiras No. 5*
Clifton Williams, *Symphonic Dance No. 3*, "Fiesta"

Unit 9: Additional References and Resources

Apel, Willi. *Harvard Dictionary of Music*. Second edition. Cambridge, MA: Belknap Press, 1977.

Rasmussen, Richard Michael. *Recorded Concert Band Music, 1950-1987*. Jefferson, NC: McFarland Press, 1988.

Rehrig, William H. *The Heritage Encyclopedia of Band Music*. Edited by Paul E. Bierley. Westerfield, OH: Integrity Press, 1991.

Smith, Norman and Albert Stoutamire. *Band Music Notes*. Third edition. San Diego, CA: Kjos West, 1982.

Contributed by:

James Popejoy
Doctoral Associate
University of North Texas
Denton, Texas

Teacher Resource Guide

Daydream

Timothy Mahr
(b. 1956)

Unit 1: Composer

Timothy Mahr was born on March 20, 1956 in Reedsburg, Wisconsin. He earned a Bachelor of Music degree in Theory and Composition and a Bachelor of Arts degree in Music Education from St. Olaf College in Northfield, Minnesota. In 1983 he completed a Master's degree in Trombone Performance at the University of Iowa and then in 1995 a Doctor of Musical Arts in Instrumental Conducting from the same institution. For three years Mahr taught instrumental music at Milaca High School in Milaca, Minnesota. Well known as a composer, Mahr is the 1991 American Bandmasters Association Oswald Award winner for his composition *The Soaring Hawk*. Mahr was elected to membership in the American Bandmasters Association in 1993.

Unit 2: Composition

Daydream was premiered on November 11, 1989. Written on a request from Miles "Mity" Johnson, the selection was intended as a quiet tune for the Festival Band at the 1989 St. Olaf College Festival of Bands. This musical daydream is, in the words of the composer, intended to "elicit mood changes and shifting images, while conjuring up in the listener the sense one perceives when he or she 'pulls out' of a daydream, returning to reality after a transient mental trip to places of flight and fancy." The composition is fifty-nine measures in length and approximately four minutes in duration.

Unit 3: Historical Perspective

The compositional techniques of the twentieth century have expanded the performing capabilities of both ensembles and performers. With the advent of the twelve-tone system, serialism, minimalism, atonality, aleatoric music, and electronic music, among others, the composer has a new vocabulary of sounds and colors that may be incorporated into contemporary compositions. It is only within recent decades that the band world has enjoyed this expanded array of sonorities and hues, but the number of works that utilize such techniques is continuing to grow. These nontraditional usages of instruments and performers add a special dimension to programmatic works, providing the composer with an ever-expanding array of descriptive devices.

Unit 4: Technical Considerations

The composition utilizes standard instrumentation for developing bands in that the scoring includes parts for piccolo, flutes I and II, oboe, bassoon, clarinets I, II, and III, alto clarinet, bass and contra bass clarinets, full saxophone section, trumpets I, II, and III, pairs of horns and trombones, baritone, tuba, string bass, piano, and five percussion parts. The horn parts generally are *tutti* and doubled throughout in other voices. The *tessitura* in the horns is from written middle C-flat to top line F-sharp. Although the rhythms and technical demands are generally simple, the exposed nature of the lines, coupled with the use of *pianissimo* dynamics, will challenge younger players. The five percussion parts contribute an array of sound effects including wind chimes, coin scrapes, and the use of a variety of mallets on various common percussion instruments. There is an eight-measure section of randomly repeated notes in the piano, flute, oboe, clarinet, and percussion parts. The scoring is fairly sparse but the doublings allow all parts to be heard while contributing to the security of the players. All orchestration considerations work together to allow students to perform this style of music with confidence and will develop the ensemble's awareness of tonal colors.

Unit 5: Stylistic Considerations

All aspects of the piece are well suited to teaching developing bands to perform quiet music at a slow tempo. The composer suggests ca. 60-66 with various *ritardando* measures. The composition exudes a mysterious quality that will require the band to strive for control while conveying the utmost in musical expressiveness. The section of randomly repeated notes should emulate the sound of popcorn popping as the initial sparse poppings gradually increase to a rapid-fire burst of sound.

Unit 6: Musical Elements

The primary aspect of this composition is its strong use of color. There is no key signature and melodic lines tend to blur any sense of tonality due to the use of tritones and well-conceived chromaticism. Much of the harmony is quartal although there are sections that convey a tonal center. The final chord is a tone cluster. All harmonic elements work together to enhance the dream-like quality of the composition.

Unit 7: Form and Structure

The work is a fine example of through-composed music.

MEASURES	EVENTS AND SCORING
1-4	Mysteriously (*p*): introduction, percussion and piano
5-16	Mysterious melody (*pp-mf-ppp*): clarinets, horns, trombones, baritone
17-21	Gentle and quiet (*pp-p*): woodwinds, trumpet duet, piano, and some percussion
22-35	Becoming agitated (*pp-ff*): randomly repeated notes in upper woodwinds and percussion, generally sustained support by the rest of the band, leads to one of the dynamic climaxes of the work in m. 31
36-45	Quiet but growing (*pp-ff-p*): staggered entrances to full band and another dynamic climax in m. 45 (*ffff* in piano)
46-59	Tranquil (*pp-mf-f-ppp*): randomly repeated notes in piano, repeated sixteenth-note pattern in flutes, melodic material in brass with pedal-like configuration in basses and low woodwinds, variety of percussion effects

Unit 8: Suggested Listening

Timothy Broege, *The Headless Horseman*
Thomas Duffy, *Crystals, Snakes*
Adolphus Hailstork, *American Guernica*
David Maslanka, *A Child's Garden of Dreams*
Joseph Schwantner, *and the mountains rising nowhere*
Jack Stamp, *Remembrance of Things to Come*
Fisher Tull, *A Passing Fantasy*

Unit 9: Additional References and Resources

Neil A. Kjos Music Company, San Diego, California.

Rehrig, William H. *The Heritage Encyclopedia of Band Music.* Westerville, OH: Integrity Press, 1991.

Thomson, John. "Of Conducting and Composing: An Interview with Timothy Mahr." *The Instrumentalist*, XLIX March 1995, 10-15.

Contributed by:

Susan Creasap
Assistant Director of Bands
Morehead State University
Morehead, Kentucky

Teacher Resource Guide

A Downland Suite
John Ireland
(1879–1962)

arranged by
Ray Steadman-Allen (b. 1922)

Unit 1: Composer

John Ireland was born in Cheshire, England. He received his formal musical training at the Royal College of Music, and was awarded an Honorary Doctorate of Music from the University of Durham in 1932. He taught music at the Royal College of Music, and among his more prominent students was Benjamin Britten. His works include music for orchestra, chorus, chamber groups, and brass band. The arranger is Ray Steadman-Allen (b. 1922). Allen is also known as a composer of brass band music, primarily for the Salvation Army. He has composed over 250 works for brass bands, and has composed and arranged for concert band, orchestra, and choir.

Unit 2: Composition

A *Downland Suite* was originally written for brass band and was commissioned by the British National Brass Band Championships of 1932. This arrangement is by Ray Steadman-Allen and was published in 1985. It is a work in four movements: "Prelude," "Elegy," "Minuet," and "Rondo." The composer adapted the "Elegy" and "Minuet" for string orchestra, and the outer movements were also adapted for strings by another of Ireland's students, Geoffrey Bush.

Unit 3: Historical Perspective

The British brass bands have a long tradition of musical excellence. There have been and still are numerous community and regional brass bands which perform for the public and compete both locally and internationally. By 1900, there were 40,000 amateur brass bands in England alone. There is a great deal of music that was originally written for brass bands that has now been arranged and adapted to the full band.

Unit 4: Technical Considerations

There are recurring octave leaps used as thematic material throughout. The first movement is colored with moving sixteenth notes compound meter, broken up by several divisions or combinations of these compound rhythms. There are soli lines for the oboe and tenor saxophone, and oboe and clarinets. There are solo lines for the trumpet, horn, oboe, and trombone. The second movement features solos and soli from the oboe, cornets, euphonium, and tenor saxophone. "Minuet" features solos by oboe, bassoon, euphonium, horns, and alto saxophone. "Rondo" features only brief solo lines mixed with ensemble passages in somewhat homophonic textures.

Unit 5: Stylistic Considerations

Thematic ideas must flow throughout the work. An overall unity of themes between movements gives the work its cohesion. There should be distinction between the different articulation markings which change frequently. There are frequent dynamic changes as well as shifting of textures from brass to woodwinds. Rhythms shift from compound to syncopation giving the effect of *hemiola*. The second movement is in direct contrast to the opening movement. Marked *Lento Espressivo*, everything should be smooth, long, and connected. The third movement is a minuet which should be lightly articulated. The melody flows from section to section smoothly and is always in the same character. Here the melody leaps an octave frequently. The final movement, "Rondo," is in 2/2 and uses earlier themes in conjunction with new material. The octave leap is expanded, and there is a combination of earlier articulations, *legato* lines, and ideas.

Unit 6: Musical Elements

There are numerous solo lines throughout the four movements. There is frequent juxtaposition of melodic and thematic ideas. The overall character of lines changes often, and is marked both by dynamic and terminology directions. Articulations are distinctly marked. Solo lines push the instrumental ranges somewhat, but never to their limits. The four movements should have distinct sounds and characters, but maintain continuity through recurring ideas.

Unit 7: Form and Structure

The score gives a solid description of the overall form and structure of the work. It is structured classically. The "Prelude" is in a somewhat sonata form. The "Elegy" is more song-like and briefly strophic. The "Minuet" has full repeats and a full trio. The "Rondo" follows the formal rondo framework of a recurring theme which reappears in different keys. The first movement is in C minor, the second in E-flat major, the third is in B-flat major, with the trio in B-flat minor, the last opens in G minor, but ends in G major. Throughout the work, phrases reach over bar lines. An example is in the "Minuet" where the opening eight-bar phrase is answered by nine bars.

Unit 8: Suggested Listening

John Ireland, *Comedy Overture*, City of London Wind Ensemble, Geoffrey Brand Conducting, British Masters Volume 2.

Unit 9: Additional References and Resources

Battisti, Frank and Robert Garofalo. *Guide to Score Study*. Ft. Lauderdale, FL: Meredith Music Publications, 1990.

Craggs, Stewart R. and John Ireland. *A Catalogue, Discography, and Bibliography*. Compiled by Stewart R. Craggs. With an introduction by Geoffrey Bush. Oxford, England: Clarendon Press; New York: Oxford University Press, 1993.

Kostka, Stefan and Dorothy Payne. *Tonal Harmony*, New York: McGraw-Hill, Inc., 1995.

Searle, Muriel V. and John Ireland. *The Man and His Music*. Tunbridge Wells: Midas Books, 1979.

Contributed by:

Otis French
U. S. Army Field Band
Ft. Mead, Maryland

Teacher Resource Guide

Dreams and Fancies

Timothy Broege
(b. 1947)

Unit 1: Composer

Timothy Broege was born in 1947 in Belmar, New Jersey. In 1969 he was awarded a Bachelor of Music degree with Highest Honors from Northwestern University. As well as teaching in Illinois public schools, Broege has held positions as an instrumental music teacher in New Jersey, organist and Director of Music at the First Presbyterian Church in Belmar, and served on the faculty of Monmonth Conservatory of Music, New Jersey.

The music of Timothy Broege ranges from educational work to major works in the wind literature. His series of *Sinfonia* include works that use conventional and unconventional instrumental techniques, while the *Concerto for Piano and Wind Orchestra* is a virtuosic showcase for both the ensemble and soloist. Broege has been a recipient of many grants and commissions from such organizations as diverse as the Tidewater Music Festival, Gruppoe Nova of Western Germany, and the Indianapolis Children's Choir.

Unit 2: Composition

Dreams and Fancies is a four-movement work with a performance time of five and three-quarter minutes. Published by Hal Leonard, the work includes parts for oboe or flute II, optional E-flat clarinet, and writing for horn I and II and trombone I and II. The percussion writing is on two parts, with many "toys" featured prominently. There is little cross-cueing, but many doublings. Nevertheless, competent soloists are required on flute, clarinet, alto sax, and trumpet; strong bassoons or baritone saxophones are needed as well. Technically, the work places few demands on most players (with the exception of a not-to-difficult 5/4 last movement), but musically players require an understanding of line and shape.

Unit 3: Historical Perspective

The use of the word "Fancies" harks back to baroque terminology. The *Harvard Dictionary of Music* describes a fancy as "the sixteenth and seventeenth-century English manifestation of the fantasia." A fantasia in this sense is a description of contrapuntal techniques, as demonstrated by such early composers as Adrian Willaert (c. 1490-1562), and later in much more complicated forms by Frescobaldi (1583-1643) and Gibbons (1583-1625). A fantasia involves the development through such techniques as inversion, augmentation, diminution, and thematic transformation through fragmentation. Early works were fantasias based upon another work.

"Dreams" is derived from a handful of English baroque works that used this term. They are all short, quiet, reflective works.

While the composer uses baroque terms in naming this work, it is not at all baroque in substance.

Unit 4: Technical Considerations

This work is variously listed as a Grade Three or Four work. In grading it at the lower level, the appraiser is offering an insight into the technical difficulty. The trumpet I part does not extend above written G, the second and third clarinet parts rarely rise above the break, and rhythmically the work remains straightforward, extending the performers only in the 5/4 last movement.

The work does require a full instrumentation. The bassoon and bass clarinet, while doubled in the baritone, provide a necessary color in the lower woodwinds. There are short (optional) solos for trumpet, alto saxophone, and flute at the opening of the second dream, and important lines in the first dream lie within the lower clarinet and lower horn parts.

Percussion writing is extensive for this level, and very important. The writing, while rhythmically not more challenging than the wind lines, requires careful counting, particularly in the slow movements.

Unit 5: Stylistic Considerations

Stylistically, *Dreams and Fancies* offers great variety. Each movement is somewhat different in character. Both "Dreams" are reflective; however, the first is tonally unsettled and replete with gestures, while the second is more melodic. The key to these movements is the shapes that are not indicated in the score. The two "Fancies" are lighter in character. The second is, as you would expect of a closing movement, the weightiest of the work. Its 5/4 syncopated nature belies the "unequal" nature of the meter, and is a jaunty exploration of a theme.

Unit 6: Musical Elements

The work makes many musical demands on players. The "Dreams," particularly the first, demand of the players a clear sense of line and direction. Indeed, melodic and rehearsal difficulties conspire to make the first movement in many ways the most difficult to perform. The "First Fancy" alternates between a *staccato* melody and a flowing *legato* line. While no instrument is called upon to make the change with a measure's rest, most instruments are called to play in both styles. The "Second Dream" features a hocketed melody that appears in two-beat snippets at the opening (in common time), and reappears complete at m. 17. The second melody is a broad stately in 3/4 that often hides the bar line. As with the "First Dream," the key here is control and a sense of line. The final movement is a jaunty 5/4 movement that explores *staccato* throughout. The middle section features a canon based on the main melody.

Unit 7: Form and Structure

SECTION AND EVENTS	MEASURES
"First Dream"	
A	1
A1	5
Transition	8-9
Climax	13
percussion transition	14
A2	18
"First Fancy"	
A	1
B	7
A	13
Coda	18
"Second Dream"	
A: Introduction	1
B	9
A	17
Coda based on B material	21

"Second Fancy"

A1: Introduction	1
A	8
A	16
A	24
Episode based on A in imitation	30
Episode based on inverted A	37
Episode based first two bars of A	43
A	50
Coda	56

Unit 8: Suggested Listening

J. S. Bach/arr. Goldman, *Fantasia in G Minor*
Dave Brubek, *Take Five*
Frescobaldi/arr. Slocum, *Toccata*
Peter Tchaikovsky, *Symphony No.* 6, Movement 2

Unit 9: Additional References and Resources

Delaney, Jack Lee. "Timothy Broege: His Contributions to the Wind Band Repertory with an Emphasis on 'Sinfonia III' and 'Sinfonia V'." DMA Dissertation, Order No. AAC 8627572, University of Cincinnati, 1987.

Rehrig, William H. *The Heritage Encyclopedia of Band Music.* Edited by Paul E. Bierley. Westerville, OH: Integrity Press, 1991.

Smith, Norman and Albert Stoutamire. *Band Music Notes.* Third ed. Lake Charles, LA: Program Note Press, 1979.

Contributed by:

Alan Lourens
Indiana University
Bloomington, Indiana

Teacher Resource Guide

Fantasy on "Sakura, Sakura"
Ray E. Cramer
(b. 1940)

Unit 1: Composer

Ray E. Cramer gained his undergraduate degree in Music Education at Western Illinois University, where he studied composition with Forrest Suycott, and a Masters degree in Trombone Performance and Composition at the University of Iowa, where he studied with Bezanson.

After teaching in Illinois and Iowa high schools, he joined the faculty of the Indiana University School of Music in the fall of 1969. In 1982, Cramer was appointed Director of Bands. Under his leadership the Indiana University Wind Ensemble has earned an international reputation for outstanding musical performances, including the 1982 ABA Convention in Indianapolis; the joint 1984 ABA/JBA Convention in Tokyo; the 1988 MENC National Convention in Indianapolis; the 1991 National CBDNA Convention in Kansas City; the 1994 National MENC Convention in Cincinnati; the 1995 ABA Convention in Lawrence, Kansas; the 1997 CBDNA National Convention in Athens, Georgia and other regional and state conventions. In addition to his administrative responsibilities as Department Chair, Cramer teaches courses at the graduate level in wind conducting, history, and literature, and conducts the Wind Ensemble and University Orchestra.

Cramer is actively involved in clinics and guest conducting engagements throughout the United States and foreign countries. He has served as a guest conductor on the faculty of the Musashino Academia of Music in Tokyo, Japan in the fall of 1990, and the summers of 1992, 1995, and 1998. In December, 1991, he was presented with an Honorary Doctorate of Humane Letters from his alma mater of Western Illinois University.

Unit 2: Composition

Beginning in the early 1990s, Ray Cramer was invited to guest conduct the Mushashino Academia Musicae Wind Ensemble in summers and during his sabbatical leave from Indiana University. The *Fantasy on "Sakura, Sakura"* was written for that group, to be performed as an encore while touring Japan, and dedicated to the memory of Koichi Onodera, the Mushashino Academia band manager who died suddenly in 1991.

The setting is simple, with a straightforward melody, yet demands great control and range of dynamics as well as beauty from all members of the ensemble. In keeping with the traditions of Japanese music, the setting calls for a strong percussion section and demands of them much melodic and atmospheric work.

The work is about three minutes long, and is published by TRN Music Publisher.

Unit 3: Historical Perspective

The western world has long had a fascination with the culture of Japan. In music, this fascination first started to show itself in music around the turn of the twentieth century, with *Madame Butterfly* by Puccini. The influence of eastern traditions on the work of Debussy is well documented. Indeed, the use of the pentatonic scale became a major element of impressionistic music.

"Sakura, Sakura" is a well-known Japanese folk song, a short statement about the beauty and short life of the blossoms on a cherry tree. In typical Japanese style, the song is very succinct. Loosely translated, it is as follows:

> Cherry Blooms, Cherry Blooms!
> All across the third month sky,
> Far as any eye can see,
> Mist and clouds are everywhere.
> And the blossoms' fragrance wafts.
> Well, I say, Well, I say!
> Let us go and see.*

Unit 4: Technical Considerations

Melodically and rhythmically, this work is very straightforward. However, a number of technical problems conspire to make this a more difficult work to put together. In keeping with the Japanese tradition, the percussion writing is extensive and mostly very exposed, with a single cadenza-like bar for the vibraphone. The trumpets have one entry on a high B, and since the layering of sounds is an oft-used effect, players must have the independence to enter in the middle of phrases.

The style is *legato* throughout, though sometimes with the addition of accents. The work closes with a long-held clarinet note, fading away (*niente*);

a rich, dark tone would be a great asset here.

The work is scored for a large ensemble, with solos for cor anglais, bassoon, flute, clarinet and horn. Percussion forces include timpani, percussion I (marimba, vibes, chimes, bells), percussion II (gong, metal wind chimes), and percussion III (suspended cymbal, crash cymbal).

Unit 5: Stylistic Considerations

This work is extremely broad throughout. From the opening bars, consisting of a D pedal point, the harmonies of this work are quite static. Impetus forward is added by the melody, and by dynamics, which range from *ppp* to *ff* and back within the first fourteen bars. Eighth notes should always be flowing and broad, and care should be taken to balance the dynamics against the pitch; where the eighth notes ascend they will naturally be heard, but the difficulty will be in being heard across all pitches.

Unit 6: Musical Elements

The effectiveness of *Sakura, Sakura* revolves around the dynamic contrasts. The composer has often asked the group to *crescendo* and *diminuendo* within a single bar, and in several places changes the dynamics from *pp* to *ff*, or vice versa, within an extremely small amount of time. It is these changes that make this setting very dramatic, and require great control from any ensemble, both to avoid overblowing and to produce resonance at the lower dynamic levels.

Unit 7: Form and Structure

SECTION	MEASURES	EVENTS AND SCORING
Introduction	1-14	One-bar phrase based on melody, opens with percussion, gradually builds to full ensemble.
False beginning	15-20	Based on opening phrase of the melody, it is really a second introduction.
Melody	21-34	The melody "Sakura, Sakura" is presented melodically almost unchanged.
Coda	35-42	Extended last line of the melody is used as a *coda*.

Unit 8: Suggested Listening

Bernard Rogers, *Three Japanese Dances*, Movement 2

Unit 9: Additional References and Resources

Julliard School. *Julliard Repertory Library*. Cincinnati, OH: Canyon Press, 1970.

Rehrig, William H. *The Heritage Encyclopedia of Band Music*. Edited by Paul E. Bierley. Westerville, OH: Integrity Press, 1991.

Smith, Norman and Albert Stoutamire. *Band Music Notes*. Third ed. Lake Charles, LA: Program Note Press, 1979.

Zajec, Victor. *The First Fifty Years: Mid-West International Band and Orchestra Clinic*. Dallas, TX: Taylor Publishing Co., 1996.

Contributed by:

Alan Lourens
Indiana University
Bloomington, Indiana

Teacher Resource Guide

Fantasy on "Yankee Doodle"
Mark Williams
(b. 1955)

Unit 1: Composer

Mark Williams's extensive experience with young musicians has made him one of the most popular writers of music for school bands and orchestras. Co-author of *Accent on Achievement*, Williams served as a full-time elementary band director for twelve years, during which time he was also director of the Spokane All-City Band program. Williams holds Bachelor of Arts in Education and Master of Education degrees from Eastern Washington University. He has toured Europe and the Pacific as a woodwind performer and Chief Arranger for the 560th Air Force Band, and currently performs on cornet with the Spokane British Brass Band. Williams has earned several awards, including the Western International Band Clinic's Gralia Competition. In addition to his composing, Williams serves as String Editor for Highland/Etling, a division of Alfred Publishing.

Unit 2: Composition

Fantasy on "Yankee Doodle" was commissioned by, and premiered at, the Bethlehem Central School District Band Festival in Delmar, New York on March 16, 1995, with the composer conducting. This festival features a massed performance of combined elementary through high school students; thus the piece carries an unusual option of allowing the participation of a beginning band starting at m. 136. The piece falls in the Grade Three category, but some points in the work may be more along the lines of a Grade Four. The piece is published by Alfred Publishing Company and is approximately six and one-half minutes in length.

Unit 3: Historical Perspective

The tune "Yankee Doodle" is one of the best known tunes of the American Revolutionary War period. It first appeared in print in 1782, yet was well known far before this time. In fact, it was used in the opera *The Disappointment* in 1767, but was not written out as the performers sang printed words. The text is anonymous and several sets exist. It was originally sung by the British to make fun of the Yankees, who later, paradoxically, sang it when the British surrendered at Yorktown.

Unit 4: Technical Considerations

Although this piece is placed in the Grade Three category, it requires several key ingredients from the ensemble. The ensemble must possess good soloists on tuba, alto saxophone, and cornet. It must also have good percussionists as the score calls for extensive auxiliary percussion as well as the normal complement of traditional percussion instruments. Williams uses rhythms that are challenging, and also sneaks in some meter changes. The second variation uses 7/8 extensively. Ranges are good for all instruments and Williams hides F minor by writing in the D-flats as accidentals.

Unit 5: Stylistic Considerations

The style changes from each variation, and by following tempos, articulations, and dynamics, these changes should be evident. The introduction should sound vigorous in nature, with the saxophone and horn calls prominent in the texture. The main theme should be playful, as one does not expect the main theme of a work to be presented by solo tuba. Variation 1 should be dark and moody; the minor-mode feel will help this. Variation 2 feels a little like the introduction. In some ways, this should be played in the style of Copland; it should be light and playful after the fanfare-like opening. Variation 3 should be reflective and solemn. Variation 4 should have two styles at once. The percussion ensemble should promote the feeling of energy while the ensemble projects power in its fragments. Variation 5 and the *coda* should be powerful as the work draws to a close. One can hear the influences of Holst, Elgar, and contemporary film scores.

Unit 6: Musical Elements

This piece presents a musical challenge to students. It requires them to execute both technical and lyrical passages. Don't be fooled by the title. This piece is an excellent tool to teach theme and variations to the high school band and requires some musical maturity in order to come off effectively. Harmonically speaking, the work is largely tertian, with sections in major and minor including occasional use of bitonality, added tones, and chords with quartal influences. It features several tempo and meter changes, and requires performers to play both light and with careful articulation as well as lyrically and with *sostenuto*. There are several places in the score where the conductor must listen carefully for good balance as well as execute good cues and clear patterns in the 7/8 section.

Unit 7: Form and Structure

The form of the work is that of a theme and variations and is structured as such.

SECTION	MEASURES	EVENTS AND SCORING
Introduction	1-8	Fanfare-like introduction involving the full ensemble. Main theme is fragmented in cornets.
Main Theme	9-24	The main theme, "Yankee Doodle," is presented in a most humorous manner in the solo tuba. At m. 17 it is passed to solo oboe, two measures later to solo cornet, two measures later to solo euphonium, and back to the tuba for the last two measures.
Variation 1	25-44	Solo alto saxophone presents minor-mode melody with flute countermelody. Full ensemble enters with flowing eighth-note lines.
Variation 2	45-88	This *allegro* variation features the full ensemble with fragments of the theme found in nearly all of the instruments. 7/8 meter is featured in much of this section.
Variation 3	89-119	Expressive variation with solo cornet to start. Transparent scoring with *soli* clarinets and flutes. More instruments added in m. 105 as the music builds to climax in m. 115. Section ends softly.
Variation 4	120-135	Percussion-ensemble-like writing begins this section with fragments of the theme injected by the full ensemble.
Variation 5	136-152	This is the section where the option of a beginning band is employed. The main theme is presented in augmentation by the full ensemble with woodwind, xylophone, and bell *stretto* entrances. Percussion writing still very active.

| *Coda* | 152-End
(10 mm.) | *Maestoso coda* with full ensemble to climactic close. |

Unit 8: Suggested Listening

Gustav Holst, *Second Suite in F for Military Band*
William Schuman, *Chester Overture for Band*
Mark Williams, *Southgate Fantasy, Variants on a Nautical Hymn*
John Zdechlik, *Chorale and Shaker Dance*

Unit 9: Additional References and Resources

Ferris, Jean. *America's Musical Landscape*. Dubuque, IA: William C. Brown
    Publishers, 1990.

Additional notes provided by Mark Williams.

Contributed by:

Rodney C. Schueller
Indiana University
Bloomington, Indiana

Teacher Resource Guide

Homage

Jan Van der Roost
(b. 1956)

Unit 1: Composer

Jan Van der Roost was born in Duffel, Belgium. He was introduced at a very young age to influential music and people within the wind, fanfare, and brass band world. He soon felt a desire to compose himself. At the Lemmons Institute in Leuven, Belgium, Van der Roost received a triple laureate diploma in Trombone Performance, Music History, and Music Education. In 1979 he continued his studies at the Royal Conservatory of Ghent and Antwerp, graduating with a diploma in Composition. Van der Roost presently teaches at the Lemmons Institute, where he conducts the choir, brass, and wind bands. He is also active composing, arranging, and working as an adjudicator. A versatile composer, his original compositions for band include *Puszta, Four Old Dances, Mercury,* and *Flashing Winds,* among others. His works have been performed by such distinguished groups as the Belgian Broadcasting Corporation, the Tokyo Kosei Wind Orchestra, and the Canadian Brass.

Unit 2: Composition

The word "homage," in its most literal sense, means anything given or done to show reverence, honor, etc. This work is in honor of Jan de Haan's twentieth anniversary as conductor of the top Dutch brass band, Soli Deo Gloria. The ensemble commissioned the work as a surprise gift to the conductor. Jan Van der Roost found inspiration in the chorale motive from the *Maestoso* section of Camille Saint-Saëns' organ symphony, *Symphony No. 3*, a piece with which de Haan holds a special bond. Apart from the chorale motive, *Homage* is also based upon note names taken from "Jan de Haan," and

"Soli Deo Gloria," resulting in the *cantus firmus* DEGAH (H being German for B-natural). As this piece was originally conceived for brass band, this *cantus firmus* has been transposed down a major second to concert C major, resulting in the pitches CDFGA. These five notes appear often throughout the composition, often in a different order, or with one pitch repeated or omitted. Composed in 1994, this single-movement work is approximately five and a half minutes in duration.

Unit 3: Historical Perspective

Homage uses two principle themes, each representing a very different musical technique. The chorale arranges preexisting material whose history will follow, and the opening uses the technique *sogetto cavato*. This refers to a subject "carved from words." Using this technique, a musical subject, or *cantus firmus*, is derived from solmization syllables of a text. Here, a musical subject is carved from the name Jan de Haan. Perhaps the most famous early example of *sogetto cavato* is Josquin Des Prez' *Missa Hercules dux Ferrarie* (ca. 1502) which was written for the Duke of Ferrara and is derived from his name. Ron Nelson's *Passacaglia: Homage on B-A-C-H* uses this technique in deriving a melodic motive based on the name of J. S. Bach. Camille Saint-Saëns (1835-1921) was a child prodigy as gifted as a young Mozart or Mendelssohn. By age six he was composing, and completed his first symphony at age fifteen. As a founding member of the Société Nationale de Musique, Saint-Saëns encouraged music of order, clarity, and restraint, countering Wagnerism. Saint-Saëns' *Third Symphony* (1886) certainly reflects these aesthetics. The motive from the *Maestoso* used in *Homage* is an example of four-part *divisi* chorale writing. This section is reminiscent of Bach chorales in its smooth contrapuntal writing.

Unit 4: Technical Considerations

Homage is based primarily in C major; however, harmonic development throughout the piece requires the ensemble to also be familiar with F, E-flat, and A-flat major, as well as A harmonic minor scale. Everyone should be able to play C major in sextuplets at 66 beats per minute, and woodwinds should have facility in all the scales listed above at that tempo. Scored for a full wind ensemble, this work includes piccolo, E-flat clarinet, English horn, string bass (doubling basses), and a percussion section with timpani, bass drum, cymbals, tam tam, and glockenspiel. Piccolo, flute I, and trumpet I play several 8va sections which are just outside the normal intermediate range. Rhythmic demands include sextuplets, dotted sixteenth/thirty-second-note (double dotted) figures, and a section of five over three with five eighth notes to a measure in the ensemble over three quarter notes to a measure in the timpani. The chorale sections pose no rhythmic challenges with half and quarter notes; however, this section does alternate between 9/4 and 6/4 measures.

Unit 5: Stylistic Considerations

In emulating an "organ-style," rich, full, sonorous tones are required, especially of the brass during the chorale sections. Woodwinds should pay close attention to unison rhythms in the sextuplet motive, and those with sustained pitches should be careful not to cover these flourishes. A sustained style with *legato* articulations is appropriate throughout the work. Players should lift off the dots of dotted rhythms for greater clarity.

Unit 6: Musical Elements

The introduction outlines the basic harmony of the work, moving from tonic to dominant and back to the tonic of C major. It also presents two motives: the sextuplet flourish (Motive 1), and the polyphonic chorale (Motive 2) which foreshadows the excerpt from Saint-Saëns (beginning at D), and are derived from the *cantus firmus* mentioned above. Marked *senza misura* (without measure/meter), mm. 3-5 provide an opportunity for the conductor to use *rubato* in shaping the phrase, increasing the flexibility of the musicians. The third motive is the Saint-Saëns chorale which is introduced in m. 37 in C major. It interacts with Motive 1 and is interrupted at E with a 5:3 section repeating the *cantus firmus* in quintuplets over a quarter-note pulse in the timpani. The harmony digresses as Motives 1 and 2 reappear before returning to C major and the second statement from the Saint-Saëns. The *coda* returns the piece decidedly to C major.

Unit 7: Form and Structure

Section	Measures	Events and Scoring
Introduction	1-2	Motive 1-sextuplet figure in woodwinds and baritone based on notes from the *cantus firmus*, here: CDCGADG
	3-5	*Senza misura* (*poco rubato*), tenor and baritone saxophone, baritone chorale based on *cantus firmus*, over sustain C pedal in trombone
A	6-7	Baritone, saxophones, bassoon pyramid entrances on GCDF from *cantus firmus* and sustain to form a harmonic structure, cornet I and upper woodwinds with Motive 1
	8-11	Motive 2 begins in clarinets and saxophones then moves to brass, *ritard*, and *crescendo* builds tension towards arrival

	12-15	Arrival tutti C major chord, timpani *crescendo*
	16-30	*Energico*, Motive 1 in woodwinds and baritone, augmented (eighth note) variation in brass
	30	Transition Motive 2 in brass with *poco ritard*
C	31-36	A *Tempo*, introduction based on variation Motive 1 cascading down through the woodwinds to baritone over C pedal in sustained pitches and timpani
D	37-43	Saint-Saëns chorale in trombones and baritone alternating measures with Motive 1 in the clarinets
E	44-53	5:3 section, one eighth-note quintuplet per measure based on *cantus firmus* over three quarter notes per measure in the timpani on C
	54-55	Motive 1 begins in low woodwinds and climbs to upper woodwinds
	56-57	Motive 2 begins in brass, moves to *tutti* statement
	58-59	Woodwinds and baritone motive one with flutes and piccolo 8va over C major sustain chord
F	60-66	Saint-Saëns chorale returns in cornet and trombone this time alternating measures with a dotted quarter two sixteenth accompaniment figure in horn, baritone, and tuba; m. 66 climax: tutti chorale statement, *fortissimo* with *poco ritard*
Coda	67-76	Motive 1, 2, and the dotted rhythm from F return
	77-80	Più lento, full chorale finale whole-note C major chords, *fortissimo* over timpani, to one final statement of Motive 1

Unit 8: Suggested Listening

The Band of the Royal Netherlands Air Force, *The Music of Jan Van der Roost*. DHM Records 10.001-3.

Ithaca College Wind Ensemble, *The Centennial Recording*. Mark Records MCBS-35891.

Josquin Des Prez, *Missa Hercules dux Ferrarie*

Nelson, Ron, *"Homage to B-A-C-H." Postcards*. Cincinnati College-Conservatory of Music. Klavier Records KCD-11058

Camille Saint-Saëns, *Symphony No. 3 in C minor, Op. 78*. Boston Symphony Orchestra, RCA 60817-2-RG.

Jan Van der Roost, *Homage. Inspiration*. Band of the Royal Netherlands Air Force, DHM Records 2.016-3.

Unit 9: Additional References and Resources

Cummings, David, ed. *International Who's Who in Music and Musicians Directory*, 13th ed. Cambridge: Melrose Press Limited, 1992.

Morgan, Robert. *Twentieth Century Music*. New York: W.W. Norton & Company, Inc., 1991.

Saint-Saëns, Camille. *Symphony No. 3 in C minor*. New York: International Music Company, 1950.

Saint-Saëns, Camille, ed. for band by Earl Slocum. *Finale: Symphony No. 3* (Organ Symphony). Texas: TRN Publishing, 1974.

Contributed by:

Jennifer McAllister
Berkner High School
Richardson, Texas

Teacher Resource Guide

I Am

Andrew Boysen, Jr.
(b. 1968)

Unit 1: Composer

Andrew Boysen, Jr. began composing for piano at age nine and has written works for concert band, full orchestra, brass choir, brass quintet, and horn
choir. He received his Bachelor of Music degree from the University of Iowa,
and has received commissions from the Herbert Hoover Presidential Library,
the University of Minnesota-Duluth, the University of Nebraska-Omaha,
Cedar Rapids Prairie High School, Andrews High School, and the Cedar
Rapids Metropolitan Orchestra Festival. He won the University of Iowa
Honors Composition Prize and the 1992 Claude T. Smith Memorial Band
Composition Contest for his work I Am.

Unit 2: Composition

I Am was commissioned by Craig Aune and the Cedar Rapids Prairie
High School Band of Cedar Rapids, Iowa in February, 1990. It was written in
memory of Lynn Jones, a baritone saxophone player in the band who was
killed in an auto accident during that winter. The work is basically tonal in
nature, but includes extended techniques such as an aleatoric section and
singing from members of the ensemble. The words "I Am" are taken from a
poem that Jones wrote days before his death.

Unit 3: Historical Perspective

Despite the tragic nature of the accident, I Am does not attempt to serve
as an elegy, but rather a celebration or reaffirmation of life. The poem reads:

I Am

Life, Music, Competition.

I like exciting things, and doing good for others.

Beauty, Successfulness and Smartness are important to me.

I like to achieve recognition.

I can succeed if I really put my mind to it.

I am very set in my ways,

But I can change when I realize my ignorance.

I like a simple nonchalant lifestyle.

I hate ignorance.

I hate structuredness.

This is me. I am!

-Lynn Jones

Another important piece for winds that is dedicated to a past student is Warren Benson's *Passing Bell*. It was written in 1974 after the death of a former student who played in the Luther College Band. These are two important pieces of the repertoire—one for younger band and one for more advanced players—that both provide a sense of closure and reflection.

Unit 4: Technical Considerations

I Am was written for a baritone saxophone player; therefore, it is essential that this instrument be used. While range is not a major concern, the score contains an aleatoric section that requires the players in the ensemble to improvise motives placed within a specific time frame. The instrumentation utilizes standard concert band instrumentation. The work incorporates many percussion instruments including timpani, wood block, snare drum, tom-tom, crash cymbals, suspended cymbal, chimes, bass drum, marimba, triangle, bells, tam-tam, and vibraphone. In case of an absence of bassoon players, the bassoon part is often doubled between the bass clarinet and baritone saxophone parts. *I Am* does not follow standard tertian harmony, but contains the tonal areas of B-flat, E-flat, and A-flat. Finally, the ensemble is required to sing an interval of a major second (B-flat to C) to the words "I Am" at the end of the piece.

Unit 5: Stylistic Considerations

I Am essentially alternates between a sense of affirmation and celebration. This contrast of style is reflected in the composer's use of slow versus fast tempos. Timbral contrast is achieved through twentieth-century techniques and variations of the melodic material. In the slow sections, a softer, more reflective tone should permeate throughout the texture. The work's single, predominating idea should be played with thoughtful expression in the slow sections, and the more melodic usage of this idea in the faster sections should be more of a celebratory nature.

Unit 6: Musical Elements

The entire piece centers around the first statement presented in the clarinet. This idea follows the first "scraping" sound in the tam-tam and is six bars in length. This simple six-measure idea is used in a variety of tempos and styles, lending itself to imitation, canon, augmentation, diminution, and motivic manipulation. In addition, the chord progressions in *I Am* often move upward an interval of a major second, either alternating between major/minor or remaining major. *I Am* employs twentieth-century techniques such as minimalism, pointillism, ensemble singing, and music set within a time frame. These compositional devices correspond to sections within the overall form and provide a variety of textures.

Unit 7: Form and Structure

SECTION	TEMPO	EVENTS AND SCORING
A	Slowly	One time: generative theme presented in clarinet (all of the following themes are based on this single idea). Two times: theme used in imitation with the clarinet; rhythmic *ostinato* enters texture at the end of the phrase. mm. 1-36
B	Fast	One time: theme in clarinet with alternating E-flat major/A-flat major chords with added seconds. Two times: theme in flute with new accompaniment in brass and percussion; opening theme occurs in middle of phrase rhythmically displaced and in augmentation. Three times: theme in canon in upper woodwinds; opening theme occurs again in the middle of the phrase rhythmically displaced and in augmentation.
A	Much slower	Second part of theme stated in baritone saxophone over rhythmic ostinato. Pointillism is used in this section while the theme is played in diminution.

C	*Senza misura*	Aleatoric section that represents morning of crash; contains motives derived from beginning statement.
B	Fast	Represents the accident.
A	Slowly	Reference to poem with ensemble singing "I Am" over an A-flat pedal.
B	Much faster	Restatement of theme in the brass.
A	Slowly	Singing returns with theme in its original form down a major second with answer in baritone saxophone; piece ends with the ensemble singing a unison C as baritone saxophone sustains an A-flat.

Unit 8: Suggested Listening

Andrew Boysen, Jr., *Distorted Images: A Jazzman's Nightmare*, *The Four Horsemen*, *Casus*

Warren Benson, *The Passing Bell*

Bruce Yurko, *In Memoriam*

Unit 9: Additional References and Resources

"The Basic Band Curriculum: Grades I, II, III." *BD Guide*, September/October 1989, 2-6.

Duarte, Leonard P., Daniel S. Hiestand, Carol Ann Prater, and Doy E. Prater. *Band Music That Works*. Volume 1. Burlingame, CA: Contrapuntal Publications, 1987.

Duarte, Leonard P., Daniel S. Hiestand, Carol Ann Prater, and Doy E. Prater. *Band Music That Works*. Volume 2. Burlingame, CA: Contrapuntal Publications, 1988.

Dvorak, Thomas L., Cynthia Crump Taggart, and Peter Schmaltz. *Best Music for Young Band*. Edited by Bob Margolis. Brooklyn, NY: Manhattan Beach Music, 1986.

Garofalo, Robert J. *Instructional Designs for Middle/Junior High School Band*. Fort Lauderdale, FL: Meredith Music Publications, 1995.

G. Schirmer Music Company (publisher of *The Passing Bell*).

Kreines, Joseph. *Music for Concert Band*. Tampa, FL: Florida Music Service, 1989.

Neil A. Kjos Music Company, San Diego, California.

Contributed by:
Keelan McCamey
Heritage of America Band
Langley Air Force Base
Hampton, Virginia

Teacher Resource Guide

In Memoriam: Kristina

Bruce Yurko
(b. 1951)

Unit 1: Composer

Bruce Yurko has composed more than a dozen works for large wind ensemble or band. Performances at three regional and four national wind conductors' conferences have included his works. In 1978, his *Chant and Toccata* received the first prize at the Virginia CBDNA and Southeastern Composers League Symposium III for New Band Music.

Yurko holds a Bachelor of Science degree in Music Education from Wilkes University in Wilkes-Barre, Pennsylvania, where he studied horn with Douglas Hill. Although Wilkes offered no composition classes, Yurko completed fifteen works there, including three for full wind ensemble. While at Wilkes, he began a correspondence with Vincent Persichetti. Yurko sent Persichetti scores and tapes of his works, and Persichetti responded with letters commenting on them. He said of the *Horn Concerto*, "You and I agree on how to write for percussion." Yurko earned a Master of Music degree in horn performance with a composition minor from Ithaca College in New York. There he was a composition student of Karel Husa. Yurko liked Husa's aggressive treatment of brasses.

Yurko's mature works for wind ensemble include *Concerto for Wind Ensemble* (1973-74), *Concerto for Horn and Wind Ensemble* (1975), *Chant and Toccata* (1975-76), *Sinfonia No. 3* (1976-77), *Concerto for Trombone and Wind Ensemble* (1977), *Danza* (1979-80), *Divertimento* (1980), *Incantations* (1984, rev. 1988), *Night Dances* (1993-94), *Rituals* (1995), *Aria* (1996), and *In Memoriam: Kristina* (1995). Most of Yurko's earlier works were complicated and appropriate for performance by the most professional wind ensembles.

With *Incantations*, and especially *Night Dances*, Yurko's style has become simpler, triadic, and more accessible to school bands at both the middle-school and high-school levels. Recently, Ludwig Music has published *Night Dances* and *In Memoriam: Kristina.*

Yurko directs the wind ensembles at Cherry Hill East and West High Schools in New Jersey. Yurko was assistant director of bands at Fairleigh-Dickenson University in Madison, New Jersey after directing the bands at Madison High School from 1974-81. For nine years Yurko also played horn in the Philharmonic Society of Northeastern Pennsylvania and the North Jersey Wind Quintet.

Unit 2: Composition

Early in the summer of 1995, two of Bruce Yurko's horn students, Kristina Damm and a high school classmate, took their last lessons before each left on vacation trips. After two weeks passed, Yurko telephoned Kristina's classmate to remind him that lessons would begin again. The classmate responded by asking Yurko if he had heard the sad news: on her camping trip, Kristina was struck by lightning and died. The news hit Yurko very hard; Kristina had been one of his most enthusiastic and hardest working students. When he assigned her one Kopprasch étude, she returned the next week with four prepared études.

As soon as he hung up the telephone, Yurko sat down to the piano and began playing. By late evening he was writing down sketches. Three days later, Paul Tomlin, Kristina's high school band director, called Yurko to commission a work for the Clearview Regional High School Concert Band in her memory. "It's already written," Yurko replied, "I only need to orchestrate it." Yurko refused the commissioning fee, specifying that the money go toward a scholarship in Kristina's name.

In Memoriam: Kristina is approximately four minutes in length.

Unit 3: Historical Perspective

Beginning with Mendelssohn's *Trauer Marsch* (1836) and Berlioz's *Symphonie funèbre et triomphale* (1840), many composers have chosen large groups of winds and percussion to remember the dead. There are *Requiems* by Henry Brant, Julius Fucik, Paul Gerhardt, Quincy Hilliard, Alan Hovahness, Vaclav Nelhybel, Sepp Thaler, Fisher Tull, and Urato Watanabe. Grieg's *Trauermasche* and Wagner's *Trauermusik (Trauersinfonie)* are notable among the many funeral marches composed for bands.

In the twentieth century, the genre includes Warren Benson's *The Passing Bell*, Andrew Boysen's *I Am* and *Conversations with the Night*, Jacob Druckman's *Paean* and *In Memoriam Vincent Persichetti*, Walter Hartley's *In Memoriam*, David Holsinger's *Consider the Uncommon Man*, Martin Mailman's *For precious friends hid in death's dateless night* and *A Simple Ceremony-In*

Memoriam John Barnes Chance, W. France McBeth's *Kaddish*, Frank Ticheli's *Amazing Grace* and *Postcard (to Meadville)*, and Bruce Yurko's *In Memoriam*, all composed in memory of individuals. Larry Austin's *In Memoriam: John F. Kennedy*, James Curnow's *J.F.K. In Memoriam*, and Ronald Lo Presti's *Elegy for a Young American* were composed in memory of the fallen president.

Works in memory of fallen soldiers make up an important subgenera: James Barnes's *Lonely Beach*, Daniel Bukvich's *Symphony No. 1 (In Memoriam Dresden-1945)*, David Gillingham's *Heroes Lost and Fallen*, John Paulson's *Epinicion*, and James Swearingen's *The Light Eternal*. Mark Camphouse, John Barnes Chance, Gustav Holst, Karen Husa, Bin Kaneda, James Morissey, Roger Nixon, and Jack Stamp all have composed works with the term "elegy" in the title.

Rare among these are works that remember women. Ticheli's *Postcard* and Yurko's *In Memoriam: Kristina* are the only ones listed here.

Unit 4: Technical Considerations

Yurko's instrumentation is for extended full band: four flutes, two oboes, six clarinets (all three parts *divisi*), bass clarinet, E-flat contrabass clarinet, two bassoons, four saxophones (AATB), three trumpets, four horns, three trombones, baritone horn, tuba, and piano. The score requires six percussion players to play the following parts: timpani, bass drum (head up), gong, chimes, orchestral bells, and vibraphone (motor on). To balance the pyramids in the *arpeggio* section, a piano is essential. Yurko is preparing a string bass part that will double the contrabass clarinet. The work is in 4/4 throughout, and there are frequent *ritardandos* and *a tempos*. The slow tempos specified range from quarter note=60 to quarter note=84. Percussionists must play four sixteenths on the beat followed by a rest. Yurko has composed an optional trumpet part to replace the difficult syncopation at the end of the *arpeggio* section. The score is in concert pitch. There are no key signatures in the score or the parts. However, the tonal center is D-flat/C-sharp. All parts are within normal ranges for most bands.

Unit 5: Stylistic Considerations

In all but the *arpeggio* sections, Yurko specifies "let vibrate" for the piano and percussion. He intends that *sostenuto* pedals on chimes, vibraphone, and piano never be released in these sections. Although Kristina Damm's name inspired the three-shorts-and-a-long subphrases in the horn theme and the hymn, Yurko's performances of this work emphasize phrases of eight notes. He always asks for a *crescendo* on the first long note, followed by tapering on the next four pitches. To facilitate breathing through these phrases, the tempo must not be too slow. Some conductors place the horn soloist offstage, leaving an empty chair onstage. Yurko approves of this practice; but in his own performances, he prefers to have eye contact with the hornist. In the *arpeggio* section, the contrabass clarinet and bassoon must give fairly strong downbeats to balance the rest of the pyramids, especially after the saxophones enter. As each instrument in the pyramid sustains, it must reduce immediately in volume to allow the rest of the pyramid to come through. In measures 78-83, the *espressivo* three-note motive in the oboe, the flute, and solo clarinet must predominate, notwithstanding the *diminuendo* to *n*. (Yurko's abbreviation for "nothing").

Unit 6: Musical Elements

Yurko prefers a monochromatic or whole consort approach to orchestration. At the beginning of *In Memoriam: Kristina*, the piano is a member of the percussion consort. Then, after the horn solo, we hear the clarinet consort, the saxophone consort, the low brass, etc. At m. 84, the consort of four flutes recapitulate the hymn. Yurko also layers consorts, notably in the *arpeggio* section beginning with clarinets doubling piano, adding the flute section, and then the saxophones. Except for an occasional passing chord, a combination of the D-flat major and C-sharp minor triads (i.e., a chord on C-sharp with both major and minor thirds) generates most of the work. The hymn melody suggests C-sharp natural minor, but the harmony consists entirely of three major chords: on D-flat (tonic with a raised third), A (sub-mediant), and B (sub-tonic). Yurko chooses C-sharp as the tonal center because "C" would be for "Christina." C-sharp is for the more sharply pronounced "K" in "Kristina."

Unit 7: Form and Structure

Arch form

SECTION	MEASURES	EVENTS AND SCORING
A Section	1-38	
Bell Theme	1-5	Four-note bell motive, ringing out the four syllables "Kris-ti-na Damm." Played three times.
Horn Theme	6-9	Horn solo, espressivio.
Bell Theme	10-13	Played four times.
Horn Theme	14-17	Clarinet section with gong.
Horn Theme & Bell Theme combined		
	18-26	Saxophones, low brasses, tutti. Build to climax at m. 23, then diminuendo.
Ending motives of Horn Theme with Bell Theme		
	27-31	Clarinet section. Bell Motive played twice.

Horn Theme ending with Bell Theme

| | 32-38 | Horn Solo. Bell Motive played twice. |
| B Section: Hymn | 39-57 | Four-note subphrases in the brasses, again intoning the four syllables "Kris-ti-na Damm." |

C Section: Arpeggio Theme

	58-83	Clarinets, brasses, tutti, woodwinds, clarinets.
B Section: Hymn	84-102	Flutes; brasses without horns; horns and tuba; clarinets, flutes, and piano; trombones and tuba.
A Section	102-118	
Bell Theme	103-106	Played four times.
Horn Theme	107-113	Horn solo with gong.
Coda	114-118	Low brass chord with percussion.

Unit 8: Suggested Listening

Bruce Yurko, *Chant and Toccata.* Eugene Corporon, West Virginia University Wind Ensemble. Tawes Theatre, College Park, MD. Crest CBDNA-77-2.

Bruce Yurko. *Chant and Toccata.* Visions of the Twentieth Century. Eugene Corporon, The Symphonic Band of the University of Wisconsin School of Music at Madison. Century KM-1932.

Bruce Yurko. *Chant and Toccata.* IUP Concert Bands-1966. Jack Stamp, Indiana University of Pennsylvania Wind Ensemble.

Bruce Yurko. *Divertimento for Wind Ensemble.* Eugene Corporon, University of Northern Colorado Wind Ensemble. Crest CBDNA-81-2.

Bruce Yurko. *Divertimento for Wind Ensemble. Reflections.* Eugene Corporon, University of Northern Colorado Wind Ensemble. Soundmark R-972.

Unit 9:   Additional Reference and Resources

"Bruce Yurko: *Night Dances.*" *Teaching Music through Performance in Band.* Compiled and edited by Richard Miles. Chicago: GIA Publications, Inc., 1997.

Tower, Ibrook. *Bruce Yurko's Concertos for Wind Ensemble (1973-74), for Horn and Wind Ensemble (1975), and for Trombone and Wind Ensemble (1977).* Ann Arbor, MI: UMI Company, 1995.

Yurko, Bruce. *In Memoriam.* Photocopy of autographed score, 1995.

Yurko, Bruce. *In Memoriam: Kristina.* Cleveland, OH: Ludwig Music Publishing Company, 1997.

Yurko, Bruce. Telephone interview by Ibrook Tower. Glassboro, NJ, February 9, 1997.

Contributed by:

Ibrook Tower
Director of Bands
Elizabethtown College
Elizabethtown, Pennsylvania

Teacher Resource Guide

An Irish Rhapsody
Clare Grundman
(1913–1996)

Unit 1: Composer

Clare Grundman has left a tremendous legacy as a composer of literature for the wind band. He has composed over sixty works and has arranged numerous orchestral works for band. He received a Bachelor of Science degree in Education and a Master of Arts degree from Ohio State University. His teaching career began with teaching high school instrumental music in Ohio and Kentucky; he later return to Ohio State, this time to teach orchestration, bands, and woodwinds. He has written music at all difficulty levels and has received numerous awards and recognition for excellence. His more popular musical settings are based on folk and popular melodies. Other works for band include *The Blue and the Gray, Northwest Saga, Fantasy on American Sailing Songs, Burlesque for Band,* and his *American Folk Rhapsody Nos. 1, 2, and 3.*

Unit 2: Composition

An Irish Rhapsody was composed in 1971 and highlights popular Irish folk music. The work includes the melodies "The Moreen (The Minstrel Boy)," "I Know I'm Going" (from *Irish Country Songs* by Herbert Hughes), "Shepherd's Lamb Reel," "Cockels and Mussels," "The Rakes of Mallow," and "Kathleen O'More."

Unit 3: Historical Perspective

A rhapsody is defined as originally being a section of a Greek epic or a free medley of such sections sung in succession. Musicians, principally in the nineteenth century as well as today, have used the term with different meanings, such as free fantasies of an epic, heroic, or national character. Clare Grundman had a passion for taking folk music and creating settings that depict the heart of these melodies. The American culture is made up of a diverse group of different cultures, each with their own special folk music and history. All of these groups have made an impact on the development of folk music as well as music of other forms in America. Some of the most spirited and moving folk melodies have come to us from Ireland and are beautifully arranged here for band.

Unit 4: Technical Considerations

The work moves through the key areas of B-flat major, F major, E-flat major, and B-flat minor. There are *soli* sections for the cornets and trumpets, low brass, woodwinds, horn I and III, flute I, oboe and piccolo, horns and alto sax. There is a short solo line for cornet I. The percussion have key parts for the snare drum, cymbals, and timpani during the introduction and in a recap of the introduction in m. 166. The tempo marking at the introduction is listed as quarter note=approximately 100, *Allegro Moderato*. This remains constant throughout the work but does go through sections of *rubato* and *moderato*. There are short sections in the woodwinds with sixteenth notes, and there is a recurring use of dotted eighth-sixteenth throughout the ensemble. There is brief use of the eighth note to dotted quarter syncopation during the "Kathleen O'More" melody.

Unit 5: Stylistic Considerations

A singing and lyrical sound quality from the solo and soli instruments is necessary. The folk melodies should be clearly heard and the articulations should never be too heavy. The melodies appear in a variety of instrumental combinations and sections. Careful consideration of balance between instruments as well as the background instruments is necessary. The dynamic range is *p* to *ff*, with various entrances and lines marked in relation to these. There must be a clear distinction between the short and marked articulations and the smooth *legato* lines.

Unit 6: Musical Elements

Each of the melodic themes is presented after brief concluding sections from each previous theme. Grundman writes the melodic ideas in whole, then juxtaposes parts of the theme in different instrumental groupings for variety of color and texture. Although the tempo marking remains constant throughout, there are numerous musical directions given such as lightly, quietly, with motion, moderately, and *rubato*.

Unit 7: Form and Structure

There is an eight-measure introduction which utilizes the second half of the "Rakes of Mallow" theme. This material recurs at m. 166. The overall form is built around the statement of new themes. The following themes are introduced: "The Moreen," mm. 9-28; "I Know Where I'm Going," mm. 29-60; "Shepherd's Lamb Reel," mm. 61-94; "Cockels and Mussels," mm. 95-138, "The Rakes of Mallow," mm. 139-173; "Kathleen O'More," mm. 174 to the end.

Unit 8: Suggested Listening

Salute to Percy Grainger, English Chamber Orchestra, Ambrosian Singers, conducted by Benjamin Britten and Stuart Bedford. London Records, 1989.

Unit 9: Additional References and Resources

Battisti, Frank and Robert Garofalo. *Guide to Score Study*. Ft. Lauderdale, FL: Meredith Music Publications, 1990.

Colwell, Richard. *The Teaching of Instrumental Music*. Second Edition. Englewood Cliffs, NJ: Prentice-Hall, Inc., 1992.

Kostka, Stefan and Dorothy Payne. *Tonal Harmony*. New York: McGraw-Hill, Inc., 1995.

Rehrig, William H. *The Heritage Encyclopedia of Band Music*. Edited by Paul E. Bierley. Westerville, OH: Integrity Press, 1991.

Whitwell, David. *History and Literature of the Wind Band and Wind Ensemble*. Northridge California Winds. 9 Vols. Northridge, CA: University of California Press, 1982-1984.

Contributed by:

Otis French
U.S. Army Field Band
Ft. Mead, Maryland

Teacher Resource Guide

Irish Suite

Stanley Applebaum
(b. 1922)

Unit 1: Composer

Stanley Applebaum was born in Newark, New Jersey on March 1, 1922. He studied with several private tutors, including Wallingford Riegger. In addition to his career as an arranger for Benny Goodman, Tommy Dorsey, Harry James, Raymond Scott, and the E. H. Morris Publishing Company, he has also arranged and conducted music for recordings and Broadway shows. In 1962 and 1963, Applebaum was Eastern Artists and Repertoire Director for Warner Brothers.

Unit 2: Composition

Irish Suite is an original work for band in three movements. While this work has not borrowed from the folk melodies of Ireland, it is certainly in the style of popular folk traditions. The names of the movements are "Fisher Boat's Home," "Nighttime," and "The Festival."

Unit 3: Historical Perspective

Stanley Applebaum's *Irish Suite* (1977) was written during a time when a great wealth of literature was being added to the wind ensemble repertoire. Compositions such as Schuman's *New England Triptych* (1975), Joseph Schwantner's *...and the mountains rising nowhere* (1977), and Leslie Basset's *Sounds, Shapes, and Symbols* were changing the way composers approached and scored for bands. Other compositions by Applebaum during this time include *Danza Bolercina* (1973), *Suite of Miniature Dances* (rev. 1972), *Spring Magic* (1960), and *Voices from Kaluga* (1976).

Unit 4: Technical Considerations

The scales of F major, C major, G major, E-flat major, D major, and G minor are required for the full ensemble. The rhythmic demands are very basic, and the time signatures remain compound duple (6/8) for all three movements. Each movement is scored so that the comfortable, playable range of each instrument is not exceeded. For example, the melodies presented usually stay within the range of a fifth. In addition, a multitude of cross cues provides more than the usual options for the conductor, allowing him or her to perform the work with a severely cut roster of instruments.

Unit 5: Stylistic Considerations

Careful attention to phrasing, dynamics, and attacks/releases will aid in the presentation of this work. The tune should always come through the texture, and close adherence to *crescendos* and *diminuendos* will aid in the direction of the melodic line. A lilted "bounce" to the pulse should predominate the outer movements, while the middle movement should contain a more tranquil character. The movements may be programmed individually, or played without pause, one after the other, at the discretion of the conductor.

Unit 6: Musical Elements

Irish Suite maintains a primarily homophonic texture throughout each movement. It uses the key areas of F major, C major, D major, E-flat major, and G minor. The melodic lines are often in a narrow range and contain periodic phrase structure. The composition also incorporates standard tertian harmonies with the use of suspensions and modal treatment of the melodies. In addition, timbral contrast is achieved by scoring each repetition of the melody with different instrumental families.

Unit 7: Form and Structure

SECTION AND EVENTS	KEY	MEASURES
Movement I: "Fisher Boat's Home"		
Introduction	F major	1-4
First statement	F major/ G minor	5-32
Transition	C major	33-43
Second statement	F major/	44-69
Coda	G minor	70-77

Movement II: "Night time"

Introduction	D major	1-4
First statement	D major	5-12
Second statement	D major	13-20
Third statement	E-flat major	21-28
Fourth statement	E-flat major	29-36

Movement III: "The Festival"

A Theme	G minor	1-16
B Theme (from first movement)	G minor	7-32
A Theme	G minor	33-48
B Theme (with extention)	G minor	49-60 61-83
Coda	G minor	84-91

Unit 8: Suggested Listening

Stan Applebaum, *Danza Boleriana, Suite of Miniature Dances, Spring Magic, Voices from Kaluga*

Barry Kopetz, *Americana Folk Suite*

Ralph Vaughan Williams, *English Folk Song Suite*

Unit 9: Additional References and Resources

American Society of Composers and Publishers, 4th ed., s.v. "Applebaum, Stanley."

Anderson, E. Ruth. *Contemporary American Composers*. Boston: G.K. Hall, 1982.

"The Basic Band Curriculum: Grades I, II, III." *BD Guide* September/October 1989, 2-6.

Duarte, Leonard P., Daniel S. Hiestand, Carol Ann Prater, and Doy E. Prater. *Band Music That Works*. Volume 1. Burlingame, CA: Contrapuntal Publications, 1987.

Duarte, Leonard P., Daniel S. Hiestand, Carol Ann Prater, and Doy E. Prater. *Band Music That Works*. Volume 2. Burlingame, CA: Contrapuntal Publications, 1988.

Dvorak, Thomas L., Cynthia Crump Taggart, and Peter Schmaltz. *Best Music for Young Band*. Edited by Bob Margolis. Brooklyn, NY: Manhattan Beach Music, 1986.

European American Music Corporation, Clifton, New Jersey.

Garofalo, Robert J. *Instructional Designs for Middle/Junior High School Band*. Fort Lauderdale, FL: Meredith Music Publications, 1995.

Kreines, Joseph. *Music for Concert Band*. Tampa, FL: Florida Music Service, 1989.

Rehrig, William H. *The Heritage Encyclopedia of Band Music*. Edited by Paul E. Bierley. Westerville, OH: Integrity Press, 1991.

Contributed by:
Keelan McCamey
Heritage Band of America
Langley Air Force Base
Hampton, Virginia

Teacher Resource Guide

Renaissance Suite

Tielman Susato
(1500–1564)

arranged by
Jim Curnow (b. 1943)

Unit 1: Composer

Tielman Susato, a native of Cologne, Germany, was a town trumpeter, instrument dealer, and music printer in Antwerp. In a book of polyphonic songs published in 1543, he introduced himself as "printer, and music proofreader, domiciled in Antwerp, close by the new Money Market." He played an important role in the diffusion of music and had a great influence on his contemporary composers.

James Curnow is a native of Huron, Michigan, and was educated at Wayne State University and Michigan State University. Among his teachers were Leonard Falcone (euphonium) and Harry Begian (conducting). He has taught instrumental music on all levels, including college teaching, and currently resides in Wilmore, Kentucky where he is a full-time composer and arranger. He has well over 250 compositions and arrangements to his credit, as well as many awards for band composition.

Unit 2: Composition

The dances in this arrangement are taken from the *Dansery, Het derde Musyck boexken* (*Dances, the third little book of music*), compiled, edited, and published by Tielman Susato in 1551. The arrangement, while updated with modern instruments, is designed to introduce younger players to the musical language and style of early instrumental music. The total timing of the piece is six minutes and fifteen seconds, with repeats.

Unit 3: Historical Perspective

"La Mourisque" is a lively duple dance in the spirit of a *branle*. "Mille Regretz" was a popular tune (*chanson*) by the first master of the high Renaissance style, Josquin Desprez (c. 1440-1521). The pavane in this setting is taken from the original tune, as many pavane melodies were. "La Bataille" contains imitating trumpet calls and drums, a loose program for the two opposing sides in a battle.

Unit 4: Technical Considerations

"La Mourisque" is keyed in concert B-flat, and is scored *tutti* throughout. While there are a few instances of inner moving parts, the rhythmic and harmonic motions are almost exclusively homophonic. The percussion parts are regular and repetitive. The upper ranges include flutes up to F6 and the trumpets to G5, but otherwise there are no significant demands on players' ranges. "Mille Regretz" is a slower paced, more lightly articulated, yet regal style, requiring control of tempo and rhythmic subdivisions. The key centers are D minor, D major, and B-flat major. The scoring of woodwind and brass families creates new opportunities for balance adjustments, as does the *tutti* in the final section. There is more polyphonic movement as well as individual lines to challenge all players, and phrase shaping is an issue in all parts. The final section has some *tutti* phrase markings, which need to be lifted appropriately so as to give the preceding note full length. "La Bataille" returns to the more *marcato* march style, with primarily homophonic scoring. The first two sections, both in B-flat major, are scored with full instrumentation. Suspensions and modal harmony (created with accidentals) add some spice to the music. The third section is an antiphonal chamber section, with different players on the repeat. Balance and intonation must be carefully monitored. The full ensemble joins together for the finale, and breath support should be full and articulation crisp, but not overblown or biting.

Unit 5: Stylistic Considerations

In "La Mourisque," attention must be given to the light, bouncy *tutti* rhythms throughout the movement. Inner parts must be heard in balance with the melody, and the percussion must maintain a regular pulse, adjusting to the dynamic changes with the winds. Note length agreement and articulation are major issues in the "Mille Regretz" pavane, and moving lines must blend carefully with the melody and harmonization. Similarly, the third movement, "La Bataille," contains constantly changing instrumental combinations which present the conductor with many challenges in balance, blend, and intonation.

Unit 6: Musical Elements

Homophony, polyphony, ABA, through-composed sectional form, phrasing, major/minor, picardy third, dance suite, pavane, *basse dance*, *branle*, terraced dynamics, Renaissance period. The director should play recordings of period instruments playing the original settings (recorders, crumhorns, shawms, curtals, serpents, lutes, et al.).

Unit 7: Form and Structure

SECTION	MEASURES	EVENTS AND SCORING
"La Mourisque"		
Introduction	1-2	tom-tom only
A	3-10	*tutti* march melody, repeated, B-flat major
B	11-18	*tutti* second theme, repeated, B-flat major
A	20-27	*tutti* march theme again, one time only *rallentando* to final cadence, B-flat major
"Mille Regretz"		
A	1-8	first strain, processional melody in woodwinds, repeated, D minor to D major
B	9-16	second strain, new melody in brass, repeated, B-flat major to D major
C	17-24	third strain, new *tutti* melody, repeated, B-flat major to D minor, *forte* to *piano*
"La Bataille"		
Introduction	1	percussion only
A	2-9	first strain, first time brass only, second time *tutti* B-flat to F
B	10-17	second strain, first time in woodwinds, second time brass, F to B-flat
C	18-27	third strain, first time flute/clarinet *vs.* bassoon/low clarinet and low saxophone, second time trumpet *vs.* low brass, B-flat, soft

D   28-36   fourth strain, first time brass, *marcato*, second time *tutti*, *marcato*, *fortissimo*, B-flat

Unit 8: Suggested Listening

Claude Gervaise, *Suite de Dances* (1557)
Guillaume de Machaut, *Remede de Fortune* (c. 1340)
Giorgio Mainerio, *Il primo Libro Di Balli* (1578)
Jacques Moderne, *Danseryes* (sixteenth century)
Michael Praetorius, *Terpsichore* (1612)
Tielman Susato, *Danseryes* (1551)

Other sixteenth-century *canzoni* and instrumental dances of Vecchi, Banchieri, Agostini, Bottegari, Willaert, de Rore, Bassano, Crecquillon, and anonymous music from the Chilesotti and Bottegari Lutebooks.

Unit 9: Additional References and Resources

Brown, Howard M. *Instrumental Music Printed Before 1600: A Bibliography.* Cambridge, MA: Harvard University Press, 1965.

Jackson, Roland. *Performance Practice Medieval to Contemporary: A Bibliographic Guide.* New York: Garland, 1988.

Randel, Don Michael, ed. *The New Harvard Dictionary of Music.* Cambridge, MA: The Belknap Press of Harvard University Press, 1986.

Roche, Jerome. *A Dictionary of Early Music from the Troubadour to Monteverdi.* London: Faber, 1981.

Contributed by:

Scott A. Stewart
Indiana University
Bloomington, Indiana

Teacher Resource Guide

Retreat and Pumping Song

David Stanhope
(b. 1952)

Unit 1: Composer

David Stanhope has been a professional French horn player, concert pianist, and conductor. As a conductor with the Australian Opera Company, Stanhope has become an expert in the performance of twentieth-century opera, and is a regular guest conductor for the six orchestras of the Australian Broadcasting Corporations.

David Stanhope's compositions have quickly gained recognition around the world. While he is best known for his works for wind band, Stanhope also has many works for brass band, a three-act opera, and a symphony recently recorded by the Western Australian Symphony Orchestra.

Unit 2: Composition

Retreat and Pumping Song started life as a shorter work for horn octet. In that form the work won the ensemble section of the International Horn Society in 1979. It was reset by the composer in the early 1990s, and was premiered by the Australian Children's Wind Orchestra in New Orleans in 1996 at the NBA conference.

The composer notes " 'The Retreat' has a contemplative mood throughout, hence the title. There are many opportunities for *rubato*, so that the music doesn't hurry at all, except in the one place where it moves towards the central climax. The 'Pumping Song' is a jolly extrovert contrast, the title springing from my desire to reflect something of the spirit (if not the shape) of old sea shanties. It is not a folk tune, however."

The work is about six minutes in length, and is published by H L Music (Australia).

Unit 3: Historical Perspective

The use of folk song, or near folk song, is one of the earliest strong influences on the works of wind ensembles. The modern literature begins with such works as Vaughan Williams's *Folk Song Suite*, O'Donnell's *Songs of the Gael*, and the suites of Gustav Holst, which draw clearly from the folk music of Britain.

The idea of writing in a folk idiom without using folk song is also not without precedent. The German Nationalist opera *Die Freischutz* by Carl Maria von Weber was written with folk melodies in mind, and the rise in nationalist movements at the end of the eighteenth century saw a generation of composers who were heavily influenced by folk music. Dvorak's *Slavonic Dances* and Brahms's *Hungarian Rhapsody* all display folk melodies. In the wind medium, it is often difficult to distinguish from those works of Grainger that are based on folk song, and those that are original melodies. His *Colonial Song* is one of his best known purely original works, not based on any preexisting folk song.

David Stanhope has taken a keen interest in the works of Grainger. His four suites *Folksongs for Band* (dedicated to Grainger) display many "Graingeresque" characteristics; however, it is in scoring as well as his use of folk-like melodies that Stanhope most borrows Grainger's technique. While Grainger explored the boundaries of tonal music, Stanhope pushes them further. His use of extended chords and harsh dissonance while remaining firmly in a key area offer both the comfort of a home key with the variety of new tonalities.

Unit 4: Technical Considerations

The technical demands of this work are not extremely great. The opening "Retreat" demands of all players careful counting. The difference between the 6/4 and the 3/2 are often blurred with ties in some voices hiding the natural pulse. The trumpets do not extend higher than a written A-flat, and no instrument is asked to play outside of its normal range for this level.

The work is written for a large ensemble, including piccolo, E-flat clarinet, alto clarinet, contrabass clarinet, two bassoons, and soprano saxophone. However, extensive cross-cueing makes this work performable by even a small ensemble. Percussion writing is for timpani, percussion I (glockenspiel, crash cymbals) and optional percussion II (tubular bells, bass drum, one player on four drums, tam-tam, and suspended cymbals).

Unit 5: Stylistic Considerations

The work falls into sections with contrasting styles. The "Retreat" is long and flowing, with broad harmonies that require great balance from the ensemble. Imitation has been used, particularly in the middle section of the main theme, and performers will need to bring out their thematic lines before blending back into the texture.

The "Pumping Song" is quite different. The shanty-like melody is presented in both a bouncy quarter-eighth figure and a broad flowing feel in the middle sections. Accents have been added to much of the accompaniment, and the *fortissimo* sections should be carefully controlled to avoid a ponderous feel.

Unit 6: Musical Elements

The "Retreat" requires a delicate touch and great musicianship. The harmonies frequently take an unusual turn, although the composer has been quick to mark these with swells and added instrumentation. The harmony often grows from imitative entries, and the construction of the "Retreat" is concise and logical. Entries frequently follow long rests, and an ensemble will need to exhibit independence for a successful performance.

The "Pumping Song" opens with an offstage trumpet, in the difficult-to-master compound "bouncy" style. Agreement will need to be carefully negotiated for the length of the quarter note, and a difference between the dotted quarter note of the opening, and the quarter note followed by a rest later in the work may be difficult to differentiate. Later, the composer juxtaposes the *staccato* style and the flowing style, offering the conductor great teaching opportunities.

Unit 7: Form and Structure

Section and Events	Measures
"Retreat"	
a	1-8
b	9-16
a	17-27
b	28-35
Coda	36-end
"Pumping Song"	
Strophe 1	1-4
a	
a1	5-8
b	9-12
a	13-16
Strophe 2	17-20
a	
a1	21-24

b	25-29
a	30-32
Strophe 3	33-36
a	
a1	37-40
b	41-44
a	45-48
Development (Thematic Variation)	49-52
a varied	
a varied	53-55
b varied	56-60
a varied	61-64
Strophe 4	65-68
a	
a1	69-72
b	73-77
a	78-79
Introduction to last strophe	80-83
Strophe 5	84-87
a	
a1	88-91
b	92-95
a	96-97
Coda	98-end

Unit 8: Suggested Listening

Percy Grainger, *Lincolnshire Posy, Colonial Song*
David Stanhope, *Folksongs for Band, Set 3*
Ralph Vaughan Williams, *Folk Song Suite*
Antonín Dvořák, *Slavonic Dances*
Johannes Brahms, *Hungarian Rhapsody*

Unit 9: Additional References and Resources

Rehrig, William H. *The Heritage Encyclopedia of Band Music*. Editor Paul E. Bierley. Westerville, OH: Integrity Press, 1991.

Smith, Norman and Albert Stoutamire. *Band Music Notes*. Third ed. Lake Charles, LA: Program Note Press, 1979.

Contributed by:

Alan Lourens
Indiana University
Bloomington, Indiana

Teacher Resource Guide

Rhosymedre

Ralph Vaughan Williams
(1872–1958)

Unit 1: Composer

Ralph Vaughan Williams is considered one of the preeminent English composers of the first half of the twentieth century. His compositions for band, orchestra, organ, solo voice, film, and choir, as well as opera and ballet, are marked by a distinctive style stemming from the English folk song tradition. Vaughan Williams received his primary composition training at the Royal College of Music where he studied with Sir Hubert Parry. Following his graduation, he pursued further degrees at Cambridge. In 1896, he went to Berlin to study composition with Max Bruch. Upon his return to England, Vaughan Williams joined the Folk Song Society whose members included Gustav Holst, and eventually Percy Grainger. It was through the Folk Song Society that Vaughan Williams was exposed to the music that was to help shape his compositional output. In 1919, he began teaching at the Royal College of Music, and other than a brief time spent studying with Ravel in Paris and three trips to the United States, he remained in England for the rest of his life. Included among his major works are the *Fantasia on a Theme by Thomas Tallis* (1908), *London Symphony* (1914), and the *Sinfonia Antarctica* (1952). While Vaughan Williams' early style can be characterized by use of folk song material, he progressed over the course of his nine symphonies to use complex and often dissonant harmonies, rich melodies, and wide-ranging emotions. In his autobiography, Vaughan Williams pays tribute to his friend and fellow composer, Gustav Holst, whom he identifies as a mentor and important influence on his musical direction.

Unit 2: Composition

In 1920, Vaughan Williams wrote three organ preludes based on Welsh hymn tunes. Of these, *Rhosymedre*, sometimes known as "Lovely," became the best known. The original hymn tune, written by J. D. Edwards, is primarily composed of whole and half notes. These act as a *cantus firmus* around which Vaughan Williams provides a three-voice contrapuntal texture. The hymn tune is heard twice in its entirety during the course of the work. In addition, there is a partial entry of the tune that occurs near the end. The counterpoint is well planned, providing beautiful melodic contours and countermelodies to the hymn tune. In this arrangement for band by Walter Beeler, the woodwinds—with the exception of the oboe, the tubas, and occasionally the flutes—are assigned to the counterpoint. The oboes, trumpets, horns, trombones, and baritones perform the hymn tune, with the baritones migrating to the counterpoint during the second half of the hymn repetition. The percussion is limited to the use of chimes and a brief entrance by the timpani at the end of the work. The arrangement, which is fifty-three measures long, was published in 1972, coinciding with the one hundredth anniversary of the composer's birth.

Unit 3: Historical Perspective

The use of English folk songs and hymn tunes is prevalent in the music of Vaughan Williams and Holst during the early part of the twentieth century. While *Rhosymedre* is not an original work for band, it reflects the composer's interest in English folk songs and their use in his early compositions. The work of the Folk Song Society proved important to both Vaughan Williams and Holst, as well as Grainger. All of these incorporated and preserved the heritage of English folk music in their works for band, including Vaughan Williams's *Folk Song Suite*, Holst's *First Suite in E-flat* and *Second Suite in F*, and Grainger's *Lincolnshire Posy*.

Unit 4: Technical Considerations

The meter of the composition is 4/2. This offers some difficulty as does the syncope of the bass voice. Once these are mastered, it is important that each line maintains rhythmic integrity so that the contrapuntal nature of the work is transparent. While the score shows that each note of the hymn tune is to be tongued, this should be accomplished in a manner that does not interrupt the flow of the line.

Unit 5: Stylistic Considerations

The independent nature of the counterpoint requires close attention to the ebb and flow of each line. This needs to be carefully balanced with the hymn tune so that all lines are audible to the listener. The work begins at *mp*, and can be effectively performed as a *crescendo* from the beginning to the climax at m. 40, with a momentary *diminuendo* before the second entry of the hymn tune. The piece *diminuendos* from m. 41 to the end. Beeler uses layering of instruments to help accomplish the building and receding motions of the music. This is true to the original Vaughan Williams scoring for organ.

Unit 6: Musical Elements

The key of the arrangement is F major (originally G major). *Rhosymedre* remains primarily in this tonal center with brief motion to the relative minor in measures 29 and 30 and the use of a G major to C major to F major motion in measures 34 and 35. These are the only measures of the piece containing accidentals outside of F major. The sixteen-measure hymn tune is asymmetrical, formed by a 4 + 4 + 3 + 5 measure construction.

Unit 7: Form and Structure

The form of the piece utilizes the Welsh hymn tune as the main organizing feature. The phrase structure of the tune is AABC with the overlying counterpoint composed in eight-measure phrases. The free-standing melody, first heard in the first and second clarinets, appears three times during the piece. This acts as a secondary point of unification. Beeler changes the instrumentation of the Welsh hymn at the beginning of each phrase, providing a colorful and changing sound fabric for the listener.

SECTION	MEASURES	EVENTS AND SCORING
Introduction	1-8	Woodwind counterpoint (clarinet melody)
First Entry	9-24	Hymn tune plus original woodwind counterpoint (modified form)
		Hymn Tune Instrumentation: A (horns and baritone) A (trombone and baritone) B (oboe, horn, and baritone) C (oboe, horn, trombone, and baritone)
Second Entry	25-downbeat of 40	Hymn tune plus newly composed counterpoint
		Hymn Tune Instrumentation: A (flute, oboe, and cornet) A (horn, trombone, and baritone) B (flute, oboe, cornet, horn, trombone, and chimes) C (cornet, horn, and trombone)

Cadential extension	40-44	Original counterpoint (modified) plus hymn tune
		Hymn Tune Instrumentation: Partial entry of C (42 beat 3-downbeat of 45; horns and trombones)
Coda	45-53	Original woodwind counterpoint (clarinet melody)

Unit 8: Suggested Listening

Gustav Holst, *First Suite in E-flat, Second Suite in F*
Percy Grainger, *Lincolnshire Posy*
Ralph Vaughan Williams, *Folk Song Suite*

Unit 9: Additional References

Dickinson, A.E.F. *Ralph Vaughan Williams*. London: Faber and Faber, 1963.

Foss, Hubert. *Ralph Vaughan Williams*. New York: Oxford University Press, 1950.

Kenned, Michael. *The Works of Ralph Vaughan Williams*. London: Oxford University Press, 1964.

Williams, Ursula Vaughan. *R.V.W.: A Biography of Ralph Vaughan Williams*. Oxford: Clarendon Press, 1964.

Contributed by:

Robert Meunier
Director of Bands/Associate Professor of Percussion
Drake University
Des Moines, Iowa

Teacher Resource Guide

Uganda Lullaby

Heskel Brisman
(b. 1923)

Unit 1: Composer

Heskel Brisman was born in New York City in 1923, and studied music at Juilliard, Yale, and Columbia. Additional studies were at Tanglewood with Ernest Toch, and with Luigi Dallapiccolo in Italy. He spent much of his life abroad, where he scored for documentary films in Italy and arranged for theater and radio in Israel. While in Israel, he was also the director of the Joseph Achron Conservatory. He returned to the United States in 1967. His music has been performed throughout the United States and abroad, and his commissions have included a cantata, *Don't Listen to the Wind* by the Ars Music Chorale and Orchestra, and *Concerted Music for Piano and Percussion* by the Paul Price Percussion Ensemble. Awards include the Berlin Prize for film scoring, two Harvey Gaul awards, and grants from the NEA and the Martha Baird Rockefeller Foundation. Brisman's *Concerto for Piano and Strings* was recorded on the MMC label, and his *Sinfonia Concertante for Viola and Orchestra* is due for release. Heskel Brisman currently resides in New Jersey.

Unit 2: Composition

Uganda Lullaby is a two-minute composition intended for junior high bands. It is based on an East Central African chant, and a version for chorus is also available. It is scored for reduced and flexible instrumentation, so bands with incomplete instrumentation will find the doublings to be generous. There are only two trumpet and clarinet parts, and one horn and trombone part. The composition itself is short, and consists of two presentations of the chant; it is very suitable for junior high or smaller high school ensembles.

Unit 3: Historical Perspective

Composed in 1973, this composition was written at a time of increasing awareness of multiculturalism in the Unites States. The Tanglewood Symposium of 1967, a discussion regarding the arts and education, viewed as a "critical issue" the teaching of music to inner-city youth. In 1973, the writings of Ellsworth Janifer in the journal *Black Manifesto for Education* explained how all children could learn from the musical heritage of African-Americans. At the same time, popular culture saw an increase in musical and artistic endeavors dealing with African traditions. In the literature for band, compositions such as *Afronetic Dance* by Robert Martin and *Mozambique* by Emanuelina Pizzutio were composed during this decade.

Unit 4: Technical Considerations

The major challenge in this composition is the use of shifting time signatures: 5/8, 6/8, 7/8, and 8/8 time are all represented. The rhythms themselves are not complex, but considerable time must be spent introducing irregular meters—especially involving the sixteenth-eighth-sixteenth note pattern—prior to rehearsing this composition. The range demands are quite easy with three exceptions: in m. 21, cornet I must play high A at a *piano* volume; in m. 20, the alto sax must play low B; and tubas must play high G frequently. The tuba part may need to be rewritten. The composition remains firmly in the concert key of G major throughout, which may be unfamiliar to some students. There are no accidentals until the last six measures. Percussion have only two parts, both on (suggested) African drums or congas.

Unit 5: Stylistic Considerations

Articulations are fairly easy and constant throughout. Consistent interpretation of the sixteenth-eighth-sixteenth note pattern is the only concern. Phrases are of regular lengths, either two or four measures. Block dynamics are used throughout and are mostly at the softer end; some additional interpretation of phrasing may be necessary. The melody is mostly *legato* and simplistic, but is never in the trumpets, so balance will be an issue throughout. The texture is usually *tutti* scoring, with certain woodwind sections having the melody; however, the baritones and tenor sax have important lines throughout and frequently double the melody. The overall stylistic effect throughout is a calm, continuous line.

Unit 6: Musical Elements

The composition stays within the key of G major throughout. The harmonies used are very simple—mostly tonic and dominant seventh chords. Mild dissonances of a major second are occasionally found in the clarinets. The primary melodic motive is found in the sixteenth-eighth-sixteenth-note figure; it can be found throughout. The melody is never found in the highest

voices, but in the clarinets or saxes or baritones. The resulting timbres are usually dark. Since there are many repeated notes in the melody, the primary areas of interest are rhythmic activity and the irregular meters used.

Unit 7: Form and Structure
Strophic Form (A^1, A^2, with introduction and codetta)

SECTION	MEASURES	SCORING AND FORM
Introduction	1-2	Key of G major all except reeds
A^1	3-20	4+4+4+4+2
A^2	3(second time)-22	4+4+4+5
Codetta	23-26	

Unit 8: Suggested Listening
Jerry Bilik, *Drums of Africa*
James Curnow, *African Sketches*
Quincy Hilliard, *Variations on an African Hymnsong*
Paul Jennings, *African Road*

Unit 9: Additional References and Resources
Anderson, William, and Joy Lawrence. *Integrating Music into the Classroom.* Second edition. Belmont, CA: Wadsworth Publishing Company, 1985.

Brandel, Rode. *The Music of Central Africa: An Enthnomusicological Study.* The Hague, Netherlands: Nijhoff Publishing, 1973.

Mark, Michael L. *Contemporary Music Education.* Second edition. New York: Macmillan, Inc., 1986.

May, Elizabeth, ed. *Music of Many Cultures: An Introduction.* Berkeley, CA: University of California Press, 1980.

Contributed by:
Jeff Emge
Assistant Director of Bands
East Texas State University
Commerce, Texas

Teacher Resource Guide

Variations on "Scarborough Fair"
Calvin Custer
(1939–1998)

Unit 1: Composer

Calvin Custer received Bachelor of Fine Arts degrees in Music Performance and Music Composition from Carnegie Mellon University. He earned a Master of Arts degree in Music Composition from Syracuse University. In his twenty-four-year association with the Syracuse Symphony Orchestra, he served as hornist, pianist, bassist, chief arranger, librarian, associate conductor, and resident conductor. Custer was an active composer and arranger writing primarily for instrumental music education.

Unit 2: Composition

This piece is a fanfare/introduction, theme, a set of four variations, and coda based on the English folk song "Scarborough Fair."

Unit 3: Historical Perspective

Variation forms (consisting of a theme with a certain structure, followed by a series of distinct "pieces" with the same or similar structure) are some of the most basic formal designs known to a wide distribution of musical cultures.

Unit 4: Technical Considerations

Maturity is needed for the flute, alto saxophone, and horn solos, as well as the vibes/bell accompaniment. There is a good deal of rhythmic interest in all parts, and most lines are either doubled or cued in other instruments. Woodwinds have several quickly-fingered passages in addition to the fugue in the last variation. The key centers around D most of the time. There are interesting percussion parts—melodic, harmonic, soloistic, and colorful.

Unit 5: Stylistic Considerations

The fanfare demands bold, separated *marcato* notes, and good control of dynamics. In the opening theme, the percussion should phrase with the soloists for maximum musical presentation, and the soloists (duettists) should balance each other in rehearsal. The punctuated notes in the second variation should be long enough to hear tone and chord, but powerful enough to make a sound impact. As fugue subjects enter, previously entered voices should back away so that the new entrances can be heard with clarity.

Unit 6: Musical Elements

Theme and variations, fanfare, fugue, shifting meters, folk song.

Unit 7: Form and Structure

SECTION	MEASURES	EVENTS AND SCORING
Introduction	1-12	fanfare, led by trumpets, followed by tutti cadence on B-flat/F major bichord (could be heard as B-flat major ninth)
Transition	13-16	D minor established in horns and low brass, piano, vibes, and bells begin *ostinato* accompaniment
Theme	17-33	"Scarborough Fair" in flute, accompanied by percussion only
	34-51	"Scarborough Fair" in alto saxophone solo, solo flute takes over counterline, accompanied by percussion and solo horn, add clarinets/horns/low woodwinds at end of phrase
Variation I	52-72	folk song material in brass choir piccolo/flute/clarinet/alto saxophone counterline
Variation II	73-93	*marcato* punctuations in all voices except upper woodwinds, who have rapid counterline *ritardando*
Variation III	94-119	folk song material in euphonium and oboe solo, accompanied by woodwind choir and tuba, held notes build up to

275

		next section by adding voices and volume
Variation IV	120-138	4/4 fugue variation of melodic material (alto saxophone/clarinet, flute/oboe, low woodwinds, bass voices)
Transition	139-143	*tutti* buildup
Ending	144-157	3/4 and 4/4 alternating by four measures, several layers of musical activity, D major established at m. 153 with exciting build to the end

Unit 8: Suggested Listening

Folk song, "Scarborough Fair"

Compositions by Calvin Custer:
Bluemond Overture, Empire Overture, Festive Jubilee, Intrada and March, Passacaglia, A Renaissance Faire, Washington Heights March

Other "theme and variations" forms:
Johann Sebastian Bach, *Goldberg Variations*
James Barnes, *Fantasy Variations on a Theme by Paganini*
Ludwig van Beethoven, *Eroica Variations*, op. 35
Johannes Brahms, *Variations on a Theme by Haydn*
John Barnes Chance, *Variations on a Korean Folk Song*
Edward Elgar, *Enigma Variations*
Wolfgang Amadeus Mozart, *Variations on "Ah! Vous dirai-je, Maman,"* K. 300e
Arnold Schoenberg, *Theme and Variations*, op. 43a

Unit 9: Additional References and Resources

Catalogue of English Folk Song Books. Boston: Longwood Press, 1977.

Dean-Smith, Margaret. *A Guide to English Folk Song Collections*. Liverpool: University Press of Liverpool, 1954.

Contributed by:

Scott A. Stewart
Indiana University
Bloomington, Indiana

Teacher Resource Guide

With Quiet Courage
Larry Daehn
(b. 1939)

Unit 1: Composer

Larry Daehn was born in Rosendale, Wisconsin in 1939. He received his bachelor's degree from Wisconsin State University-Oshkosh and a master's degree from the University of Wisconsin-Platteville. For thirty-five years, Larry Daehn directed elementary and high school bands, including twenty-seven years at New Glarus High School in Wisconsin. He has done considerable research on the life and music of Percy Aldridge Grainger, having traveled to Melbourne to study at the Grainger Museum. Since 1987 he has dedicated his life to composing and arranging for the wind band medium as owner of Daehn Publications.

Unit 2: Composition

The following is from correspondence with the composer:

With Quiet Courage was written in memory of my mother, Lois Daehn. She inspired many people because of her grace, kindness, and strength. She was born humbly, grew up poorly in the Depression; she didn't get many "breaks" in life. In mid-life she was struck by many health problems. She lost much of her eyesight and both legs to diabetes. But as one of the speakers at her funeral said, "I never thought of her as handicapped."

She wanted no pity. She was more concerned about those around her; that her misfortunes might worry them. There is not a day that I don't think of her, and others tell me that they also remember her often. She inspired many of us. Whenever we face great obstacles, we think of the courage and determination of Lois Daehn, and we know that we can go on and face just about anything, because she did; because she courageously lived her life and faced her death with quiet courage.

I tried to make the music like her; simple, with strength, nobility, and beauty.

A poem contained in the full score reads:

Lois Daehn

Her life was heroic, but without fanfare.
She worked and hoped and inspired.
She loved and was loved.
Her life was a noble song of quiet courage.

Unit 3: Historical Perspective

With Quiet Courage is one of several works by Larry Daehn composed or arranged for concert band. Notable arrangements include: *I'm Seventeen Come Sunday* by Percy Grainger; *Themes from "Green Bushes"* by Grainger; *Walking Tune* by Grainger. Two original works for band are *As Summer Was Just Beginning* and *Renaissance Trilogy*. *With Quiet Courage* was premiered by the U. S. Navy Band on September 16, 1995.

Unit 4: Technical Considerations

With Quiet Courage is composed for large symphonic band instrumentation, exhibiting modest technical demand but affording considerable musical reward. The first key center will allow ensembles to explore D-flat major with confident results. Modest instrument ranges make the work accessible to a wide array of musical ensembles. Dotted eighth-note figures must be played *tenuto* and should never be rushed. The *ritardando* in the final four measures of the work should be clearly subdivided with each eighth note played *tenuto* in soft reflection.

Unit 5: Stylistic Considerations

With Quiet Courage is a masterful study in *legato* writing. The work demonstrates wide use of *molto cantabile* style with no written accents and requires careful application of *rubato* and *tenuto*. Each melodic line and phrase calls for clear musical direction allowing for the teaching of linear shaping and ensemble expression. Sweeping countermelodies in horn, alto saxophone, and euphonium at mm. 33 and 49 provide interest and variety in this four-and-a-half minute composition.

Unit 6: Musical Elements

The work is written for large symphonic band with two trumpet, two horn, and two trombone parts. Percussion parts are limited to bells, vibraphone, chimes, suspended cymbal, and timpani. *With Quiet Courage* is tonal and highly melodic, blending warm sonorities through changing instrumental timbres and colors. Suspensions are found throughout the work, presenting educational opportunities in demonstrating the aesthetic of musical tension and release.

Unit 7: Form and Structure

SECTION	MEASURES	THEME	SCORING
A	1-8	1	*Andante e legato*
	9-16	1	
	17-24	1	
Section B	25-32	2	
Section A'	33-40	1	
Section C	41-48	3	
Section A"	49-54	1	*Maestoso*
Coda	55-58		*Ritardando/Largo*

Unit 8: Suggested Listening

Daehn, *As Summer Was Just Beginning*
Holsinger, *On a Hymnsong of Philip Bliss*
Lo Presti, *Elegy for a Young American*
Thompson/Buckley, *Alleluia*
Tschesnokoff/Houseknecht, *Salvation Is Created*
Van der Roost, *Canterbury Chorale*

Unit 9: Additional References and Resources

With Quiet Courage is recorded on:
Band Music of Distinction, Volume 1. New Glarus, WI: Daehn Publications. The Indiana University of Pennsylvania Wind Ensemble, Jack Stamp, conductor.

Contributed by:

Glen J. Hemberger
University of North Texas
Denton, Texas

Teacher Resource Guide

Ye Banks and Braes
o' Bonnie Doon

Percy Aldridge Grainger
(1882–1961)

Unit 1: Composer

Percy Aldridge Grainger, the noted Australian pianist and composer, left behind a rich legacy of wind music. His intense interest in folk music and performance practice led to many compositions based on British melodies. He called folk singers "kings and queens of song...lords in their own domain—at once performers and creators."

Unit 2: Composition

Grainger's original 1901 setting of this Scottish folk melody was for "Mixed Voices, Whistlers, and Harmonium." The wind band version dates from 1932. The full tune is heard twice, and the duration of the entire piece is about two minutes.

Unit 3: Historical Perspective

Robert Burns's poem "The Banks o' Doon" is the basis for the folk song.

> Ye banks and braes o' bonnie Doon,
> How can ye bloom sae fresh and fair?
> How can ye chant, ye little birds,
> And I sae weary fu' o' care?
> Thou'lt break my heart, thou warbling bird,
> That wantons thro' the flowering thorn:
> Thou minds me o' departed joys,
> Departed never to return.

Aft hae I roved by bonnie Doon,
To see the rose and woodbine twine;
And ilka bird sang o' its love,
And fondly sae did I o' mine.
Wi' lightsome heart I pu'd a rose,
Fu' sweet upon its thorny tree;
And my fause lover stole my rose,
But ah! he left the thorn wi' me.

Unit 4: Technical Considerations

This highly tonal setting is centered in F. The meter is a "slowly flowing" 6/8, most likely conducted in six. Harmony is mostly functional, with a few chromatic alterations in the second half of the piece.

Unit 5: Musical Considerations

The pentatonic melody should be phrased in the same smooth, unbroken manner as a vocalist/folk singer, with a fair amount of give and take in the tempo. The main challenge of this deceivingly complex piece is balance. The saxophones are the only instruments to keep the tune throughout, so the full texture of the wind ensemble must balance carefully against that section. The "Scotch snap" rhythmic should not be rushed or harshly accented, but rather given weight with air and then relaxation on the resolving note. Dynamics and swells are clearly marked and should be balanced well within the overall warm, dark sound of the piece.

Unit 6: Musical Elements

Ye Banks and Braes contains elements of folk song, pentatonic scale, functional harmony, 6/8, and Scotch snap.

Unit 7: Form and Structure

The form of the setting follows the exact structure of the poetry: ABAB.

VERSE	SECTION	SCORING
1	A	oboe, English horn, clarinets, saxophones, low cornets, horns, and trombones; piano
	B	*forte*
2	A	add piccolo, flute, E-flat clarinet, cornet I; *pianissimo*

B	tutti; chromatic movement, climax at m. 29; piano cadence (from *gliss*) on F major

Unit 8: Suggested Listening
Other works by Percy Grainger:
Lincolnshire Posy, Colonial Song, Children's March, Irish Tune from County Derry, Molly on the Shore

Unit 9: Additional References and Resources
Bird, John. *Percy Grainger.* London: Faber, 1982.

Fennell, Frederick. "Ye Banks and Braes o' Bonnie Doon" in *The Instrumentalist*, September 1981, 29-32.

Contributed by:
Scott A. Stewart
Indiana University
Bloomington, Indiana

Grade Four

Teacher Resource Guide

Africa: Ceremony, Song and Ritual

Robert W. Smith
(b. 1958)

Unit 1: Composer

Robert W. Smith received a Bachelor of Music Education degree from Troy State University and a Master of Music degree from the University of Miami. He is currently Director of Bands at Troy State University. With over 300 publications to his credit, he is one of the most prolific composers of concert band literature today. He has been awarded numerous commissions from ensembles of all levels, including middle school and high school bands, as well as university and professional military bands. *The Inferno* and *The Ascension* from his symphony entitled *The Divine Comedy*, have received worldwide critical acclaim. As a conductor and clinician, Smith has performed throughout the United States, Canada, Japan, and the United Kingdom.

Unit 2: Composition

Africa: Ceremony, Song and Ritual is based on the primitive folk music of Western Africa. Commissioned by the New Trier High School Band of Winnetka, Illinois, the piece was inspired by the recording and research of Stephen Jay. The work features traditional ceremonial music for dance and entertainment, as well as dynamic percussive invocations and historical songs. Folk songs used in the work include: OYA "Primitive Fire," which recreates man's conquest of fire; the "Ancient Folk Song," which originates from Ghana, situated in the tropical belt of West Africa, an area that became known as the Gold Coast; the folk song "Marilli," which is added as a secondary melody in the final statement of the "Ancient Folk Song;" and the chant to the God of Thunder "Shango," which brings the work to a frenzied conclusion. The work is approximately six minutes and forty-five seconds in length. Published by Belwin Mills in 1994, the piece is currently listed by music retailer J. W. Pepper as the most popular work for the concert band at the medium-advanced level.

Unit 3: Historical Perspective

The use of folk songs as material for composition has been an important and popular element in twentieth-century band music. Selection of a work such as this provides an excellent opportunity to explore and appreciate the musical history of cultures from around the world. The techniques learned from performing this type of music can provide excellent training for musicians. For Africans, music is tightly woven into the very fabric of their existence. The composer states in his program note:

> African musicians feel that they bring life to their instruments just as God gives life to the musician. As a result, individual instruments are believed to possess consciousness and are treated with the same respect and reverence given to an honored living person. The drum, the featured section in this work, is considered a sacred object as well as a musical instrument. It is believed to be endowed with a mysterious power which has been incomprehensible to the many missionaries and early travelers on the African continent. As one listens, the mind experiences a wide range of emotions including joy, fear, hope, and grief.

Unit 4: Technical Considerations

The piece utilizes the keys of C minor, G minor, G major, and D minor. Meter signatures used include 4/4, 3/4, and 12/8. Tempos range from quarter note=60 to quarter note=152. Ensemble members will need a strong command of various articulations, and dynamics are stretched to the extremes. Syncopated rhythms are the rule rather than the exception, and upper woodwinds have several sixteenth-note runs. All wind players are asked to vocalize, including humming and "primal screams." Solos are indicated for flute, oboe, English horn (optional), bassoon (optional contra-bassoon), euphonium, and percussion. The trumpet section will need harmon mutes. A major consideration for selecting this composition is preparing the percussion section for performance. Eight percussionists (two of whom will be mallet players) will be required to cover the parts, and the composer encourages the use of additional players performing offstage as well. The percussion instrumentation is conga drums, log drums, large tom-toms, bass drum, timpani, finger cymbals, suspended cymbals, crash cymbals, gong, wind chimes, cowbells, claves, castanets, beaded gourd, shaker, flexatone, bells, marimba, and chimes.

Unit 5: Stylistic Considerations

The composition is essentially a medley of African folk songs; therefore, the piece is structurally put together with many transitions and style changes. Strong rhythmic precision from all ensemble members is essential in order to present the proper style of these African folk songs. While the parts are clearly notated with articulations and phrase markings, familiarity with authentic African music would greatly enhance the performance of this work. The percussion section must be strong enough to not only present independent solo lines and balanced section work, but must present a comfortable "groove" for the ensemble to play over. The wind players will be asked to imitate "horn calls" and other sounds to emulate the music of Africa.

Unit 6: Musical Elements

The composer utilizes key signatures for the entire work with the exception of the introduction. The tonal centers of C minor, G minor, G major, and D minor are used. G major is presented with a C major key signature and the accidental F-sharp indicated as needed. The work employs some dissonance and extremes in dynamic ranges. The scoring includes opportunities for exposed solo and small ensemble playing as well as *tutti* ensemble work. The use of vocalizations and the percussion writing will help to set the "atmosphere" of the work. The rhythms of the 12/8 section will require attention from all players, and include some duplet playing against the 12/8 feel. The percussion section will need to play many rhythmic patterns including triplet and sixteenth variations, and will need to interconnect the parts to create a whole.

Unit 7: Form and Structure

Section	Measures	Events and Scoring
Introduction	1-13	Powerful ensemble figures including horn calls. Bells and chimes play three against two repetitive figures.
Transition	14-23	Conga solo leads to full percussion section setting up the "groove" for first song.
Song I	24-37	Key change. Piccolo and bass clarinet soli first time; add flute, oboe, clarinet, alto clarinet, alto saxophone, tenor saxophone on repeat, along with wind accompaniment.

	38-48	Meter changes to 3/4. Melody continues in same voices as above, eventually becoming *tutti* ensemble "hits."
	49-64	Return to 4/4. Melody in horns and euphoniums.
	65-67	Slow tempo down. Section ends as started with conga drum solo.
Transition	68-74	Solos for bassoon, flute, oboe, and bass clarinet. Band vocalizes "Sh" (à la wind).
Song II	75-90	English horn solo; band humming.
	91-102	Meter change to 12/8. Two-measure percussion set-up; followed by unison melody rhythm in band with counter-line from horns and euphonium on repeat. Euphonium solo m. 100.
Transition	103-106	Meter change to 3/4. Percussion *ad-lib* solos.
Song III	107-126	Key change to D minor. Unison horn melody over percussion. Low brass take melody m. 115; section ends with horn call in 4/4.
	127-144	Meter change to 12/8. Four-measure percussion set-up. Melody all saxophones, horns, and euphoniums; answer figures in trumpets and trombones.
	144-149	Meter change to 4/4. Tempo change to quarter note=144-152 (with wild abandon!). Percussion set-up. Band *ad-lib* "native" vocals.
	150-170	Key change to C minor. Full ensemble; unison woodwind melody m. 162. Brass *ad-lib* vocals, screams, etc. (as primal as possible!), m. 166.

Coda	171-184	Tempo change to quarter note=88. Repeat of introduction; includes two measures of whole notes with band indicated to "pick a note."

Unit 8: Suggested Listening

Samuel Taylor Coleridge, *Rhapsodic Dance "Bamboula"*
Karl A. Forssmark, *Three African Songs*
Quincy Hilliard, *Variations on an African Hymnsong*
Ernesto Lecuona, *La Comparsa, Carnival Procession from "Danzas Afro-Cubanas" Suite*
H. Owen Reed, *La Fiesta Mexicana*
John Philip Sousa, *Tales of the Traveler: "The Kaffir on the Karoo"*
Robert Washburn, *Kilimanjaro—An African Portrait*

Unit 9: Additional References and Resources

Rasmussen, Richard Michael. *Recorded Concert Band Music, 1950-1987*. Jefferson, NC: McFarland Press, 1977.

Rehrig, William H. *The Heritage Encyclopedia of Band Music*. Edited by Paul E. Bierley. Westerfield, OH: Integrity Press, 1991.

Smith, Norman and Albert Stoutamire. *Band Music Notes*. Third edition. San Diego, CA: Kjos West, 1982.

Contributed by:

James Popejoy
Doctoral Associate
University of North Texas
Denton, Texas

Teacher Resource Guide

Autumn Walk

Julian Work
(1910–1986)

Unit 1: Composer

Julian Work (b. 1910) began his early music training at Fisk University in Nashville, Tennessee. He has composed several works for band, chorus, and orchestra. In addition, he served as an arranger for vaudeville, radio, and television, and was a staff arranger for CBS radio, television, and recordings.

Unit 2: Composition

Autumn Walk was composed in 1958 and represents Work's sixth composition for band. His previous works for band include *Portraits from the Bible: Moses*, *Portraits from the Bible: Ruth*, *Portraits from the Bible: Shadrach, Meschach and Abendego*, *Driftwood Patterns*, and *Processional Hymn*.

Unit 3: Historical Perspective

Autumn Walk is just one of many pieces that were composed for winds by African-American composers during the middle part of the twentieth century. Among these many works are:

In Memoriam Zach Walker	T. J. Anderson (b. 1928)
Crispus Attucks	Arthur Cunningham (b. 1928)
Concert Sketches	Ulysses Kay (b. 1917)
Three Jazz Moods	John Lewis (b. 1920)
Symphony #6	Julia Perry (b. 1927)
Somersault	Hale Smith (b. 1925)
From the Delta	William Grant Still (b. 1895)
Pastorale	Fred Tillis (b. 1930)

Unit 4: Technical Considerations

There are many unison passages employed in this work that could create difficulty with precision of movement. This precision difficulty is caused by the slow tempo marking (quarter note=88). These unison sections are often divided into woodwinds alone, brass alone, and both combined. It is in the combined sections where balance between the woodwind and brass timbres becomes a challenge. There are several bassoon, oboe, and E-flat clarinet solo passages in the work, but they are all cross-cued in other instruments. The English horn plays an important timbral role in the work, sometimes being the only woodwind combined with a unison brass section. However, these English horn passages are cross-cued into different instruments. There are a few sections that call for one on a part playing, requiring individual soloistic skills. Several sextuplets exist in the work: some are simply chromatic passages, while others move by different intervals. The relatively slow tempo should allow the ensemble to single-tongue these figures instead of using multiple tonguing techniques. Finally, the work as a whole has a limited dynamic range, with the emphasis on softer dynamic levels (*pp* to *mf*). This would create the opportunity for an ensemble to develop subtleties at the soft end of the dynamic spectrum.

Unit 5: Stylistic Considerations

Autumn Walk is full of timbral, textural, and dynamic subtleties which require careful attention to detail in order for them to be effective. Much of the work is dedicated to sustained sounds that are interrupted by tongued or slurred sextuplets, creating a variety of textures. Several meter changes exist in this piece, often placed in the middle of a sustained passage. A controlled, sustained sound will not draw attention to these changes. The greater the contrast between the dynamic subtleties, the articulations, and balance, the more effective the presentation will be.

Unit 6: Musical Elements

This work uses several twentieth-century compositional techniques that were used by the composers of the impressionistic school, chiefly Claude Debussy and Maurice Ravel. These include planing, chordal extensions of the ninth and eleventh, and non-tertian harmony.

Unit 7: Form and Structure

Autumn Walk could best be described as having a fantasia form. The form is dictated by the changes in sonority and harmonic movement rather than motivic development. Section 1 is texturally dense and is harmonically adventurous. The following two sections become gradually more diatonic and texturally thinner.

SECTION	MEASURES	SCORING
1	1-44	G major
2	45-80	G-flat major
3	81-103	G major

Unit 8: Suggested Listening

David Diamond, *The Enormous Room*
Claude Debussy, *Prelude to the Afternoon of a Faun*
Maurice Ravel, *Le Tombeau de Couperin*

Unit 9: Additional References and Resources

ASCAP Biographical Dictionary. Fourth Edition. New York and London: Jaques Cattell Press, 1980.

Berry, Lemuel L. *Biographical Dictionary of Black Musicians and Music Educators*. N.p.: Educational Book Publishers, 1978.

De Lerma, Dominique-Rene. *Bibliography of Black Music*. 4 volumes. Westport, CT: Greenwood Press, 1981.

Everett, Thomas. "Concert Band Music by Black-American Composers." *The Black Perspective in Music*, 6 (2), 143-150, 1978.

Floyd, Samuel A. Jr. and Marsha J. Reisser. *Black Music in the United States: An Annotated Bibliography of Selected Reference and Research Materials*. Millwood, NY: Kraus International Publications, 1983.

Gray, John. *Blacks in Classical Music: A Bibliographical Guide to Composers, Performers and Ensembles*. Westport, CT: Greenwood Press, 1988.

Meadows, Eddie S. *Theses and Dissertations on Black American Music*. Beverly Hills, CA: Front Music Publications, 1980.

Rehrig, William H. *The Heritage Encyclopedia of Band Music*. Edited by Paul E. Bierley. Westerville, OH: Integrity Press, 1991.

Skowronski, JoAnn. *Black Music in America: A Bibliography*. Metuchen, NJ: Scarecrow Press, 1981.

Southern, Eileen. *Biographical Dictionary of Afro-American and African Musicians*. Westport, CT: Greenwood Press, 1982.

Spencer, Jon Michael. *As The Black School Sings: Black Music Collections at Black Universities and Colleges with a Union List of Book Holdings*. Westport, CT: Greenwood Press, 1987.

Tischler, Alice. *Fifteen Black American Composers: A Bibliography of Their Works*. Detroit: Information Coordinators, 1981.

Contributed by:

Jason Worzbyt
Assistant Professor of Bassoon and Music Theory
Morehead State University
Morehead, Kentucky

Teacher Resource Guide

Color

Bob Margolis
(b. 1949)

Unit 1: Composer

Bob Margolis (b. 1949, Staten Island, New York) studied at Brooklyn College and at the University of California before founding the publishing firm of Manhattan Beach Music in 1981. Active also as a composer and arranger, he has published a series of band works which explore the rich history of instrumental dance music of the Renaissance, all with a trademark ear for interesting sonorities and idiomatic writing. In addition, Margolis has composed several pieces in a more contemporary style, including *In the Big Apple* and *Fantasia Nova*. His work *Terpsichore* took Honorable Mention in the ABA Ostwald Composition contests in 1982 and 1983.

Unit 2: Composition

Color is a five-movement work based on English country dance tunes. For his source material, Margolis used two collections of unaccompanied Renaissance melodies: John Playford's *English Dancing Master* (published in 1651), and Jacob van Eyck's *Der Fluyten Lust-Hof* (published in 1646). As in their sources, the individual movements are titled "Stanes Morris," "Stingo," "Daphne," "Argeers," and "The Slip."

The title of the work as a whole stems from the composer's emphasis on the instrumentation and accompaniment to the tunes. In his notes in the score, Margolis states that the "focus of this music is not the melody, but the setting...the texture, the color, and the harmony." The present version, published in 1984, is a revision of an earlier version dating from 1982. The work is dedicated to Donald George and the University of Wisconsin-Eau Claire Symphony Band, who performed the premiere on April 8, 1984.

Unit 3: Historical Perspective

John Playford (1623-1686) was an English music publisher whose virtual monopoly on the publication of printed music in Europe lasted from 1651 until 1684. His collection, the *English Dancing Master,* contains both dance tunes (a mix of folk songs and composed tunes) and information on the performance of the dances that went with the tunes. It was one of the first music collections aimed at use by the general populace, and remains our single largest source of ballad airs. Upon Playford's death, the eminent English composer Henry Purcell wrote an elegy in his honor. A facsimile edition was published by Schott & Co. in 1957. "The Slip" is the final tune in the collection, and the dance for it involved couples leaving the floor one by one until no one is left.

Jacob van Eyck (1589 or 1590-1657) was a Dutch composer and performer who also taught carillon performance and made important contributions to the theory of carillon bell construction and design. *Der Fluyten Lust-hof* is a two-volume set of 144 pieces for treble recorder, mostly organized into sets of variations on Dutch popular tunes. It is still popular today with recorder performers and teachers, and exists in a modern edition of three volumes, published in 1957 by Muziekuitgeverij Ixijet. The melody for "Daphne" comes from this collection, where its full title is "Doen Daphne D'Over Schoone Maeght."

Unit 4: Technical Considerations

In terms of notes and fingerings, *Color* presents relatively few difficulties. The second movement, "Stingo," calls for several short runs in the woodwinds, and the third, "Argeers," has a rapid articulation pattern for two *soli* trumpets. But on the whole, the challenge lies primarily in ensemble and sectional playing. One of the most intriguing, refreshing aspects of *Color* lies in the numerous short passages scored for soli sections or solo instruments—almost all sections are exposed at one time or another. There are particularly exposed solos for piccolo ("Stingo") and oboe ("Argeers").

The percussion writing is especially effective and varied, calling for four players minimum and a variety of auxiliary instruments, including a sizzle cymbal and tuned water glasses. The glasses need not be crystal, and doubling or tripling the glass players may be necessary for the color to be heard.

The score also calls for an alto clarinet, which is cross-cued or doubled at all points, except for eight bars at the beginning of the third movement. Here, rewriting the line for B-flat clarinet or bassoon is possible if needed.

Unit 5: Stylistic Considerations

It is important to keep in mind during rehearsal that this is, at its heart, dance music. Even with its contrasting moods and tempos, a tone of movement and propulsion should prevail. For example, the air of mystery in "Daphne" should also be underpinned by a sense of urgency, of motion towards the resolution, the revealing of what is only hinted at in the opening bars. Overall, detached style in the faster movements and careful attention to dynamic levels in the slower will help keep the work from bogging down.

In addition, don't overlook the considerable humor and playfulness of Margolis's scoring—the saxophone and bassoon smear at the end of "Stingo," the comic brevity of the last two bars of "The Slip," the brass solos in "Argeers." If anything, err on the side of broadness in depicting these elements, in keeping with the lively and quasi-burlesque atmosphere of the work as a whole.

Unit 6: Musical Elements

Margolis uses four tonal centers in *Color*—G minor for Movements 1 and 2, F major for Movement 3, D minor for Movement 4, and A-flat major for Movement 5. But the quality of the melodic material, recurrent use of open fifths in accompaniment, and use of accidentals give the work a strong modal flavor as well. The major/minor melody of "Stanes Morris" gives ample opportunity to explore the effect of accidentals on tonal centers and implied harmonies, as does the raised third in the ending of "Daphne" and the tone cluster chord at the finish of "Argeers."

Unit 7: Form and Structure

SECTION AND EVENTS	MEASURES
"Stanes Morris"	
Introduction	1-6
A Section of melody	7-14
B Section of melody	15-18
C Section of melody	19-22
Repeat of C with variation	23-29
Return of introduction fragment	30-32
"Stingo"	
Introduction	1-5
A Section of melody	6-9
Transition	10-11

Variation of A Section	12-20
Transition	20-21
Repeat of A	22-25
B Section of melody	26-29
Coda	30-35

"Daphne"

A Section of melody	1-9
B Section of melody	10-17
C Section of melody	18-29

"Argeers"

Introduction	1-8
A Section of melody	9-16
B Section of melody	17-26
Free variations	27-39
Coda	40-67

"The Slip"

A Section of melody	1-8
B Section of melody	9-16
Repeat of B with variation	17-24

Unit 8: Suggested Listening

Thoinot Arbeau/arr. Margolis, *Belle Qui Tiene Ma Vie*
Pierre Attaingnant/arr. Margolis, *Fanfare Ode and Festival*
Jan Bach, *Praetorius Suite*
Gordon Jacob, *The Battell, William Byrd Suite*
Michael Praetorius/arr. Margolis, *Terpsichore*
Frank Ticheli, *Fortress*

Unit 9: Additional References and Resources

Dvorak, Thomas L., Robert Grechesky, and Gary Ciepluch. *Best Music For High School Band*. Edited by Bob Margolis. Brooklyn, NY: Manhattan Beach Music, 1993.

Grout, Donald J. *A History of Western Music*. Third edition. New York: W.W. Norton and Co., 1980.

Munrow, David. *Instruments of the Middle Ages and Renaissance*. London: Oxford University Press, 1976.

Rehrig, William H. *The Heritage Encyclopedia of Band Music*. Edited by Paul Bierley. Westerville, OH: Integrity Press, 1991.

Sadie, Stanley, ed. *New Grove Dictionary of Music and Musicians*. London: MacMillan Publishers Limited, 1980.

Contributed by:
Doug Norton
Director of Bands
American School in London
London, United Kingdom

Teacher Resource Guide

Dreamcatcher

Walter Mays
(b. 1941)

Unit 1: Composer

Walter Mays received his Doctor of Musical Arts degree from the University of Cincinnati College-Conservatory of Music, where he studied composition with Felix Labunski and Jeno Takacs, and chamber music with Walter Levin. He also worked briefly with John Cage and Krzysztof Penderecki. Various awards include a Naumburg Recording Award, a Composers Award from the Martha Baird Rockefeller Fund for Music, and a Tanglewood Commission from the Fromm Musical Foundation at Harvard. His *Six Invocations to the Svara Mandala* for percussion ensemble won first prize in the 1974 Percussive Arts Society National Composition Contest and has been performed by many percussion groups throughout the United States. In 1981, the oratorio *Voice from the Fiery Wind*, commissioned by the Omaha Symphony, was nominated for a Pulitzer Prize. *Dreamcatcher* for winds and percussion was recognized as the winner of the 1996 National Band Association/William D. Revelli Memorial Band Composition Contest. In addition, his *Rhapsody for Bassoon and Piano* was the winner of the 1997 Music Teachers National Association first prize among MTNA commissioned works, and Mays was named "MTNA Shepherd Distinguished Composer of the Year."

Six Invocations to the Svara Mandala and *Concerto for Alto Saxophone* appear on CRI Recordings. The music of Walter Mays is handled by G. Schirmer. Mays is currently a member of the composition faculty at Wichita State University.

Unit 2: Composition

The composer offers the following program note in the score:

> According to the Ojibwe People, dreams, both good and bad, float about in the night air. Above the sleeper hangs a magic hoop delicately crisscrossed with animal sinews and decorated with feathers. The good dreams, knowing the way, pass through the woven designs freely. The bad dreams, not knowing the way, become entangled in the dreamcatcher and are dissolved by the first light of day.
>
> The opening and closing sections of the composition are inspired by the light, aerial nature of the dreamcatcher, and by the restfulness of sleep. The middle section suggests a recurring nightmare. Many rhythms and melodic motives have been influenced by Native American music. Most can be traced back to the opening oboe solo. *Dreamcatcher* was commissioned by Victor Markovich and the Wichita State University Concert Band for the 1996 Music Educators National Convention.

Unit 3: Historical Perspective

Native American cultures are based on the belief that we are surrounded by good spirits and bad spirits. Each tribal community has a shaman, or medicine man, who possesses great spiritual and magical powers. So in essence, the dreamcatcher is a religious device, created by a shaman or another strong spiritual leader of the community, with magical powers to ward off the bad spirits and welcome the good. As each sinew is crisscrossed across the hoops, a prayer is said. In addition to Mays's interest in the dream state and the struggle between good and bad dreams, an important inspiration for the work was the poetic idea of the dreamcatcher itself—each one a uniquely individual artistic creation.

Although Mays used a traditional Ojibwe melody as the compositional basis for the piece, the idea and use of the dreamcatcher was not limited to the Ojibwe nation (also known as the Chippewa). Many of the tribes that once occupied the area of North America that is now southern Canada and the northern United States developed beliefs, legends, and customs that involved the use of the dreamcatcher to bring a peaceful night for the sleeper.

Unit 4: Technical Considerations

The successful performance of this piece will require the technical facilities and musical maturity of advanced players. The composer has written for an expansive array of instruments that includes, in addition to the traditional concert band instrumentation, a bass flute, contrabassoon, soprano saxophone, a second tenor saxophone, bass trombone, piano/celesta, and harp (the composer suggests that the harp, contrabassoon, or the celesta could be successfully replaced by a synthesizer, if the acoustic instruments and/or performers are not available). Many timbral colors afforded by this expanded instrumentation are exploited as the performers are at times required to perform in extreme registers. Isolated solo passages require mature tone quality and independent musical lines from many of the ensemble members. Of crucial importance is a soprano saxophone *cadenza* early in the third formal section of the piece.

Multilayered rhythmic textures and many changing metered passages create additional challenges and demands for individual players and the ensemble. In addition, the full battery of percussion does not function merely as a rhythmic complement to the winds, but rather as an important melodic, harmonic, and timbral component of the piece. Mays has referred to the combination of mallet percussion with piano, celesta, and harp as a "gamelan" section.

Unit 5: Stylistic Considerations

The opening and closing sections of this three-part work are very impressionistic. Each of the solo passages should be approached freely and played with an element of *rubato*. The floating lyrical lines, suggesting the restfulness of a peaceful sleep, should blend together seamlessly and explore many different levels of quiet playing.

Major seventh chords play an integral role in the harmonic language of the piece. Passages of instrumental choirs moving from one major seventh chord to another in fluid or parallel motion are an important structural element of the composition, and dynamic shape and timbral changes should be emphasized each time they occur. It is especially important to balance and tune these chords carefully.

The middle section suggests a recurring nightmare, and the style becomes much more articulated, with a driving *ostinato* eighth-note pattern and multi-metered passages that create a highly punctuated rhythmic energy. Timbral color is also affected by the use of mutes in the brass voices and stopped horns.

Extra care must be given to create the effect that the composer intended at the end of the piece. The final release of the winds, keyboard percussion, and the harp in m. 231 is clearly written and should fade to *niente*. There is a *fermata* over the following measure (232) that should last only five or six seconds. At the end of this measure, the conductor should release the bass flute. The rain stick solo comes two beats after the release and should last about four seconds. At this point, the only remaining sounds should be the steady eighth-note *ostinato* of the muffled bass drum and sleigh bells. The long fade out should last at least fifteen seconds, and it should not *diminuendo* too soon.

Unit 6: Musical Elements

The opening oboe solo in m. 5 is a traditional Ojibwe melody. All of the other themes and motives are the composer's own, and some symbolize important elements or characters in this musical portrait of the dreamcatcher. The "Dreamcatcher motive" is first heard in the flute and piccolo at letter A, from m. 8 to m. 12. The "Medicine Man motive" is highlighted in the bass flute after letter F, mm. 57-60. There are two "Nightmare motives." The first is heard in the piccolo at letter H from m. 72 to m. 75, and the second, lower "Nightmare motive," is presented by a choir of low woodwinds in mm. 84-87. These alternate in a rondo design throughout the middle section.

The repeated use of sequential major seventh chords is an important compositional element of the work, and according to the composer, they suggest "dreams floating about in the night air." This "Floating Dreams motive" can be found in the low brass at m. 37, where the melody consists of a seven-note row, and the major seventh chords all move in parallel motion. An inversion of this motive is heard earlier in the upper woodwind voices after letter B in mm. 24 and 25. After letter F in mm. 60 and 61, muted trumpets play major seventh chords in a symmetrical sequence at the culmination of the "Medicine Man motive" in the bass flute. Near the end of the nightmare section, the timpani solo at letter Q outlines a major seventh chord. An interesting harmonic moment occurs in mm. 193-195, when the ensemble plays the repeated chord that introduces the soprano saxophone *cadenza*. That repeated chord is made up of three superimposed major seventh chords on B-flat, F, and C.

The *Senza misura* section at letter V is a musical vignette straight from the composer's backyard. Mays was searching for the appropriate transition material to follow the soprano saxophone *cadenza* when he decided to record all of the bird songs that he heard in his backyard on an August morning. The piccolo represents a bluejay, the flutes are house wrens, and the oboe imitates a flycatcher. The call of a Baltimore oriole is heard in the E-flat clarinet, above the caw of a crow in the vibraslap, and the chattering knock of the woodpecker played by percussion and bass clarinet. The line in the piano part is representative of a cardinal.

At the beginning of the *coda* section, the flutes and piccolos begin a sequence of arpeggiated major seventh chords (at letter X, m. 205). The arpeggiated chords continue to build into a pyramid through other voices of the ensemble. The most settling and sonorous sounds in the piece happen at letter Z as the last five chords in the sequence of major seventh chords are extended into ninth chords by adding a third below each seventh chord. This peaceful sonority, which brings a cadential element to the piece, is repeated in mm. 229 and 231.

Unit 7: Form and Structure

Three-part form, ABA

Section and Events	Measures	Rehearsal Markings
A Section	**1-66**	**Beginning to G**
Introduction and Ojibwe melody	1-7	Beginning to A
Dreamcatcher motive	8-18	A to B
Dreams floating about in the night air motive	19-44	B to E
Canon based on Ojibwe melody	45-55	E to F
Medicine Man motive	56-65	F to G
B Section	**66-197**	**G to W**
Introduction to the Nightmare	66-71	G to H
First Nightmare motive	72-82	H to I
Second Nightmare motive	83-89	I to J
Development (motives from A and B)	90-179	J to T
Transition	180-185	T to U
A1 Section	186-end	U to end
Dreams floating about in the night air	186-195	U to cadenza
Cadenza (based on Ojibwe melody)	196	cadenza to V
Backyard vignette (senza misura)	197	V to W
Canon based on Ojibwe melody	198-204	W to X
Coda		
Major seventh chord sequence	205-218	X to Y
Dreams floating in air	219-225	Y to Z
Major ninth chords and fade	225-end	Z to end

Unit 8: Suggested Listening
Claude Debussy, "Fêtes" and "Nuages" from *Nocturnes*

Walter Mays, *Six Invocations to the Svara Mandala* (CRI), *Concerto for Saxophone and Chamber Ensemble* (CRI)

Olivier Messiaen, *Oiseaux Exotiques*

Florent Schmitt, *Dionysiaques*

Igor Stravinsky, *Firebird Suite*

Edgar Varese, *Ameriques, Hyperprism, Integrals*

Unit 9: Additional References and Resources
Campbell, Joseph with Bill Moyers. *The Power of Myth.* New York: Doubleday, 1988.

Campbell, Joseph, ed. *Myths, Dreams, and Religion.* New York: E. P. Dutton, 1970.

Densmore, Frances. *Indian Action Songs: A Collection of Descriptive Songs of the Chippewa Indians.* Boston: C.C. Birchard, 1921.

Densmore, Frances. *The American Indians and Their Music.* New York: The Womans Press, 1926.

Mays, Walter, composer. Interview by Brian Lamb, 17 April 1997.

Contributed by:
Brian Lamb
Director of Instrumental Studies
Southwest Baptist University
Bolivar, Missouri

Teacher Resource Guide

Elegy for a Young American
Ronald LoPresti
(b. 1933)

Unit 1: Composer

Ronald LoPresti was born in 1933 in Williamstown, Massachusetts. He graduated from the Eastman School of Music and received several Ford Foundation grants to young American composers, having also served as a Ford Foundation "composer-in-residence." LoPresti, a clarinetist, taught at Texas Technical University, Indiana State College (now Indiana University of Pennsylvania), and finally at Arizona State University in Tempe (hired in 1964). His works include *A Festive Music*; *Introduction, Chorale, and Jubilee*; *Pageant Overture*; *Prelude*; *Suite for Winds*; *Tribute*; and *Tundra*.

Unit 2: Composition

The *Elegy for a Young American* was written in 1964 and is dedicated to the memory of President John F. Kennedy. It received its premiere in April of that year by the Indiana University of Pennsylvania Wind Ensemble, conducted by Daniel DiCicco. The tempo of the work is a slow *adagio*, with the exception of a ten-measure *allegro* near the end. A simple scalar motif in the opening clarinet develops melodically and harmonically throughout the elegy, giving the listener a full musical experience of pain, grief, and loss. Solo instruments alternating with small sectional groupings and the tutti wind ensemble provide contrast and balance. In a brilliant stroke by Lo Presti, the final knells of the funeral chimes leave the listener not with despair and emptiness, but rather a sense of growth and inner peace.

Unit 3: Historical Perspective

An elegy is a sorrowful or melancholy musical setting in remembrance of a person who has died. Other names for works of mourning are lament, planctus, tombeau, apotheosis, and dump.

Unit 4: Technical Considerations

Many instruments explore a wide range of diatonic and chromatic pitches in this piece, and octave/major seventh leaps will need to be addressed. Dynamics on each extreme, as well as the middle, will also be found, so phrasing control in rising, falling, and climaxes must be in the mind of all at all times. Additionally, tuning at extremely loud and soft extremes will require careful listening and adjusting by all players. There are limited meter changes, melodic figures which occur on shifting beats, and *hemiola* under quickly moving parts. Percussion is used sparingly, but effectively.

Unit 5: Stylistic Considerations

The tempo is marked at quarter note=54-56, a challenge in itself. The conductor must work to communicate connectedness of notes and long, meaningful phrases which ebb and flow. The conductor has many decisions to make regarding phrasing; several meaningful interpretations are certainly possible. Some of the close harmonies demand careful balancing and tuning by all players. The first climax (rehearsal 2) begins from a *pianissimo* entrance at rehearsal 1. Some *rubato* is allowed, and certainly the moving quarters at rehearsal 2 should be stretches; also, the *decrescendo* should not happen too quickly. The eighth note on the end of four—two measures before rehearsal 3—should be *tenuto*, and the cadence chord at 3 should be as well, with a release prior to the trombone entrance. Bring out the trombone echo and timpani rearticulation after rehearsal 4. At 7, make sure that the long note sustains long enough to resolve the suspension in the horns and clarinets. The balance at 7 with the *fugato* figures is challenging, as the rising figures in the brass (opening motif) must be heard as well. The *stringendo* at 8 continues this *crescendo* to the *allegro* at 9. Accented notes should be accented by space, not harsh attack. The climax of the piece (four after rehearsal 10) requires great power and control at the same time, with a controlled *decrescendo* after the cymbal crash and syncopated low brass/wind chord over the sustained tones. At 12, conduct each entrance instead of beating time.

Unit 6: Musical Elements

Elegy, phrasing, cluster, consonance/dissonance, suspension, tension/resolution, full dynamic range, *tenuto, rubato, stringendo, poco più mosso, hemiola*, motif, rising action/falling action, climax, *maestoso*, inversion, augmentation.

Unit 7: Form and Structure

SECTION	MEASURES/ REHEARSAL MARKINGS	EVENTS AND SCORING
First	mm. 1-8	Rising motif in clarinets, suspension/resolution, twice add saxophones, then low clarinets
Second	reh. 1	Development of rising motif, add flutes and trombones, then gradually all other voices build up
Third	reh. 2	Explosive climax, gradual falling patterns and removal of voices to B-flat major cadence at reh. 3
Fourth	reh. 3	Trombone choir, timpani, rising motifs, cadence in B-flat major by full low brass section
Fifth	reh. 4	Unison rising clarinet octave/ seventh motif, echo in trombone solo, B-flat pedal in tuba and timpani, transition from A-flat to E-flat at reh. 5
Sixth	reh. 5	Full woodwind choir and horns, development of rising motif, florid passage/thick harmonies
Seventh	reh. 6	*Tutti, poco più mosso*, rising motif further developed, slight ritardando to reh. 7
Eighth	reh. 7	Rising motif in trombones and euphonium, superimposed inverted flute octave/ seventh motif, add clarinets in *fugato*, then alto saxophone
Ninth	reh. 8	Brass and low woodwinds continue with rising motif, woodwinds continue *fugato* figures with octave/ seventh motif, with *stringendo*
Tenth	reh. 9	Allegro, sustained accented chords in trumpets and saxophones, delayed shifting block chords in low

		voices, moving line in upper woodwinds, counterline in horns, *cesura*
Eleventh	reh. 10	*Molto maestoso*, explosive concert G, augmented rising octave/seventh motif, full and sustained to climax (five after reh. 10), gradual die down, removal of voices through reh. 11
Twelfth	reh. 11	E-flat pedal in timpani, trombones, low woodwinds, horn/clarinet two suspension figures, then E-flat major chords in woodwinds, funeral bell (chime/stopped horn), another chord with added trumpet and funeral bell, then a pedal release, upper woodwind E-flat major chord, then lower voices join at *ppp*, with a final chime and dying away to *niente*

Unit 8: Suggested Listening

Works by LoPresti:

A Festive Music; *Introduction, Chorale, and Jubilee*; *Pageant Overture*; *Prelude*; *Suite for Winds*; *Tribute*; *Tundra*

Other elegies:

Alban Berg, *Concerto for Violin* (in memoriam Manon Gropius)
John Barnes Chance, *Elegy*
Paul Hindemith, *Trauermusik* (in memoriam King George V)
Igor Stravinsky, *Elegy for JFK*
Richard Wagner, *Trauermusik* (burial of Carl Maria von Weber)

Unit 9: Additional References and Resources

Wallace, David and Eugene Corporan. *Wind Ensemble/Band Repertoire*. Greeley: University of Colorado School of Music, 1984.

Contributed by:

Scott A. Stewart
Indiana University
Bloomington, Indiana

Teacher Resource Guide

Four French Songs
Robert Hanson
(b. 1946)

Unit 1: Composer

Robert Hanson earned Masters and Doctorate degrees in Music Composition from Northwestern University, where he also received the Faricy Award for Excellence in Music. While at Northwestern, he studied composition with Anthony Donato. He founded the Elgin Area Youth Orchestra in 1976 and served as the Elgin Choral Union director from 1978 to 1993. Hanson also served as music director of the Lake County Chamber Orchestra and the Liberty-Fremont Chorus from 1974-1979. Hanson currently serves as music director and conductor of the Elgin Symphony Orchestra in Elgin, Illinois, a post he has held since 1983. In 1988, the ESO was honored as the Illinois Orchestra of the Year. He also currently serves the Traverse Symphony Orchestra as artistic advisor and principal guest conductor. He continues to guest conduct many orchestras, choruses, and festivals in the midwest. Hanson's many compositions and arrangements receive critical acclaim wherever they are performed. Many of his works are regularly performed throughout the United States, Europe, and the Soviet Union.

Unit 2: Composition

Four French Songs is a composition in four movements. These are all free transcriptions/arrangements of four of the *chansons* found in the *Thirty Chansons for Three and Four Voices from Attaingnant's Collections*. The first movement, "Troubadours," is a very free arrangement of an anonymous *chanson* titled "Jamais Je N'aimerai." The second movement, "Solemn Ceremony," is an exact transcription of a *chanson* by Claudin de Sermisy titled "Gris et

Tanne." Movement Three, "Petite Dance," is an expansion of an anonymous *chanson* called "Oui de Beaux." The final movement, "Festivals," is a very free version of a *chanson* called "Un Jour" by Pierre Certon. *Four French Songs* is published by Southern Music Company of San Antonio, Texas.

Unit 3: Historical Perspective

Pierre Attaingnant was a music publisher working in Paris from about 1528 to 1553. These were exciting and important years for French music because of the advent of music publishing. For that reason, the printed collections of Attaingnant serve as a cross section of Parisian musical taste for the second quarter of the sixteenth century. Most of the *chansons* in the collection deal with love and sensuality, a favorite topic of poets and musicians in sixteenth-century Paris.

Unit 4: Technical Considerations

The rhythms contained in the work are not difficult. Basic sixteenth-note runs appear in the woodwinds with some sixteenth-note passages in the brasses which require a little dexterity on the part of the performers. The conductor should note the tricky passage in Movement One, mm. 28 through 35, that features the insertion of 5/4 and 3/2 meters. Ranges will be tested in the cornets, but most other instruments are scored in a comfortable range with a couple of exceptions. Percussion instrumentation is not complex in nature; it includes bass drum, snare, timpani, triangle, bells, tambourine, and cymbals. The score calls for a string bass and its use would greatly enhance the overall quality of the performance.

Unit 5: Stylistic Considerations

Performing a work such as this requires careful attention in regard to style. The opening movement is marked *Marcato* and the composer notes that the quarters should be detached throughout. The conductor must also assure that the dotted rhythms are crisp and rhythmically correct. When half or whole notes occur in succession, be sure not to have the same separation as the quarters. Articulating the notes in a *marcato* fashion will provide the necessary feeling of separation. Movement Two needs to have the feeling of being performed by a choir, thus the "chorale style" marking by the composer. The use of a *legato* tongue and the connection of notes will produce a most pleasing result. Perhaps the conductor may want to consider a slight separation of notes in the last five bars of the piece to add some drama and tension. Movement Three must be kept light to provide for the dance feeling, especially in the A and A' sections. A little contrast can be provided by performing the B section in a stately manner, especially mm. 31-34, marked "detached." The final movement is marked similar to the first, but should be played in a "Grandiose" fashion, as the composer requests. The fanfares will project themselves, thus players must be careful not to overblow them. When the augmented original theme appears in the woodwinds, they must play it in a *legato* and *tenuto* fashion. The conductor must not allow the ensemble to overdo the final *crescendo*.

Unit 6: Musical Elements

Dynamics play an important role in the overall presentation of this work. The conductor must reinforce the importance of playing the dynamics as they are marked for this will provide the necessary contrast. Articulations must also be handled with care from movement to movement to provide differing musical shifts. The second movement should be approached as though the band was going to sing instead of play. Performers should strive for the most rich and full sound in this movement with careful phrasing. The composer has taken steps to help assure proper phrasing with the insertion of breath marks. These must be observed and it should be noted that the notes preceding breath marks should be held full value. The appearance of accents, in general, designates that notes should be played with separation. It is more of an emphasis mark than that of an articulation marking. Harmonically speaking, the movements are modal and remain true to the harmonies of the original *chansons* with the exception of the quartal harmonies in the freely expanded sections of the first and last movements. Perhaps to provide for further understanding, some historical perspective and listening should be included in the teaching of the music. The mental images can go a long way in helping students comprehend this compositional period and its various stylistic and musical facets.

Unit 7: Form and Structure

Section	Measures	Events and Scoring
I. "Troubadours"		
A	1-20	Full ensemble scoring with slight variants on the opening two-bar theme.
B	21-41	Woodwind antecedent with brass consequent. This occurs twice until the full ensemble enters in a four-bar transition beginning in bar 38.
A	1-22	Exact repeat of A material with the first three bars of the original B section.
Coda		Short two-bar coda with the movement ending on a staccato G-minor chord.

II. "Solemn Ceremony"
  This movement is through-composed, yet develops a short theme throughout.

III. "Petite Dance"

A	1-20	This section is in 3/2 meter, with the melody first appearing in the third B-flat clarinet, the B-flat bass clarinet, and the piccolo. It is later passed to the cornets and trombones.
B	21-37	This section is signaled by the change in meter to cut-time. It also presents new thematic material with transparent scoring until the full ensemble enters in m. 31 at a *fortissimo* dynamic.
A'	38-end	This is not an exact repeat of the opening A section. There is different scoring for the melody and well as a slight variation on the theme.

IV. "Festivals"

This movement follows no formal structure.

1-20	It begins with strict adherence to the original imitative *chanson*.
21-39	This is interrupted by the appearance of fanfare figures in the brasses.
40-57	The *chanson* reappears disguised by rhythmic and melodic variations.
57-end	The principle theme is augmented and fanfare material is inserted to close the movement.

Unit 8: Suggested Listening

Thoinot Arbeau/arr. Peter Williams, *Two French Dances*
Hector Berlioz, *Grand Symphony for Band*
Anthony Donato, *The Hidden Fortress*
Gabriele Faure, *Pavane, Op. 50*
Jacques Moderne, *Musique de Joye*
Pierre Phalese, *Chorearum Molliorum*

Unit 9: Additional References and Resources

Attaingnant, Pierre. Albert Seay, ed. *Thirty Chansons for Three and Four Voices from Attaingnant's Collections*. New Haven, CT: Yale University, 1960.

Grout, Donald Jay. Claud V. Palisca, ed. *A History of Western Music*. 3rd ed. New York: W.W. Norton & Co., 1980.

Kreines, Joseph. *Music for Concert Band*. Tampa, FL: Florida Music Service, 1989.

Randel, Don Michael. *The New Harvard Dictionary of Music*. Cambridge, MA: Harvard University, 1986.

Stolba, K Marie. *The Development of Western Music*. Dubuque, IA: William C. Brown Publishers, 1990.

Contributed by:

Rodney C. Schueller
Indiana University
Bloomington, Indiana

Teacher Resource Guide

Fugue in G Minor
(Little Fugue BWV 578)

Johann Sebastian Bach
(1685–1750)

arranged by
Yoshihiro Kimura

Unit 1: Composer

Johann Sebastian Bach is now generally regarded as one of the greatest composers of all time, although his contemporaries regarded him mainly as a proficient organist (as well as organ builder) and harpsichordist. His appearance on the music scene at the height of the Baroque era synthesized the styles, forms, and conventions which had developed in sacred and instrumental music up to that time.

Unit 2: Composition

One of Bach's most popular pieces for organ (BWV 578, "Little"), this piece is frequently heard in the brilliant orchestral transcriptions of Lucien Cailliet and Leopold Stokowski. The wind ensemble is an ideal medium for transcription, most similar to an organ in that different timbres produced by air columns are manipulated in various registrations, *tessituras*, and combinations of voices.

Unit 3: Historical Perspective

Bach became highly interested in writing fantasias, preludes, toccatas, and fugues upon his appointment to the New Church in Arnstadt, where he was appointed organist in 1703 at the age of eighteen. The church's organ of two manuals and twenty-three stops offered a splendid instrument. To confirm his interest in organ music, Bach is reported to have traveled four hundred miles round-trip on foot to hear Buxtehude play. The *Little Fugue in G minor* quite possibly was composed during the time Bach spent at Mühlhausen (1707-1708), where he wrote the famous *Toccata and Fugue in D minor* (BWV 565) and the *Passacaglia in C minor* (BWV 582). The designation "Little" is utilized to distinguish it from the so-called "Great Fugue" in the *Fantasia and Fugue* (BWV 542) in the same key of G minor.

Unit 4: Technical Considerations

The piece is centered in G minor, with all of the expected modulations into the subdominant (C minor) and dominant (D) key areas, as well as some more remote ones (B-flat and F). Most players are given either subject, answer, or countersubject materials at some point, so there are some clear technical challenges throughout the work. Articulations are generally smooth and connected.

Unit 5: Musical Considerations

The initial temptation for wind players will be to play the melodic figures too heavily and the free material too loudly. The subject should be nicely shaped with the natural rise and fall of the line, and counterpoint should always be subordinate to the thematic material. Woodwinds should check for uniformly smooth articulation during technical passagework and strive to achieve a fluid line of sixteenth notes which connect from one instrument to the next. The scoring in this arrangement is highly transparent at times, signaling a clear necessity for careful listening for appropriate balance. The soft dynamics should be exaggerated, and the final chords should not be too heavy or loud.

Unit 6: Musical Elements

This is an excellent introduction to classical fugue treatment. Exposition (subject, answer, and countersubject), episode, *stretto*, free material, pedal point, cadence, modulation, fragment, and polyphony are all an important part of the structure of the piece.

Unit 7: Form and Structure

SECTION AND EVENTS	REHEARSAL MARKINGS	SCORING
Subject Entrance #1 (G minor)	beginning	oboe solo
Answer (D minor)	reh. 1	English horn (countersubject in oboe)

Answer #3 (G minor)	reh. 2	clarinet and bassoons
Answer #4 (D minor)	reh. 3	second bassoon, low clarinets, baritone saxophone, baritone, string bass
Episode	reh. 4	upper woodwinds, bassoon (circle of fifths modulation)
False Subject		horns
Subject Entrance	2 before 5	trumpets
Episode		woodwinds
Subject Entrance (F)	reh. 6	horns and saxophones
Free Material	reh. 7	
Subject Entrance (B-flat)	reh. 8	low brass and woodwinds
Episode	reh. 9	trumpet/euphonium duet, woodwinds with free material
Subject Entrance (C minor)	reh. 10	upper voices, all voices with free material, pedal G
Episode (C minor)	reh. 11	modulatory
Episode (G minor)	reh. 12	ritardando, D dominant
Final Subject Entrance (G minor)	reh. 13	low voices (pedal emulation) dominant, prolongation/pedal point cadence in G major

Unit 8: Suggested Listening

J.S. Bach, *Fugue in G Minor* ("Little")—original organ version

J.S. Bach/Donald Hunsberger, *Passacaglia and Fugue in C Minor*

Unit 9: Additional References and Resources

Marshall, Robert L. *The Music of Johann Sebastian Bach*. New York: Schirmer Books, 1989.

Smith, Norman and Albert Stoutamire. *Band Music Notes*. Lake Charles, LA: Program Note Press, 1989.

Contributed by:

Scott A. Stewart
Indiana University
Bloomington, Indiana

Teacher Resource Guide

Hymn of St. James
Reber Clark
(b. 1955)

Unit 1: Composer

Reber Clark was born in DesMoines, Iowa in 1955. He attended Arkansas Tech University where he studied composition with James Perry. After completion of a B. A. in music education, Clark taught public school music for several years. He is currently a freelance composer, arranger, and performer with compositions for concert band and wind ensemble published and distributed by Southern Music Company (San Antonio, TX); Warner Brothers Music Publishers (Miami, FL); Wingert-Jones Music Incorporated (Kansas City, MO); and Shattinger Music Company (St. Louis, MO). Clark has fulfilled many commissions for middle school, high school, and college bands. Recent works include *Siciliana*, *Mt. Hope Union*, and *Aresti Dance*. A complete catalog of Reber Clark's works is available from the composer.

Unit 2: Composition

Hymn of St. James, published in 1984, is based upon the familiar hymn, "Let All Mortal Flesh Keep Silence." The text is taken from the liturgy of St. James while the melody is a seventeenth-century French carol. The text, in four stanzas, reads:

> Let all mortal flesh keep silence,
> and with fear and trembling stand;
> ponder nothing earthly minded,
> for with blessing in his hand,
> Christ our God to earth descendeth,
> our full homage to demand.

King of kings, yet born of Mary,
    as of old on earth he stood,
Lord of lords, in human vesture,
    in the body and the blood;
he will give to all the faithful
    his own self for heavenly food.

Rank on rank the host of heaven,
    spreads its vanguard on the way,
as the Light of light descendeth
    from the realms of endless day,
that the powers of hell may vanish,
    as the darkness clears away.

At his feet the six-winged seraph,
    cherubim, with sleepless eye,
veil their faces to the presence
    as with ceaseless voice they cry;
Alleluia, Alleluia,
    Alleluia, Lord Most High!

The composer uses each of the stanzas to build a section of the work. Clark utilizes contemporary harmonies and nontraditional band techniques to bring the text to life aurally. There is an errata available by the publisher.

Unit 3: Historical Perspective

This setting of "Let All Mortal Flesh Keep Silence" uses traditional harmony complemented by techniques which are distinctly twentieth century, creating a unique sound for band.

Unit 4: Technical Considerations

The basic keys in this composition are D minor, A minor, and D major. The metaphorical conflict between good and evil is suggested through ambiguity of the key in sections of the work, with the final tonal shift to D major representing the triumph of good over evil.

The work utilizes contrasting tempos and several meter changes to create interest for the player and the listener. The articulation is mostly *legato*, but in some instances requires the brass to play in a heavy, fanfare-like style. This usually occurs with the woodwinds playing sound screens over the fanfare sections. Therefore, articulations must be precise to offer clarity. There are some exposed sections for flute, oboe, bassoon, and first clarinet. Technical challenges for the flutes include chromatic scales. The brass ranges are very safe with the first trumpet going to a B-natural above the staff and the French horn going to an A above the staff. The standard band instrumentation is used with the exception of the first flute part dividing into four piccolo parts for eleven bars of the piece. Rhythmic demands in this work are minimal.

Unit 5: Stylistic Considerations

Several nontraditional compositional techniques are used in this work. The first is a sustained cluster line. These cluster lines are often called "sound envelopes." The cluster lines result from building chords through a designated section of the band. Both chromatic and diatonic clusters are used, with the chromatic cluster built on minor seconds and the diatonic clusters built on both major and minor seconds.

The composer creates an aleatoric section by instructing the woodwinds and low brass to play freely up and down a chromatic scale beginning on A. This creates a "sea of sound," according to the composer. Riding on this sea are the trumpets and French horns stating the theme as the conductor dictates. This section shifts to a tone cluster which eventually resolves to a major tonality.

Another unique feature of the work is the requirement of the brass to blow air into their instruments while playing a notated rhythm. Additionally, piccolo and tuba are called upon to vary intonation in sustained sections, resulting in waves of sound and generated harmonics. The use of these techniques gives the piece a unique aural character and makes it a useful pedagogical tool for the ensemble.

Unit 6: Musical Elements

The composer treats the melody differently in each of the four stanza statements, at times employing a woodwind chamber group setting as well as both trumpet and French horn section statements. Even in the climatic sections at rehearsal letter K, the melody is not stated by any one group of instruments, but is woven throughout the ensemble.

Harmonically, the composer leaves the hymn in the original key and uses tonal shifts to suggest mood. Dynamics are an important consideration in this work, contributing to the layered effect of the melodic statements.

Unit 7: Form and Structure

SECTION AND EVENTS	MEASURES	SCORING
I. Introduction	1-2	marimba
A Motif	3-12	woodwinds in hocket
A Motif	13-16	horns and trumpets
B Motif	17-23	brass, saxes, and woodwinds

II.	Transition	24-27	clarinet sound screen
	A Motif	28-34	woodwinds
	A Motif	35-41	woodwinds with brass countermelody
	B Motif	42-49	full band to just woodwinds
	Transition	50-60	brass to full band
III.	Introduction	61-64	percussion with low brass
	A Motif	65-77	trumpet melody with horn fanfares
	A Motif	78-92	woodwind sound screen with low brass melody
	B Motif	93-96	aleatoric band with horn and trumpet melody
Transition		97-104	percussion and air sound
IV.			
	A Motif	105-117	trumpet melody with woodwind soundscreen
	A Motif	118-129	horns with melody
	B Motif	130-139	full band melody in hocket
	Coda	140-end	full band with horn rips

Unit 8: Suggested Listening

Reber Clark, *Into the Great Dark Ocean, Nox Invictus*

Unit 9: Additional References and Resources

Blanchette, Marc. *Study Guide on the Hymn of St. James.* Unpublished.

Clark, Reber. Interview by Brad Genevro, 21 March 1997.

Clark, Reber. "Hymn of St. James." *The Clark Catalog* 17 (No. 1, February 1997): 4.

Studio 224, c/o CPP/Belwin, Inc. Publisher of score.

Contributed by:

Brad Genevro
Assistant Director of Wind Studies
University of North Texas
Denton, Texas

Teacher Resource Guide

Japanese Tune

Soichi Konagaya
(b. 1949)

Unit 1: Composer

Soichi Konagaya, a native of Kamakura, Japan, is a well-known Japanese composer, arranger, and percussionist. He began composing while still a student at the Tokyo University of Fine Arts and Music from which he graduated in 1973. He went on to become a CBS/Sony studio arranger, writing extensively for an array of wind and percussion media. In recent years, Konagaya has undertaken numerous challenging commissions by some of the world's foremost soloists and performing groups, and was selected in 1989 as a test piece composer for the renowned annual All Japan Band Competition. He is a member and advisor of the Japan Band Clinic and currently is leader of the Ageo Citizens' Wind Band. Many of his compositions are now available in the United States through Kjos Publishing Company, including *March "The Nine"* and *Star Puzzle March*.

Unit 2: Composition

Japanese Tune was commissioned by the Zushi Kaisei High School Band and published by Molenaar in 1987. The piece actually includes three Japanese folk tunes: "The Genroku Flower Festival Danse," "Cherry Blossoms," and "Yagi Bushi." Each of the tunes is presented in a different character and with unique scoring. The approximate performance time of the work is five minutes and fifty seconds.

Unit 3: Historical Perspective

The use of folk songs as material for composition has been an important and popular element in twentieth-century band music. Selection of a work such as this provides an excellent opportunity to explore and appreciate the musical history of cultures from around the world. The techniques learned from performing this type of music can provide excellent training for musicians.

Unit 4: Technical Considerations

The piece utilizes the key signatures of C, F, and B-flat. However, as is typical of this style of music, the melodic material is based on pentatonic scales and harmonies. With the exception of two 2/4 measures, the entire work uses a 4/4 meter signature. Tempos range from *adagio* to *allegro*, with only one *andante* section marked with a specific tempo of quarter note=80. Solos are indicated for flute and a woodwind quartet of flute, oboe, clarinet, and bassoon. All wind players are asked to vocalize "Hah" several times. Trumpets, horns, and trombones will need straight mutes. The piece includes parts for E-flat clarinet, soprano saxophone (*ad lib*), and string bass. Optional parts are also included for treble-clef trombones and tubas. Percussion instruments required include several Japanese instruments (allowances are made for traditional percussion instrument substitutions). Instruments indicated are *Shime-Taiko, Oh-Taiko, Chan-Chiki*, timpani, snare drum, tom-tom, bass drum, suspended cymbal, crash cymbals, triangle, sleigh bells, glockenspiel, xylophone, and vibraphone. Seven percussionists would be needed, three with mallet skills; however the work could be performed with five players.

Unit 5: Stylistic Considerations

The study of melodic and harmonic material traditionally associated with Japanese culture, and the use of percussion instruments in this music, would greatly enhance the performance of this piece. The composer has clearly indicated articulations and dynamics throughout the work. Since the work utilizes three different folk tunes, the players will be asked to perform a variety of styles ranging from smooth, connected, *legato* playing to a very precise, rhythmic "percussive" approach.

Unit 6: Musical Elements

The use of pentatonic scales and related harmonies give this piece its traditional Japanese sound. The composer weaves counterlines and accompaniment parts with the folk song material to create variations within each section. Ensemble members will need to be comfortable playing with controlled, sustained sounds, as well as with strong, rhythmic drive and tight, *staccato* articulations. The introduction requires very high, soft playing for many of the parts along with close harmonies. Most of the rhythms required are very accessible; however, a few parts will need to play some thirty-second notes and triplet sixteenths. The piece contains a wide dynamic range. Much of the scoring is doubled, but some solo and chamber opportunities are included.

Unit 7: Form and Structure

SECTION	MEASURES	EVENTS AND SCORING
Introduction	1-15	Adagio, molto cantabile. Slow, reflective opening statement punctuated with horn calls. Melody in piccolo, oboe, clarinet I, soprano saxophone, alto saxophone, trumpet I.
Song I	16-27	Andante. Melody in low woodwinds and low brass, string bass, and timpani. Joined by upper woodwinds in m. 20.
	28-48	Allegro. Melody in piccolo, flute, oboe, E-flat clarinet, clarinet I, alto saxophone, bells, and vibraphone. Moving eighth-note accompaniment in clarinet II and III; horn I and II.
Transition	49-52	Flute solo ("Freely").
Song II	53-65	Adagio. Woodwind quartet of flute, oboe, clarinet, and bassoon.
	65-80	Piu Mosso. Melody in flute, oboe, E-flat clarinet, clarinets I, II, and III, bells, vibraphone.
Song III	81-88	Allegro. Unison Japanese and traditional drums. Winds vocalize "Hah."
	89-99	Two-measure drum set-up followed by melody in piccolo and flute, with oboe and clarinets joining on repeat. Full ensemble m. 96.
	100-116	Unison *legato* melody in oboe, clarinets, saxophones, and horns.
	117-124	Rhythmic "percussive" parts for all divided into two groups: upper and middle woodwinds and percussion; and low woodwinds and brass.

125-141	Unison *legato* melody in flute, oboe, E-flat clarinet, trumpets, trombones, euphonium, and glockenspiel.
142-145	Rhythmic "percussive" parts for all divided as above. Ends with *tutti* "Hah."

Unit 8: Suggested Listening
Toshio Akiyama, *Japanese Songs for Band*
Clare Grundman, *Japanese Rhapsody*
Robert Jager, *Japanese Prints*
Bin Kaneda, *Japanese Folk Song Suite, Warabe-Uta*
Bernard Rogers, *Three Japanese Dances*

Unit 9: Additional References and Resources
Dvorak, Thomas L. *Best Music For Young Band*. First edition. Brooklyn, NY: Manhattan Beach Music, 1986.

Rasmussen, Richard Michael. *Recorded Concert Band Music, 1950-1987*. Jefferson, NC: McFarland Press, 1988.

Rehrig, William H. *The Heritage Encyclopedia of Band Music*. Edited by Paul E. Bierley. Westerville, OH: Integrity Press, 1991.

Smith, Norman and Albert Stoutamire. *Band Music Notes*. Third edition. Sand Diego, CA: Kjos West, 1982.

Contributed by:
James Popejoy
Doctoral Associate
University of North Texas
Denton, Texas

Teacher Resource Guide

Kaddish

W. Francis McBeth
(b. 1933)

Unit 1: Composer

William Francis McBeth was born in Ropesville, Texas on March 9, 1933. He holds degrees from Hardin-Simmons University and the University of Texas and has studied with James Clifton Williams, Kent Kennan, Bernard Rogers, and Howard Hanson. Currently he is professor of music, resident composer, and chairman of the theory-composition department at Ouachita University, as well as Conductor Emeritus of the Arkansas Symphony Orchestra. McBeth has composed works for many media, including choir, orchestra, chamber, and band. Among his many awards are the Presley Award, the Howard Hanson Prize, and the Edwin Franko Goldman Award. His compositions have been consistently among the most often performed works for winds for over two decades. In 1975, McBeth was appointed Composer Laureate of the State of Arkansas by the governor.

Other compositions by Francis McBeth from his over thirty works for band include: *Chant and Jubilo* (1963), *Masque* (1968), *The Seventh Seal* (1972), *Beowulf* (1986), *Of Sailors and Whales* (1990), *They Hung Their Harps in the Willows* (1988), *Wine from These Grapes* (1994), and *Through Countless Halls of Air* (1995).

Unit 2: Composition

Kaddish, which premiered in March, 1976, was commissioned by and dedicated to Howard Dunn and the Richardson High School Band of Richardson, Texas. Howard Dunn had gained great respect from the composer for his superior musicianship and the accomplishments he had achieved as director of the Richardson High School Band.

McBeth was grieving over the serious illness of one of his college teachers when he received the request for the commission, and later secured permission from Howard Dunn to write an elegy for James Clifton Williams. The ensuing death of Clifton Williams and the nature of the title provide vital information to fully understand the character and interpretation of the work.

The *Kaddish* is a Jewish prayer for the dead recited by the bereaved each morning and evening for eleven months, then on each anniversary of the death thereafter. Profound emotion caused by the illness and death of James Clifton Williams compelled Francis McBeth to compose this powerful memorial. Four main ideas providing contrast and unity bind this single-movement work. The first is a motive made up of two details which work together for contrast as well as for unity. The characteristic nature of each of the two details in the motive is contrasting, while their recurring use throughout the composition is a unifying element. The first of the three opening statements of the motive at the beginning of the work are started very softly and grow, each one to a stronger conclusion. The statements of the motives at the end are performed *fortissimo*. The motive is also expressed as a chant that begins softly at letter B and grows in intensity as the work progresses.

The second idea is a syncopated heartbeat, a rhythmic quote from *Caccia and Chorale* by Clifton Williams. This rhythmic figure is first stated in m. 6 and continues to interrupt the work throughout.

The emotional characteristics of the work require a *rubato* tempo which enlivens the heartbeat at the end of the motive statements. The effective use of *rubato* throughout the work also portrays the prayerful chanting, the anxiety of such situations, and the strong emotion about the death of a beloved teacher and friend.

The last idea is the use of dynamics to effectively portray the series of extreme emotions felt by an individual when faced with the reality of the death of a friend. They must be performed at extreme levels of soft and loud, regardless of texture, in order to achieve the full range of feeling. The end of the work is the emotional high point, dynamically speaking. The composer writes that this work is a combination of all the emotions that surround the death of a friend—cries, shouts, resignation, and sorrow—but the work should end as an alleluia, an affirmation of life.

Unit 3: Historical Perspective

Kaddish was composed in 1976 during a period when the band repertoire was beginning to be enriched by increased commissions and performance of works by Pulitzer Prize-winning composers. The focus was on band transcriptions of works by the original composer and works considered to be of serious artistic merit. The length of band compositions in general had increased from previous years, and the instrumentation sometimes varied from piece to piece.

Kaddish follows the tradition of McBeth's Romanticism in terms of compositional technique, programmatic titles, and wide variants of dynamic levels. The emotional content of the work requires the conductor to consider the full variety of dramatic implications found in the music. The compositional devices used include modal scale formations dating back nearly 1500 years to the chant style singing in the Catholic Church. *Kaddish* in this case is a mourner's prayer from the Doxology of synagogue liturgy.

Unit 4: Technical Considerations

Kaddish is orchestrated for standard band instrumentation with much of the scoring in sections rather than solo lines. Since the score is a full, transposed score using no key signature, the tonal areas are indicated through the use of accidentals. The work uses the Phrygian scale in several keys, ascending and descending often a fifth apart and frequently coming to resolution on a major chord based on the root of the descending Phrygian scale.

This work requires tremendous sensitivity to extreme dynamic variation within the context of balance both horizontally and vertically. The full effect of the gradual and *subito* dynamic changes found throughout the composition must be controlled and properly timed in order to achieve the maximum emotional impact upon the listener. The trombone section must develop the ability to perform long sections of sustained notes at a consistent *fortissimo* without decay. The odd-numbered phrase structure is also a technical consideration that must be understood in order to achieve the dynamic timing factors.

Rhythmically, the eighth-note, triplet, and sixteenth-note figures are not difficult to perform but must be executed with utmost accuracy in terms of placement within the beat so that the dramatic quality of the work is maintained at all times. This accurate subdivision of the beat is also critical for the control of *rubato* and syncopated figures, such as the heartbeat figure reiterated throughout the work. There must also be an effort to control the dotted eighth-note patterns which nearly always use the more noble portion of the motive, based on the interval of a fifth.

The musicians assigned to the timpani and bass drum parts must not only control the dynamic and proper subdivision of the heartbeat figure, but must also perform the flams in a disciplined manner at letter G with good quality sound at a *fortissimo* dynamic level. The two chime notes in the opening three bars must be performed with equal volume, not allowing the stronger hand to gain control of volume. Since the four sets of sixteenth-note figures in the chimes and glockenspiel after letter B form the underlying pattern, both melodically and rhythmically, with which the wind parts must match their parts, it is vital that these figures be performed with discipline in order to accurately control the placement of those notes within the beat.

Unit 5: Stylistic Considerations

Kaddish is a twentieth-century romantic band work. Although the tempo of the work is marked *Adagio drammatico*—quarter note at 54-56 with only one variation of that tempo indicated about halfway through the work—the nature of the composition requires that slight variations using *rubato* be incorporated into the performance. Subtle use of the *rubato* technique will help to create the character and set the mood for the most meaningful performance.

The work should begin almost subliminally at a soft enough volume that will allow for a full range of dynamics that will most effectively portray the emotions about death, from resignation and grief, to impassioned cries and shouts, and finally to a celebration of life. The tone quality should be sonorous with careful attention to intonation.

All accents and *tenuto* markings should be performed without separation. The natural decay of the tone and subsequent articulation will make it sound as if there is almost a separation, but one should not deliberately separate these notes. This lack of deliberate separation includes all marked figures including the tuba and baritone *ostinato*-like theme after letter D.

The second part of the motive should be performed in a singing manner, with air moving through the interval leap. The formulae used in Jewish prayers were of a melodic character that imparted something of the feeling of the text and suggested more direct communication from the soul to God. Since the Phrygian portion of the motive shows a tendency toward instability, the fifth adds stability. Although during the Renaissance Josquin used the Phrygian mode as a vehicle for somber expression, the mode was more often suited to matters where bravery or power were needed and shown. In this way, the Phrygian mode might inspire enthusiasm. The melodic interval of a fifth enlivens the Phrygian aspects of the structure.

Unit 6: Musical Elements

Harmonically, the work ends clearly in the key of C major. The move toward C is haunting from the beginning of the work, but does not receive true clarity until the last five bars. At the beginning, the motive in clarinets and horns on a unison C quickly moves away through the ascending C Phrygian and descending F Phrygian scale segments to a resolution on an F major chord. The heartbeat enters in the timpani on a C. The timpani heartbeat figure always reappears on C throughout the work, as a reminder of life, and builds to a tremendous climax at the end of the work. The pedal C in the tuba part beginning briefly at letter F and again from letter I to the end also helps build this emotional high point in the work.

At letter B, new Phrygian scale segments are used, but the relationship of the motive remains the same. The texture begins to thicken at letter F and the various components of the motive are harmonized, intertwined with the melodic fifth interval, and finally settle at letter J with what McBeth calls a massive harmonization of the ascending and descending motive simultaneously. The Phrygian portion of the motive, however, eventually gives way to the melodic fifth intervals, ascending natural minor scales in fifths, major chords on C, F, E-flat, D-flat, and ultimately the final C.

The melodic structure of *Kaddish* is based on the repetitive development of the motive. The motive becomes a lyric chant scored in the tuba, baritone, and low reeds at letter E, increasing in intensity to the end of the work.

Rhythmically, the work is held together with the syncopated heartbeat figure first stated in the timpani and later incorporated into the wind parts as melodic and accompanimental design. The texture and timbral quality of the work varies from one family of instrumental groupings to the next, becoming denser as the work progresses to the end.

Unit 7: Form and Structure

MEASURES	EVENTS AND SCORING
mm. 1-17: 17 bars (2+5+5+5)	Chime and gong announce the beginning of the prayer followed by three statements of the two-part motive, each one more intense, moving through the F and C Phrygian scale segments to resolve twice in F major and the third time in C major. The heartbeat rhythmic figure enters in the timpani and bass drum on each resolution.
mm. 18-36: 23 bars (7+4+5+7)	The two-part motive becomes accompaniment in the upper woodwinds and mallet percussion until letter C, using scale segments from the G and D Phrygian scales. The low brass and woodwinds chant a melody based on the D Phrygian scale. At letter C the chanting is taken over by the upper woodwinds, followed by the trumpets, both based on the C Phrygian scale. The section ends using G Phrygian scale segments in the low brass and woodwinds. The heartbeat rhythmic figure continues the first seven bars of the section and afterwards is only present as a part of the chanting figures until it reappears in the last bar to lead into the next section.
mm. 37-46: bars (5+7+3+7)	Woodwinds enter *fortissimo* and sustain one full 22 bar at that level without a *diminuendo*. The chant-like figures continue in the low brass and woodwinds on F and C Phrygian scale segments, followed by middle voices using G Phrygian and the upper woodwinds with C Phrygian segments.

A brief descending F Phrygian segment leads into the next section.

mm. 47-69:
23 bars (7+9+7)

Simultaneously, the middle voices play a moving accented line based on the ascending G Phrygian scale, the trombones play a harmonized chorale-like setting of the descending motive using C Phrygian, the upper woodwinds play a version of the descending portion of the motive interrupted every fourth beat by a fifth interval whose roots form an ascending G Phrygian scale segment, and the tubas play a C pedal. This moves into an accelerated section in which the ascending motive is stated energetically in the trumpets, baritones, and horns, while the descending motive is harmonized in the low brass and woodwinds. All of the brass, saxophones, and low reeds join in the chant centered on a unison F.

mm. 70-96:
27 bars (6+5+4+6+6)

The beginning of this section is similar to the section above. The energized ascending motive is played in the baritone, bassoons, and alto clarinet. The chorale setting of the descending motive is in the trombones and saxophones, and the upper woodwinds play the descending motive interrupted by the interval of a fifth. The heartbeat rhythmic figure returns two bars before the C major chord at letter J. Beginning in m. 77, the ascending and descending Phrygian scale motives on C and F respectively are fully harmonized and lead to a resolution in F major in m. 80, E-flat major in m. 84, D-flat major in m. 88, and finally C major in m. 91. All of the sixteenth-note scale passages beginning in m. 80 are natural minor scales on C and G and, finally, in m. 93 there is a harmonized C major scale in the upper woodwinds leading to a pronounced C major chord three bars from the end. The emphasis on C major is stressed further by the C major triads in the horns in mm. 92-93 and the trumpet triad which builds in mm. 94-95. The scoring of the final chord includes a six-octave spread on C. Further drama is added to the final section of the work with the twenty-three bar statement of the rhythmic heartbeat in the timpani and bass drum.

Unit 8: Suggested Listening

Mark Camphouse, *Movement for Rosa, Elegy*

John Barnes Chance, *Elegy*

Elliot Del Borgo, *Do Not Go Gentle into That Good Night*

Howard Hanson, *Chorale and Alleluia*

W. Francis McBeth, *The Creative World of Francis McBeth*, Walking Frog Records

W. Francis McBeth, *Chant and Jublio, Cantique and Faranade*

James Clifton Williams, *Caccia and Chorale*

Unit 9: Additional References and Resources

Battisti, Frank. *The Twentieth Century Wind Band/Ensemble*. Fort Lauderdale, FL: Meredith Music Publications, 1995.

Dvorak, Thomas L. *Best Music for High School Band*. Brooklyn, NY: Manhattan Beach Music, 1986.

Grout, Donald Jay and Claude V. Palisca. *A History of Western Music*. Fifth edition. New York: W. W. Norton and Company, 1996.

McBeth, W. Francis. *Effective Performance of Band Music*. San Antonio, TX: Southern Music Company, 1972.

McBeth, W. Francis. *"Kaddish," The Instrumentalist*, May 1981.

Rehrig, William H. *The Heritage Encyclopedia of Band Music*. Edited by Paul E. Bierley. Westerville, OH: Integrity Press, 1991.

Sadie, Stanley, ed. *The New Grove Dictionary of Music and Musicians*. London, UK: Macmillan Publishers Ltd., 1986.

Smith, Richard James. "Theoretical Analysis and Practical Applications to the Rehearsal and Performance of Selected Wind Band Compositions by W. Francis McBeth (Volumes I-IV)." Ph.D. diss., the Louisiana State University and Agricultural and Mechanical College, 1986.

Smith, Norman and Albert Stoutamire. *Band Music Notes*. Third ed. San Diego: Kjos West, 1982.

Contributed by:

Patricia J. Hoy
Director of Bands
Northern Arizona University
Flagstaff, Arizona

Teacher Resource Guide

Masque

W. Francis McBeth
(b. 1933)

Unit 1: Composer

William Francis McBeth was born in Ropesville, Texas on March 9, 1933. He holds degrees from Hardin-Simmons University and the University of Texas and has studied with James Clifton Williams, Kent Kennan, Bernard Rogers, and Howard Hanson. Currently he is professor of music, resident composer, and chairman of the theory-composition department at Ouachita University, as well as Conductor Emeritus of the Arkansas Symphony Orchestra. McBeth has composed works for many media, including choir, orchestra, chamber, and band. Among his many awards are the Presley Award, the Howard Hanson Prize, and the Edwin Franco Goldman Award. His compositions have been consistently among the most often performed works for winds for over two decades. In 1975, McBeth was appointed Composer Laureate of the State of Arkansas by the governor.

Other compositions by Francis McBeth from his over thirty works for band include: *Chant and Jubilo* (1963), *The Seventh Seal* (1972), *Kaddish* (1976), *Beowulf* (1986), *Of Sailors and Whales*, *They Hung Their Harps in the Willows* (1988), *Wine from These Grapes* (1994), and *Through Countless Halls of Air* (1995).

Unit 2: Composition

Masque, which premiered in February 1968, was commissioned by the State College of Arkansas for the dedication of their Fine Arts Center.

In sixteenth- and seventeenth-century England, a masque was a genre of entertainment that developed around a masked dance. The genre, which originated from the disguising tradition of Renaissance festivals, included instrumental music derived from folk and court dances and vocal music from popular as well as sophisticated styles. Based on mythological and allegorical themes involving poetry and the use of elaborate staging, the disguising was performed at night on special or festive seasonal occasions by both speaking and singing actors, with dance as the culminating event. The songs of the masques had musical and dramatic significance to the spectacle as a whole, but they, like the text and staging, were secondary to the dances. The three grand masking dances (the entry, the main dance, and going-off) performed by all the maskers was the most significant portion of the spectacle. The climax was the middle section or main dance, a ballet involving symbolic figures, letters, and geometrical patterns related to the theme of the masque. McBeth's score reflects the general air of festivity of the early masques, and although there appears to be no specific musical relationship, the three sections or three grand masking dances could be considered to be the structure of the composition.

Three main ideas are used throughout the work to provide contrast and unity. The first is a three-note motive developed during the entire course of the work. There is simple contrast and unity in the use of this motive, presented in a variety of emotional settings using contrasting dynamics, articulation, phrasing, note lengths, color, tempo, and texture. The short motive contrasted with itself in an augmented and more fully developed form allows for great melodic contrast and interest. The second idea is a sixteenth-note rhythmic motive heard in the fast sections of the work. Although originating in the percussion, the rhythmic motive is used on unison and chordal sections throughout the band to increase intensity and drama, often providing a focus of C for the nontraditional harmonic structure used in the work. The last idea is the use of extreme dynamic contrast which allows for a vast emotional representation of the noble, festive, and dramatic aspects of the celebration.

Unit 3: Historical Perspective

Masque was composed in 1967 during a period when there were increasing numbers of original works being composed for the band. Many of these works, however, had not yet become a significant part of the repertoire, and conductors felt it was essential to sustain the interest of composers and publishers by programming new works and accepting them as part of the basic band repertoire. McBeth was joined in the 1960s by other important composers, including Samuel Adler, Martin Mailman, Howard Hanson, Roger Nixon, Alfred Reed, Vaclav Nelhybel, Ron Nelson, and John Barnes Chance, who also wrote works for band.

The twentieth-century romantic style of *Masque* is identified by programmatic titles and compositional technique, including fast changes in dynamic levels, dramatic markings such as *sfp*, wide dynamic range, varying tempi, the use of *rallentando, accelerando*, and *rubato*, and the use of a large palette of colors, particularly from the percussion instruments. The emotional content of the work requires the conductor to consider the balance between the three main sections of the work and the contrast each provides to enhance the overall effect of the celebration of all that is involved in the dedication of a new building.

Unit 4: Technical Considerations

Masque is orchestrated for a standard band instrumentation with nearly equal scoring dedicated to sections and full band. Since the score is a full, transposed score using no key signature, the tonal areas are indicated through the use of accidentals. The work uses extensive development of a short motive that is made up of fragments from Dorian and minor scales presented in several keys, with nearly all melodic construction using scalar intervals, the widest often a fourth. Harmonically, the students must gain an understanding of balance and blend in polychordal sections and must sense the challenge of individual linear lines moving opposite one another.

This work requires tremendous sensitivity to extreme dynamic variation within the context of balance and control. The full effect of the gradual and *subito* dynamic changes found throughout the composition must be controlled and timed in order to achieve the maximum impact of the festive occasion. Balance must be maintained on the extreme *subito* changes at letters C and L, and particularly the changes in the fast sections must be closely observed in order to reach new levels in time for the effect to occur at the right location phrasally. Melodic quarter notes must be performed full value with equal weight throughout the note. This will allow for the utmost dignity of the lyric melodies such as the one at letter A.

Rhythmically, the sixteenth-note motive must be performed accurately, without any rushing, to ensure adequate placement within the beat. A decision must be made regarding the note grouping emphasis of the sixteenth-note figures so that a consistent character may be established, also allowing the band to perform the figures together. In many portions of the fast sections, accurate performance of entrances, particularly those involving rests requiring an entrance on a weak beat of the measure, is a challenge. This is also true for sustained notes which move on weak beats of the measure. The subdivision of the beat, even on rests and sustained notes, is critical for the control of these figures.

The timing of dynamic change for *sfp* markings must be determined in order for them to achieve the maximum emotional effect. Percussion must be concerned with this marking after letter D, at E, and three bars from the end. This is also true for the full band *sfzp* after letter L. In addition, the subsequent *crescendo* following each of these markings must be timed carefully so the new dynamic is reached as marked. This is difficult at the fast performance tempo.

Unit 5: Stylistic Considerations

Masque is a twentieth-century romantic band work. There is extreme contrast in tempo between the fast sections and the slower middle section. The middle section is less than half the speed of the fast sections. This contrast is vital to the character of the work and the timing of the *rallentando* into the slow section at letter F is also critical. The middle section of the work, beginning at letter F, could be considered to be the most significant part of the work. As in the early three masking dances, this section of the music could be symbolic of the emotions of the masque theme, or, in this case, the dedication of a new Fine Arts Center on a campus. The tempo must be *rubato* and performed in a sensitive manner according to the phrase structure. Also, in order to achieve the emotional impact of the return to the opening fast section at letter I, there must not be a breath leading into this section.

The work should begin and end with the festive atmosphere of such a celebration. The tone quality could be somewhat brilliant in the fast, rhythmic sections and more rich and sonorous in the slower and more lyric sections. There are ample listings of modal ethos among medieval and Renaissance sources to indicate the early phenomenon of mode association to mood or character. The Dorian and often the minor mode used in fragments throughout this work has been associated with its capability to portray all effects, but most often corresponds with serious or noble themes. This seems appropriate for a building dedication.

As in all of McBeth's music, the accented articulation markings must be performed full value. The markings as used by this composer do not indicate a shortened note length, but rather denote only emphasis on the attack.

Unit 6: Musical Elements

Harmonically, the work ends in C major preceded by an eighteen-bar pedal F, scale passages giving the feeling of F minor, occasional F and C major chords in the harmony, a strong movement from F major chords to G-flat major leading to a false C major ending in m. 233, then on to the three-note motive and a final cadence in C major. Although the work uses twentieth-century harmonic techniques such as polychordal writing, the harmony throughout settles on C major punctuated by occasional F major.

The scale passages in the fast sections are predominantly C, with occasional moves to short Dorian or minor scale passages based on other notes. A hint of F minor and possibly even D-flat major scale passages is also present at times. The slow section uses brief developmental sections of Dorian and minor scale fragments based on the opening three-note motive.

The melodic structure of *Masque* is based on the repetitive development of the three-note motive. The motive is transformed from a short punctuated fragment, to a singing melody, and to a chorale.

Rhythmically, the work is held together by the reappearing sixteenth-note motive and the syncopated melodic figures, even in the lyric and slow sections.

The textural and timbral quality of the work varies from one family of instrumental groupings to the next. A fully scored band is used in only a little over half of the composition. The textural high point of the work occurs from N to the end with a fully scored band performing a chorale based on the three-note motive, a punctuated use of the three-note motive in the upper woodwinds, the use of a version of the sixteenth-note motive, a use of a variety of percussion instruments, and a pedal F in the bass voices.

Unit 7: Form and Structure

MEASURES	EVENTS AND SCORING
Section I (A) 1-21 21 bars (14+7)	The simultaneous use of both motives. The full band playing the three-note motive in two forms—punctuated and lyric—and the percussion playing the sixteenth-note motive. The emphasis harmonically, punctuated in the xylophone, is on C.
22-56 35 bars (8+9+6+6+6)	The three-note motive is used first as a unison chant, followed by a chorale. The timpani provides a C pedal for the chorale section. The section builds from a *pianissimo* light wood-wind texture, to the sonorous brass, to a full band scoring and a *crescendo* to *fortissimo*.
57-89 33 bars (4+9+5+6+5+4)	This section makes heavy use of the sixteenth-note motive, polychords ending on C major, and a rhythmic winding down effect of emphasis on beat four, followed by beat three, beat two, and beat one. The character changes dramatically from a fully scored *fortissimo* on an F major chord to a C major chord and finally a *pianissimo* open fifth C and G in the low brass.
Section II (B) 90-135 46 bars (16+11+13+6)	This *rubato* middle section features the development of the three-note motive using various scale fragments to arrive at C major in mm. 106 and 116, F major in mm. 119 and 128, D-flat seventh chord in m. 122, G major

chord in m. 125, finally arriving at C major at the return of the fast section.

Section III (A) 136-240 24 bars (14+10)	This section is very similar to the opening section, mm. 1-21.
35 bars (6+6+6+9+8)	This section is the reverse in terms of phrasal analysis from the equivalent section, mm. 22-56, in the first part of the work.
10 bars (6+4)	Restatement of material from the opening section. The lyric use of the three-note motive is found in the low brass and reeds, and the punctuated version of the motive is scored in the trumpets and upper woodwinds.
36 bars (9+9+8+10)	The work concludes with a *coda-like* section from letter N to the end, including a pedal F which leads to a clear conclusion in C major.

Unit 8: Suggested Listening

Howard Hanson, *Chorale and Alleluia*

W. Francis McBeth, *The Creative World of Francis McBeth*, (Walking Frog Records). *Chant and Jublio, Cantique and Faranade, Kaddish, Drammatico*

Vaclav Nehlybel, *Estampie, Festivo, Prelude and Dance, Suite Concertante*

Clifton Williams, *Caccia and Chorale, Festival, Symphonic Dance No. 2*

Unit 9: Additional References and Resources

Battisti, Frank. *The Twentieth Century Wind Band/Ensemble*. Fort Lauderdale, FL: Meredith Music Publications, 1995.

Grout, Donald J. and Claude V. Palisca. *A History of Western Music*. Fifth ed. New York: W. W. Norton & Company, 1996.

McBeth, W. Francis. *Effective Performance of Band Music*. San Antonio, TX: Southern Music Company, 1972.

Rehrig, William H. *The Heritage Encyclopedia of Band Music*. Edited by Paul E. Bierley. Westerville, OH: Integrity Press, 1991.

Sadie, Stanley, ed. *The New Grove Dictionary of Music and Musicians*. London, UK: Macmillan Publishers Ltd., 1986.

Smith, Richard James. "Theoretical Analysis and Practical Applications to the Rehearsal and Performance of Selected Wind Band Compositions by W. Francis McBeth (Volumes I-IV)." Ph.D. diss., the Louisiana State University and Agricultural and Mechanical College, 1986.

Smith, Norman and Albert Stoutamire. *Band Music Notes*. Third ed. San Diego: Kjos West, 1982.

Contributed by:
Patricia J. Hoy
Director of Bands
Northern Arizona University
Flagstaff, Arizona

Teacher Resource Guide

Of Dark Lords
and Ancient Kings

Roland Barrett
(b. 1955)

Unit 1: Composer

Roland Barrett was born May 23, 1955 in Nebraska City, Nebraska. Barrett played trumpet in the Auburn, Nebraska high school band. During that time he studied with Dennis Schnieder, Professor of Trumpet at the University of Nebraska–Lincoln. He attended Peru State College in Peru, Nebraska, where he was a student of Gill Wilson and David Edress. Following graduation from Peru State, Barrett taught in the public schools in Nebraska for six years. In 1983, he began to pursue master's degree work at the University of Oklahoma, Norman (OU). His skills as an arranger and drill designer were recognized by his teachers, and he was invited to stay at OU, where he has remained. He is presently completing doctoral work in composition at OU, while continuing his duties as assistant director of bands. Barrett is active as a composer, arranger, and clinician throughout the United States. He has written a number of works for band, including *Chants, Long Forgotten, Fanfare and Dance Segments, On Wings of the Chosen, Sentavo,* and *Symphonic Journey.* Barrett has also written numerous arrangements for marching band, as well as chamber music.

Unit 2: Composition

Of Dark Lords and Ancient Kings was commissioned by the Central Oklahoma Directors Association (CODA) for their annual Honor Band Festival. The premiere was presented by the CODA Junior High Honor Band on January 8, 1994 in Oklahoma City. The work is evocative of the title, with low sonorities darkly scored against themes which conjure up images of past splendor. Its form is episodic, with juxtaposition of sections of different tempos and themes. Barrett makes use of twentieth-century techniques including aleatory music, *ostinati*, modality, mixed meter, and extensive use of percussion. *Of Dark Lords and Ancient Kings* is 122 measures long and takes approximately six minutes to perform. It is suitable for bands who play at the Grade Three level.

Unit 3: Historical Perspective

Barrett's music is representative of an eclectic style characteristic of the late twentieth-century teaching repertoire, and reflects the high regard he has for two fellow composers; W. Francis McBeth and Claude T. Smith. The dark brass scoring in *Of Dark Lords and Ancient Kings* is inspired by the characteristic brass writing of McBeth. Barrett's use of mixed meter, particularly at cadence points, is much like that of Claude T. Smith, who is also the composer Barrett most admires for his rhythmic sense. Barrett embraces a tonal harmonic style that makes use of seventh and ninth chords. Further, Barrett makes extensive use of percussion, both as a separate sonority (the piece begins with only percussion playing) and as rhythmic reinforcement.

Unit 4: Technical Considerations

The Dorian and Ionian (major) modes are important elements in the melodic and harmonic development of this piece. The fast sections are in the Dorian mode, centered in the following keys: E, G, E-flat, and F. The slow section at the middle of the piece is written in C major, but poses no other technical challenges. These modes and scales should be practiced in eighth notes at 144 beats per minute.

Rhythmically, *Of Dark Lords* is composed of simple patterns of eighth, quarter, half, and whole notes in duple meter. However, students will need a strong sense of rhythmic independence to play this music well. Barrett layers rhythmic *ostinati* so a strong sense of ensemble pulse will be important. Further, he occasionally uses accents to give the impression of a metrical shift. None of the rhythmical challenges are beyond the capability of Grade Three players.

Unit 5: Stylistic Considerations

Of Dark Lords and Ancient Kings presents at least three challenges for middle-level players. Achieving the appropriate style in the various sections is the cardinal task of the conductor, followed by proper execution of the aleatoric section, and care in following the dynamic contour. Attention to the dark quality of the low brass scoring in the opening sections of the work will be paramount to creating a proper setting for the remainder of the work. The aleatoric section requires total independence from each player as the directions call for each player to play their phrase at a different speed from others in the section.

The main thematic section demands careful attention to articulation and dynamics from the students. There will be a tendency to play too heavily and too loudly in the *ostinato* parts. Light playing is the operative word until the dynamic level is above *forte*.

Dynamics, contrast, and balance will pose a special challenge to mid-level players. The loudest play is indicated six bars from the end of the piece. Students must be encouraged to hold back until late in the work. Percussion will need to be monitored so that they do not overpower the band.

Unit 6: Musical Elements

Of Dark Lords is centered in the keys of D minor and its relative major, F. There are also excursions to the key centers of G and E-flat minor and C major. The Dorian mode is used frequently in the themes of the minor section. The C major section is presented in approximately the middle of the work and lasts eighteen measures.

Rhythmically, the work is predominantly in a duple feel. There are, however, some deviations; one measure of 7/8 time and four measures of 3/4 time, cross-accented, give an impression of 6/8 time. The remainder of the piece is a basic pattern of rhythm in duple time. There are two sixteenth notes for the upper winds and euphonium. The snare drum part has several patterns of sixteenth notes throughout.

Barrett is sensitive to the orchestration by alternating sections of the nearly tutti playing with sections that are scored lightly. As the work progresses, the amount of full band playing increases along with the dynamics.

Unit 7: Form and Structure

There is no allegiance to any particular form in this piece; however, the work is conceived as a series of episodes. The work can be divided into three main sections: a long introductory section, a main section, and a closing section.

MEASURES	KEY	EVENTS AND SCORING
Introductory section		
1-14	D minor	Slow. Percussion and brass introduction.
15	D minor	Faster. 7/8 bar foreshadowing of main theme.
16-22	D minor	Slow. Flutes, clarinets, and euphonium present a B idea. Slightly faster than opening.
23-27	D minor	Faster. Expanse of the foreshadowing idea in m. 15.

28-32		Slow. Trumpet solo phrase which temporarily moves away from the D key center.

Main section

33-34	D minor	Slow aleatoric passage in which motives from the piece are presented.
35-48	D minor	Fast section, main idea presented (m. 37) over *ostinato*.
49-57	G major	New idea presented in woodwinds to contrast main idea.
58-68	G minor	Main idea returns, in new key, with different accompaniment. The section ends with a short transitional phrase (mm. 67-68).
69-78	C major	Slow. Contrasting theme, new key, slow tempo.
79-82	C major	A closing phrase to major idea. Moving from C major set up harmony in next section.
83-87		A trasitional phrase for woodwinds and euphonium solo.
87-95	E-flat minor	Fast. Return of main idea like mm. 41-48.
96-102	F	Restatement of main idea, different accompaniment, low brass suggests an augmentation of the main theme.
103-108	F minor	Slow. Return of material from mm. 23-27 in new key.

Closing section

109-111	D-flat major	Partial return of material from mm. 28-29, and scored tutti.
112-117	F minor	Presto. Last statement of main idea.
118-122 (end)	F minor/F major	Closing phrase built on motive from main idea. Ends in F major with percussive ending.

Unit 8: Suggested Listing

Roland Barret, *Fanfare and Dance Segments*, *Symphonic Journey*, *Chants Long Forgotten*
David Holsinger, *Liturgical Dances*, *Sinfonia Voce*
W. Francis McBeth, *Of Sailors and Whales*, *Masque*
Claude T. Smith, *Emperata Overture*, *Incidental Suite*

Unit 9: Additional References and Resources

Rehrig, William H. *The Heritage Encyclopedia of Band Music*. Vol. 3. Edited by Paul Bierley. Westerville, OH: Integrity Press 1996.

Contributed by:

Jay W. Gilbert
Doane College
Crete, Nebraska

Teacher Resource Guide

Satiric Dances
(for a Comedy by Aristophanes)
Norman Dello Joio
(b. 1913)

Unit 1: Composer

Norman Dello Joio was born in New York City in 1913. He began studying organ with his father, who had emigrated from Italy in the early 1900s, and
continued organ lessons with his godfather, the renowned organist Pietro Yon.
He went on to study composition with Bernard Wagenaar and Paul
Hindemith. He taught at Sarah Lawrence College, the Mannes School of
Music, and was Dean of Fine Arts at Boston University. Comfortable in all
idioms, his music exhibits a striking lyric inventiveness. His writing is pro-
foundly influenced by Gregorian chant, and elements of Italian grand opera
and jazz are also present. Among his other works for band are *Scenes from the
Louvre*, *Caccia*, *Variants on a Medieval Tune*, *Concertante*, and *Fantasies on a
Theme by Haydn*.

Unit 2: Composition

Satiric Dances was composed in 1975 for the town of Concord,
Massachusetts in commemoration of its Bicentennial. The commission was
funded by the Town of Concord and the Eastern National Park and
Monument Association. The work is in three brief movements: I—*Allegro
Pesante*; II—*Adagio Mesto*, and III—*Allegro Spumante*. Movements II and III
are performed without break. The entire work is about seven minutes in
length.

Unit 4: Technical Considerations

The tonal center for the first movement is A minor, with sections of modulation to C major and A major. Technical demands in this movement are relatively slight. Trumpets and saxophones must execute sixteenth-note passages based on the C octatonic scale. All brass must execute eighth-note lines in A major. Rhythmic demands are minimal. A unison melody in four octaves between piccolo, flute, oboe, bassoon, and trumpet in m. 7 will require attention. The second movement is slow and lyrical, and requires control and strength from all parts, with many interval leaps of fifths to octaves and exposed solo lines. Its tonal center is C, with much chromaticism and tonicization to other key areas. The final movement is very quick (quarter note=152), is in C minor, and requires technical agility from all parts. Trombones and horns must execute octave *glissandi* on C and G; saxophones and bassoons must execute one measure of *staccato* sixteenths; all parts require fluent chromatic technique; double tonguing is necessary in the flutes and horns; and trombones must execute the C major and C chromatic scales in *staccato* eighth notes.

Unit 5: Stylistic Considerations

Dello Joio projects the satirical qualities of the work in the outer movements through sudden dynamic contrasts and timbral shifts, harmonies and melodies based on octatonic scales, and a Mediterranean folk dance character. These elements can be enhanced by paying very close attention to stylistic markings, and by resisting the natural urge to rush, especially into weak beats. The last movement must sparkle (*spumante*); to be playable, the articulation must be light and controlled. The middle movement requires much *espressivo* playing. It is important to remember when performing these pieces that they are *dances*, with a strong emphasis on rhythm and melody.

Unit 6: Musical Elements

The texture is generally homophonic throughout the first and third movements, with occasional countermelodic activity. The second movement contains sections of polyphony, as well as homophony. Compositional techniques include the use of chromatic harmonies and melodies, especially based on octatonic scales. The form of Movement I is ABA with *coda*; Movement II is ABA; Movement III is ABA with *coda*.

Unit 7: Form and Structure

SECTION	SUBSECTION	MEASURES	TONAL CENTER	EVENTS AND SCORING
Movement I				
A	Introduction	1-6	A minor	Intro based on last four measures of "Morning Dew"

		Measures	Key	Description
	Theme I	7-19		Two statements of main themes (repeat); second time countermelody in trumpet I; "boom-chuck" accompaniment
	Theme II	20-28	C major	Clarinet solo, thinner texture; return of introduction material
	Theme I	29-33	A minor	Return of Theme I, this time *tutti* forza
B	Theme III	34-42	A minor to A major	Piu Mosso; fanfare-like Theme III introduced by chimes in minor, brass play it in major key
A	Theme III	43-46	A minor	Four-bar final statement of Theme I
		47-49	G-flat to A minor	Three-bar codetta
Movement II				
A		1-17	C	The A section introduces four brief motives; characterized by short phrases, thin textures with solos in flute, horn, clarinets I and II, bass clarinet, bassoon, and euphonium; prevalence of chromaticism in harmonies and melodies
B		18-27		First part of binary B section; contrasts with A—longer, flowing phrases, fuller textures; melody (Theme B)

				based on motive found in flute solo in m. 8
		28-34		Second statement of Theme B
A		35-52	C	Recapitulation of material and style of A section; segues directly into Movement III

Movement III

A	Introduction	1-15	C minor	Begins with bongo solo; antiphonal statements of motivic material between instrumental groups
	Exposition	16-26		Theme introduced by clarinets, oboes
		27-40		Second statement of theme, *tutti*
B	Development	41-46	A-flat minor	Brief development of ascending arpeggio motive from introduction
		47-55	G	Development of fragments of Theme I
A	Recap.	56-69	C minor	Theme I return
	Coda	70-77		Brief coda based on Theme I, picardy third in last two measures, closing in C major

Unit 8: Suggested Listening

Norman Dello Joio, *Variants on a Medieval Tune*, *Scenes from the Louvre*, *Variations on a Theme by Haydn*

Unit 9: Additional References and Resources

Sadie, Stanley, ed. *The New Grove Dictionary of Music and Musicians.* London: Macmillan, 1980.

Smith, Norman and Albert Stoutamire. *Band Music Notes.* Lake Charles, LA: Program Note Press, 1989.

Contributed by:

Robert Spittal
Director of Bands
Gonzaga University
Spokane, Washington

Teacher Resource Guide

Sea Songs
Ralph Vaughan Williams
(1872–1958)

Unit 1: Composer

Ralph Vaughan Williams is known as one of the greatest modern composers after Sir Edward Elgar in England. He graduated from the University of Cambridge and Royal College of Music in London where he studied composition under Charles Hubert Parry and Sir Charles Villiers Stanford. In addition, he was a pupil of Max Bruch and Maurice Ravel, from whom he learned extensively the technique of orchestration. He was active at various periods of his career as organist, conductor, lecturer, teacher, editor, and writer. Throughout his life he displayed a keen interest in British folk songs. His research and collection of folk songs, obtained while traveling through many parts of England, influenced his own compositions as well as twentieth-century British music. His known compositions for wind band include *English Folk Song Suite, Flourish for Wind Band, The Golden Vanity March, Toccata Marziale, Variations for Brass Band,* and *Music for the Pageant of Abinger.*

Unit 2: Composition

This work is constructed with a folk-tune-like melody and eighth-note accompaniment. The simple minuet and trio-like ternary form with clear tonality is easy to follow. Divided into three sections—"Princess Royal," "Admiral Benbow," and "Portsmouth"—this work is approximately four minutes long.

Unit 3: Historical Perspective

This quick march was composed in 1924, and premiered at the British Empire Exhibition in April, 1924. The work is based on the songs "Princess Royal," "Admiral Benbow," and "Portsmouth." The composer transcribed this work for full orchestra in 1942.

Unit 4: Technical Considerations

The melodic lines have slur, *tenuto*, and *staccato* that require precise articulation for phrasing. Since the bass lines are often eighth-note figures with *staccato*, the phrase tends to be overplayed.

Unit 5: Stylistic Considerations

When the *tutti* appears, the balance between melodic lines and accompaniment should be carefully maintained since the accompaniment is often so dense that the melodic line is easily lost. The dynamic control throughout the piece is essential for a successful performance. For instance, after the brief strong introduction, the entire ensemble is suddenly directed to play *piano*. In the trio section, a great control of *crescendo* and *decrescendo* is demanded for the effective phrasing where the composer marked *cantabile*.

Unit 6: Musical Elements

Vaughan Williams uses both folk and march idioms in this composition. Bright melodic lines remind one of folk tunes while quick two-beat motives suggest a rhythm of march. Materials and keys are changed from section to section, such as a section where stated as "Princess Royal" (opening section). Harmony stays tonal with clear traditional harmonic directions. Dominant is often emphasized underneath the melodic lines. Similar to a traditional minuet and trio form, the trio section is contrasted with the first section with more flowing texture and horizontal lines. Continuous off-beat figures contribute to keep a sense of march throughout this trio section.

Unit 7: Form and Structure

The basic tonal structure is minuet and trio-like ternary form:
A—B (Trio)—A

SECTION	MEASURES	KEY	EVENTS AND SCORING
Section A	1-70		
Intro. statement	1-4	A-flat	Short opening statement on tutti
First Theme	5-12	A-flat	Melody on upper woodwinds
First Theme repeated	13-20	A-flat	Restatement of First Theme on flutes, piccolo, oboes, and cornets

Modified First Theme	21-32	A-flat	Brief introductory statement overlapped into modified first theme; melodic lines on piccolo, flutes, and cornets
Second Theme —A	33-39	C minor	Melody on clarinets and trumpets
Second Theme —B	40-47	C minor	Melody on flutes
First Theme	48-55	A-flat	Melody on saxophones and euphoniums
Modified First Theme	56-70	A-flat	Main lines on flutes, piccolo, and clarinets
Section B, New Theme	71-104 71-88	D-flat	Melody on clarinets
New Theme repeated	89-104	D-flat	Melody at octave higher on flutes, oboes, and clarinets

The repeated A section is an exact refrain of the opening A section.

Unit 8: Suggested Listening

Gustav Holst, *First Suite in E-flat*
Percy Grainger, *Gumsuckers March*

Unit 9: Additional References and Resources

Drickinson, Alan Edgar Frederic. *Vaughan Williams*. Irvine, California: Reprint Services, 1988.

Kennedy, Michael. *A Catalogue of the Works of Ralph Vaughan Williams*. New York: Oxford University Press, 1996.

Kennedy, Michael. *The Works of Ralph Vaughan Williams*. New York: Oxford University Press, 1964.

Pittman, Daniel Sayle, Jr. "Percy Grainger, Gustav Holst, and Ralph Vaughan Williams: A Comparative Analysis of Selected Wind Compositions." Doctoral diss., Memphis State University, 1979.

Rehrig, William H. *The Heritage Encyclopedia of Band Music*. Edited by Paul E. Bierly. Westerville, OH: Integrity Press, 1991.

Vaughan Williams, Ursula. *R. V. W.: A Biography of Ralph Vaughan Williams*. New York: Oxford University Press, 1964.

Contributed by:
Yoshiaki Tanno
Indiana University
Bloomington, Indiana

Teacher Resource Guide

A Solemn Music

Virgil Thomson
(1896–1981)

Unit 1: Composer

Virgil Thomson was born in Kansas City, Missouri. He attended Harvard University, and also studied with Nadia Boulanger in Paris (1921-22). From 1925-1932 he lived primarily in Paris, where he came into contact with *Les Six* and Gertrude Stein. In 1940, he moved to New York permanently, where he was music critic for the *Herald-Tribune* until 1954. After 1954, he devoted much of his time to composition, conducting, lecturing, and writing. Debussy and Satie were major influences on Thomson, but the subject matter and tunes in many of his works are in the American nationalist tradition. He is often grouped into the category of New York composers active in the mid-twentieth century, including Schuman, Mennin, and Persichetti. His output includes works for symphony orchestra, two operas, film music, and chamber music.

Unit 2: Composition

A *Solemn Music* was composed in 1949 on a commission from the League of Composers. It was dedicated to Richard Franco Goldman, and was composed for the Goldman Band. It is a single-movement work, approximately five minutes in length.

Unit 3: Historical Perspective

A *Solemn Music* is another of many works commissioned by the League of Composers for the Goldman Band. Other works commissioned by that body include pieces by Mennin, Persichetti, Schuman, and many other leading

American composers of the period. *A Solemn Music* is unique in the repertoire, and is unlike much of the band music from the 1940s and 1950s: it is atonal, with a somber, dirge-like mood that pervades the entire work. The fact *A Solemn Music* was commissioned for one of the Goldman Band's outdoor summer concerts, at which lighter numbers were usually performed, makes it an even more extraordinary piece in the repertory.

Unit 4: Technical Considerations

The work's demands on control and musical maturity are greater than its demands on technical prowess. Harmonies are very exposed, and intonation of vertical sonorities is critical. There are many instances of unison chromatic woodwind lines that will require attention to intonation. There is substantial emphasis on sensitivity of attacks and releases. Leaps of octaves and minor ninths in the trumpet/cornet parts require sufficient control.

Unit 5: Stylistic Considerations

This is slow, expressive music. Vertical harmonies move slowly and in a homophonic style over a slowly moving *basso ostinato*. The musical intensity changes slowly, and *crescendi/diminuendi* are extended over long phrases.

Unit 6: Musical Elements

This movement is a *passacaglia* with a form of ABA with *coda*. The texture is homophonic throughout, with slowly moving chords over an eight-measure, twelve-tone *basso ostinato*. Although the *basso ostinato* melody is twelve-tone, this is tonal music, with clearly distinguishable tonal centers.

Unit 7: Form and Structure

SECTION	PHRASE	KEY	THEME
A	I	C minor	A
	II	C minor	A
	III	C minor	A, B
	IV	C minor	A, B, C
	V	C minor	A, B, C
B	VI	E-flat major	A, B1
	VII	G major	A, B2
	VIII	F major	D—transition theme
A	IX	C minor	A, E—Recap
	X	C minor	A, E[1]

XI	C minor	A, B
XII	C minor	A, B
XIII	C minor	A, B, C
XIV	C minor	D, E—Transition
XV	E-C	Coda

Unit 8: Suggested Listening
Virgil Thomson, *Four Saints in Three Acts, The Mother of Us All*

Unit 9: Additional References and Resources
Dvorak, Thomas L., Robert Grechesky, and Gary Ciepluch. *Best Music for High School Band.* Brooklyn, NY: Manhattan Beach Music, 1993.

Hoover, Kathleen and John Cage. *Virgil Thomson, His Life and Music.* New York: T. Yoseloff, 1959.

Contributed by:
Robert Spittal
Director of Bands
Gonzaga University
Spokane, Washington

Teacher Resource Guide

Suite on Greek Love Songs
Henk van Lijnschooten
(b. 1928)

Unit 1: Composer

Henk van Lijnschooten was born March 28, 1928 in the Hague, Holland. As a young man, he learned to play the clarinet and the violin. He was a member of the Royal Military Band for twelve years and graduated with honors from the Royal Netherlands Conservatory in 1956. From 1957 to 1964, van Lijnschooten was director of the Royal Netherlands Marine Band. During his tenure he made numerous recordings of European wind band music. From 1965 until 1987 when he retired, van Lijnschooten held teaching positions in wind conducting and wind instrument studies at the conservatories of Rotterdam, Arnhem, and Utrecht. He remains active as a composer and is a frequent guest conductor throughout Europe, North America, and Japan.

Since the mid-1960s, van Lijnschooten has devoted much time to the composing of wind/band music. Writing either under his own name or the pseudonyms "Michael van Delft" and "Ted Huggens," van Lijnschooten has composed over one hundred works for wind players. Most of his wind music is suitable for American high school bands. His best-known works include *Rhapsodie Francaise, Rhapsody from the Low Countries, Royal Jubilee March,* and *Overture for Fun.*

Van Lijnschooten is the recipient of nearly a dozen awards, including Knighthood in the order of the Oranje Nassau, and the prize for Dutch Wind Music.

Unit 2: Composition

Suite on Greek Love Songs was composed in 1982 and published in 1984 by Molenaar, a well-known Dutch wind/band publisher. The composition was commissioned by the Amsterdam Foundation for the Arts.

The suite consists of four movements based on four Greek folk tunes from the eighteenth century. More specifically, these songs are called mockery songs, so called because the woman mocks the man's declaration of love. Van Lijnschooten chose to use the main theme for each folk tune and then compose original material to illustrate the text. The following texts are provided for each movement in the score:

> Movement I: *Vivace Ironico*
> *I had a love once. She heartlessly only mocked me. But, for me, she will always be the only love in the world.*

> Movement II: *Andante Expressivo*
> *When I was only a boy I fell in love with a shepherdess. She kissed me and said: You are too young to love. I am grown now, but she loves another, but I can never forget that kiss she gave me.*

> Movement III: *Allegretto Patetico*
> *Your eyes are black like olives. And when I kiss you I tremble on my knees and I feel weak and nervous.*

> Movement IV: *Presto*
> *When I enter the garden of the convent I see an apple tree and in it a nun. I tell her to come down that we might build a nest. But she picks the apples and throws them at me.*

Unit 3: Historical Perspective

Greece has only recently developed a national identity as a result of outside influences, such as World War II. Geography has played an important part in the development of Greek culture. The sea (from which no city is more than a hundred miles), the mountains (which cover three quarters of the country), and the fertile lowlands, have for centuries kept the villages and cities somewhat isolated from each other. Because of these geographical and other historical factors, Greek folk music and the many traditions that surround it, cannot be isolated into specific types and styles. The majority of Greek folk music is in dance form. Many of the folk songs and texts recount important historical events. There also appears to be a folk tradition of specific songs and dances for the wedding ceremony. As in any culture, love songs are also a popular subject.

Mixed and irregular meters are an important stylistic aspect of Greek folk music, particularly dance music. The time signatures 5/4, 6/4, 7/8 (3+2+2 and 2+2+3), 8/4 (6+2), and 9/4 (4+5) are common. Modality and melodic characteristics in the folk music have been freely borrowed for Byzantine ecclesiastical music.

Unit 4: Technical Considerations

The rhythmic and tempo requirements are paramount concerns in the performance of this music. The first movement is in a fast 7/8 time (grouped 3+2+2). The rhythms are not difficult, but for ensembles unaccustomed to irregular meter, it will take some rehearsal time. The final movement is a *presto* in 2/4 time. Finding the fastest controlled tempo will be the challenge. The other movements are rhythmically straightforward and should present few problems.

Generally speaking, the melodic and harmonic writing is composed in natural minor scales in the keys of C, D, and G. Sections in C, F, and A major are interspersed throughout the movements. Some sections of the movements are original material by van Lijnschooten. While the harmonic language remains tonal, the progressions are clearly twentieth century.

The ranges are well within the overall technical difficulty of the work. The first trumpet part plays one B-flat above the staff. The first trombone is required to play G above middle C. Overall, the part writing is idiomatic and should not pose any special concerns. The percussion score requires four to five players.

Unit 5: Stylistic Considerations

According to the *Encyclopedia Britannica*, the Greeks as a people possess a vitality "that makes other European counties seem tame, even dull by comparison." Therefore, this music should appropriately reflect a high level of energy and emotion. The tempo markings should be taken literally, and the first and last movements should be performed as fast as the group can play. Accents should be well marked. Dynamic contrast should be as wide as possible. Both the second and third movements are marked to be played expressively (note that *patetico* marked in the third movements is the Italian word meaning "with great emotion").

Unit 6: Musical Elements

Each movement of *Suite on Greek Love Songs* is based on an eighteenth-century melody that has been reworked to include new material by the composer. Each movement is composed in a freely adapted form that retains elements of song form and quasi-development of new material by van Lijnschooten. The rhythms and modalities that identify this as Greek folk music are retained. The melodic and harmonic material, added by van Lijnschooten to illustrate the texts, embrace a conservative twentieth-century aesthetic.

Unit 7: Form and Structure

Section	Measures	Key	Events and Scoring

Movement I: *Vivace ironico*, 7/8 (3+2+2) throughout

I had a love once. She heartlessly only mocked me. But for me she will always be the only love in the world.

Section	Measures	Key	Events and Scoring
A	1-16	G minor	Theme played in unison in upper winds and brass. Answered by full band every two measures. Key firmly established in eighth measure.
B	17-27	D minor	A series of short statements of new material passed between brass and woodwinds, ending with full band.
C	28-38	B-flat major/ G minor	A third idea utilizing parallel triads and moving between G minor and its relative major.
A	39-56	G minor	A theme presented in upper voices and accompanied by the full band.
Closing	57-59	G minor	Closing phrase.

Movement II: *Andante espressivo*, 4/4

When I was only a boy I fell in love with a shepherdess. She kissed me and said: You are too young to love. I am grown now, but she loves another, but I can never forget that kiss she gave me.

Section	Measures	Key	Events and Scoring
A	1-16	G minor	Theme played by first clarinets. Joined by other high woodwinds in the ninth bar.
B	17-29	C major	Second theme in first trumpets, with brass accompaniment. Modulating toward next key.
A	30-45	F minor	Final return of A theme presented in upper brass and woodwinds with full band accompaniment in key of F minor.

Movement III: *Allegretto patetico*, 2/4
Your eyes are black like olives. And when I kiss you I tremble on my knees and I feel weak and nervous.

A	1-8	F major	Four-bar introduction. Theme presented by solo trumpet with lightly scored brass accompaniment.
	9-16		Closing phrase consists of a two-bar idea played four times.
A	17-22		Short recapitulation of theme and closing phrase material.
B	23-30	C major	Sixteenth-note idea in upper woodwinds. Repeated with a different embellishment.
	31-38	E/G minor	Return of motives from A material. Moving to G minor.
C	39-42	G major	New material scored in upper woodwinds, with light accompaniment.
A	43-48		Closing phrase material from m. 9. Full band accompaniment begins at m. 45.
B	49-52	B-flat major	New material closely related to m. 27.
A	53-58		Closing phrase material.
A	59-70	C major	Recapitulation of A theme and closing phrase material for the last time.
B	71-78		Material closely related to mm. 49 and 27. *Stringendo* into final section.
Closing	79-85		Closing Section. Change of time signature to 3/8. Four measures of repeated material followed by grand pause. Movement ends on unison A.

Movement IV: *Presto*
When I enter the garden of the convent I see an apple tree and in it a nun. I tell
her to come down that we might build a nest. But she picks the apples and throws
them at me.

A	1-20	D minor	Unison upper brass and wood-wind statements with answers joined by the full band every two measures.
B	21-33	G minor	Tutti scoring of B section. Melodic minor scale is used to extend phrase ending.
A variant	34-49	D minor	Altered return of A section.
B variant	50-60	G minor	Altered return of B section. New closing material, a four-measure sequence.
Transition	61-64	D major	Canonic imitation in upper brass. Momentary tonilization of D major, the dominant of the next key center.
A variant	65-76	G minor	Opening A theme fragment presented in three-part canonic imitation. Followed by another motive fragment which repeated four times. Repeated cluster chords close this section.
C	77-112	G major	Extended transitional passage of new material similar to A theme. Syncopated rhythms contrast A material. Passage is in the dominant key of next section.
A	113-128	C minor	Return of A theme. Different scoring than first statement, with theme in woodwinds.
B	129-143	C minor	Return of B. Uses sequence pattern similar to m. 57. Modulates to G.

| A variant | 144-162 | G major | Duet between clarinet and flute with light percussion accompaniment. Vacillates between G major and minor. Very sparsely scored at the end of the phrase. |
| Closing | 163-169 (end) | G major/ G minor | Tutti playing of quarters, eighths, and G minor sixteenth notes. Starts in G major. The last two measures revert to G minor, the band playing a unison downward scale passage which is derived from the A theme. |

Unit 8: Suggested Listening

Henk van Lijnschooten, *Rhapsodie Française*, *Rhapsody from the Low Countries*, *Royal Jubilee March*

Unit 9: Additional References and Resources

Ammer, Christine. *Musician's Handbook of Foreign Terms*. New York: Schirmer Books, 1971.

Anastaplo, George. "Greece," *Encyclopedia Britannica: Macropedia*. 1983 edition.

Murphy, Howard. *Form and Music for the Listener*. Camden, NJ: Radio Corporation of America, 1945.

Rehrig, William. *The Heritage Encyclopedia of Band Music*. Westerville, OH: Integrity Press, 1991.

Rehrig, William. *The Heritage Encyclopedia of Band Music*. Volume 3 (Supplement). Westerville, OH: Integrity Press, 1996.

Sadie, Stanley, ed. *New Grove Dictionary of Music and Musicians*. London: Macmillan, 1980.

Smith, Norman and Albert Stoutmire. *Band Music Notes*. San Diego, CA: Kjos, 1979.

Suppan, Wolfgang. *Das Neue Lexikon des Blasmusikwesens (Dictionary of Band Music)*. Freiburg, Germany: Blasmusikverlag Schulz, 1988.

Contributed by:
Jay W. Gilbert
Doane College
Crete, Nebraska

Teacher Resource Guide

Three Chorale Preludes
William P. Latham
(b. 1917)

Unit 1: Composer

William P. Latham retired from teaching in 1984 after a long and productive career as a professor of composition and theory that spanned five decades. Today he resides in Denton, Texas, where he continues to catalog his large output of compositions. Upon completion of this task, Latham's entire collection of compositions will be housed in the University of North Texas music library.

William Latham was born in Shreveport, Louisiana on January 4, 1917. He was educated in Kentucky, Ohio, and New York, completing degrees in composition and theory at the Cincinnati College of Music (Ohio). Later, he was awarded a Ph.D. in Composition from the Eastman School of Music at the University of Rochester (New York). His principal composition teachers were Eugene Goossens and Howard Hanson.

Latham taught theory and composition at the University of Northern Iowa from 1946 to 1965, attaining the rank of Professor of Music in 1959. In 1965 he joined the faculty of the School of Music at North Texas State University as Professor of Music and Coordinator of Composition. He was appointed Director of Graduate Studies in Music in 1969. In 1978 he was promoted to the rank of Distinguished Professor of Music, the university's highest rank. Only seven other faculty members of the university had been so honored at that time. He retired from service at NTSU in June, 1984, and he was formally designated Professor Emeritus by the Board of Regents that November.

Latham has composed over one hundred works, about half of which have been published; many have been performed throughout the United States,

Canada, Europe, and Japan. He has received numerous awards and commissions. His orchestral works have been performed by the Cincinnati Symphony, the Eastman-Rochester Philharmonic, the Dallas Symphony, the St. Louis Symphony, and radio orchestras in Brussels, Belgium, and Holland, under such well-known conductors as Eugene Goossens, Howard Hanson, Thor Johnson, Anshel Brusilow, John Giordano, and Walter Susskind.

Unit 2: Composition

Although written in the early eighteenth-century style and based on familiar chorale melodies, *Three Chorale Preludes* are not arrangements of any existing chorale preludes. They are original compositions for band. Composed in 1956, the work has recently been reissued by Warner Publications (the original edition was published by Summy-Birchard Music). Three chorale melodies are used in the complete composition:

1. "Break Forth O Beauteous Heavenly Light"—melody by Johann Schop (died ca. 1665); text by Johann Rist.
2. "O Sacred Head Now Wounded"—by Hans Leo Hassler (1564-1612).
3. "Now Thank We All Our God"—melody likely by Johann Cruger (1598-1661); text by Martin Rinckart.

Although any single movement from the *Three Chorale Preludes* can be performed separately, Latham describes the entire work as a "complementary set" that should be performed in its entirety.

Unit 3: Historical Perspective

Chorale preludes are polyphonic settings of Protestant chorales (hymn tunes) for organ. Although the tunes on which they are based are generally well known to church congregations, composers' treatments of the tunes vary considerably. The inventive skill of the composer (or the lack of it) is displayed in the contrapuntal elaboration which surrounds the principal melody (referred to as the *cantus firmus*).

Perhaps the best known and best-loved chorale preludes are those of J. S. Bach, although literally hundreds of such compositions have been written by composers from the late sixteenth century up to the present day. Many transcriptions and arrangements of these have been made for various instrumental ensembles.

1. "Break Forth, O Beauteous Heavenly Light" is a Christmas hymn, first published in Rist's *Himmlische Lieder*, 1641. The tune had been used by many composers, including J. S. Bach in his *Christmas Oratorio* (1734).

2. "O Sacred Head Now Wounded" has had several text settings. It has come to be known as the Passion Chorale, although it was originally a love song, "Mein G'muth ist mir verwirret," by Hans Leo Hassler. As such, it appeared in his collection of secular songs called *Lustgarten neuer Teutscher Gesang* (1601). Bach used the tune five times in the *St. Matthew Passion* (1729.) There have been many settings by various composers, including Johannes Brahms and Felix Mendelssohn.

3. "Now Thank We All Our God" first appeared in Johann Cruger's *Praxis Pietatis Melica* (1647). Bach used the chorale in his Cantata No. 79, *Gott der Herr ist Sonn'und Schild* for Reformation Sunday.

Unit 4: Technical Considerations

"Break Forth, O Beauteous Heavenly Light"

Key Area: F major; modulation to C major

Meter and Tempo: 6/8 (in two) at an *Andantino* tempo (metronome marking=72-80)

Instrumentation Demands: oboe/bassoon duet; oboe solo

Special Demands: eighteenth-century ornamentation; flowing eighth-note lines at a slow 6/8-duple tempo

"O Sacred Head Now Wounded"

Key Area: D minor

Meter and Tempo: 3/4 at a *Poco Adagio* tempo (metronome marking=54-60)

Instrumentation Demands: no special requirements

Special Demands: long, sustained melodic lines for horns, baritone, alto and tenor saxophones

"Now Thank We All Our God"

Key Area: F major; modulation to C major

Meter and Tempo: 2/2 at an *Allegro giusto* tempo (metronome marking=96-100)

Instrumentation Demands: trombones have melody throughout the entire movement

Special Demands: low brass and low reeds must maintain *staccato* quarter-note pulse throughout movement

Unit 5: Stylistic Considerations

In all three movements the conductor must highlight the actual chorale tune when present. Often times in chorale prelude settings, the tune itself is not necessarily the most active or prominent line in the texture. All of the musicians must be aware of where the melody is found in every phrase.

"Break Forth, O Beauteous Heavenly Light"

The chorale tune is played by the flutes, piccolo, and cornets throughout. While the tune is predominantly dotted quarter notes, the underlying triplet feel of 6/8 time must be felt by melodic musicians. The fluid eighth-note lines in the middle ground parts (clarinets, oboe, alto saxophone) must always be played with a lilting feel.

"O Sacred Head Now Wounded"

The chorale tune is played by the horns, baritone, and alto and tenor saxophones. The long, sustained melodic lines reflect the somber yet sacred character of the movement. Melodic musicians must sustain air support to the release of every phrase to accomplish the sweeping melodic lines. The *tenuto* markings in the accompanying parts indicate that each quarter note must be articulated lightly and with an extra push of air, but never separated. The timpani must take great care to never cause the tempo to drag.

"Now Thank We All Our God"

The chorale tune is played by the trombones throughout, with the horns and saxophones joining in on the final "Amen." The melody is deliberately marked with an accent on every note, so each note must be played slightly separated. The low brass and reeds must maintain the *staccato* quarter-note pulse throughout the movement by listening to and imitating the timpani's sound. The lively middle ground accompaniment in the cornets, horns, and woodwinds must be played lightly in order to achieve the *giusto* character of the tempo marking.

Unit 6: Musical Elements

"Break Forth, O Beauteous Heavenly Light"

The first movement is a pastorale—a musical representation of shepherds and maidens on a hillside setting. Both the melodic and accompanying parts are fluid and flowing lines. The melody always comprises an antecedent and consequent phrase. The echoing effect in the accompanying parts (mm. 3-6 clarinets II and III, horns, and alto saxophone, for example) must be highlighted. The climax occurs on the downbeat of m. 49. The *ritardando* in the final four measures must occur naturally and not suddenly so that the final cadence does not disrupt the flowing character of the movement.

"O Sacred Head Now Wounded"

Latham describes the seconds movement as "a serious expression of angst." The music demands a dark sonority, especially in the louder phrases. The chorale tune must be played extremely sustained and

smoothly; the *diminuendo* at the ends of phrases must occur naturally and not as a matter of musicians running out of air. The climax
occurs at m. 40.

"Now Thank We All Our God"

    The final movement is jubilant—a stark contrast to the preceding
movement. Latham describes the movement as the "Lutheran
National Anthem," indicating both the joyous and proud qualities of
the chorale tune setting. The trombone melody must be prominent
in every phrase; the accompanying figures must never overpower the
tune itself. The quarter-note pulse in the low instruments and timpani must always be played on the front side of the beat, but without
rushing the tempo. The *ritardando* in the final four measures will
effectively prepare the climax to both the movement and the entire
composition, which is the final cadence. Allow the eighth-note figures in the woodwinds to create the slowing tempo.

Unit 7: Form and Structure

SECTION	MEASURES	
"Break Forth, O Beauteous Heavenly Light"		
A	1	
A	2	(on repeat)
B	29	
A′	42	
"O Sacred Head Now Wounded"		
A	1	
A	1	(on repeat)
B	17	
B′	33	
"Now Thank We All Our God"		
A	1	
A	3	(on repeat)
B	19	
A′	36	

Unit 8: Suggested Listening

J. S. Bach, *Das Orgelbüchlein*

J. S. Bach/arr. Reed, *Komm, Süsser Tod* ("Come, Sweet Death"); *Sleepers, Awake!*

Johannes Brahms/arr. Guenther, *Two Chorale Preludes*

Flor Peeters, *Chorale Preludes on Well-Known Hymns*

William Latham, *Court Festival, Brighton Beach*

Vincent Persichetti, *Chorale Prelude: O God Unseen*; *Chorale Prelude: So Pure the Star*

Ralph Vaughan Williams/arr. Walter Beeler, *Rhosymedre*

Unit 9: Additional References and Resources

Dirst, Matthew. "Tradition, Authenticity, and a Bach Chorale Prelude." *The American Organist*, 25:3 March 1991, 59-61.

Kopetz, Barry. "Interpreting William Latham's *Three Chorale Preludes*." *The Instrumentalist*, 49:2 September 1994, 36-49.

Maliepaard, Reinier. "How to Write a Chorale Prelude." *The American Organist*. 29:8 August 1995, 54-57.

Phillips, Gordon. *Articulation in Organ-Playing*. New York: Edition Peters, 1961.

Smith, Norman and Albert Stoutamire. *Band Music Notes*. Lake Charles, LA: Program Note Press, 1989.

Stinson, Russell. *Bach: The Orgelbüchlein*. New York: Schirmer Books, 1996.

Tusler, Robert L. *The Style of J. S. Bach's Chorale Preludes*. New York: Da Capo Press, 1968.

Contributed by:

Lawrence F. Stoffel

Assistant Professor of Music/Director of Huskie Bands

Northern Illinois University

De Kalb, Illinois

Teacher Resource Guide

Toccata

Girolamo Frescobaldi (1583–1643)
Gaspar Cassado (1897–1966)
Hans Kindler (1892–1949)
Earl Slocum (1902–1994)

Unit 1: Composer

Girolamo Frescobaldi, who supposedly composed the original source for this particular work, was born in Ferrara, Italy in 1583. Recognized as one of the most progressive and leading musical locations in Europe during this time, Ferrara provided and exposed Frescobaldi to many musical experiences at an early age. During his youth, he studied organ with the famous organist Luzzaschi, the court organist for the reigning duke, Alfonso II d'Este. At fourteen years of age, Frescobaldi became organist at the Accademia della Morte in Ferrara. In 1604, he attended the Accademia di S. Celia in Rome, and three years later became the organist of S. Maria in Trastevere. At the age of twenty-five, and widely recognized as one of the greatest organists and keyboard composers of the seventeenth century, he was appointed organist at St. Peter's in Rome. There is documentation stating that approximately 30,000 spectators witnessed his debut performance at St. Peter's.

This same year, 1608, Frescobaldi published his first volume of keyboard music consisting of fantasias, with remarkable counterpoint, and a book of madrigals. In 1615, a volume of toccatas and partitas was published showing his mastery of improvisation, incorporation of unusual harmonies, and turns of phrase. Frescobaldi's capriccios of 1624, along with his toccatas of 1627, demonstrate his maturity as a master craftsman, and represent the spirit of Italy in the early Baroque period.

He served as organist at St. Peter's until 1628, at which time he left Rome to become organist at the Florentine court of Ferdinand II de' Medici. During his six years of employment with the court in Florentine, Frescobaldi wrote two books of *Arie musicali* (published 1630), which consisted primarily of compositions for solo voice. In 1634, he returned to Rome and once again served as organist at St. Peter's until his death in 1643.

Gaspar Cassado was born in Barcelona, Spain in 1897. His father, Joaquin, was a notable musician who was an organist, composer, and choir director at several churches in Barcelona. Gaspar Cassado studied cello with March in Barcelona and with Casals in Paris, from the age of nine. A recognized performer and composer of cello works, he made several tours of Europe and the United States, making his debut in New York City in 1936. Several of Cassado's arrangements for cello include the *Mozart Horn Concerto* and the *Weber Clarinet Concerto*. Cassado composed the *Toccata for Cello and Piano— Like Frescobaldi* in 1925.

The most well-known controversy surrounding the original Frescobaldi *Toccata* involves Cassado and will be discussed in Unit 2.

Hans Kindler was born in 1892 in Rotterdam, Holland. He studied cello at the Rotterdam Conservatory where he received first prize for his performance on cello and piano in 1906. In 1911, he was appointed professor at the Scharwenka Conservatory in Berlin, Germany. At this time, he also performed as first cello with the Berlin Opera. For the next two years, he toured Europe performing on his cello. In 1914, he moved to the United States and became principal cellist with the Philadelphia Orchestra. Thirteen years following his arrival to Philadelphia, he became conductor of the Philadelphia Orchestra. In 1931, he organized and founded the National Symphony Orchestra in Washington, DC and remained involved with the symphony as conductor until his resignation in 1948.

In 1942, Hans Kindler, having heard a performance of the Frescobaldi *Toccata*, decided to transcribe the Cassado *Toccata* for orchestra.

Earl Slocum was born in Concord, Michigan on June 17, 1902. He attended the University of Michigan where he studied flute with John Wummer. Slocum was appointed director of bands at the University of North Carolina–Chapel Hill in 1933, and held this position until his retirement in 1967. Slocum retired to Florida and became the director of the Little Symphony in Deland, Florida. He was inducted into the American Bandmasters Association in 1941. He served as president of this prestigious organization in 1962, and was elected to life membership in 1986.

Slocum transcribed many orchestral works for band including the "Frescobaldi" *Toccata* , Elgar's *Enigma Variations*, and Liszt's *Piano Concerto in E-flat*. Earl Slocum contributed several "standards" to the band repertoire prior to his death in 1994.

Frescobaldi works transcribed for band:
Canzona in Quarti Toni, Kendor/arr. Anzalone, 1972
Galliard and Courante
    a. Rubank/arr. C. Johnson, 1957
    b. Saga/arr. E. Smedvig, 1981
Preambulim and Canzona, Kalmus/arr. Gray, 1981
Preludium and Fugue, Chappell/arr. L. J. Brunelli
Suite Ancienne, Staff/arr. M. Gardner, 1963

Unit 2: Composition

There are many different theories regarding the origin of Frescobaldi's *Toccata*. The first-known edition of the *Toccata* for band can be traced back to a work written for cello by Gaspar Cassado entitled *Toccata for Cello and Piano—Like Frescobaldi*. This work was copyrighted in 1925, and led to the orchestral adaptation in 1942 by cellist-conductor Hans Kindler. An article was published in the *American String Teacher* by Walter Schenkman entitled, "Cassado's Frescobaldi, A Case of Mistaken Identity Or Outright Hoax." John Burk, who was the program note writer for the Boston Symphony (1955), contacted Cassado regarding the original Frescobaldi source. The results of this conversation brought the following remarks from Burk:

> An inquiry sent to Mr. Cassado in Siena, Italy has just brought a reply. Mr. Cassado explains that the *Toccata* which he has arranged for cello was discovered by him in the archives of La Merced, the Conservatory of Music at Barcelona. The score bore the title *Toccata* and the name Frescobaldi, and was presumably a copy originally written for organ solo. Mr. Cassado adds: "I cannot be absolutely sure whether it was Frescobaldi or another author who did the rest, though in some passages one can easily find some characteristic 'frescobaldiane'."

According to Schenkman's article, one can refer to the twelve toccatas of the *First Book of Toccatas, Partitas,...* or to the eleven toccatas of the *Second Book of Toccatas, Canzonas,...* from which exist original Frescobaldi toccatas. Both of these collections of Frescobaldi's compositions were written and published in 1637, during Frescobaldi's lifetime, and all have autographed scores and are authentic. The theory that Frescobaldi did not compose this *Tocatta*, is plausible when Cassado's *Toccata* is compared with the books of toccatas from 1637. There are two distinctly different styles between Cassado's writing and Frescobaldi's.

CHARACTERISTICS OF THE COMPOSERS' TOCCATAS:

Frescobaldi
modality
contrapuntal
motivic
limited range of line
four independent parts (texture)
fragmented contrapuntal ideas

Cassado
tonality
homophonic
thematic
unlimited range of line
five and six parts
expansive counterpoint

In an article from *The Instrumentalist* magazine (May, 1992) entitled, "Frescobaldi's Toccata, An Interpretive Analysis," Barry Kopetz states that "three principles guided the style of early Baroque music: sectional form, variation in melodic procedures, and a distinct polarity between the bass line and the upper voices." These facts reinforce the idea that Frescobaldi in all likelihood did not provide the original material for this band transcription.

Another source attributes the original toccata to Muzio Clementi (1752-1832). In the book, *Music for Piano* by Freundlich and Friskin, there is reference to a 1920 article written by Benevuti which states that Mario Castelnuovo-Tedesco wrote the original work, which was later arranged for orchestra by Hans Kindler. Though there is uncertainty to the original source for this particular *Toccata*, this work has found its niche and has become one of the standard works in the band repertoire.

Unit 3: Historical Perspective

The word "toccata" is derived from the Italian word "toccare" meaning "to touch," and refers to performing a keyboard work characterized by "rhapsodic sections with sustained chord, scale passages, and broken figurations." The Frescobaldi *Toccata* for band is a work recognized as a repertoire classic with both technical and musical demands. According to *Band Music Notes*, the publisher Breitkopf and Härtel published a total of sixty-eight of Frescobaldi's compositions.

As a transcription of Kindler's orchestral adaptation, this work has been a mainstay for the band repertoire since its publication by Mills Music, Inc. in 1956. From an educational standpoint, this is a composition that most high school bands can perform (Grade Four). Since the work is credited to Frescobaldi, this is an opportunity for your band to perform a work characteristic of the Baroque period and to talk about the music from the seventeenth century.

Unit 4: Technical Considerations

According to *Music for Concert Band*, by Joseph Kreines:

The slow, sustained introduction (*Grave*, C minor, 4/4) requires

expressive *legato*, careful balancing of voices, and well-controlled intonation. The succeeding *Allegro* is lively and rhythmic; the horns state
the main theme along with intricate sixteenth-note passages in the
woodwinds. Later, the theme is taken up by the trumpets and trombones, and brought to a climax with a return of the opening section.
A fantasia section follows featuring flutes and clarinets playing thirty-
second-note scales while the oboe (cued trumpet) plays a sustained
ascending line. The work concludes with a final statement of the
Allegro in full band scoring.

Unit 5: Stylistic Considerations

In Barry Kopetz's "Interpretative Analysis" of the Frescobaldi *Toccata*, the
following guidelines are recommended:

> The challenge of the *Grave* is to maintain the musical tension at the
> tempo indicated. The ornamental grace notes in measure 10 need to
> be placed on the beat. This music also has many diminished fourths,
> tritones, and augmented triads, most often in the first inversion, thus
> creating tension. Adding a *ritardando* to measure 17 will help bring
> out the climactic moment of the *Grave*. A slight pause just prior to
> the *Allegro giusto* will bring closure to the opening section, and will
> help with setting up the new tempo. Horns and saxes, as well as all
> others, when playing this new motif need to use a "dah" syllable for a
> softer entrance as opposed to a harsher "tah" attack. Conductors
> should have an exact tempo and intention in mind to begin the
> *Tranquillo* in measure 52. Slow the *Pesante* at measure 57, not overdo-
> ing the accents in the cornets, trumpets, and baritone. A clear
> separation before the new tempo makes bridging the two sections—
> measure 61—relatively easy. Conduct the *Grave* in four, stretching
> out each pulse in measure 69. Once the tempo is established at mea-
> sure 80, the music plays itself. In the *Allegro giusto dramatic*, the
> fanfare concert E-flat in the first cornets and trumpet at measure 85
> adds a bit of bravura to this restatement and should be heard both
> here and again at measure 89 where it joyously heralds the piece's
> conclusion.

Unit 6: Musical Elements

Grave

The work begins with a *Grave* section in the key of C minor and in 4/4.
A *fermata* on a C minor chord sets the mood for this opening section. Theme
A begins at m. 2. The B theme occurs at m. 12, and a two-bar coda of theme
A returns at m. 18.

Allegro giusto

At m. 20, the *Allegro giusto* introduces theme A. Measure 31 to the *fermata* in m. 43 is the B theme. There is a transition at m. 39. A restatement of theme A in C minor occurs at m. 44. A transition takes place at the *Tranquillo*, m. 52. The *Pesante* at m. 57 is in A-flat major and is theme A prime. A development section follows from the *Allegro giusto* at m. 61. The *Grave* section in C minor is theme A (from the beginning). A transition takes place during the next six bars. Harmonically, there is an ascending line moving step-wise for the first four bars in the oboe and saxes. In the last two bars, the oboes and saxes are in *hemiola* with a descending E-flat major scale pattern over a pedal B-flat in the basses. Measure 80 is a transition in E-flat major very closely related to theme A. The recapitulation of the theme A occurs in m. 84 as the work concludes with a brilliant E-flat major chord.

Unit 7: Form and Structure

The *Grave* and *Allegro giusto* are treated as two entirely separate sections for this exercise. Therefore, Theme A in the *Grave differs* from Theme A in the *Allegro giusto*.

SECTION AND EVENTS	MEASURES	SCORING
Grave		
Fermata	1	
Theme A	2-11	
Theme B	12-17	
Coda (A)	18-19	
Allegro giusto		
Theme A	20-30	
Theme B	31-38	
Transition	39-43	
Restatement (A)	44-51	
Transition	52-56	*Tranquillo*
A′	57-60	*Pesante*
Development	61-68	*Allegro giusto*
Theme A (Grave)	69-73	
Transition	74-79	
Transition (related to theme A)	80-83	
Recapitulation (A, *Allegro giusto*)	84-93	

Unit 8: Suggested Listening

Sempre Italiano. Frescobaldi's Toccata. Tokyo Kosei Wind Orchestra, Frederick Fennell, conductor. Tokyo Kosei TKWO-804.

Educational Record Reference Library 8. Frescobaldi's Toccata. The University of Illinois Concert Band, Mark Hindsley, conductor. Franco Columbo Publication BP-108.

On Tour. Frescobaldi's Toccata. The University of Kansas Symphonic Band, Robert E. Foster, conductor. Audio House AHS 4672.

Stokowski-Shostakovich, Bloch, et al. *Il Secondo libro di toccate: Gagliard.* Leopold Stokowski, conductor. EMI Symphony of the Air.

Heritage—The Antiphonal Music of Gabrielli. Toccata in D and *Toccata in G.* Boston Symphony Orchestra Brass, E. Power Biggs, organist. Sony Classical Masterworks MHK 62353.

Verdi: Quattro pezzi Sacri/Ferenc Fricsay. Toccatas. Allessandro Scarlatti Orchestra, Sergia Celibidache, conductor. Laudis Records Suite STE 7001.

Frescobaldi: Begli orchi io non provo/Leller Coker. Toccate d'intavolatura di cimbalo: ballett(i). Ensemble de' Medici, Keller Coker, conductor. RCM 19401.

Castelnuovo-Tedesco, Ben Haim: Violin Concertos/Perlman. Concerto for Violin No. 2, op. 66. Israel Philharmonic Orchestra, Zubin Mehta, conductor. EMI Classics CDC 54296.

Castelnuovo-Tedesco, Guitar Concertos 1 & 2/Yamashita. Concerto for 2 Guitars, op. 201. London Philharmonic Orchestra, Kazuhito Yamashita, guitar, Leonard Slatkin, conductor. RCA Victor Red Seal 2RC 60355.

Clementi: Orchestral Works Vol. 1-2, Symphonies, Concertos. Concerto for Piano in C. ASV DCA 802. Philharmonia Orchestra, Pietro Spada, piano, Francesco D'Avalos, conductor.

Muzio Clementi: Piano Trios op. 27 & WO.6/Trio. Sonata (3) for Keyboard, Violin, and Cello, op.27, no.2 in D. Gabriel Faure Trio, Sergio Bonfanti, cello. Dynamics CDS 19.

Cassado: Works for Cello and Piano/Spanoghe, De Groote. Danse du diable vert. Andre De Groote, conductor. Talent Records DOM 291025.

In Memoriam Pau Casals. Requiebros. Barcelona Cellists Ensemble, Lluis Claret, cello. Auvidis Valois V4733.

Cello and Organ/Rostropovich, Tachezi. Toccata for Cello and Piano, Like Frescobaldi. Mstislav Rostropovich, cello. Teldec 2K 77308.

This work by Cassado is identical to the Frescobaldi Toccata for band version by Earl Slocum. It is exactly the same!

Unit 9: Additional References and Resources

Grout, Donald Jay. Edited by Claude V. Palisca. A History of Western Music. Third ed. NY: W.W. Norton & Co., 1980.

Kopetz, Barry E. "Frescobaldi's Toccata, An Interpretive Analysis." The Instrumentalist, May 1992.

Kreines, Joseph. Music for Concert Band. Tampa, FL: Florida Music Service, 1989.

Rehrig, William H. Edited by Paul R. Bierley. The Heritage Encyclopedia of Band Music. Vol. 2. Westerville, OH: Integrity Press, 1991.

Sabin, Robert. The International Cyclopedia of Music and Musicians. Ninth ed. New York: Dodd, Mead & Company, 1964.

Sadie, Stanley, ed. The New Grove Dictionary of Music and Musicians. London: Macmillan Publishers Limited, 1980.

Schenkman, Walter. "A Case of Mistaken Identity Or Outright Hoax." American String Teacher.

Smith, Norman and Albert Stoutamire. Band Music Notes. Rev. ed. San Diego, CA: Kjos, 1979.

Contributed by:

Robert E. Foster, Jr.
Associate Director of Bands
Texas Christian University
Fort Worth, Texas

Teacher Resource Guide

Trail of Tears

James Barnes
(b. 1949)

Unit 1: Composer

As a member of both the Band and Theory-Composition faculties at the University of Kansas, James Barnes teaches orchestration, arranging, and composition, and conducts the Wind Ensemble and Concert Band. He also teaches graduate conducting and band and orchestral literature classes. His numerous publications for concert band are extensively performed in the United States, Europe, and the Pacific Basin. His works have been performed at Tanglewood, Lincoln Center, Carnegie Hall, and the Kennedy Center in Washington, DC. Barnes has twice received the coveted American Bandmasters Association Ostwald Award for outstanding contemporary wind band music. He has been the recipient of numerous ASCAP Awards for composers of serious music, the Kappa Kappa Psi Distinguished Service to Music Medal, and numerous other honors and grants. He has completed three commercial compact disc recordings of his music with the famed Tokyo Kosei Wind Orchestra. In recent years he has been commissioned to compose works for all five of the major military bands in the Washington, DC area. Barnes has traveled extensively as a guest composer, conductor, and lecturer throughout the United States, Australia, and Japan. He is a member of the American Society of Composers, Authors, and Publishers, the American Bandmasters Association, and numerous other professional organizations and societies. Since 1984, his music has been published exclusively by Southern Music Company of San Antonio, Texas.

Unit 2: Composition

Trail of Tears, a Grade Four programmatic work, was composed in the summer of 1989. This tone poem for symphonic band was written to commemorate the 150th anniversary of the "Trail of Tears" (1839-1989). It uses several contemporary compositional techniques such as free-time with pseudo-improvisational solos, the tramping of feet, whispering, speaking, and shouting. It is published by Southern Music Company of San Antonio, Texas.

Unit 3: Historical Perspective

On *Trail of Tears*, the composer writes:

[This] tone poem for wind band describes the 150th anniversary of one of the most cruel, unjust, and embarrassing official actions in the history of the United States government. In 1838-39, federal troops rounded up many members of the "Five Civilized Indian Tribes" who were living in the Southeastern U. S.: Cherokees, Choctaws, Creeks, Chickasaws, and Seminoles. Despite a landmark decision rendered by the legendary Supreme Court Justice John Marshall stating that the members of these tribes could not be moved off their sovereign lands because of a prior treaty granting them this territory, troops were ordered to move all of these Native Americans by forced march in the dead of winter over 1,500 arduous miles to what was then known as "Indian Territory," now the eastern portion of the state of Oklahoma. On this tragic journey, more than 4,000 Native Americans perished from starvation, exhaustion, and exposure to the elements. It is an event that will be forever ingrained in the memory of our Native Americans; tragic sequences of events inflamed by political pressure, the greed of white settlers for more land, an irrational fear of Indians, and downright racial bigotry.

Unit 4: Technical Considerations

This piece employs some contemporary compositional techniques. The use of "Tramping Feet" is optional but encouraged if the piece is performed on a stage with a wooden floor. It also employs chant which should be rehearsed separately from the music. This will insure proper rhythm and inflection. Percussion writing includes snare drum, bass drum, suspended and crash cymbals, timpani, triangle, and bells. The use of the optional parts for xylophone, chimes, and vibraphone is highly encouraged. Ranges are comfortable for nearly all instruments, although flutes must be able to control sound and pitch in the lower register.

Unit 5: Stylistic Considerations

It is important to keep in mind the programmatic elements of this composition. The *adagio* section that begins the work should be played *sostenuto*

and with feeling as the composer is portraying the "non-aggressive nature of these 'Five Civilized Tribes,' who simply wished to be let alone and allowed to live in peace on their ancestral hunting grounds". The section following the *adagio*, marked *Allegro Vivo—ma non troppo*, should project strength as this "portrays the strife between the Indians and the encroaching settler." The closing of the work should be played in a sustained and powerful style, depicting the agony of the march itself. The chant included in this section must be taken seriously and should emulate the "recitation of a mournful poem in the Cherokee language."

Unit 6: Musical Elements

The ensemble is required to perform passages that are both lyrical and somewhat technical. Proper articulation and close adherence to dynamics will produce a most pleasing performance. Dynamics change rapidly within nearly every musical line. The conductor must balance rhythmic parts against the melodic elements in each section. A majority of the work is in D minor but the close of the work modulates to D major. It uses two principal themes and continually develops them throughout.

Unit 7: Form and Structure

The piece follows no formal structure. It is a tone poem for concert band that paints a musical portrait of this event in history.

Unit 8: Suggested Listening

James Barnes, *Spitfire Overture, Yorkshire Ballad*
Andrew Boysen, *I Am*
Carl Busch, *A Chant from the Great Plains*
James D. Ployhar, *Variations on a Sioux Melody*

Unit 9: Additional References and Resources

Ehle, John. *The Trail of Tears: The Rise and Fall of the Cherokee Nations*. New York, NY: Doubleday, 1988.

Walters, Elizabeth L. and Joan Thatcher. *The Trail of Tears: An American Indian Experience*. Valley Forge, PA: Fund of Renewal, 1974.

Additional notes by James Barnes.

Contributed by:

Rodney C. Schueller
Indiana University
Bloomington, Indiana

Teacher Resource Guide

Watchman, Tell Us of the Night
Mark Camphouse
(b. 1954)

Unit 1: Composer

Mark Camphouse is Associate Professor of Music and Director of Bands at Radford University in Virginia. A native of Chicago, Camphouse received his formal musical training at Northwestern University. His active guest conducting schedule has taken him to eighteen states, Canada, and Great Britain. His principal commissions include the United States Marine Band, the United States Army Band, the Florida Bandmasters Association, and the St. Louis Youth Wind Ensemble. Some of his other principal works for band are *Elegy, A Movement for Rosa, Tribute,* and *To Build a Fire.*

Unit 2: Composition

Watchman, Tell Us of the Night was commissioned by the St. Louis Youth Wind Ensemble, Milton Allen, Conductor. The work was written in 1994 and received its premiere in 1995. It was written as part of a project to commission works that represent some aspect of the human situation. Camphouse wrote *Watchman, Tell Us of the Night* as a musical tribute to survivors of child abuse. It is often dream-like in nature, as seen through the eyes of a child. The work is intended to be a portrait of the loneliness, loss of innocence, and yet enduring hope, and not as a graphic portrayal of abuse. The title is taken from John Bowring's 1825 text setting of George Elvey's church hymn, also known as the Thanksgiving Hymn, "Come Ye Thankful People Come."

Unit 3: Historical Perspective

Camphouse did extensive research into the topic of child abuse with the

assistance of the Department of Health and Human Services, and the National Center for Child Abuse and Neglect. It is amazing that the problem of abuse is so widespread and affects so many people. The impact on a child who has suffered abuse can reach far into the individual's adult life. But there is hope, and it is this hope that drew the composer to write this composition.

Unit 4: Technical Considerations

The work calls for four percussion groups (five players minimum, six preferred), and also an acoustical grand piano. The percussion writing is complex. There are numerous exposed solo lines including piano. There is the use of a *senza misura* (without measure) section with a repeating pattern for the ensemble. There is the use of vocalization for select individuals during the closing section of the work. Although not marked in the score, the composer intended for the vocal character to be that of *falsetto* to depict the child-like quality. There are subtle instrumental combinations and groupings that call for close attention to balance and blend. There are transparent textures that are frequently juxtaposed. The hymn section calls for full ensemble moving in a homophonic texture, with precise breath marks for phrasing. There are numerous meter changes and subtle changes in tempo and dynamics.

Unit 5: Stylistic Considerations

Stylistically, Camphouse writes in a very orchestral manner, and intends for lines to be performed *molto sostenuto* (full bow). He chooses instrumental solo lines and combinations with much thought and careful consideration of each color and texture. There are no notes written without some relation to the overall scheme. Often there are tone clusters or chords that are harmonic versions of melodic ideas or motives. The composer uses numerous performance directions throughout the work such as *grave, stringendo molto, subito molto allargando,* freely, and *trattenuto*. These are all specifically chosen to create moods or sounds. The concept is long, sustained, flowing, melodic lines. There is a recurring child-like playful theme throughout. Each time it appears, be careful of overall balance in relation to the rest of the ensemble.

Unit 6: Musical Elements

The work is made up of the hymn, child-like theme, and fragmentation of each in textural variation. Throughout the work the ensemble is called upon to flow in and out of textural settings. The three sections of the piece call for three distinct moods. There are numerous dynamic shifts which allow the themes to change from being in the background to moving forward. The work calls for individual expression, solid ensemble playing in homophonic textures, and control of both rhythmic and dynamic variation.

Unit 7: Form and Structure

According to Camphouse, he does not compose with a particular form in mind. The compositional technique he uses consists of a long period of time in which ideas are developed and sketched, instrumental combinations are chosen, and individual themes and motives are realized. There are three distinct sections which are clearly divided by double bars. The first section lasts until m. 103 and is intended to be a dream-like section. The second section is mm. 103 to 214. This section includes the homophonic hymn section and the greatest use of rhythmic ideas. The final section is a brief ethereal section from mm. 214 to the end. The first full statement of the hymn does not occur until some thirty-eight measures into the middle section. The child-like theme first appears in the trumpet in m. 27.

Unit 8: Suggested Listening

Keystone Wind Ensemble, Jack Stamp Conducting, Citadel Records, 1997.
Orchestral works of Samuel Barber and Aaron Copland
Symphonies of Ralph Vaughan Williams

Unit 9: Additional References and Resources

Battisti, Frank and Robert Garofalo. *Guide to Score Study*. Ft. Lauderdale, FL: Meredith Music Publications, 1990.

"A Nation's Shame: Fatal Child Abuse and Neglect in the United States." A report of the United States Advisory Board on Child Abuse and Neglect, April 1995. United States Department of Health and Human Services, 1-800-394-3366, 200 Independence Avenue SW, Washington, DC 20201.

Kostka, Stefan and Dorothy Payne. *Tonal Harmony*. New York: McGraw-Hill, Inc., 1995.

Weisberg, Arthur. *Performing Twentieth-century Music: A Handbook for Conductors and Instrumentalists*. New Haven and London: Yale University Press, 1993.

Contributed by:

Otis French
U.S. Army Field Band
Ft. Mead, Maryland

Grade Five

Teacher Resource Guide

Al Fresco

Karel Husa
(b. 1921)

Unit 1: Composer

Karel Husa maintains a world-renowned career as a distinguished conductor and composer of many media. Born on August 7, 1921 in Prague, part of what is now known as the Czech Republic, Husa studied at the Prague Conservatory and the Academy of Music. Upon the completion of his studies in the former Czechoslovakia, he moved to the flourishing musical environment of Paris where he received degrees from the *Ecole Normale de Musique* and the Paris National Conservatory. Husa's long list of distinguished teachers includes Nadia Boulanger, Jaroslav Ridky, and Arthur Honneger. Husa emigrated to the United States and became a naturalized citizen in 1959. On the faculty of Cornell University since 1954, Husa maintained an active and successful academic career until his retirement in 1992. During his tenure at Cornell, Husa also guest lectured at Ithaca College regularly from 1967 to 1986. His honors and awards are numerous. In 1969, he won the Pulitzer Prize for his *String Quartet No. 3*. Husa also received awards from the American Academy and Institute of Arts and Letters, a Guggenheim Foundation Fellowship, Koussevitzky Foundation commissions, the Lili Boulanger Award, the Czech Academy for Arts and Sciences Prize, and grants from the National Endowment for the Arts and UNESCO. Husa's latest work for winds, *Les Couleurs Fauves*, was premiered during the 1996 Midwest Band and Orchestra Clinic.

Unit 2: Composition

Al Fresco is a work that juxtaposes the harmonic conventions of the twentieth century with traditional form and flowing, beautiful melody. It is well balanced and beautiful, yet at the same time shocking and violent. Perhaps the nature of the artwork that inspired the piece is the reason. In the opening note of the score, the composer writes:

> *Al Fresco* has no programmatic content. However, the title indicates my admiration for the art of painting, especially mural painting on wet plaster. I have always been greatly moved by the forceful, even grandiose and rough, mysterious pictures dealing with primitive life, war, and pageantry.

Unit 3: Historical Perspective

Al Fresco was commissioned in 1975 by the Ithaca College Band as the first of the Walter Beeler Commission Series. It was premiered by Ithaca on April 19, 1975 at the Music Educators National Conference convention in Philadelphia with Husa conducting.

Interestingly, a small amount of the material for *Al Fresco* was used in an earlier work called *Three Frescos for Orchestra* (1946). This work was confiscated by the Czech government.

Unit 4: Technical Considerations

Al Fresco appears more difficult than it actually is. The players must familiarize themselves with a few twentieth-century notational devices like unspecified pitches and quarter-tone accidentals. Husa clearly explains these in the forward of the score. Husa also states the following in the score's foreword:

> This work is intended to be performed by young, high school musicians. Some of the passages in mm. 219-238 may seem difficult and although the pitches and rhythms are written out, they do not need to be played exactly. The performers are given freedom in expressing the ascending as well as descending lines and may perform the speed of the rhythmic figures according to their abilities. The conductor may be helpful in suggesting easier possibilities. Also, it is necessary that the conductor clearly indicate the tempi of mm. 235, 236, and 239, so that all those who are playing the *ad lib* passage can enter again in the tempi of the strict measures.

Clearly, Husa, while striving for precision, is emphasizing effect. It should be noted that there are several points where the reeds are asked to tongue quickly and with precision. The ranges are not outrageous, although the horns are asked to play a couple quick scalar passages to B-flat and C-sharp. Intervals in the low brasses are wide and atonal, so some drill will be needed. Overall, however, *Al Fresco* is quite playable.

Unit 5: Stylistic Elements

Close attention should be paid to dynamics and articulation. There are moments of sweeping lyricism as well as dry and brittle accompaniments. Attention to the details will help to intensify the drama. *Pianissimos* should be whisper quiet and *fortissimos* deafening, within good taste, of course. *Staccatos* should be quite short in places for the desired effect. At many points throughout the piece, traditional "classical" style is surprisingly effective in much of the figuration. It gives the work a haunting expressiveness.

Unit 6: Musical Elements

Al Fresco is thematically linked and grows and develops with an efficient organization. The opening begins with the marimba rolling a *ppp* C-sharp which the third trombone joins. The trombone expands through a slow *glissando* to a D. This type of handing off continues and the first theme grows and is stated completely for the first time by the flute. The curious conductor could literally spend hours on a motivic treasure hunt that will yield numerous examples of themes and accompaniments that grow from each other. Themes should be very expressive and the conductor should look for the tension and arrival points. Some of the phrases are quite long and diagramming them is often helpful.

Texture is also a very important element. Clarity should be sought and balance is critical. In most cases, Husa is striving for an overall effect and he gives clear indications on how sections should be balanced.

Unit 7: Form and Structure

Though a twentieth-century work tonally, *Al Fresco* is in *sonata-allegro* form reminiscent of the first movement of a seventeenth-century symphony. The introduction is slow and gradually lays out the thematic material of the work. The *allegro* begins at m. 37 and contains two primary themes. The B theme enters at m. 89 and progresses through some transitional material to the development section at m. 120. There is a short, but dramatic recapitulation at m. 219 leading to a *coda* at m. 238. The piece winds down and ends as it began. It literally starts quietly, gradually building its themes and sections. At the climax, the work is very violent and dramatic, but it soon gives way and recedes into softness again. *Al Fresco* is a magnificent arch both formally and texturally. Like many of his Eastern European contemporaries, Husa's music develops as much by texture as it does anything else. Each section is episodic in nature, but all themes tend to be quite interrelated. Though this is an oversimplification, the basic formal schematic may be expressed like so:

SECTION AND EVENTS	MEASURES
Introduction	1-19
A theme introduced	20-36
Exposition	37-45
Episode 1	46-68
Episode 2	69-79
Episode 3 with transition	80-88
B theme	89-111
Transition	112-119
Development A theme	120-132
(Episode 1)	133-152
(Episode 2)	153-157
B theme	158-191
Transition	192-218
Recap (aleatoric)	219-235
Climax	236-238
Coda—A theme	239-264
B theme	265-270
Intro material	271-281

Unit 8: Suggested Listening

Karel Husa, *Al Fresco, Music for Prague 1968, Apotheosis of This Earth, Concerto for Alto Saxophone, Smetana Fanfare, Concerto for Wind Ensemble, Les Couleurs Fauves*

Gyorgy Ligeti, *Atmospheres*

Krzystof Penderecki, *Threnody in Memory of Victims of Hiroshima*

Any Haydn or Mozart symphony (for a classical example of sonata form)

Unit 9: Additional References and Resources

Baker, Theodore. "Karel Husa," *Baker's Biographical Dictionary of Musicians.* Sixth ed. Revised by Nicholas Slonimsky. New York: Schirmer, 1984.

Corporon, Eugene. Unpublished personal files. Denton, TX.

Randel, Don Michael, ed. *The New Harvard Dictionary of Music.* Cambridge, MA: Harvard University Press, 1986.

Smith, Norman and Albert Stoutamire. *Band Music Notes*. San Diego: Neil Kjos, 1979.

Watkins, Glenn. *Soundings*. New York: Macmillan, 1988.

Contributed by:

Edwin Powell
Director of Bands
McLennan Community College
Waco, Texas

Teacher Resource Guide

American Salute
Morton Gould
(1913–1996)

transcribed by
Philip J. Lang (b. 1911)

Unit 1: Composer

Morton Gould published his first composition *Just Six* when he was six years old. Two years later, he began playing for radio broadcasts, and he began to study theory and composition at the Institute of Musical Arts (now the Juilliard School). After leaving the Institute, Gould's most important teachers were Abby Whiteside (piano) and Vincent Jones (composition). During the Depression, the teenager worked in New York's vaudeville and movie theaters. Gould became staff pianist at Radio City Music Hall at age eighteen. By the age of twenty-one, he was conducting for WOR Mutual Radio. There, Gould's music, combining classical and popular idioms, gained national prominence. During the 1940s, Gould moved to CBS, reaching an audience of millions. At the same time, his symphonic music was being recorded and performed by Leopold Stokowski, Arthur Rodzinski, and Arturo Toscanini. Gould composed in many genres, including music for Broadway, films, television, and ballet. Always open to new styles, he composed a *Tap Dance Concerto* in 1952, and in the '90s he incorporated a rapper/narrator into *The Jogger and the Dinosaur*. Gould composed more than a dozen works for band, including his *West Point Symphony* (1952).

Gould received the Kennedy Center Honors Award from President Clinton in 1994 and the Pulitzer Prize in Music for *Stringmusic* in 1995. In 1986 he was elected to the American Academy of Arts and Letters. In addition, Gould received twelve Grammy nominations and a Grammy award in 1966 for his recording of Charles Ives's music with the Chicago Symphony.

After long service on the board of the American Society of Composers, Authors, and Publishers (ASCAP), his colleagues elected him to its presidency in 1986, a post he held until 1994. However, his favorite musicians were students; he was a frequent guest conductor of school bands and orchestras and lecturer on the art of composition.

Philip J. Lang transcribed *American Salute* for band. Lang, Gould's colleague at WOR Mutual Radio, has orchestrated more than seventy Broadway musicals, and also has arranged for Arthur Fiedler, Andre Kostelanetz, and Alfred Wallenstein.

Unit 2: Composition

During World War II, Gould composed several settings of marching tunes from the allied nations. These were to be performed by a full orchestra on a March, 1943 United States Government Radio program. The tunes included the *Red Cavalry March* (from the USSR), *New China March*, and *American Salute* (variations on *When Johnny Comes Marching Home*). Gould composed *American Salute* overnight, starting at dinner time and finishing it in time for a 9:00 a.m. broadcast. In the same year, Philip J. Lang prepared the band transcription under the composer's supervision. *American Salute* is approximately four and a half minutes long.

Unit 3: Historical Perspective

Patrick Gilmore (1829-1892), the "Father of the Concert Band," published "When Johnny Comes Marching Home" in 1863 under the pseudonym "Louis Lambert." Whether or not the Irish native Gilmore actually composed the song is a matter of controversy. Some believe its jig-like rhythm reveals it to be of Irish folk origin.

According to Gould, "In the 1920s and 1930s, even if your works were performed by symphony orchestras, it was unlikely that you would receive any kind of fee....For that reason I chose to shape part of my career around income-producing possibilities, and at that time radio was an important one. I became active in live radio, conducting programs of light music that I arranged and sometimes composed." "Light music" in the early '40s meant incorporating elements of jazz, folk, and military band music into the sound of the symphony orchestra. The text "When Johnny Comes Marching Home" carried hope to Gould's World War II home-front audience. Although *American Salute* could have remained a period piece appropriate only for wartime use, it has become a light classic, one of the most often-performed works by bands and orchestras alike.

Unit 4: Technical Considerations

Although the parts are heavily cross-cued, it is difficult to do justice to the work without at least two of the three bassoons called for in the score.

(This transcription substitutes the third bassoon for the bass clarinet in the original orchestral score.) The entire first variation (letter C) is devoted to an English horn solo. An alto saxophone can substitute here. Cornets and trumpets, horns, and trombones all need straight mutes.

The percussion parts call for four timpani, snare and bass drums, steel bells, xylophone, marimba, chimes, large gong, and cymbals. Three musicians can cover the parts. Although the orchestral score calls for harp, piano, and guitar, it would not be particularly advantageous to use them in the band transcription.

While the ranges are not extreme, the score calls for virtuoso tonguing and fingering in all parts. The piece changes key for each variation. It uses the following keys: E minor, D minor, F minor, E-flat minor, and G minor. At letter G (variation four), the key signature changes to no flats or sharps in all parts. Performers see the accidentals as they go.

Errata

All parts: key signatures are shown only where they change. They are not repeated at the beginnings of staves.

MEASURES	AFTER	BEAT	CORRECTION
First Flute:			
9	Beginning	1	Four-measure rest
2	F	1	"simile" (staccato)
Second Flute:			
6	D	2	Add reminder flats
2	F	4	Change final D to fourth-space E-flat
7	I	2	">"
5-6	P		"8va"
C Piccolo:			
7	I	2	">"
1	M	3	Make eighth note dotted
E-flat Clarinet:			
7	I	2	">"
10	L	1	Slur into downbeat of M
First B-flat Clarinet:			
1	Beginning	1	["tacet"]
2	C	1	"tutti"
6	G	3	">"
4	P		Change "ff" to "fff"

MEASURES	AFTER	BEAT	CORRECTION
Second B-flat Clarinet:			
1	beginning	1	["tacet"]
2	C	1	"tutti"
2	C	2	Add dot to quarter rest
4	D	3	Replace rests with fourth-space D tied over quarter
2	F	4	Change final E to first-space F
7	I	2	">"
1-2	J		Divisi pitches difficult to read
Third B-flat Clarinet:			
4	D	3	Replace rests with third-line B-flat tied-over quarter
7	I	2	">"
2	P	1	Tie over fourth-space E from previous measure
3	H	1, 3	Change third-space C to C-sharp
7	H	1, 3	Change third-space C to C-sharp
E-flat Alto Clarinet:			
3	H	1, 3	Change second-line G to G-sharp
7	H	1, 3	Change second-line G to G-sharp
B-flat Bass Clarinet:			
8	C	4	">"
9	C	1, 2, 3	">"
3	H	1, 3	Change middle C to C-sharp
7	H	1, 3	Change middle C to C-sharp
12	H	2	Change D below staff to D-sharp
First Oboe:			
4	D	3	Replace rests with C above staff tied-over quarter
5	D	3	Reminder flats

MEASURES	AFTER	BEAT	CORRECTION
6	D	3	Reminder flats
7	I	2	">"

Second Oboe:

4	D	3	Replace rests with A-flat above staff tied-over quarter
5	D	3	Reminder flats
6	D	3	Reminder flats
7	I	2	">"

First Bassoon:

8	C	4	">"
9	C	1, 2, 3	">"
2	H		">" on every beat
3	H		"simile"
1	1		Move "pp" to beat 2

Second Bassoon:

8	C	4	">"
9	C	1, 2, 3	">"
2	H		">" on every beat
3	H		"simile"
1	L	1	Move "pp" to beat 2

First E-flat Alto Saxophone:

3	H	1, 3	Change second-line G to G-sharp
7	H	1, 3	Change second-line G to G-sharp
7	I	2	">"

Second E-flat Alto Saxophone:

3	H	1, 3	Change second-line G to G-sharp
7	H	1, 3	Change second-line G to G-sharp
7	I	2	">"

B-flat Tenor Saxophone:

3	H	1, 3	Change third-space C to C-sharp
7	H	1, 3	Change third-space C to C-sharp

MEASURES	AFTER	BEAT	CORRECTION

E-flat Baritone Saxophone:

3	H	1, 3	Change second-line G to G-sharp
7	H	1, 3	Change second-line G to G-sharp
1	J	2, 3	Change third-space Cs to C-sharps

First B-flat Cornet:

12	I	1	"Hand in Bell"
13-14	K		decrescendo
4	M		"tutti"

Second B-flat Cornet:

12	I	1	"Hand in Bell"
4	J	4	Change third-line B-sharp to fourth-line D-sharp
13-14	K		decrescendo
4	M		"tutti"

Third B-flat Cornet:

| 10 | I | 1 | staccato dot |
| 12 | I | 1 | "Hand in Bell" |

First and Second B-flat Trumpets:

| 12 | I | 1 | "Hand in Bell" |

First and Second Horns in F:

9	C	4	"open"
2	H		">" on all notes
3	H		"simile"

Third and Fourth Horns in F:

2	H		">" on all notes
3	H		"simile"
1	I	1	Change Fourth Horn first-space F to first-line e

First Trombone:

2	H		">" on all notes
3	H		"simile"
6	K	4	"ff"
13-14	K		decrescendo

Second Trombone:

| 2 | H | | ">" on all notes |

MEASURES	AFTER	BEAT	CORRECTION
3	H		"simile"
10	O	3	Change D to C above staff

Third Trombone:

2	H		">" on all notes
3	H		"simile"

Baritone (Bass Clef):

6	G	1	">"
2	H		">" on all notes
3	H		"simile"

Baritone (Treble Clef):

6	G	1, 3	">"
2	H		">" on all notes
3	H		"simile"

Basses:

2	L	4	"Bass Clarinet"

String Bass:

5	E	4	slur

SCORE

MEASURES	AFTER	STAFF	BEAT	CORRECTION
1-9	Beginning	1		"piccolo 8va"
1-2	Beginning	2		Add Ds below the staff to all chords
7-8	Beginning	2		Add Ds below the staff to all chords
5	A	note	2	"Steel bells" Add third-line B and B above treble-clef staff
5	A	note	4	Add second-space A and A above treble-clef staff
6	A	note	2	Add second-line G and G above treble-clef staff
7	A	note	4	Add first-space F-sharp and top-line F-sharp

Measures	After	Staff	Beat	Correction
7	B	3	4	Horns "(muted)"
6-8	C	1		slur
3	C	1	1	Add fourth-line D whole note "Bells"
6	C	1	1, 3	"oboes: quintuplets"
9	C	3	1	Move "Basses, Bar., Horns. Sax's [sic], Alto + Bass Cls." to beat 4
9	D	1		"Piccolo 8va first flute"
5	D	2	4	Change B below staff to B-flat; change E below staff to E-flat
2	E	3	4	Change B to B-flat above staff
5	E	2	1	Change quarters to dotted quarters
6	E	1	1	"Cornets" add D below staff and first-space F and fill rest of measure with rests
6	E	2	1	"Marimba"
9	F	1	3	Change fourth-space Cs to third-line B-double-flats
9	F	3	1	"Clarinets 2-3 8va"
11	F	1	1	"Clarinets 8va"
11	F	1	1	"Clarinets 8va"
11	G			"Key change to no flats in all parts"
11	G	1		"Piccolo 8va First Flute"
11	G	3	2	Slur into next measure

MEASURES	AFTER	STAFF	BEAT	CORRECTION
11	G	3	1, 2	Add cymbal crashes
4	G	2	2-4	crescendo
5	G	1	1	"Clarinets 8va"
6	G	1		"All woodwinds"
6	G	3	1, 2	Add cymbal crashes
6	G	2, 3	2	">"
8	G	3	1	"Horns 8va"
10	G	3	4	"Baritone" add fourth-space E-flat eighths
11	G	3	3	"Bassoons"
11	G	3	1	Add fourth-space E-flat quarter
11	H	1		"Piccolo 8va First Flute"
3	H	2	1	Add reminder natural to third-line B
3	H	3		"simile"
4	H	2	4	Change B-natural above staff to B-flat
7	H	2	1	Add reminder natural to third-line B
9	H	2	2	Change B-natural above staff to B-flat
12	H	1	2	"Oboes"
12	I	1		"Piccolo 8va First Flute"
12	I	3	1, 3	Add cymbal crashes
12	I	3	1	"f"
3	I	3	2	Add second-space C half note

Measures	After	Staff	Beat	Correction
4	I	3	1	Add second-space C quarter
5	I	1	1	"Alto Clarinet 8va basso, Bass Clarinet 15ma basso"
5	I	3	1	Add D below staff quarter
5	I	3	1, 3	Add cymbal crashes
7	I	1	2	">"
7	I	3	2	Add second-space C quarter
10	I	1	1	"Saxophones 8va basso"
10	I	3	1	"Horns"
1-2	J	2		Add Third Clarinet pitches (see part)
2	J	1		Add reminder natural to third-line B
2	K	2	4	Add reminder natural on first-line space E
2	K	3	4	Add reminder natural on fourth-space E
2	K	3	1	Add third-line D quarter
13-14	K	1		decrescendo
3	K	3	1	"Chimes"
5	K	3	1	"Chimes"
5	L	2	1	Add G below staff
10	L	1	4	Slur into M
10	M	1		"piccolo 8va first flute"
10	M	3	1	"Bass Clarinet"

MEASURES	AFTER	STAFF	BEAT	CORRECTION
4	M	2	4	stem down chord: staccato dot
7	M	1	4	Add G below staff
7	M	3	4	"Bassoons, Alto, and Bass Clarinets, Saxophones"
7	M	3	4	Add first-line G, change FF to low GG in ledger lines below staff
8	M	1	1-4	Add As below staff
8	M	3	1-4	Add first-line Gs, change FFs to low GGs in ledger lines below staff
8	N	1		"Piccolo 8va First Flute"
9-11	O	3		Add Timpani part (see part)
7-8	O	1		trill to B-flat over tied note
9-10	O	3		Add second Horn and Baritone parts (see parts)
2	O	1		"Piccolo, E-flat Clarinet 8va"
3	O	3	1, 3	Add third-line D
4	O	3	1, 3	Add third-line D
5	O	3	1, 3	Add third-line D
6	O	3	1	Add third-line D
11	O	3	1	Add F below staff dotted quarter
11	O	3	4	Add fourth-line A dotted quarter

MEASURES	AFTER	STAFF	BEAT	CORRECTION
11	P	2	4	Change last pitch E to second-line G
2	P	2	1	Add fourth-line D eighth to down beat
5	P	1	3	"Oboes"
14	P	3		Add middle C to all chords

Unit 5: Stylistic Considerations

The day before his death, Gould attended a morning rehearsal of the U. S. Military Academy Concert Band, giving tips and guidance on performing his music. He rehearsed the band on *American Salute*, which he was scheduled to conduct that evening at the newly opened Disney Institute in Orlando, Florida. After the rehearsal, Gould became ill. He attended the concert, but was not able to conduct. According to the band's commander and conductor, LTC David H. Deitrick, "He was extremely pleased with the concert, and couldn't say enough about how happy he was with the way the band performed his music." In the rehearsal, Gould's opening tempo (dotted quarter note=140) was considerably faster than the tempo of the 4/4 at letter K (quarter note=128). He returned to the original tempo at two measures after O.

Gould reminded the band to exaggerate the dynamics. The theme begins with a *pianissimo* Morse-code accompaniment at m. 13. Gould asked the clarinets to remain tacet on this until letter C. After the soft bassoon trio, the piece builds to a *forte* climax at letter E. After a short *diminuendo*, the high woodwinds begin variation three at letter F, again *pianissimo*. Variations four and five and the first phrase of variation six are *fortissimo*. The second phrase is an echo of the first, and the work builds from letter N to the end.

In several articles, Gould was adamant about avoiding indiscriminate doublings, especially in flutes and brasses:

> Undue weighting of flutes negates the unique quality of the instrument. Capricious doublings or triplings of brass scatters tonal impact rather than focusing....this weighting diffuses rather than concentrates sound. But, most important, fast, precise tonguing is practically impossible by more than one player to a part.

In spite of the extensive cross-cueing in Lang's arrangement, Gould was equally insistent about substitutions. "Tuned percussion must be played with finesse and precise articulation. Bells are not substitutes for vibraphones, or xylophones for marimbas." This statement begs the question, "Are the 'steel bells' called for in both scores the same as orchestra bells?" Gould's term probably distinguishes the steel orchestra bells from the alloy bell-lyres once used in marching bands, and also from brass tubular bells, or "chimes," also used in both versions.

Unit 6 Musical Elements

Gilmore's song consists of four phrases:

When Johnny comes marching home again, Hurrah! Hurrah!
We'll give him a hearty welcome then, Hurrah! Hurrah!
The men will cheer, the boys will shout, the ladies they will
    all turn out;
And we'll all feel gay, When Johnny comes marching home.

The first three lines are a verse for a soloist. The chorus sings the "Hurrahs" at the ends of the first two lines and the entire last line as a refrain. The first two phrases make up a parallel period, and the two occurrences of the text "When Johnny comes marching home" have a similar rhythm and melodic contour.

Beginning with the opening chord, the influence of jazz on *American Salute* is evident. Woodwind syncopations give laughing jazz answers to the heavy low brass octaves in Variation Five (letter H), and who could miss the levity of the jazz cornet "doo-wah doo-wah," one measure before J?

Throughout the work, Gould uses "thickened-line" jazz voicings: a section of the band follows a melody in closely spaced parallel chords. This voicing first shows up in the exchanges between cornets and low brasses at m. 3, and the bassoons' statement of the theme at letter A. Occasionally, Gould adds an additional voice in contrary motion, for example the lowest voice in the fifth measure of letter B. Sometimes two thickened lines oppose each other in contrary motion (letter J). When Gould wants a big, driving sound, he doubles the thickened line at the octave (horns and trombones, seven measures after O).

Jazz is not the only style affecting this work. In Variation Six (letter K), a mysterious, marching *ostinato* begins in the horns with interpolations by the large gong and bass clarinet. Over this, cornets and first trombone sound two phrases of the theme in augmentation, first nearby, then muted, from a distance. Woodwinds and xylophone follow with the third phrase in macabre dotted rhythms that could have come from a Beethoven symphony. Finally, the full brass section reassures us with a rousing version of the fourth phrase, ending the variation with five nasty horn and clarinet tritones.

The three notes on the words "Johnny Comes" provide the unifying motive for the introduction, episodes, and *coda*. The descending scale, "all feel gay, When," in the seventh measure of the 12/8 tune provides the source for the marching *ostinato* of Variation Six (at K). It also provides an ending for Episode Two (four and five measures after E). In augmentation, the motive is

the accompaniment (oboe and bells four and five measures after C) for the English horn line, "The men will cheer, the boys will shout, the ladies they will all turn out," in Variation One.

Unit 7: Form and Structure

Theme and Variations

SECTION	LETTER	EVENTS AND SCORING
Introduction		G7sus4 in 12/8
Theme	A	Bassoon trio in E minor
Episode 1	B	Antiphonal muted brasses and woodwinds
Variation 1	C	English horn in D minor with bassoon ostinato
Variation 2	D	Low brasses and woodwinds in F minor
Episode 2	E	Brasses and timpani
Variation 3	F	Staccato woodwinds in E-flat minor
Variation 4	G	Alla breve tutti in C minor
Variation 5	I	Tutti in D minor with more syncopation
Variation 6	K	Cornets and trombone in G minor over 4/4 ostinato
Episode 3	N	Antiphonal high woodwinds and low brasses 12/8
Variation 7	O	Tutti in D minor
Coda	P	Antiphonal woodwinds, snare drum, and timpani; builds to ending on D7sus4

Unit 8: Suggested Listening

Morton Gould. *American Salute*. Arthur Fiedler, Boston Pops. RCA Gold Seal (Papillon Collection) 6806-2-RG (CD),6806-4-RG8 (tape), 11-7862B (LP).

Morton Gould. *American Salute*. Arr. Philip J. Lang. American Variations, Eugene Corporon, Cincinnati Wind Symphony. Klavier KCD-11060.

Morton Gould. *American Salute*. Morton Gould's Orchestra. Columbia ML5874, ML4218.

Morton Gould. *American Salute*. Arr. Philip J. Lang. United States Air Force Band. An American Tribute, USAF-163.

Morton Gould. *American Salute*. Arr. Philip J. Lang. Harry Begian, University of Illinois Band. University of Illinois IL-76.

Morton Gould. *American Salute*. Arr. Philip J. Lang. Belwin Concert Band Classics #1. Ed Peterson, The Washington Winds.

Unit 9: Additional References and Resources

BMG Music. "Morton Gould: Conductor." Classics World Biography. 1995-97: photo, 6 pars., sound clips. Online: internet address http://www.classicalmus.com/artists/gould.html (April 19, 1997).

Center for New Media at Columbia University, The. "The Pulitzer Prize Board Presents the 1995 Pulitzer Prize Winners: Prize in Music." Columbia Journalism Review. "Winners." 1995: 3 par. Online: internet address: http://www.pulitzer.org/winners/1995/winners/music.html (April 19, 1997); "Biography." 1995: 1 par., photo.

"Composer/Conductor Morton Gould Dies at 82." ASCAP *Playback Magazine*. January-February 1996: photo, 12 pars. Online: internet address http://www.ascap.com/playback/1996/february/gould.html (April 19, 1997).

Deitrick, LTC David H. West Point, NY Telephone interview by Ibrook Tower, March 28, 1997.

Evans, Lee. "Morton Gould: His Life and Music." Ed.D. diss., Columbia University Teachers College, 1978.

G. Schirmer Promotions Department. "Around the Year with Morton Gould." New York: G. Schirmer, Inc., 1988.

G. Schirmer/AMP Promotion Department. "Morton Gould," October 7, 1996: photo, 11 pars. Online: internet address http://www.schirmer.com/composers/gould_bio.html (April 19, 1997).

Gilmore, Patrick. "Music Lyrics: When Johnny Comes Marching Home." St. Andrew Civil War Reenactment Club. 1997: 4 pars. Online: internet address http://scooby.cheney.net/~braxton/music2.html (April 27, 1997).

Gould, Morton. *American Salute*. Transcribed for band by Philip J. Lang. New York: Mills Music, 1943.

Gould, Morton. "*American Salute* with Remarks by Mr. Gould." LTC David H. Deitrick, conducting the U.S. Military Academy Band. Disney Institute, Orlando, FL, February 20, 1996. Sound Cassette.

Gould, Morton. "The Sound of a Band." *Music Educators Journal*, 48, April-May 1962, 36-46.

Howard, John Tasker and George Kent Bellows. *A Short History of Music in America*. New York: Apollo Editions, 1967.

Marrocco, W. Thomas and Harold Gleason, ed. *Music in America*. New York: W.W. Norton and Company, 1964.

"Morton Gould." The Kennedy Center Honors. 1994: photo, 7 pars. Online: internet address http://kennedycenter.org/explore/honors/html/1994/gould.html (April 19, 1997).

"Morton Gould Remembered." *Instrumentalist*, July 1996, 52-55.

"Morton Gould: Symphony for Band 'West Point.' " *Teaching Music through Performance in Band*. Compiled and edited by Richard Miles. Chicago: GIA Publications, Inc., 1997.

"Morton Gould: Works for Band Available from G. Schirmer, Inc." *Schirmer News*, February 1993, 80th Birthday Celebration.

Neidig, Kenneth L. "*American Salute*: An Interview with Morton Gould." *Instrumentalist*, October 1978, 19-22.

Phillips, Harvey. "Morton Gould Reflects: From ASCAP to *American Salute*." *Instrumentalist*, January 1995, 29-32.

Popular Songs of Nineteenth Century America. Introduction and notes by Richard Jackson. New York: Dover Publications, Inc., 1976.

Rehrig, William. *The Heritage Encyclopedia of Band Music*. Edited by Paul E. Bierley. Westerville, OH: Integrity Press, 1991.

Renshaw, Jeffrey. "The Legacy of Morton Gould." *Instrumentalist*, July 1996, 17-20.

Russo, William. *Composing for the Jazz Orchestra*. Chicago: University of Chicago Press, 1961.

Sadie, Stanley and H. Wiley Hitchcock, eds. *New Grove Dictionary of American Music*. London: MacMillan Press, 1986.

Sadie, Stanley, ed. *New Grove Dictionary of Musical Instruments*. London: MacMillan Press, 1984.

Smith, Norman and Albert Stoutamire. *Band Music Notes*. Third ed. Lake Charles, LA: Program Note Press, 1989.

Stone, Thomas. "Morton Gould: Champion of the Band." *BD Guide*, January-February 1995, 2-5.

Swetnam, Staff Sgt. LaDonna L. "Morton Gould: An American Composer." United States Military Academy Band. July 2, 1996: photo, 10 pars. Online: internet address http://www.usma.army.mil/Band/gould.htm (April 19, 1997).

Contributed by:
Ibrook Tower
Director of Bands
Elizabethtown College
Elizabethtown, Pennsylvania

Teacher Resource Guide

An Outdoor Overture
Aaron Copland
(1900–1990)

Unit 1: Composer

Aaron Copland belongs to the generation of composers that put American music on an equal footing with contemporary developments in European modernism. He is perhaps the most honored and best-known American composer of the twentieth century. Few contemporary composers have had their music heard in places as disparate as the concert hall, the opera and ballet stage, movie theaters, television, commercials, as well as several rock and roll albums. Copland's early works combined jazz elements with advanced harmonies and rhythms; among these are *Music for the Theatre* and his *Piano Concerto*. In 1936, Copland began to change his style, concentrating on folk themes. During this middle period, he composed his best-known works, including *Fanfare for the Common Man, Rodeo*, and music for the film *The Red Pony*. In the 1950s, Copland lost interest in his American folk style. He turned to serialism in the *Piano Quartet*, *Music for a Great City*, and *Inscapes*, his last major orchestral work. *Emblems*, composed for band in 1964, is more conservative in style. Copland received many awards, including the 1949 Academy Award for Best Dramatic Film Score for *The Heiress*, and the 1944 Pulitzer Prize for *Appalachian Spring*. Lyndon Johnson presented him with the Presidential Medal of Freedom. He received the National Medal of Arts in 1986.

Unit 2: Composition

According to Copland's note, he composed *An Outdoor Overture* in 1938 for Alexander Richter and the school orchestra of New York City's High

School of Music and Art. After hearing a performance of his high school opera *The Second Hurricane* in 1937, Richter decided that Copland should compose an orchestral work that would open the high school's campaign "American Music for American Youth."

Copland found the idea so irresistible that he interrupted work on his ballet *Billy the Kid* to finish the overture in two and one-half weeks. He completed its orchestration a week later. Richter suggested "a single-movement composition somewhere between five and ten minutes in length…rather optimistic in tone, which would have a definite appeal to the adolescent youth of this country." When Richter first heard Copland play the nine-and-one-half-minute overture from the piano sketch, he pointed out that it had an open-air quality. Together they hit upon the title: *An Outdoor Overture*.

In *Modern Music*, Elliott Carter complained that music critics ignored the work: "*An Outdoor Overture*…contains some of his finest and most personal music. Its opening is as lofty and beautiful as any passage that has been written by a contemporary composer. It is Copland in his prophetic vein which runs through all his works…never before…has he expressed it so simply and directly." London Philharmonic annotator Cecil Smith wrote in 1954, "Youth and freedom and tireless energy are the subject matter of the *Overture*. This is music without poetizing, without introversion."

Copland arranged *An Outdoor Overture* for band in 1941 in response to a request by Dr. Edwin Franko Goldman. In June, 1942, the Goldman Band introduced the arrangement in New York. Copland conducted. Boosey and Hawkes did not publish the arrangement until 1948.

Unit 3: Historical Perspective

In his autobiography, Copland discussed *An Outdoor Overture* in a chapter entitled "Music for Use." As the world economic and political crisis deepened and war approached, the artistic populism of the 1930s changed Copland's artistic direction. He composed for popular venues: *An Outdoor Overture* for high-school orchestra, the "school opera" *The Second Hurricane*, and music for theater, ballet, and films. The extraordinary development of the American public high school orchestra had convinced Copland that composers could and should supply these groups with a music matching their enthusiastic young members' emotional and technical capacities, building future audiences for new American music. Perhaps *An Outdoor Overture* reflects the general optimism demonstrated by the preparations for the New York World's Fair of 1939. Copland composed music for a puppet show, *From Sorcery to Science*, given at the fair's Hall of Pharmacy, and music for his first film, *The City*, a documentary shown at the Science and Educational Building.

Unit 4: Technical Considerations

Copland orchestrated *An Outdoor Overture* for the expanded concert band of the 1940s: three flutes (third doubling piccolo), E-flat clarinet, two oboes, six clarinet parts (solo, first, divided second, divided third), alto clarinet, bass clarinet, four saxophones (AATB), a part (probably optional) for bass saxophone and B-flat contrabass clarinet, two bassoons, four horns, four cornets (solo and first on one part, second and third on another), two trumpets, three trombones (first, second, bass), euphonium, basses (divided), string bass, timpani, snare and bass drums, cymbals, xylophone, triangle, and glockenspiel. Three musicians can cover all of the percussion parts. All brasses except euphoniums and tubas need straight mutes.

The overture needs a strong cornetist to play the twenty-measure solo following the introduction. The score also requires depth in the cornet/trumpet section, with *stretto* entrances on high A above the staff. The clarinet parts are very high, the solo and first clarinets reaching high A in ledger lines above the staff. The second clarinets on several occasions go to high G a step lower. It takes a baritone saxophonist with a quick tongue and a delicate touch to play the soft, repeated-note solos at mm. 106 and 130. The parts are heavily cross-cued, providing an opportunity to use the first bassoon on those solos. However, this may make the solo bassoon entrance at m. 134 less effective. There are also important solos for clarinet and oboe.

The score contains mixed meters and the following concert key signatures: no flats, two flats, one flat, three flats, no flats, two sharps, no sharps, four sharps, and no sharps. Although phrases are irregular in length, none of the syncopated rhythms should present any great problems. Copland provides tempo markings throughout the score. The score and the parts contain many errors. Correcting them before the first rehearsal should save time in achieving Copland's style.

Errata

PARTS

MEASURES	BEATS	CORRECTION
Concert Flutes and Piccolo:		
1	1	Label second staff "Piccolo"
14	1	Piccolo: "to Flute III"
33	1	Piccolo: "take Flute III"
39-42		*"poco a poco accel."*
43	1	Flute III: "to Piccolo"
50	3	">"
95	1	Flutes: ">"
184-185	1, 2	Slurs missing
187-188	3, 1	Flute and Piccolo: break ties between measures
213	1	Flute: "a2"
224		Change "8ves" to "8va"

MEASURES	BEATS	CORRECTION
253	4	">"s on dotted eighth and sixteenth

E-flat Clarinet:

5	1	*"marcato"*
52	1	Remove slur
55	1	*"f"*
77	1	Remove ">"
102-103		Make single *crescendo* mark
123-125		Add lower slurs as in Piccolo part
144	1	"<"
189		Remove lower slur
208	1	Add reminder natural to fourth-space E
253	4	">"s on dotted eighth and sixteenth

Oboes:

5	1	*"marcato"*
11	3	"<"
33	4	"solo, unless no Alto Clarinet"
35	4	"a2"
39-42		*"poco a poco accel."*
50	3	"<"
104	1	*"Un poco meno mosso"*
165	2	Change ">" to *staccato* dot
169-170		*"rit."*
188	1	"solo"
206	2	Remove "a2"
231-233		Add lower slurs as in Piccolo part
239-242		Add lower slurs as in Piccolo part
253	4	">"s on dotted eighth and sixteenth

Solo B-flat Clarinet:
2 (first complete measure)

	2	*"sf"* on eighth note D above staff
32-33		Remove lower slur
41	4	Add quarter-note rest to end of measure
77	1	remove ">"
88	2	">"
113	2	second eighth should be fourth-space E
113-115		Remove lower slurs
176-186		Remove lower slurs
188-196		Remove lower slurs
216	1	Remove *"mf"*

MEASURES	BEATS	CORRECTION
253	4	">"s on dotted eighth and sixteenth
254	1	">"
255	3	">"
256	3	">"
257	1, 3	">"
258	4	">" and "*sff*"

First B-flat Clarinet:

32		Remove lower slur
39-42		"*poco a poco accel....*"
50	1	">"
76	1	Add "*subito*" to "*f*"
77	1	Remove ">"
88	2	">"
94	1	">"
104	1	"*Un poco meno mosso*"
122		remove lower slur
169-170		"*rit.*"
171	2	Remove "//" (no full stop)
176-186		Remove lower slurs
188-196		Remove lower slurs
196		Remove existing slur, add slur over whole measure
198	1	remove "*poco accel.*"
199-204		"*poco a poco accel....*"
250-253		"*cresc.*"
258	4	">"

Second B-flat Clarinet:

49	1	">"
59	1	">"
61	1	">"
76	1	Remove ">"
83	1	">"
95	1	">"
99	1	*Più Allargando*
140	1	Replace "*molto*" *legato* with "*non*" *legato*
176	4	Remove lower slur
179-181		Remove lower slurs
183-185		Remove lower slurs
187-192		Remove lower slurs
196		Replace existing slur with slur over entire measure

Measures	Beats	Correction
208	1	Key signature change to two sharps
210	1	Remove key signature change
250	1-2	Change fifth-line F-sharp to F-natural
252	1	Add reminder F-sharp
253	4	">"s on dotted eighth and sixteenth
260	4	">"

Third B-flat Clarinet:

50	1	">"
52	1	Remove slur
74-75		Slur over both measures in stems up part
75	2-3	Add tie in stems down part
77	1	"f"
94	1	">"
99	1	*Più Allargando*
167	2	Replace ">" with *staccato* dot
188-194		Remove lower slurs
196		Replace existing slur with slur over entire measure
253	4	">"s on dotted eighth and sixteenth
254	1	">"

E-flat Alto Clarinet:

16	3	"*mp*"
33		Remove lower slur
50	3	">"
65	1	Remove ">" on dotted quarter after beat
144	3	">"

B-flat Bass Clarinet:

39-42		"*poco a poco accel....*"
50	3	">"
76	1	"*sub. f*"
116	1	four-measure rest
120	1	two-measure rest
144	3	">"
174		">"
199-204		"*poco a poco accel....*"
228-233		*staccato* dots on all notes

First E-flat Alto Saxophone:

5	3	"*marcato*"

MEASURES	BEATS	CORRECTION
65	2	change pitch to first-space F
95	1	">"
99	1	*Più Allargando*
144	3	">"
253	4	">"s on dotted eighth and sixteenth
254	1	">"

Second E-flat Alto Saxophone:

5	3	*"marcato"*
50	3	">"
95	1	">"
144	3	">"
252	1	reminder "#" on fourth-space C
253	4	">"s on dotted eighth and sixteenth
254	1	">"

B-flat Tenor Saxophone:

164	1	no *staccato* dot
253	4	">"s on dotted eighth and sixteenth

E-flat Baritone Saxophone:

39-42		*"poco a poco accel...."*
96	1	">"
129	4	take dot off dotted quarter
162	1	*staccato* dot
206	1	no key change
208	1	key change to two sharps
228	1	*"mf"*

B-flat Bass Saxophone and B-flat Contrabass Clarinet:

15	3	*"sub. mp"*
39-42		*"poco a poco accel...."*
96	1, 2	">"
97	1	">"
104-116		*staccato* dots on quarters
123-129		*staccato* dots on quarters
141	2, 4	">"
142	4	*crescendo*
143	1	">"
144	1	">"
167	1	*"ff"*
199-204		*"poco a poco accel...."*
212	1	">"
228	1	*"mf"*

MEASURES	BEATS	CORRECTION
228-233		*staccato* dots on quarters
243	1	"*ff*"
250-253		*crescendo*
253	4	">"s on dotted eighth and sixteenth
254	1	">", "*fff*"
255	1	">"
256	1	"<"

First Bassoon:

39-42		"*poco a poco accel….*"
50	3	">"
96	2	">"
106		"*pp*" "*espressivo*"
130		"*p*" "*espressivo*"
144	3	">"
169	1	"*ff*"
253	4	">"s on dotted eighth and sixteenth

Second Bassoon:

50	3	">"
95	4	">" on second eighth
144	3	">"
148	1	change "*mf*" to "*sub. p*"
169	1	"*ff*"
212	1	"*f*" ">"
253	4	">"s on dotted eighth and sixteenth

First and Second Horns in F:

8	2	">" Horn I
15	3	">"
39-42		"*poco a poco accel….*"
42		remove "*poco accel.*"
60		"note stem direction"
142	2	">"
172	4	">"
175	1	"*p*"

Third and Fourth Horns in F:

39-42		"*poco a poco accel….*"
40		remove "*poco accel.*"
60		"note stem direction"
97	3-4	*crescendo*
143	1	"*ff*"
154	2	"*f*"

MEASURES	BEATS	CORRECTION
179	1	"con sordino" "Horn III"
191	3	"con sordino"

Solo and First B-flat Cornets:

77	1	remove ">"
99	1	Più Allargando
138		"Senza sordino"
253	4	">"s on dotted eighth and sixteenth

Second B-flat Cornet (relabel part "Second and Third B-flat Cornets"):

4	4	"a2"
7		Whole rest above staff
7	2	"3rd Cornet"
13		Whole rest below staff
13-14		Reverse stems
14	1	Half rest below staff
14	3	"a2"
14	3, 4	Stems up
15	2	"divisi"
76	1	Remove ">"
96	4	">"
99	1	Più Allargando
99	4	Change "1st Solo" to "2nd Solo"
100	4	Change "2nd Solo" to "3rd Solo"
101	2	"p"
102	1	remove "p"
210	3	"p"
212		crescendo
213		"f"
235		"solo"
236		"tutti"
236		Third Cornet "Senza sordino"
253	4	">"s on dotted eighth and sixteenth

B-flat Trumpets:

3	3, 4	">"
12	3	">"
39-42		"poco a poco accel...."
50	1	Change "sf" to "ff"
97	3	">"
98	2	">"
98	3	">" on second eighth
103		Divide two-measure rest
138		"a2"

MEASURES	BEATS	CORRECTION
253	4	">"s on dotted eighth and sixteenth

First Trombone:

3	3, 4	">"
97-98		*crescendo*
98	2	">"
98	3	">" "*fff*" on second eighth
144	1	"*ff*"
151	4	"*mf*"
241	3	Change C above staff to tied-over A
253	4	">"s on dotted eighth and sixteenth

Second Trombone:

3	3, 4	">"
50	1	"*ff*"
55	4	"*f*"
88	3	Remove ">"
99	1	*Più Allargando*
151	4	"*mf*" "*marcato*"
250	1	"*f*"
250-253		*crescendo*
253	4	">"s on dotted eighth and sixteenth
254	1	"*fff*"

Bass Trombone:

3	3, 4	">"
50	1	Remove "*sf*"
91	1, 3	">"
104		"*Un poco meno mosso*"
142	4	"*Senza sordino*"
250	1	"*f*"
250-253		*crescendo*
253	4	">"s on dotted eighth and sixteenth
254	1	"*fff*"

Euphonium Bass Clef (Baritone):

8	4	"*marcato*"
39-42		"*poco a poco accel....*"
50	1	"*ff*"
97-98		*crescendo*
98	3	"*fff*" on second eighth
139	2	">"
143	1	"*ff*"
149	4	Remove "*f*"

MEASURES	BEATS	CORRECTION
167	4	Move "*ff*" to beat 1
226	1, 4	"*>*"
227	3	"*>*"
228	1	Move "230" rehearsal number to beginning of four-measure rest
244	1	Change "*f*" to "*ff*"
253	4	"*>*"s on dotted eighth and sixteenth
254	1	"*fff*"

Euphonium Treble Clef (Baritone):

8	4	"*marcato*"
39-42		"*poco a poco accel....*"
50	1	"*ff*"
60	1	Change "*f*" to "*ff*"
97-98		*crescendo*
98	3	"*fff*" on second eighth
143	1	"*ff*"
149	4	Remove "*f*"
226	1, 4	"*>*"
227	3	"*>*"
244	1	Change "*f*" to "*ff*"
253	4	"*>*"s on dotted eighth and sixteenth
254	1	"*fff*"

Basses:

11-14		"press forward"
39-42		"*poco a poco accel....*"
40		remove "*poco accel.*"
52	4	"*>*"
53	4	"*>*"
78	1	"*>*" stems up part
80	1	"*>*" stems up part
86	1	"*>*" stems up part
87	1, 4	"*>*" stems up part
88	3	"*>*" stems up part
91	2	"*f*"
94	4	"*>*"
96	2	"*>*"
97	1	"*ff*"
97	1, 3, 4	"*>*"
97-98		*crescendo*
98	3	"*>*" on both eighths
98	3	Move "*fff*" to second eighth

MEASURES	BEATS	CORRECTION
104-115		*staccato* dots
135-139		Mark as string bass cue
135-139		*staccato* dots
210-211		*staccato* dots
212	1	">" "*marcato*"
228	1	">"
228	2	"*mf*"
234	1	"*f*"
244	1	"*ff*"
253	4	">"s on dotted eighth and sixteenth
254	1	"*fff*"

String Bass:

6	2	begin upbow, change "*f*" to "*ff*"
15	3	"*sf*"
15	4	Move "*pizz.*" to beat 3
15-43		*staccato* dots
39-42		"*poco a poco accel....*"
40		remove "*poco accel.*"
52	4	">"
53	4	">"
77	1	"*f*"
91	2	"*f*"
94	4	">"
96	2	">"
97	4	">"
98	2	">"
98	3	">" both eighths
138	4	"*mf*"
145	2	upbow
146	2	"*pizz.*"
175-197		*staccato* dots
210	1	Remove "*arco*"
253	4	">"s on dotted eighth and sixteenth
261	4	"*ff*"
262	1	"*sff*"

Timpani:

11-14		"press forward"
15	3	Change "*sff*" to "*ff*"
97		*crescendo*
98	3	"*fff*" on second eighth
146-163	1	*staccato* dots on downbeats

MEASURES	BEATS	CORRECTION
213	1	*"marcato"*

Drums, Cymbal, Xylophone, Triangle, and Glockenspiel:

2	2	"two plates" "let vibrate"
11-14		"press forward"
39-42		*"poco a poco accel...."*
70	1	*"legato"* change "*p*" to "*mp*"
94	2	">"
98	3	">"
100		Divide five-measure rest into four measures and one measure
104		*"Un poco meno mosso"*
110		*"L'istesso tempo"*
143	1	*"sf"*
174	3	add quarter rest
202		Divide three-measure rest into two measures and one measure
204	1	"Tempo I, Allegro"
222	1	">"
254	1	*"fff"* under lower staff
254	2	*"ff"* under upper staff
254	4	">" on dotted eighth and sixteenth on lower staff
258	4	Remove "*sff*"
261	1	Change snare drum half note to whole note

SCORE

MEASURE	BEATS	INSTRUMENTS	CORRECTION
1		Piccolo (Flute III)	Label second staff "Piccolo (Flute 3)"
1	4	Flutes	"a2"
1	4	Oboes	"a2"
5	1	Second B-flat Cornet	Remove half note rest
6	2	String Bass	begin upbow
15	3	B-flat Contrabass Clarinet and Bass Saxophone	*"sub."*
37	4	Second B-flat Cornet	*"Senza sordino"* Third Cornet

MEASURE	BEATS	INSTRUMENTS	CORRECTION
50	3	Oboes, E-flat Alto Clarinet	">"
55	4	Second Trombone	"f"
61	1	Second B-flat Cornet	">"
61	1	Solo and First B-flat Cornet	">"
73	4	2nd B-flat Clarinet	First-space F-sharp does not tie over into next measure
78	1	Basses	">"
80	1	Basses	">"
83	1	Oboes, E-flat Clarinet, Solo, First, Second B-flat Clarinet	">"
85	1	Oboes, E-flat Clarinet, Solo, First, Second B-flat Clarinet	">"
88	2	Oboes, E-flat Clarinet, Solo, First, Second B-flat Clarinet	">"
90	1	First and Second, Third and Fourth Horns	"senza sordino"
92	2	Bass Drum	">" "f"
96	1	B-flat Contrabass Clarinet and Bass Saxophone	">"
96	2	E-flat Baritone Saxophone, B-flat Contrabass Clarinet, and Bass Saxophone	">"
97	3-4	First and Second, Third and Fourth Horns	crescendo
97	2	First Trombone	crescendo
97	4	Second Trombone	"ff"
97	1, 4	B-flat Contrabass Clarinet and Bass Saxophone	">"
98	2	First Trombone	">"

MEASURE	BEATS	INSTRUMENTS	CORRECTION
98	3	First Trombone	">" on second eighth
99	4	Second Cornet	Change "1st Solo" to "2nd Solo"
100	2	Second Cornet	"*f*" 2nd Solo Player
100	4	Second Cornet	Change "2nd Solo" to "3rd Solo"
104-116		B-flat Contrabass Clarinet and Bass Saxophone	staccato dots on quarters
119		Piccolo (Flute III)	"Take flute"
121	1	Piccolo (Flute III)	"Flute solo"
123		Solo B-flat Clarinet	"*tutti*"
123-125		E-flat Clarinet	Add lower slurs as in piccolo part
123-129		B-flat Contrabass Clarinet and Bass Saxophone	staccato dots on quarters
127-129		Solo and First B-flat Clarinet	Add lower slurs as in piccolo part
138	1	Oboes	"a2"
138	4	String Bass	"*mf*"
138	4	String Bass	"*mf*"
141	2, 4	B-flat Contrabass Clarinet and Bass Saxophone	">"
142		Bass Trombone	"*Senza sordino*"
142	4	B-flat Contrabass Clarinet and Bass Saxophone	*crescendo*
143	1	B-flat Contrabass Clarinet and Bass Saxophone	">"
144	1	First Trombone	"*ff*"
144	1	B-flat Contrabass Clarinet and Bass Saxophone	">"
145	2	String Bass	slur over entire beat, "*ff*" upbow

MEASURE	BEATS	INSTRUMENTS	CORRECTION
148-152		E-flat Alto, B-flat Bass Clarinet	note staccato dots above stems
165	2	Second B-flat Cornet	*staccato* dot
169	1	B-flat Contrabass Clarinet and Bass Saxophone, First, Second Bassoon	"*ff*"
169-170		B-flat Contrabass Clarinet and Bass Saxophone, First, Second Bassoon, Second, Bass Trombone, Euphonium, Basses	">" on every note
172	3	Oboes	"a2"
174	3	Flutes and Piccolo	Tie into m. 175
177		E-flat Alto Clarinet	Remove tie into next measure
179	1	Third and Fourth Horns	"*con sordino*"
181	1	First and Second Horns	"*con sordino*"
188	1	First Trombone	"open"
188	1	Second Trombone	"open"
188	1	Oboes	"solo"
204	2	Solo and First B-flat Cornet	"*Senza sordino*"
205		Second E-flat Alto Saxophone	"2 Solo"
211	4	Solo and First B-flat Cornet	"*f*"
212	1	Solo and First B-flat Cornet	*crescendo*
212	4	Oboes	Remove unnecessary stems down
218	1	Oboes	Remove unnecessary "a2"
226	4	Euphonium	">"
227	3	Euphonium, Xylophone	">"
228	1	E-flat Baritone Saxophone, B-flat Contrabass Clarinet, and Bass Saxophone	"*mf*"

MEASURE	BEATS	INSTRUMENTS	CORRECTION
228	2	Basses	"*mf*"
228-233		E-flat Alto, B-flat Bass Clarinet	note *staccato* dots above stems
228-233		B-flat Contrabass Clarinet and Bass Saxophone	*staccato* dots on quarters
231-233		Solo and First B-flat Clarinet	Add lower slurs as in piccolo part
231-242		Oboes	Add lower slurs as in piccolo part
234	1	Basses	"*f*"
235	1	Second B-flat Cornet	"solo"
239-242		Second and Third B-flat Clarinet	Add lower slurs as in piccolo part
240	1	Bass Trombone	"*f*"
241		Solo and First B-flat Cornet	tutti (note: solo cornet since m. 204)
242	1	Second Bassoon	"*ff*"
244	1	B-flat Contrabass Clarinet and Bass Saxophone, Euphonium, Basses	"*ff*"
250	1	First Trombone	"*f*"
250	1	Second Trombone	"*f*"
250	1	Bass Trombone	"*f*"
250-253		First, Second, Bass Trombone	*crescendo*
251	1	Second B-flat Cornet	"*f*"
251	1	Solo and First B-flat Cornet	"*f*"
253	4	Flutes and Piccolo, Oboes, E-flat, Solo, Second, Third B-flat, B-flat Contrabass Clarinet and Bass Saxophone,	

		First, Second Bassoon, Solo and First, Second, Third B-flat Cornet, B-flat Trumpets, First, Second, Bass Trombone, Euphonium, Tuba, String Bass	">"s on dotted eighth and sixteenth
261		Second Trombone	bass clef
262	1	Oboes	Remove unnecessary stems down

Unit 5: Stylistic Considerations

One of the most important questions concerning the style of this overture is how long the eighths should be. The two-eighth descending fifth in the horns and second cornet at the beginning and the *marcato* marking in m. 4 suggest a short eighth ending the opening three-note motive. The downbeat of m. 2 should also be short to bring out the syncopated quarter following it on the same pitch. Because Copland composed them originally for *pizzicato* strings, the slurred *staccato* markings beginning in m. 15 should be well tongued.

At mm. 153, 157, and 163, Copland originally marked consecutive downbows for the cellos on beats one and two. For this reason, trombones should leave a slight break between these notes as well. When theme four returns at m. 234 and later, the orchestral strings have no special bowings. It should then be performed more *legato*.

In the orchestral version, Copland marks the *ostinato* parts at m. 152 *non legato*. This passage returns unmarked at m. 235. The orchestral piano part that enters at m. 244 is marked *non legato*, confirming that the recapitulation should be performed with the same articulation.

Tempo is also an important consideration. The overture begins *Maestoso* (quarter note=69-72), presses forward at m. 11, and arrives at a tempo no faster than quarter note=76 in m. 15. This measure is confusingly marked "Tempo I." Copland probably means that, after speeding up, the tempo should slow immediately to a tempo slightly faster than the introduction. The slightly faster metronome marking is to accommodate the long trumpet solo.

The *Più mosso* (quarter note=96) at m. 32 is only an intermediate tempo, as an *accelerando* begins at m. 39, arriving at *Allegro* (quarter note=144) at m. 43. This is the overture's fastest tempo. It is maintained through only a part of the exposition, until the *Più allargando* at m. 99, and never returns (if one observes the metronome markings rather than the Italian tempo markings).

The *Più allargando* ends at m. 104, *Un poco meno mosso* (quarter note=132). This is still a fast tempo, and it is the one Copland specifies in the fast part of the recapitulation (mm. 204-end). It is easy for this tempo to slow down through the baritone saxophone solos, originally composed for cello, at mm. 106 and 130, especially with the *legato l'istesso* tempo between them. Perhaps, as suggested above under "Technical Considerations," substituting the more agile first bassoon will help preserve the tempo. It is the *l'istesso* tempo at m. 134 that will reveal whether the tempo has been maintained. If it is too slow, this bassoon passage simply will not work. The conductor then must ignore Copland's marking and change tempo.

At m. 205 of the recapitulation, Copland marks "Tempo I *Allegro* (quarter note=132)." However, Copland's initial *allegro* tempo is quarter note=144. The conductor must decide which tempo is more effective.

Copland composed parts for piano and celesta in the original orchestral version. The glockenspiel parts at mm. 70-75 and 228-234 in the band version replaced the celesta. Copland doubled the glockenspiel line one octave lower in the first passage, and one and two octaves lower in the second passage, in which he marked the use of the celesta *ad lib*. Obtaining and using the published orchestral piano part will add a color that a listener who knows the earlier version would miss.

If the augmentation of Theme 3 in mm. 122-132 sounds too heavy or screechy, a solo flute could replace the piccolo, and the clarinets could remain *tacet*. For the same reason, the *pianissimo* passage in the recapitulation at mm. 188-200 may be played one-on-a-part, possibly eliminating the E-flat clarinet.

Unit 6: Musical Elements

The introduction contains the overture's principal melodic motives (descending and ascending root position triads, rising perfect fourths and fifths, and descending four-note scales) and rhythmic motives (two sixteenths and an eighth, and an eighth and a quarter followed by an eighth tied over). The phrases are irregular: seven beats, five beats, six beats, four beats, six beats, five beats, four beats, four and a half measures. The trumpet solo uses the principal motives.

An accompanying *ostinato* begins in woodwinds, trombones, then back to woodwinds. The higher instruments alternate B-flat tonic and supertonic chords. At the same time, the basses swing back and forth between dominant and tonic. This makes the chords on beats two and four sound like supertonic and tonic at the same time.

The bridge uses short woodwind motives from the introduction, changing colors quickly. Theme 1 also includes the descending four-note scale. Each time the complete Theme 2 enters, it is in a different mode. Note the partial entrance of the trumpets at m. 66, the soft, homophonic texture at m. 70, and the *stretto* at m. 76. Copland reverses the traditional "oom-pah" accompaniment to "pah-oom."

Based on Theme 1, the first part of the episode builds up to a rhythmic canon between high and low instruments at m. 94. The second part of the episode begins with the grandiose theme and ends with Theme 1. With a slow "pah-oom" accompaniment in D, the Theme 3 melody in A is modally ambiguous, using both G and G-sharp above the staff, and it avoids the third. Note the augmentation in mm. 122-125.

The second transition is based on Theme 1. Theme 4 in D Mixolydian appears first in parallel thirds, then in parallel major chords. The accompaniment is an *ostinato* of descending four-note scales in C Mixolydian.

The recapitulation bridge is an *ostinato* in G major with repeated horn triads in E minor and D minor. Over the *ostinato* are triadic outbursts from various instruments, interrupted for a short time by Morse code in flutes and piccolo. The time between outbursts gets shorter and shorter. In the recapitulation of Theme 2 the accompaniment changes to "oom-pah." The *coda* begins in C, but suddenly changes to F in the last three measures.

Among the many errors in the score and parts are the numerous omissions of accents on the first notes of the two eighth-note motives beginning at m. 47, and repeated many times throughout the work. Carefully observing all of the accents in the overture greatly improves the listener's chance of perceiving this gesture.

Unit 7: Form and Structure

Sonatina form

Section	Measures	Tonal Centers and Quotations from Score
Exposition	1-133	
Introduction	1-15	C to B-flat. *"The piece starts in a large and grandiose manner."*
Trumpet Theme	16-31	B-flat. *"A theme that is immediately developed as a long solo for the trumpet."*
Bridge	32-42	F. *"A short bridge passage in the woodwinds less imperceptibly leads to the first theme of the allegro section."*
Theme 1	43-59	F to E-flat. *"The first theme of the allegro section, characterized by repeated notes."*
Theme 2	60-91	E-flat, A, G Mixolydian, C Mixolydian, A Mixolydian. *"Shortly afterwards, these same repeated notes, played broadly, give us a second snappy, march-like theme, developed in cannon [sic] form."*

SECTION	MEASURES	TONAL CENTERS AND QUOTATIONS FROM SCORE
Episode	92-109	
	92-98	C.
	99-109	C to D. *"There is an abrupt pause, a sudden decrescendo."*
Theme 3	110-129	Accompaniment in D, melody in A. *"and the third lyric theme appears, first in the [clarinet], then the [oboe], and finally, high up in the [piccolo and E-flat and B-flat clarinets]."*
Transition	130-145	G minor to B-flat major to C minor. *"Repeated notes on the [baritone saxophone] seem to lead the piece in the direction of the opening allegro."*
Theme 4	146-170	D Mixolydian, accompaniment in C Mixolydian. *"Instead a fourth and final theme evolves—another march theme, but this time less snappy, and with more serious implications."*
Recapitulation	171-253	
Introduction	171-174	A tritone higher, in F-sharp, without modulation. *"There is a build-up to the opening grandiose introduction again."*
Trumpet	175-197	A half step higher, in B. *"continuing with the trumpet solo melody, this time sung by [piccolo, flutes and clarinets] in a somewhat smoother version."*
Bridge	198-212	Ostinato in G major. *"A short bridge section based on a steady rhythm."*
Theme 2	213-227	Begins a minor third lower, in G and C Mixolydian; the melody is a step lower than before, in G, *ostinato* in C. *"brings a condensed recapitulation of the allegro section."*
Theme 3	228-233	

| Themes 1, 2, 3, and 4 | 234-253 | The *ostinato* in C Mixolydian continues, Theme 3 in G, Theme 2 in D minor, Theme 4 in G, B-flat. "*As a climactic moment, all the themes are combined.*" |
| Coda | 254-262 | C to F. "*A brief coda ends the work on the grandiose note of the beginning.*" |

Unit 8: Suggested Listening

Aaron Copland, *Outdoor Overture*. *American Dreams*. Eugene Corporon, Cincinnati Wind Symphony. Klavier KCD 11048.

Aaron Copland, *Outdoor Overture*. Eric Kunzel, Cincinnati Pops. Telarc CD-80117.

Aaron Copland, *Outdoor Overture*. Gerard Schwarz, Seattle Symphony Orchestra (6/92). Delos DE 3140.

Aaron Copland, *Outdoor Overture*. Aaron Copland, London Symphony Orchestra. Sony Classical 3-SM3K 46559.

Aaron Copland, *Outdoor Overture*. Donald Hunsberger, Eastman Wind Ensemble. Toshiba EMI-TA-72044.

Aaron Copland, *Outdoor Overture*. Symphonic Songs for Band. Frederick Fennell, Tokyo Kosei Wind Orchestra. TKWO 110.

Unit 9: Additional References and Resources

"Aaron Copland: *Down a Country Lane*" and "Aaron Copland: *Emblems*." *Teaching Music through Performance in Band*. Compiled and edited by Richard Miles. Chicago: GIA Publications, Inc., 1997.

"Aaron Copland." *The Kennedy Center Honors*. 1979: photo, 7 pars. Online: internet address http://kennedy-center.org/explore/honors/html/1979/copland.html (April 19, 1997).

"Aaron Copland: American Composer." *Lucidcafé Library*. January 3, 1997: photo, 5 pars. Online: internet address http://www2.lucidcafe.com/lucid-cafe/library/95nov/copland.html (April 19, 1997).

Austin, William. "Aaron Copland." In *The New Grove Twentieth-Century American Masters*. New York: W.W. Norton & Company, 1988.

Berger, Arthur. *Aaron Copland*. Da Capo Press Music Reprint Series. New York: Da Capo Press, 1990.

Butterworth, Neil. *The Music of Aaron Copland*. New York: Universe Publications, 1986.

Carter, Elliott. "Once Again Swing; Also American Music." *Modern Music*, 16:2, January-February 1939, 102-103.

Copland, Aaron. *An Outdoor Overture*. New York: Boosey and Hawkes, Inc., 1940, 1948.

Copland, Aaron and Vivian Perlis. *Copland: 1900 through 1942*. New York: St. Martins/Marek, 1984.

Daum, Gary. "The Orchestral Tradition in the Twentieth Century: Aaron Copland (1900-1991)." *Music: A User's Guide for the Beginner*. 1994-1996: 6 pars. Online: internet address http://leonardo.gprep.pvt.k12.md.us/~music/musikbok/chap16.html (April 19, 1997).

Parkany, Steve. "An Outdoor Overture." In *Band Music Notes* by Norman Smith and Albert Stoutamire, third ed. Lake Charles, LA: Program Note Press, 1989.

Schwartz, Steve. "Aaron Copland." *Classical Net Home Page*. March 1, 1997: photo, 14 pars. Online: internet address http://www.classical.net/music/comp.lst/copland.html (April 19, 1997).

Skowronski, Joann. *Aaron Copland: A Bio-Bibliography* (Bio-Bibliographies in Music No. 2). Westport, CT: Greenwood Publishing Group, 1985.

Venezia, Mike. *Aaron Copland* (Getting to Know the World's Greatest Composers). Danbury, CT: Children's Press, 1995.

Contributed by:
Ibrook Tower
Director of Bands
Elizabethtown College,
Elizabethtown, Pennsylvania

Teacher Resource Guide

Chester Overture for Band
William Schuman
(1910–1992)

Unit 1: Composer

William Howard Schuman, one of America's most famous composers, was born in New York City. He studied at the Malkin Conservatory in New York, the Teachers College of Columbia University, and the Mozarteum Academy in Salzburg. After completing his studies, Schuman became music instructor at Sarah Lawrence College and later president of the Juilliard School of Music. His composing career received national acclaim when the Boston Symphony, under the direction of Koussevitsky, performed his *American Festival Overture* in 1939. Schuman was awarded the first Pulitzer Prize in music for the secular cantata, *A Free Song* (1942), composed on a text of Walt Whitman. He was a strong supporter of modern dance and composed several pieces for Martha Graham. His musical output also includes an opera, six symphonies, concertos, choral works, chamber music, and of course, music for the concert band. Schuman composed five original band works from 1940 to 1980 with *Newsreel* (1941) as the first venture into the medium. Like his teacher, Roy Harris, Schuman uses long, flowing melodies; emotional tension is accomplished through chromaticism and polytonality. His rhythms tend to be more irregular and syncopated than Harris's, relating more closely to the popular music scene.

Unit 2: Composition

Chester was originally the third movement of an orchestral work, *New England Triptych: Three Pieces after William Billings* (1956), commissioned by

Andre Kostelanetz. According to Joseph Machlis, Schuman explained his impetus for writing the *Triptych* thus:

> William Billings is a major figure in the history of American music. The works of this dynamic composer capture the spirit of sinewy ruggedness, deep religiosity and patriotic fervor that we associate with the Revolutionary period. I am not alone among American composers who feel an identity with Billings, and it is this sense of identity which accounts for my use of his music as a point of departure.

When Pi Kappa Omicron commissioned Schuman to write a piece for band in 1956, the composer rescored and adapted *Chester* for the concert band. Billings' original work was composed as a church hymn but was later employed by the Continental Army and it is this duality that Schuman so aptly weaves into a classic work for band. The initial *Religioso* opening section explores the simplicity and majesty of the early American hymn tune, but once its religious roots are revealed, Schuman presents the melody as a marching song, now in memory of its relationship to the early militia. Throughout the composition, Billings' tune goes through a series of transformations, fusing the character and musical genius of both composers into a wonderfully conceived masterwork. Due to many additions and deletions the work does not fit into the category of a transcription. The 249-measure piece is approximately nine minutes in duration and has become one of the cornerstones of the concert band repertoire.

Unit 3: Historical Perspective

A native of Boston, William Billings (1746-1800) is one of the most prominent figures in early American music. A member of a group of composers known as the Yankee Tunesmiths, Billings had traded his career as a tanner to devote his time entirely to musical endeavors. Generally a self-taught musician, he served as a teacher, conductor, composer, publisher, and promoter of music. His musical output includes hymns, canons, anthems, and other such compositions. The tune "Chester" first appeared in 1778 in a collection of tunes and anthems entitled *The Singing Master's Assistant*.

Traditionally the nineteenth-century overture is a single-movement work in either sonata or free form. This Romantic era version of the overture was no longer tied to a larger work such as an opera. With the Mendelssohn *Overtüre für Harmoniemusik*, Opus 24 (1926); Berlioz's *Roman Carnival Overture* (first concert performance *sans opera*, 1844), and the Brahms *Academic Festival Overture* (1881), the form found a life of its own.

Schuman's use of this tune in an overture for band is not unusual since the overture is a particularly popular form for works for band. While transcriptions of orchestral overtures were common during the first half of the twentieth century, later composers have found it to be the perfect vehicle for their creativity. Whether entirely based on original material, or, as in the case of *Chester*, developed from a known tune, the overture has become a mainstay of the concert band repertoire.

Unit 4: Technical Considerations

Chester has no written key signature, relying instead on accidentals to convey the various tonal centers. Players should be familiar with the scales of G major, E-flat major, D major, C major, and D-flat major. Although the difficulty of key is not a major concern, the brisk tempo and asymmetrical phrasing may present difficulties that are not readily apparent from the score. The ensemble will need to perform sixteenth-note passages with clarity and should use light articulations. The opening hymn, presented in traditional four-voice harmony, must be properly balanced so that the hymn tune is predominant over the moving eighth notes. While the polychordal harmony may be a potential source of intonation problems, allowing the students to hear each chord separately will help them to develop a sense of what voices to listen to and how to adjust the tuning within their section and chord. There are no mallet percussion parts, and although there are numerous sections of exposed instruments, the only solo is found in the timpani part.

Unit 5: Stylistic Considerations

The opening chorale in the woodwinds—marked *Religioso* with the tempo quarter=c. 72—should be performed at a dynamic level that allows for a full and rich woodwind sound. All dynamics are relative. Conductors should emphasize cadence points and non-harmonic tones. The brasses should listen for moving eighth-note lines in their statement of the hymn tune. The *Allegro Vivo* (quarter=160) should be crisp and rhythmically accurate. As with any work, even accented eighth notes by themselves should have some body and tone. This part of the overture should be light and should emphasize the syncopation and many varied entrances.

Unit 6: Musical Elements

Following the opening statements of the hymn tune, first by the woodwinds and followed by the brass, Schuman creates five variations and a *coda* based on the melodic and motivic material of Billings' early American tune. By carefully studying the form of the work, conductors will have a good sense of phrasing and style. The woodwind chorale begins in G major with a marking of *dolce legato*. Make sure to sustain all notes and place a slight taper at the ends of phrases. The brass entrance in E-flat major should enter with vigor at the written *forte* dynamic level. Again the four-bar phrases are clearly felt but it is the addition of the timpani rolls that provide a sense of continuity and drive into the subsequent phrase. Players need to be aware of the lyrical lines that are above the punctuated passages in the *Allegro Vivo* section. Careful attention to articulation, dynamics, and rhythmic precision will provide for a very exciting and stirring performance.

Unit 7: Form and Structure

The work is in arch form. After the initial double statement of the hymn there are five variations and a *coda*.

SECTION	MEASURES	EVENTS AND SCORING
Chorale	1-16	G major chorale in woodwinds with four distinct four-measure phrases.
Chorale	17-37	E-flat major chorale presented by the brasses in four phrases, each is four measures long with exception of the last which is five with both brass and woodwinds.
Variation 1	38-101	Begins with eight-bar introduction in saxes and brass, then four phrases each four measures long with melody in woodwinds; phrase four is repeated in hocket style starting at m. 62 with the full ensemble. Centered in G major.
Variation 2	102-141	Begins with brass and low woodwinds, polychordal in tonality, four total phrases with phrases three and four somewhat connected, fourth phrase repeats.
Variation 3	142-170	Clarinet, saxophone, trumpet, and bassoon carry phrase one with phrase two in woodwinds, phrase three in woodwinds and trumpet, and full ensemble in phrase four. This development begins in a pantriadic manner and eventually settles in D major.
Variation 4	171-211	D-flat major parallelism, four phrases in length with phrase three repeating; second time through phrase three is D-flat major with phrase four being monochordal.

| Variation 5 | 232-249 | Begins in C major but by the third phrase modulates to D-flat major once again. Four phrases plus a coda which features the entire ensemble to close. Coda is a repeat of phrase one material. |

Unit 8: Suggested Listening

Paul Creston, *Celebration Overture*
Joseph W. Jenkins, *American Overture for Band*
Andreas Makris, *Aegean Festival Overture*
Felix Mendelssohn, *Overture for Band*
William Schuman, *Be Glad Then, America, Circus Overture, Dedication Fanfare, George Washington Bridge, When Jesus Wept*
Claude T. Smith, *Overture on an Early American Folk Hymn*
John Zdechlik, *Chorale and Shaker Dance*

Unit 9: Additional References and Resources

Apel, Willi. *Harvard Dictionary of Music.* 2nd ed. Cambridge, MA: The Belknap Press of Harvard University Press, 1970.

Battisti, Frank. "William Schuman: *When Jesus Wept.*" *BD Guide,* January/February 1990, 17.

Brown, Michael Ray. "Analysis: *American Hymn*—Variations on an Original Melody by William Schuman." *Journal of Band Research,* XXVII/2, Spring 1992, 67-79.

Brown, Michael Ray. "The Band Music of William Schuman: A Study of Form, Content, and Style." Diss., University of Georgia, 1989.

Brown, Michael Ray. "Conducting Schuman's *Chester Overture.*" *The Instrumentalist,* XLVIII November 1993, 29-36.

Brown, Michael Ray. "Enduring Wisdom from William Schuman, An Unpublished 1986 Interview." *The Instrumentalist,* XLVIII November 1993, 26-29.

Fennell, Frederick. "William Schuman: *George Washington Bridge.*" *BD Guide, March/April 1993,* 33.

Grimes, Ev. "Conversations with American Composers: Ev Grimes Interviews William Schuman." *Music Educators Journal,* 72/8, April 1986, 46,47, 50-54.

Hitchcock, H. Wiley. *Music in the United States.* 3rd ed. Englewood Cliffs, NJ: Prentice Hall, 1988.

Machlis, Joseph. *The Enjoyment of Music*. 4th ed. New York: W.W. Norton & Co., 1977.

Merion Music, Inc. Bryn Mawr, Pennsylvania.

Smith, Norman and Albert Stoutmire. *Band Music Notes*. Lake Charles, LA: Program Note Press, 1989.

Rhodes, Stephen L. "A Comparative Analysis of the Band Compositions of William Schuman." Diss., University of Northern Colorado, 1987.

Rhodes, Stephen L. "William Schuman: Chester Overture for Band." *BD Guide*, March/April, 1989, 32, 35-36, 38.

Whitwell, David. "Schuman—His Music for Winds." *The Instrumentalist*, XXI January 1967, 40-41.

Contributed by:

Susan Creasap
Assistant Director of Bands
Morehead State University
Morehead, Kentucky

Rodney C. Schueller
Associate Instructor
Indiana University
Bloomington, Indiana

Teacher Resource Guide

Dance of the Jesters
Peter (Piotr) Ilyich Tchaikovsky
(1840–1893)

arranged by
Ray Cramer (b. 1940)

Unit 1: Composer

Peter (Piotr) Ilyich Tchaikovsky was born on May 7, 1840. The son of a relatively well-to-do mining inspector, he showed no significant talent until he enrolled in the newly-formed conservatory in Saint Petersburg, where he studied composition with Zaremba and Rubinstein. After winning the silver medal for a cantata, he became professor of composition at the Moscow Conservatory, where he began to prodigiously compose. His first compositions there showed little promise, but by 1868 he began to formulate the essential elements of his own style: overtly emotional music with fatalistic hints, a proclivity for writing in minor keys, and a strong rhythmic interest. Besides composing and teaching, Tchaikovsky was also a music critic, traveling frequently and writing about music. Although very famous, he had considerable financial difficulties until a wealthy widow, Nadezhda von Meck, learned of Tchaikovsky's talent and agreed to sponsor him to the sum of 6000 rubles each year. They wrote frequently, but never met in person; von Meck's sponsorship continued thirteen years. Although very popular in some respects, Tchaikovsky was haunted throughout his life by personal torments, which included a disastrous marriage and frequent criticism of his music. He died from cholera in Saint Petersburg. Interestingly enough, his death was the subject of fantastic speculation including a false story about a suicide pact. Today he is best remembered for his symphonies, piano concertos, and ballets.

Unit 2: Composition

Dance of the Jesters is one part of the incidental music to the play *The Snow Maidens*. In 1873, Ostransky commissioned a play based on folk legends and asked Tchaikovsky to write the music. This selection is known as Number 13 in Act Three. In other sources, this number is referred to as the "Dance of the Tumblers." It was written in three weeks, and Tchaikovsky received 350 rubles for the commission. In a letter to his patroness von Meck, Tchaikovsky wrote: "I think you can feel in this music the happy, spring-like mood which possessed me at the time." Rubinstein conducted the first performance, and it was not well received at the time, especially by the well-known composer Cui. In this rare happy glimpse of Tchaikovsky, the music seems to foreshadow some of the (years later) work of Shostakovich. The composition is four and one-half minutes in duration.

Unit 3: Historical Perspective

At the time this composition was written (1873), the Romantic era of music history was at its peak. The music of Johannes Brahms and Guiseppe Verdi dominated Western Europe, while a strong nationalistic movement was in place in Russia. Especially prominent were the so-called "Mighty Five"—Borodin, Cui, Mussorgsky, Balakirev, and Rimsky-Korsakov—the circle of prominent composers who were crucial in this nationalistic development. The prominence of Tchaikovsky came just after the peak of the "Five." At this time in music history, most of what little music written specifically for band was usually for military band; therefore, what band music we do have is in the form of marches or transcriptions of symphonic music. This era produced music that is still popular today, and much of it has been transcribed for band.

Unit 4: Technical Considerations

The keys of C major, B minor, E-flat major, G major, and A-flat major must be very familiar to the ensemble. The key signature stays the same throughout, but the tonal centers change for significant portions of the composition. The major technical demands on the ensemble come from the tempo (184 beats/minute) and the frequent use of sixteenth-note runs. Piccolo, flutes, clarinets, cornet I, and euphoniums must play slurred diatonic and chromatic sixteenth-note passages. Range demands are moderate for this composition; clarinet I must play high F-sharp and cornet I must play high B, but otherwise, all ranges are reasonable for the difficulty of this composition. There are short duets between solo clarinet and alto sax, but most of the composition has generous doublings. There are several *soli* clarinet sixteenth-note runs which are very difficult. All in all, careful practice at slower tempos is necessary to align the sixteenth-note runs with frequently syncopated accompanimental lines.

Unit 5: Stylistic Considerations

Articulations throughout should be imitative of orchestral styles, especially in the accompanimental voices. In typically Romantic style, articulation should be related to string bowing, especially in the use of *staccato* and separated eighth notes. Some explanation to the group of the purpose of this composition (incidental music from the orchestra for a dance) will be helpful in understanding the composition. Dynamics are more exuberant and less restrained here. However, the brasses will need to be controlled when the clarinets play material borrowed from the violins (i.e., sixteenth-note runs). The frequent syncopated lines should be playful and lightly separated.

Unit 6: Musical Elements

The harmony used is moderately complex, as would be expected of the later Romantic era. There are more frequent major-minor and diminished seventh chords present. There are not many strong dissonances, but there are frequently unusual chord progressions, as is typical of Tchaikovsky. The basic melody of the A theme is diatonic, but the secondary themes and sixteenth-note runs are quite chromatic at times. Rhythms are quite active, with frequent eighth-note syncopations and sixteenth notes throughout. There are no complex rhythms, however. The composition is totally written in 2/4 meter. There is a lot of full ensemble scoring in the A sections, but a wide variety of textures are present in the contrasting sections and transitions. Traditional band scoring is used throughout.

Unit 7: Form and Structure

Modified rondo form

SECTION		MEASURES	TONAL CENTER
A		1-74	
	a^1 (twice)	1-16	C major
	$a^2 + a^1$	17-32	G major and C major
	b^1 (twice)	33-48	B minor
	b^2 (transition)	49-58	
	a^1 (twice)	59-74	C major
B		75-122	
	a (twice)	75-90	A-flat major
	b (twice)	91-106	E-flat major
	a (twice)	107-122	A-flat major
A		123-196	
	a^1 (twice)	123-138	C major
	$a^2 + a^1$	139-154	G major and C major
	b^1 (twice)	155-170	B minor

b^2 (transition)	171-180	
a^1 (twice)	181-196	C major
C	197-228	
a^1 + a^2 (twice)		G major
D	229-264	
introduction	219-232	C major
a (twice, no upper WW or trombone)	233-248	
a (twice, tutti)	249-264	
E	265-296	
a (twice)	265-280	A minor
a (with countermelody)	281-296	
D	297-342	
a (per 233-248)	297-312	C major
a (plus transition)	313-326	
transition (using D motive)	327-342	
A (serves as *coda*)	343-358	C major

Unit 8: Suggested Listening

Alexander Borodin, *Polovetzian Dances* from *Prince Igor*
Modest Mussorgsky, *Pictures at an Exhibition*
Dimitri Shostakovich/Reynolds, *Folk Dances*
Piotr Ilyich Tchaikovsky, *The Snow Maidens, Romeo and Juliet, Symphony No. 6*

Unit 9: Additional References and Resources

Brown, David. *Tchaikovsky: The Early Years 1840-1874.* New York: W.W. Norton & Co. Inc., 1978.

Newmarch, Rosa. *Tchaikovsky: His Life and Works, with Extracts from his Writings, and the Diary of His Tour Abroad in 1888.* New York: Greenwood Press, 1969.

Orlova, Alexandra. *Tchaikovsky: A Self-Portrait.* Translated by R. M. Davidson. New York: Oxford University Press, 1990.

Slonimsky, Nicolas, ed. *Baker's Biographical Dictionary of Music and Musicians.* Eighth edition. New York: Macmillan, Inc., 1992.

Contributed by:
Jeff Emge
Assistant Director of Bands
East Texas State University
Commerce, Texas

Teacher Resource Guide

Exaltations, Op. 67

Martin Mailman
(b. 1932)

Unit 1: Composer

Martin Mailman was born in New York City on June 30, 1932. He received his B.M., M.M. and Ph.D. from the Eastman School of Music where he studied composition with Louis Mennini, Wayne Barlow, Bernard Rogers and Howard Hanson. Mailman is the recipient of many awards and commissions including the Edward Benjamin Award (1955), prizes from the Birmingham Arts Festival (1966), Willamette University (1966), Walla Walla Symphony (1967), NEA grant (1982), Queen Marie-Jose Prize (1982), Shelton Excellence in Teaching Award (1982), the Annual ASCAP Award, the American Bandmasters Association/NABIM award (1983), the National Band Association/Band Mans Award, and the American Bandmasters Association/Ostwald Award (1989). He has been a guest conductor, composer, lecturer, and clinician at numerous international, national, regional, and state meetings as well as universities, high schools, and festivals. He has over ninety compositions to his credit, involving genres such as chamber music, band, choir, orchestra, film scores, television music, and opera. Some of his other works for band include *Geometrics for Band*, Op. 22; *Liturgical Music for Band*, Op. 33; *For precious friends hid in death's dateless night*, Op. 80; *Bouquets*, Op. 87; and *Secular Litanies*, Op. 90.

Unit 2: Composition

Exaltations was commissioned in 1981 by the Manatee High School Band, Bradenton, Florida, Howard Lerner, conductor, and was premiered by that group in May of 1982. The piece later won the ABA/NABIM Award in 1983,

442

and was performed at the American Bandmasters Association convention in Kansas City, Missouri by the United States Air Force Band, Colonel Arnold D. Gabriel conducting. The piece is in one movement, is a Grade Five difficulty, and lasts about eight minutes.

Unit 3: Historical Perspective

Mailman belongs to a generation of late-twentieth-century composers that includes Ron Nelson and Fisher Tull. He was one of the composers selected to participate in the Ford Foundation Project, which was an important vehicle for several aspiring musicians. He is currently in demand as composer, conductor, and clinician, and his works are already highly respected as is evidenced by his *For precious friends hid in death's dateless night* being the first piece to ever win both the ABA/Ostwald Prize and the NBA/Band Mans Award in the same year.

Unit 4: Technical Considerations

The piece has no key signatures so accidentals abound. There is a significant metric modulation without pause into the second large section. The tempos remain consistent within the movements. There are both *staccato* and *legato* articulations, so contrast is important. All instruments have several exposed sections and several solos as does the percussion section. Ranges and scalar passages are not difficult. The E-flat clarinet has some difficult parts, and the timpanist has several solos. The piece gives the entire percussion section a great deal to play. The entire middle section is in 5/4 meter; the measures are both 2+3 and 3+2; the conductor must decide which grouping to use based on the phrasing, and this must be carefully explained to the ensemble.

Unit 5: Stylistic Considerations

Articulations should be crisp, uniform, and march-like. All markings in the score support this. Each section has its own style but a certain drive should propel the work throughout. The intensity and movement of the music should be equal to the phrasing, articulation, rhythms, and principles of the line. This is a twentieth-century work with twentieth-century sounds; it should be approached with a twentieth-century interpretation. Part of the great appeal of this piece is Mailman's use of metrically strong beats in the measure on beats other than one or three. Many important accents and "hits" occur on beats two and four. An ensemble would need to be able to feel metrically strong beats anywhere in the measure.

Unit 6: Musical Elements

The entire piece rhythmically is an exchange between various rhythmic levels of twos and threes. Half notes, quarter notes, and eighth notes are in constant struggle and interplay with dotted half notes, dotted quarter notes, and triplets. Even the meters demonstrate the twos and threes: 3/4, 4/4, and 5/4 (2 + 3). The single unifying rhythm of two eighth notes (usually punctuated by percussion) is found in all arrival moments in the outer sections, and is so important that the entire piece ends with the rhythm.

The piece is in three sections; the first begins with an energetic triplet pattern exchanged between timpani solos and the ensemble. The horns enter, establishing the central theme of the piece, and "murmuring" running triplets are heard in the lower woodwinds. The melody of the second section is first established in the solo trumpet, accompanied by woodwinds and bell-like percussion. This theme is gradually expanded into a full brass choir. When the third section begins, it sounds like an exact repeat of the beginning, but quickly diverges. After a statement of the principal theme (a 3/4 theme written in 4/4 time), the "brass chorale" theme from the second section is displayed in counterpoint with running triplets and material from the second-section accompaniment combined and then divided between the upper woodwinds and the percussion. All themes from the first and second sections are used simultaneously in a later phrase. The piece concludes with a full unison statement of the primary triplet theme from the beginning which leads to a five-measure coda that "tonicizes" the final unifying rhythm of two eighth notes. All of the piece's melodic and harmonic construction is based on the four pitches (and their intervals) played by the timpani (F, A, B, and E).

Unit 7: Form and Structure

SECTION	MEASURES	EVENTS AND SCORING
Section I ($\quarternote$=126-132)	1-19	Main triplet theme, percussion and timpani solos
	20-38	Principal theme, French horn section with chimes
	38-55	Statements of unifying rhythm, build to fanfare theme, murmuring triplets
	56-60	Unifying rhythm used for first big arrival point, fanfare theme in brass
	61-88	Principal theme with running woodwinds
	89-97	Transition to Section II, metric modulation begins m. 96
Section II $\dottedhalf$. = $\quarternote$ ($\quarternote$=88)	98-106	Theme II, trumpet solos with shimmering woodwinds

	107-120	Theme II in brass chorale
	121-124	Stacking chords to woodwinds entrance
	125-131	Woodwinds closing Theme II
	132-142	Transition to Section IA
Section IA ($\downarrow$=126-132)	143-154	Opening repeated, main triplet theme, percussion and timpani solos
	155-171	Principal theme in low muted brass
	172-175	Transition
	176-194	"Brass chorale" with triplets and second section accompaniment
	195-204	Unifying rhythm, fanfare theme *tutti*
	205-210	Stacking chords with running woodwinds
	211-219	All themes combined
Coda	220-230	Use of all themes, unifying rhythm featured in last five measures

Unit 8: Suggested Listening

Howard Hanson, *Chorale and Alleluia*

Martin Mailman, *For precious friends hid in death's dateless night, Op. 80; Liturgical Music for Band, Op. 33; Secular Litanies for Band, Op. 90*

Matthew Mailman, *Effects for Symphonic Band*

Ron Nelson, *Rocky Point Holiday*

Unit 9: Additional References and Resources

Baker, Theodore. "Mailman, Martin," *Baker's Biographical Dictionary of Musicians*. 6th ed., revised by Nicolas Slonimsky. New York: Schirmer Books, 1984.

National Band Association Selective Music List for Bands.

Rehrig, William H. *The Heritage Encyclopedia of Band Music*. Westerville, OH: Integrity Press, 1991.

Contributed by:
Matthew Mailman
Director of Bands
Oklahoma City University
Oklahoma City, Oklahoma

Teacher Resource Guide

Festivo

Edward Gregson
(b. 1945)

Unit 1: Composer

Edward Gregson was born in Sunderland, England. A student of Alan Bush, he studied at the Royal Academy of Music in London from 1963-1967. He has worked with British brass bands as well as contemporary wind ensembles. Gregson is currently Principal Lecturer at Goldsmith's College, University of London, and teaches composition at the Royal Academy of Music. He is also highly regarded as a conductor of contemporary music.

Unit 2: Composition

Festivo is a concert overture which has replaced a traditional middle slow portion with a quick minimalistic section. It is a fresh, jubilant, driving composition which utilizes the instruments of the contemporary wind ensemble in soloistic, chamber, and tutti idioms.

Unit 3: Historical Perspective

Festivo was commissioned in 1985 for the tenth anniversary of the Bolton Youth Concert Band with funds provided by the Trustee Savings Bank. It was premiered by that same group (conducted by Nigel Taylor) in Kortrijk, Belgium, at the Conference of the World Association of Symphonic Bands and Wind Ensembles in July, 1985.

Unit 4: Technical Considerations

C major is the central key area of the piece, although frequent modulations occur throughout. Constantly shifting meters (simple and compound) and a wide array of rhythmic figures will keep the conductor and players alert, and the half-beat altered accompaniment at rehearsal 2 requires confidence on behalf of all the brass players. Significant technique is displayed in the woodwind and mallet percussion parts throughout. The trumpets and horns have large range requirements, and there must be depth in each section. Strong soloists are needed for the many motivic solo spots. This is a short six-minute work, but highly demanding in terms of individual and ensemble playing skills.

Unit 5: Stylistic Considerations

The opening fanfare figures should be full value but separated. The *allegro* 8/8 figures must be played lightly and accented on the strong beats, as must the Lydian scale figures must be accented on 1, the "and" of 2, and 4. In general, articulation should be quite light on all of these technical passages. The fanfare figures before 3 and in subsequent passages are also long and spaced apart. When multiple layers of musical activity stack up in various places, the conductor will have to ensure that parts are equally balanced. The softer section after rehearsal 5 must calm down significantly, lapsing into a relaxed flowing section. Syncopated *ostinati* should be long notes, lightly separated. The festive mood is reestablished at rehearsal 7. Unison passages should not be overplayed after rehearsal 8. The minimalistic section beginning four before 9 should gradually increase in intensity as the various instruments and motifs begin to accumulate. The unison descending minor third at rehearsal 12 should forceful, but not be too loud. Bell tones should be equally balanced and prominent before 13, and recede into the background at 13. At *Giocoso*, both the horn call and the scalar motifs should be heard equally. The last note should be full value and energetic.

Unit 6: Musical Elements

Musical elements include: compound meter, shifting meter, *stretto*, displaced rhythms, Lydian mode, motif, syncopation, superimposition of themes, minimalism, overture, and quartal pattern.

Unit 7: Form and Structure

SECTION	MEASURES/REH. MARKS	EVENTS AND SCORING
Introduction	1-10	Majestic opening horn motif (A) and presentation of melody based on A (fourth, second, fourth), timpani sixteenths, A motif in stretto, cadence in C major
Transition	reh. 1	Shifting compound meter, soft

		sustained clusters percussion, scalar/descending triadic motif (B) in solo oboe, flute, bass clarinet, clarinet, bassoon, piccolo, E-flat clarinet
First section	reh. 2	Displaced downbeat/offbeat pattern Lydian scalar melody (C) in clarinets, echoed in alto and tenor saxophones, C major
	2 before 3	Fanfare figure (D) in woodwinds and horns
Second section	reh. 3	Trumpets with C, echoes in bassoon/baritone, melody taken over by upper woodwinds.
	5 after 3	D in trumpets and trombones, developed and extended, bass voices added
Third section	reh. 4	D motif developed in brass and saxophones with *stretto* in upper woodwinds
Transition	5 after 4	C in *stretto* in woodwinds and mallets, A motif in horns and trumpets, modulatory with A motif
Fourth section	6 after 5	Light texture, syncopated accompaniment in bassoons and clarinets, solo variations of A motif (fourths, fifths, seconds) in clarinet, oboe, tuba, contra-bass clarinet, flute, alto saxophone, baritone, bassoon, later added upper woodwinds/ trumpets to build
Fifth section	reh. 7	Horns/trombones with synco-pated punctuations, C in clarinets, echoed in flutes, C in oboes and clarinets, then trumpets

Sixth section	4 before 8	Block legato chords in brass, responded to by C in woodwinds and percussion
Transition	3 after 8	C in woodwinds, then shift to B motif, and gradual descent to sustained pedal A in stopped horns/baritone/saxophones
Seventh section	4 before 9	Two harmonies: D and E-flat, alternating minimalistic increase in rhythmic action, voices, and melodic/harmonic layering, downbeat/afterbeat figures, clarinet sixteenths, muted trumpet sixteenths, sustained pedals in bassoons/tubas, punctuated descending thirds and fifths in oboes and upper clarinets, sixteenths in flutes and saxophones, rising fourths in horns, snippets of A, sixteenths in mallets and woodwinds, alternating punctuated descending intervals in brass (increasing in frequency and closeness), displaced, build to unison descending minor third at 12
Eighth section	reh. 12	Timpani sixteenths to recapitulation of A motif
Ninth section	3 before 13	Bell tones in brass, B in piccolo/flute/clarinet, A in muted trumpets, add clarinets on B, horns and tenor saxophone on B, build
Tenth section	reh. 14	D in woodwinds, flourish
Eleventh section	5 after 14	Downbeat/afterbeat accompaniment under A in alto voices/C in piccolo/flute/clarinet, echo in trumpet and baritone

| Twelfth section | reh. 15 | D in brass, extended 2 before 16, two more measures of super-imposed A and C |
| Ending Section | reh. 16 | C in *stretto* in woodwinds and mallets, A motif in horns and trumpets, extended A motif with final cadence in C major (with timpani sixteenths) |

Unit 8: Suggested Listening

Music by Edward Gregson:
Metamorphoses
Prelude for an Occasion
Concerto for Tuba and Band
Concerto for Trombone and Band
The Sword and the Crown
Celebration
The Kings Go Forth

Unit 9: Additional References and Resources

British Orchestral Music. London: Composers Guild, 1958.

Fanerc, Karen, ed. *Catalog of the American Music Center*. Volume III. Washington: American Music Center, 1975-83.

Military and Brass Band Music in the Australian Music Center. Sydney: Australia Music Center, 1977.

Suppan, Armin. *Repertorium der Märsche für Blasorchester*. Tutzing: H. Schneider, 1982.

Contributed by:

Scott A. Stewart
Indiana University
Bloomington, Indiana

Teacher Resource Guide

Four Scottish Dances
Malcolm Arnold
(b. 1921)

arranged by
John Paynter (1928–1996)

Unit 1: Composer
Malcolm Henry Arnold was born on October 21, 1921, in Northampton, England. Arnold was the product of a family with strong musical roots. His father, although a shoemaker, was an active amateur pianist, and his mother was an accomplished keyboard performer. His early musical training came from his mother who encouraged him to study the drum set, the violin, and finally the trumpet. It was the trumpet, however, which most interested the young Arnold. During his early years of study, he became fascinated with the jazz style of Louis Armstrong. Arnold's formal studies came at the Royal College of Music in London between 1938 and 1940, where he studied trumpet, conducting, and composition with Gordon Jacob. In 1941, he joined the London Philharmonic Orchestra and was soon promoted to the principal seat. In 1948, Arnold went to Italy to devote his full energies to the study of composition. Upon returning to England in 1949, he had completed his first of nine symphonies. Since that time, Malcolm Arnold has written for almost every musical idiom. In 1968, he received an Oscar for his film score to *The Bridge on the River Kwai*.

Unit 2: Composition
Four Scottish Dances was composed in 1957 and was dedicated to the British Broadcasting Corporation's Light Music Festival. Arnold states, "They are based on original melodies but one, the melody of which was composed by Robert Burns." The composition utilizes a number of rhythms, motives, and

harmonies frequently associated with Scottish folk music. Originally for orchestra, the work was transcribed for wind band in 1978 by John P. Paynter.

Unit 3: Historical Perspective

The *Four Scottish Dances* is one of five dance suites composed by Malcolm Arnold. The other compositions in this genre include the *English Dances Set One and Two* (1950), the *Cornish Dances* (1966), and the *Irish Dances* (1986). The movements of these suites are individual musical cameos, each developing its own musical sentiment. Many movements may stand alone as pictorial miniatures in the same spirit as Dvorak's *Slavonic Dances* or Brahms's *Hungarian Dances*. Arnold's musical style, however, draws its roots from those masters of English folk music including Vaughan Williams, Holst, and Jacob. Arnold's original music for wind bands include *H.R.H. The Duke of Cambridge* (1957), *Overseas* (1960), *Water Music* (1964), *Little Suite #1* (brass band, 1965), *Little Suite #2* (brass band, 1966), *The Padstow Lifeboat* (brass band, 1967), and *Travelyan Suite* (wind ensemble, 1967).

Unit 4: Technical Considerations

FIRST MOVEMENT

Rhythmic accuracy is of prime importance during the first movement. Arnold motivically uses the dotted eighth- and sixteenth-note figure throughout the movement. Exact precision on the single sixteenth is critical. Rhythmic complexities occur in the woodwinds when moving from sixteenth notes to triplet sixteenths in accompanimental passages. The *poco più mosso* in m. 21 requires accurate triple tonguing in the trumpets and trombones. This passage is punctuated with rapid two-octave *glissandi* in the horns requiring all four parts to hit a B above the staff. Syncopated triplets are used against an eighth-note scalar passage in m. 30 to return to the A material in m. 31. Demands on precision and technique are placed upon the woodwinds, horns, euphonium, and tuba in a sixteenth-note *accelerando molto* into the movement's final *pesante* statement.

SECOND MOVEMENT

This movement, marked *Vivace* with the quarter note at 160, places technical demands upon all instruments. Of special note is the need for experienced bassoons and clarinets throughout. During the brief sixty-five measures of this movement, Arnold modulates six times, moving through the keys of E-flat, E, F, G-flat, G, and returning to E-flat. All players must be able to negotiate rapid, technical passages in these keys. Diatonic trill fingerings may pose a problem in many of the woodwind parts. Accurate articulations, coupled with the requirement of a light *staccato* technique make this movement truly a "tour de force" for the ensemble.

THIRD MOVEMENT

The third movement is an example of Arnold at his lyric best. This movement will require a keen sense of intonation, beautiful characteristic tone, and control within the softest dynamic *tessituras*. A *pianissimo* three-part flute and clarinet *divisi* opens this movement in sustained closed position triads. The primary solo instrument used throughout the movement is the oboe. If one does not have a mature oboist, it would be wise to place the solo material in the flute, which was Arnold's original selection in the orchestral setting. The harp is important to this movement. If no harp is available, the use of synthesized harp, a piano, or celesta is recommended. Technical problems in this movement revolve around control and intonation. Groups of instruments are regularly required to enter and exit at very soft dynamic levels. Technical concerns may occur with trills and their ornamental resolution (mm. 20, 52, 59, 60).

FOURTH MOVEMENT

The tempo marking for this movement is *con brio* with the quarter note marked at 144. Paynter has scored the original violin parts in the first and second alto saxophones only. The parts play kaleidoscopic sixteenths which must clearly project over the harmonic drone in the brass. Starting in the third measure, rhythmic precision will be a problem in the upper woodwinds. It is critical for the woodwinds to accurately and consistently release and separate after the *staccato* eighth-note. At m. 19, it is important to emphasize the cross-rhythms in the bass line which must be in balance with the horns, trombones, and euphonium. Balance at mm. 27 through 43 is important to allow moving percussion lines to clearly project over the ensemble. Sustained material between mm. 43 and 50 must be kept at a soft dynamic level to maximize the timbral and dynamic contrast. It is important to keep the eighth note as the constant rhythmic pulse when the 6/8 in m. 49 is executed. Attention should be given to the *accelerando* and the *forte-piano* marking at m. 67, since both tempo and dynamic pacing are critical as the ensemble moves into the closing *presto* in m. 77.

Unit 5: Stylistic Considerations

FIRST MOVEMENT

In writing about the first movement, Arnold states, "The first dance is in the style of a slow strathspey—a slow Scottish dance in 4/4 meter—with many dotted notes, frequently in the inverted arrangement of the 'Scotch snap'. The name was derived from the Strath Valley of Spey." Throughout the movement, clarity must be given to both the dotted eighth and sixteenth figures, as well as when the accented sixteenth note occurs on the beat. Abrupt contrasts are an important element in Arnold's musical style. The *poco più mosso* in m. 21 should have a lighter, more fleeting style than the surrounding strathspey material. The trumpet and trombone fanfare used throughout this section should have a crisp brilliance. The *coda*, mm. 49-51, should be performed in a heavier *tenuto* manner, giving the music an almost drunken style.

SECOND MOVEMENT

Regarding this movement, Arnold states, "The second, a lively reel, begins in the key of E-flat and rises a semi-tone each time until the bassoon plays it, at a greatly reduced speed, in the key of G. The final statement of the dance is at the original speed in the home key of E-flat." The melody for this movement was originally a portion of Arnold's film score, *The Beautiful Country of Ayr.* This movement should have a crisp, athletic character to its style. As the music modulates by half step with each variation, the character of each new section should seem increasingly energized (this is Arnold playing musical "one-upmanship"). Attention should be given to the changes in orchestration; all instruments are used very soloistically and shifts in instrumental colors should be emphasized. Although each variation has its unique character, the fifth variation (mm. 41-56) is in augmentation in the bassoon. This variation should be interpreted in a rhythmically freer manner, again giving an almost drunken character to the music. Rhythmic precision should be emphasized throughout the final thematic statement (mm. 57-65), since Arnold has hocketed the melodic material in the last three measures.

THIRD MOVEMENT

In his discussion of the third movement, Arnold states, "The third dance is in the style of a Hebridean song, and attempts to give an impression of the sea and the mountain scenery on a calm summer's day in the Hebrides." The Hebrides are a group of islands just off the coast of Scotland. The weather on these islands ranges from calm to very stormy, but usually a gentle breeze is present most of the year. Mendelssohn attempted to set this landscape to music in his *Hebrides Overture* (1832). The melody of this movement should have a sustained, sweeping quality. Like an unpredictable breeze, the conductor should shape and stretch the line to give added contour to the melody. A rhapsodic quality to the music should be sustained throughout the movement. Attention to timbral shifts in the accompanimental material should be highlighted. Transitions between each statement of the melody should be stretched, with particular care given to trilled woodwind material with ornamental resolutions.

FOURTH MOVEMENT

Arnold states, "The last dance is a lively fling which makes a great deal of the use of the open string pitches of the violin." In this arrangement, the two alto saxophones are given this "fiddle tune;" care should be taken to help this line project. The movement should maintain a buoyant, fleeting character. The musical drones in the lower brass and woodwinds should be emphasized (Arnold "bagpipe" signature) but should not cover the light-hearted melody in the upper woodwinds. A sharp dynamic and stylistic

contrast should be evident in mm. 11-18, as the more *pesante* second theme is introduced. Arnold alternates these two ideas, with the first stylistic shift occurring in m. 43. Care should be taken to keep all sustained material at a soft level to allow the "child-like" thematic treatment to easily be heard. Starting in m. 67, an *accelerando* adds excitement and energy which must be carried through to the final note.

Unit 6: Musical Elements

FIRST MOVEMENT

The opening movement is in ternary form (ABA) with an added *coda*. The A theme is repeated three times in the first section with the addition of two countermelodies. The first countermelody is a florid sixteenth-note line stated in the upper woodwinds, with the second entering in a two-voice canon in m. 9. The B section, mm. 21-29, is characterized by fanfare-like figures in the trumpets and trombones over a dominant pedal. After a brief transition in m. 30, the A section returns with four thematic repetitions with alternating drone and countermelody 1 and 2 overlays. A scalar sixteenth-note transition leads to the *coda* which presents a slower, comical conclusion to the movement.

SECOND MOVEMENT

The second movement is a theme and variations. The unaccompanied theme is stated in the unison bassoon and clarinet followed by six variations. The first variation simply restates the theme with an accompaniment with all following variations ascending by a half step. In the first four variations, contrast is provided by altering the instrumentation and texture of the accompaniment. Variation five offers the first "character variation" with the theme in augmentation played by the bassoon. A final return to the original key and tempo concludes the movement with the theme split between the clarinet and bassoon.

THIRD MOVEMENT

The third movement is in a strophic variation form. Arnold uses one unifying melody, mm. 5-12 in the oboe, answered by a secondary theme in the trumpet (mm. 13-20). The movement contains three complete statements of the two melodies, once in F major, A major, and D-flat major. A single statement of the A theme with an added *coda* closes the movement.

FOURTH MOVEMENT

The final movement is again in a strophic variation form. After a brief introduction establishing the A minor tonality, the composer introduces the A theme in the upper woodwinds set against a tonic-dominant pedal. The B theme is a hocketed line, alternating a dotted eighth and sixteenth figure with an accented sixteenth-note passage. There are two complete statements of the

A and B themes before Arnold inserts a variation of the A material in mm. 43-50 prior to the third B theme statement. A final statement of the A material leads to a closing section which is based upon segments of the A and B themes. An *accelerando* propels the movement into a nine-measure *coda* marked *Presto*.

Unit 7: Form and Structure

First Movement: *Pesante*

Section	Measures	Tonal Center	Events and Scoring
A	1-8	A minor	A theme with drones
	4-8		Countermelody added in woodwinds
A^1	9-16		A theme with countermelody 2 in low brass and low woodwinds
Transition	16		
A^2	17-20		A theme with countermelody 2 in low brass and low woodwinds
B	21-29	E minor	Fanfare figures in trumpets and trombones over a dominant pedal
Transition	30		
A	31-34	A minor	A theme with countermelody 2
A^1	35-37		A theme, drone-like accompaniment
Transition	38		
A^2	39-42		A theme with countermelody 1
A^3	43-45		A theme with tonal-dominant pedal
Transition	46-48		Sixteenth-note
Coda	49-51		Slow *pesante*, new material

SECTION	MEASURES	TONAL CENTER	EVENTS AND SCORING
Second Movement: *Vivace*			
A	1-8	E-flat	Unaccompanied theme in clarinet and bassoon
A¹	8-16	E-flat	Restatement of theme with accompanimental material
A²	17-24	E	Melody in clarinet, trumpet, and alto saxophone, thicker accompaniment
A³	25-32	F	Melody in flute and clarinet with the second half in the trumpet; sixteenth-note accompaniment
A⁴	33-40	G-flat	Melody in flutes, clarinet, and oboe; drone-like accompaniment
A⁵	41-56	G	Slower tempo; melody in augmentation in the bassoon; light accompanimental figures
A⁶	57-65	E-flat	Original tempo; return to original key; melody in clarinet with second half in bassoon
Third Movement: *Allegretto*			
Introduction	1-4	F major	Chordal opening with moving harp line
A	1-12		Melody in oboe, homophonic accompaniment
B	13-20		Musical answer to A, B theme in brass with triplet accompaniment figure
Modulatory transition	19-20		
A	21-28	A major	A theme with triplet accompaniment

SECTION	MEASURES	TONAL CENTER	EVENTS AND SCORING
B	29-36		B theme in woodwinds
Modulatory transition	35-36		
A	37-44	D-flat major	A theme in oboe; triplet accompaniment
B	45-52		Melody in horn and English horn; chordal accompaniment
Modulatory transition	51-52		
A	53-61	F major	Melody in oboe; simple homophonic accompaniment
Coda	62-68		Chordal material in upper woodwinds

Fourth Movement: *Con Brio*

Introduction	1-2	A minor	Sixteenth-note figure in saxophones with drone accompaniment
A	3-10		Melody A in upper woodwinds
B	11-18		Hocketed melody between woodwinds and brass
A	19-26		A theme with drone accompaniment
B	27-34		Variation of B theme
A	35-42		A theme in woodwinds and cornets; light accompanimental figures
A variation	43-50		Light "child-like" statement of A theme with rhythmic extensions; tonic pedal
B	51-58		Hocketed woodwind and brass exchanges

SECTION	MEASURES	TONAL CENTER	EVENTS AND SCORING
A	59-66		Return to opening setting
Closing	67-77		Closing section based on an overlay of segments of A and B themes with an *accelerando*
Coda	77-85		*Presto*

Unit 8: Suggested Listening

Malcolm Arnold, *Cornish Dances, English Dances, Irish Dances*
John Corigliano, *Gazebo Dances*
Ralph Vaughan Williams, *Folk Song Suite*
Guy Woolfenden, *Illyrian Dances*

Unit 9: Additional References and Resources

Arnold, Malcolm. *Arnold Dances*. The Philharmonia conducted by Bryden Thomson. Chandos CHAN 8867. Notes by Christopher Palmer.

Arnold, Malcolm. *Arnold for Band*. Dallas Wind Symphony conducted by Jerry Junkin. Reference Recording RR-66CD. Notes by Frank Byrne.

Sadie, Stanley, ed. *The New Grove Dictionary of Music and Musicians*. London: Macmillan, 1980.

Slonimsky, Nicolas. *Baker's Biographical Dictionary of Musicians*. New York: Macmillan, 1992.

Smith, Norman and Albert Stoutamire. *Band Music Notes*. Lake Charles, LA: Program Note Press, 1989.

Contributed by:

Edward Harris
Director of Bands
California State University/Stanislaus
Turlock, California

Teacher Resource Guide

Illyrian Dances

Guy Woolfenden
(b. 1937)

Unit 1: Composer

Guy Woolfenden was born at Ipswich, England in 1937. Educated at Christ's College, Cambridge, and at the Guildhall School of Music, London, he has been Head of Music for the Royal Shakespeare Company at Stratford-on-Avon for many years, and has written more than 150 scores for its productions. His interest in incidental music for theatrical productions and in ballet has taken him to other countries, most notably Australia, where he has arranged and conducted productions with the Australian Ballet, and Russia, where he has appeared with the Kirov Ballet in St. Petersburg. Also active as a conductor, Woolfenden was artistic director of the Cambridge Festival from 1986 to 1991, and has given orchestral concerts in England, Canada, Germany, and France. He is the founder of the Ariel Music Publishing Company. Woolfenden has made a significant contribution to the repertoire for wind instruments. His chamber works for winds, and the concertos for oboe and clarinet have been well received. *Suite Française* for wind octet is frequently performed. A number of his scores for productions of the Royal Shakespeare Company employ winds and percussion only. His band works include *Gallimaufry* and *SPQR*.

Unit 2: Composition

Illyrian Dances, commissioned by the British Association of Symphonic Bands and Ensembles, was first performed at Warwick University, on September 26, 1986, during the fifth annual BASBE conference. Illyria is a mythical country invented by Shakespeare as the setting for *Twelfth Night*.

461

According to the composer, Shakespeare was not interested in a precise geographical location for Illyria, but was attracted by the resonance of the word itself and by the lure of far-away, make-believe places. Woolfenden considers Illyria to be Never Never Land, and was intrigued by the idea of writing dances for such a place. The score is prefaced with a quotation from the first act of *Twelfth Night*:

Viola: What country, friends, is this?
Captain: This is Illyria, lady.

The work has three movements: "Rondeau," "Aubade," and "Gigue." All three are based on scores written by Woolfenden for earlier productions of the Royal Shakespeare Company. The "Rondeau" draws on the music of a 1967 production of *Romeo and Juliet*, while the other two movements, "Aubade" and "Gigue," are based on incidental music composed in 1977 for *A Midsummer Night's Dream*. The music for both of these productions was originally scored for winds and percussion only. *Illyrian Dances* is approximately ten minutes long.

Unit 3: Historical Perspective

Because this music was conceived with Shakespeare in mind, it is Neoclassical in concept, reflecting musical practices that are approximately contemporary with the great English author. All three dance types (*rondeau, aubade,* and *gigue*) are associated with the seventeenth century, and Woolfenden has carefully reflected the style and form of these dances, while the harmony, rhythm, and scoring are of this century. In the seventeenth-century *rondeau*, a refrain alternated with contrasting episodes that explored closely-related keys. Refrain and episodes were constructed of clearly-marked and regular phrases. Woolfenden's "Rondeau" replicates the refrain-episode structure of its model, but, while contrasting keys are explored, timbral variety is much more important. Phrasing is well marked, but the refrain (in 2/4 time) and most of the episodes are seven bars long and have a measure of 6/8 as their sixth bar, creating a delightful rhythmic nuance. The *aubade* of the seventeenth century was quiet music played at the *levées* of royal personages. No specifics of form and content seem to have been practiced, and the term has since come to denote any music associated with morning. Woolfenden's "Aubade," which clearly reveals its theatrical origin, is a sensitive and atmospheric description of the onset of day. Seventeenth-century *gigues* were fast dances in compound meter that featured melodies with wide leaps and uneven phrase lengths. Textures were highly imitative. In his "Gigue," Woolfenden reflects all of these characteristics in a transparent scoring that approaches pointillism in several places.

Unit 4: Technical Considerations

The first movement is in 2/4 meter, *Allegro moderato*, quarter note=120. It has a key signature of one flat, but the harmony is modal, precipitating many accidentals. The refrain and its variants are transposed to a number of pitch levels. Ranges are moderate except for a few high notes in the horns, and some important melodic material in the low register of the flutes that is difficult to project. All sections have exposed solos. Easy solos for timpani and oboe appear, as well as a challenging tuba solo. Woodwinds and xylophone have a number of short passages in sixteenth notes. Rhythmically demanding for all players, this music incorporates numerous shifts between 2/4 and 6/8, syncopation, and multiple layers of subdivision.

The second movement is in 3/4, *Andante con moto*, quarter note=80. Modally conceived melodies and harmonies again precipitate numerous accidentals. Rhythmically sophisticated, this movement features *hemiola*, an important aspect of the melodies and the accompaniment in every section, and a metric modulation from 3/4 to 6/8 and back to 3/4. Horn, oboe, clarinet, flute, and trumpet have exposed solos.

The third movement is simpler harmonically and rhythmically than either of the previous movements. Tonally centered on C, it is in 6/8 meter, *Allegro giocoso*, dotted quarter note=92. The melodic material features many wide skips at fast tempos, and high woodwinds encounter a few very rapid sixteenth-note passages. The highly contrapuntal texture requires careful counting. Oboe, piccolo, two flutes, clarinet, trumpet, timpani, xylophone, and snare drum have exposed solos.

In addition to the challenges of pitch and rhythm identified above, Woolfenden's motivic counterpoint and the especially transparent scoring of this work require that constant attention be focused on balance, articulation, listening, and musical sensitivity.

Unit 5: Stylistic Considerations

Since these movements are dances, care must be taken to establish and maintain a light, buoyant style, with particular concern assigned to pulse. Seventeenth-century models provide the inspiration for the imitative counterpoint and the frequent shifts between full-band and chamber-ensemble textures that recall the structure of the *concerto grosso*. Precise and consistent articulation are essential if melodic relationships are to be clearly projected. Also reflecting older musical procedures is the extensive use of ornamentation, which is either written out or marked using traditional symbols. Interpretation of these symbols should follow established practices. As might be expected in a twentieth-century composition, dynamic changes, often by small increments, are used to define phrases. Even the slightest alterations, especially those immediately preceding cadences, must be perceivable by audiences.

Unit 6: Musical Elements

MOVEMENT ONE

The first movement begins with a timpani solo that might be heard as calling dancers to the stage. It is followed by a nine-bar introduction that draws on motives from the refrain theme. The refrain arrives at m. 12, played first by brass only. Instead of alternating the refrain with contrasting episodes as would be the usual practice, Woolfenden repeats it, initially with little alteration to the tune, in a series of highly variable scorings. Later he constructs variants on the primary theme. However, all repetitions are clearly separated by cadences that are preceded by a 6/8 bar. Most are seven bars long. After thirteen statements of the primary theme in its various guises, the timpani solo from the opening bars returns to usher in a *coda* that is at a faster tempo. In the *coda*, the refrain is restated exactly as it first appeared, then is repeated and extended to create an effective ending.

MOVEMENT TWO

The composer describes this movement as "ternary form with a hint of the dawn chorus at the close." The initial A has two subsections: A-1 and A-2. Both employ the same melodic motives constructed from fragments of modal scales and harmonic pyramids in the accompaniment. However, a new melody appears in A-2 that incorporates wide skips and later includes numerous hesitations, meter changes, and much *hemiola*. B is very delicately scored with solo textures much in prominence. The melodies are also modal fragments and immediately establish a 6/8 feel against the 3/4 meter. The final part of this section leads into the climax of the movement, which features a metric modulation from 3/4 to 6/8 and back. The second A begins with the A-2 theme in canon, and later sets motives from A-1 and A-2 against each other in counterpoint. The "dawn chorus" mentioned by the composer is inserted into this section, and serves as a dramatic contrast to earlier music. A low-register sound cloud is established through the superimposing of several levels of subdivision. Over this gently pulsating background, flute, oboe, and first clarinet play birdcall figures. The movement concludes with a restatement of the music with which it began, altered only to provide a cadence.

MOVEMENT THREE

Like the first movement of this work, the "Gigue" is an unconventional *rondo*, Intro.-A-B-A-B-C-D-Coda (B-A). However, the divisions of the form are not clear-cut, since all thematic material contains fragments from A or are developments of motives from the primary theme. Also, in the *coda*, the musical elements are stated in reverse order, B-A, and the closing segment recalls the textures and scoring of the introduction, giving the complete movement a sense of arch form. Like the "Rondeau," this movement opens with a percussion solo and an introduction based on fragments of the primary theme. A arrives at m. 16. Its first phrase is played by solo piccolo; flutes/oboe complete the tune. B has the character of a fanfare, but it incorporates a motive from A, and introduces a *hemiola* figure. The second A uses only the first phrase of the theme. Hints of B appear in the accompaniment. C employs part of A adapted to incorporate the *hemiola* from B. It also introduces a new theme that is derived from A. The rhythm in the accompaniment relates to B. D is similar to C in construction. It uses fragments from A and presents another new melody built from the opening notes of the primary melody. A climactic segment follows that also clearly displays its relationship to A, and leads to the *coda*. As in the first movement, the *coda* begins with a percussion solo. At the return of A, the music abruptly modulates to D-flat, but gradually reverts to C in the closing bars.

Unit 7: Form and Structure

SECTION	MEASURES	EVENTS AND SCORING
Movement One: "Rondeau"		
Intro.	1-11	Timpani solo, ensuing bars are based on motives from the theme of the refrain; establishes the metric shift to 6/8 within 2/4 meter
R(efrain)-1	12-18	Brass only
R-2	19-26	Full band; extended by one bar
R-3	27-33	Melody in clarinet I; very simple accompaniment; flutes play a rhythmically simplified and decorated version of the melody
R-4	34-40	Melody in horn I; accompaniment similar to R-3; new motive played imitatively in high woodwinds
R-5	41-47	Fuller scoring; trumpet soli; melody doubled by flutes, clarinet I
V(ariant)-1	48-55	First variant on tune in flutes/piccolo for one phrase, finished by clarinets; inversion of tune as accompaniment; section extended by one bar
V-2	56-62	New variant in clarinet I; simple accompaniment
V-1	63-70	First variant played by solo tuba; simplified inversion in accompaniment

SECTION	MEASURES	EVENTS AND SCORING
R-6	71-77	Melody in solo oboe; simple accompaniment
V-1	78-85	Melody in flutes and clarinet I; section extended one bar by timpani solo
V-3	86-92	New variant; trombone soli
V-4	93-100	New variant; flutes; section extended by one bar
V-5	101-107	New variant; flutes/oboes
V-5	108-114	Fuller scoring
Coda	115-118	Timpani solo; accelerando to più mosso
R-1	119-125	
R-7	126-138	Melody in horns; cadential extension

Movement Two: "Aubade"

A	1-8	A-1; chord in fourths built as a musical pyramid in clarinets; melodic fragments in flute, horn, clarinet I, and oboe based on segments of modal scales (mostly Aeolian)
	9-20	A-2; harmonic structure A-1; new melody in flutes constructed around wide skips; variant of horn motive from A-1 in clarinet I and oboe; second part separated into short phrases by fermatas; much hemiola
B	21-38	New melodic idea, also modal; solo and duet textures
	39-46	Metric modulation and climax
A	47-66	A-2; melody in canon; melodic ideas from A-1 and A-2 in counterpoint after m. 54
"Dawn chorus"	67-78	Sound cloud in accompaniment; birdcalls in flute, oboe, and clarinet I
	79-88	Mm. 1-8 with two-bar cadential extension

SECTION	MEASURES	EVENTS AND SCORING
Movement Three: "Gigue"		
Intro.	1-15	Motives from primary theme; gradual textural accumulation
A	16-31	Primary theme stated twice: first time played by solo piccolo and flutes with simple accompaniment; second time full band
B	32-40	Secondary idea; fanfare that incorporates motives from A
A(1)	41-48	Contrapuntal development of first phrase of A
B(1)	49-58	Development of fanfare
C	59-74	Fragments of A in piccolo, oboe, and E-flat clarinet; new theme in flutes and clarinet I that is based on A; accompaniment related to B
D	75-90	New theme in solo trumpet (later clarinets as well); motive from A in flutes and piccolo; rhythmic figure from B in horns and oboes
T	91-100	Transitional and climactic material; motives from A
Coda	101-113	Timpani solo; recall of B; modulation to D-flat
	114-121	Recall of A
	122-133	Cadential extension; motives from A; textural recession; modulation to C

Unit 8: Suggested Listening

Francis Poulenc, *Suite Française*
Ottorino Resphigi, *Ancient Aires and Dances* (Three Suites)
Guy Woolfenden, *Gallimaufry, SPQR, Suite Française*
Archangelo Corelli, George Frederick Handel, Johann Sebastian Bach: *concerti grossi* and orchestral suites.

Unit 9: Additional References and Resources

Apel, Willi, ed. *Harvard Dictionary of Music*. Second ed. Cambridge, MA: The Belknap Press of the Harvard University Press, 1972.

Dvorak, Thomas L., Robert Grechesky, and Gary Ciepluch. *Best Music for High School Band*. Brooklyn, NY: Manhattan Beach Music, 1993.

Cummings, David M., ed. *International Who's Who in Music and Musician's Directory*. Fourteenth ed. Cambridge: Melrose Press Ltd., 1994.

Gooch, Bryan N. S., and David Thatcher. *A Shakespeare Music Catalogue*. Oxford: Clarendon Press, 1991.

Rehrig, William H. *The Heritage Encyclopedia of Band Music*. Edited by Paul Bierley. Westerville, OH: Integrity Press, 1991.

Sadie, Stanley, ed. *The Norton/Grove Concise Encyclopedia of Music*. New York: W.W. Norton & Co., 1988.

Contributed by:

Keith Kinder
Associate Professor of Music
McMaster University
Hamilton, Ontario, Canada

Teacher Resource Guide

Incantation and Dance
John Barnes Chance
(1932–1972)

Unit 1: Composer

John Barnes Chance was born in Beaumont, Texas. He began studying composition at the age of fifteen and had several performances of his works while he was still a high school student. Chance earned both his bachelor and master of music degrees at the University of Texas where he studied composition with Kent Kennan, Clifton Williams, and Paul Pisk. In 1956 he was awarded the Carl Owens Award for best compositional work by a student. Although commonly known as a composer, Chance also performed as timpanist for the Austin Symphony Orchestra and served as an arranger for the Fourth and Eighth United States Army Bands. From 1960 to 1961 Chance was composer-in-residence at Greensboro Senior High School in North Carolina with the Ford Foundation Young Composers Project. Chance enjoyed a short but successful career as a composer of works for band, chorus, orchestra, solo instruments, and chamber groups. Chance died at the age of forty on August 16, 1972, a victim of electrocution.

Unit 2: Composition

Incantation and Dance is the first composition for band by John Barnes Chance. It was composed for the Greensboro Senior High Band and Director Herbert Hazelman and was premiered on Wednesday, November 16, 1960. The original title for the work was *Nocturne and Dance*, but when Chance later revised the composition, he not only deleted thirty-one bars, but changed the name to its current title. The "Incantation" section of the work formally serves as an introduction and presents a thirteen-measure theme from which all other melodic material is derived. The "Dance" section begins quietly with the building of a complex and driving rhythmic pattern in the percussion. As the rest of the band enters, the music becomes more and more frenzied, continuing its wild dance with complete abandon up to the final measure. *Incantation and Dance* is 235 measures in length and approximately seven and one-half minutes in duration.

Unit 3: Historical Perspective

Incantation is defined as "words chanted in magic spells or rites." Composers have often been drawn to create musical renditions of supernatural or magical happenings. Throughout music history there are prime examples of art songs, operas, tone poems, and the like based upon subjects that exceed the accepted limits of religious and social belief and wander into another realm. Chance's work for band virtually takes the listener into another time period for a chanting ritual or mystic celebration. From the *misterioso* opening of the "Incantation" to the wild presto of the "Dance," this composition creates a visual and aural image of a magical ceremony.

Unit 4: Technical Considerations

Rhythm is perhaps the most important element of the work and presents the greatest technical challenge. Students will need to count carefully and make entrances with confidence and security. The sixteenth-note runs and the *hemiola* feel in the dance theme provide a special challenge. Students must strive to attain rhythmic precision while conveying the freedom and frantic energy of the musical ideas. Conductors must concern themselves throughout with proper attacks, releases, and articulations. Precision will significantly impact the final product. Woodwinds are required to perform lengthy trills and great leaps in pitch. Because of the extremely loud dynamic levels, brasses will need to work on pitch and tone control. Range is also a concern as both the brass and woodwind parts have wide *tessitura*. The percussion is scored in six parts and requires the use of bass drum, gong, maracas, claves, gourd, temple blocks, timbales, timpani, whip, cymbals, tambourine, and bongos. Given the many technical considerations *Incantation and Dance* richly deserves the Grade Five level of difficulty bestowed upon it.

Unit 5: Stylistic Considerations

The "Incantation" section is both *largo* and *legato*. Strive for fluid, well-conceived phrasing while maintaining the *piano* dynamic level. Trumpets will need hats to achieve the tone color desired by the composer in m. 26. Due to the rhythmic intricacies of the piece, the conductor needs to be concerned with rhythmic execution and accent placement. Staccatos should be dry yet have some body and tone. The marked short, hard accents should not be hammered, but need to be given emphasis. Space between notes in the quarter-note triplets is essential to properly convey the phrase. Chance's score markings are quite specific in reference to articulation and dynamic levels.

Unit 6: Musical Elements

The first theme of the "Incantation" is in Phrygian mode and subsequent melodic entrances continue to use the initial four notes of this scale. Pedal tones help to establish a tonal base while contributing to the *misterioso* quality of this introductory section. Fragmentation seems to be the prevailing concept in the "Dance" portion of this work. Virtually all instruments in the ensemble play at least a portion of the theme. Careful attention to balance is necessary to hear important lines. The composer made a note in the original score concerning accents:

> Because there is no musical notation to indicate a "non-accent," it may be necessary to caution the players against placing any metric pulsation on the first and third beats of the syncopated measures of the dance; to accent these beats in the accustomed way will destroy the intended effect.

Unit 7: Form and Structure

The "Incantation" portion of this work functions as an introduction. The "Dance" portion is divided into two parts with a coda.

SECTION	MEASURES	EVENTS AND SCORING
"Incantation"	1-25	Flutes with low reeds accompanying clarinets with counterline in bassoon, contrabass clarinet, and tuba at the marked *Poco più mosso*.
	26-32	Full ensemble enters with thematic material in trumpets, trombones, and baritones.
"Dance" Section I		Introduction of thematic material via fragmentation.
	35-52	Presentation of five different rhythmic motives in percussion.
	33-129	Portions of theme appear in nearly all instruments as the dance progresses with a constant intensity.
Section II	130-225	Recapitulation; percussion rhythmic motives. Original "Incantation" theme returns in *stretto* and expands throughout the ensemble.

Coda	226-End	Portions of all motives are used in conjunction with a flourish of sixteenth-note runs in the woodwinds to create an exciting *coda* that builds upon the intensity created in Sections I and II.

Unit 8: Suggested Listening

Hector Berlioz, *Symphonie fantastique*

John Barnes Chance, *Blue Lake Overture*, *Elegy*, *Variations on a Korean Folk Song*

Paul Dukas/Winterbottom; Hindsley, *The Sorcerer's Apprentice*

Clifton Williams, *Caccia and Chorale*, *Fanfare and Allegro*

Unit 9: Additional References and Resources

Anthony, Donald Allen. "The Published Band Compositions of John Barnes Chance." Diss., University of Southern Mississippi, 1981.

Boosey & Hawkes, Inc. New York, NY.

Fennell, Frederick. "John Barnes Chance: Variations on a Korean Folk Song." *BD Guide*, (Sept.-Oct., 1989), 15.

Kopetz, Barry E. "An Analysis of Chance's Incantation and Dance." *The Instrumentalist* (October, 1992), pp. 34-38, 40, 42, 44, 46, 107-08.

Smith, Norman and Albert Stoutmire. *Band Music Notes*. Lake Charles, LA: Program Note Press, 1989.

Contributed by:

Susan Creasap
Assistant Director of Bands
Morehead State University
Morehead, Kentucky

Rodney C. Schueller
Associate Instructor
Indiana University
Bloomington, Indiana

Teacher Resource Guide

"Lads of Wamphray" March
Percy Aldridge Grainger
(1882–1961)

Unit 1: Composer

Percy Aldridge Grainger was born in Brighton, Melbourne, Australia on July 8, 1882. His mother, Rose, encouraged his study of the piano at an early age. By the age of twelve, Grainger had musically progressed so quickly that he and his mother moved to Germany for more advanced musical studies. While in Germany, the young Grainger took an interest in composition and was befriended by such notable composers of the era as Cyril Scott, Herman Sandby, Roger Quilter, Balfour Gardiner, and Norman O'Neill. In 1902, the family moved to London, where Grainger established a successful concert career performing throughout Europe, South Africa, and Australia. Grainger's talents were brought to the attention of Norwegian composer Edvard Grieg, who selected Percy to premiere his *Concerto in A* in 1907. In 1915 Grainger made his American debut and enlisted in the U.S. Army shortly after the outbreak of World War I. While in the military, Grainger was assigned to the Army School of Music where he became familiar with a number of wind instruments, especially the saxophone. After becoming a U.S. citizen in 1919, Grainger served for a period as head of the Music Department at New York University. Grainger became noted for his eccentric life-style as well as his music. On August 9, 1928, he married the Swedish poet Ella Viola Strom in the Hollywood Bowl before 22,000 people in attendance at one of his concerts. Grainger's musical style was highly progressive, utilizing many techniques which predate Stravinsky, Bartók, and Varèse. His musical language, however, remained conservatively post-romantic with a strong belief in

traditional harmony and melody. Grainger was one of the first composers to embrace the wind band as a serious concert medium.

Unit 2: Composition

Although Grainger composed a wealth of music, he frequently took months, years, and even decades to complete a work to his satisfaction. Grainger freely rewrote, edited, and rearranged much of his own music throughout his life, and the *"Lads of Wamphray" March* is a product of this process. His first setting of *"Lads of Wamphray" March* was completed in 1904 and was set for men's chorus and orchestra or men's chorus and two pianos. Grainger rescored the work for wind band in 1905, and was pleased to have England's Coldstream Guard Band read the work. Grainger wrote to a friend, "This morning the 'Coldstreams' played thru my Wamphray March....Lots of it sounded splendid and some didn't. My feeling is that it is successful...but that it is fearfully badly scored." In December of 1936, Grainger received a commission from the American Bandmasters' Association for two new works to be performed at their convention the next year. After considerable revisions, he submitted the *"Lads of Wamphray" March* and a new composition, *Lincolnshire Posy*, for performance. Inspired by a text drawn from Sir Walter Scott's *Minstrelsy of the Scottish Border*, this work expresses the devil-may-care character of the cattle-riding, swashbuckling English and Scottish "borders" of the fourteenth through sixteenth centuries. The composition's title comes from the following portion of Scott's poem:

> For where'er I gang, or e'er I ride,
> The lads of Wamphray are on my side;
> And of a' the lads I do ken,
> A Wamphray lad's the king of men.

Unit 3: Historical Perspective

Although Grainger, like Bartók, became noted for his interest in folk music, *"Lads of Wamphray" March* contains only original material. During the period of 1901-1904, while developing thematic material for this work, Grainger composed *Hillsong #1*, *Marching Song of Democracy*, and his orchestral work *English Dance*. Prior to starting his revisions in 1937, Grainger completed the entire *Lincolnshire Posy* in just over one week. During the early years of the twentieth century, critics were hesitant to acknowledge Grainger's ability as a composer since much of his music consisted of short, folk-song oriented works. *"Lads of Wamphray" March* held an important place for Grainger, since it was his first large-scale composition.

Unit 4: Technical Considerations

"Lads of Wamphray" March requires a fairly high level of technical skill

throughout the ensemble. All parts contain melodic material and are of interest to the individual. The work is 421 measures in length, with few rests in many parts. Endurance will be a factor in the programming of this work. Low woodwinds play an important role in the "reedy" sound which Grainger desired in this composition. As with many of his wind works, a full saxophone family including soprano and bass (which could be doubled with a contrabass clarinet) is required. Typically, Grainger has scored independent baritone and euphonium parts. Unlike many of his works, however, he has avoided the "tuneful" mallet percussion, relying upon a more compact percussion battery.

Unit 5: Stylistic Considerations

Balance will pose a concern for conductors, especially in *tutti* passages, where chordal voicing is close and contrapuntal material abundant. A strong sense of musical independence is needed from players who are frequently required to perform contrasting styles against the full ensemble. As in his other works, Grainger utilizes abrupt dynamic and stylistic shifts throughout. A very short *staccato* style is required to permit articulated passages to project through densely scored passages. A strong sense of rhythm is required of all players to maintain the crisp rhythmic vigor of the march. The conductor must assure a sense of melodic flow for the lyric lines especially when set in highly contrapuntal textures.

Unit 6: Musical Elements

Grainger often referred to many of his works as "rambles." Frequently these rambles started with several melodic ideas which Grainger would mold together and develop, and like the trunk of a new tree, he was never certain where the branches might lead. The tone-poem *"Lads of Wampray" March* structurally falls into this category. The form is divided into five large sections resembling a double rondo-variation form, with each rondo consisting of three principal themes. The first set of rondo themes, mm. 1-84, utilizes a crisp, detached style while the second set of rondo themes, mm. 85-317, is lyric in nature. Grainger sets the first rondo statement in B-flat major and moves to the subdominant, E-flat, for the second rondo set. A repeat follows, of both sets, back in B-flat major. The final section of the work, mm. 359-421, freely develops earlier material while adding one final new theme in m. 376. Throughout *"Lads of Wamphray" March*, Grainger proves himself to be the master of motivic and thematic development. Large sections of transitional material are based upon sequential treatment, as well as other developmental techniques. Grainger also demonstrates his craft in the art of counterpoint, particularly in the final section of this work, where three melodies are sustained above accompanimental material.

Unit 7: Form and Structure

SECTION	MEASURES	TONAL CENTER	EVENTS AND SCORING
I-A	1-19	B-flat	Homophonic setting; theme A in woodwinds
B	20-35		Homophonic setting; theme B in woodwinds
C	36-67		Homophonic settings; theme C in brass/woodwinds
Transition	60-67		Motivic development
A	68-84		Homophonic setting; theme A in woodwinds/brass
II-D	85-96	E-flat	Homophonic setting; theme D lyric styles in woodwinds
E	97-107		Homophonic setting; theme E lyric style set in woodwinds
F	108-117		Polyphonic setting; theme F lyric style in woodwinds, countermelody 1 in trumpets/horns
E	118-131		Homophonic setting; theme E lyric style in brass
D	132-135		Homophonic setting; theme D in saxophones/brass, brief statement
E	136-140		Homophonic setting; theme E lyric style in woodwinds; brief statement
D	141-144		Variant of theme D; brief statement
Transition	145-158		Motivic development

SECTION	MEASURES	TONAL CENTER	EVENTS AND SCORING
III-A	159-176	B-flat	Homophonic setting; theme A in woodwinds/ brass
B	177-192		Homophonic setting; theme B in woodwinds
C	193-224		Homophonic setting; theme C in brass
A	225-241		Homophonic setting; theme A in woodwinds; lyric statement of A in saxophones
IV-D	242-254		Homophonic setting; theme D in woodwinds
E	255-268		Homophonic setting; theme E in woodwinds
E	269-276		Polyphonic setting; theme F in woodwinds; counter-melody 1 in horns
E	277-290		Homophonic setting; theme E in woodwinds, *marcato* statement in brass
Transition	291-294		Motivic development
E	295-317		Homophonic setting, theme E with develop-ment
Transition	318-358		Deceptive transition with motivic development
IV-closing	359-391		Polyphonic setting; thematic development of themes D and E in woodwinds
G	376-391		Introduction of new theme G in cornet; highly polyphonic with two countermelodies

SECTION	MEASURES	TONAL CENTER	EVENTS AND SCORING
D	392-395		Brief restatement of theme D—*forte*
E	396-411		Brief restatement of theme E—*piano*
Transition	412-413		Sixteenth-note flurry in woodwinds
Coda	414-421		Development of theme D with rhythmic interjections

Unit 8: Suggested Listening

Percy Grainger, *Children's March, Lincolnshire Posy, Marching Song of Democracy, Hillsong #1 and #2*

Unit 9: Additional References and Resources

Dreyfus, Kay. *The Farthest North of Humanness: Letters of Percy Grainger 1901-1914.* Saint Louis, MO: MMB Music, 1985.

Lewis, Thomas P. *A Source Guide to the Music of Percy Grainger.* White Plains, NY: Pro/Am Music Resources, 1991.

Sadie, Stanley, ed. *The New Grove Dictionary of Music and Musicians.* London: Macmillan Inc., 1980.

Slattery, Thomas. *Percy Grainger: The Inveterate Innovator.* Evanston, IL: The Instrumentalist Co., 1974.

Slonimsky, Nicolas, ed. *Baker's Biographical Dictionary of Musicians.* New York: Macmillan Inc., 1992.

Smith, Norman and Albert Stoutamire. *Band Music Notes.* Lake Charles, LA: Program Note Press, 1989.

Contributed by:

Edward Harris
Director of Bands
California State University/Stanislaus
Turlock, California

Teacher Resource Guide

A Movement for Rosa
Mark Camphouse
(b. 1954)

Unit 1: Composer

Mark Camphouse is Associate Professor of Music and Director of Bands at Radford University in Virginia. A native of Chicago, Camphouse received his formal musical training at Northwestern University. His active guest conducting schedule has taken him to eighteen states, Canada, and Great Britain. His principle commissions include the United States Marine Band, the United States Army Band, the Florida Bandmasters Association, and the St. Louis Youth Wind Ensemble. Some of his other principle works for band are *Elegy, Watchman Tell Us of the Night, Tribute,* and *To Build a Fire.*

Unit 2: Composition

A Movement for Rosa was commissioned by the Florida Bandmasters Association. It was composed and orchestrated over a period of three months, from August to November, 1992. It is approximately eleven and a half minutes in length, and is in a single movement. It is a quasi-tone poem in three distinct sections. This work was written in honor of the civil rights heroine Rosa Parks, and in memory of Mark Camphouse's mother Esther Camphouse.

Unit 3: Historical Perspective

Camphouse provides historical and background information in score. The work recalls the contributions made by Rosa Parks to the cause of civil rights. On December 1, 1955, Rosa Parks was arrested for refusing to give up her seat to a white man on a segregated city bus in Montgomery, Alabama. She earned the title, "Mother to a Movement" for this act of personal courage, and sparked the civil rights movement of the 1950s. The Rev. Dr. Martin Luther King, Jr. inscribed the following words on the frontpiece of his book, *Stride Toward Freedom*: "To Rosa Parks, whose creative witness was the great force that led to the modern stride toward freedom."

Unit 4: Technical Considerations

The work calls for exposed solo lines in the flute, bassoon, alto saxophone, clarinet, euphonium, and piano. There should be careful attention to instrumental balances and groupings so that the character of each line can be realized. The marked dynamics should be monitored to allow hidden lines to come through. There are frequent and numerous meter changes throughout, along with tempo changes that are sometimes very subtle. The dynamic range is *ppp* to *ff*. Rhythmically, there is great diversity throughout, particularly in the middle section, mm. 127-158. The percussion writing is complex and also contributes a melodic element as well as colors and textures. There are numerous dynamic and subtle tempo changes. Instrumental ranges are extended and pushed in places.

Unit 5: Stylistic Considerations

This work is programmatic and is vividly pictorial. Each note has importance and every musical idea has relevance to the overall work. Stylistically, Camphouse writes in a very orchestral manner and intends for lines to be performed *molto sostenuto* (full bow). He chooses instrumental solo lines and combinations with much thought and careful consideration of each color and texture. There are transparent textures that are frequently juxtaposed. The use of tone clusters and chords are tied to melodic ideas. An example is the piano part, left hand, three measures from the end. The pitches here are the same pitches found in the theme that is segmented in the ensemble. The composer utilizes the themes "We Shall Overcome" and the rhythmic representation of a chant by protesters, "Freedom, Freedom Now," throughout the work. There should be careful balance and attention to rhythmic pulse to hear each of the fragments from these two ideas.

Unit 6: Musical Elements

Camphouse carefully chooses instruments for solo and soli lines. The melodic fragmentation of the themes discussed above are used as foreshadows of later full statements. There are vivid contrasts in textures and sounds with instrumental combinations and *tessitura*. The meter changes should be smooth and allow for a flow and completion of ideas. The composer uses terminology such as "Heroically," "Violently," and "*Nobilmente*" in the score and parts to assist with the overall concept of sound and approach.

Unit 7: Form and Structure

The work has three distinct sections, each of which depicts a different aspect of Rosa Park's life and experiences. The first section, mm. 1-76, represents her early years, from her birth in February, 1913, through her marriage in 1932. The opening theme in the flute is Rosa's theme. Section Two, mm. 77-180, represents years of racial strife in Montgomery and the quest for social equality. The third section, mm. 181 to the end, depicts quiet strength and serenity. The final measures of the work serve as a reminder of racism's lingering presence. Throughout the first and second sections, the "We Shall Overcome Theme" is foreshadowed. The first complete statement of this theme is in the horn at m. 187. The first complete principle theme occurs at m. 44. The second enters at m. 55. Section Two begins with the rhythmic and melodic statement of the "Freedom, Freedom Now" theme. The third section utilizes the full statement of "We Shall Overcome" and a variety of texture changes to contrast the second section. The work ends reflectively.

Unit 8: Suggested Listening

Joseph Schwantner, *New Morning for the World: "Daybreak of Freedom,"* for Speaker and Orchestra, with text drawn from the words of Dr. Martin Luther King, Jr.

Mark Camphouse, *A Movement for Rosa.* Indiana University Symphonic Band, ABA Conference, 1995, conducted by Mark Kelly of Bowling Green, Ohio.

Mark Camphouse, *A Movement for Rosa.* Indiana University of Pennsylvania, Jack Stamp, Conductor.

Orchestral works of Samuel Barber and Aaron Copland.

Symphonies of Ralph Vaughn Williams.

Unit 9: Additional References and Resources

Battisti, Frank and Robert Garofalo. *Guide to Score Study.* Ft. Lauderdale, FL: Meredith Music Publications, 1990.

Kostka, Stefan and Dorothy Payne. *Tonal Harmony.* New York: McGraw-Hill, Inc., 1995.

Parks, Rosa with Him Haskins. *Rosa Parks: My Story.* Dial Books, 1992.

Weisberg, Arthur. *Performing Twentieth-Century Music: A Handbook for Conductors and Instrumentalists.* New Haven and London: Yale University Press, 1993.

Contributed by:

Otis French
U.S. Army Field Band
Ft. Mead, Maryland

Teacher Resource Guide

Orient et Occident Grande Marche

Camille Saint-Saëns
(1835–1921)

edited by
Timothy Reynish (b. 1938)
and Bruce Perry (b. 1969)

Unit 1: Composer

Camille Saint-Saëns, French composer and pianist, was one of the most prolific composers of the Romantic era. Born in Paris, Saint-Saëns was heralded as a child prodigy, composing his first piano piece at age three and studying composition at age seven. In 1848 he entered the Paris Conservatoire and at age eighteen composed his *Symphony No. 1 in E-flat*. He was a friend of Gounod, Rossini, and Berlioz; it was Franz Liszt who called Saint-Saëns the greatest organist in the world. His over 300 compositions encompass many genres from opera to sacred and from keyboard to chamber music. His most noted works include the *Symphony No. 3*, "Organ," the opera *Samson et Dalila*, *Piano Concerto No. 4*, and *Le carnaval des animaux*.

Unit 2: Composition

The *Orient et Occident* (East and West) *Grande Marche* was composed in 1869 and is dedicated to Théodore Biais and l'Union Centrale des Arts Appliqués á l'Industrie. Settings of the work exist for piano (four hands), military band, and orchestra. First performed October 21, 1878, the eight-minute *Grande Marche* was the first of four marches written for military band by Saint-

Saëns. Reminiscent of an overture in three large sections, the "Occident" is characterized by a bold, sweeping melody in E-flat major complete with march-like trio in A-flat. The middle section, "Orient," is a slow, controlled *moderato* utilizing colors of unison woodwinds above the *ostinato* pulse of triangle, snare drum, cymbal, and gong. The "Occident" returns in a brief *fugato* and a derivation of the "Orient" material is heard before *Orient et Occident* closes with an energetic, deliberate *coda*.

Unit 3: Historical Perspective

The French Revolution had a profound effect, and not least on that of the eighteenth-century military band. The *Harmonie* chamber music of Beethoven, Haydn, Mozart, and Krommer (most often an octet of wind instruments) was expanded in 1789 when Bernard Sarette introduced the band of the Garde Nationale, a group of some forty-five players. The evolution of the large band was further developed through "revolutionary" symphonies and marches by such composers as Catel, Jadin, and Reicha. The 1995 edition of *Orient et Occident*, published by Maecenas Music and edited by Timothy Reynish and Bruce Parry, sought to achieve authenticity and accessibility in its scoring. The editors have included several optional parts to accommodate contemporary ensemble instrumentation but suggest that, for an authentic performance of the work, optional parts be omitted.

Unit 4: Technical Considerations

The *Grande Marche* offers considerable challenges for the woodwinds, especially in technique and intonation throughout the middle section. Eight original parts for cornet, trumpet, and bugle have been reedited for five cornet/trumpet parts, each of which carries notable range and articulation demands. Valuable footnotes by the editors are found throughout the full score reflecting stylistic interpretation and original articulation, phrasing, and dynamic markings.

Unit 5: Stylistic Considerations

In keeping with nineteenth-century French performance practice, the brass must approach the *Grande Marche* with a light style of playing. The middle section, marked *Moderato assai Sostenuto* (quarter note=54), must maintain its tempo with confidence without allowing sixteenth- and thirty-second-note figures to rush. The *Animato* segment should reflect forward motion while allowing clarity of articulation and lightness of style to prevail.

Unit 6: Musical Elements

Balance of melodic lines, preservation of lightness of style, and integrity of unison pitch in the "Orient" make this work a challenge to a wide range of ensembles. Tutti chords must be carefully tuned and balanced and woodwind lines reflecting the "Orient" themes should be granted dynamic priority in the final section of the *Grande Marche*. The original "Occident" theme must be dominant throughout the brief *fugato* segment.

Unit 7: Form and Structure

SECTION		MEASURES	EVENTS AND SCORING
1	A	1-133	2/2; half note=116
		1-24	First theme; E-flat
		25-40	Second theme
		41-71	First theme
		72-133	Trio; A-flat
2	B	134-183	3/4; "Orient;" G/pentatonic; quarter note=54
3	A′	184-345	2/2; half note=116
		184-230	Fugato; E-flat
		231-254	*Crescendo e stringendo*
		255-279	First theme
		280-303	Animato
		304-325	Bridge
		326-345	Coda

Unit 8: Suggested Listening

Ludwig von Beethoven, *March No. 1 in F* (1809)

Hector Berlioz, *Grand Funeral and Triumphant Symphony* (1840)

Anton Bruckner, *E Minor Mass* (1869)

Camille Saint-Saëns, *Piano Concerto No. 5 'Egyptian'* (1896), *Marche Militaire Française* (1880)

Ludwig Spohr, *Notturno for Turkish Band* (1817)

Unit 9: Additional References and Resources

Dvorak, Thomas L., Robert Grechesky, and Gary Ciepluch. *Best Music for High School Band*. Brooklyn, NY: Manhattan Beach Music, 1993.

Smith, Norman E. *March Music Notes*. Lake Charles, LA: Program Note Press, 1986.

Contributed by:
Glen J. Hemberger
University of North Texas
Denton, Texas

Teacher Resource Guide

Paris Sketches

Martin Ellerby
(b. 1957)

Unit 1: Composer

Martin Ellerby was born in Worksop, England and studied with Joseph Horowitz, W. S. Lloyd Webber, and Wilfred Josephs. He received the Arts Council Dio Fund Award for young composers, an Allcard Award from the Worshipful Company of Musicians, and various composer-in-residencies, resulting in many commissions. His range of compositions includes works for choir, orchestra, chamber ensembles, brass bands, and wind ensemble. In 1988 he was appointed Professor of Music at the London College of Music.

Unit 2: Composition

This fifteen-minute composition is a four-movement tribute to the French capital. Each movement pays homage to some part of Paris and to other composers who lived, worked, or passed through it. The presence of bells—a prominent feature of Parisian life—runs through the work as a unifying theme.

Unit 3: Historical Perspective

Paris Sketches was commissioned under the auspices of the British Association of Symphonic Bands and Wind Ensembles Consortium Commissioning Scheme. It was premiered in July, 1994 at Ripon Cathedral by the Cleveland Youth Wind Orchestra, conducted by John MacKenzie. This set of "homages" to other composers is reminiscent of Maurice Ravel's *Tombeau de Couperin*. Both combine historical references with contemporary gestures and techniques, making clear allusions to well-known musicians' styles while adding their own creative voice.

I. "SAINT-GERMAIN-DES-PRÉS"

This is the Latin Quarter, famous for its artistic associations and bohemian life-style. This is a dawn tableau haunted by the shade of Ravel: the city awakens with the ever-present sound of morning bells.

II. "PIGALLE"

This is the Soho of Paris, a burlesque with scenes cast in the mold of a balletic scherzo—humorous in a kind of "Stravinsky meets Prokofiev" way. The bells here are car horns and police sirens!

III. "PERE LACHAISE"

This is the city's largest cemetery, the final resting place of many a celebrity who had once walked its streets. The movement concludes with a quotation of the "Dies Irae" chant. The mood is one of softness and delicacy; the bells are gentle, nostalgic, and wistful.

IV. "LES HALLES"

This is the fast, bustling finale. The bells are triumphant and celebratory. Les Halles is the old market area, a Parisian Covent Garden. The climax quotes from Berlioz's *Te Deum*, which was first performed in 1855 at the church of St. Eustache—actually in the district of Les Halles.

Unit 4: Technical Considerations

Paris Sketches requires confident, advanced playing in all wind instrument families, as well as in percussion, string bass, and piano.

I. "SAINT-GERMAIN-DES-PRÉS"

This movement is quasi-impressionistic, with a tonal center of D. Solo voices penetrate the multilayered texture, which is highly consonant and rich. Meters (with a combination of two and three divisions) change frequently, and tempo fluctuation is common. The opening horn motif is heard throughout the movement, as are other suggestions of bells and morning awakening. The drag triplet figure is prominent.

II. "PIGALLE"

This spirited movement is based on the harmonic progression established in the opening *staccato* figures (V-I of a key to V-I of a key one tri-tone away). The constantly changing meters and quick exchanges of thematic materials among many instruments makes for great excitement. Rapid woodwind figures and soloistic writing are present in most parts, including tuba and multiple percussion. Flutter tonguing, stopped effects, and muting are required. The movement is tonal, also centered in D.

III. "Pere Lachaise"

This soft and delicate movement evokes Satie's *Gymnopedie*. Alto and tenor saxophone, glockenspiel, vibraphone, oboe, and flute are all featured as soloists. The piece moves from A minor to D major.

IV. "Les Halles"

Range and flexibility are required in the horns, trumpets, and trombones for this triumphant movement. Frequently changing compound meter, often challenged by duple figures, is found throughout. The flute and oboe have extensive solo work. The key is centered around E-flat major.

Unit 5: Musical Considerations

I. "Saint-Germain-des-Prés"

The thick scoring could cover solo voices, so players will need to be sensitive to balance at all times. Articulations and rearticulations should be smooth, and moving figures should be played with full value and made distinct. Dynamic feathering is crucial as different voices enter and exit with various fragments and motifs. Accents should be played with weight, not force. The cross-rhythms can create challenges, especially at points of *ritardando*.

II. "Pigalle"

All of the quick figures must be played lightly and crisply. The style is *secco*—very much in the tradition of Prokofiev and Stravinsky. Tempo maintenance is vital. The sweeping melody at rehearsal G requires *legato* phrasing. The *fugato* quarter-note figures at rehearsal I should be separated and held back in the texture as new voices are added.

III. "Pere Lachaise"

Accompaniment must be subordinate to solo melodies. The glockenspiel part must not be buried. Articulation is smooth and phrases should be well supported. The "Dies Irae" quote should be brought out seven measures prior to rehearsal L.

IV. "Les Halles"

Accompanying triplet figures must be played in a smooth and even manner. The fanfare-like thematic material must be *marcato* and separated. Intonation will be an issue with the many chords which are built in a pyramidal-cluster method. *Hemiola* patterns must be separated and brought to the fore (e.g., after rehearsal C in the bassoons). The Berlioz "Te Deum" quote (rehearsal I) should have a "choral" sound: rich, *legato*, and blended.

Unit 6: Musical Elements

Paris Sketches is an example of programmatic and referential music. The contrasting movements allow for discussions of multiple/changing meters, motifs, episodic (vs. thematic) writing, quotations, canon, Impressionism, scherzo, waltz, and fanfare. Additionally, the very title evokes interest in the history, geography, and music of Paris and France.

Unit 7: Form and Structure

I. "SAINT-GERMAIN-DES-PRÉS"

The movement is through-composed. The generating motif is built on an ascending fourth plus and ascending fifth. This is passed around from voice to voice in an ever-changing texture of varying instruments. A climax occurs at E with the "ringing" of the morning bells. The movement begins and ends quietly.

II. "PIGALLE"

This episodic movement is based on the harmonic progression of D and A-flat. Dry *staccato* figures, short flourishes, "oom-pah" accompaniments, quick fanfares, rollicking march figures, wild syncopation, extreme lyricism, and good humor mix and intermingle throughout this jovial section.

beginning	Introduction
reh. D	Section 1 ("march" and other episodes)
reh. E	Section 2 (lyrical thematic material)
reh. H	Return of Section 1 material
reh. I	*Fugato* build-up (D/A-flat harmony)
reh. K	Pyramidal build-up; block chords; final D major chord

III. "PERE LACHAISE"

The simple Satie-like accompaniment endures the entire movement, while soloists play the dreamy thematic material.

beginning	Introduction
reh. A	Theme 1 in alto saxophone—oboe—alto saxophone
reh. E	Theme 2 (*tutti*)
reh. F	Theme 1 in alto saxophone— oboe/clarinet/alto saxophone/horn
reh. H	Theme 1 in flute/clarinet motifs; fragments of theme to end

IV. "Les Halles"

beginning	Fanfare figures in brass
reh. A	Theme 1 in clarinets (descending pyramidal cluster)
reh. B	Theme 1 in trumpets (rhythmic counterpoint in horns)
	transition
reh. C	Theme 2 in flute solo (based on fanfare)
reh. D	Transition Theme 1 (and inversion) in saxophones and bassoons
reh. E	Theme 2 in oboe
reh. F	Transition, build-up
reh. I	Slower tempo; quote from Berlioz's *Te Deum*
reh. K	*A tempo*, percussion add-on section
reh. L	Fanfare figures return in brass
reh. M	*Coda*—broad figures (plus reference to first movement climax) and *a tempo*; final chord on E-flat major

Unit 8: Suggested Listening

Louis-Hector Berlioz, *Te Deum*
Achille-Claude Debussy, *Nuages*
Jacques Offenbach, *La Gaieté Parisienne*
Sergei Prokofiev, *Symphony No. 1, Romeo and Juliet* Suite
Maurice Ravel, *Le Tombeau de Couperin*
Erik Satie, *Gymnopedie*
Igor Stravinsky, *Octet*

Unit 9: Additional References and Resources

Stolba, K Marie. *The Development of Western Music*. Dubuque, IA: William C. Brown Publishers, 1990.

Contributed by:

Scott A. Stewart
Indiana University
Bloomington, Indiana

Teacher Resource Guide

Ricercare a 6
Johann Sebastian Bach
(1685–1750)

arranged by Clark McAlister
edited by Frederick Fennell (b. 1914)

Unit 1: Composer

The biographical details of the life of Johann Sebastian Bach are detailed and well known. Considered to be one of the master composers of his time, Bach received only regional fame in his lifetime, and it was not until the nineteenth century, when a revival group led by Felix Mendelssohn came to the fore, that Bach was elevated to the position akin to deity in Western music.

The outline of Bach's life displays the development of a master musician. With many musical family members in his past, Bach studied music from a young age, and developed proficiency in both the violin and clavier before moving on to the organ. He was appointed organist at Arnstadt at the age of eighteen, where be began to study the art of composition. He held the same position in Mühlhausen for one year before becoming court organist at Weimar in 1708. From 1717 to 1723 Bach served as court Music Director at Cöthen and then became the Cantor in Leipzig at the St. Thomas School where he remained for the rest of his life. It was during these years in Leipzig that Bach composed most of the works for which he is known. His musical output is extensive and includes cantatas, concertos, chamber ensemble music, fugues, motets, suites, masses, and organ music; music for every occasion, composed, in general, to fulfill the requirements of each job situation. His compositions reflect the energy, genius, dedication, and vision of this revered composer.

Unit 2: Composition

In his notes on the score, Clark McAlister details the history of the *Musical Offering* (1747), from which the *Ricercare a 6* is taken. When Bach appeared before King Frederick "the Great" of Prussia (where Bach's son Carl Philip Emmanuel Bach was employed as court accompanist), the King offered a theme upon which the elder Bach could improvise on all the *fortepiano* instruments at the Potsdam Stadtschoâ. Upon his return to Leipzig, Bach pursued the theme and proceeded to write a series of works that were later published as the *Musical Offering*. Based upon the King's theme, the piece is a collection of thirteen compositions for different instruments with instrumentations ranging from a single instrument to groups as large as four instrumentalists.

The *Ricercare a 6* is a six-part fugue written for harpsichord, a most difficult task as the King's theme does not readily offer itself to treatment of this kind. Written two years prior to *The Art of Fugue*, the *Ricercare* is an object lesson in fugal writing, mixing strict adherence to form with the textural contrast.

Clark McAlister states in the score that the transcription was undertaken at the request of Frederick Fennell. The *Ricercare a 6* is approximately six to seven minutes in duration, and is published by Ludwig Music as part of their Fennell Editions series.

Unit 3: Historical Perspective

The canonization of Johann Sebastian Bach in Western music literature is often attributed to Felix Mendelssohn. It was Mendelssohn's work in the early nineteenth century that brought the forgotten composer back into prominence. Bach was known in his own time as a great keyboard performer with exceptional skills in improvisation. Since Mendelssohn's campaign, the name "Bach" has become associated with the highest technical and artistic compositions of the eighteenth century. The *St. Matthew Passion* has become an Easter tradition in many parts of the world while Bach's chorales and cantatas are oft performed in both their original sacred settings and as art music at secular occasions.

The *Musical Offering*, like *The Art of Fugue*, is a textbook example of strict and free counterpoint. The *Ricercare a 6* is strict in its form, and is a fine example of the blending of artistic considerations with functional construction.

Unit 4: Technical Considerations

In the preparation of this work, blend and balance are key elements in achieving a successful performance. The inevitable overlapping of melodic ideas creates considerable problems for an ensemble that may not have been faced by the original solo performer. Although the technical demands on the performers are not vast beyond the rhythmic difficulties created by the 4/2 time signature, the contrapuntal nature of the work demands attention to vertical rhythmic alignment. In typical Bach fashion, there is much syncopation and entry on off-beat rhythms.

McAlister's transcription is masterful. He has crafted Bach's masterpiece into a work that permits artistic concerns to supersede technical demands. As such, the trumpet parts (all of which double flügelhorn) progress into the upper register on a regular basis, requiring confident and mature players.

Unit 5: Stylistic Considerations

Many transcriptions assume a life away from the original; this one cannot. The eighteenth-century performance on the original keyboard instruments allows for much *rubato* and band conductors must understand this in order to arrive at an authentic stylistic interpretation. The intertwining of ideas calls for the prioritizing of melodies; there should be a marked difference between subject *piano* markings and countersubject *piano* markings.

Intonation can be a significant problem. The opening statement, shared as it is between clarinet II and tenor saxophones, poses difficult pitch problems because of the *tessitura* of the saxophone.

Unit 6: Musical Elements

The musical demands of this complex fugue are many. Besides the prioritizing of lines, players are faced with sometimes difficult doublings, and must know how their parts fit into the work as a whole. The lines are clear and demand shaping from the performers. Melodic movement is often created by the harmonies; therefore players should emphasize the harmonic movement, both the unexpected and expected. Suspensions are an integral part of this language, and performers must emphasize the tension they add to the harmonic motion.

In listening to keyboard performers perform this music, one often hears an emphasis on particular cadences. The performer's interpretation helps to break the work into clearly defined sections. Shifting the strength of the various cadences will create different sections, therefore the conductor should explore the options before rehearsing this work. The tempo indication on the score is 60-66. Although close to the tempo typically selected by keyboard performers, this is indeed a challenging tempo for the large ensemble.

Unit 7: Form and Structure

MEASURES	EVENTS	SCORING
Exposition		
1	Subject	Clarinet II, tenor sax

5	Answer	(On Dominant) clarinet I, alto saxophone
	Countersubject	Clarinet II, III
9	Subject	Bass clarinet, bassoons
	Countersubject	Clarinet I
13	Answer	Horns
	Countersubject	Bass clarinet, bassoons
17	Cadential Extension	
19	Subject	Flutes, piccolo, oboes
23	Cadential Extension	
25	Countersubject	Low voices
29	Episode I	Sequential ascending layering
40		Sequential descending layering
48	Answer	Trombones
52	Episode II	
58	Subject	Horns (in sub-dominant)
62	Cadential extension	
66	Subject	Clarinet I (in sub-dominant F major)
70	Countersubject	Soprano sax
73	Answer	Tenor sax, baritone (in B-flat minor)
79	Episode III	Based on material from Episode I
86	Answer	Trumpets (in G major—to accent V-i)
90	Juxtaposition of Subject and Countersubject	
99	Subject	Tutti (tonic key)

Unit 8: Suggested Listening

Johann Sebastian Bach, *Musical Offering, Little Fugue in G Minor, The Art of Fugue, Toccata and Fugue in D Minor, Passacaglia and Fugue in C Minor*
Houston Bright, *Prelude and Fugue in F Minor*
Benjamin Britten, *The Young Person's Guide to the Orchestra—Fugue and Finale*

Jaromir Weinberger, *Polka and Fugue* from *Schwanda the Bagpiper*

Unit 9: Additional References and Resources

Apel, Willi. *Harvard Dictionary of Music*. 2nd ed. Cambridge, MA: The Belknap Press of Harvard University Press, 1970.

Ludwig Music. Cleveland, OH

Rehrig, William H. *The Heritage Encyclopedia of Band Music*. Edited by Paul E. Bierley. Westerville, OH: Integrity Press, 1991.

Smith, Norman and Albert Stoutamire. *Band Music Notes*. 3rd ed. Lake Charles, LA: Program Note Press, 1979.

Contributed by:

Alan Lourens
Indiana University
Bloomington, Indiana

Susan Creasap
Assistant Director of Bands
Morehead State University
Morehead, Kentucky

Teacher Resource Guide

Russian Christmas Music

Alfred Reed
(b. 1921)

Unit 1: Composer

Alfred Reed was born in Manhattan, New York on January 25th, 1921. He began his formal music training on trumpet at the age of ten and was playing professionally by the time he reached high school. It was at this time that he took up the study of theory and composition with John Sacco and later became a scholarship student of Paul Yartin.

After three years at the Radio Workshop in New York studying with Vittorio Giannini, he enlisted in the Army during World War II and became a member of the 529th Army Air Force Band. During the three and a half years in this organization, Reed produced nearly 100 compositions and arrangements.

Following his release in 1946, he enrolled at the Juilliard School of Music in New York in order to continue his study with Giannini. In 1948 he became an arranger and composer at NBC and subsequently at ABC in New York, where he wrote and arranged music for radio and television, as well as for record albums and films.

He has held the positions of conductor of the Symphony Orchestra at Baylor University in Waco, Texas, editor at Hansen Publications, Inc. in New York, and appointments in Theory-Composition, Music Education, Music Media and Industry, and Conductor and Music Director of the Symphonic Wind Ensemble at the University of Miami. He retired from the University of Miami in 1993 and continues to serve as a regular guest conductor of the Tokyo Kosei Wind Orchestra, the Osaka Municipal Symphonic Band, and the Bisai Civil Wind Orchestra in Japan where he has appeared in some seventy-one Japanese cities to date. His work as a guest conductor and clinician has taken him to forty-nine of the fifty United States, as well as to eighteen other countries including Europe, Asia, South America, Mexico, Canada, and Australia.

With more than 250 published works for Concert Band, Wind Ensemble, Orchestra, Chorus, and various smaller chamber groups, Reed is one of the nation's most prolific and frequently performed composers. He continues to serve on the Board of Advisors of *Instrumentalist* magazine and writes a column, "South of the Border," for the Canadian Band Journal. Reed has resided in Coral Gables, Florida since 1968.

Unit 2: Composition

Russian Christmas Music, a Grade Five composition, was originally written for a special concert in December, 1944, and is dedicated to Harwood Simmons. The piece is in four distinct sections: "Children's Carol," "Antiphonal Chant," "Village Song," and "Cathedral Chorus." It uses the ancient Russian Christmas Carol "Carol of the Little Russian Children" as its basis, although it also incorporates original material. The musical impression is that of Old Russia, well before World War II, during the Christmas season. The version we know today is different from the original and represents several revisions done by the composer in order to better fit the symphonic band and wind ensemble. The piece is approximately twelve minutes in length and is published by Sam Fox Publishing Company.

Unit 3: Historical Perspective

From a historical standpoint, it is important to note that the music contained in the *Russian Christmas Music* is based on the liturgical music of the Eastern Orthodox Church. In Orthodox services no instruments are permitted to play as it is the belief that God should be worshipped with only human means and no mechanical contrivances of any kind. Reed tells the story of the production of the composition:

> The concert in 1944 was a present from the City Fathers to the people of the city of Denver for having over-subscribed their quota in the Sixth or Seventh (I forget which) War Bond Drive that year. It was conceived and administered by the noted American composer Roy Harris as a tribute to friendship between the Russian and American people at the time, fighting together in World War II, and was to consist entirely of new Russian and new American works as the highlight. Harris transcribed the second movement of his Sixth Symphony (the Abraham Lincoln Symphony, as it was known at the time) for band, and when no new Russian band piece could be located, asked me (practically ordered me!) to produce something along

this line...in just two weeks before the concert date! When I tried to protest what I thought was an impossibility (at least for me), he just said, "Well, don't make it too long then...only about fourteen or fifteen minutes." So there was no alternative (being in the service and having been commanded to do so by my commanding officer as well) and I produced the score in just eleven days, with a squad of six copyists following along as I sent in whatever I had completed each day and churning out the parts in time for rehearsals on the two days before the concert...and a coast-to-coast broadcast over NBC as well!

Unit 4: Technical Considerations

The opening of the work presents the challenge of playing passages softly with control of pitch. Performers must be able to effectively execute both *legato* and *marcato* passages. Woodwinds have difficult sixteenth-note patterns throughout the work, yet must also be able to play extended musical phrases with a full sound. Brasses must posses the ability to double-tongue as well as the ability to control pitch in various ranges at both loud and soft dynamic markings. As in other Reed compositions, more players should cover the trumpet parts as they represent the upper voices of the brass choir while the cornets function as the lower, more mellow voice. Instrumentation balance in the brass section is critical and should be well thought-out. A string bass is truly essential for this work, especially considering the soli *pizzicato* line beginning at m. 118. The composer suggests that this line be ignored should no string bass be available. Percussion writing is extensive and must be handled with great care and attention to proper musical execution.

Unit 5: Stylistic Considerations

Because of the vocal nature of the music, the band or wind ensemble must take strides to play even the fast tempi and powerful climaxes in the most lyrical and *sostenuto* style. The conductor must be able to change style from one section to the other, yet have cohesiveness in the overall work. Most stylistic elements appear on the page, whether it is a dynamic, articulation, phrase, or tempo mark. When a style change is needed, chances are it appears on the part or in the score.

Unit 6: Musical Elements

The carol of the first section is slightly altered from the modern version by Hawley Ades. Reed, however, does not change the melodic line. The composer notes that tempo markings are given simply as a guide, and can be altered slightly given the ability of the group and/or the musical taste of the conductor. The composer states:

The harmonic approach to all of the material used in this piece, both traditional and original, was what I would call "extended modality" with basically tertian chords constructed on the steps of the scales derived from the individual melodic lines, and not restricted to just seven or eight. This greatly expands the resources available to the composer, provided, however, that he can still manage to convey a feeling of traditional modality despite the enlarged scales and the increased number of chords thereby erected on them.

Balance is of great concern, and *crescendos* and *decrescendos* must be handled with care by the conductor. This is especially true in the powerful closing section as fanfare figures and horn calls can be easily lost in the *fortissimo* and sustained parts of the other brass.

Unit 7: Form and Structure

SECTION	MEASURES	EVENTS AND SCORING
Introduction	1-3	Chimes and string bass play a sustained three-bar introduction.
"Children's Carol"	4-31	Clarinets and low reeds present the "Children's Carol" in a low and sustained manner. Brasses are added and the section builds to a climax in m. 20. The opening material is repeated again and the section ends softly in m. 31.
"Antiphonal Chant"	32-117	The trombones proclaim the "Antiphonal Chant" starting in m. 32. It is repeated by the woodwinds and then is passed back to the trombones. The full ensemble enters in m. 47 with this material. M. 55 presents a tempo change as the chant is now in stretto. This section continues with the chant appearing in various voices with fanfare interjections. The tempo slows at m. 86 and features an English horn solo with woodwind accompaniment and horn calls. The section ends softly, with flute and piccolo sixteenths.
"Village Song"	118-165	This section features the woodwinds as they have the sustained and sonorous melody throughout. The string bass has

		an extended soli starting in m. 118. An English horn solo is featured in the last seven bars of the section.
"Cathedral Chorus"	166-end	The final section begins in a similar manner to the first, with a sustained pedal before the chimes enter with a "church bell" passage. There is no doubt that the brass dominate the closing section with both fanfare and the juxtaposition of the main melody. The full ensemble is featured in a majority of this section, although the clarinets do present the closing theme beginning in m. 200. By m. 219 the full ensemble is back and closes the work with a rich, powerful, and beautiful sound. Motifs from the first three sections can be heard throughout the entire fourth section.

Unit 8: Suggested Listening

Reinhold Gliere, *Russian Sailors Dance*
David Holsinger, *Liturgical Dances*
Alfred Reed, *A Festival Prelude*, *Armenian Dances, Pt. I*
Dmitri Shostakovich/arr. Donald Hunsberger, *Festive Overture*

Unit 9: Additional References and Resources

Dvorak, Thomas L., Robert Grechesky, and Gary M. Ciepluch. *Best Music for High School Band*. Brooklyn, New York: Manhattan Beach Music, 1993.

Kreines, Joseph. *Music for Concert Band*. Tampa, FL: Florida Music Service, 1989.

Smith, Norman and Albert Stoutmire. *Band Music Notes*. Lake Charles, LA: Program Note Press, 1989.

Contributed by:

Rodney C. Schueller
Indiana University
Bloomington, Indiana

Teacher Resource Guide

The Solitary Dancer

Warren Benson
(b. 1924)

Unit 1: Composer

Warren Benson, born in Detroit, Michigan on January 26, 1924, has been an influential composer in the development of a serious repertoire for the wind band. A percussionist, he played timpani with the Detroit Symphony, earned two degrees from the University of Michigan, taught in Greece on two successive Fulbright grants, and authored *Creative Projects in Musicianship* as a result of his involvement with the Contemporary Music Project. His forty-year college and university teaching career (1953-1993) included fourteen years at Ithaca College, where he founded one of the first percussion ensembles on the east coast, followed by twenty-six years at the Eastman School of Music. He has appeared as a guest composer, conductor, and lecturer throughout the United States, Canada, Mexico, South America, and Europe. His music has been described as combining "sinewy sparseness with a pervasive concern for lyricism in compositions that are varied, selective, and non-doctrinaire in their technique and style."

Unit 2: Composition

The Solitary Dancer is certainly "non-doctrinaire." It was commissioned in 1966 by the Clarence, New York Senior High School Band, Norbert J. Buskey, Director, and is dedicated to Bill Hug. A one-sentence program note is printed on the score: "*The Solitary Dancer* deals with quiet, poised energy that one may observe in a dancer in repose, alone with her inner music." This is a masterpiece, an ensemble work dealing with quiet intensity representing stored energy, imagined dance moves, and a dancer's emotional/thoughtful interaction with her "inner music." The entire piece feels reflective or anticipatory. Its duration is six minutes, twenty-five seconds, is in 4/4 time, and is marked "with quiet energy throughout, quarter note=140-144." Published by MCA Music in 1970, it is now available from Carl Fischer.

Unit 3: Historical Perspective

The Solitary Dancer was the first composition of its kind for wind ensemble. It was at the time, and perhaps remains, the only fast-quiet piece in the repertoire. Benson had previously been involved with the Contemporary Music Project, had been composing on commission since 1958, and had been instrumental in the development of the now renowned commissioning project of Frank Battisti's Ithaca High School Band. Scottish writer Neil Butterworth, commenting on Benson's two symphonies for winds, calls them "landmarks in band music," and goes on to say that they "demonstrate the huge potential that is offered by the concert band of today." In Acton Ostling's 1978 Dissertation, "An Evaluation of Compositions for Wind Band According to Specific Criteria of Serious Artistic Merit," no less than fourteen works of Warren Benson were listed—*more than any other composer*—of which *The Solitary Dancer* was the most well known by the twenty university wind band conductors surveyed. By 1993, eighteen of Benson's works were listed (in Jay Gilbert's replication study) and *The Solitary Dancer* still was among his best known and most highly respected compositions (along with *The Leaves Are Falling* and *The Passing Bell*). It remains his most performed piece.

Unit 4: Technical Considerations

The Solitary Dancer was composed for a wind ensemble of forty-five players, with each part expected to be played by a single performer "with the exception of first, second, and third B-flat clarinets, E-flat alto clarinet, and tuba, which are to be played by two players each." Instrumentation includes parts for soprano saxophone, piano, two flugelhorns, and six percussionists. Clarinet players are required to do some clapping; most others contribute to important unison singing near the end. There are independent, significant parts for E-flat clarinet and the two alto clarinets. Trumpets are muted throughout, with first trumpet range extending to written C above the staff (at *mezzo piano*!); other parts are mostly mid-range. Percussion parts include timpani, bass drum, snare drum, suspended cymbal, triangle, bells, marimba, vibraphone, bongos, gourd, and "brushes on paper."

The composer asks for a variety of sounds from the percussion section: bass drum on the rim, timpani on bowl, suspended cymbal played "with light wood sticks," "soft sticks," or "small wood sticks," and snare drum played with fingers instead of sticks. At the required tempo, percussion fatigue can be a factor, as can conductor fatigue. Care must be taken to ensure that the metronome marking be maintained.

Exactness of execution is critical. Repositioning the ensemble is recommended, with piano, string bass, and percussion grouped in a central location. Good articulation is essential to the syncopated rhythms that comprise an important part of the piece, and good breath control is needed to sustain the vitality of the long tones. Players must listen carefully for rhythmic precision, tonal blend, balance, and good intonation. Dynamics are almost exclusively on the soft side, mostly ranging from *pianissimo* to *mezzo piano*. Although the piece may not look like more than a Grade Four technical challenge, the cumulative artistic level of the piece, especially in terms of concentration and endurance, is Grade Six. This is a very sophisticated composition.

Unit 5: Stylistic Considerations

Soloists or consorts of instrumental groupings are often used, with syncopated rhythms pitted against a background of sustained harmony. Long tones, while quiet, need to preserve their intensity. The timbre evolves, rarely changes. Subtleties must be noticed and brought out, such as the shape of releases, attention to the details of articulation, uniformity of *staccato*, *tenuto*, and *legato*, and dynamic shadings. Rhythmic vitality and exactness of execution are necessary for a successful performance. Timbral effects, such as one group of instruments fading out while another group enters quietly and *crescendos*, need to be diligently rehearsed. Unison singing of the "din" syllable will need attention, especially with regard to accents and slurs and a rather jazz-like quality.

Unit 6: Musical Elements

This quiet-but-energetic, sophisticated composition was one of the first to employ aspects of what has come to be called "minimalism." Subtle changes and nuance are often the main event. It has been called "a tempest in a tutu." Themes are understated, as the title and program note suggest. Percussion playing requires care and discipline. The continuous sixteenth-note figure in bongo/snare drum lasts 190 measures, and serves as a background for the interplay between sustained and syncopated wind parts. Melody often takes the form of combining these two elements. Textural sonorities and isorhythms lend variety and interest. The key signature is two flats, with a tonal center of D, making it sound Phrygian.

This composition will compel performers to become involved in a unique way, especially as regards pitch, balance, style, dynamics, and coming to terms with imagery through a gentler kind of music-making. Matching pitch, for example, is less a "listen down" experience than a "listen across" one. As with much of the repertoire, the publisher has printed boxed numbers every five bars; therefore it is essential that the conductor carefully mark parts or teach the students how to mark their parts to indicate the arrivals of musically significant events.

The conductor must be diligent in keeping the tempo constant, bringing out the syncopations and creating a seamless chordal background.

Unit 7: Form and Structure

This soft, reflective piece is through-composed, with virtually all elements introduced in the first fifteen bars. Rhythmically active gestures frequently end in long tones, as if imagined leaps, turns, or other dance movements drift into memory. Of importance throughout is the interplay between the ascending-descending minor third fragment (mm. 4-5 in soprano saxophone, for example) and the syncopated motive which often ends with a descending half step (mm. 7-9 in piccolo). Combinations of these two elements form melodies, typically growing out of or ending with sustained notes. For most of the piece, continuous sixteenths are present in percussion.

MEASURES	EVENTS AND SCORING
1-15	Introductory material. Tonality of D minor (Phrygian); melodic fragment of minor third in soprano saxophone; syncopated motive in piccolo ending with descending half step; preview of continuous sixteenths in suspended cymbal; rhythmic dialog in percussion.
16-26	Beginning of development (i.e., combining, altering, enlarging of introductory ideas). Sustained harmony becomes syncopated motive becomes melody in flute and first clarinet. Other developmental ideas will include harmonic shifts and constant, almost prismatic mutation of instrumentation.
27-44	Harmonic transition: seven bars of E-flat minor, nine bars of E minor, two of C minor. Continuous sixteenths (which will last 190 bars) beginning at m. 27, are joined by a syncopated quarter-eighth pattern at m. 29 (which lasts 67 bars).
45-64	Return to D minor. Soprano saxophone, oboe solo over sustained trombones. At m. 55, piccolo takes melody, then is joined by piano.
65-69	Brief harmonic shift to E-flat minor. Trumpet solo over clarinet syncopation, dynamic increases to *mezzo piano*.
70-85	Return to D minor. Ostinato bass line begins in piano, string bass. Melodic fragment gets tossed about.
86-95	Harmonic shift to E-flat minor. Ostinato continues while melody moves to clarinet section.

96-105	Return to D minor. Ostinato ends, percussion sixteenths transferred from bongo to snare drum played by fingers.
105-139	New bass line combines melodic fragment with syncopated motive. Trumpet melody is first *mezzo forte* of the piece. Ostinato returns briefly in bass clarinet (m. 117) against piccolo/piano melody.
136-145	Harmonic transition: four bars of D-flat, two bars of E-flat, two bars of F, two bars of G, with suspensions that need to be clarified, and a resolute, syncopated D in the piano part that extends from mm. 126-204.
146-172	Return to D minor (in 6/4 position, initially). Bongo reentry signals move to final section, as percussion instruments are added under upper woodwind melody. At m. 164 it is important to observe that the only *forte* in the score is there to achieve a penetrating balance, to bring out the bassoon/bass clarinet figure, while isorhythms in several parts accompany the flute/oboe/trumpet melody.
173-192	Clapping begins in clarinet section; it is imperative that players make considerable contrast between accented and unaccented notes. In m. 177 unison singing begins, builds via tessitura and inflection (not dynamic) to become the climax of the piece, then subsides. The timbre of the "din" syllable is such that articulation is emphasized above tone projection.
193-225	Brief harmonic shift to C and back to D, fade to conclusion. The snare drummer needs to be encouraged to play the diminuendo by moving to the very edge of the head in order to achieve the effect of disappearing into silence.

Unit 8: Suggested Listening

Claude Debussy, *Nocturnes*
Steven Halpern and Gloria Kelly, *Ancient Echoes*
Vincent Persichetti, *Chorale Prelude: O God Unseen*
Steve Reich, *Drumming*
Eric Satie, *Trois Gymnopedies*

Unit 9: Additional References and Resources

Benson, Warren. *The Leaves Are Falling.* Donald Hunsberger and the Eastman Wind Ensemble, Centaur Records.

Benson, Warren. Telephone conversation with Robert Halseth, July 26, 1997.

Butterworth, Neil. *The American Symphony*. London: Scholar Press, 1998.

Copland, Aaron. *Music and Imagination*. New York: Harvard University Press, 1952.

George, Roby Granville, Jr. "An Analysis of the Compositional Techniques Used in Selected Wind Works of Warren Benson." DMA thesis, University of Cincinnati, 1995.

Gilbert, Jay Warren. "An Evaluation of Compositions for Wind Band According to Specific Criteria of Serious Artistic Merit: A Replication and Update." DM diss., Northwestern University, 1993.

Harbison, William G. "Analysis: *The Passing Bell* of Warren Benson." *Journal of Band Research* XXI/2 (Spring 1986): 1-8.

Hunsberger, Donald. "Discussions with Warren Benson: *The Leaves Are Falling*." *College Band Directors National Association Journal* I/1 (Spring 1984): 7-17.

Ostling, Acton Jr. "An Evaluation of Compositions for Wind Band According to Specific Criteria of Serious Artistic Merit." Ph.D. diss., University of Iowa, 1978.

Renshaw, Jeffrey. "Conducting Warren Benson's *The Leaves Are Falling*." *The Instrumentalist*, XLVII (March 1993) 30-34.

Wallace, David and Eugene Corporon, eds. *Wind Ensemble/Band Repertoire*. Greeley, CO: University of Northern Colorado School of Music, 1984.

Contributed by:

Robert Halseth
Director of Wind Studies
California State University
Sacramento, California

Teacher Resource Guide

Soundings

Cindy McTee
(b. 1953)

Unit 1: Composer

Cindy McTee is currently Professor of Music Composition at the University of North Texas. She is from a family of amateur musicians who encouraged her interest in music and the arts. In the course of her undergraduate studies at Pacific Lutheran University, she spent a year in Poland studying with Krzysztof Penderecki. She credits Penderecki as both a musical and a professional influence. She continued her studies, earning a master's degree from Yale University and a Doctor of Philosophy in Music Composition from the University of Iowa. Professionally, she has developed an excellent reputation with performances by major American and international orchestras. She has also received several prestigious commissions, including a fellowship from the National Endowment for the Arts. In 1992 her work was recognized by the American Academy of Arts and Letters with the Goddard Lieberson Award.

Unit 2: Composition

Soundings was commissioned by the Big Eight Band Directors Association and completed in 1995. The premiere was given by the Oklahoma University Wind Symphony, William Wakefield, conductor, at the College Band Directors National Association Southwestern Division Regional Convention in 1996. It consists of four movements entitled "Fanfare," Gizmo," "Waves," and "Transmission." After *Circuits* and *California Counterpoint: The Twittering Machine*, both of which have orchestral counterparts, *Soundings* is McTee's third work for wind ensemble, but the first conceived originally and exclusively for winds. McTee provides a minimum instrumentation, but the work

was written with the expectation that parts would be doubled and is designated for "band."

Unit 3: Historical Perspective

McTee's music is part of an eclectic trend of the late twentieth century. Her works use materials associated with many different movements. The influence of minimalists can be seen in *ostinato*. Jazz and jazz-like elements infuse both the harmony and the orchestration. The "Waves" movement in particular reflects McTee's work in the electronic studio. Philosophically, McTee seeks to write music that connects to the audience on multiple levels. She interacts with the intellect in using organized structures and humor, and engages the body with motion and dance-like movements.

Unit 4: Technical Considerations

Soundings is a demanding work written for mature players. Although the technical requirements are high, the parts are idiomatically written and well suited to the instruments. Subtle dynamic and musical shadings, from inaudible entrances and releases to imaginative solos, call for substantial individual musicianship. The percussion is treated as an equal choir with the woodwinds and brass. The "Fanfare" movement demands especially sensitive playing from both the brass and the percussion. The brilliant colors of the "Waves" movement depend upon exquisitely sensitive control of intonation and timbre.

Unit 5: Stylistic Considerations

McTee's music displays a colorful stylistic palette, and *Soundings* is the most stylistically complex of her works for winds. Familiarity with jazz articulations and inflections are required. A mature lyricism and sensitive soloistic playing are particularly evident in the third movement, but are demanded in other movements as well.

Unit 6: Musical Elements

Soundings makes use of several harmonic languages. The first movement is quintal, centering around an F/C fifth. The third movement is triadic in some respects (the solos are octotonic), but not functionally tonal. The tertian sounds are derived from the harmonic series. The second and fourth movements have a variety of harmonic material, much of it derived from jazz. McTee also creates harmony with parallel major scales at half steps a fourth apart. This creates an interval content similar to her earlier works that were based on octatonic scales, but which is more idiomatic for winds. Like her earlier works, much of *Soundings* is based on juxtaposing musical ideas and musical layers.

Unit 7: Form and Structure

Soundings is in four movements.

SECTION	MEASURES	EVENTS AND SCORING
MOVEMENT I: "FANFARE"		
Introduction	1-24	Percussion
A	24-52	Brass, quintal harmony centering around an F/C fifth
a.	25-37	Two phrases, percussion stops at second phrase
b.	38-45	One phrase transposed to E-flat/B-flat fifth
c.	46-52	Return to F/C fifth
B	53-95	Constructed in two layers:
Layer 1	53-95	Four brass phrases alternating F/C and E-flat/B-flat
Layer 2	72-86	Woodwind counterpoint to brass on F/C (mm. 86-95), woodwinds converge with brass on E-flat/B-flat
A	96-102	Return on F/C
Coda	103-105	A material on F/C

MOVEMENT II: "GIZMO"

The form of this movement is a deceptively simple binary, ABAB. However, with one exception—a repeated chord in the brass derived from the octatonic scale—all the musical materials in both A and B are the same. The form is defined by silences between the sections, the use of the brass chord in the B section, and the way the materials are layered.

SECTION	MEASURES
A	106-125
B	126-146
A	147-166
B	167-191

MOVEMENT III: "WAVES"

Also a simple form, ABABAB, the "Waves" movement is constructed in three layers. The background layer consists solely of a C major chord. The form is defined by the alteration of the second and third layers. Layer 1 is percussion rolls, with tuned instruments rolling a C/G fifth and winds that enter inaudibly and crescendo and diminuendo on C major chord tones. Layer 2 is independent flute, oboe and clarinet solos which do not play rhythmically exactly in order to achieve a result of flexibility and independence. Layer 3 is a tutti lyrical line in various scorings and a variety of muted colors with occasional counterpoint. A consists of Layers 1 and 2; B consists of Layers 1 and 3.

SECTION	MEASURES
A	192-201
B	202-208
A	209-218
B	219-225
A	226-231
B	232-238
A	239-248
B	249-256

MOVEMENT IV: "TRANSMISSION"

McTee chose the title for the double meaning of information from a transmitter and the mechanical transmission of an automobile. She views the process of metric or temporal modulation as analogous to a driver smoothly shifting gears. This movement uses a process that juxtaposes ideas to create a complex and multidimensional form. This analysis will describe two views to make its shape more obvious.

The first view concerns the temporal structure. The movement goes through a series of metric modulations which represent the smooth gear shifting described by McTee.

SECTION	MEASURES	SCORING
1	257-278	Quarter note=108
2	279-286	Quarter note=216 (eighth note=quarter note)
3	287-358	Quarter note=144 (dotted quarter note=quarter note)
4	358-365	Quarter note=108 (triplet eighth note=sixteenth note)

| 5 | 366-488 | Quarter note=144 (sixteenth note=triplet eighth note) |

The second view, a larger structural view based on motivic structure, is that Transmission is in three parts.

A	257-368	Encompassing 1 through 4 of the temporal structure and introducing motivic material
B	369-418	New material in Part 5 of the temporal structure
C	419-488	More contrasting material and a return of earlier material from A and B.

Unit 8: Suggested Listening
John Adams, *A Short Ride in a Fast Machine*, *Grand Pianola Music*
Cindy McTee, *Circuits*, *California Counterpoint: The Twittering Machine*

Unit 9: Additional References and Resources
McTee, Cindy. *Circuits*. Eugene Corporon and the University of Cincinnati College-Conservatory of Music Wind Symphony, 1992. Compact Disk KCD-11042.

McTee, Cindy. *California Counterpoint: The Twittering Machine*. Eugene Corporon and the University of North Texas Wind Symphony, 1995. Compact Disk KCD-11070.

McTee, Cindy. *Soundings*. Eugene Corporon and the University of North Texas Wind Symphony, 1997. Compact Disk KCD-11084.

This study guide was prepared with material from an unpublished DMA Thesis (in progress) by Matthew McInturf entitled "The Wind Music of Cindy McTee: *Circuits*, *California Counterpoint: The Twittering Machine*, and *Soundings*," including an interview and materials from Cindy McTee. Both are used by permission.

Contributed by:
Matthew McInturf
Director of Wind Studies
Florida International University
Miami, Florida

Teacher Resource Guide

Symphony No. 1, "The Lord of the Rings"

Johan de Meij
(b. 1953)

Unit 1: Composer

Johan de Meij was born on November 23, 1953 in Voorburg, Holland. He received his musical training at the Royal Conservatory in The Hague where he majored in band conducting and trombone performance. Although the *Symphony No. 1, "The Lord of the Rings,"* brought the composer into international prominence as a composer of band works, de Meij had, in fact, already established a reputation for himself as a distinguished arranger and trombone soloist. He has performed in several ensembles including the Dutch Brass Sextet, the Amsterdam Trombone Quartet, Orkest De Volharding, and the Amsterdam Wind Orchestra. De Meij is the recipient of numerous composition awards and commissions and is in demand as a guest conductor and clinician.

Unit 2: Composition

Symphony No. 1, "Lord of the Rings" is Johan de Meij's first work for band. It was the 1989 winner of the prestigious Sudler International Wind Band Composition Competition, having been selected from 143 entries representing twenty-seven countries. In addition the composer was honored in 1990 by the Dutch Composers Fund for this work. The symphony is a large, majestic work in five movements. Broadly programmatic, it is based on the literary trilogy by J.R.R. Tolkien (1892-1973) of the same title. Tolkien's work is a fantasy set in the mythical land of Middle-earth, a place where hobbits, dwarves, elves, men, ents, orcs, and wizards reside. Since the 1937 publication of *The Hobbit*, readers have been fascinated by the author's masterful development of this imaginary land and time. Tolkien worked on *The Lord of the Rings* from 1936 to 1949, although the complete trilogy did not go to publication until 1955. From that year on, the characters of Middle-earth have been discovered anew by each generation.

De Meij's symphony was composed over a period of three years, from 1984 to 1987. Each of the five movements musically illustrates either a character or an important event from the book:

I. "Gandalf" is a wise and powerful wizard, who battles the forces of darkness and evil, often astride his noble stallion "Shadowfax."

II. "Lothlórien" is the Elvenwood, home to the rulers of the Elven Kingdom, a place of woodlands, birds, and peace.

III. "Gollum" ("Sméagol") is a monstrous creature, once a simple hobbit whose greed has set a series of events into motion that ultimately lead to the battle between good and evil.

IV. "Journey in the Dark" is a description of the journey through the dark Mines of Moria, and the battle on the bridge of Khazad-Dûm.

V. "Hobbits" is a musical portrait of the little people of Middle-earth, happy, carefree folks with furry feet.

Symphony No. 1, "Lord of the Rings" was premiered in Brussels on March 15, 1988 by the Groot Harmonie Orkest van de Gidsen conducted by Norbert Nozy. Its Dutch premiere occurred on June 2, 1988 with Pierre Kuijpers conducting the Royal Military Band. This performance was a part of the advanced festivities for the 1989 World Music Competition at Kerkrade. The work is approximately forty-three minutes in duration, and is published by Amstel Music.

Unit 3: Historical Perspective

Although programmatic ideas may be found in music of the seventeenth and eighteenth centuries (and earlier), the beginnings of nineteenth-century program music are rooted in Beethoven's *Pastoral Symphony* (1807-08). Unlike "absolute" music, which has no descriptive ties, program music is specifically designed to convey nonmusical ideas. Works such as the Berlioz *Symphonie fantastique* (1830-31), Listz's *Les Préludes* (1845), Debussy's *Prélude à l'après-midi d'un faune* (1894), and Richard Strauss's *Alpensinfonie* (1915) all convey a particular story, poem, or description of some event or person. Works that are multimovement compositions are generally called program symphonies, while shorter, single-movement pieces are termed symphonic poems, or tone poems. *Symphony No. 1, "The Lord of the Rings"* therefore falls into the cate-

gory of program symphony. In this powerful piece de Meij conveys all the wonder and wizardry of its literary namesake while artfully constructing a work of depth and beauty that appeals to both artists and audiences.

Unit 4: Technical Considerations

Scored for full band, the *Symphony No. 1, "The Lord of the Rings"* includes demanding solos for clarinets, soprano saxophone, and trombone. The instrumentation also requires flügelhorn (second and fifth movements), piano, and extensive percussion. There are rich and beautiful solos for virtually every instrument of the band; most of the solos are more musically demanding than technically rigorous. However, the overall rhythmic, dynamic, and musical constraints are such that the work is best performed by mature, experienced players (although the "Gandalf" and "Hobbits" movements are within the performing abilities of finer younger ensembles). The full tonal range of most instruments is utilized and the sheer length of the composition may create endurance problems, particularly in the upper brass. The work remains firmly tonal throughout, and as such, most parts are not difficult to tune. While many time signatures are used, there is little of the constant shifting between time signatures that can create difficulties. The rhythmic complexity of the symphony varies with each movement, with the inner movements providing the most challenge. Multiple tonguing technique will be a necessity for the trumpet section during the third movement. Throughout the work dynamic contrast and ensemble balance will demand the utmost in professional performance from the ensemble members.

Unit 5: Stylistic Considerations

Within the forty-plus minutes of this symphony, many styles are explored. Overall, the work is extremely orchestral in its concept and timbre. The scoring provides a dark orchestral color with rich resonance from all instruments. Style changes occur within each movement and with each subsequent musical description. The first movement, "Gandalf," should convey the power and nobility of the great wizard, a truly majestic characterization. Strive to bring out the rich, dark, somber color of the brass chords through careful attention to balance. After the initial *forte* opening, solo euphonium and trumpet lines need to predominate the texture of the stately opening. All notes should be sustained to full value, always maintaining a *maestoso* style. The "Shadowfax" section of this movement should gallop, creating the visual image of a stallion racing over the land, its feet barely touching the ground as it races faster than the wind. The brass bursts should punctuate the line without blasting or shattering the texture. As the movement returns to the primary noble theme, work to maintain clarity of all melodic lines while creating a deep, dark, rich texture in the accompaniment by bringing out the lower woodwind and brass voices.

The second movement begins with solo clarinets, delicately supported by a variety of sustaining voices. In contrast to the first movement, the style of "Lothlórien" is reminiscent of the elegance of the Renaissance period, with some very definite twentieth-century twists. The overall texture should be quite light. Listen to a recording of Darius Milhaud's woodwind quintet, *La Cheminée du Roi René*. This small ensemble example may serve as a model for establishing proper balance, style, and texture. The beautiful brass hymn section must be choral-like in nature with carefully constructed balance throughout.

The third movement opens with a virtuoso soprano saxophone solo characterizing the many twists and turns in the personality of the pitiful creature "Gollum." A solo trombone later picks up the solo line. The complexities of the character's psychological makeup are aptly portrayed by a continual shift in the musical styles and textures of this movement.

Through the tunnels of the dark Mines of Moria, the wizard Gandalf leads his companions. The opening timpani sets the tempo and haunting mood of the fourth movement. Low brass, percussion, and piano help to establish the sense of dread and foreboding as the company trudges ever more deeply into the Mines. Maintain a steady tempo throughout the introductory section while working to convey a sense of dread and underlying fear. The flight from the Orcs and the confrontation on the bridge of Khazad-Dûm pits the wizard against the monstrous Balrog, a musical battle erupts with the final measures of the movement imparting the sad outcome. Work with the woodwinds to maintain a steady drive in the punctuated rhythm of the repeated pitches. The departure from the Mines after the battle must be *piano*.

The final movement, "Hobbits" is a fitting conclusion to the work. It begins with the opening theme of "Gandalf" but quickly proceeds into a happy, lilting folk dance expressing the optimism and exuberance of the Hobbits. The hymn that follows plays tribute to the resilience and fortitude of the little people of Middle-earth. This theme is *dolce* and *legato*, and while it begins quietly, it evolves into a full ensemble chorale. The *andante* tempo and *sostenuto* style must be maintained throughout this section. The movement ends with yet another statement of the "Gandalf" theme before settling into a peaceful conclusion as Gandalf and Frodo sail away to the Grey Havens and disappear.

Unit 6: Musical Elements**

While this work does not tackle any aleatoric or experimental notation, most musical elements from the Western art music tradition are present. From the fanfare opening to the cheeky nature of "Gollum," performers will have to deal with mixed meter, places in which many notes appear in the bar, and frequent stylistic changes.

The most difficult considerations are those of balance. Similar to a work for orchestra, this work requires the brass to exhibit combinations of restraint while accompanying and full volume in peak brass sections. Ensembles should work to develop in this work a "shimmer" from the woodwinds that is only occasionally overshadowed by the power of the brass.

Unit 7: Form and Structure

This work is programmatic. While formal constructions and cyclic features are evident, they must be read in conjunction with the programmatic elements they represent.

SECTION	MEASURES	EVENTS AND SCORING
Movement One: "Gandalf"—Arch Form ABCBA		
A	1-5	Opening Fanfare
B	6-14	a
	15-23	a
	24-35	a^1
C	36	*Allegro vivace*; "Shadowfax—The Grey Horse"
	36-59	Introduction (i)
	59-69	a
	69-77	Transition
	78-90	i^1
	91-100	a
	101-107	a
	107-110	Transition
	111-118	*Maestoso*; b with snippets of a
B	123-131	a
	132-139	a
	140-147	a^1
A	148-165	Fanfare
Movement Two: "Lothlórien"		
A	1-10	a
	11-18	b

SECTION	MEASURES	EVENTS AND SCORING
B	19-22	*Allegretto grazioso;* Introduction
	23-34	a; "The Mirror of Galadriel"
	35-47	a
	48-51	b (related to small b above)
	52-57	Transition
A	58-68	a
B	69-76	Introduction
	77-88	a
C	89-105	a "Mythrandir Chorale"
B	106-116	a
	117-124	Transition
	124-149	*Piu Mosso;* development of a
	149-178	Coda

Movement Three: "Gollum"

Intro	1-13	Three important ideas: a—six-note gesture at opening b—half step descending line c—syncopated fourths
Cadenza	14-32	Soprano saxophone—three main ideas
A	33-60	*Allegro;* bright 6/8 humorous march
A	61-72	Melody in piccolo
	73-78	Transition
Dev.	78-89	Development; rhythmic section, with melodic interjections (a) from the opening cadenza
	90-118	Continued development of cadenza ideas; addition of long descending idea (b)
	119-142	*Presto Agitato;* rhythmically dense, layering of melodic ideas from opening

SECTION	MEASURES	EVENTS AND SCORING
	143-161	Rhythmic drive continues. Addition of sextuplet idea (a)
Trans.	162-168	Transition based on falling triplet from opening (b)
Dev. II	169-193	Based on the long *glissando* (b)
A	194-224	March from m. 33
Dev.	225-244	Development based on (c)
A	245-271	March
Coda	272-294	Based on six-note idea (a)

Movement Four: "Journey in the Dark"
A. "The Mines of Moria"

Intro	1-16	Plodding, heavy introduction
A[1]	17-27	Melodic/harmonic idea presented in horns/bassoons
A[11]	28-36	Melodic ideas presented in English horn, clarinet, trumpet
A[111]	37-42	Melodic ideas presented in trombones, flutes horns, soprano saxophone, and clarinet
A	43-53	Ideas coalesce into a coherent melodic idea. The opening can be seen as a kind of reverse development, moving towards a complete melody.

B. "The Bridge at Khazad-Dûm"

Movement Five: "Hobbits"

Intro	1-12	Long sustained tones, based on opening fanfare idea from Movement One
Fanfare	14-22	Opening fanfare from Movement One
Intro	23-38	Introduction to the "March of the Hobbits"
A March	39-55	"March of the Hobbits." A bright melody in the form aaba[1]
A	56-71	

SECTION	MEASURES	EVENTS AND SCORING
A	72-90	Low brass melody
A	91-106	Full ensemble
Trans.	107-131	Transition to the "Hobbits Hymn"
B	131-146	"Hobbits Hymn" based on the march; at first very restrained in the clarinets
B	147-162	Hymn with added low brass
B	163-183	Hymn (repeated), full ensemble plus added countermelody second time
Trans.	183-193	Transition
Fanfare	194-205	Opening fanfare from Movement One. Fanfare finally comes to rest at m. 208. Pedal point on C, repeated C major chords.

Unit 8: Suggested Listening

Ludwig von Beethoven, *Symphony No. 6, (Pastoral)*
Hector Berlioz, *Symphonie fantastique*
Paul Dukas, *The Sorcerer's Apprentice*
Johan de Meij, *Symphony No. 2, The Big Apple*; *Aquarium, Loch Ness*
Felix Mendelssohn/arr. Hindsley, *Les Préludes*
Darius Milhaud, *La Cheminée du Roi René*
H. Owen Reed, *The Awakening of the Ents*
Richard Strauss/arr. Hindsley, *Till Eulenspiegel, Ein Heldenleben*

Unit 9: Additional References and Resources

Amstel Music, The Netherlands.

Apel, Willi. *Harvard Dictionary of Music*. 2nd ed. Cambridge, MA: The Belknap Press of Harvard University Press, 1970.

Grout, Donald Jay. *A History of Western Music*. 3rd ed. New York: W.W. Norton & Co., 1980.

"The Lord of the Rings." Liner notes. The Hague, the Netherlands: KMK & Ottavo Recordings, 1989.

Margolis, Bob, ed. *Best Music for High School Band*. New York: Manhattan Beach Music, 1993.

Tolkien, J.R.R. *The Lord of the Rings*. New York: Ballantine Books, Inc., 1965.

Contributed by:

Susan Creasap
Assistant Director of Bands
Morehead State University
Morehead, Kentucky

Alan Lourens
Indiana University
Bloomington, Indiana

Teacher Resource Guide

Toccata Marziale
Ralph Vaughan Williams
(1872–1958)

Unit 1: Composer

Ralph Vaughan Williams is acknowledged as one of England's most well respected and admired composers. He graduated from the University of Cambridge and the Royal College of Music in London. His principal teachers included Charles Hubert Parry, Sir Charles Villiers Stanford, and Maurice Ravel. It was the latter who taught Vaughan Williams to orchestrate for color and texture. Although primarily known as a composer, Vaughan Willliams also was active as an organist, conductor, lecturer, teacher, editor, and writer. From 1904 to 1906 he was the musical editor of the new *English Hymnal* and continued his editorial work with the *Songs of Praise* (1925) and the *Oxford Book of Carols* (1928). A believer in the amateur musician, Vaughan Williams was affiliated with the Leith Hall Music Festivals, serving as the conductor of these amateur singers and players from 1909 to 1953. In addition to his conducting duties, he composed a number of works for these musicians. His interest in English folk songs led the composer on a journey through the country in search of melodies, texts, and historical information. This fascination with the music of his country influenced his musical output and British twentieth-century music as well. Vaughan Williams wrote symphonies, music for film, operas, choral works, hymns, music for choir and orchestra, and other instrumental pieces. His compositions for wind band include *English Folk Song Suite*, *Flourish for Wind Band*, *The Golden Vanity March*, *Sea Songs*, *Variations for Brass Band*, and *Music for the Pageant of Abinger*.

Unit 2: Composition

The second work for wind band by Vaughan Williams, *Toccata Marziale* was written in 1924 and premiered during that same year by the Royal Military School of Music Band conducted by Lt. H. E. Adkins. The performance took place in London at Wembley Stadium as a part of the British Empire Exposition. Even with such an auspicious premiere, the work did not enjoy great popularity in its native land. Scored for full wind band including soprano and bass saxophones, cornets and trumpets, the instrumentation is the same as that of the 1924 Sousa Band. Written in 3/4 meter with a tempo indication of *Allegro maestoso*, *Toccata Marziale* is 157 measures in length and is approximately five minutes in duration.

Unit 3: Historical Perspective

The word "toccata" is taken from the Italian *toccare* meaning "to touch." This connection is readily apparent when one considers that the early toccata referred to a composition for a keyboard instrument. The typical toccata was set in a free style with full chords and running passages, often scalar in nature. Although often virtuosic in character, the early toccatas included expressive passages that were intended to be played in a free tempo, *rubato*. By the mid to late sixteenth century, the toccata had evolved into a composition that altered free, typical keyboard writing with fugal sections. As the genre moved into the next century, the toccata experienced further changes. According to Willi Apel, the Frescobaldi toccata was written "in a series of short sections, exhibiting a variety of moods in rapid succession." By the early eighteenth century, the form had become a virtuoso piece for keyboard instruments that was often devoid of any true musical intent, serving rather as a showpiece for performers. These perpetual motion works demanded strict adherence to a tempo and began to take on the character of an étude rather than a concert work.

In Germany the toccata followed one of two paths. While the South German composers chose to continue to write these works in the standard style of the Italians, it was in the hands of the North Germans that an all-new and improved model was created. The toccatas of Matthias Weckmann (1619-74), Dietrich Buxtehude (c. 1637-1707), and Johann Sebastian Bach (1685-1750) went beyond the Italian model into a more rhapsodic style.

The term "toccata" was also employed in the early seventeenth century to indicate a brass fanfare.

Unit 4: Technical Considerations

The rhythmic complexity of the *Toccata Marziale* is derived from its contrapuntal nature. It is this aspect of the composition that presents the biggest challenge. Since all melodic and contrapuntal material is developed from a single motive that is both melodic and strictly rhythmic in character, the successful performance of this work is dependent on both rhythmic accuracy and melodic clarity. Fennell suggests that a tempo of quarter note=104-112 throughout will be most conducive to a musical, concise performance.

The wind parts all require mature, technically proficient performers who have command of the full range of their instruments. Sixteenth-note passages occur in all parts and must be played with precision. The dynamic aspects of the composition offer a particular challenge. Within the span of one beat (m. 15), Vaughan Williams asks the ensemble to *decrescendo* from *forte* to *piano*. Because of the contrapuntal texture of the work, great care must be taken in the long, sustained *crescendos* and *diminuendos* to maintain proper balance. Work to allow melodies and countermelodies to predominate the texture.

Vaughan Williams studied orchestration with Maurice Ravel and it was this association that enhanced the former's appreciation of tonal color. The score of the *Toccata Marziale* calls for both trumpets and cornets. An authentic rendition of the work will be most likely if the conductor elects to use these two instruments since Vaughan Williams composed with these specific timbres in mind (two-thirds of the trumpet part is not duplicated in the cornet part). The bass clarinet part is of particular interest since it is used in conjunction with the upper saxophone parts and is often scored higher than the upper clarinets.

An errata is available in the Fennell article of the *Conductor's Anthology* (see Unit 9).

Unit 5: Stylistic Considerations

W. Francis McBeth has stated that "the initial statement of the motive will indicate the style of the work." Never has this been more true than in the *Toccata Marziale*. From a single two-bar motive, Vaughan Williams has masterfully created countermelodies, melodic echoes, and accompaniment figures. According to Fennell the style of the piece will be established by the articulation of the opening two notes. This ascending fourth, from F to B-flat, should be executed with a slight hesitation. The conductor would do well to give counts two and three before the opening up-beat eighth note. Make sure to keep the sixteenth notes *staccato* while maintaining both a slight separation and a *tenuto* length in the eighth notes. Work consistently to observe a definite contrast among the indications of *staccato*, *marcato*, and *legato*.

Avoid doubling the solo line in m. 22 by selecting either the oboe or the cornet. Further suggestions for the interpretation of this piece are well defined in the excellent article by Frederick Fennell located in the *Conductor's Anthology*, Vol. 2 (see Unit 9).

Unit 6: Musical Elements

Built on a single two-measure motive, the composition exudes a dynamic energy that permeates all sections of the music. Although the key signature of B-flat major is maintained throughout the piece, the use of accidentals clearly establishes other key areas and segments based on pentatonic (mm. 65-68) and whole tone scales (mm. 69-90, 153-157). The return of the A theme is in G-flat major. Aside from the initial main motive, there are five musical ideas and the traditional Vaughan Williams folk-like melodies. The use of parallelism contributes to the density of the texture (G-flat to B-flat to C to B-flat).

Unit 7: Form and Structure

Toccata Marziale is written in simple ternary form: ABA.

SECTION	MEASURES	EVENTS AND SCORING
A	1-52	Main motive, contrapuntal texture, harmonized in thirds and triads
	1	Idea I in clarinets, trombones, and horns
	5	Idea II in woodwinds
	8	Transitional
	9	Idea III in woodwinds, cornets, and trumpets, *mezzo forte legato*, supporting background material based on opening motive, bass line will be used in about one-third of the piece
	14	Idea IV in flutes
	22	Idea V in oboes and cornets, then passed around the ensemble with snippets of Idea II (m. 27)
	48-50	Closing section of A
B	53-90	Folk-song-like melody, use of Ideas II, III, IV
	53	Folk melody in alto reeds and euphonium
	58	Folk melody in cornets
	61	Folk melody in trombones, main motive in clarinets
	69	Idea IV in woodwinds

Section	Measures	Events and Scoring
	75	Idea IV in low brass
	78	Idea IV in flutes and bassoons
A	91-146	Return of main motive now in G-flat major, literal transposition, then embellished; use of melodic ideas I, II, III, IV, V
	91	Main motive in basses; Idea I in clarinets, saxophones, and bassoons
	93	Folk-song melody in flutes, clarinets, cornets, and trombones
	96	Main motive in trumpets and horns; Idea II in flutes, oboes, clarinets
	97	Folk melody in cornets and euphoniums
	100	Idea III in clarinets and euphoniums
	101	Folk melody in horns and cornets
	103	Folk melody in basses
	106-116	Derived from Idea IV and folk melody
	117	Idea V in flutes, clarinets, cornets, and trumpets
	120	Restatement of Idea V from m. 26-39
	147-end	*Codetta*, fragments of main motive

Unit 8: Suggested Listening

Johann Sebastian Bach, *Toccata and Fugue in D Minor*
Robert Jager, *Chorale and Toccata*
Percy Grainger, *Molly on the Shore*
Jack Stamp, *Chorale and Toccata*
Ralph Vaughan Williams, *Sea Songs, English Folk Song Suite*

Unit 9: Additional References

Apel, Willi. *Harvard Dictionary of Music.* Second ed. Cambridge, MA: The Belknap Press of Harvard Univesity Press, 1970.

Boosey and Hawkes Music Publishers, New York.

Drickinson, Alan Edgar Frederic. *Vaughan Williams*. Irvine, CA: Reprint Services, 1988.

Erickson, Frank W. "A Composer Discusses Music." *School Musician*, August/September 1967, 70-72.

Fennell, Frederick. "Vaughan Williams' *Toccata Marziale*." *Conductors Anthology*, vol. 2, second ed. Northfield, IL: The Instrumentalist Company, 1993.

Grout, Donald J. *A History of Western Music*, Third ed. New York: W.W. Norton & Co., 1980.

Kennedy, Michael. *A Catalogue of the Works of Ralph Vaughan Williams*. New York: Oxford University Press, 1996.

Kennedy, Michael. *The Works of Ralph Vaughan Williams*. New York: Oxford University Press, 1964.

McBeth, W. Francis. "*Kaddish*." *Conductors Anthology*, vol. 2, second ed. Northfield, IL: The Instrumentalist Company, 1993.

Pittman, Daniel Sayle, Jr. "Percy Grainger, Gustav Holst, and Ralph Vaughan Williams: A Comparative Analysis of Selected Wind Compositions." Doctoral diss., Memphis State University, 1979.

Rehrig, William H. *The Heritage Encyclopedia of Band Music*. Edited by Paul Bierley. Westerville, OH: Integrity Press, 1991.

Vaughan Williams, Ursula. *R.V.W.: A Biography of Ralph Vaughan Williams*. New York: Oxford University Press, 1964.

Contributed by:

Susan Creasap
Assistant Director of Bands
Morehead State University
Morehead, Kentucky

Yoshiaki Tanno
Indiana University
Bloomington, Indiana

Grade Six

Teacher Resource Guide

and the mountains rising nowhere
Joseph Schwantner
(b. 1943)

Unit 1: Composer

Joseph Schwantner was born in Chicago on March 22, 1943, and is currently Professor of Composition at the Eastman School of Music of the University of Rochester where he has taught since 1970. He has also served on the faculty of the Julliard School and was the 1987-88 Karel Husa Visiting Professor of Composition at Ithaca College, Ithaca, New York. Schwantner received his musical and academic training at the Chicago Conservatory and at Northwestern University, where he completed a doctorate in 1968. From 1982 to 1985, Schwantner served as Composer-in-Residence with the Saint Louis Symphony Orchestra as part of the Meet the Composer/Orchestra Residencies Program funded by the Exxon Corporation, the Rockefeller Foundation, and the National Endowment for the Arts. He has been the subject of a television documentary entitled *Soundings*, produced by WGBH in Boston for national broadcast. His work *Magabunda: Four Poems of Agueda Pizarro* which was recorded by the Saint Louis Symphony, was nominated for a 1985 Grammy Award in the category "Best New Classical Composition," and his *A Sudden Rainbow*, also recorded by the Saint Louis Symphony, was nominated for "Best Classical Composition."

Unit 2: Composition

And the mountains rising nowhere was commissioned by the Eastman Wind Ensemble with a grant from the National Endowment for the Arts. The premiere was given by the Eastman Wind Ensemble, Donald Hunsberger conducting, at the National Conference of the College Band Directors

Association in 1977. It is published by Helicon Music Corporation and distributed by European American Music Distributors.

And the mountains rising nowhere is dedicated to Carol Adler, whose poem, taken from a collection entitled *Arioso*, was used as a generator.

> arioso bells
> sepia
> moonbeams
> an afternoon sun blanked by rain
> and the mountains rising nowhere
> the sound returns
> the sound and the silence   chimes

And the mountains rising nowhere was Joseph Schwantner's first work for wind band. In 1980 Schwantner completed his second wind band composition, *From a Dark Millennium*, and in 1996 *In Evening's Stillness* became the final composition of his wind band trilogy.

The eleven-minute work calls for six flutes (I-IV double on piccolo), two B-flat clarinets, four oboes (III and IV double on English horn; all oboes double on glass crystals), four bassoons, four trumpets in B-flat, four horns in F, four trombones (fourth is bass trombone), one tuba, one contrabass, piano (amplified, *sostenuto* pedal required), percussion I (vibraphone, bell tree, timbales, three tom-toms, two suspended cymbals, tam-tam with contrabass bow required for *arco* playing of vibes and tam-tam), percussion II (marimba, glockenspiel, water gong, bass drum, two suspended cymbals, two triangles), percussion III (vibraphone, xylophone, four tom-toms, bass drum, two suspended cymbals, two triangles with contrabass bow required for *arco* playing of vibes), percussion IV (glockenspiel, tubular bells, water gong, two suspended cymbals, two triangles) percussion V (xylophone, crotales, bass drum, tam-tam, four tom-toms, two suspended cymbals, and also plays tubular bells of percussion IV; contrabass bow required for *arco* playing of tam-tam and crotales), percussion VI (four timpani).

Unit 3: Historical Perspective

And the mountains rising nowhere has become a landmark composition in the wind band repertoire. Contributing to this significance were the creative sounds that Schwantner introduced through his orchestration and stylized approach to musical materials. In an interview in 1991, Schwantner commented that,

> [And the mountains rising nowhere] was completed at a time when I was writing chamber music for such groups as the Contemporary Chamber Ensemble, the Boston Musica Viva, the Twentieth Century Consort, and the New York New Music Ensemble. I wanted to explore ways small ensembles produce sound by giving individual

musicians more to do. For example, a clarinetist might play other instruments such as crotales, triangles, or crystal goblets. This idea of augmenting performers' roles led to a similar strategy with concert band in which musicians sing and whistle. The amplified piano and large percussion section are treated equally with winds and brass and state many of the work's primary musical elements.

Unit 4: Technical Considerations

And the mountains rising nowhere incorporates a number of contemporary notational concepts. A number of these devices include:

X = Cancels meter. Music is time-framed in seconds. Rhythm is interpreted by the relative spatial placement of notes.

= Duration of pitch in X sections is determined by length of the beam.

= fast as possible

= accel.   = rall.

= 4 sec. fermata

Almost all of Schwantner's works are composed in Micro notation. Time signatures of 2/8, 3/8, 4/8, 5/8, 7/8, 5/16, 6/16, and 4/dotted eighth note are used with subdivisions as small as a sixty-fourth note. Spatial notation, *senza mizura*, and time line notation are also used. Instrumental ranges are in the highest *tessitura* for most instruments. The piano part is integral to the entire work. In many respects this becomes a quasi=piano concerto with most programs listing the pianist's name as soloist. All wind players and double bass are required to either sing or whistle. All four oboes double on glass crystals. Percussion set-up is extremely important in regard to dynamic balances within the entire ensemble and equipment shared amongst the percussionists. Many sections

include intricate episodes of "shared monody."

Unit 5: Stylistic Considerations

Schwantner states that some of his intentions in composing the work included creating a work for winds and percussion that did not sound "like a band piece." He was further interested in writing a work: 1) where the percussion section would be on an equal footing with the woodwinds and brass; 2) to further exploit the process of synthesis between tonal and non-tonal musical materials; 3) to expand the sonorous timbral and articulative resources of a large ensemble by having performers engage in "extra performance activities," such as singing, whistling, and playing glass crystals. Some of the key stylistic elements are the way in which he utilizes the elements of rhythm, timbre, and texture in a number of contemporary and traditional techniques. Rhythm is treated in spatial notation in Sections 3, 8, and the *coda*, which form the A parts of the large ABA[1] structure. Asymmetric meters are used in Sections 4 and 7 while traditional, regular rhythm is used in Sections 6 and 9.

An example of rhythmic transformation is the bass drum and timpani rhythm in Section 7. Each measure is a transformation of one basic rhythmic pattern. The accents are always on beats 1, 2, and 4 whether the time signature is 5/16 or 6/16.

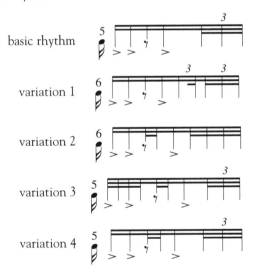

This eight-bar *ostinato* is repeated three times. This motive consists of five rhythmic elements (a, b, c, d, e) that are presented in the pattern a-b-a-c-a-d-b-e.

Percussion Motive–Section 7

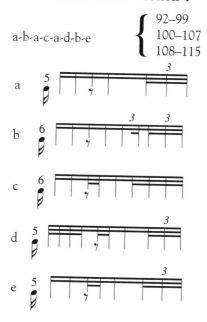

Timbre serves to outline the form of the work. The glass crystals, which appear at the beginning and end of the composition, outline the arch form. The percussion motives serve as bridges between sections. Motive 1 at the start of the introduction and the end of Section 3 sets off the first large A section.

Schwantner also uses a timbre and textural technique he refers to as "shared monody." This is a melodic idea that is shared by partial doublings among several instrumental voices. According to Schwantner, this technique is a single linear event that is melodically shared by many players with each single player entering and sustaining a different pitch of the theme in order. These notes becomes a single line in which many participate as differentiated from a single player on a solo line.

Unit 6: Musical Elements

The basic harmonic, melodic, and rhythmic materials of *and the mountains rising nowhere* are developed from transformations or expansions of six motives and two motivic variations. These eight cells can be traced throughout the work as both derivative and connecting materials.

MOTIVE 1

The first motive is a non-pitched percussion motive which opens the work. The motive consists of seven strokes marked *fortissimo, crescendo, sforzando* and followed by their resonance decay. This quick *crescendo* serves as an upbeat into six of the formal sections.

Motive 1

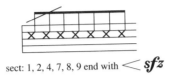

sect: 1, 2, 4, 7, 8, 9 end with $<$ **sfz**

(upbeat into the quiet opening of a new section)

MOTIVE 2

The second motive is presented by the glass crystals in the introduction, Section 1, and into Section 2. They return again in Section 8 through the *coda*. B-natural is heard as the pitch of emphasis because it is the first pitch sounded and is the lowest note. The pitch materials form the modal scale of B Aeolian which is also pitch-class set 7-35.

Motive 2

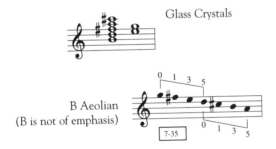

Glass Crystals

B Aeolian
(B is not of emphasis)

7-35

MOTIVE 3

Motive 3 is derived from Motive 2 since it is a subset of 7-35 (5-20 [0 13 7 8]). This chord also appears in Schwantner's *Sparrows* (1979), for soprano and chamber ensemble, repeatedly on the word "bell." There may be an association with the word "bells" from the first line of Carol Adler's poem.

Motive 3

5-20

Derived from Mot. # 2

(Bells from poem "Arioso" and from "Sparrows")

MOTIVE 4

This quintuplet motive is based on the octatonic scale and pitch-class set

8-28. It first appears in the piano and is later transformed using other rhythms and patterns.

Motive 4

(0134679A) 8–28 octatonic scale
N.B., minus G-natural

MOTIVE 5

Motive 5 appears in three forms: 1) untransposed with B as the lowest note; 2) transposed at T9 with A-flat as the lowest note; and 3) in canon at the tenth. Cynthia Folio observes that "the juxtaposition of A-flat and B reflects, on a motivic level, a larger structural idea: the two main tonal areas of the composition are B and A-flat. The canonic statement of Motive 5 occurs before the A-flat section as a kind of transition and again at the very end of the composition as a kind of summary."

Motive 5

B Dorian / superimposed 5ths

MOTIVE 6

This motive introduces the third important pitch-class, 7-34 [0 1 3 4 6 8 A].

Motive 6

intro's: 7–34 (013468A)
(not arranged symetrically)

MOTIVE 2A
    Motive 2A is first used in Section 2.

Motive 2A

Sect 2: 5x in pno/4x w/ flute, perc added 7-35 (B
Aeolian) actually var. of Motive 2 later transposed
at T9 w/ A as bottom

MOTIVE 3A
    The last motive to be introduced, Motive 3A, first appears in Section 4
and is the basic material for the entire section.

Motive 3A

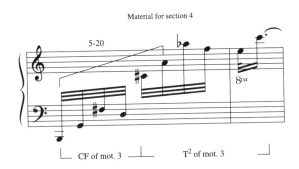

Unit 7: Form and Structure

And the mountains rising nowhere is comprised of eleven sections that
begin with an introduction and end with a coda-like section. The introduction is presented as spatial notation in the glass crystals, piano, and percussion.
Motives 1, 2, 3, 4, 5, and 6 are introduced and set the atmosphere for Section
1. This section builds tension using Motives 3 and 2, culminating in a "resonant" four seconds of silence.
    The second section introduces Motive 2A along with the previously stated Motives 2, 4, and 5. Whistling and singing textures are layered over
percussion and piano which builds to a *sforzando* chord in m. 37. Section 2
elides with the beginning of Section 3. This area is again in time-controlled
spatial notation and serves as a *coda*-like section to the introduction and
Sections 1 and 2.
    Section 4 begins at m. 38 and is based upon Motive 3A material. This
passage builds to a high point in m. 52 through the use of rhythmic activity,

fortissimo dynamics, and increased register, followed by a sudden dynamic change at the beginning of the longest of the meter areas, Section 5 (33 measures). A-flat becomes the pitch center of this section leading into the brass chorale in Section 6. Section 7 is built on the transposed pitches in Motives 3 and 4 with a increasing predominance of the bass drum and timpani.

Section 8 recapitulates the glass crystals and whistler motives with contrasts of dynamics and a multilayered texture. This section uses similar material as found in the introduction and Section 1, as well as time notation. Section 9 is a return of B as a pitch center and builds from m. 121 to a point of tension in m. 133 which resonates through the *coda*.

These eleven sections can be grouped into a larger form as:

A: Introduction through Section 3

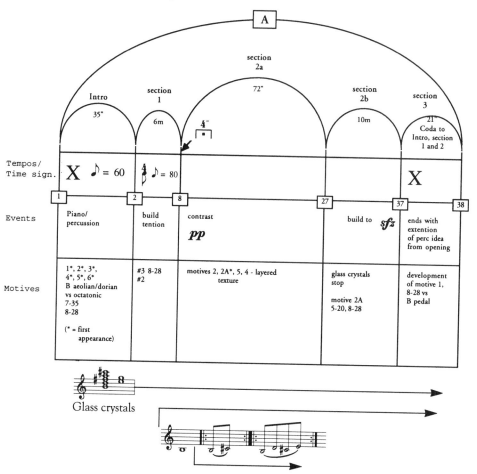

B: Section 4 through Section 7

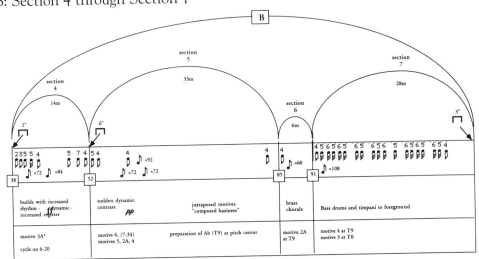

A^1 Section 8 through the *coda*

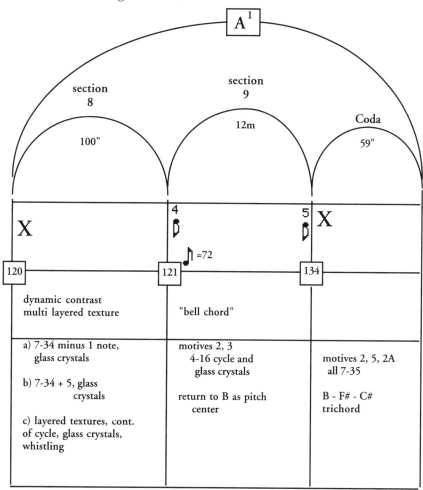

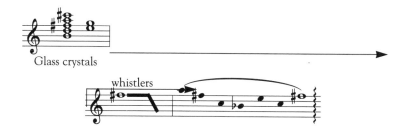

Glass crystals

whistlers

The work begins with an emphasis on B and shifts to A-flat and returns again to B. The glass crystals reinforce the idea of returning "home" to the pitch area B; Schwantner even wrote "Back home on B" on the last page of his annotated score. Folio further states that: "Motives #5 and #2A appear transposed from B in the first and the last parts to A-flat in the second part, to strengthen further the sense of 'modulation.' Both A parts are framed by sections using time-free notation: part A is framed by the introduction and Section 3, A^1 by Section 8 and the *coda*." Further support can be found in the note that Schwantner wrote over m. 37 in his annotated score: "acts as a *coda* to Introduction, and Sec. 1 & 2."

Unit 8: Suggested Listening
Works by Joseph Schwantner:
and the mountains rising nowhere
From a Dark Millennium
Music of Amber
Aftertones of Infinity
Sparrows
New Morning for the World
Elixir
A Sudden Rainbow

Unit 9: Additional References and Resources

Folio, Cynthia. "An Analysis and Comparison of Four Compositions by Joseph Schwantner: *and the mountains rising nowhere; Wild Angels of the Open Hills; Aftertones of Infinity;* and *Sparrows.*" Doctor of Philosophy Dissertation, University of Rochester, Rochester, New York, 1985.

Renshaw, Jeffrey. "Conducting Analysis: Joseph Schwantner's *And The Mountains Rising Nowhere.*" *The Instrumentalist*, Vol. 45/6, January 1991.

Renshaw, Jeffrey. "Conducting Analysis: Joseph Schwantner's *From A Dark Millennium.*" *The Instrumentalist*, Vol. 44/2, September 1989.

Renshaw, Jeffrey. "Interview with Joseph Schwantner." *The Instrumentalist*, Vol. 45/10, May 1991.

Contributed by:
Jeffrey Renshaw
Director of Bands
University of Connecticut
Storrs, Connecticut

Teacher Resource Guide

Aspen Jubilee
Ron Nelson
(b. 1929)

Unit 1: Composer

Ronald J. Nelson has made significant contributions to the music world through his numerous compositions for band, orchestra, and chorus. He was born in Joliet, Illinois on December 14, 1929, and began composing at the age of six. He studied at the Eastman School of Music with Howard Hanson and Bernard Rogers, and in Paris under a Fulbright grant. He has received numerous awards from a variety of universities and national cultural organizations. His list of compositions include seven works for orchestra, over forty choral works, and works for band.

Unit 2: Composition

Aspen Jubilee was commissioned by the Manatee High School Band, Bradenton, Florida, Howard Lerner and Joseph Powell, musical directors. It was published in 1988 by Boosey & Hawkes. The work features a unique addition—a solo soprano vocal part intended to add an entirely new timbre to the instrumental ensemble.

Unit 3: Historical Perspective

Composers for any type of ensemble search for new sounds, instrumental or vocal combinations, or effects. Nelson has consistently displayed the capability to write for a variety of media while continuing to develop new and fresh ideas in the areas of ensemble texture, melodic and harmonic structures, and the use of percussion. In all of his many works there is a dedication to preserving the atmosphere of artistic ideas that he intends to convey.

Unit 4: Technical Considerations

Aspen Jubilee gives the ensemble and conductor a number of challenges. There are a number of difficult syncopated rhythmic figures throughout the ensemble, some of which are similar to jazz rhythmic ideas. The percussion parts are written for nine players to include a piano/celeste combination. The composer suggests that if there are not enough players the conductor should select the most vital parts to be covered. The work calls for a solo soprano vocalist who sits within the ensemble to add a new and unique timbre. The part requires solid and extended range up to E-flat above the staff, and is intended for a vocalist with a pure tone and harmonics. There are numerous short solo lines that must blend together to form the overall structure. The horn line in particular requires a solid lower register. There are numerous meter shifts throughout the work, and a constant juxtaposition of ideas through the ensemble. The tempo is fast in the opening and closing sections which further complicates the performance of the rhythmic figures.

Unit 5: Stylistic Considerations

There are a variety of textures and solo lines that must be heard throughout the performance. The composer gives some suggestions in the score for the vocal solo line treatment. The performance of the first theme clarinet duet in m. 27 is listed as "acorney tones" and should convey a light and playful atmosphere. The solo voice can be amplified but must blend carefully with the ensemble. The vocal part also has additional lines that are not marked or notated in the score. The composer suggests that these be performed. The meter shifts should be smooth and allow for a connected flow of the fragmented themes and lines. The middle section is marked *arubatos* and can be treated in different ways. The melodic ideas of this section will return in the closing section similar to a *coda*. This gives the conductor the opportunity to show diversity in the performance styles of these sections. Throughout the work, the ensemble must carefully balance solo lines and ideas with the accompaniment, and execute difficult rhythmic patterns smoothly.

Unit 6: Musical Elements

The melodic ideas are fragmented and juxtaposed throughout. There are numerous meter and rhythmic changes to enhance the themes as well as the accompaniment. All melodic and accompaniment material is derived from very basic elements or fragments which combine to create the overall form and structure. The percussion and in particular the celeste play an important role throughout the work.

Unit 7: Form and Structure

The overall form is in three basic sections with an introduction and closing section or *coda*. The work begins with an introduction utilizing fragments of the thematic material used throughout the composition. This segues direct-ly into the first section which has two basic melodic ideas: the first in the fast opening meter and the second in triple meter performed in one to a bar. The slow middle section is highlighted by the solo soprano with the ensemble. This section develops and comes to a climax then transitions back into a restatement of the opening introduction and first sections completely. The theme from the slow middle section returns in the closing section which is similar to a *coda*. This theme is now treated in the same fast manner as the opening section with syncopated and pulsed rhythms as accompaniment.

Unit 8: Suggested Listening
Mushashino Academia Musicae Wind Ensemble, Frank Bencriscutto and
    Ray E. Cramer, Conductors, Mid-West International Band and
    Orchestra Clinic, 1995. (MW95MCD-30).
Orchestral works of Ron Nelson

Unit 9: Additional References and Resources
Battisti, Frank, and Robert Garofalo. *Guide to Score Study*. Ft. Lauderdale,
    FL: Meredith Music Publications, 1990.

Weisberg, Arthur. *Performing Twentieth-Century Music: A Handbook for
    Conductors and Instrumentalists*. New Haven and London: Yale University
    Press, 1993.

Contributed by:
Otis French
U. S. Army Field Band
Ft. Mead, Maryland

Teacher Resource Guide

Bacchanalia for Band
Walter S. Hartley
(b. 1927)

Unit 1: Composer

Walter Hartley is a prolific and eclectic composer of music for a variety of media. He has given us some of the most interesting and rewarding solo and ensemble music composed for wind instruments. Born in Washington, DC in 1927, he studied with Bernard Rogers and Howard Hanson at Eastman, and received his Ph.D. in 1953. Hartley taught at the National Music Camp (1956-60), at Davis Elkins College in West Virginia, and at SUNY-Fredonia.

Unit 2: Composition

The Bacchanalia was the Roman festival in honor of Bacchus, the god of wine and revelry. A related term is the *bacchanal*, which was a dance or song in honor of Bacchus; music associated with it is unrestrained, passionate, and wild in character.

Composed in 1975, the work is written for full concert band (a note in the score says that "the parts provided in this set conform to the recommendations of the Published Music Committee of the National Band Association"). It is 241 measures in length and takes five and a half minutes to perform; it is published by Accura Music, Inc.

Unit 3: Historical Perspective

Perhaps the best known *bacchanal* is from Saint-Saën's opera *Samson et Dalila*. Tales of pagan ceremony, accompanied by ecstatic and unrestrained passion, have inspired Western poets, painters, and musicians throughout history. In music, only the *tarantella* can compare with the *bacchanal* for the use of the most extreme passions. The music is dance-like and typically characterized by powerful rhythmic *ostinatos*, rapid tempo, sharp melodic materials, and often a compound meter.

Unit 4: Technical Considerations

The work is written for virtuoso band, with prominent solos in most of the leading parts. There are noteworthy solos in the mallet percussion and timpani. Passages of rapidly moving articulated notes are frequent. Dynamics shift instantly from the loudest to the softest. The accompanying figures are syncopated with frequent cross-rhythms. Starting at m. 204 part of the band is in 2/4 while the rest is in 6/8.

Unit 5: Stylistic Considerations

Keeping a proper balance between passion and control is essential for the proper performance of this work. The tempo is brisk—*Allegro*, but not *con fuoco*. Too fast and the syncopations will have less impact, too slow and *the party runs out of wine!* Care must be taken that the *staccato*, accented, *ostinato* accompanying figures not obscure the *legato* lyrical figures which fade in and out of the texture. The dynamics are carefully indicated, and the quieter sections must not lose momentum and drive. The writing for the various choirs of the band is superb, but care must be taken that the brass and percussion not overly dominate the texture.

Unit 6: Musical Elements

Music form consists of repetition, contrast, and variation. The *Bacchanalia for Band* is in three sections which contrast in terms of meter and complexity. The parts are idiomatically well written for the instruments, the *tessitura* being quite appropriate for the level of player required to play the piece.

Unit 7: Form and Structure

The first section is in common time. The tempo is *Allegro*, and the opening texture consists of the combination of *staccato fortissimo* syncopations in the brass, over quiet dark clarinet *tremolos*. There are three primary musical ideas: 1) a *staccato* sixteenth-note melodic figure; 2) a slurred, syncopated, disjunct contrasting melodic pattern; 3) strong, syncopated eighth-note *ostinato* patterns. The composer works them out in varying combinations and in isolation.

The second section is from m. 83 through m. 141. The quarter note is constant but it is in 3/4 time. The opening sounds like a waltz, with the low brass playing a typical "oom-pa pa" pattern, which accompanies the alto saxophone solo, in a lyrical, slurred, syncopated melody. This is answered by the trumpet. The waltz feel fades away, with the syncopated melody carrying on

in chordal style at a *pianissimo* dynamic level. The brass break in with a *fortissimo staccato* figure. The waltz returns but fades away into the final section.

The work closes with a *Più Mosso* section in 6/8 time, which has some feeling of a *tarantella*. The woodwind parts are slurred, while the brass are articulated. Dynamically the closing section starts very softly and builds to very loud at the close. Rhythmically the section is very striking with syncopations and the mixture of 2/4 and 6/8 in different sections of the band.

Unit 8: Suggested Listening

Camille Saint-Saëns, *Bacchanal* from the opera *Samson et Dalila*
Carl Orff, *Carmina Burana*

Unit 9: Additional References and Resources

Graves, Robert. *I Claudius*. New York: Random House, 1961.

Garnscy, Peter and Richard Saller. *The Roman Empire: Economy, Society, Culture*. Berkley: University of California Press, 1987.

Contributed by:

Jim Klages
Indiana University
Bloomington, Indiana

Teacher Resource Guide

Blue Shades
Frank Ticheli
(b. 1958)

Unit 1: Composer

Prize-winning composer Frank Ticheli is Professor of Composition at the University of Southern California and Composer-in-Residence of the Pacific Symphony Orchestra. He holds degrees from Southern Methodist University and the University of Michigan, where his teachers have included William Albright, George Wilson, Leslie Bassett, and William Bolcom.

Ticheli has won both the Goddard Lieberson Fellowship and the Charles Ives Scholarship from the American Academy and Institute of Arts and Letters, and first prize in the eleventh annual "Symposium for New Band Music" in Virginia. Ticheli's works for other media, including several orchestral compositions, have also met with critical acclaim.

Unit 2: Composition

Blue Shades was written in 1996, the result of a consortium commission of thirty high school and university bands under the auspices of the Worldwide Premieres and Commissioning Fund, Inc. This eleven-minute work is a three-part episodic composition based on jazz-influenced motifs and themes, treated within the context of soloists, chamber groupings, and tutti wind ensemble.

Ticheli's notes for *Blue Shades* indicate that it grew out of a previous work, *Playing with Fire*, for traditional jazz band and orchestra, and is an attempt to reflect his love of jazz through his own musical voice.

Unit 3: Historical Perspective

Jazz has had an impact on "classical" music since the beginning of the twentieth century. The Europeans, particularly the French and composers working in Paris, were the earliest to knowingly incorporate jazz (what we think of today as "ragtime") into their work. Stravinsky was enamored with this early American jazz and incorporated it into his style with significant works like *L'Histoire du Soldat* and the *Octet for Wind Instruments*. Subsequent composers approached incorporating jazz in different ways. Gershwin began from a popular base and grafted "classical" form and orchestration onto the music. Gunther Schuller identified jazz elements and sought to merge the styles. Now at the end of the twentieth century, composers like John Harbison are treating jazz materials more organically than ever before. Jazz artists like John Coltrane, Wynton Marsalis, and Arturo Sandoval are also moving in directions that organically incorporate processes that have been traditionally considered "classical." As the twenty-first century arrives the popular and the classical, from third stream to minimalism, seem to be moving closer together.

Unit 4: Technical Considerations

Blue Shades is a technically demanding work requiring strong playing from all sections. Extroverted solos, especially clarinet, bass clarinet, and oboe, are featured. Like most of Ticheli's works, the rhythmic structure is intricate. Syncopations, *hemiola*, and cross-rhythms are used prominently. Extended techniques, such as *glissando*, flutter tongue, and pitch-binding, are also called for in various instruments. The percussion are used as an equal voice with the woodwinds and brass. With the exception of the extended clarinet solo, the instrument ranges are not extreme. The dynamic range, however, is wide and requires mature playing from all performers. The key is centered around G "blues," which fluctuates between major and minor.

Unit 5: Musical Considerations

The entire piece makes use of the minor-third motif and other short themes. The outer fast sections must maintain a "front of the beat" feel, while the slow middle one calls for a "laid back" sort of tempo control. While many of the syncopated patterns are written in exact triplet mensural notation, players must be familiar with the "swing eighths" feel. There are several special effects (e.g., flutter tonguing, *glissando*, Doppler effect, muting, etc.) incorporated throughout the piece. Players will need to exhibit distinct differences among "regular," accented, *staccato*, and *marcato* notes. The "dirty" section must remain tasteful (yet edgy) in terms of tone quality.

Unit 6: Musical Elements

The elements of jazz which are integrated into the classical form include blues scales (and "blue notes"), swing feel (vs. straight), syncopation, walking bass, call and response, and improvisation. Other musical elements worth dis-

cussing with students are minor third, ABA form, motif, theme, *hemiola*, and modality.

Harmonically, *Blue Shades* uses pitches traditionally thought of as "blue notes:" flat thirds, fifths, and sevenths, and harmonies that could be analyzed as pentatonic. Ticheli does not use traditional "blues" progressions, but captures the harmonic color with the chordal structure. The process of the work takes the basic material through a variety of jazz styles.

Unit 7: Form and Structure

The overall form of the piece is ABA (fast-slow-fast). Within each division are clearly delineated episodic sections which develop the motifs and themes presented early in the piece.

MEASURES	EVENTS AND SCORING
A Section (allegro)	
1	m3 motif (G)
14	swing-eighth motif (clarinets)
34	transition—lyrical theme/ascending/additive
46	bass motif (based on m3)
50	m3 and blues figures
54	bass motif
59	blues figures/ascending
69	"sultry" m3 motif/M2 ascending motif saxophone runs (based on blues scale)
96	intensity build/glisses/m3 motif/runs/horn duple figures
108	new m3 motif (D-flat)
116	repeated section—new horn theme (2 vs. 3)
126	tone painting, *gliss (portamento)*, *hemiola*, train reference, Doppler effect (m3 motif)
140	funk section with cowbell/blues run/syncopated patterns
149	fragment of bass motif
153	saxophone m3 motif/more soundings of motif
173	"minimalistic" section/*staccato* fragments/tone colors/ D pedal (dominant prolongation)/emphasis on thirds/ layering/convergent rhythmic patterns

MEASURES	EVENTS AND SCORING
209	G major established
214	building section/m3 motifs/layers
228	bass motif (F)
234	blues scales/additive layers/lyrical theme
249	syncopation/layering/*hemiola*/blues (G) dominant (D)
265	cadence theme (G)/horn rips
271	6/8 flute solo/clarinet solo/bass clarinet solo/tuba solo

B Section (slow blues)

284	free bass clarinet solo (sounds improvised) call and response in flute/bassoon (based on m3), B-flat clarinet solo, syncopated figures passed around, layering of voices, build up
304	"Dirty" (bump-and-grind) section—climax
308	Transition—*accelerando* to fast section (m3 motif, saxophone runs)

A' Section (allegro)

321	extended B-flat clarinet solo (high register, *klezmer* and Benny Goodman influence), accompanied by marimba, staccato bass line, and frequent punctuations from the other winds
376	"new horn theme" in B major/flourishes in flutes, dominant
388	bass motif over B-flat pedal/fugal treatment of bass motif/layering/build-up
400	rapid passagework over walking bass, "wail" of clarinet solo and train reference in *hemiola*, switch to D major (as dominant)
417	climax of section—cadence theme (G)

Coda

422-433	culminates in a light-hearted ending
423	*hemiola* marcato quarter notes (emphasis on m3)— G major

MEASURES	EVENTS AND SCORING
430	woodwinds blues flourish—cadence on G major, last interval is M3 in flutes only (Ray Cramer adds a cymbal splash for the very last note!)

Unit 8: Suggested Listening

Classically-based works with jazz influences:
Leonard Bernstein, *Three Dances from "On the Town"*
Timothy Broege, *No Sun, No Shine*
George Gershwin, *Concerto in F*
John Harbison, *Three City Blocks*
Sergei Prokofiev, *Jazz Suite No. 1*
William Grant Still, *Afro-American Symphony*

Other Ticheli compositions:
Amazing Grace
Cajun Folk Songs
Concertino for Trombone and Band
Portrait of a Clown
Fortress
Gaian Visions
Music for Winds and Percussion
Pacific Fanfare
Postcard

Unit 9: Additional References and Resources

Miles, Richard, ed. *Teaching Music through Performance in Band.* Vol. 1. Chicago: GIA Publications, Inc., 1997.

Stolba, K Marie. *The Development of Western Music.* Dubuque, IA: William C. Brown Publishers, 1990.

Contributed by:

Scott A. Stewart
Indiana University
Bloomington, Indiana

Teacher Resource Guide

Celebration: Praeludium for Wind, Brass, Percussion, Harp, and Piano

Edward Gregson
(b. 1945)

Unit 1: Composer

Edward Gregson was born in Sunderland, England in 1945. He studied composition at the Royal Academy of Music with Alan Bush and won a number of important prizes. He is currently Principal Lecturer at Goldsmith's College, University of London and teaches composition at the Royal Academy of Music. Although active in all areas of composition, he is particularly acclaimed for his contributions to the wind and brass repertoire. Some of his other works for band include *Festivo*, *The Sword and the Crown*, and *Metamorphoses*.

Unit 2: Composition

Celebration is one of many works for band composed by Gregson. The piece was commissioned by the Royal Liverpool Philharmonic Society to mark its one-hundred and fiftieth anniversary. It was first performed by the Royal Liverpool Philharmonic Orchestra, conducted by Libor Pesek at Philharmonic Hall, Liverpool on March 21, 1991, in the presence of H.M. The Queen. The piece has one movement, is a Grade Five difficulty, and lasts about seven minutes.

Unit 3: Historical Perspective

The composer writes:
"I was particularly pleased to receive the invitation to write this

piece as it gave me an opportunity to compose a work which would celebrate not just the birthday of a great orchestra, but the skills of a fine group of players, allowing them to demonstrate both their virtuosity and their capacity for sustained, sensitive playing. It seemed appropriate to make it a sort of miniature *Concerto for Orchestra* (albeit without the strings), and despite its brevity I have highlighted each department of the ensemble in turn before bringing them together at the end."

Unit 4: Technical Considerations

The piece has no key signatures, so accidentals abound. There are many meter changes. There are both *staccato* and *legato* articulations, so contrast is important. All instruments have several exposed sections and several solos. Ranges and scalar passages are difficult for the entire ensemble, and the score does specify one on a part. Rhythms occur on many levels and are difficult. Although only three percussionists are called for, they each have many instruments to play. The piece does not use saxophones or euphoniums. The piano has to play octave triplets at quarter note=138.

Unit 5: Stylistic Considerations

The piece plays continuously, but sections are clearly distinguishable. Articulations should be uniform and stylistically appropriate. All markings in the score support this. Each section has its own style. Although in the classical overture vein, this is a twentieth-century work with twentieth-century sounds; it should be approached with a twentieth-century interpretation. The intensity and movement of the music should be equal to the phrasing, articulation, rhythms, and principles of the line.

Unit 6: Musical Elements

The piece opens with a fanfare (announced by three spatially separated trumpets and tubular bells), essentially exuberant music which plays an important part later in the work. This leads into the second section, basically scherzo-like, but with an expressive central passage. A brief *tutti* ushers in a simple chorale. The development follows, often highly-charged rhythmically, and using material from the first two sections plus a new idea heard on trumpets. The music rises to a climax which moves directly into a reprise of the chorale, in combination with the opening fanfare, to bring the work to a triumphant conclusion. The piece is centered around the key of D major.

Unit 7: Form and Structure

SECTION	MEASURES	EVENTS & SCORING
Jubilantly! (D major)	Beginning to 4	fanfare, features brass, percussion and piano
Scherzando (D major)	4 to 13	features wind trios, harp and percussion
Molto sostenuto	13 to 14	various related keys chorale, features all winds only
Development	14 to 19	various related keys based on fanfare and chorale, *tutti*
Climax (D major)	19 to end	opening fanfare and chorale combined, full ensemble

Unit 8: Suggested Listening

Edward Gregson, *Festivo, Metamorphoses, The Sword and the Crown*
Martin Mailman, *Exaltations, Op. 67, The Jewel in the Crown:*
    A Ceremonial March
Ron Nelson, *Rocky Point Holiday, Savannah River Holiday*
Philip Sparke, *Celebration, Jubilee Overture, Op. 19*

Unit 9: Additional References and Resources

National Band Association Selective Music List for Bands

Rehrig, William H. *The Heritage Encyclopedia of Band Music.* Westerville, OH: Integrity Press, 1991.

Westrup, J. A. and F. L. Harrison. *The New College Encyclopedia of Music.* Revised by Conrad Wilson. New York: W.W. Norton & Co., 1981.

Contributed by:

Matthew Mailman
Director of Bands
Oklahoma City University
Oklahoma City, Oklahoma

Teacher Resource Guide

Circus Polka

Igor Stravinsky
(1882–1971)

Unit 1: Composer

Perhaps the most seminal mind in music composition of the twentieth century, Igor Stravinsky exhibited many influences and style changes in his long career. Nearly every genre and form was touched by Stravinsky, from the Russian folk-saturated melodies of *The Firebird*, to the primitivism of *The Rite of Spring*, to the dissonant pointillism of *L'Histoire du Solda*, and the neoclassical reverence in *The Rake's Progress*.

A native of Oranienbaum, Russia, Stravinsky first studied with Rimsky-Korsakov. In 1909, he began his successful collaboration with choreographer Serge Diagilev and the Paris-based *Ballets Russes*. He lived in Switzerland during World War I, in Paris from 1920-1939, and then moved to the United States in 1940. He taught composition at the University of Southern California and died in New York in 1971.

Unit 2: Composition

The piece is subtitled "For a Young Elephant." It is a brief work of carefree liveliness, with only a hint of the characteristic traditional polka rhythms appearing in the piece.

Unit 3: Historical Perspective

In 1941, George Balanchine was originally commissioned by the Ringling Brothers of Barnum and Bailey's Circus to provide music for a Ballet of Elephants. Balanchine immediately telephoned Stravinsky and the legendary conversation ensued:

Stravinsky:	"What kind of music?"
Balanchine:	"A polka."
Stravinsky:	"For whom?"
Balanchine:	"Elephants."
Stravinsky:	"How old?"
Balanchine:	"Young."
Stravinsky:	"If they are very young, I'll do it."

Stravinsky finished the piano score in 1942, and contacted Robert Russell Bennett to orchestrate the piece for circus band. He was unable to take on the project, and referred Stravinsky to David Raksin, who would later achieve major success in composing for television and movies. The Barnum and Bailey Band had considerably more brass players, so Raksin suggested that the Hammond organ which traveled with the circus be used to reinforce the woodwind parts.

Unit 4: Technical Considerations

This is a six-minute work with "nonstandard" scoring: three flutes, four solo clarinets, four clarinets, alto saxophone, baritone saxophone, four solo cornets, six cornets, two baritones, four horns, four trombones, two tubas, two snare drums, two cymbals/bass drum, and Hammond organ. This unusual grouping produces a different wind ensemble timbre and will bring balance issues to the attention of the conductor. There are tonal gestures (with key signatures venturing into F-sharp major, for example) and even key centers at times, but certainly an absence of functional harmony.

Unit 5: Musical Considerations

This is a technically and musically demanding selection. Extreme flexibility in range and performance of awkward intervals is required by the brass section, and advanced facility is necessary in all wind parts. The passagework is rapid, frequently disjunct, and non-diatonic at times. As with much of Stravinsky's music, meters shift frequently, accents displace strong beats, and irregular rhythms challenge the structure of the barline. *Staccato* notes should be played with a very dry separation.

Unit 6: Musical Elements

Polka, circus music, consonance/dissonance, irregular rhythm, syncopation, quotation, and asymmetry are all elements of the Stravinsky *Circus Polka*.

Unit 7: Form and Structure

The formal structure of the piece is loosely pieced together by recognizable themes and returns, although there is no regard to symmetry or harmonic function.

Section	Measures	Events and Scoring
Introduction	1	Dense texture/chromatic/disjunct tonal analog, but not discernible mixed meter, irregular rhythms
A	15	Disjunct horn/saxophone/clarinet melody (ten measures)—accompanied by downbeats
B	25	Baritone saxophone/baritone/tuba/ organ chromatic theme
	33	*Tutti* outburst (fragmentation and variation of B theme)
A	45	Return of first theme
	51	Transition
C	56	*Tutti* march-like theme
	62	Transition (static harmony)
D	68	Pointillistic, sparse scoring/short, dry punctuations, different groupings of instruments
	94	Transition
A	97	Return of first theme, accompanied by downbeats and upbeats
B'	119	Fragmented presentation of B thematic elements
	139	Transition—dissonant, harsh
E	143	Quotation from *Marche Militaire* by Schubert (Theme 1)—accompanied by polka figures
E'	152	Second quotation from *Marche Militaire* (Theme 1)
	159	Overlap of *Marche Militaire* (Theme 2)

Brief coda and final note on E unison

Unit 8: Suggested Listening

Recordings of the University of North Texas Wind Symphony, Eugene
    Corporon, Conductor

Other wind works by Stravinsky:
Octet
Symphonies of Wind Instruments
Concerto for Piano and Wind Instruments
Ebony Concerto
Ragtime

Other polkas:
Malcolm Arnold, *Sarabande and Polka*
Jaromir Weinberger, *Polka and Fugue from "Schwanda the Bagpiper"*

Other "circus" music:
Karl King, *Barnum and Bailey's Favorite*
William Schumann, *Circus Overture*

Unit 9: Additional References and Resources

Stravinsky, Igor. *Themes and Conclusions.* Berkley, CA: University of
    California Press, Inc., 1966.

White, Eric Walter. *Stravinsky: The Composer and His Works.* University of
    California Press, Inc., 1966.

Contributed by:

Scott A. Stewart
Indiana University
Bloomington, Indiana

Teacher Resource Guide

Concerto for
Twenty-Three Winds

Walter S. Hartley
(b. 1927)

Unit 1: Composer

Walter S. Hartley, born in Washington, DC on February 21, 1927, is an American composer/pianist of Scottish and Lancastrian heritage. He began composing at age five and became seriously dedicated to the "art of composing" at age sixteen. Hartley spent a great deal of his youth in the Washington, DC area where he received his early education from the public schools. All of his college degrees are from the Eastman School of Music, University of Rochester. He received his Ph.D. in composition in 1953, and studied with Burril Phillips, Thomas Canning, Herbert Elwell, Bernard Rogers, Howard Hanson, and Dante Fiorillo. Hartley is recognized by many as a "neo-classical" composer with numerous instrumental compositions to his credit. Hartley additionally refers to his compositional style as "neo-classic," which he describes as incorporating "classical forms and counterpoint into his compositions, but in a twentieth-century way with regards to harmony; some use of polychords and bi-tonality."

In a recent interview when asked how Hartley would describe his composition style as perceived by other colleagues, he stated the following:

> I have been called a "traditional contemporary" composer, which sounds contradictory, and yet is essentially true. Although I am a university teacher, I do not fit the common stereotype of "ivory tower" or Ivy League university composers (one who writes only for fellow composers). Rather, primarily for performers, and through them, for audiences; to give them music that is challenging, and yet enjoyable.

According to Hartley, the majority of his performances are for educational circumstances, and that the music he has written has never deliberately been aimed in that direction for commercial purposes. He states that his compositions have been written in more of a "response to need," and especially a particular need of repertoire for instruments which do not have a long and illustrious tradition of many masterpieces. Hartley goes on to say that much of his music "has been called into being by persuasive friends who are fine musicians. The resulting music has, in turn made more friends, and called forth more music: over a hundred pieces primarily for winds and/or percussion, over forty of which feature the family of saxophones." Several important individuals who have approached Hartley to compose, and brought to his attention the need for compositions for saxophone, include Robert Resnik, Sigurd Rascher, Frederick Hemke, and Donald Sinta.

Additionally, there is an interesting relationship between Percy Grainger and Hartley. Hartley's primary inspiration to become a composer and performer on the piano came to him at the age of seventeen when he enrolled at the National Music Camp at Interlochen, Michigan and studied piano with Percy Grainger. This was his first contact with Percy Grainger and according to an article from the "Percy Grainger Journal" by Harry R. Gee titled "Walter S. Hartley's Music for Band," Grainger was the first "famous" musician Hartley ever met and the "one who crystallized his desire to become a pianist and composer." Additionally, it is not uncommon to find Hartley and Grainger compositions frequently programmed together, much due to their unique approach to writing for the saxophone family. Hartley said that he appreciates Grainger for his "sensitivity to linear and coloristic relationships," but his interest in writing for the saxophone family is purely coincidental.

Hartley states that his primary composite influence is the Western Art Music tradition as a whole, "with its emphasis on unity balanced with variety, repetition balanced with contrast, and proportionate design and relationship of melodic, harmonic, rhythmic and timbral factors organized in time and space." Additionally, he states that he does not downgrade the validity of non-Western or avant-garde musical concepts and practices, but only points out their relative lack of interest to him as a composer.

> I could not write a piece based on tone-colors and dynamics only, or one disclaiming all linear or vertical relationships whatever, or one consisting of seemingly endless unvaried repetition. I do not doubt that such things can be done well, but I have no desire to do them at all. The usual label for such views is "conservative," but I would prefer to be called a "conservationist" of values I do not wish to see disappear, whatever others might prefer; values such as craftsmanship, seriousness of purpose, and aesthetic integrity.

Hartley has held teaching positions at several different universities including King's College (Delaware), Longwood College (Virginia), Hope College (Michigan), and Davis and Elkins College (West Virginia); currently he is Emeritus Professor of Music and Composer in Residence at State University of New York College at Fredonia (New York). He additionally taught piano, theory, and composition at the National Music Camp, Interlochen, Michigan from 1956-1964.

A prolific composer, Hartley has more than 200 compositions (most published) dating from 1949 to the present. His works are for nearly every instrumental and vocal medium, though he is best known for his compositions for brass instruments and saxophones. He has been guest composer at the World Saxophone Congress in Toronto (1972) and the First International Tuba Symposium and Workshop. His music has been performed by many ensembles, including the National Symphony Orchestra, Oklahoma City Symphony, Eastman-Rochester Orchestra, and the Eastman Wind Ensemble. His *Chamber Symphony* (1954) was commissioned by the Koussevitsky Foundation, his *Concert Overture* for orchestra received a prize from the National Symphony Orchestra (1955), and his *Sinfonia No. 3* (1964) for brass choir won the Conn Award. More recently, Hartley has received numerous commissions from college and high school musical organizations including his *Symphony No. 3* written for the Greater Buffalo (NY) Youth Orchestra, and a *Fantasia for Tuba and Chamber Orchestra* (1989) for Scott Watson and the University of Kansas Orchestra.

Unit 2: Composition

In a recent interview with Hartley, I learned that in 1957 he was approached by Frederick Fennell and the Eastman Wind Ensemble to compose the *Concerto for Twenty-Three Winds*. According to Hartley, Fennell approached a large number of composers to write original works for different instrumentation than the "standardized" music in existence for concert bands. This bold idea and pursuit for new music by Frederick Fennell (who had recently founded the Eastman Wind Ensemble on September 20, 1952) had a tremendous impact on bands greatly influencing today's musical ensembles and concert bands. Performing works with smaller and varying instrumentation evolved into a "new performance medium" in the 1950s called the "wind ensemble." Hartley and his concerto are a vital part of the history and advancement of the wind ensemble movement.

The *Concerto for Twenty-Three Winds* was completed September 2, 1957, and dedicated to Fennell and the Eastman Wind Ensemble who premiered it on May 3, 1958 for the Eastman School's twenty-eighth annual Festival of American Music. It is also interesting to note that this was Walter Hartley's *first* large work for winds. Hartley feels that his writings for winds have helped him to break into the standard repertoire, and even though he has written numerous compositions for the orchestral and voice media, he is convinced that his best compositions are for wind instruments. This concerto was originally published in 1959 by Rochester Music Publishers, Inc., but was assigned to Accura Music, Inc. in 1978 and revised by Accura in 1982.

This concerto was greatly influenced by several composers and their works, most prominently Igor Stravinsky, from his neo-classical period. Hartley stated that the reason he chose to compose a work for twenty-three instrumentalists and no percussion was because Stravinsky's *Symphonies of Wind Instruments* had been written for this same instrumentation. Other works which influenced the concerto are Stravinsky's *Symphony in C*, and the *Concerto for Piano and Winds*. Hartley continues by adding that he was also inspired by the First Movement from Bela Bartok's *Piano Concerto, No. 2*, and by the compositions of Paul Hindemith.

In a note to Frederick Fennell, Hartley wrote the following comments describing his concerto:

> It is in four movements roughly corresponding to those of the classical symphony or sonata in form, but is textually more related to the style of the Baroque concerto, being essentially a large chamber work in which different soloists and groups of soloists play in contrast with each other and with the group as a whole. The color contrasts between instruments and choirs of instruments are sometimes simultaneous, sometimes antiphonal; both homophony and polyphony are freely used, and the musical interest is distributed widely among these components of the wind section of a symphony orchestra. The first and last movements make the most use of the full ensemble; the second, a scherzo, features the brass instruments, and the slow third movement, the woodwinds. The harmonic style is freely tonal throughout. There is a certain three-note motif (ascending G-A-D) which is heard harmonically at the beginning and dominates the melodic material of the last three movements.

Unit 3: Historical Perspective

Hartley writes:

> *The Concerto for Twenty-Three Winds* occupies a special place in my compositional output. It was my first work for a large wind ensemble in response to Frederick Fennell's invitation to a large number of composers to write for the newly founded Eastman Wind Ensemble. It is the only one of my thirty wind ensemble works to use orchestral wind instrumentation only (3, 3, 3, 3, 4, 3, 3, 1), omitting the saxophone family, euphonium, and contrabass clarinet found in most of my other wind ensemble works. It is also the only one to use three oboes and three bassoons which, along with its ensemble difficulties, has limited

the number and type of performing groups that can play it.

Until recently, this concerto was only available through rental which limited the exposure and therefore the number of performances. The old Mercury recording of Fennell and the Eastman Wind Ensemble, playing the *Concerto for Twenty-Three Winds*, was the only commercial LP recording made. It was also the first of all of Hartley's compositions ever to be recorded. However, thirty-nine years following the completion of this concerto, it has "made enough firm friends among college band directors to be considered part of the standard repertory."

The instrumentation is the same as that of the revised 1947 version of Stravinsky's *Symphonies of Wind Instruments*, although Hartley writes that the "music itself is more influenced by other works of Stravinsky."

The *Concerto for Twenty-Three Winds* was originally written to be performed either by a reduced orchestra or band, but in fact the first orchestral performance known to Hartley was a performance by the wind section of the National Symphony Orchestra under Frederick Fennell on September 2, 1983. Coincidentally, this was twenty-six years to the day after the work's completion. On the occasion of the 1983 Fennell performance, which occurred in the Kennedy Center, the following statement was revealed to Hartley which had been made shortly after the concerto's world premiere in Rochester by the late American composer and Eastman faculty member Lyndol Mitchell to Frederick Fennell on April 23, 1958.

There are three kind of pieces:
1. the composition is so good that the performance is not critical;
2. the composition is such that the performance is critical before that compositional excellence will be apparent;
3. there are compositions where the piece is so good that the performance is *extremely critical*; Hartley's *Concerto for Winds* is one of these pieces.

Unit 4: Technical Considerations

The *Concerto for Twenty-Three Winds* is written for twenty-three players, each with an independent part. This composition requires a mature performer/ensemble since each part is treated as a "solo". Additionally, as stated earlier, this work requires three bassoons and three oboes, so there are some important instrumentation demands and considerations before even playing the first note.

When I presented Hartley with what he considered to be challenging and technically difficult with this composition, he replied that the "main technical difficulties are not the individual parts, but putting it all together." Additionally, he feels that "there could be ensemble problems due to the level of musicianship and discipline necessary to perform a work of this nature."

Unit 5: Stylistic Considerations

Hartley has provided the conductor with an extremely detailed score and has eliminated most of the guesswork with regards to the conductor selecting styles, tempos, etc. The stylistic markings, meter changes, tempo changes, dynamics, phrasing, *crescendos*, *decrescendos*, accents, and articulations are well notated. With much attention to the texture and varying the instrumentation groupings throughout each of the movements, Hartley takes full advantage of the players at hand, as he has established great contrast between the solo/chamber sections and the larger *tutti* ensemble scoring.

There are several phrase endings, however, without written in *ritards*. When added, these can enhance the overall interpretation of the movements. One place to consider adding a slight *ritard* is in Movement III, m. 34 which can enhance this phrase ending by "stretching" the previous phrase ending, before introducing the new theme which follows in the next measure. Another place to consider a little "artistic expression" is in Movement IV, m. 142 with the transition into the English horn solo, and a *ritard* and brief pause in mm. 156-157 which will help set up the abrupt tempo/stylistic change introduced by the trombones.

Unit 6: Musical Elements

As referred to in Unit 2, Hartley has incorporated contemporary harmony practices into his "neo-classical" concerto with the use of polychords and bi-tonality, while the work is "classical" with regards to form and counterpoint.

Unit 7: Form and Structure

The *Concerto for Twenty-Three Winds* consists of four movements set in the classical symphony or sonata form:

Movement I   *Andante* (Sonata form-slow intro)   4:20

Movement II   *Vivace* (Extended A-B-A form)   2:38

Movement III *Lento* (A-B-A-C, Rondo form)   4:30

Movement IV *Allegro molto* (Rondo form + *coda*)   3:00

Total playing time: 14:30

Each of the four movements is based on a three-note motif consisting of concert G, A, and D. This motif is disguised and less obvious in Movement I, but can be easily identified in the remaining movements.

MOVEMENT I

The first movement is written in sonata form, and opens with a slow intro. The opening is marked *Andante* (quarter note=92), with the melodic material primarily occurring in the woodwinds. The solo horn enters in m. 4, imitated later by the oboe, followed by new melodic material introduced by the solo clarinet in m. 21. This is the exposition consisting of the first and second themes. In m. 27, the tempo picks up—*Allegro non troppo* (quarter note=108) as the horns introduce the "frolicking" sixteenth-note motif, based on the three-note motif. Hartley takes this rhythmically exciting motif, exploring many different uses of it through counterpoint with a variety of different instrumentation combinations throughout the movement. This motif additionally serves as the melodic material and as an accompaniment pattern throughout the development section of the movement. The movement concludes with the recapitulation of solos from the slow intro recurring in the solo oboe in m. 118, English horn in m. 122, and in the bassoon and horns in m. 132, intertwined with the "frolicking" motif restated by the horn in m. 124, bringing this movement to a peaceful resolution.

MOVEMENT II

The second movement, marked *Vivace* (dotted quarter note=120), is written in an extended A-B-A form, based on the three-note motif (G, A, and D) which is initially introduced in m. 1 by the horns (Theme A). The solo trumpet in m. 22 states the "main melody" of the A Section. In the development of the A Section, the trumpet solo restates Theme A in m. 37, later imitated and developed by the flute solo in m. 62, the trumpet solo in m. 67, and with the flute and oboe through counterpoint in m. 71. Hartley continues to develop use of notes G, A, and D by introducing a new motif (Theme B) in m. 77 with the trombone. Theme B next appears in m. 83 in the solo trumpet, trumpet II in m. 85, and the horns in mm. 90-91. The B Section of the movement occurs in m. 101 with a contrasting melody occurring throughout the woodwinds by extensive counterpoint. (This two-bar motif [Theme C] additionally is the subject material used in the fourth movement as its opening statement by the trumpets.) Throughout this section of the movement, Theme C is passed from the woodwinds to the brass as the melodic material used in counterpoint, as well as in the woodwinds as an accompaniment figure. The main melody of the A Section, originally stated by the trumpet, recurs with the solo clarinet in m. 121, as well as the oboe in m. 127. The opening statement (Theme A) is reintroduced by the solo horn in m. 136, followed by Theme B in the woodwinds in m. 147 building to a climactic ending. This movement rhythmically speaking is very exciting as Hartley has made optimal use of the three notes G, A, and D by creating exciting motifs, developing each motif with counterpoint, then incorporating the different motifs as the subject material through even more counterpoint.

MOVEMENT III

The third movement, marked *Lento* (quarter note=60-66), is described by Hartley as an aria, in rondo form (A-B-A-C) based on the three-note motif.

The solo oboe in the first measure introduces Theme A, next to be played in m. 9 by the oboe. Theme B is stated in m. 12 by the flute, with the development and outgrowth of the original theme in the oboe, m. 18, and with the second flute in m. 22. A new motif (development) is introduced by the horn in m. 27. Theme A reappears with the flute in m. 35 with the motif treated in retrograde in m. 40. The Section C of this movement begins with a new theme in the flute, m. 48, and is developed. The flute duet in m. 59 restates Theme A's development from m. 6. The original theme is restated one last time by the oboe in m. 63, and the movement ends leaving a question in the listener's mind, as bi-tonal sequencing to the end by the flutes requests a resolution, but is denied.

MOVEMENT IV

The fourth movement is marked *Allegro molto* (quarter note=144) is in rondo form that ends with a *coda*. According to Hartley, there are many "echoes of previous movements" which provide the material for this energetic movement. The three-note motif (G, A, and D) is stated in the opening thorough counterpoint between the solo trumpet and solo trombone, which can also found in Movement II, m. 101. An outgrowth of Theme A is then introduced in unison by the woodwinds in m. 9, and m. 15 by the horns before it becomes the melodic material in counterpoint between two horns, two trumpets, and two trombones in mm. 18-25. The notes G, A, and D next recur in the oboes in m. 32, soon to be passed on to the trombones. The B Section begins with the trumpet solo in m. 36 which is a reflection of the previous movement. The flute enters in m. 50 with the second half of Theme B which is stated earlier in m. 44 by the solo horn. Development follows with several extensions of previous material. Measure 81, the descending passage introduced by the trombone, is a variant of the extension of Theme B, and used in counterpoint between the trombones, trumpets, and horns. A rhythmic variation of Theme A is reintroduced in counterpoint with the flutes and clarinets in m. 97. The oboe in m. 105 restates a variant of Theme B, originally stated in m. 36 by the solo trumpet. Development of previous material follows and brings us to the first of three parts to the *coda* at m. 143 (*Andante*). The beginning of the *coda* is a restatement of a variation of Theme A by the English horn. The middle section of the *coda* begins with an earlier motif, in m. 158 treated in counterpoint; first introduced by the trombones, followed by the horns, oboes, and trumpets. Measure 165 is the extension of Theme B in the horns superimposed with the Theme A in the flutes. The final section of the *coda* begins in m. 173, with varied restatements of Theme A by the trumpets and trombones used in counterpoint. The trumpets, piccolo, flute, and clarinet beginning in m. 187 have a variation from the original three-note motif. Thematic material borrowed from Movement III follows in m. 198 in the trumpets and trombones. There is a chord progression from m. 201 to the end as this movement concludes with a "vibrant" G major chord with the added second scale degree. The significance of this chord is that this is also the first chord introduced in Movement I, and the second scale degree additionally is the second note of the three-note motif.

Unit 8: Suggested Listening

Concerto for Twenty-Three Winds, the Eastman Wind Ensemble, Frederick Fennell conducting. Mercury Records (LP).

Concerto for Twenty-Three Winds, the Cincinnati Conservatory Wind Ensemble, Eugene Corporon conducting. Klavier Recording (CD).

Concerto for Twenty-Three Winds, the Tokyo Kosei Wind Orchestra, Frederick Fennell conducting. Brain-Co., Ltd., BOCD-7506 (CD).

Concerto for Alto Saxophone and Band, Ithaca College band, Donald Sinta, soloist. Golden Crest Records (LP).

Hallelujah Fantasy, Langley Air Force Band, Lt. Col. Lowell Graham conducting. U.S.A.F. Promotional Recording.

In Memoriam (*In Memory of Walter Beeler*), the Ithaca College Band, Edward Gobrecht conducting. Golden Crest Records (LP).

Miniatures, the British Tuba Quartet. Polyphonic Reproductions LTD. QPRZ013D (CD).

Petite Suite, Jamal Rossi, Alto Saxophone. Open Loop, 016 (CD), Dorn.

Sinfonia No. 3, the Fredonia Brass Choir, C. Rudolph Emilson conducting. Mark Records (LP).

Sinfonia No. 4, the Tokyo Kosei Wind Orchestra, Frederick Fennell conducting. Kosei Publishing Company, KOCD-3569 (CD).

Sinfonia No. 4, the Fredonia Wind Ensemble, Donald Hartman conducting. Mark Records (LP).

Sinfonia No. 6. for Saxophones, the South German Saxophone Chamber Orchestra, Linda Bangs-Urban conducting. Orgon Records ORG 25761 (CD).

Sinfonia No. 9 and Chautauqua Overture, "New Classics for Wind Band," the University of Kansas Symphonic Band, Robert E. Foster conducting. Vestige Records (CD).

Sonata Euphonica, Steven Meade, euphonium and Joyce Woodhead, piano. Polyphonic Reproductions Ltd., QPRZ O14D (CD).

Southern Tier Suite, the Fredonia Symphonic Band, Herbert Harp conducting. Mark Records (LP).

Symphony No. 2 (for Large Wind Ensemble), the Crane School of Music Wind Ensemble, Anthony Maeillo conducting. Silver Crest Records (LP).

Unit 9: Additional References and Resources

Gee, Harry R. "Walter S. Hartley's Music for Band." *Winds*, V (No. 3 1990): 36-37.

Hartley, Walter S. "Bio-Sketch File of Walter S. Hartley." Wingert-Jones Music, Inc., 1996.

Hartley, Walter S. "Catalog of Compositions." Hartley File, 3-9-93.

Hartley, Walter S. "Lecture to Theory Class." Hartley File, 6-30-88.

Mitchell, Lyndol. "Letter to Frederick Fennell." Hartley File, 4-23-58.

Rehrig, William H. Edited by Paul Bierley. *The Heritage Encyclopedia of Band Music*. Vol. 1. Westerville, OH: Integrity Press, 1989.

Smith, Norman and Albert Stoutamire. *Band Music Notes*. Rev. ed. San Diego, CA: Kjos, 1979.

Votta, Michael. Edited by Frank Cipolla and Donald Hunsberger. *The Wind Ensemble and Its Repertoire*. Rochester, NY: University of Rochester Press, 1994.

Interviews with Dr. Hartley via phone on June 20, July 3, July 5, and July 7, 1996.

Additional information for this project was acquired from the program notes for Mercury Record MG50388/SR90388, Frederick Fennell conducting the Eastman Wind Ensemble.

Contributed by:

Robert E. Foster, Jr.
Associate Director of Bands
Texas Christian University
Fort Worth, Texas

Teacher Resource Guide

Dance Movements
Philip Sparke
(b. 1951)

Unit 1: Composer

Philip Sparke was born in London, England and received his formal education at the Royal College of Music. While at the Royal College, he studied composition, piano, and trumpet. While in school and upon the urging of his composition teacher, Philip Cannon, he began studying and writing for bands. Sparke's first published composition was *Concert Prelude* published in 1975. Since then, Sparke has written for bands in Europe, America, and the Pacific Rim.

Unit 2: Composition

Dance Movements was commissioned by the United States Air Force Band and premiered at the Florida Music Educators Association Convention in January, 1996. The work is cast in four movements played without a break. The second movement features just the woodwinds and the third movement just the brass. These two movements showcase the unique colors and capabilities of these families of instruments. All four movements of this piece are dance inspired; however no specific dance rhythms were used. The composer notes this is the first time that he has written a band composition that used a piano: "although it is by no means a 'solo' part, its presence did tend to colour my thinking throughout, and the music somehow centered on it in terms of colour and rhythm." The four movements are entitled "Ritmico," "Molto Vivo," "Lento" and "Molto Ritmico." *Dance Movements* was published in 1997 by the Studio Music Company in London, England.

Unit 3: Historical Perspective

Dance Movements is a contemporary work in the English band tradition of quality literature, like those of Holst, Jacob, and Vaughan Williams. Sparke compared his use of the piano and harp to that of the two instruments used in the *Symphony in Three Movements* by Igor Stravinsky. *Dance Movements* was inspired by dance rhythms, although there were no specific dance rhythms used. The first movement with its use of xylophone, cabasa, tambourine, and wood block has a Latin American feel or color. The woodwind movement is, in the composer's words, "in the style of an English country dance." Although the brass movement is without any specific dance analogy, it can be, in Sparke's words, "seen as a love duet in a classical ballet." The last movement, which is the longest, is owed to Sparke's fascination with the music of Leonard Bernstein. Sparke admits, "I hope I cured my ten-year fascination, almost obsession, with the music of Leonard Bernstein and will readily admit that it [the fourth movement] owes its existence to the fantastic dance music of *West Side Story*." This piece is very much eclectic because it draws not only from music of England but also music from the United States, making this piece a culturally diverse piece with a British band sound.

Unit 4: Technical Considerations

First Movement

The movement begins with a multi-meter introduction which moves from 4/4 to 5/8 to 3/4 to 5/8 and back to 4/4. There are piccolo, clarinet, oboe, flute, and trumpet solos intermixed within the rhythmic texture set by large chords and *ostinati*. There are many syncopations throughout the movement, along with scalar passages in the woodwinds, which move through a variety of modes. This piece is orchestrated for standard band instrumentation with additions being harp, piano, string bass, and English horn. The ranges of the brass instruments are extreme in places. Trumpets play to a written C-sharp above the staff, French horns play to a written B above the staff, and the euphoniums play to a B-flat above the staff.

Second Movement

Again in the second movement there are many soloistic passages. The solos include piccolo, flute, oboe, English horn, soprano sax, and clarinet. There is a contrabassoon solo, but it is cued in the bassoon part. This movement is written for the woodwinds with piano, harp, and keyboard percussion intermixed. The piccolo player, in this particular movement, doubles on flute. The first and second flute parts are written above the staff in thirds which makes it a challenge to play in tune. Clarity with articulation is vital for the performance of this movement. The clear articulation enhances the rhythmic flow. The orchestration assigns the melody to a variety of individual parts making it essential for articulation and rhythmic execution to be consistent.

THIRD MOVEMENT

The third movement is orchestrated for just brass and percussion. The brass are all required to have mutes. There are soloistic passages written for the French horn and trombone. Brass ranges are not a concern. None of the range demands are extreme. There are rhythmic concerns in the introduction and conclusion of the movement. There are groups of five set against groups of two. Along with this, Sparke also breaks up the groups of five so all five notes are not played by the same individuals. There are no drastic tempo changes or meter changes in this movement.

FOURTH MOVEMENT

A canonic percussion introduction begins the fourth movement. The movement is connected with melodic motifs that are orchestrated in hocket. These passages are orchestrated so that the melody is handed between the woodwinds and brass. Syncopations throughout the movement require rhythmic clarity to keep the piece from slowing down. The tempo in this movement stays consistent throughout until it moves into 2/2 time near the conclusion of the piece. The woodwind writing is full of scalar passages that require clarity to give the movement direction. Attention to the balance between the melody and the massive band accompaniment is also important for the success of this piece.

Unit 5: Stylistic Considerations

MOVEMENT ONE

Energy is a key ingredient in each movement, some being rhythmic and some emotional. The first movement is full of rhythmic energy. Above all the energetic rhythmic motifs there are *legato* melodic lines that soar above the rhythmic energy. Although there is a lot of *tutti* writing in this movement, these sections have a light, driving feel.

MOVEMENT TWO

This movement is full of soloistic passages that set the style of this movement. The melodic line is played over a light, but present *ostinato* giving it a dance-like feel. Articulation throughout this movement needs to be accurate and dry to create the appropriate feel. The movement suggests an English folk dance. A *legato* oboe solo interrupts the rhythmic energy but the percussion keyboards take over an *ostinato* until the recapitulation occurs.

MOVEMENT THREE

Unlike the first two movements, the third is not a rhythmically energetic piece. This movement's impact is derived from emotional energy. The composer likened it to a love duet in a classical ballet. This movement, however, was not composed with a specific dance analogy in mind. The horn and trombone soloists carry on a conversation, which is interrupted by the full brass

and percussion who, in turn, relinquish the melody back to the soloists. This movement is very *legato* in style with long sustained lines. This movement is very challenging because of the long line which needs to be played without breaks.

MOVEMENT FOUR

This particular movement needs the ensemble's best "West Side Story Dance Music Feel" to accurately perform it. This movement is full of powerful tutti sections with a driving *ostinato* while melodic lines flow above them. This movement is eclectic in that the composer uses styles from the earlier movements to create the overall feel of this one. This movement requires technique from the woodwind players and if it is not present this will prohibit the movement from taking shape stylistically.

Unit 6: Musical Elements

MOVEMENT ONE

The first movement, according to the composer, has a Latin feel which is portrayed by the use of xylophone, cabasa, tambourine, and woodblock. The opening motif is played by the French horns and alto saxophone while the ensemble accompanies with stabbing, angular chords. A gentler motif then evolves within the texture of the ensemble being much leaner and lighter than the initial introduction. The main theme finally arrives in m. 37 with several different *ostinato* figures accompanying it. Each time the main theme recurs it changes its tonal center. The theme is connected with transitional segments that propel the listener into the next return of the main theme. Each recurrence is accompanied with a change in the orchestration or the *ostinato* patterns that underlie the entire movement. The movement derives much of its energy from the *ostinato* patterns within this movement.

MOVEMENT TWO

The second movement has a great deal of textural contrast from the first movement in that it is written for just woodwinds and percussion. The oboe states the initial theme which is then taken over by a clarinet and bassoon duet. A full *ostinato* occurs at rehearsal number 14 while the full clarinet section continues with the initial melodic material. This particular section is centered around the key of F major. This section progresses through many textural changes created through orchestration. The flow of the movement is then interrupted with a keyboard *ostinato* that sets up an oboe solo that soars above the *ostinato*. The low reeds and clarinet then expand upon the melodic material to this point by adding a syncopated motif that eventually turns into an *ostinato* passage as well. The opening theme then returns over the syncopated *ostinato* in the low reeds and clarinets. The piece then recaps the opening melodic theme along with the first *ostinato* passage. The final statement of the theme is played in hocket by several soloists from top to bottom in score order.

MOVEMENT THREE

The third movement is likened, by the composer, to a classical ballet love story. The two characters are represented by the French horn and trombone soloists who take part in a call-and-response motif. This is preceded by an introduction of trumpet and percussion setting the less rhythmically energetic, *legato* section. The soloists are then interrupted by the full section of the brass which takes the melodic statements of the soloists and expands upon them until a melodic and orchestration climax is reached. After that, the composer starts reducing the instrumentation until the last melodic statement you hear is played by the lone trombone soloist which then leads into the return of the introduction material that brings the movement to a close.

MOVEMENT FOUR

This movement bursts into a percussion canon that drives the piece into a full-band "shout chorus" which eventually subsides into a low reed *ostinato* that begins at number 45. The dotted motif that has been present throughout the whole piece then appears in the upper woodwinds as it did in the first movement. As this motif is played, the texture is thickened and leads the piece into another full-band tutti where a robust French horn and alto saxophone melody emerges. This is overtaken once again by the "sinister" music from earlier in the movement. A passive, more *legato* section appears in the woodwinds that is accompanied with a low woodwind *ostinato*. The movement then shifts to the brass and percussion sections that eventually builds into another full-band tutti. After several restatements of the theme, the piece turns into a flurry of passage writing that eventually leads the movement into a triumphal brass fanfare that brings the movement to a close. This movement is eclectic in that Sparke uses orchestration and themes from the first three movements as well as the melodic motifs to tie the whole piece together making it cyclical in form.

Unit 7: Form and Structure

SECTION	MEASURES	SCORING
Movement 1		
Opening Theme	1-11	French horn and saxophone full band accompaniment
Second Theme	12-21	piccolo and clarinet duet
Transition	22-26	oboe and flutes
Second Theme	27-34	oboe and flute section

SECTION	MEASURES	SCORING
Main Theme	35-46	woodwinds
Development	47-65	full band
B Theme	66-84	ostinato with brass theme
A Theme	85-94	chamber woodwind setting
A Theme with Second Theme	95-103	full band
False Recapitulation	104	
Recapitulation of Opening Theme	105-111	full band
Recapitulation of Main Theme	112-End	full band

SECTION	SUBSECTION	MEASURES	SCORING
Movement 2			
	Introduction	1-4	flutes and percussion
A	A Theme	5-12	oboe solo
	Restatement of Intro.	13-16	same with soprano saxophone
	A Theme	17-24	solo clarinet and bassoon
	Secondary Theme with Ostinato	25-40	high and low woodwinds
	Development of Main Theme	41-72	full woodwinds and percussion
B	Introduction	73-74	keyboards
	B Theme	75-97	oboe solo with ostinato
	B Theme	98-120	saxophone with full woodwinds
	Secondary B Theme	121-163	syncopated woodwinds
	B Theme over Secondary Theme	164-189	oboe solo with syncopated woodwinds

SECTION	SUBSECTION	MEASURES	SCORING
	A Theme over Syncopation	190-205	piccolo solo with woodwinds
A	Recapitulation of A Theme	206-214	oboe and bassoon solos
	A Theme and Secondary Theme	215-265	full woodwinds
	Transition	266-273	full woodwinds
	A Theme	274-End	hocket through woodwind parts

SECTION	MEASURES	SCORING
Movement 3		
Introduction	1-8	trumpets and percussion
Statement of A Theme	9-12	French horn solo
Response of A Theme	13-16	trombone solo
Call	17-18	French horn solo
Return of Intro	19-20	trumpets
Response	21-22	trombone solo
B Theme	23-29	horns and low brass
B Theme	30-46	full brass
Return of A Theme	47-55	French horn and trombone sections
Return of Introduction	56-End	trumpets and percussion

SECTION	MEASURES	SCORING
Movement 4		
Introduction	1-9	percussion in canon
Melodic Motif A	10-21	full band
Rhythmic Theme from First Movement	22-46	woodwinds with ostinato
Melodic Motif B	47-55	full band

SECTION	MEASURES	SCORING
Main Theme	56-79	French horn and saxophone full band accompaniment
Melodic Motif C	80-92	woodwind melody with brass accompaniment
Melodic Motif D	93-117	brass melody with woodwind interjections
Recapitulation of A Motif	118-129	full band
Recap. of Rhythmic Theme	130-154	brass with woodwind interjections
Recap. of Melodic Motif B	155-167	full band
Recap. of Melodic Motif C	168-178	woodwinds in canon
Transition	179-204	woodwind scalar passages
Melodic Motif E	205-210	brass fanfare over woodwinds
	211-229	brass with woodwind ostinato
Coda	230-end	full band

Unit 8: Suggested Listening

Malcolm Arnold, *English Dances*

Leonard Bernstein, "Symphonic Dance Music" from *West Side Story*

Philip Sparke, *Celebration, Yorkshire Overture, London Overture, Jubilee Overture*

Unit 9: Additional References and Resources

Sparke, Philip. *Dance Movements*, "Excursions." Washington, DC 1996. Compact Disc BOL-9602C.

Studio Music Company, London, England. Publisher of Score.

Contributed by:

Brad Genevro

Assistant Director of Wind Studies

University of North Texas

Denton, Texas

Teacher Resource Guide

Dance of the New World
Dana Wilson
(b. 1946)

Unit 1: Composer

Dana Wilson is a composer, jazz pianist, clinician, and conductor who is currently Professor of Composition at Ithaca College in New York, a position once held by Warren Benson. He holds a doctorate from the Eastman School of Music, has several commissioned works to his credit, and has received arts grants from the New England Foundation, New York State Council, National Endowment for the Arts, Arts Midwest, and Meet the Composer. His music has been performed in the United States, Europe, Australia, and Asia. His composition *Piece of Mind* won both the Sudler Wind Band Competition and the ABA/Ostwald Award.

Unit 2: Composition

Dance of the New World was commissioned by the Belmont High School Symphonic Band of Belmont, Massachusetts, Fred Harris, director, with funding from the New England Foundation for the Arts, Meet the Composer, the Massachusetts Cultural Council, the National Endowment for the Arts, and the Boston Company. It is in 6/8 and 4/4 time, with a duration of ten minutes and fifteen seconds. Composed in 1992, it was published by Ludwig Music in 1996.

Unit 3: Historical Perspective

The composer writes:

Dance of the New World was composed during the months that, exactly 500 years earlier, Columbus was on his historic voyage, and I wanted to capture in the piece the spirit of awakening and burgeoning that resulted from his journey. The piece begins almost imperceptibly and gradually evolves (though, as in American history, not without difficulty and need for reflection) to an exuberant climax. Because of where in the western hemisphere he landed, I decided to employ aspects of Latin American music to represent the many cultural syntheses that have since evolved.

On his first trip, Columbus landed on what is now the Bahamas and later on the Dominican Republic ("Hispaniola"). Subsequent trips (he made four in all) took him to Puerto Rico, Jamaica, Cuba, Trinidad, Honduras, Nicaragua, Costa Rica, and Panama. Rhythms of these countries set the mood of the piece.

Unit 4: Technical Considerations

Wind instrumentation is standard; the percussion section calls for six members playing nineteen instruments, many of which help create the Latin American flavor of the composition (bongos, cowbell, tom-toms, small cabasa, maraca, claves, and wood block). The percussion section is an integral part of the piece, absent in only 34 of the 419 measures. Parts are written with skilled players in mind. Ability of all players to perform together a large variety of rhythms in 6/8 time may be the biggest technical challenge. Because of the importance of the percussion section, it is strongly recommended that their parts be perfected before beginning full band rehearsals. Since it generates an enormous amount of energy, it is important that it not get too big too soon. A long and important oboe solo is the feature of the slow 4/4 section at m. 243.

Unit 5: Stylistic Considerations

Inspired by Columbus, *Dance of the New World* is heavily influenced by one of the new world's musical contributions: Latin American jazz. It is mostly written in 6/8 (several jazz educators have suggested that jazz should be written in 6/8, to more accurately convey the triplet feel and the syncopated rhythms) and has a jazz feel, with grace notes and other melodic inflection bringing to mind the blues. In this style, melodies are usually *legato* and accompaniments often are *staccato*.

Unit 6: Musical Elements

Percussion playing requires care and discipline. All rhythms are dependent on an articulate and ongoing percussion section. There is no key signature, but the key scheme suggests an ascent in thirds (G—B-flat—C-sharp—E—G) to reflect that aspect of the melodic structure. Open fifths abound, and there is a kind of minor/major uncertainty that keeps the tonality in a state of flux. The tonic/dominant relationship often feels like a variety of tritone substitution common in jazz (for example, A-flat7 replacing D7 as a dominant chord in the tonal center of G). Melodies are often built around the intervals of the minor third (m3), half step (m2) and tritone (d5). Syncopation and *hemiola* establish the Latin jazz flavor of the composition. Phrases are of uneven lengths.

All themes are derived from the opening melodic material, first heard in mm. 43-48 in the flutes and designated Theme I. It uses the intervals of m3, m2, and d5 to create a feeling of forward motion and uncertainty. Theme II is first heard in mm. 57-65, and is more active rhythmically, also using m3 and m2. Theme III (bar 129) is more of an accompanying motive, consisting of a two-measure figure, the first bar of which uses ascending m3 followed by descending m2; the second bar uses M3 and m2. Theme IV (m. 133) deals primarily with the half step in a manner that sounds improvised, each time varied.

Unit 7: Form and Structure

In macroanalytic terms, this piece is constructed in A-A'-B-A form, with the A sections in 6/8 time and the A' and B sections in 4/4.

SECTION	MEASURES	EVENTS AND SCORING
A	1-194	6/8 (dotted quarter note=108-112*)
	1-42	Percussion instruments enter one at a time, building a complex rhythmic fabric that changes minimally from m. 31 to m. 100
	43-56	Theme I introduced in flutes, repeated, tonal center of G (minor, mostly, moving to D-flat tritone)
	57-65	Theme II in flutes (nine bars) in tonality of F (moving to B tritone)
	66-92	Repeat of 43-65, with added instrumentation and Theme II in canon at m. 80
	93-99	Percussion interlude
	100-128	Theme I in brass/saxes, harmonized in open fifths, reduced percussion, Theme II in oboe/clarinet (m. 114), canon in piccolo

SECTION	MEASURES	EVENTS AND SCORING
	129-153	Shift in energy, Theme III (ascending two-bar figure in low woodwinds) in G, Theme IV at m. 133 in horns
	154-176	Move to B-flat, Theme IV in alto saxophones
	177-194	Fragmentation (four bars) and expansion (wider skips) of Theme I, reduction of percussion activity, leading to concluding motive in m. 189 (descending eighth notes, seconds and thirds, semi-chromatic)
A'	195-300	4/4 [quarter note=162-168*]
	195-207	Shift in energy to 4/4, C-sharp minor, second inversion, Theme IV variation in tuba
	208-215	E minor, Theme IV variation in trombone
	216-221	Theme IV transfers to clarinets, harmony changes to G minor, with a raised seventh and ninth
	222-233	Theme II variation explores m3 in clarinet/trumpet (some notation errors in this section, see Errata below), Theme III is inverted and augmented in tubas, et al.
	234-242	Theme IV in upper woodwinds over static D minor harmony
B	243-271	"Slow, static" [half=quarter] Tempo here should be quarter note=81-84* This section of the piece gives great opportunity for slow, expressive playing. Rubato recommended mm. 252-265 to achieve a sense of freedom in the extended oboe solo. Needs to feel improvisitory in keeping with the character of the piece. Solo part

SECTION	MEASURES	EVENTS AND SCORING
		explores m3, half step (C/E-flat/D, F/A-flat/G) over slowly moving progression of open fifths built on B-flat, D-flat, G, and E. Reentry of tom-toms in m. 266 coincides with beginning of a twenty-bar B-flat drone and prefaces return to faster section.
	272-285	Tempo Primo 4/4 [quarter note=108-112*] This acts as a retransition back to A. Oboe solo extends, active percussion returns, harmony is static on B-flat drone
	286-300	Theme I is inverted and augmented in woodwind dialogue with percussion for fifteen bars (eight bars of E-flat, seven bars of E), diminuendo leads to return of rightside up original theme, bongo part prepares 6/8 percussion transition
A	301-end	6/8 [dotted quarter note=108-112*]
	301-316	Return to opening meter, tempo, Theme I with augmented middle returns in trombones (8+8), tonal center of F
	317-325	Theme II variation in saxophones, clarinet canon in m. 321, tonal center of E-flat, m3 motive in low brass
	326-343	Another variation of Theme II in quiet unison woodwinds, building to the return of...
	344-357	Theme I in G (expanded duplicate of mm. 100-113),with low brass canon and upper woodwind commentary
	358-369	Theme II with canon (shorter, busier duplicate of mm. 114-128, notice rhythmic variety of accompaniment)

SECTION	MEASURES	EVENTS AND SCORING
	370-390	Theme I in trumpets, Theme III in low woodwinds for four bars, followed by a tritone bass line in hemiola in trombones (7+7+7), first seven bars ornamented with flute sixteenths, next seven less active with oboes, last seven adds quadruplets in saxophones
	391-399	Shortened four-bar version of Theme I, tritone harmony of G, followed by open fifths on B-flat and D-flat, as piece moves toward ending, frequency of chord changes increases, ideas come faster
	400-405	Six-bar closing theme (like 189, but with fuller instrumentation)
	406-end	Coda (thirteen bars of A-flat), building in rhythmic complexity and dynamic to climax on last bar, a final tutti open fifth on G

Errata**

MEASURE, BEAT	PART	CORRECTION
224, "and" of 2	Clarinet I, II	C-sharp
"and" of 3	Clarinet I, II	C-natural
227, "and" of 2	Clarinet I, II	C-natural
228, "and" of 2	Oboe	B-flat
234, downbeat	Oboe	A-flat

*Note: metronome markings do not accurately reflect the metric relationships. The opening marking [dotted quarter=108] results in quarter=162 [*not* 168] when eighth=eighth at m. 195. One alternative would be to keep the marking at m. 195 but change the initial tempo (and therefore the tempi at mm. 272 and 301) to 112. The following suggestion offers more flexibility and makes sense mathematically:

MEASURE	METRONOME MARKING
1	dotted quarter note=108-112

195   quarter note=162-168

272   quarter note=108-112

301   dotted quarter note=108-112

**The composer indicates that Ludwig now includes a complete errata sheet with the score; none came with mine, however.

Unit 8: Suggested Listening

Leonard Bernstein, "America," from *West Side Story*
Carlos Chavez, *Chapultepec for Band*
Aaron Copland, *El Salon Mexico*
Esteban Pena Morell, *Anacaona, Sinfonia Barbara*
H. Owen Reed, *La Fiesta Mexicana*
Clifton Williams, *Symphonic Dance No. 3: "Fiesta"*
Dana Wilson, *Piece of Mind, Sang!, Shakata,* and *The Shifting Bands of Time*

Unit 9: Additional References and Resources

Ferrari, Lois. "Two Symphonic Wind Ensemble Compositions of Dana Wilson: *Piece of Mind* and *Shakata: Singing the World into Existence.*" Doctoral diss., Eastman School of Music of the University of Rochester, 1995.

Gilbert, Jay Warren. "An Evaluation of Compositions for Wind Band According to Specific Criteria of Serious Artistic Merit: A Replication and Update." DM diss., Northwestern University, 1993.

Mathes, James. "Analysis: *Piece of Mind* by Dana Wilson." *Journal of Band Research* XXV/2 (Spring 1990): 1-12.

Slonimsky, Nicolas. *Music of Latin America.* New York: Da Capo Press, 1972.

Thompson, Donald, and Annie F. Thompson. *Music and Dance in Puerto Rico from the Age of Columbus to Modern Times: An Annotated Bibliography.* Metuchen, NJ: The Scarecrow Press, 1991.

Wilson, Dana. Letter to Robert Halseth, 7/11/97.

Contributed by:

Robert Halseth
Director of Wind Studies
California State University
Sacramento, California

Teacher Resource Guide

Divertimento in "F"
Jack Stamp
(b. 1954)

Unit 1: Composer

Jack Stamp was born in Washington, DC in 1954, and grew up in the nearby Maryland suburbs. He received a BS degree in Music Education from Indiana University of Pennsylvania in 1976, a MM degree in Percussion Performance from East Carolina University in 1978, and a DMA degree in Wind Conducting from Michigan State University in 1988 where he studied with Eugene Corporon. His primary composition teachers were Robert Washburn and Fisher Tull. More recently he has worked with Joan Tower, David Diamond, and Richard Danielpour.

Stamp is currently Professor of Music at Indiana University of Pennslyvania where he conducts the Wind Ensemble, Symphony Band, and Concert Band, and teaches courses in conducting and percussion. He is founder and musical director of the Keystone Wind Ensemble, a professional recording group dedicated to the advancement of American concert band music.

Unit 2: Composition

Divertimento in "F", composed in 1994, was commissioned by Frank Wickes and the Louisiana State University Bands in celebration of their seventy-fifth anniversary.

The title does not refer to key centers, but to the fact that the movement titles all begin with the letter "F": "Fanfare," "Fate," "Fury," "Faith," and "Frolic." Each movement is dedicated to a person or persons important to the composer. The "Fanfare" is dedicated to Fisher Tull (one of Stamp's composition teachers); the "Fate" movement is subtitled "In Memoriam William Schuman" (Stamp calls himself a "Schumaniac", and learned much about composition from studying his scores); "Fury" is dedicated to Joan Tower (the movement was written during Stamp's brief study period with her); "Faith," the only movement not dedicated to a musician, is dedicated to four North Carolina Baptist ministers whom Stamp considers influential in his spiritual life; and "Frolic," dedicated to the great American composer David Diamond (written during a brief study period with the composer).

Unit 3: Historical Perspective

The *divertimento*, an instrumental composition dating back to the Classical era, is rooted in the wind music of Haydn and Mozart. The form, usually entertaining in design, is comprised of rather short, contrasting movements.

Unit 4: Technical Considerations

The work is the most technically challenging to date in the composer's catalog. Instrumentation requirements alone expand the tonal pallet of the everyday ensemble. The inclusion of two English horns (though one is cross-cued in saxophone), string bass, electric bass (final movement), as well as an extended battery of percussion, make this work demanding from an instrumentation perspective alone.

I. "FANFARE"

Consists of many meter changes with difficult syncopation occurring within those changes. First trumpet range extends to a high D above the staff.

II. "FATE: IN MEMORIAM WILLIAM SCHUMAN"

Requires the timpanist to use snare sticks on the timpani and execute a multiple bounce roll. There is an extended duet for bassoon and oboe.

III. "FURY"

This movement is the most difficult of the five and a rhythmic challenge for the conductor as well as the ensemble. Not only are there extreme ranges (both high and low) for woodwinds and brasses, but the rhythmic complexities demand careful study by the players and conductor. The illusion of tempo changes through meter and rhythm is a highlight of this movement. These tempo variations are much like metric modulations but occur without a change in the basic pulse.

IV. "FAITH"

Instrumentation is a requirement of this movement with much exposed writing for the double reeds. In particular, there is a request for two English horns (crossed-cued in alto sax).

V. "FROLIC"

This highly contrapuntal movement requires electric bass. There are range demands on the horn section at the end of the work, and the rhythmic complexities which are prevalent throughout the work continue.

Unit 5: Stylistic Considerations

As the title suggests, *Divertimento in "F"* is a five-movement work of contrasting styles. The outer movements are highly contrapuntal and rhythmic in nature and require precision and clarity throughout the ensemble. The second and fourth movements are more lyrical in quality and require secure solo playing as well as careful attention to ensemble balance and timbre. The middle movement, "Fury," requires the most flexibility from the ensemble. The wide range of dynamics (including some fairly brutal playing) coupled with extreme rhythmic complexities force the ensemble members to be independent and yet move with ensemble precision and power.

Unit 6: Musical Elements

This work is filled with a wide variety of compositional techniques which will educate the players to the creative process of the music of their time.

"Fanfare" explores a variety of textures and styles including quartal and quintal harmony, "wrong note" bass techniques, canon and fugue, minimalism, and augmentation.

"Fate" explores the *passacaglia* and is a study in polychords. There is also a brief quote from William Schuman's *Third Symphony*.

"Fury" is an adventure in rhythm. The illusion of *accelerando* and *ritard* is created through meter change and the even distribution of a rhythmic pattern within those changes.

"Faith" is based on the Scottish hymn "Dundee." It is a chorale with five variations and a *coda*. The movement is treated much like a *chaconne* with each variation presenting a different compositional setting of the hymn tune. Variation 4 (m. 38) is an example of a modal harmonization.

"Frolic" returns to the contrapuntal texture of the first movement. A *fugato* section based on the "Frolic" theme ensues. The device of "cyclicism" appears where the theme of the "Fanfare" appears as a double *fugato* with the

"Frolic" theme. The minimalistic section of the "Fanfare" also returns with the "Fanfare" theme in augmentation while the trumpets play the "Frolic" melody.

Unit 8: Suggested Listening
David Diamond, *Tantivy*
William Schuman, *String Symphony, When Jesus Wept*
Jack Stamp, *Chorale and Toccata, Cheers!, Prayer and Jubilation*
Joan Tower, *Silver Ladders*
Fisher Tull, *Accolade, Final Covenant*

Unit 9: Additional References and Resources
Dvorak, Thomas L., Robert Grechesky, and Gary M. Ciepluch. *Best Music for High School Band*. Edited by Bob Margolis. Brooklyn: Manhattan Beach Music, 1993.

Rehrig, William H. *The Heritage Encyclopedia of Band Music*. Edited by Paul E. Bierley. Westerfield, OH: Integrity Press, 1991.

Contributed by:
Jack Stamp
Conductor of University Bands
Professor of Music
Indiana University of Pennsylvania
Indiana, Pennsylvania

Teacher Resource Guide

Fantasy Variations on a Theme by Niccolò Paganini for Symphonic Band

James Barnes
(b. 1949)

Unit 1: Composer

James Barnes was born in Oklahoma in 1949, and has degrees in Theory and Composition from the University of Kansas where he is Associate Professor of Theory and Composition and Assistant Conductor of Bands. A prolific composer for band, he has twice won the Ostwald Composition Award. Prominent works include *Brookshire Suite*, *Centennial Celebration Overture*, *Heatherwood Portrait*, *Invocation and Toccata*, and *Yorkshire Ballad*.

Unit 2: Composition

The *Fantasy Variations on a Theme by Niccolo Paganini* was commissioned by the President's Own United States Marine Band in 1988 for use on its national tour. The work is written for large concert band and features each section. The writing is very difficult yet effective. The work is published by Southern Music Company.

Unit 3: Historical Perspective

Variation is one of the basic elements of musical form. Contrast, repetition, and variation bring coherence, direction, and drama to a musical work. Variations on a theme have been used through the ages, both as light works for diversion and profound works of the highest significance. Two important examples are the *Goldberg Variations* of Bach and the *Thirty-Three Variations on a Waltz by Diabelli* of Beethoven.

Niccolò Paganini and Franz Liszt wrote virtuoso compositions for their own use, which exploited the technical and expressive possibilities of their instruments. The variation form was seen as a congenial vehicle for this. In an extended work the character of the theme could be dramatically modified, yet thematic unity would provide coherence. Variations may be organized into groups of differing character, tempo, meter, and mode which creates a large composite form.

The theme chosen by Barnes has been used by many composers for extended treatment. The theme is that of the last of Paganini's *Twenty-Four Etudes-Caprices for Violin*. Brahms was the first to write his own variations on it (Liszt and others had made arrangements of Paganini's showpiece). Since the time of Brahms dozens of composers have produced variations on this theme: solo pieces, jazz, ballet, and orchestra. Perhaps the most famous orchestral setting is by Rachmaninoff.

Unit 4: Technical Considerations

The work is taxing for the musicians to play; therefore sectional rehearsals could be helpful. Precise ensemble playing between widely separated soloists can be problematic. Great care must be given to observe the tempo, dynamic, and articulation markings. Care must be taken to see that the solo line is always clearly audible through the texture.

Unit 5: Stylistic Considerations

The variations are organized in groups of differing tempo, meter, dynamic, and instrumentation. The larger sections must maintain coherence internally and within the larger structure. The music makes many references to other works and composers which should be brought out. This work is an example of character variation technique.

Unit 6: Musical Elements

The melodic and harmonic vocabulary is that of the late Romantic period. There are many musical references to works of Tchaikovsky and Rachmaninoff. The work is of symphonic scope and of great musical weight and seriousness. Tremendous emotional range, from passion to humor, is brought out in the various variations. The full coloristic resources of the symphonic band are fully exploited.

Unit 7: Form and Structure

SECTION AND EVENTS	SCORING
Introduction	*Allegro risoluto* 2/4; full band
Tema	Oboe with woodwind accompaniment

Section and Events	Scoring
Variation I	Full band; theme in woodwind and brass
Variation II	*Un poco più mosso*; theme in clarinet section
Variation III	*Andante misterioso* 3/4; C. B. Theme in clarinet with trombone accompaniment
Variation IV	*Presto* 2/4; theme in flute
Variation V	*Moderato assai* 3/4; tuba with baritone accompaniment
Variation VI	*Allegro moderato* 2/4; bassoon duet
Variation VII	*Andante moderato* 4/4; oboe with clarinets
Variation VIII	*L'istesso tempo*; saxophone quartet
Variation IX	*Allegro vivo* 6/8; clarinets accompanied by bassoon, horn, and tuba
Variation X	Add flute, oboe, and vibraphone
Variation XI	2/4; cornet and trumpet theme
Variation XII	*Meno mosso*; trombone theme
Variation XIII	*Più mosso* 3/4; horn theme
Variation XIV	4/4; full band, trumpets state theme. There is a grand pause followed by a tempo marking of *Adagio* and an oboe solo which serves as transition to the next variation.
Variation XV	*Un poco più mosso*; lyrical variation featuring the bassoon, E-flat alto saxophone, horn, and baritone
Variation XVI	*Adagio-ma non troppo.* This variation changes meter from 4/4 to 5/4 to 6/4 and so on in a style reminiscent of Tchaikovsky, and first features the English horn, later the entire ensemble.
Variation XVII	*Allegro giocoso* 2/4; features the percussion
Variation XVIII	Continues with the percussion but brings in the rest of the band

| Variation XIX | Starts with the brass, then builds to the full ensemble |
| Variation XX | Finale—*a tempo primo*; the full band returns in a powerful close; the last seven measures are marked *più vivo* |

Unit 8: Suggested Listening

Johannes Brahms, *Paganini Variations*
Niccolò Paganini, *Twenty-Four Etudes-Caprices for Violin*
Sergei (Vassilievich) Rachmaninoff, *Rhapsody on a Theme of Paganini*

Unit 9: Additional References and Resources

De Courcy, G. I. C. *Paganini the Genoese*. Two vols. Norman, Oklahoma: 1957.

Contributed by:

Jim Klages
Indiana University
Bloomington, Indiana

Teacher Resource Guide

Fiesta Del Pacifico

Roger Nixon
(b. 1921)

Unit 1: Composer

Roger Nixon was born in Turlane, California in 1921. He studied at Modesto Junior College (1938-40) and took clarinet lessons from a former member of the Sousa Band, Frank Mancini. He furthered his education at the University of California at Berkeley, receiving a B.A. (1941) and an M.A. (1949) in Composition. Among his teachers were Arthur Bliss, Ernest Bloch, and Arnold Schoenberg. He served on the Modesto College faculty while working on his Ph.D. in Education from 1951-59, and then joined the San Francisco State College teaching staff in 1960. He was elected to the American Bandmasters Association in 1973.

Unit 2: Composition

Nixon's virtuosic composition is a colorful depiction inspired by the moods and events of the festival by the same name. While no particular folk songs are employed, various unmistakable "Spanish" musical elements weave their way in and out of the various themes. It was dedicated to the San Francisco State College Symphonic Band (Edwin Kruth, Director) and published first in 1960.

Unit 3: Historical Perspective

Fiesta Del Pacifico is one of several festivals held annually in various communities in California which celebrate the Old Spanish Days of the state. This particular festival is held in San Diego for twelve days in the summer and features a play on the history of the area with a cast of over a thousand, a parade, a rodeo, and street dances.

Unit 4: Technical Considerations

The quick tempo of the entire work combined with multiple rhythmic layers, shifting meters, syncopation, and virtuosic technique create a challenging work for advanced groups. All woodwind players will find quick fingerwork throughout this piece. Brass players have light quick articulation, and ranges extend up to high B-flat in trumpets and high G-sharps in horns. Instrumental color demands require that specified instruments be used, including confident soloists in piccolo, flute, E-flat clarinet, B-flat clarinet, oboe, English horn, bassoon, alto saxophone, trumpet, horn, timpani, castanets, celesta, and xylophone. There are four divided cornet parts and a string bass part as well. Percussion and harp parts add nicely to the virtuosity and color of the music.

Unit 5: Stylistic Considerations

Articulation in all instruments must remain light in order to accommodate the quick tempo. Scoring is quite heavy at times, so players must use caution when playing tutti rhythms or melodic patterns. Phrasing of the melodic/thematic lines should be matched in the accompaniment. Accented quarter notes (e.g., rehearsal 30) and all syncopated patterns should be full value but separated. Woodwinds must play softly so that the English horn solo is not buried at m. 107. Make sure that trills at the *tempo di valse* end on the lower note, and fade into the tied beat. This section should be conducted in one. The exciting finale to the piece still demands control by each member of the ensemble.

Unit 6: Musical Elements

"Spanish" musical elements, program music, motif, impressionism, compound meter, shifting meter, solo, soli, tutti, ABA form.

Unit 7: Form and Structure

Motif key:

sixteenth motif	= A	(see m. 4)
Spanish motif	= B	(see m. 11)
scalar passage	= C	(see m. 19)
trumpet dance	= D	(see m. 41)
3/4 dance motif	= E	(see m. 45)
lyrical dance	= F	(see m. 107)
waltz melody	= G	(see m. 231)

SECTION	MEASURES	EVENTS AND SCORING
A *Allegro*		
Introduction	1	Fanfare in cornet/snare drum
First section	4	fanfare + A (woodwinds) over 1-5-5-1 bass line (F)
	11	B in clarinets and baritone
	16	fanfare + A (woodwinds) over bass line
	19	B in clarinets and baritone
	23	Fanfare (higher) + A (keyed in G-flat)
Transition	26	C in solo clarinet and bassoon, add oboe (snippet of E motif to end phrase), brass downbeat/afterbeat response
	34	Repeat of C with B rhythm repeat of response
	40	Flourish in woodwinds and harps to D in trumpet tutti, punctuations in other winds and percussion
	48	5/8 section, dance section varied, punctuations
Second section	57	Flourish in woodwinds and harp to A in one-measure canon (saxophones and low clarinets vs. upper woodwinds)
	61	E-flat clarinet disjunct solo (transitional)
	65	Repeat of A in one-measure canon
	69	Repeat of E-flat clarinet solo— *rallentando*
Third section	74	A *tempo* E in bassoon/tuba/string bass, afterbeat accompaniment in clarinets
	83	E in bass/baritone/baritone sax/bass clarinet, afterbeat accompaniment in clarinets/oboe
	90	E in bass voices (add trombones), afterbeat accompaniment (add flute/trumpets, then saxophones)

SECTION	MEASURES	EVENTS AND SCORING
	98	Transitional material (swells), bassoon/xylophone solo/echo
Fourth section	107	F in English horn solo (downbeat/afterbeat pattern in bassoon/clarinet), flute coloring baritone countermelody in m. 123
	143	E in basses, afterbeats in horn/trombone punctuations in clarinets
	151	F in alto saxophone, then trumpet solo
	159	E in basses, afterbeats in horn/trombone punctuations in clarinets
	167	F in oboe, then flute solo clarinet run
	175	B in canon (flute/oboe/trumpet vs. tenor saxophone/baritone/bassoon), eventually becomes tutti build
	183	Timpani solo (2/4, 5/8, 7/8)
	185	Tutti B with syncopation accompaniment, timpani solo continues under fortepiano
	192	Repeat of tutti B with timpani
	199	C in woodwinds, answered by trumpet/horn/trombone afterbeats
	205	Repeat of C
	211	D in woodwinds/xylophone punctuations in brass/snare drum rim shots
	220	5/8 section (snippets of E)
	227	Castanet solo (transitional)
B *Tempo di valse*	231	Flute duet melody accompaniment in clarinet I trills, celesta, and harp, glockenspiel/piccolo answer (m. 244)
	247	Oboe duet melody with glockenspiel/piccolo answer (m. 260)

SECTION	MEASURES	EVENTS AND SCORING
	263	Clarinet duet melody, English horn decorative line, answers in oboe duet, flute duet
Transition (A materials)	281	B in xylophone, then in *stretto* with trumpet 1/2, oboe, clarinet, flute, and E-flat clarinet
	289	Punctuations in brass, B in bassoons and baritones 5/8, fragments of E, more punctuations, more 5/8
	305	*Ritardando*, open fifths fragment of B in bassoon/baritone, *a tempo* at m. 307
Transition (E materials)	307	E in tuba/baritone/bass clarinet, snippets of A in flute/oboe/clarinet/trumpets building throughout—increases in rhythmic activity, instrumentation, volume, and intensity
	346	Climax and drop-out of all voices

A' *Allegro* (recapitulation/truncation)

	347	Opening fanfare in trumpets/horns
	351	Tutti, F dominates, counterline referenced to B in flute/clarinet/oboe, building in intensity
	375	Extension of F in trumpets and trombones (sustained line), much activity in all voices (moving lines, portions of B, fanfare figures, 1-5-5-1 bass lines, afterbeats)
	393	*Subito pp* syncopation plus B motivic figures building to 400
	400	Cadence figure in C, scales build in all voices to final chord (F major)

Unit 8: Suggested Listening

Other pieces by Roger Nixon:
Academic Tribute
Centennial Fanfare-March
Elegy and March
Pacific Celebration Suite
Psalm for Band

Other pieces with Spanish folk elements:
Emmanuel Chabrier, *España*
Manuel De Falla, *The Three-Cornered Hat*
Ernesto Lecuona, *Andalucia*
Maurice Ravel, *Aldoraba Del Gracioso*
Alfred Reed, *El Camino Real*, *Second Suite for Band*

Unit 9: Additional References and Resources

Rehrig, William H. *The Encyclopedia of Band Music*. Edited by Paul R.
    Bierley. Westerville, OH: Integrity Press, 1991.

Contributed by:

Scott A. Stewart
Indiana University
Bloomington, Indiana

Teacher Resource Guide

Gazebo Dances for Band
John Corigliano
(b. 1938)

Unit 1: Composer

John Corigliano was born on February 16, 1938 in New York City. He studied composition with Otto Luening at Columbia College, Vittorio Giannini at the Manhattan School of Music, and Paul Creston. His first widely recognized composition was the *Sonata for Violin and Piano* which won First Prize in the 1964 Spoleto Festival Competition. He later composed an oboe concerto in 1975, a clarinet concerto in 1977, and the film score for *Altered States* in 1980 which has been condensed into a concert suite entitled *Three Hallucinations for Orchestra*. He has served as composer-in-residence with the Chicago Symphony Orchestra where he premiered his *Symphony No. 1* in May, 1990 to critical acclaim.

Unit 2: Composition

The composer notes:

Gazebo Dances was originally written as a set of four-hand piano pieces dedicated to a certain one of my pianist friends. I later arranged the suite for orchestra and concert band, and it is from the latter version that the title is drawn. The title *Gazebo Dances* was suggested by the pavilions often seen on village greens in towns throughout the countryside, where public band concerts are given on summer evenings. The delights of that sort of entertainment are portrayed in this set of dances, which begins with a Rossini-like Overture, followed by a rather peg-legged Waltz, a long-lined Adagio, and a bouncy Tarantella."

Gazebo Dances for Band was scored for wind ensemble in 1973 and was premiered by the University of Evansville (Indiana) Wind Ensemble, Robert Bailey, conductor. As noted above, the piece contains four movements and is approximately seventeen minutes in length. The piece is available via rental from G. Schirmer, Inc.

Unit 3: Historical Perspective

This piece was written with one certain historical element in mind: a summer band concert in the gazebo of a park. It certainly is a wonder that the composer did not originally write the piece for the concert band as historically it was this medium that was noted for its summer concerts. Conductors should have some knowledge of the touring bands such as those of Patrick Gilmore and John Philip Sousa. The history of the concert band would be significantly different if these groups would have never existed. Each movement in this piece conjures the same basic memories of those touring bands, yet each is contrasting in musical content. From the viewpoint of the band, the overture functions perhaps as recognizing the use of transcribed overtures from the orchestral repertory. The waltz was a popular dance in the era of gazebo concerts and was sure to be found on the program. As I state later, the *Adagio* movement almost could relate to the frequent use of soprano soloists on band programs in the Sousa era. The word "tarantella" does have a specific meaning in a historical context. It is a dance in either 3/8 or 6/8 time that alternated major and minor keys. It often used repeated notes and diatonic motion with regular phrase structure. The dance was typically accompanied by a tambourine or castanets and used an *accelerando* as it progressed. This should be kept in mind when performing the final movement of this work as one can plainly see that this is exactly what the composer had in mind as these elements, as well as a modified rondo form, close the piece.

Unit 4: Technical Considerations

If one looks at the work as a whole one quickly realizes that this is a piece worthy of the Grade Six label. Players must be able to play nearly all major and minor scales in addition to having a grasp on modality. Listed below is a brief technical overview of each movement.

OVERTURE

The overture presents many problems to even the most advanced ensembles. The use of mixed meter forces the conductor to set the subdivisions between triple, duple, and compound meters so the group has a strong metronomic feeling. Rhythmically the movement is not overly difficult, but players will need to execute sixteenth-note passages flawlessly. Articulation and accent placement are very critical to giving a good performance.

WALTZ

The composer continues to write exposed solo lines and use transparent scoring. The conductor is faced with the *hemiola* effect in the 3/4 waltz and later the 5/4 waltz presents problems all its own. This movement certainly requires good soloists on a variety of instruments.

ADAGIO

This movement requires maturity in lyrical performance. Once again the transparent scoring and solo writing challenge the conductor to carefully balance the ensemble. One may almost consider this movement an oboe solo as this line dominates a majority of the movement. The movement does contain mixed meter but the rhythms are not overly difficult with the exception of some sixteenth-note triplets and a few thirty-second-note runs in woodwinds. Players must have control and be able to play soft dynamics in tune.

TARANTELLA

The tempo of a dotted quarter note=138-144 will present players with some technical challenges. This is eased somewhat by the diatonic writing of the composer. Once again Corigliano employs mixed meter but no overly difficult rhythmic passages. Players must once again have control in soft passages and must also be able to perform long tones in soft passages.

Unit 5: Stylistic Considerations

Gazebo Dances for Band, although considered to be a piece that conjures similar thoughts and emotions of summer concerts in the park, presents four movements of contrasting styles. The conductor and ensemble must be able to "shift gears" and move from one style to the next. Listed below are some stylistic considerations for each movement.

OVERTURE

The composer has called the overture "Rossini-like," but this reviewer fails to see many connections with that particular composer's style. This overture is very unique and full of zest like those of Rossini, but the compositional elements are fresh and speak of a different era. Contrast is probably a good word to describe the various elements contained within even the first movement. The conductor needs to make sure that *staccatos* remain light, yet accented notes need to have body and tone along with space between notes. I consider the A and B sections to be similar in that they are light and playful in nature. The C section contrasts the previous material by bringing about an air of strength and power. *Staccatos* serve to provide space between notes, not shorten the length. The trombone and tenor sax lines need to have strength and all solo lines are of utmost importance.

WALTZ

I believe conductors should have some knowledge of the many dance bands that performed regularly in the '30s and '40s. This waltz is almost in a style that brings about recollections of the Guy Lombardo Orchestra or similar groups. The composer has called this waltz "peg-legged" and the performers should keep that in mind as this movement is almost tongue-in-cheek. However, performers should not take the movement lightly as it may be the most difficult to perform as an ensemble. Performers must strictly adhere to all markings to give a good performance.

ADAGIO

This movement allows for expressive and lyrical performance by not only the soloists, but the entire ensemble. One might even draw the connection between this movement and John Philip Sousa's use of a soprano soloist on his concerts as this movement certainly has that feel with the oboe being the predominate voice. The freedom of expression and the use of *rubato* with good musical execution could provide a very romantic feeling.

TARANTELLA

From a listener's point of view one may draw the connection between this movement and the fourth movement of the Holst *Second Suite in F.* Given the information in Unit 3, this dance-like movement needs to remain light and bouncy with perhaps a bit of aggressiveness in the C section of the movement.

Unit 6: Musical Elements

OVERTURE

The form of this movement is ABACABCA and sections are, for the most part, clearly defined. The overture is mostly homophonic and uses tonal and modal harmonies and melodies and mixed meter.

WALTZ

The form of this movement is ABA with a *coda*. The composer writes the waltz in 3/4 meter in the A section and in 5/4 in the B section while juxtaposing them in the return of A. The *coda* employs the compositional technique of fragmentation. The texture is rather transparent for most of the movement and requires good soloists.

ADAGIO

This movement employs the structure of theme, fantasia, theme, and *coda.* One could roughly associate this with ABA *Coda,* but it does not fall strictly into those lines. The composer once again employs fragmentation and develops several motives and themes in a highly lyrical and *legato* movement.

TARANTELLA

This movement employs a modified rondo form of ABACABDA and alternates between C major and C minor while also employing modality. The movement features much diatonic motion and antecedent and consequent writing along with the use of an *ostinato.*

Unit 7: Form and Structure

SECTION	MEASURES	EVENTS AND SCORING
"Overture"		
A	1-21	Full ensemble, modes of G and C Lydian with C as central tonality, thematic material in piccolo, bassoon, E-flat clarinet, B-flat bass clarinet, and baritone saxophone. Very rhythmic and accented in nature.
B	22-48	Mostly tonal with some modal implications—still centered in C. Solo lines in horn and trumpet with arpeggiated accompaniment from flute, piccolo, baritone, and tuba. Other woodwinds eventually enter and share melodic fragments.
A	49-64	Very similar to original A section.
C	65-89	Tonal section; pedal lies in bass with trombone and tenor sax antecedent, full ensemble consequent.
A	90-107	Repeat of mm. 1-21.
B	108-147	Same melodic material as first B, only this time it appears in E-flat clarinet and solo first and second B-flat clarinets. Arpeggiated accompaniment in bassoon with melodic fragments in trumpet.
C	148-177	Repeat of mm. 65-89.
A	178-191	Final repeat of A section functions as a coda. Material is similar with eight-measure ending featuring scalar passages, block chords in brasses, and closing on a staccato, accented eighth note.
"Waltz"		
A	1-34	3/4 waltz with use of several tonalities: major, minor, and modal. Passing solo lines in woodwinds and trumpet.

B	35-70	5/4 waltz; use of full ensemble; tonalities spelled enharmonically; presentation of new melodic material.
A	71-123	Juxtaposition of 3/4 and 5/4 to create hemiola effect; return of A material with B material interwoven; much solo and soli writing.
Coda	124-153	Exclusive use of 3/4; melodic fragmentation in full ensemble.
"Adagio" Main Theme	1-14	B-flat Lydian; theme presented in oboe with ostinato in clarinets and alto saxophones; use of 7/4, 3/4, 3/8 meters.
Fantasia	15-44	Divided into two sections: I–mm. 15-30, and II–mm. 31-41; Section I uses several themes, motives, and an ostinato with much employment of fragmentation; second section returns to a fragmented version of the original theme uses full ensemble.
Main Theme	45-51	Return of main theme with different scoring and use of fragmentation.
Coda	52-53	Two-bar extension with continued fragmentation of the main theme to the close.
"Tarantella" Introduction	1-2	6/8 meter; C major tonality; rhythm defined by trumpets, horns, and bells (quarter - eighth).
A	3-16	C major with some modal implication; solo line in clarinet that is mostly diatonic with a few leaps; eventually repeated in oboe; accompaniment in lower voices.
B	17-27	Use of both C major and C minor; continued diatonic motion with antecedent and consequent lines between high woodwinds and brass.

SECTION	MEASURES	EVENTS AND SCORING
A	28-41	C major tonality; melody presented in horns, then passed to trumpets before appearing in flutes and piccolo; melody also fragmented in B-flat and E-flat soprano clarinets.
C	42-84	Alternating tonality/modality; contrasting material with use of 9/8 meter along with the 6/8; repeated notes (eighths) in diatonic motion. Block chord scoring bridges the gap back to the A section; ostinato in high woodwinds.
A	85-98	Return of A material and C major tonality; continued diatonic motion with melody presented in flute and piccolo, then in the trumpet and oboe on repeat.
B	99-109	Use of C major and C minor; similar to mm. 17-27 with some changes in orchestration.
D	110-151	Alternating tonality/modality. This section uses material from both Section A and Section C as both the diatonic theme of A and the repeated note material of C appear.
A	152-177	Return of C major tonality and A theme; extension of material functions as the coda.

Unit 8: Suggested Listening

Paul Creston, *Celebration Overture, Prelude and Dance*
Vittorio Giannini, *Symphony No. 3*
Gustav Holst, *Second Suite in F for Military Band*

Unit 9: Additional References and Resources

G. Schirmer Inc., 866 Third Ave., New York 10022.

Olfert, Warren D. "An Analysis of John Corigliano's Gazebo Dances for Band." *Journal of Band Research* 29/1 (Fall, 1993); 25-43.

Humphrey, Mary Lou. "John Corigliano." New York: G. Schirmer, 1989.

Schwandt, Erich. "Tarantella," *The New Grove Dictionary of Music and Musicians*. 18: 575-76.

Smith, Norman and Albert Stoutmire. *Band Music Notes*. Lake Charles, LA: Program Note Press, 1989.

Contributed by:

Rodney C. Schueller
Indiana University
Bloomington, Indiana

Teacher Resource Guide

Huntingtower Ballad

Ottorino Respighi
(1879–1936)

Unit 1: Composer

Ottorino Respighi was born in Bologna, Italy on July 9, 1879. At the age of twelve, he studied violin and viola at the Liceo Musicale of Bologna with Federico Sarti and shortly thereafter began studying composition with Luigi Torchi and Giuseppe Martucci. In 1900, at twenty-one years of age, he went to St. Petersburg, Russia to study composition privately with Nicolas Rimsky-Korsakov and to play first viola and violin in the Imperial Opera Orchestra. In 1908 he moved to Germany to study with Bruch and to absorb the rich musical environment of Berlin. Respighi's compositions up to this time were influenced by Rimsky-Korsakov, Martucci, Ravel, Sgmambati, and Strauss. In 1910, with his compositions of *Nebbie*, *Nevicata*, and *Stornellatrice*, he is credited with abandoning the styles of his predecessors and contemporaries and thus developing his own unique style.

Returning to Rome in 1913, Respighi was appointed Professor of Composition at the Liceo (later Conservatorio) di Santa Cecilia. He also was very active performing in orchestras as a violinist and violist. Respighi was appointed director of Liceo di Santa Cecilia in 1924, but resigned in 1925 to devote his work specifically to his compositions. He earned a reputation for his interest in early music, especially neglected Italian music, and for his work as a teacher. His music depicts a celebration and a determined effort to revive nationalism in Italy during this period of time. Respighi was very active in the later part of his life as a conductor, composer, and teacher. He toured Europe, as well as the United States in 1925-26 and 1932, conducting his compositions and accompanying his wife and singer, Elsa Olivieri-Sangiacomo.

Ottorino Respighi is known as one of the "masters" of modern Italian music with regards to orchestration. He is recognized for having the ability to evoke the "Italian scene" and to "hold audience interest." His numerous musical compositions include opera, ballet, choral and orchestral works, chamber music, band work, and songs. Many of his works are based on church modes and plainchant. Respighi's music is described as romantic-impressionist because the melodies are extended and fully developed while the orchestral sound is impressionistic in nature. His greatest success was achieved by his two symphonic poems, *The Fountains of Rome* and *The Pines of Rome*. These landmark compositions, and the advocacy of many well-known conductors including Toscanini, made Ottorino Respighi the most respected Italian composer of the early twentieth century. Respighi passed away in Rome, April 18, 1936.

Unit 2: Composition

In 1929, the American Bandmasters Association (A.B.A.) was organized. The purpose of this organization was to "promote better music through the instrumentality of the concert band" while its objectives were to:

> secure the adoption of a universal band instrumentation so that band publications of all countries "could" be interchangeable; to induce prominent composers of all countries to write in the large forms for the band; to establish for the concert band a higher standard of artistic excellence than has been generally maintained in the past, and thus gain for the band the artistic recognition which it rightly merits.

According to *The Concert Band* written by Richard Franko Goldman, during the 1930s there was a strong attempt by the A.B.A. to have the best European and American composers write music specifically for the wind band medium. It is interesting to note that during this era, Paul Hindemith, Ernst Krenek, Jaromir Weinberger, Sergei Prokofiev, Nikolai Miaskovsky, Florent Schmitt, Albert Roussel, and Ottorino Respighi each composed at least one work specifically for band. The tremendous impact that these composers had in attracting other great composers to write compositions for band is astonishing. The band movement during the 1940s attracted even more great composers including Arnold Schoenberg, Igor Stravinsky, Darius Milhaud, Roy Harris, Paul Creston, William Schuman, Samuel Barber, and Morton Gould to write works for band.

In a meeting with fellow A.B.A. committee members to set up the Third Annual American Bandmasters Association meeting to be held in Washington, DC, Edwin Franko Goldman listed the accomplishments of the previous two meetings and stated the following:

It will be the intent of the Association to arouse interest of European composers to the extent that they will join with the better-known American composers in preparing and submitting papers adding to the general interest and knowledge of band music. It is intended to use the three large service bands....with well-known composers of band music playing their own compositions. (Benter, 1931)

The A.B.A. had success and failure in encouraging European composers to write band works for the 1932 convention. Goldman was successful in commissioning two of the most prominent European composers, Gustav Holst and Ottorino Respighi, to have their works premiered at the convention. Holst composed *Prelude and Scherzo "Hammersmith"* and Respighi composed *Huntingtower Ballad.* Sir Edward Elgar did not share the same enthusiasm when asked to write a work for band, and declined the invitation. Nevertheless, the A.B.A. had made significant achievements in the quest to attract extremely reputable orchestral composers to write for bands. In his comments to fellow A.B.A. members during his address at the 1932 convention in Washington, DC, Goldman made the following remarks:

In the past, the band was ignored by the great composers....For our convention this year, Ottorino Respighi, Italy's most famous composer, has written a special number, as has Gustav Holst, one of England's greatest composers....For next year's convention the great French composer, Maurice Ravel has promised to write a work for band. We can safely say now that the band will soon have a repertoire of its own. Perhaps more real composers have written directly for band the last two years than ever before...

Unit 3: Historical Perspective

Ottorino Respighi was commissioned by Edwin Franko Goldman, president of the American Bandmasters Association and band leader of the Edwin Franco Goldman Band, to write a composition for the "Tribute" concert at Constitution Hall, in memory of John Philip Sousa for the A.B.A. Convention in Washington, DC, April 17, 1932. The work was inspired during a sojourn at a small place called Huntingtower in Scotland. Huntingtower is a castle in Scotland where Respighi visited on several different occasions. The Scottish theme introduced toward the middle of the work is based on an old Scottish ballad. Respighi completed the work in February, 1932 and it was premiered several months later by the United States Marine Band, under the baton of Captain Taylor Branson. The importance of this work is that the American Bandmasters Association, along with the Edwin Franko Goldman Band, was able to attract one of the best European composers, Ottorino Respighi, to write a work specifically for band. *Huntingtower Ballad* along with Gustav Holst's *"Hammersmith"*, were two early twentieth-century works written specifically for band, which in turn led to more great European composers to write compositions for band.

Unit 4: Technical Considerations

Huntingtower Ballad is written with a transposed score and for standard band instrumentation. There are several parts noted as "optional" parts in the score which are for the English horn, soprano sax, bass sax, three trumpet parts, and string bass. It is also important to realize that the baritone part and the euphonium part are independent of each other. The written ranges of all of the instruments are very practical.

The first challenge that the players will encounter is the fact that this work is written in a key that many young bands don't commonly experience. The work is written in E-flat minor, tonality will vary from section to section, and there are numerous meter changes as well as tempo changes. The opening section with the rhythmic motif stated by the bass voices poses a challenge due to the exposure of the line and the doublings. The *tutti* section three bars before rehearsal number 2 presents the same problems with consistency of matching note lengths and style. The next rhythmic motif two bars prior to rehearsal number 4 will present problems with clarity as seven different instruments play this line, marked *pp*. Due to the texture of this developmental section, with so many different musical ideas occurring simultaneously and overlapping, spatial separation is needed to "clean" individual lines. At rehearsal number 6, the dynamics are *ff* and this is a trouble spot with regards to balance with only two trumpets playing the Scottish melody versus trills in the woodwinds, seven voices playing the rhythmic motif (horse galloping), and a descending chromatic line in the horns, baritone, and euphonium. Rehearsal number 8, *Andante*, presents problems with tuning due to the doublings and the thickness of scoring with the melody. The accompaniment unison descending modal scales can present problems with regard to pitch. Coincidentally, Respighi incorporates significant pedal pitches of B-flat and E-flat throughout the work. More often than not, the pedal does not function as the bass voice or "foundation" of the chords, so it is vitally important to determine the "role" and purpose of these notes and to not overlook their importance. Dynamics throughout the composition play a very important part in bringing this work to life due to all of the different "episodes," their individual character, and in drawing contrast of all of the high and low sections with emotion and intensity. When played correctly, *Huntingtower Ballad*, though very somber in nature, can be an extremely powerful and emotionally moving selection.

Unit 5: Stylistic Considerations

Respighi composed *Huntingtower Ballad* the same as he would an orchestral work. The form, as is typical with his compositions, is unconventional.

As can be found in many of his orchestral compositions, there are many disjunct episodes through the development, overlapping musical ideas,
incorporating folk songs (Scottish), use of modern modality, and deceptive
resolutions. Additionally, the scoring of romantic chords, simple melodies
which are expanded throughout the work, along with the driving rhythmic
motifs, are very characteristic of Respighi's compositions. Careful attention to
tempo markings, dynamic contrast, transitions from one meter to the next,
and attention to balance will enhance the overall performance of this work.

Unit 6: Musical Elements

As referred to in Unit 7, this work is based upon the first eight measures
of the composition. The rhythmic motif and simplistic melody are the basis for
this composition. Romantic chords, a chorale at rehearsal number 3, along
with use of a variety of different modes and pedal points, make this work harmonically very interesting. The instability and random shifting from one key
to the next and extensive use of modality build tension for the listener. The
Scottish folk song found in the middle of the selection shows Respighi's fond-
ness for Scotland and folk songs. The different sections tend to be "episodic"
and somewhat unrelated, but all come together for a climactic conclusion.

Unit 7: Form and Structure

Huntingtower Ballad can be broken down into three distinct sections: the
opening, development, and closing section. Within this framework, it can be
broken down even more.

Section A:	Melody and rhythmic motif; beginning to two bars before rehearsal number 4.
Section B:	Development (horse gallop + modality); two bars before rehearsal number 4 to nine after rehearsal number 5.
Transition:	3/4 (melody + rhythmic motif + Section B rhythmic motif).
Section C:	Development (Scottish Theme); rehearsal number 6 (6/8) to four bars prior to rehearsal number 7.
C′:	Four bars prior to rehearsal number 7.
Transition:	(Scottish Theme); rehearsal number 7 to rehearsal number 8.
Section D:	Development (4/4, new material); rehearsal number 8 to rehearsal number 9.
D′:	Rehearsal number 9 to five bars before rehearsal number 10.
Section A:	Recapitulation ; five bars before rehearsal number 10 to the end.

ANALYSIS

Huntingtower Ballad is not conventional with regards to form, although the outer sections tend to have standard romantic chords in terms of harmony while the episodic middle sections harmonically make use of modern modality. This work is centered around E-flat minor, but is very unstable as Respighi uses very few cadences to reinforce the key, incorporates many deceptive resolutions, and through modality and brief key changes creates tension and uncertainty for the listener. The first Section A begins with the rhythmic motif in the low reeds and brass which is mysterious and haunting sounding, while the melody is introduced in the clarinets, bassoons, baritone sax, and baritone. The first eight bars are the essential melody and rhythmic ideas, which are then explored and expanded as they are developed throughout the work. At rehearsal number 3, a "new episode" occurs: an eight-bar chorale is stated by the woodwinds in G-flat major, but then suddenly returns to E-flat minor.

Two bars before rehearsal number 4, Section B begins with the driving/static rhythm in the low reeds, brass, and timpani. I feel this rhythmic motif resembles a horse gallop for the hunt. Up to this point, the tonal center has been oriented around E-flat minor, but then has shifted to a series of different tonal centers before finally returning to E-flat minor. At rehearsal number 4, the importance of E-flat is still present in the bass voices and timpani. However, due to the bass line C-flat pedal and the ascending scale patterns played by the oboes, clarinets, and saxes, the tonality has shifted to the C-flat Lydian mode. This section, with voices fading in and out, along with the movement in the bass voices and persistent rhythmic pulse, create a sense of tension and instability. The texture throughout this section tends to be overlapping, which is commonly found throughout Respighi's compositions.

A transition begins in the 3/4, nine measures after rehearsal number 5. Respighi overlaps the low brass rhythmic motif from Section A, with the opening melody, this time stated by the trumpets in diminution (G-flat minor), along with the driving rhythmic (horse gallop) from Section B.

Rehearsal number 6 in 6/8, is the start of Section C as the trumpets introduce the Scottish theme. The previous transition has delivered us from G-flat minor to the B-flat Mixolydian mode. Four bars prior to rehearsal number 7, C prime begins with the mode shifting to E-flat Mixolydian. Rehearsal number 7 serves as a transition to rehearsal number 8. The linear motion of the descending bass line from D-flat to F leads us into new melodic material in the B-flat Mixolydian mode.

Section D begins at rehearsal number 8, with the bass line pedal B-flat, along with the descending scale patterns to establish the B-flat Mixolydian mode, before shifting to the E-flat Mixolydian mode five bars later. The melody in the flutes, oboes, clarinets, and alto sax is entirely new material.

This section uses many "color scales" and changes modes frequently, going from Mixolydian, Lydian, and Ionian modes. Rehearsal number 9 is D prime, incorporating ascending scale patterns while continuing to explore the various modes. This section is building tension and leading up to the climax of the composition. The tempo picks up slightly, due to the score marking *Animando* before reaching a *rallentando*.

The cadence, a B-flat dominant seventh chord, resolves back to the key of E-flat minor, and a recapitulation of Section A which occurs five bars prior to rehearsal number 10. From this point forward, there is finally stability with the key of E-flat minor. This section, marked *a tempo*, is very similar to the opening section of the composition with regards to tempo, the accompaniment of the rhythmic bass line, along with the melodic material. This section builds for fourteen measures, with many highs and lows. A *molto rallentando*, along with a series of E-flat minor chords, builds tension and increases the intensity, eventually leading to the final E-flat minor chord which concludes the work.

Unit 8: Suggested Listening

Band arrangements of Respighi's compositions:

Ancient Airs and Dances (Ricordi, arr. J. S. Howgill)

The Fountains of Rome (Ricordi, 1920, arr. Ranalli)

Huntingtower Ballad (Ricordi, 1932, Maecenas Music, 1991. This is an original work for band.)

The Pines of Rome
      a. (Belwin, 1974, arr. G. Duker)
      b. (Ricordi, 1926, arr. A. d'Elia)
      c. (Ricordi, 1966, arr. G. Duker)
      d. (Ricordi, 1948)

Roman Festivals
      a. (Ricordi, 1930, arr. A. d'Elia)
      b. (Ricordi, 1976, arr. W. Schaefer)

Somber Misti (Rubank, 1957)

Ottorino Respighi compositions

Adagio con variazoni for Cello and Orchestra, Supraphon Records. CD 11-1940, Czech Philharmonic, Andre Navarra, cello, Karel Ancerl conducting.

Ancient Airs and Dances, Sets 1 & 2, EMI Angel CDC 47116. Los Angeles Chamber Orchestra, Sir Neville Marriner conducting.

Ancient Songs-Stornellatrice, Capriccio Records 10272. Edemire Arnaltes, pianist.

Aretusa, Marco Polo 8.223347. Slovak Radio Symphony Orchestra
  Bratislava, Faridah Subrata, mezzo soprano, Adriano conducting.

Aubade for Violin & Piano, Opus 111 OPS44-9202. Fabio Biondi, violin.

Autumn Poem, Koch International Classics KIC 7215. San Diego Chamber
  Orchestra, Igor Gruppman, violin, Donald Barra conducting.

Belfagor Overture/Pines of Rome, EMI Classics CDFB 69358. Los Angeles
  Chamber Orchestra, Sir Neville Marriner conducting.

Berceuse for Strings, Chandos Records Chan 9415. Sinfonia 21, Richard
  Hickox conducting.

Brazilian Impressions, Dorian DOR 90182. Dallas Symphony Orchestra,
  Eduardo Mata conducting.

Carnival Overture, Marco Polo 8.223348. Czech-Slovak Radio Symphony
  Orchestra Bratislava, Adriano conducting.

Church Windows, Telarc Records CD 80356. Cincinnati Symphony
  Orchestra, Jesus Lopez-Cobos conducting.

Fountains of Rome/Pines of Rome/Roman Festival, Sony Classical Essential
  Classics SBK 48267. Philadelphia Orchestra, Eugene Ormandy conducting.

Fountains of Rome, RCA Victor Gold Seal 61401. Chicago Symphony
  Orchestra, Fritz Reiner conducting.

Gli uccelli "The Birds," Mercury Living Presence 2PM 432-007. London
  Symphony Orchestra, Antal Dorati conducting.

Huntingtower Ballad, Belwin, Inc. (Educational Record Reference Library)
  Stereophonic BP117. The University of Texas Symphonic Band,
  William J. Moody conducting.

La boutique Fantasque, Mercury Living Presence 2PM 434-322. Eastman
  Wind Ensemble, Frederick Fennell conducting.

Nebbie, Eklipse EKRCD13. Ezio Pinza, bass, Donald Voorhees conducting.

Nevicata, Gallo CD731. Ruben Amoretti, tenor.

Pines of Rome, EMI Classics ZDMB 65427. Symphony of the Air, Leopold
  Stokowski conducting.

Roman Festival, RCA Victor Gold Seal 2RG 60262. NBC Symphony
  Orchestra, Arturo Toscanini conducting.

Small Pieces (6) for Piano 4 Hands, Aca Digital CM 20009. Tony Lenti, piano.

Songs, Elan Recordings CD2280. Sofia Chamber Orchestra, Burjana Antonova, mezzo soprano, Emil Tabakov conducting.

Trittico botticelliano, EMI Classics CDFB 69358. Academy of St. Martin in the Fields, Sir Neville Marriner conducting.

Work(s), Legend LGD138. New York Philharmonic Orchestra, Arturo Toscanini conducting.

Unit 9: Additional References and Resources

Davis, Alan L. A *History of the American Bandmasters Association*. 1987.

Goldman, Edwin F. *Band Betterment*. New York: Carl Fischer, Inc., 1934.

Goldman, Edwin F. Edited by Ernest Hutcheson. *The Concert Band*. New York-Toronto: Rinehart & Company, Inc., 1946.

Rehrig, William H. Edited by Paul Bierley. *The Heritage Encyclopedia of Band Music*, Vol. 1. Westerville, OH: Integrity Press, 1989.

Ressler, Mike. US Marine Band Library Notes. (Marine Band Librarian) Marine Barracks, 8th & I Streets, S.E. Washington, D. C. 20390-5000.

Sadie, Stanley, ed. *The New Grove Dictionary of Music and Musicians*. London: Macmillan Publishers Limited, 1980.

Smith, Norman and Albert Stoutamire. *Band Music Notes*. Rev. ed. San Diego, CA: Kjos, 1979.

Interviews with Col. John Bourgeois, Emeritus Commander/Director of the United States Marine Band, and Robert Foster, Director of Bands at the University of Kansas, via phone, April, 1997.

Thanks to Dr. Blaise Ferrandino, Professor of Music Theory/Composition at Texas Christian University.

Contributed by:

Robert E. Foster, Jr.
Associate Director of Bands
Texas Christian University
Fort Worth, Texas

Teacher Resource Guide

The Leaves Are Falling
Warren Benson
(b. 1924)

Unit 1: Composer

A composer of international stature, Warren Benson promotes the notion that even the most renowned musician must be, in part, responsible for the education of young musicians. With his own catalog of band compositions (Grades Three through Six), Benson firmly believes that music education begins "with the literature. There is no other place to start...without that there is nothing" (Norcross, p. 56).

His life has revolved around centers of significant band activity this half of the twentieth century. After graduating from the University of Michigan (BM 1949, MM 1951), he served as Composer-in-Residence at Ithaca College (1953-1967) and then as Professor of Composition at the Eastman School of Music (1963-1993). While his band compositions are highly regarded and respected, Benson remains largely a composer best known for his vocal works.

In describing his musical style, Warren Benson himself prefers to quote the words of Wilma Salisburg, distinguished critic of the *Cleveland Plain Dealer*: "Benson's music...is undeniably 'romantic,' generally a word of condemnation in regard to new music. But Benson's romanticism, free from maudlin sentiment and embarrassment, is a welcome expression of something true-felt and communicated in contemporary terms."

Unit 2: Composition

The work was inspired by the poem *Herbst* (Autumn) from *Buch der Lieder* (Book of Songs) by Rainer Maria Rilke, the Austro-German poet and novelist (1875-1926). Benson explains: "Rather than attempting the impossi-

ble, namely to describe with words what could only be expressed with music, the poem itself [serves better] in lieu of any other form of introduction."

Autumn

The leaves are falling, falling from way off,
as though far gardens withered in the skies;
they are falling with denying gestures.

And in the nights the heavy earth is falling
from all the stars down into loneliness.

We all are falling. This hand falls.
And look at others: it is in them all.

And yet there is one who holds this falling
endlessly gently in his hands.

Unit 3: Historical Perspective

Composed in 1963-1964, *The Leaves Are Falling* represents a period of changing attitudes toward the artistic possibilities of concert band music. Warren Benson was among a growing number of composers and conductors seeking to develop a more meaningful repertory of concert band works.

Benson describes his compositional process as "essentially a layering process. I tend to write a work all the way through..." (Hunsberger, p. 7). But the order of events when writing *The Leaves Are Falling* did not follow his typical routine. The first half of *The Leaves Are Falling* originates from a sketch which had been set aside incomplete. Not until the fateful events of November 22, 1963 did Benson return to this manuscript. Struck by the assassination of President John F. Kennedy, Benson was able to complete the unfinished sketch piece within a month's span.

A student brought Rilke's poem *Autumn* to Benson. The composer was struck by the poem, it captured the mood of the nation: "...everything was going to pot, and the upbeat spirit of the Kennedy administration...had just been blown away" (Hunsberger, p. 10). *The Leaves Are Falling* eulogizes an entire generation as well as the spirit of what some called "The Camelot Years."

Unit 4: Technical Considerations

Two significant technical challenges are present in the composition: an extremely slow tempo throughout, and a polymeter in the second section (mm. 61-121).

Benson wrote that "the creation of something original...involves an element of risk" (Benson, p. 38). From a conducting perspective, considerable risk is involved with the performance tempo of *The Leaves Are Falling*. The indicated tempo is quarter note= 32-34 in *alla breve*. The instructions provided by the composer ("with steady rhythm") dictate that the meter must be duple (*not* subdivided into four) and the extremely slow pulse not waver. While a clearly defined ictus from the conductor will assist in performance, ensemble precision at this tempo will be achieved only when the musicians rely upon listening and responding to each other, rather than on the conductor's baton (or as Benson states, "...give them [the] responsibility and stand back" [Norcross, p. 55]).

In the second half of the composition, the Martin Luther chorale tune, *Ein feste Burg ist unser Gott* (1529), is introduced. Rather than injecting the chorale melody in the established *alla breve* meter, Benson writes the melody in a compound meter (6/4) to highlight the melody's agogic accents. The result is a polymeter of 6/4, *both* in duple meter.

Unit 5: Stylistic Considerations

Donald Hunsberger describes the performance challenges:

> *The Leaves Are Falling* is undoubtedly one of the most difficult works in the wind repertoire to perform due to the demands, both musical and emotional, imposed upon the conductor and the ensemble....The infinite control required of each performer produces situations seldom seen in traditional large scale band writing and focuses attention on basic performance techniques such as tone control, extremely quiet entrances and exits, graduated crescendi, intensity and projection of individual and section lines and, at all times, rhythmic control. (Hunsberger, p. 8)

Unit 6: Musical Elements

The Leaves Are Falling is constructed upon dual characteristics of the pitch D-flat/C-sharp. Motion from this single pitch tends to move toward both C and D. The D-flat is the upper leading tone to the dominant C of F, and the C-sharp is the leading tone to D. Musical contrast is achieved between the pull toward F and the pull toward D minor.

Three pitch sets are employed to create all of the melodic material employed in the work: 1) G-F-E; 2) G-F-E-flat-D; and 3) D-A-A-flat.

Both elements (the pitch sets and the D-flat/C-sharp) are used in an *ostinato* (an "incessant pulse") which initiates the composition and persists through all but the last sixteen measures.

Unit 7: Form and Structure

One of Benson's goals in composing *The Leaves Are Falling* was to fill that which he described as a gap in the band repertory. In the 1960s, he observed that the band repertory lacked pieces of any significant length; three to six minutes duration was standard for a band composition. But no single-movement work of profound length, comparable to an orchestral tone poem, was available.

The Leaves Are Falling is accurately described as a long, continuous, unbroken line comprising two distinct but similar sections. The first section (mm. 6-60) employs an original theme (first stated by a solo flute, mm. 6-18) which is developed through fragmentation. The second section (mm. 61-160) combines the first theme fragments with a second, well-known melody, the chorale tune *Ein feste Burg ist unser Gott* (A Mighty Fortress Is Our God).

SECTION	MEASURES	EVENTS AND SCORING
Introduction	1-5	Claves/chimes pulse (*ostinato* begins)
Section 1		
A^1	6-45	Melodic fragments passed among various instruments, but all based upon solo flute (mm. 6-18)
A^2	46-60	Repeat of melodic fragments from A^1 with new instrumental combinations
Section 2		
B^1	61-121	Melodic fragments of Section 1 combine with series of chorale melody phrases in succession
B^2	122-160	Repeat of melodic fragments and chorale melodic phrases from B^1 with 1) new instrumental combinations, and 2) increasing overlapping and complexity of multiple phrases
Coda	161-182	Chorale melody unaccompanied (*ostinato* pulse ends)

Unit 8: Suggested Listening

Johann Sebastian Bach, *Cantata*, BWV 80

Johann Sebastian Bach, Chorales, "*Ein feste Burg ist unser Gott*," BWV 302 and 303

Johann Sebastian Bach, Chorale Prelude "*Ein feste Burg ist unser Gott*," BWV 720

Warren Benson, *The Passing Bell*

Leonard Bernstein, *Kaddish, Symphony No. 3*

William Kraft, *A Kennedy Portrait*

Ronald Lo Presti, *Elegy for a Young American*

Felix Mendelssohn, *Symphony No. 5 "The Reformation"*
Claude T. Smith, *Eternal Father, Strong to Save*
Igor Stravinsky, *Elegy for JFK*

Unit 9: Additional References and Resources

Benson, Warren. "The Creative Child Could Be Any Child." *Music Educators Journal*, 59:8 (April 1973): 38-40.

Benson, Warren. *Creative Projects in Musicianship*. Washington, DC: Music Educators National Conference, 1967.

Buszin, Walter E. *Luther on Music*. Saint Paul, MN: North Central Publishing Co., 1958.

Hunsberger, Donald. "A Discussion with Warren Benson: *The Leaves Are Falling*." CBDNA *Journal*, 1:1 (Spring 1984): 7-17.

Norcross, Brian. "Spotlight on American Band Education." *Music Educators Journal*, 78:5 (January 1992): 53-58.

Norton, M. D. Herter. *Translations from the Poetry of Rainer Maria Rilke*. New York: W.W. Norton & Co., Inc., 1938.

Renshaw, Jeffrey. "Conducting Warren Benson's *The Leaves Are Falling*." *Instrumentalist*, 47:8 (March 1993): 30-38.

Contributed by:
Lawrence F. Stoffel
Assistant Professor of Music/Director of Huskie Bands
Northern Illinois University
De Kalb, Illinois

Teacher Resource Guide

Profanation

Leonard Bernstein
(1918–1990)

arranged by
Frank Bencriscutto (b. 1928)

Unit 1: Composer

Leonard Bernstein was one of America's best-known conductors, as well as being internationally recognized for his skills as a composer, teacher, and pianist. As a composer, Bernstein was equally versed in both symphonic and popular styles. His diverse output includes *West Side Story, Candide, On the Town, On the Waterfront, Slava!, Chichester Psalms, Mass,* and three symphonies. All are marked by rhythmic vitality and a mixture of traditional and jazz harmonies. Bernstein's musical training began at age ten with piano lessons. His teachers included Susan Smith and Boston's foremost piano teacher, Heinrich Gebhard. In 1935 Bernstein entered Harvard University, where his teachers included Walter Piston, and in 1939 he entered the Curtis Institute where he studied with Randall Thompson and Fritz Reiner. He also studied conducting with Koussevitzky during the summers of 1940 and 1941 at the Berkshire Music Center where he was named assistant conductor in 1942. His rise to prominence as a conductor occurred in 1943, when, as an assistant conductor with the New York Philharmonic Orchestra, he substituted for a suddenly ill Bruno Walter for a nationally televised concert. His performance was reviewed by newspapers nationally, including the *New York Times* and he became an instant celebrity. From 1945 to 1948, Bernstein was the music director of the New York City Symphony Orchestra and began to appear on the international scene as guest conductor. After Koussevitzky died in 1953, Bernstein became head of the orchestra and conducting departments at Berkshire. During that year, he also became the first American to conduct at La Scala. After serving as co-director of the New York Philharmonic during 1957, he became its first American-born music director 1958. He remained in that position until he retired as conductor laureate in 1969. Bernstein was elected to the American Academy and Institute of Arts and Letters in 1981 and received the Academy's Gold Medal for Music in recognition of his work as a composer in 1985.

Unit 2: Composition

Profanation is the second of three movements from Bernstein's *Symphony No. 1, "Jeremiah."* Written in 1942 and premiered by the Pittsburgh Symphony Orchestra with the composer conducting in January, 1944, the *Jeremiah Symphony* won the New York Music Critics' Circle award as the best American work of that year. The symphony, dedicated to Bernstein's father, was not intended to have literal programmatic meaning; rather, it attempted to create emotional quality (Bernstein, 1944). *Profanation* is the *scherzo* movement of the work. It depicts the chaos and destruction brought about by the pagan corruption within the priesthood and the people (Bernstein, 1944). As *scherzo* suggests, the movement is fast paced, with the eighth note receiving the pulse. It is marked by extensive use of mixed meter. The emotional quality of the work ranges from light and uplifting to dark and heavy. The arrangement for band by Frank Bencriscutto, written in 1952, preserves the integrity of Bernstein's work. Bencriscutto provides a helpful rhythmic analysis as a prologue to the work that depicts the various eighth-note grouping used in the movement.

Unit 3: Historical Perspective

Bernstein's long-standing relationship with Aaron Copland helped to shape his compositional language. The late 1930s and early 1940s saw the development of the "American sound," particularly in the music of Piston and Copland's *Outdoor Overture* (1938), *Billy the Kid* (1938) and *Rodeo* (1942). This sound, featuring the use of perfect fourths, fifths, and octaves, as well as bitonality, is commonly found in music dating from that time period. In addition, the music is marked by rhythmic drive contrasted by lyricism.

Unit 4: Technical Considerations

One of the primary performance considerations is rhythmic accuracy and drive. The work demands consistent eighth-note subdivisions throughout. The tempo is quarter note=144, with the eighth note receiving the pulse. The constant use of mixed meter requires the performer and conductor to remain aware of rhythmic groupings as well as time signatures. The movement must maintain forward momentum through the precise beat placement. Accents are a prominent feature and must be brought out in order to aid the syncope

of the line. Range requirements include written high Cs in all horn parts.

Unit 5: Stylistic Considerations

The movement must flow easily with great attention given to overall pacing and the inherent character of each theme. Tonguing should be light so that the music remains buoyant. Dynamics and balance are key considerations, especially when inner voices perform thematic material.

Unit 6: Musical Elements

The tonality of *Profanation* is based on shifting harmonies between major and minor modalities. These are often supported by open fifths, octaves, and/or pedal point, allowing the composer freedom to explore both types of tonality. The overall key of the work is A minor. This is based on the use of the movement from G-sharp to A in the opening theme and the 3-2-1 (C-B-A) motion used for the final notes of the piece. Bernstein often uses distant key relationships in order to create surprise. The movement is a four-part form (Introduction-A-B-C-D) which uses two main theme groups (A and B). The opening theme is heard during the introduction in its original key (A minor). The theme cadences in E major, which is confirmed at the beginning of part A. The opening theme is then heard in D minor which moves to A major. The section ends in E major. Part B develops Theme Group A. It begins in E but quickly moves through a series of distantly related key centers. It is brought to a close with Theme 1 partially stated in D minor. Part C introduces and develops an entirely new theme group (Theme Group B). It begins with an abrupt motion to and from E-flat. Again, the harmony proceeds through distant key relationships as it did in part B. Part D begins with the return of Theme 1 in the original key and proceeds to act as a recapitulation of themes from both theme groups.

THEME GROUP A

Theme 1   The first entrance of Theme 1 occurs in mm. 1-7 in the flute, piccolo, and clarinet I. It is based on a six-note scale of A-B-C-D-E-G-sharp, making it possible for the composer to shift between minor tonality using the pitches C, G-sharp, and A, and major tonality using E and G-sharp. The perceived harmonic movement is from i to V. The phrase construction is A-B with a C phrase added in mm. 15-18. The C phrase serves as a transition to the beginning of Part A.

Motive 1   The first entrance of Motive 1 occurs in mm. 25-26 in alto sax II and clarinet III. It is thirteen notes long (8/8 + 5/8) and based on the language of Theme 1. Motive 1 appears as an accompanying figure throughout the work. It is also used with its measures reversed (5/8 + 8/8) as Motive 1a.

Theme 2	Theme 2 first appears in mm. 29-34 in the oboe, horn, flute, and piccolo, providing contrast to Theme 1 by use of longer note values and differing harmonic construction. It is fourteen notes long and marked by the use of ascending and descending half steps and perfect fifths. The phrase construction is A-B.
Theme 3	Theme 3 first appears in mm. 38-50 and is the closing theme of Part A. The phrase construction is A-B with the A phrase newly composed and the B phrase composed of the first four pitches of Theme 2 and Motive 1a.
Motive 2	The first entrance of Motive 2 occurs in m. 63 and is based on the first seven notes of Theme 1.

THEME GROUP B

Motive 3	Motive 3 first occurs in mm. 116-118 in clarinet I. It is a seven-note motive comprised of the range of a perfect fourth. This serves as the major source of ideas for Part C.
Theme 4	Theme 4 first appears in flute I in mm. 124-126, providing contrast to the half-step motion of Motive 3 by using quartal harmony.
Theme 5	Theme 5 first appears in a fully developed form during mm. 135-153. The eight measures that comprise this theme are found in mm. 177-184. It is the lyrical theme found in the flute, piccolo, and clarinet parts.

Unit 7: Form and Structure

SECTION	MEASURES	EVENTS AND SCORING
Introduction	(1-14)	
	1-7	Theme 1 (flute, piccolo, clarinet I)
	8-14	Theme 1 repeated (oboe, bassoon, bass clarinet)
Part A (| |: 15-50 : | |) [Theme Group A]		
	15-18	Transition (c phrase added to Theme 1)
	19-25	Theme 1 transposed
	25-28	Motive 1/transition (alto sax II, clarinet III)
	29-33	Theme 2 (oboe, horn, flute, piccolo)

SECTION	MEASURES	EVENTS AND SCORING
	4-37	Theme 2 transposed (woodwinds)
	38-50	Theme 3 (tutti)

Part B (51-115) [Development of A]

	MEASURES	EVENTS AND SCORING
	51-62	Development of Motive 1 and Theme 2 (first four beats) [four measures with one exact repetition and one transposed repetition]
	63-65	Motive 2 (development theme 1)
	66-70	Transition
	71-78	Development of Theme 2 (first five pitches)
	79-94	Motive 2 (development of Theme 1)
	95-106	Development of Theme 2
	107-115	Theme 1 [(a) phrase + combination of (a) and (b) phrases with (a) cadential figure]

Part C (116-246) [Episode/Development based on Theme Group B]

	MEASURES	EVENTS AND SCORING
	116-123	Motive 3 (English horn, clarinet I and II, bassoons)
	124-129	Theme 4 (flutes, oboes, clarinet I and II)
	129-134	Development of Motive 3
	135-145	Development of Theme 5 (flutes)
	146-152	Transition (rhythm of Motive 3, harmonic language of Theme 5)
	153-176	Development of Motive 3
	177-192	Theme 5 (eight measures with one transposed repetition)
	193-212	Development of Motive 3
	213-217	Theme 4 (one repetition + one partial repetition)
	17-226	Development of Motive 3

SECTION	MEASURES	EVENTS AND SCORING
	227-234	Theme 4 (horns) [augmentation]
	235-246	Development of Motive 3
Part D (247-313) [Recapitulation]		
	247-253	Theme 1
	253-280	Repeat of mm. 51-79
	281-287	Theme 3 [(a) phrase transposed down a major third; rebarred]
	288-289	Theme 4
	289-295	B phrase added to Theme 4
	296-297	Motive 2 (cornets, trumpets, trombones)
	298-304	Transition based on Motive 2
	305-310	Theme 3 (Phrase B only) 3
	12-313	Final cadence

Unit 8: Suggested Listening

Leonard Bernstein, *Jeremiah Symphony*, *Slava!*, *Overture to Candide*
Aaron Copland, *An Outdoor Overture*
David Holsinger, *Liturgical Dances*

Unit 9: Additional References and Resources

Bernstein, Leonard. *The Infinite Variety of Music*. New York: Simon and Schuster, 1966.

Bernstein, Leonard. *The Unanswered Question*. London: Harvard University Press, 1976.

Gruen, John. *The Private World of Leonard Bernstein*. New York: Viking Press, 1968.

Peyser, Joan. *Bernstein*. New York: Beech Tree Books, 1987.

Secrest, Meryle. *Leonard Bernstein: A Life*. New York: A. A. Knopf, 1994.

Contributed by:

Robert Meunier
Director of Bands/Associate Professor of Percussion
Drake University
Des Moines, Iowa

Teacher Resource Guide

Shakata: Singing the World into Existence

Dana Wilson
(b. 1946)

Unit 1: Composer

Dana Wilson was born in 1946. He is associate professor at Ithaca College where he teaches theory, composition, and jazz courses. He holds a doctorate from the Eastman School of Music, and is active as a composer, jazz pianist, clinician, and conductor, with several commissioned works and grants to his credit. His compositions and arrangements have been performed in the United States, Europe, and Australia, and many have also been published. He was a Yaddo Fellow at the artists' retreat in Saratoga Springs, New York and a Fellow at the Society for the Humanities, Cornell University. Wilson is also a Charles A. Dana Research Fellow in composition. His work for band *Piece of Mind* won the Sousa Foundation's 1988 Sudler International Wind Band Composition Competition and the 1988 ABA/Ostwald Prize. He also wrote *Time Cries, Hoping Otherwise* for band.

Unit 2: Composition

The Australian Aboriginals believed that the countryside and the world did not exist until the ancestors sang it, and that still, to be perceived, it must be conjured by descendants following ancestral songlines. *Shakata: Singing the World into Existence* is a collective ritual whereby the ensemble conjures up the earth and its various aspects from within. The term "shakata" has no literal significance, thereby allowing it to be a trans-lingual (or pre-lingual) intonement. The piece is in one movement and is a Grade Six difficulty.

Unit 3: Historical Perspective

Dana Wilson belongs to a recently-discovered new generation of band composers. His background in several different genres of music has influenced his music composition by displaying a variety of styles, textures and rhythms. He is currently in demand as composer and clinician, and his works are already highly respected as is evidenced by his *Piece of Mind* winning the Sousa Foundation's 1988 Sudler International Wind Band Composition Competition and the 1988 ABA/Ostwald Prize.

Unit 4: Technical Considerations

The piece has no key signatures, so accidentals abound. There are several meter changes, and there is quite a bit of shifting of the metrical "feel." The tempos remain consistent within the large sections. Saxophones must play lip *glissandi*. At a few points, players are called upon to sing "ah" as warmly as possible without *vibrato*. All instruments have both soli and exposed sections and several solos as does the percussion section. Ranges and scalar passages are quite difficult at times, mainly due to the accidentals containing both sharps and flats.

Unit 5: Stylistic Considerations

Articulations should be interpreted exactly; all markings in the score support this. Each section has its own style. The intensity and movement of the music should be equal to the phrasing, articulation, rhythms and principles of the line. Several different musical styles are required, from a driving modern technique to "bluesy" or jazz. This is a twentieth-century work with twentieth-century sounds; it should be approached with a twentieth-century interpretation.

Unit 6: Musical Elements

Much of the music is composed in small cells, so attention must be paid to making these cells connect and relate to each other. These cells generally feature a certain set of pitches that Wilson uses for a time and then adds or changes notes to a different cell. Wilson combines jazz elements in the music with blocks of sounds. The ensemble must chant, shout, and murmur the vocalizations with confidence, intensity, and sincerity to make the chant sections work.

Unit 7: Form and Structure

SECTION	MEASURES	EVENTS AND SCORING
With driving energy ♩=100		continually shifting tonalities
Introduction	1-31	opening with several solos
	32-57	piano solo with slowly building winds

	58-67	sixteenth-note pulse with long chords
Slowly ♩=60		
	68-88	chant with flute solo
♩ = ♩. (= 60)		
Bluesy, intense	89-98	brass and saxophones in 12/8 meter
Out of tempo	99	tutti chant
Tempo primo ♩=100		
	100-107	tutti chant
	108-115	tutti chant with additive instruments
	116-132	tutti rhythms
	133-146	tutti chant
Closing	147-172	tutti in 3/4

Unit 8: Suggested Listening

Anthony Iannaccone: *Apparitions*
Martin Mailman: *Bouquets for Band, Op. 87, Effects for Symphonic Band*
Dana Wilson: *Piece of Mind, Time Cries, Hoping Otherwise*
Gregory Youtz: *Fireworks, Scherzo for a Bitter Moon*

Unit 9: Additional References and Resources

National Band Association Selective Music List for Bands.

Rehrig, William H. *The Heritage Encyclopedia of Band Music.* Westerville, OH: Integrity Press, 1991.

Westrup, J. A. and F. Ll. Harrison. *The New College Encyclopedia of Music.* Revised by Conrad Wilson. New York: W.W. Norton & Co., 1981.

Wilson, Dana. *Contemporary Choral Arranging.* Prentice-Hall.

Contributed by:

Matthew Mailman
Director of Bands
Oklahoma City University
Oklahoma City, Oklahoma

Teacher Resource Guide

Symphonic Metamorphosis on Themes of Carl Maria von Weber

Paul Hindemith
(1895–1963)

arranged by Keith Wilson (b. 1916)

Unit 1: Composer

Paul Hindemith was born on November 16, 1895 in Hanau, Germany. He began to show interest in music at the age of nine by studying the violin, and at fourteen he entered the Hoch Conservatory in Frankfurt. By the time Hindemith was twenty, he was concertmaster of the Frankfurt Opera, and he also played viola in various string quartets. As a composer, he joined the modern movement and was an active participant in the contemporary music concerts at Donaueschingen. From 1927 to 1937 Hindemith taught at the Berlin School of Music, after which, due to conditions surrounding World War II, he emigrated to the United States. Hindemith promoted the philosophy in composition of *Gebrauchsmusik*—music for practical use rather than music for art's sake, and he was concerned with the furtherance of active music-making among amateurs, a movement called *Hausmusik*. From 1940 to 1953, Hindemith was a member of the Yale University School of Music faculty. He wrote music of all types for all instrumental combinations, including a series of sonatas for each orchestral instrument with piano. Hindemith composed original works for band: *Concert Music* (1926), and the monumental *Symphony in B-flat* (1950).

Unit 2: Composition

Symphonic Metamorphosis on Themes of Carl Maria von Weber was composed in 1943 while Hindemith was at Yale University. Hindemith had earlier collaborated with the dancer/choreographer/impresario Léonide Massine, and it was the choreographer who suggested that Hindemith investigate the music of Carl Maria von Weber as possible material for a ballet. Hindemith initially liked the idea, and made a few sketches based on some of Weber's themes, but Massine found them "too personal" for the production he envisioned. Hindemith also had misgivings about the project when he learned that Salvador Dali would be designing the sets and costumes. Dali, it seems, had been responsible for a staging for Massine of the Bacchanal from Wagner's *Tannhäuser* filled with what Hindemith felt were "a series of weird hallucinatory images...[that were] quite simply stupid." By mutual consent, composer and choreographer abandoned the plan. Practical musician that he was, however, Hindemith did not let the work done on the ballet go to waste. He took up the sketches again in 1943 and gave them the final form as the *Symphonic Metamorphosis* for orchestra.

The work's four movements are organized loosely around the traditional model of the symphony. Each movement is based on a separate theme of Carl Maria von Weber (1786-1826): three on miniatures for piano duet and one on an Oriental melody from incidental music for a play. The first movement is based on the fourth of Weber's *Huit Pièces*, Op. 60, for piano duet. The second movement is a *scherzo* using a melody from the overture Weber contributed to the incidental music for Schiller's play *Turandot*. The theme of the third movement is an arrangement of a gentle *siciliano* from Weber's *Pièces Faciles* for Piano, Four Hands, Op. 3, Book 2. The vibrant fourth movement theme is derived from No. 7 of Weber's *Huit Pièces*, Op. 60. Hindemith has altered and elaborated on all themes. Performance of the four movements totals approximately twenty-one minutes in length (I: four minutes, II: seven minutes, III: four minutes, IV: five minutes).

Unit 3: Historical Perspective

Hindemith felt strongly that this work should be available in a version for band and asked his colleague at Yale, Keith Wilson, to do the transcription. Not until 1960 was permission received from Hindemith's publishers, and then the work took one and a half years to complete. There are hundreds of major orchestral works that have been transcribed for band. Some have been transcribed by the composer; Aaron Copland's *An Outdoor Overture* and William Schuman's *New England Triptych* are two popular examples. Hindemith apparently felt that he did not have the time to transcribe his work, so he entrusted the operation to Wilson.

The fact that Hindemith's composition is based on music originally written for piano is not unusual. Many orchestral works have been based on pieces originally written for piano. One well-known transcription is Modeste Moussorgsky's *Pictures at an Exhibition*. Some of Franz Liszt's *Hungarian Rhapsodies* were later transcribed for orchestra. Karel Husa's *Divertimento for Band* was composed with melodies from some of his piano music.

The compositional idea of using music and melodies from other composer's works as a basis for new compositions goes back in history to techniques used in the Middle Ages and the Renaissance. During the fourteenth and fifteenth centuries, borrowed melodies were used in the *paraphrase* technique. Beginning in the sixteenth century a more complex technique of borrowing began that is called the *parody* technique. Throughout history many composers have borrowed themes from others on which to base new orchestral compositions. Works for band have also followed this technique. Norman Dello Joio wrote *Fantasies on a Theme of Haydn*; James Barnes wrote *Fantasy Variations on a Theme of Niccolò Paganini*; Fisher Tull composed *Sketches on a Tudor Psalm* (a psalm melody by Thomas Tallis); Richard Wagner wrote *Trauermusik*, based on melodies from Carl Maria von Weber's opera *Euryanthe*.

Unit 4: Technical Considerations

The tonal centers of this work include A minor, F major, B-flat major, and B-flat minor. Along with chromatic scales and passages, there are Lydian and Dorian modal scales as well. All movements contain running scalar passages for woodwinds that are quite challenging. The second movement has an eighty-five-measure passage in triplets that begins in the lower woodwinds. The flutes, clarinets, saxophones, and low woodwinds have these triplets in alternating passages until the line is scored for clarinet I in what is one of the most difficult ten-measure sections of the piece. All standard rhythmic values are used in the work, in both simple and compound times. There are thirty-second-note runs in woodwind parts with eight, eleven, and twelve notes per beat. There is an abundance of trills for both woodwind and brass instruments with the upper accidental sometimes indicated and sometimes not indicated. Syncopated rhythms play a major role in both melodic lines and accompaniment figures, especially in the second movement. One of the more challenging metrical passages occurs at the end of the second movement. Beginning two measures before rehearsal letter Z, there are thirty-two beats in a section that is written as eight *alla breve* measures for the percussion. The rest of the ensemble plays rhythms in alternating 2/2, 3/4, and 3/2 meters. Ranges are extreme for all instruments, primarily in the principal parts. In the first movement, there is major solo for oboe. The second movement begins with solos for flute, piccolo, and clarinet. The sustained F concert in the muted cornets and trumpets at this point is sometimes doubled in or given to the clarinets. The third movement has solos for clarinet and bassoon, with a demanding solo for the flute. The fourth movement calls for some heroic playing by the brass, especially by the horns. The scoring is for full symphonic band including English horn, contrabass clarinet, and contrabassoon. The percussion is not extensive (timpani, snare drum, bass drum, tom-tom, tambourine, triangle, small gong, crash and suspended cymbals, chimes, glockenspiel, and woodblock), but the parts are rhythmically challenging.

Unit 5: Stylistic Considerations

The tempos marked are: Movement I—quarter at 108; Movement II—quarter at 132, then half at 96; Movement III—eighth at 96-100; Movement IV—half at 80. The conductor will have to decide for him/herself, but there have been many very effective performances of this work with tempos taken slower than marked, especially in the first three movements. Typical of Hindemith is his use of a "motor rhythm" accompaniment line. Great care must be taken that this *ostinato* type of accompaniment does not become too weighty and overpowering and that the melody is still heard as the prevailing dominant line. For example, the opening melody is scored only for oboes, E-flat clarinet, and clarinet I. Playing accompaniment are flutes, clarinets II-III, alto clarinet, bass clarinet, contrabass clarinet, bassoons, contrabassoon, alto and baritone saxophones, muted trumpets, horns I-II, tuba, and timpani. With most emphasis on the melody, one may still want to coax the syncopated line in the saxes and horns, and even highlight the tritone between the saxes and horns. This requires very careful balancing, indeed! The beginning of the fourth movement also illustrates this concern. The melody is scored for oboe I, English horn, and alto saxophones. The interesting accompaniment in the bass voices and muted brass could very easily prevail. This is another instance when the conductor must act as judge and decide the proper balance of the various forces.

Unit 6: Musical Elements

The tonality centers around A minor, F major, B-flat major, and B-flat minor. There are some modal and chromatic areas as well. The harmony is very tonal and the melodies are very lyrical. The basic rhythms are not unusually difficult. The meters in each movement are, for the most part, constant. With frequent doubling of lines in the scoring, performing the rhythms accurately as an ensemble may provide challenges.

Unit 7: Form and Structure

SECTION	MEASURES	EVENTS AND SCORING
Movement I		
Theme 1	1-14	Oboe, clarinets (repeated)
Theme 1	15-32	Motives in upper woodwinds, oboe solo
Theme 1A	33-42	Flutes, oboes

Section	Measures	Events and Scoring
Theme 1A	43-52	Cornets, trombones
Theme 1B	53-60	Brass (repeated)
Theme 1B (repeated)	61-68	Woodwinds (rhythmic diminution)
Theme 1B	69-82	Motives in brass and woodwinds
Theme 1C	83-98	Oboe solo (altered inversion of Theme 1B)
Theme 1C	99-114	Piccolo, clarinet I, oboe I
Theme 1C	115-123	Motives in low woodwinds, oboe, English horn
Theme 1	124-131	Piccolo, flute I, English horn, clarinet I
Theme 1	132-139	Upper woodwinds
Theme 1	140-151	Motives in upper woodwinds
Theme 1	152-160	Piccolo, oboes, English horn, E-flat clarinet, alto clarinet, alto sax, cornets
Coda	160-168	Theme 1 motives
Movement II		
Theme 2	1-27	Four phrases change voices—flute, piccolo, clarinet I
Theme 2	28-44	Low woodwinds
Theme 2	45-61	Upper woodwinds, with changing voices
Theme 2	62-78	Horns, cornet, clarinet II, alto clarinet
Theme 2	79-95	Trombones, baritones
Theme 2	96-112	Trumpets, woodwinds
Theme 2	113-129	Four phrases change voices—clarinets, low brass
Theme 2	130-146	Four phrases change voices—cornets, horns, baritones
Transition	147-159	Brass fanfare and clarinets continuing accompanying triplets

Section	Measures	Events and Scoring
Theme 2A	160-162	Trombones (syncopated variant)
Theme 2A	163-166	Horns
Theme 2A	167-169	Cornets
Theme 2A	170-172	Tuba
Theme 2A	173-177	Motives in brass
Theme 2A	178-194	Six statements continue changing voices in brass
Theme 2A	195-203	Timpani solo
Theme 2A	204-233	Eleven statements continue changing voices in woodwinds
Theme 2A	234-245	Three statements in timpani and percussion
Theme 2	246-249	Low woodwinds—Phrase 1 only (with 3/2 measure)
Add Countermelody 1	250-253	Horn I, trombone I
Theme 2, Countermelody 1	254-257	English horn, tenor sax, cornets join CM 1
Add Countermelody 2	258-261	In trumpets
Theme 2, Countermelody 1, Countermelody 2	262-265	Add flutes, oboes to CM 1
Theme 2, Countermelody 1, Countermelody 2	266-269	Add saxes, clarinets
Theme 2, Countermelody 1, Countermelody 2	270-273	Tutti scoring
Theme 2	274-280	Brass in rhythmic augmentation
Theme 2	280-304	Motives in percussion in rhythmic variation
Movement III Phrase a	1-4	Clarinet I
Phrase a	5-8	Bassoon I

SECTION	MEASURES	EVENTS AND SCORING
Phrase b	10-13	Horn, clarinet, flutes, cornets
Phrase a	14-17	Woodwinds, trumpets, horns
Phrase c	18-21	Clarinets, saxes
Phrase c	22-25	Flutes, oboes, clarinets, alto saxes
Phrase d	26-28	Clarinets, low woodwinds
Phrase c	29-32	Flutes, English horn, bassoons, saxes, horns, baritones
Phrase a	33-36	Clarinet I with flute solo
Phrase a	37-40	Bassoon I with flute solo
Phrase b	41-44	Horn, clarinet, flutes, cornets with flute solo
Phrase a	45-49	Woodwinds, trumpets, horns with flute solo
Movement IV Introduction	1-5	Motive in trumpets, trombones
Theme 3	6-20	Woodwinds (repeated)
Motivic tag	21-26	
Motivic tag extended	27-33	
Introduction Motive	34-37	Trumpets, trombones, flutes, clarinets
Theme 3	38-44	Woodwinds
Motivic tag	45-50	
Theme 3A	51-59	Horns
Theme 3A	59-67	Horns
Theme 3A	68-73	Woodwinds
Theme 3A	74-81	Flutes, clarinets, saxes, baritones then in brass
Introduction Motive	82-87	Piccolo, flutes, clarinet I, bassoons (rhythmic augmentation)

SECTION	MEASURES	EVENTS AND SCORING
Theme 3	88-105	Trombones
Motivic tag	106-110	
Theme 3	110-124	Brass
Theme 3	125-132	Horns
Introduction Motive	132-142	Brass
Cadence	143-144	B-flat major

Unit 8: Suggested Listening

Paul Hindemith, *Concert Music, Op. 41, Mathis der Maler, Symphonic Metamorphosis on Themes of Carl Maria von Weber* (orchestral version), *Symphony in B-flat*

Carl Maria von Weber, *Huit Pièces, Op. 60, Pièces Faciles for Piano, Four Hands, Op. 3*, Book 2

Unit 9: Additional References and Resources

Anderson, Gene H. "Analysis: Musical Metamorphosis in Hindemith's March from *Symphonic Metamorphosis on Themes of Carl Maria von Weber*." *Journal of Band Research* 30, No. 1 (Fall 1994): 1-10.

Baker, Theodore. *Baker's Biographical Dictionary of Musicians*. Eighth ed. Revised by Nicolas Slonimsky. New York: Schirmer, 1992. S.v. "Paul Hindemith."

Hindemith, Paul. *A Composer's World, Horizons, and Limitations*. Cambridge: Harvard University Press, 1952.

Hindemith, Paul. *The Craft of Musical Composition*. Fourth ed. New York: Schott, 1945.

Paulding, James E. "Paul Hindemith: A Study of His Life and Works." Ph.D. diss., University of Iowa, 1974.

Randel, Don Michael. *The New Harvard Dictionary of Music*. Cambridge, MA: Harvard University, 1986.

Rehrig, William H. *The Heritage Encyclopedia of Band Music*. Westerville, OH: Integrity Press, 1991.

Smith, Norman and Albert Stoutamire. *Band Music Notes*. Lake Charles, LA: Program Note Press, 1989.

Stolba, K Marie. *Development of Western Music*. Dubuque, IA: Brown and
    Benchmark, 1990.

Contributed by:

Kenneth Kohlenberg
Director of Bands
Professor of Music
Sinclair Community College
Dayton, Ohio

Teacher Resource Guide

Tunbridge Fair

Walter Piston
(1894–1976)

Unit 1: Composer

Considered one of the most influential teachers in American music of the twentieth century, Walter Piston was also renowned for his compositional skill in combining contemporary musical materials with neo-classical counterpoint and form. Born in Rockland, Maine in 1894, Piston began his studies in art, but switched to music after service in a Navy band in World War I, where he played saxophone. He graduated from Harvard University in 1924, and like many of his musical contemporaries, went to Paris to study with the great French teacher Nadia Boulanger.

Upon returning to the U. S. in 1926, Piston joined the faculty of Harvard, where he taught until 1960. Through his compositions, his teaching, and his extensive educational writings on compositions, orchestration, and theory, he influenced a broad range of later composers, including Leonard Bernstein, Irving Fine, and Daniel Pinkham. In describing his own works, Piston defined his goal as a composer as striking "the perfect balance between expression and form." Perhaps his most popular work is the ballet suite *The Incredible Flutist* (1938). Along with Samuel Barber, he is the only composer to win the Pulitzer Prize for Music twice—for his *Symphony No. 3* in 1948, and for his *Symphony No. 7* in 1961.

Unit 2: Composition

Piston's only work for band, *Tunbridge Fair* was written in 1950 on a commission from the League of Composers (at the behest of Edwin Franko Goldman). This short, one-movement work stands as a marvel of concise, painstaking craft combined with an energetic and lyrical spirit of expression, a synthesis of two major threads in all of Piston's compositions. Unlike his serial compositions, this piece is solidly tonal in nature, but with a fluid and flexible harmonic nature.

Originally titled *Intermezzo for Band*, the title was changed at his publisher's insistence. Piston took the nearby country fair in Tunbridge, Vermont as inspiration for the requested title, and reluctantly appended a programmatic description linking the piece to the events and spirit of such a fair:

> People from all walks of life are jostled together in the gay riotous turmoil that is Tunbridge Fair—the back-country folk of soil mingle with people from the metropolitan districts; world travelers eat hot dogs at the same booth with native Vermonters; schoolteachers from Iowa, lumbermen, truck drivers, state officials, country storekeepers, college boys, school girls, bankers and laborers are caught alike in the hilarious whirl.

The world premiere of the work took place on June 16, 1950, with the composer conducting the Goldman Band. In the *New Grove Dictionary*, the list of Piston's works mistakenly includes *Tunbridge Fair* and *Intermezzo for Band* as two separate works. They are the same piece.

Unit 3: Historical Perspective

At the time of the commission for *Tunbridge Fair*, the band world was deep in an era of tremendous growth and change. Before the 1940s, few composers had taken the medium of the concert band seriously as a voice for their compositions. Outside of transcriptions of orchestral pieces and a handful of original words, there was little serious concert music available.

But at this time in America, through the leadership of bandmasters such as Edwin Franko Goldman, Frederick Fennell, and William Revelli, the image of the concert band as a distinct and much inferior relative to the orchestra underwent dramatic change. The high standards of performance and musicianship of these and other bandsmen of the time focused attention on establishing a repertoire of compositions written for band. Leading American composers accepted commissions for band works and quickly discovered the unexplored musical and coloristic potential of large wind groups. Along with *Tunbridge Fair*, important American works of this critical period of growth include Samuel Barber's *Commando March* (1942), Arnold Schoenberg's *Theme and Variations* (1943), Morton Gould's *Ballad for Band* (1946), and Vincent Persichetti's *Divertimento* (1950).

Unit 4: Technical Considerations

Rhythmic feel is a crucial element of *Tunbridge Fair*, a factor complicated by Piston's dense arrangement of counterpoint and polyphony. The score is

marked with a very moderate (and flexible) quarter note=ca. 92, but there is considerable octave and chromatic doubling within families, and the rhythmic complexity may require a mediation between desired tempo and practical performance speed.

With the complicated texture in the first theme areas, clarity of line also becomes problematic, requiring extra care in balancing and listening for the thematic material. Brass writing is bright and often high in the register, especially for the horns and repeated notes, and figurations require a delicate, detached articulation at all volumes. All parts have intricate chromatic passages, and Piston also makes use of a complex, hocket-like division in the upper woodwinds, which complements the second theme material. This division demands independence and rhythmic confidence from all parts, particularly the clarinets. Percussion requires five players to cover the parts, and the writing is simpler than that of the winds, usually punctuating melodic statements.

Unit 5: Stylistic Considerations

In his liner notes to the first recording of the work, David Hall describes the first theme as "a kind of 'yokel' jazz." Despite its thick rhythmic texture, *Tunbridge Fair* carries in it a mood of unfettered and gymnastic enjoyment. This quality of pulse and vitality, always important but especially critical here, must be maintained in a delicate balance with the need to play at a speed which does not overwhelm the players. Experiment with tempo, but once you find one that seems to "lock in" the best, stick with it—players will need to be able to find the groove quickly.

A key rhythmic cell in the first theme is the syncopated sixteenth-eighth-sixteenth. Work for a loose, ragtime feeling in this motif, carefree and joyous without being sloppy. The tendency will be toward heaviness because of the thick scoring, so keep conducting gestures light to communicate this to your players. In rehearsal, break sections down to their component lines and let the players hear what is going on in the other parts, and let them discover which lines are the most important and how that should affect their playing.

The contrasting second theme has a quality of grand nostalgia. Howard Pollack suggests the tune resembles an old-fashioned sentimental song, and the scoring suggests a melodeon or reed organ similar to those played at the fair in Vermont. Pay close attention to balance when this theme is layered in a canon-like process near the end of each B section. This presents a great opportunity for playing "who-has-the-melody-now" games to sharpen listening skills. Use the lyricism of the second theme to ask questions of your players: what is difference between the two themes, how they can highlight these differences in their playing, why is there a need for contrast at all.

Unit 6: Musical Elements

One of the more notable elements of *Tunbridge Fair*, though typical of Piston's style, is the breadth of its melodic material. Each note gives rise to the next in an entirely natural manner and creates long, spun-out phrases of logical, yet expressive, shape and clarity. Give these lines their proper feel with careful markings of phrase length and shaping of dynamic quality. Isolate melodies and have players perform them with different phrasings, leading them to the reasons for longer phrases that require more breath control.

Compositional techniques that could be discussed include canon, melodic fragmentation and re-combination, and chord construction using dissonant seconds and ninths, which gives the piece much of its harmonic bite, and open fourths and fifths, which gives it a spacious feeling. Though the piece runs through several tonal centers, there is no key signature in score or parts. Accidentals are simply written in where needed.

Unit 7: Form and Structure

The form of *Tunbridge Fair* is a clear-cut ABABA.

SECTION	MEASURES
A	1-23
B	24-44
A	45-66
B	67-87
A	88-116

Unit 8: Suggested Listening

Gustav Holst, *Hammersmith*

Walter Piston, *Symphony No. 3* (1948), *Symphony No. 4*, fourth movement, (1950), *Toccata for Orchestra* (1948)

Unit 9: Additional References and Resources

Austin, William W. *Music in the Twentieth Century*. New York: W.W. Norton & Co., 1988.

Grout, Donald J. *A History of Western Music*. Third edition. New York: W.W. Norton & Co., 1980.

Eastman Wind Ensemble. *American Concert Band Masterpieces*. Frederick Fennell, conductor; liner notes by David Hall. Record MG40006. Mercury, 1953.

Pollack, Howard. *Walter Piston*. Ann Arbor, MI: UMI Research Press, 1982.

Randel, Don, ed. *New Harvard Dictionary of Music*. Cambridge, Massachusetts: Harvard University Press, 1986.

Sadie Stanley, ed. *Norton/Grove Concise Encyclopedia of Music*. New York: W.W. Norton & Co., 1988.

Smith, Norman and Albert Stoutamire. *Band Music Notes*. San Diego, CA: Kjos, 1979.

Contributed by:

Doug Norton
Director of Bands
American School in London
London, United Kingdom

Teacher Resource Guide

Winds of Nagual
A Musical Fable for
Wind Ensemble on the
Writings of Carlos Castaneda

Michael Colgrass
(b. 1932)

Unit 1: Composer

Michael Colgrass was born on April 22, 1932 in Chicago, Illinois. He received his Bachelor of Music degree from the University of Illinois in 1956. Colgrass studied composition with Lukas Foss at the Berkshire Music Center and Tanglewood Summer Festival in 1952. He also studied with Darius Milhaud at the Aspen Music Festival in 1953, with Wallingford Reiger from 1958 to 1959, and with Ben Weber from 1959 to 1962. As a free-lance percussionist, Colgrass performed as a member of the Modern Jazz Quartet, New York Philharmonic Orchestra, and the Columbia Recording Orchestra with Igor Stravinsky.

Michael Colgrass has received wide recognition and several awards for his compositions. In 1964 and again in 1968 he was awarded a Guggenheim Fellowship. In 1969 he was the recipient of a Rockefeller grant and in 1972 a Ford Foundation grant. In 1978 he won a Pulitzer Prize in Music for *Déjà Vu* (for four percussionists and orchestra) and was awarded an Emmy 1982 for *"Soundings:" The Music of Michael Colgrass*. He has composed over forty works for stage, chamber ensembles, orchestra, and band. Colgrass has two original scores for band, *Winds of Nagual* (1985) and *Arctic Dreams* (1991). He has also transcribed *Déjà Vu* for wind ensemble (1986).

Unit 2: Composition

The *Winds of Nagual* is a tone poem in the tradition of the late nineteenth-century composer Richard Strauss. Drawing his inspiration from Strauss, Colgrass utilizes thematic transformation as a principle means of telling a story through sound. Based on *Tales of Power*, authored by Carlos Castaneda, the *Winds of Nagual* is about Castaneda's fourteen-year apprenticeship with Don Juan Matis, a Yaqui Indian sorcerer from Northwestern Mexico. Castaneda met Don Juan while researching hallucinogenic plants for his master's thesis in Anthropology at UCLA. Juan became Castaneda's mentor and trained him in pre-Columbian techniques of sorcery, the overall purpose of which is to find the creative self, what Juan calls the *nagual*.[1]

This "musical fable" roughly parallels the events which occur in *Tales of Power*, the first book in Castaneda's trilogy. While the listener need not have read the book to appreciate the music, the musical experience is heightened enormously if one is familiar with the trilogy. Colgrass uses a wide array of compositional techniques to transform the musical themes and reflect the personal transformation that the main characters of the book undergo.

Each of the characters has a musical theme: Juan's is dark and ominous, yet gentle and kind; Carlos' is direct and unsure. We hear Carlos' theme throughout the piece from constantly changing perspectives, as Juan submits him to long desert marches, encounters with terrifying powers, and altered states of reality. A comic aspect is added to the piece by Don Genero, a sorcerer friend of Juan's who frightens Carlos with fantastic tricks like disappearing and reappearing at will.[2]

Unit 3: Historical Perspective

Winds of Nagual was commissioned by the New England Conservatory Wind Ensemble on a grant from the Massachusetts Council on the Arts and Humanities, and was premiered at Jordan Hall in Boston on February 14, 1985, with Frank Battisti conducting. This is a landmark composition for several reasons. The craft is of the highest quality and the writing is orchestral in nature, which means there is little or no doubling of parts. The textures and timbres displayed in the work will serve as a model of orchestration for generations. Finally, the melodic inventiveness stands out as some of the most creative writing in the modern repertoire for band.

Unit 4: Technical Considerations

The technical challenges presented in *Winds of Nagual* are numerous. It is a highly rhythmic piece filled with complex meters, changing meters, and tempos. *Hemiola* is often used to create a variety of musical effects.

The tonal language is exotic. Colgrass integrates tonal music with atonal music in a seamless fashion and moves effortlessly between several modes. It is Colgrass' ability to combine this tonal language with a wide array of rhythmic devices that enables the melodies to become transformed and parallel the characters in Castaneda's books.

The part writing is at times virtuosic, requiring excellent performers in every section. Harp, piano, celeste, and contrabassoon are indispensable, and experienced soloists on alto flute, soprano sax, E-flat clarinet, and flügelhorn are essential. The brass writing moves to extreme ranges in all parts and covers a wide range of dynamics. As with most of Colgrass' writing, the percussion section plays a prominent role in the overall sound of the music.

The instrumentation is as follows: six flutes (six double piccolo, two double alto flute), E-flat clarinet, six B-flat clarinets, bass clarinet, B-flat contrabass clarinet, contrabassoon, soprano sax, alto sax, six trumpets (two double cornet), flugel horn, six horns, six trombones, two euphoniums, two tubas, two contrabasses, celesta and piano (one player), harp, and six percussion players playing Parsifal bells, vibraphone, crotales, chimes, xylophone, marimba, bass drum, three gongs, four large suspended cymbals, three large pairs of crash cymbals, one pair eight-inch crash cymbals, five cowbells, temple blocks, bongos, timbales, snare drum, tenor drum, field drum, and four timpani.

Unit 5: Stylistic Considerations

Winds of Nagual is a tone poem, and is a highly romantic work drawing on the universal theme of personal transformation. In the beginning of the work the styles and sounds of the two main themes (Don Juan and Carlos) are clear and distinct from one another. By the end of the composition the themes are entwined in a way that makes them nearly indistinguishable from one another. This thematic transformation not only reflects the content of *Tales of Power*, it also reflects the wide interpretive demands placed on the performers and the conductor.

The character of Carlos must be presented as an insecure and naive student, as a person in a psychedelic trance, a warrior who "asserts his will," and finally as a student who has come to understand the ways of sorcery. The character of don Juan is presented as dark, ominous and distant, gentle and kind, and possibly even as a loving teacher.

A successful performance of this composition is very much dependent on the insight the conductor/teacher can bring to the rehearsal. Without well-formed opinions, insight, and musical judgment, the performers and the conductor run the risk of making *Winds of Nagual* sounding merely difficult and missing the work's greatness altogether.

Unit 6: Musical Elements

There is a wide palate of musical colors employed in this piece. While much of it can be attributed to orchestration alone, there is equal use of various scalar and harmonic devices contributing to the sound and texture of the composition. There are sections that are strictly tonal (e.g., in a definite key and consequently subject to traditional tonal relationships) and many passages that can best be described as utilizing "tonal nonfunctional harmony." Colgrass intermixes pentatonic scales with bitonal harmonizations and freely moves between major, minor, and Aeolian modes. He shifts his harmonic language rapidly between, polychords, sound mass harmonization, tone clusters, and *klangfarbenmelodie* techniques. Much of the melodic language is derived from whole tone scales, synthetic scales, and pentatonic scales. The frequent use of a harmonic pedal unifies this diverse harmonic and melodic language. Consequently, much of the music sounds tonal despite the many nonfunctional harmonic techniques. Hence the term, "tonal nonfunctional harmony."

The rhythmic language of the composition is equally complex but easier to grasp. There are numerous tempo changes that reflect the constant "thematic transformation." Changing meters and complex meters abound in addition to *hemiola*. The work is highly contrapuntal in the sense that there are always multiple layers of counterpoint at any given tempo.

Unit 7: Form and Structure

MEASURES	EVENTS AND SCORING
"The Desert"	
1-25	*Quasi recitative* Introduction of melodic and rhythmic motifs that are used frequently throughout the composition. The pentatonic scale is used to provide a tonal framework while the harmony is essentially free use of "sound mass" techniques, with vertical sonorities being derived from melodic material. Use of an E-flat pedal lays harmonic foundation in the final four measures leading to D Aeolian in the next section.
26-58	*Don Juan emerges from the mountains* First statement of Don Juan's theme based on Aeolian mode.
59-70	*Carlos approaches Don Juan* First statement of Carlos' theme. Freely moving between F major and D minor while sustaining a C-sharp pedal through many of the phrases.
71-78	*Don Juan shows Carlos a new concept of himself* Fragmentation of Don Juan's theme in B major with a lighter character. The section closes with a final statement of Carlos' theme in mm. 77-78.

MEASURES	EVENTS AND SCORING
79-83	*Don Genaro appears* Introduction to the next section, loosely derived from rhythmic motives introduced in mm. 1-25.

84-109	*Genaro clowns for Carlos* Both *Genaro clowns for Carlos* and *Genaro satirizes Carlos* are derived from Carlos' theme. The music in mm. 84 through 109 is actually *Genaro satirizes Carlos* in fragmentation. The fragmentation is accomplished by use of hocket between E-flat clarinet and piccolo. The melody is further disguised by altering intervals of the melody which will occur, in earnest, between mm. 110-125. Measures 96 through 109 are a tone painting of the antics of Genaro as described by Castaneda in *Tales of Power*. The harmonic techniques are once again sound mass technique, drawing pitches and intervals from melodic material.

110-125	*Genaro satirizes Carlos* This is a dance section based on the style of a Mexican dance and a serenade. The theme is presented without fragmentation. The dance serves as a unifying element for the composition as a whole because of its thematic and stylistic connection to *Juan clowns for Carlos* (mm. 418-517).

126-127	Transition

128-160	*Genaro laughs and leaps to a mountain top, and disappears* Atonal phrases using a wide variety of scalar techniques. This is again a tone painting of actions and events from *Tales of Power*. It is loosely connected, motivically, to earlier music but is not based on either of the two main themes.

"Carlos Stares at the River and Becomes a Bubble "

161-178	*Carlos stares at the water…is transfixed…mesmerized by…and becomes a bubble.* This movement begins with long introduction based on rhythmic and melodic fragments. The use of vibes, harp, and celeste in highly chromatic passages is intended to convey "ripples on the water."

MEASURES	EVENTS AND SCORING
179-201	*...and travels with the water* Hyper-augmentation of Carlos' theme (alto flute) by use of extreme chromatic ornamentation. Wide variety of scalar techniques used in winds, harp, celeste, and vibes used to convey the intensification of "ripples on the water."
202-208	*Carlos tumbles in cascades of water* Rapid scalar passages, with tone clusters bringing the tone painting of water to a close.
209-213	*Juan jolts Carlos awake with a shrill voice* Closing theme based on motivic material from "The Desert" (introduction).
214-222	*Carlos feels euphoric...climbs out of the water* *Codetta* based on Carlos' theme (harp). Motivically derived static harmony built on A-flat. Cadence in D-flat minor.

"Gait of Power"

223-240	*Don Juan shows Carlos how to leap between boulders in the dark* While this movement sounds like new material, it can also be viewed as rhythmic fragmentation of music presented in The "Desert" movement. This point of view is, however, intended only to identify the source of the musical material.
241-270	*Something moves in the dark* Juxtaposition of tone clusters, against rhythmic and melodic motifs and chordal harmonizations. This section can be viewed as a developmental treatment of the prior section.
271-281	*A terrifying creature leaps at Carlos...it grabs his throat* Juxtaposition of rapid scalar passages, polychordal harmonization, and rhythmic motifs leading to the following section.
282-296	*Carlos exerts his will* Polychordal harmonization of Carlos' theme. Cadence on A-flat major followed by a G minor polychord transition to next movement.

| MEASURES | EVENTS AND SCORING |

"Asking Twilight for Calmness"

297-303
Carlos calls to the desert from a hilltop
Bitonal introduction based on melodic motifs from "The Desert."

304-334
Carlos dances
Slow dance based on Carlos' theme. The use of *hemiola* implies triple meter while moving between 7/8, 5/8, and 2/4 time signatures; bitonality continues.

335-337
Carlos meditates
Augmentation of the "slow dance" theme. Free arpeggiated accompaniment in F Aeolian without *hemiola*.

374-399
Carlos moves again
Measures 374 to 386 are a restatement of the material presented at m. 304. Measures 387 to 392 are a brief rhythmic interjection based on the bitonal introduction of this movement. Measures 393 to 400 are the final statement of the "slow dance," with *hemiola*, in E-flat Aeolian.

400-409
He feels a deep calm and joy
Development of the melodic style formulated in the "slow dance." Again based on Carlos' theme, aria-like melody in A-flat.

410-417
Nightfall
Closing theme which is a continuation of the prior phrase with homophonic accompaniment. Cadence in E-flat minor.

"Juan Clowns for Carlos"

418-517
A Mexican dance that is formed from a compilation of elements in both Carlos' and Don Juan's themes. The second theme of this dance is drawn from the second theme of *Genero Satirizes Carlos*. The humorous aspect of this section is conveyed by using "hyper-octave-displacement and rhythmic similar to "Gait of Power."

"Last Conversation and Farewell"

518-566
A lyric "conversation" between winds and brass based on the themes of Carlos and Don Juan. Tonal chord succession that culminates in a brief chorale in mm. 556-558. Measures 559-565 are a harmonic and rhythmic dissolution of the chorale.

566-588   *Carlos leaps into the abyss…and explodes into a thousand views of the world*
Three "leaping" musical gestures made up of descending scales and *arpeggios* result in tone clusters that lead to the final statement of Carlos' theme. The final statement is made of a combination of polychords, sound mass, and rhythmic fragmentation. The piece comes to final climax at m. 574 with an "explosion of sounds" made up of a massive brass chord and fragments of melodic material. The remaining measures are a gradual dissolution of an E-flat diminished ninth chord, culminating in silence at m. 588.

Unit 8: Suggested Listening
Michael Colgrass, *Arctic Dreams*
Richard Strauss, *Till Eulenspigel, Don Juan*

Unit 9: Additional References and Resources

Bohle, Bruce, ed. *The International Encyclopedia of Music and Musician.* New York: Dodd, Mead, and Company, 1985.

Cummings, David, ed. *International Who's Who in Music and Musicians Directory.* Cambridge, England: Bath Press, 1992.

Castaneda, Carlos. *Tales of Power.* Simon and Schuster, 1974.

Colgrass, Michael. *Winds of Nagual.* New York: Carl Fischer, 1987.

Mathes, James. "Analysis: *Winds of Nagual* by Michael Colgrass." *Journal of Band Research* 23, Number 1 (Fall 1987).

Contributed by:
Mitchell J. Fennell
Director of Wind Studies
California State University/Fullerton
Fullerton, California

[1] Michael Colgrass, *Winds of Nagual*, A Musical Fable for Wind Ensemble on the Writings of Carlos Castaneda, (New York: Carl Fischer, Inc., 1987).
[2] Ibid.

Index by Publisher/Distributor for Teaching Music through Performance in Band: Volume 2

Index by Publisher/Distributor for Teaching Music through Performance in Band: Volume 1

This index lists all the titles discussed in the first volume of the *Teaching Music through Performance in Band* series along with the name of the publisher.

Index by Composer, Arranger, Transcriber

Index by Title